Bob Backenforth's

CIVITAS IN BEERO ET PUBBI FIDELIS

Worcester Pubs

Then.
And now.

Bob Blandford

Worcester Pubs Then and Now is published by:

The Whole Picture Publishing Co.,
Addison Road, Beechwood Park, Worcester WR3 8EA

© Bob Blandford and The Whole Picture Publishing Co
http://www.the-whole-picture-publishing.co.uk

ISBN 978-0-9927418-0-8

9 780992 741808 >

Printed and bound in the United Kingdom by Page Bros, Norwich

Worcester
Pubs
Then
And now

Bob Blandford

Contents

Notes on 'Worcester Pubs Then.

racing the precise location of many of Worcester's 'ancient' pubs – particularly those in the City's mediaeval heart and those on the west side of the river – is not the doddle many might think it to be. Even that ace chronicler of all things Worcester, 'Rambler' John Noake. on the subject of the history of the City's inns, taverns, ale-houses and gin palaces said as far back as 1877:

> *'...sorry I am that the fragments of the history of this institution of Worcester are so scanty as to afford little beyond a dry list of names. But slight as this is, I deemed it worth preservation in the hope that some friendly correspondents might be enabled to throw further light upon the ancient Vigornian victualling fraternity'.*

...enter **this** friendly correspondent and fully-paid up member of the ancient Vigornian victualling fraternity'!

Though there's no shortage of maps outlining the changing shape of Worcester over the years – many of them lovingly drawn and prepared with such consummate artistry and mathematical precision I'm left humbled with admiration and wonder at how those first cartographers quite managed to pull it off without the benefit of aerial photography or modern technical gizmos – none were so precise as to show the location of anything so lowly as a tavern or inn, and the first to do so was the Ordnance Survey of 1886.... which is, frankly, less than useless if you're looking for the location of some long-lost Worcester pub that painstaking research has unearthed, as in some cases here, for the first time in 250 years!

Resorting to the simple device of an address also amounts to a thankless task... first off, the mass's general inability to read, at least up to the mid-19th century, rendered numbering houses and properties a futile exercise – and even then, many inns and taverns might be listed under half a dozen different property numbers in a ward or parish that changed its boundaries twice or three times, in a street that might have been blessed with four of five different names. Today's Tybridge Street is typical: it could have been listed as any of Torcae, Turkey, Turkey Street, Clement Street, St Clements Street and even on rare occasions the unlikely 'Tybridge Street'.

Nor does valuable drinking time squandered in poring over pre-pubco wills or even early census returns reveal very much as regards an establishment's specific location – trust me, I found out the hard way!

All of which is a long-winded way of saying that while every care has been taken to log each pub in its actual location, in some cases a small element of guesswork has had to be applied, while in those few worst-case examples when all there is to go on is the name of the parish in which it lay, a much larger dose of guesswork has been drummed-up and pressed into action.

Despite all that, unless otherwise stated, you can take it as pretty much Gospel that where you see the pointy circle in any one of the maps in this book, it's indicating as near as dammit that pub's actual location and thus marks the spot. Meanwhile, if the sign is a circle, it means the spot can be deemed 'approximate': like 'The Rambler' before me, sorry I am that there's more circles than I might have liked, but as the modern idiom has it, 'there you go' – right, Mister Noake sir?

And now'

In similar vein, while even more potential drinking time has been sacrificed in the pursuit of listing a complete, unbroken, line of owners and licensees for each hostelry, chances of missing out a name or two are all but unavoidable. Curiously, this is especially true of later years when the rapid turnround in tenants and especially managers made it a thankless task even to attempt it – though I am grateful to Tony Stevens for filling in swathes of the inevitable gaps from information compiled by his late father, Derrick.

So yes, there will be Es and Os *(errors and omissions)* but then, we all make mistakes: as someone else once memorably remarked, no-one's inflammable! (Spell-checked, OK). What I *will* say is that where the occasional oversight bubbles through, my apologies are unreservedly offered.

As regards the photographs, the modern stuff is mine. Not that you will be much impressed by that – and why should you be? The skilful stuff and the archive stuff is the work of others and my indebtedness to them is recorded in the 'Contributors' section towards the end of this book. Throughout this work, copyright has been duly acknowledged and dues settled, but in the inadvertent and unwitting case of failure to a) trace and b) acknowledge ownership, please feel free to notify me of such.

No history of any aspect of Worcester would be complete without at least a nod in the direction of two acknowledged titans in the field, Dr. Pat Hughes and Bill Gwilliam, and my thanks – in the first case directly and in the second via his successors – to them for the occasional 'lifted' quote (and recorded as such). If yours is even a passing interest in this great City of ours, the work of both authors is eminently worth further attention and I would readily recommend **'The Story of Worcester'** *(Logaston Press – ISBN 978 1 906663 57 5)* by Pat Hughes and Annettte Leach, and of course Bill Gwilliam's evergreen **'Old Worcester: People and Places'** *(Halfshire Books ISBN 0-9513525 8 X).*

Thanks are also due in no small measure to, among others, Worcester Heritage Amenity Trust (at Tudor House) for access to the Changing Face of Worcester Project archive which embraces the collection of Clive and Malcolm Haynes, staff at The Hive, Greg Warner, Jim Panter, John Jordan, Malcolm Price, Worcester Source, Steve Agg, The Trumpet, Berrows Worcester Journal, Worcester News and other newspaper publishers for printing my sweated-over pubs-related editorials in the first place; friends and followers of the **Worcester Pubs Then and Now FB page**, https://www.facebook.com/groups/worcesterpubsthenandnow and an endless list of Worcester pub landlords who over the past half century had the time, patience and forebearance to hear-out someone whose mood was up and down like a 'ore's drawers but whose gratitude was always there, if never always adequately voiced.

Oh yes, and especial thanks to the legion of like-minded fellow pub-goers that make any study of Worcester pubs such a delight. Over the years, chances of you and me having already passed the time of day in some mutually-favoured bar are high. If, sadly, we didn't, maybe we can have put that to rights by the time the next volume comes out. I can only hope so.

Bob Blandford *(aka Bob Backenforth)*
Worcester 2013

1: Bob... er, who?

I t's with some confidence that I can state, pretty much categorically, that my on-going and fully consummated love affair with British pubs in general and Worcester pubs in particular began on Sunday, January 18th 1948 at **The Albion** in Bath Road.

Not only was it the first pub I ever ventured into, but it was also the first pub I was carried out of. What's more, I'd be on reasonably safe ground to add that this was the first time a goodly whack of the customers in there had ever set eyes on me before, and while I can't be absolutely certain on this one, there's a more than a fair chance I made my feelings noisily known, followed by, as like as not, either nodding-off in a corner or throwing-up over someone. Possibly both.

Not for the last time, either, did I come away with no recollection whatsoever of having been there – but at least, here I can offer mitigating circumstances...

The occasion, you see, was the little family gathering following my very own christening in the nearby St Mark's Church, and the day was only my twentieth on God's green earth *(which, while we're on the subject of days, reminds me: I've since had something in the region of 24,000 more on which to continue attending to my devotions as set on that particular day – precious few of which, it pleases me no end to relate, saw the opportunity missed. Praise be for that)*

The upshot to all this is that this book is a complete, total, one-hundred-per-cent LOL – no, not in the current computer-speak idiom as per 'lottsa love' or even less so, 'laughing out loud'... more in the style of a pre-computer-speak Labour of Love, the sole object of my undimmed and almost exclusive attention in the non-human direction being the pub and the mild and bitter memories generated therefrom.

Despite the best efforts of the breweries, various employers, insistent pals, idols, my genes, a fairly gregarious nature, an unusually benevolent HMRC, the in-built inability to resist temptation, and God Almighty – all of whom have mercifully left my memory abnormally undimmed – I can also recollect with deeply satisfying clarity **The Sandpits** *(later The Bedwardine)*, **The Swan** and **The Angel** in St Johns, and more especially **Heenans' Club** all in the 1950s, leaving me, like many of you I suspect, drooling with nostalgia for the hours spent sitting outside, juggling a Vimto in one hand and bag o' Smiths potato crisps with the blue twist of salt in the other, hoping to be asked to join in the noisy games or to make friends with the other kids similarly left to their own devices *outside* while parents, guardians and sundry other relatives charged

St Marks Church, Cherry Orchard (CCMH/CFOW)

ST. MARKS CHURCH, CHERRY ORCHARD.

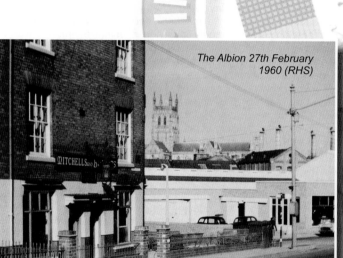

The Albion 27th February 1960 (RHS)

with our well-being did whatever-it-was-they-did on the smoky fairytale-land *inside*.

My crystal clear 1950s memory bank is also vivid with the inerasable image of everybody within earshot singing their austerity hearts out after a couple of drinks – almost always to the tinkling background of an out-of-tune honky-tonk played by a crumpled vamper who was invariably fag-ash speckled and always seemed to have half a dozen pints if it was a *him*, and a similar number of Cherry Bs or Babychams if it was a *her*, lined up on the discordant and equally bashed-about old joanna.

Moving on to the 1960s, more haloed memories have survived intact of Worcester's pubs of the day... hot'n'bothered evenings spent canoodling in cosy alcoves in **The Swan with Two Nicks** or **The Feathers** or **The Talbot** in The Tything, hoping not to be upbraided and unceremonially booted-out for being woefully under-age... lowering my voice half an octave and growling for my 'alf in the macho **Woolpack** and the hairy-armed **Duke of York** *(as if the barman/maid hadn't sussed me out the minute I'd walked in!)*... the smell of brand new wood varnish in the shiny new and oddly-named **Glovers Needle**... half-time drinks in **The Bell** in Droitwich Road or **The Sebright** or **The Halfway House** in Fernhill Heath while laying down a mean bass-line with various bands thinking we were God's gift... **The Crown** in Droitwich Road, **The Mug House** way out in the rural sticks, beef and dripping rolls in **The Raven**, the table footie in **The Pheasant** *(and aforementioned **Raven**)*, bar billiards in **The Great Western**... oh yes, and the wobbly stone-flagged floor of **The Farriers Arms** in Fish Street – the first and only pub I ever queued up outside waiting to be let into, the occasion being July 1966 when as George Best lookalike I was given the choice of either getting my hair cut or returning for my final three days at my highly regarded *(though whether the reverse is true remains debatable)* school, Worcester Royal Grammar – another location the tiniest details of which my memory has preserved like flowers pressed into a book.

That July day – a sunny, summery Monday I recall – I opted to bid farewell to what had been my

educational home for the previous seven years and to treat four more soon-to-be-ex-WRGS pupils to a few pints in **The Farriers** which had by then been our Saturday night regular for both our 'A' level years anyway. I won't mention their names for fear of embarrassment or recriminations: suffice to say, one went to America to seek his fortune *(and, I gather, succeeded)*; another became a respected headmaster and Chief Secretary of the National Association of Headmasters and Union of Women Teachers; the third a teacher of German in a school that I gather had a relaxed attitude to pretty much everything including education; and the fourth a high-ranking Officer with Ordnance Survey – who, incidentally, I gratefully thank for allowing me to use some of their pioneering works to pinpoint the precise location of quite a few otherwise-forgotten Worcester pubs.

And then there was me....

Having shown precious little interest in anything involving chemicals, glass jars, numbers, mathematical symbols, tools, dissection dishes, balls *(cricket, rugby or football)*, words with curious accents, map reading or anything even vaguely involving physical exertion, I was at least rabid about spelling and grammar and could spin the odd phrase to often comical effect, alongside an ability to draw folks' likenesses with an uncanny degree of similarity as well as to forge often important people's signatures to generally lucrative effect. Thus, here at least was a glimmer of what the future might hold. I even drew and occasionally painted the odd canvas for some small financial gain and even illustrated one Master's published text books, but just as soon shrank away from a fancied, though scarcely realistic career as a pro portrait painter when I realised that Pietro Annigoni was never going to wake up one morning quaking in his **stivali** *(boots)* over the threat some bright, if essentially lazy paintbrush-wielding embryo master-forger and composer of smutty verse posed to his status as master of the craft.

So it was that I turned to my second choice to eke out a crust – words, initially 'filling in the grey lines' the layout artists had kindly allowed for us copywriters on Kays catalogue, then as newspaper reporter locally, then regionally, then *nationally*, even progressing to the unlikely status of leading newshound on some national titles and later editor of several regional magazines and newspapers.

In time, and now with highly viable sidelines of handling 'the meejah' (of which I was a fully paid-up member) for the likes of Avis, Bovis, Gulf Oil, Babcock, Kawasaki and a role I relished more than maybe I should have, Ansells *(in turn leading to Banks's, M&B and Home Breweries in Nottingham)* this was a key period of professional scribing, designing, film-making and photography that had not only given me the opportunity to hold a glass or two alongside A-lister pop and film stars, stage actors and actresses, film directors, TV personalities, politicians and royalty as well as the good, the bad and the downright pug-ugly, but had also given me the opportunity, not to mention the far-from-negligible wherewithall, to get to see the inside of hundreds of pubs in every county in England, Wales and much of Scotland and too...

by Bob Backenforth

I never was a CAMRA member, but being on the road for hundreds of solitary hours a year, I always managed to find comfort – and occasionally my way home – from the CAMRA Beer Guide, and a recent chance discovery of my 1980 edition reveals I visited 138 different pubs in 39 of the 49 English counties that year alone, each one graded on overall merit.

WORCESTER
WORCESTER/
DROITWICH EDITION

SOURCE

Issue 359
OCTOBER 21st, 1982

DISTRIBUTED WEEKLY FREE OF CHARGE TO 54,110 • HOMES AND BUSINESSES IN SOUTH WORCESTERSHIRE (• Audited Figure)

Inside This Week
FEATURE ON
MALVERN
PAGES 8 & 9

STA UPPER TYTH
WORCESTER
TEL. 23312

...the only time my writing got me compared to Shakespeare: barred.

My memory still retains picture-perfect images of **The Merton Arms** in Bootle, **The Black Swan** in Uttoxeter, **The Commercial** in Ashton-in-Makerfield, **The Garden Gate** in Leeds, **The Fleece** in Northallerton, **The Royal Oak** in Gretton, and **The Black Lion** in Leighton Buzzard *(where my darts partners were either Butch, Duke or P'nut of the Barron Knights)* among hundreds of those I called in en route to somewhere else, either as a diversionary destination or merely in passing.

Closer to home, recollections of Ma Pardoe's or **The Coachmaker's Arms** in Wednesbury remain vibrant and undimmed. Interesting to note, thirty-three years on, that a fair whack of those that I hadn't visited that year may well also have been looked in on during any of the previous gadabout years... and all this on those fine works of fiction I penned and submitted with clockwork regularity month-in, month-out: exes *(or to those unexposed to the temptation of petty thievery, expenses)*.

Come 1981 and by now thoroughly hacked-off *(no pun intended – oh, I don't know though)* with scarcely being around for my two daughters who never ceased to impress me by always being prepared to be shown the inside of some ever more distant pub or other even though I'm sure they'd far rather have been elsewhere instead, I gave up the roving life and settled back in what had always been home: my town, God's own Worcester.

The 80s was the time of setting down proper roots with, for the first time ever, a true local that I could call my own and a second home. This was **The Barbourne** in New Bank Street, and if you could bottle whatever magic it had in those early 80s years, you'd end up a rich man indeed. It was also the time of territorial warfare in terms of pub games: darts for teams I played so badly for I've chosen not to remember, cricket for **The Coach and Horses**, crib for **The Barbourne** *(naturally – though by now, I was captain)* and quiz for **The Old Greyhound, The Halfway House** and **The Mug House**.

I could never quite get the hang of dastardly dominoes though – and as for snooker and pool, it was unfair to pit me against the ball-potting wizards I saw playing for other pubs on account of they'd end up choking on their beer from laughing. Quoits, bridge, phat and other pub games just left me cold.

his, though, was the time **Bob Backenforth** fist saw light of day...

As freelance journalist and sole editorial/photographic staff of the weekly *'Worcester Source'* between June 1981 and February 1983 *(when I was unceremoniously sacked for ~~remonstrating with, talking to,~~ bopping someone who thought it'd be clever to change my words)* I wrote and photographed not only the news, but also threw-in film and theatre reviews, restaurant reviews and something I thought might, just might, take off as I didn't think it had been done before, least of all in Worcester. This was **The Bob Backenforth Good Beer Guide** and it lasted from June 1981 to November 1982 by which time I'd pretty much exhausted every pub that'd have me.

Even so, it not only got me on the inside of the better part of 200 Worcestershire pubs in eighteen months, but it also proved beyond a shadow of doubt that yes, you can mix business and pleasure.

It's a verifiable fact and maybe also a matter of public record that I got to drink beer – again on exes, no questions asked – **and** get paid for the pleasure of so doing. Not only that, but through some extraordinary benevolence on the part of HMRC *(either that or they were just glad to get rid of me)* I was also allowed £500 a year – that's £10 a week when a pint was about 42p – tax allowance for that self-same purpose, and there ain't many can say that. The same today would be about £6,000.

It's certainly no understatement to add that the Bob Backenforth beer guide had quickly attracted a coterie of regular followers who'd tried to make a point of visiting both the pubs I featured each week *(the paper was published on a Friday)*: I know this because I'm still occasionally reminded of it – and much humbled I am too to have memories re-kindled and occasionally even thanked for, over a piece of whimsy I wrote mostly for my own amusement more than 30 years ago.

It was also the only time my writing got me compared to Shakespeare... *barred.*

That said, for all the friends it made, it conjured-up some enemies too – and, but for LVA chairman, long-standing mate Mike Stevens who I'd known long before he substituted his original craft of printing for what seemed to me the far riskier business of the pub trade, I'd likely have found myself with a blanket ban from **all** the Worcester pubs, as had already happened with the Malvern and Upton LVA.

And as if all that wasn't bad enough, I also signally upset the gay fraternity at **The Pear Tree** after warning customers who dropped their change to leave it there – a bit naïve and puerile with hindsight, though it prompted a titter from some, alongside threats of dire deeds being done with a Guinness bottle from others.

There was also **The Long Stop** saga whose beer *(Ansells)* I described as being 'so soupy you could stand a spoon up in it...'

Not only did it prompt the LVA's retained solicitor David Wright to threaten me with repeating the alleged feat in court with severe penalties if I failed, but it also spurred two heavies from the pub to visit the *Source* office intent on a quiet word with whomsoever had maligned them by slagging-off their cherished local. If I'd called their wives whores and their kids ugly I'd have been on safer ground.

As it happened, it was the self-same Bob Backenforth, now only an infrequent visitor to the office as he/I was doubling his/my salary at the time freelancing for other titles, that greeted their request for a quiet chat *'wiv that there Bob Backinforff'* – a move that demanded some lightning-quick thinking...

"Sorry, sunshine, not here at the minute" he/I lied, sussing the situation in a flash and already sensing a painful penalty if they realised just who it was they were actually talking to.

"Wurzeegonthen?" demanded the rougher and more tattooed of the two. And so he/I splurged out the totally fabricated tale that he/I had gone to his/my karate class and would be back later – throwing-in the entirely unsolicited and erroneous pay-off that he/I was a nasty piece o' work who took his killer karate seriously and'd do for you as soon as look at you, before adding the falsely helpful kiss-off of promising to ask him/me to call them if only they'd leave their names on this 'ere scrap o' paper.

Self-preservation being the most powerful of a whole armoury of natural instincts, I suspect the proof that the hastily cobbled-together ruse proved ultimately effective is attested-to by the fact that my nose and jaw-line are still roughly the same shapes today as they were then – all of which goes to show a) the passion and high regard with which Worcester folk hold their favourite pub, and b) that there's no accounting for taste.

I was only once asked to write about a certain pub – and that was **The Punch Bowl** in Ronkswood whose licensee at the time kindly offered me the services of a minder for the duration of the interview/ beer-sampling session *(honest)*!

There was also the time that...   ...but no, this book isn't about Bob Backenforth or about:

Instead, it's about my Worcester and its fine heritage of places in which to meet, drink, socialise, chat, jest, leg-pull, play games, piss-take and see and be seen in – *every single one of which I can state with absolute conviction to have visited on at least a dozen occasions.* Suffice to say that what with the drink driving laws and the virtually guaranteed arrival of two letters a week from the no doubt miffed and by now overpressed LVA solicitor, the aforementioned David Wright of Messrs Parkinson Wright – plus getting bored with at best having pub doors slammed in my face and being 'shown the door' *(for which read 'ticketted and told to bugger off' or words to that effect)*, I considered it prudent to call time on my own party.

It had been good while it lasted and since then, it's been an up'n'down – mostly up – whirligig of more newspapers, hacking *(in the scribing sense, not as per current computer-speak)* video, local and national awards and being asked by a range of clients including Worcester City and Worcestershire County Council to make 'em look good in the press, on TV and radio, and in their publicity material. I even got paid for it most of the time.

It was in this period of generally fun-filled semi-employment *('remunerated f*nnying around' is how I've described it on more than one occasion)* that the idea of penning the definitive book on the rich heritage of Worcester's pubs took hold and grew. After all, it'd be a cryin' shame to see all those years of dedicated beer-quaffing, thirst-quenching, people-watching, friends-making, pub critique-ing and getting gently out of it for an hour or two – not to mention a high-res memory bank that's almost full to capacity, but not quite – go to waste.

So here it is: a short year on the drawing board (okay then, Apple Mac) but far and away the better part of three score years and ten in the gathering. Or put another way, half a century of dedicated re*(hic)*search that remains as work-in-progress and still has a long way to go, even though this volume is already on the streets.

It's already foregone that you won't get anywhere near as much pleasure from reading this book that I did from researching it – and for that I offer no apologies whatsoever. But if you care even half a jot for Worcester and its history, you will derive at least a measure of satisfaction that there's a minimum two of us – 'ee and me – ready and willing, if not entirely able, to do our bit to preserve the memory of Worcester Pubs Then and Now. 'Tis enough to make you wail into your ale when you consider that at the rate they're disappearing, that's all that'll soon be left to us: memories – which, I trust this book will go some small way to keeping alive, at least in the short-term.

So for now, here's to English pubs in general and Worcester pubs in particular. A forlorn hope it might be, but long may what's left of them continue to reign...

Cheers!

Rule, Beertannia

(...or, the Brits and the booze)

2: **Rule, Beertannia** (or, the Brits and

I n the Beginning was the Word. And the word was *'tavern'*.
Given the title of this chapter and the undeniable fact that we Brits have always enjoyed a special relationship with the booze, it'd be more than satisfying to say that we invented not only that glorious little six-letter gem of a word and every other little *bon mot* associated with the supremely pleasurable pastime of drinking a foaming pint or several of English ale in the company of like-minded Brits within a cosy abode where the only rule is 'drink and be merry'.

Sadly, no. Not only did we not invent – or more accurately, discover – ale or beer, but we were also beaten to all of the words most commonly associated with it: all except one...

Take the aforementioned *'tavern'* for instance. Brit? No – Roman latin, from *'taverna'* meaning a hut or shop. Booze, then? No – Dutch, the intransitive verb büsen: effectively, 'to drink excessively or to get drunk'. How about 'inn'? Nope, 12th century Norse 'inni' meaning a dwelling.

'Beer' has to be ours surely? 'Fraid not. Old High German 'bior' first known use before the 12th century. Ale's ours though? Wrong again. Those cursed Norsemen beat us to it with their 'ol' or possibly the Lithuanians with their 'alus'. Pint? Mais non... either French *(pinte)* or more likely latin *'picta'* (ie painted) from the practise of painting a line on the side of a drinking vessel roughly equating to the standard measure in force to this day.

Now, 'tippler' we *can* lay claim to: it comes from the Middle English 'tipler' – effectively an alehouse keeper, but not only is it something of a non-word anyway, it's also a bit of a late-comer, appearing several hundred years behind all the others and so loses some of its impact as a result.

But at least the word 'pub' is ours – *and for me, that's the best of the lot.*

Etymologically (that is, the study of words – and for more of the same, a look at the Merriam-Webster Dictionary is an illuminating exercise http://www.merriam-webster.com/dictionary) rocket science it ain't: it's simply an abbreviation of the term public house '...denoting a house that's open to the public, as opposed to a private house' *(Wikipedia)* and it was first coined as recently as 1859.

So...

While we Brits didn't necessarily invent the institution of the pub per se, nor were we first off the mark to discover what today is reckoned to be the world's third largest-consumed beverage next to tea and coffee, it's to our everlasting credit that we first coined the term 'pub' and then tossed a heady dose of uniqueness into the mix by elevating a) the craft of keeping one, and b) the joy of using one, into a high art-form and justifiable source of national pride.

Both monumental achievements have proved so marked and successful over the years that the rest of the world has torn its collective hair out trying to copy the concept of 'the English *(for which, also read Scottish, Welsh, Irish and to a lesser degree, Australian and New Zealand)* pub' and turn it into its own.

But what Pierre, Fritz, MIguel and even Elmer Foreigner have so signally failed to grasp is that the institution is unique, quintessentially ours, doesn't travel well and is not to be tampered-with – though,

the booze)

in their favour it might be added that their inability to emulate what we gave the world owes more to the British nature and appetite for somewhere handy to meet, chat, relax, drink, make new friends and put the world to rights in, than any shortcomings on their part.

The incontrovertible upshot is while we fall woefully short of being first past the post in the creation of the words, the resulting product – the English pub – was, is, and will ever remain, unique, special, exclusively red-white-and-blue and the envy of the world. That the last few years has also seen us do our level best to undo all the good that's been done and to destroy what we spent centuries creating is a different issue altogether – of which more in later on.

So yes, the love affair between the Brits and the booze is, in that sense at least, a healthy one: as Queen Victoria is reputed to have so nobly put it, '...give my people plenty of beer, good beer, and cheap beer, and you will have no revolution among them'.

Hence the title of this chapter: *Rule Beertannia*.

There will, rest assured, be more quotes abut beer as we progress through his merry romp over the love:love relationship between the Brits and a goodly pint of foaming ale, but for now, let's revel in the unarguable certainty that the English pub is unique. And long may it remain so.

The inescapable fact is that we Brits are a nation of boozers – and proud of it. Not only that, but our traditions of drunkenness have been around since the year dot and shows no signs of abating. They might like to think they did, but today's 18/20 Brits abroad didn't invent the concept of binge-drinking: it's in-bred, it's part of our make-up and it's been recorded in history since the eighth century at least.

So what of this remarkably long-lived institution that we didn't perhaps initiate, but certainly fine-tuned, honed and developed into what has shaped the British character more than any other influence save perhaps, the weather and the sea, and has to take a rightfully prominent place in any social history of a Britain that is, in every sense of the word, 'Great'?

The origins and history of the English pub have been written about and analysed ad pukeam elsewhere – and the local lending library, bookshops, Google and Wikipedia are awash with just that colourful tale, albeit largely from a 'New World' standpoint *(for which read 'pea-green envious')*.

But by way of introduction to this all-too brief over-the-shoulder glance at English pubs in general and Worcester pubs in particular, an easy-going look at how the English pub came about and blossomed into something special and unique mightn't go amiss here for starters...

ubs are like people. Young or old. Warm or indifferent. Rich or poor. Brash or introverted. Popular or unwelcome. Clean or shabby. Stick-in-the-mud or fun-to-be-with. Fresh or downright unsavoury. Welcoming or cold. Generous or mean. Placid or volatile. Well-fed or undernourished. Cosy or uncomfortable. Competitive or complacent. Plain or flashy. Classy

or trashy. Loud or sshhh.... Safe or dangerous. You love them or you hate them. They love you or hate you. They blow hot or cold. They can be your best friend or your worst enemy. They're 'in' or they're 'out'. They come and they go.

Apply any adjective you can coin or find in a dictionary and it will fit some pub, somewhere.

Not only that, but nowhere else on God's green earth is – or sad to relate, was – the pub so central to each community's way of life as Britain: nor is there anywhere else that one man's perception of what a pub should be is so often diametrically at odds with the next man's.

Take what for many represents the mirror image of contemporary real life: the soaps... The East End pub *(The Queen Vic)*, The Yorkshire Dales pub *(The Woolpack)*, The Inner Manchester pub *(The Rover's Return)*, and the rural Worcestershire pub *(The Bull at Ambridge)* have all been represented in TV and radio and seen and heard the world over – and while they're all fictional and exist only in a studio, each is not only based on somewhere that actually exists in real life, but can also be said to have a character as different to any of the others as mild is to bitter.

Despite the best efforts of architects, marketeers, pubcos, local authorities, planners and the modern tendency towards house styles and formulaic 'out-of-the-box solutions', no pub is the same as any other. And long may that remain so.

Like people: every one is unique and the essential difference is character.

Take this from that most English of writers, H. G. Wells – whose description of an English inn from his enchanting book **'The History of Mr Polly' (1908)** is probably the closest yet penned to what many still believe pubs should be...

> *'The nearer he came to the place the more he liked it… the green tables outside were agreeably ringed with memories of former drinks and an extensive grape vine spread level branches across the whole front of the place… (Mr. Polly) went up three steps to the glass panelled door and peeped into a broad, low room with a bar and beer engine, behind which were many bright and helpful looking bottles against mirrors and great and little pewter measures, and bottles fastened in brass wire upside down with their corks replaced by taps and a white china cask labelled 'Shrub' and cigar boxes and boxes of cigarettes, and a couple of Toby jugs and a beautifully coloured hunting scene framed and glazed, showing the most elegant and beautiful people taking Pipers Cherry Brandy and cards such as the law requires about the dilution of spirits and the illegality of bringing children into bars and satirical verses about swearing and asking for credit, and three very bright red-cheeked wax apples and a round shaped clock. But these were the mere background to the really pleasant thing in the spectacle, which was quite the plumpest woman Mr. Polly had ever seen, seated in an armchair in the midst of all the bottles and glasses and glittering things, peacefully and tranquilly, and without the slightest loss of dignity, asleep'*

...not a sports-roaring telly, juke-box, food menu, piped music, bandit, quiz machine, sweetie dispenser, charity collection box, poppy tray, games console, coffee maker or fag/nut/darts-scorer machine in sight and a gobby barmaid so skinny you could use her as a pull-through. But then, there are those for whom a sports-roaring telly, juke-box, food menu, piped music, bandit, quiz machine, sweetie dispenser, charity collection box, poppy tray, games console, coffee maker or fag/nut/darts-scorer machine in sight and a gobby barmaid so skinny you could use her as a pull-through represent everything a pub *should* be.

Like I said, there's no accounting for taste. Opinions vary, and so do pubs.

Not only that, but what was 'in' one year is very much old-hat the next and the very nature of pubs has shown dramatic change over the centuries, much of it shaped not so much by public opinion and patronage as by meddling and interference of officialdom at every level. As we shall soon see...

Every civilization, even the earliest as they emerged out of their caves to a dinosaur feast, had found a way to brew something intoxicating out of the local weeds and sundry other floral resources readily at hand.

Most works on the subject both scholarly and flimsily lightweight, place the origins of beer *(ale was a later European addition being the combination of beer with hops to assist both its flavour and its preservative qualities as outlined later)* on the Egyptians and Arabs, with a date of around 3000BC, and it'd be pleasing to think of some ancient Egyptian or Arab waking up one sunny morning and saying 'I know, today I'll invent beer!'

Sadly, like the etymology of all things booze-related, the facts of its discovery are nowhere near so exciting as the fanciful dream: the truth is that the discovery of beer was entirely accidental – the serendipitous result of wild yeast naturally present in the air fermenting with cereal.

That said, the charming image of that first lucky Egyptian or Arab who saw what had happened and took the first draught of the resulting concoction is somewhat easier to envisage – as might be his first word, the Egyptian or Arabic version of 'whoo' coming firmly to mind...

To their eternal credit – as we can confidently infer from the fact that they had the words before we did *(and let's be honest about this, a word is of no use whatsoever without something to apply it to)* – all of the north European tribes had found ways of making their own heady beer-like brews out of the cereal crops growing wild and plentiful around them, and as time progressed, they evolved their own brewing techniques. Then, as successive invaders and would-be colonizers, they found like-minded civilizations and cross-pollinated the essential ingredients, skills and refinements that down the years metamorphosed into a) beer as we now know it, and b) the pub as we now know it.

In often-invaded Britain, it was malted barley, water and yeast flavoured with heather, myrtle, sage or ivy that had given the earliest brews their essential character – later mixed-in with flavours and techniques brought by successive marauding Celts, Norsemen and Germanics.

By the time the Romans came, saw and conquered, the Brits' production of beer was comparatively refined and though the latest invaders' local flora had been grapes – with the result that they'd evolved into a nation of wine drinkers – that didn't stop them setting about Italicising the rough libation they found working its magic in far-off Albion which, of course, sparks-off the classic image of John Cleese demanding of his little tribe in **'The Life of Brian'** just what the Romans had done for them...

Well, as regards Britain, aside from the creation of an admirable roads system *(note: 'roads system' refers to the great Roman highways, Ermine Street, Fosse Way and Watling Street and their like, not the back roads and country lanes as referred-to in the phrase 'the rolling English drunkard made the rolling English road')* they're credited with bringing the notion of an organised drinking house, or

taverna, to these shores – for which we collectively owe them a debt, and I personally owe them the opening line of this chapter.

But as if that wasn't enough, there's more... because it was the Romans that also gave us the concept of using some kind of external visual device so as to mark it out from its neighbours. And thus began the tradition of hanging out a sign to proclaim to the passing world that by stepping over the portal under which it lay, therein you'll find something cool, amber and refreshing and, taken in sufficient quantities, enough to give the world a golden glow and to consign all its troubles and woes to tomorrow.

The first signs were probably images of vine leaves: fast-forward eight hundred years or so, and the Anglo-Saxon alewife would have maintained the self-same tradition thus set by putting up put a green bush on a pole to let people know her brew was ready – and given that few of the population had yet mastered the art of reading, resorting to such a device worked wonders in helping the population at large to identify where to get a goodly sup of the latest draught.

For a libation fit for Royalty – as William Shakespeare pithily noted, 'a quart of ale is a dish for a king' ('A Winter's Tale') – it's also barely surprising that successive English monarchs also played their regal part in the development of English pubs...

King Edgar, ruler of England from 959 to 975 (and interestingly, one of the few places you'll ever see any tribute to the monarch also called 'The Peaceable' *though some say 'The Spoilsport' might be a more fitting sobriquet* is Worcester where his pensive statue takes pride of place on the Tower that still bears his name) had already intervened in what was rapidly becoming a popular institution by decreeing that there should be just one ale-house per village.

Others reckon that our very own King John whose last mortal remains reside not a hundred yards from Edgar's Tower takes the credit for having standardised the measure of a pint in 1215 though there's as much confusion about this as there is about what the precise measure of a pint should be. In 1277, at the Assize of Bread and Ale, the lawmakers laid down that '...no brewster henceforth to sell except by true measures, the gallon, the pottle (half a gallon) and the quart, and that the tun be 150 gallons and sealed'.

Back to the subject of signs, Richard II who ruled between 1377 and 1399 it was who followed the Romans' example and demanded all landlords put up some kind of recognitive device outside his or her premises – on the seemingly harsh penalty of forfeiting all of his, or her, ale if he or she failed to do so.

round this time too, the first moves to restrict drinking hours also came about – though less for reasons of promoting sobriety, more to prevent thieves and other ne'ers-do-well having a place to hide after dark:

'..whereas misdoers going about by night have their resorts more in taverns than elsewhere and there seek refuge and watch the hour for misdoing we forbid that any Taverner or Brewer keep the door of his Tavern open after the hour of curfew'.

The scallywags aside though, by the Middle Ages, we Brits were a comparatively happy and contented race... after all, the production of beer was honed and refined and every peasant drew his ration of home-brewed beer from the manor. Even young children had a ration of two quarts – perhaps luckily so for our continued future, as by then beer was a healthier drinking option than water as rivers had become evilly polluted. At the time, beer's health-restoring qualities were put down to its ingredients, but science later corrects that misconception as being the impact of simply boiling the water.

Even so, the implication is clear: the members of many a mediaeval household would likely have spent their entire waking lives from breakfast to bed time, slightly squiffy because of the staple diet of beer... thus, the image of the boozy Brit first came about. *(Note: the lovely little word 'squiffy' comes from descriptions of former Prime Minister Herbert Henry Asquith (1852-1928) known to enjoy a tot or two!)*

By now, though, there was a growing number of outlets where those that could afford the paltry price could gather and put the world to rights. Thus, the scene was set for the impact of two all-powerful influencing factors – the effects of both still a) being felt today and b) very much in existence today... Enter left, commercialism and consumerism, enter right, officialdom.

Human nature being what it is, it was at this point that the peace of this happy scenario was shattered by the first example of out-and-out consumerism...

By this time, the producers of the better beers had found a ready market within their own localised community and were extending the boundaries of their sales area. Cue 'the brewery'.

In this respect, the monks were well ahead of the game. First off, they had the time, the resources and the fiscal savvy to create new and better beers via new and better production methods. They were also among their own best customers: the daily ration for monks was a gallon day.

Accordingly, it wasn't just the word of God they spread but also the word of grog, and following the monks' lead, a gallon a day soon became normal fayre for many a mediaeval Brit.

Even when Henry VIII dissolved the monasteries, he couldn't banish those that had made them what they'd been, so the ex-monks simply carried on doing what they'd always done, but now without the cloak of religiosity. Hence was created a new breed of businessman, the professional brewer, whose market-place was no longer limited merely to the Church and all its pilgrims, but additionally to the village, town or City at large. The move spelled the beginning of the decline of home brewers – many of whom were women rejoicing in the charming description of 'alewives'.

At a stroke, it also sparked a distinct switch away from the small-time house in favour of a better quality brew in the company of those of like-minded outlook: the tavern.

What the Romans had initially initiated, the Brits had turned into something unique – though it had taken 1500 years to pull it off.

It was about this time – circa 1500 – that rampant commercialism also raised its perhaps not so ugly head. Some of the foreign brewers, notably our near-neighbours and the great sea-going merchants of the world, the Dutch, had introduced hops to their brews. English beer had by tradition been low gravity, bitter and prone to rapid souring. The new-fangled 'ale' with the addition of hops was an altogether sweeter and stronger brew that, tellingly, kept much longer.

For a while, there were two distinct schools of thought on this issue – on one hand the purists for whom the very thought of tampering with the beer was anathema *(enter the Middle Ages equivalent of CAMRA),* and on the other, those progressives who were promising stronger, lighter beers with a later 'best before' date or whatever the official 1500s equivalent might have been.

The furore created in its wake had produced a major split within the ranks of the growing number of brewers but inevitably commercialism won the day, thereby setting a pattern that was to be repeated again and again during the history of beer and brewing... that you'll have what the brewers say you'll have.

Despite this, the two sides forgot their differences and agreed to work together to the better good.

But this was also the time the heavy hand of officialdom came crashing down – and it's this factor, probably more so than any other that has shaped the look of 'the pub' as we now know it.

To that end, let's return to the fascinating subject of signs...

I n an early piece of legislation, Richard II's 1393 decree that '...whosoever shall brew ale in the town with intention of selling it must hang out a sign, otherwise he shall forfeit his ale' was yet another example of the official meddling in the by-now burgeoning drinks trade: *interesting to note that hanging out a sign was voluntary in every other line of business.*

One of the next pieces of legislation was the creation of official ale-tasters or 'conners' – on the face of it created to preserve the quality of the ale or beer for the common man, but more realistically to determine the amount of tax that should be levied on different brews: the stronger

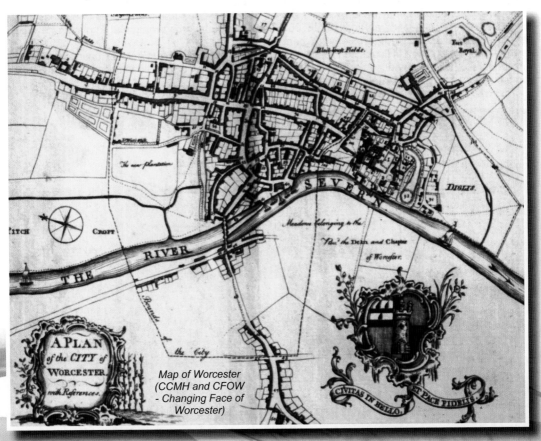

Map of Worcester
(CCMH and CFOW
- Changing Face of
Worcester)

the brew, the higher the tax. *(Sounding familiar?)*

Though essentially, if indirectly, tax-collectors, the conners did provide a tangible benefit though: brewers caught short-measuring could expect to be dragged through the streets and publicly disgraced if they were found guilty of tampering with the beer or trying to flog a below-par brew. Of course, the tavern sign had by now come into its own by way of making alehouses easily visible to passing inspectors: according to *Wikipedia*, William Shakespeare's father John held down such a role.

 t was Government intervention that also pointed the way towards the next key development in the now blossoming industry...

They decided to make a clear distinction between the differing types of establishments abundantly springing up, based on what it was legally allowed to provide. Thus, an **ale house** was little more than that: a house, probably also someone's home and as like as not the kitchen or parlour that was limited to serving ale and not much more. One step up the ladder, **taverns**.

Here, travellers could expect to find a room for the night and could also expect to be fed as well as to have his fill of the local potion. And at the top, the **inn** – coaching or otherwise, often, though by no means exclusively – located at some handy stopping-off point in the country or a town between the great cities and where every convenience including stabling and fodder for horses was afforded, at a price of course.

The early-1500s also witnessed more Government attempts to limit the number of outlets in a move to combat increasing levels of drunkenness. London was allowed to keep 40; the great cathedral see of York a long way behind at nine; the seafaring port of Bristol six, but Worcester, Hereford, Lincoln, Southampton and Oxford were all limited to just three.

Even so, within a few years, the brewers had become so successful that their increasing demand for wood to make barrels 'created a scarcity of that useful article' and in the first year of Edward VI's reign *(1547 when he was aged 9)* an order was made that '...from the Fest of All Saints to Fest of Purificac'on *(sic)* neither bakers nor brewers shall buy noo wood by the cobbull lode', severe penalties awaiting those that tried.

By 1557 the drinks industry was booming. Probably because of demand, restrictions on the number of outlets had been significantly eased – to the point that it's reckoned that the number of alehouses had shot up to 13,000, alongside an additional 2,000 inns and 400 taverns throughout England and Wales: effectively one establishment for every 200 people.

Small wonder the idea of licensing crept in. It was about now that the first Act was passed demanding innkeepers to pay for a licence in order to sell beer, whether of their own making or commercially bought on an increasingly open market.

The idea is, of course, as 'in force' today as it was then.

The Brits have always enjoyed a strong relationship with the booze. As Queen Victoria herself once memorably said: '...give my people plenty of beer, good beer, and cheap beer, and you will have no revolution among them'. Hence the title of this chapter: Rule Beertannia.

The 1600s

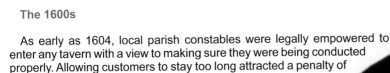

As early as 1604, local parish constables were legally empowered to enter any tavern with a view to making sure they were being conducted properly. Allowing customers to stay too long attracted a penalty of 10/- (50p), which was then given to the poor.

And, of course, more ways of fleecing the landlord and his customers came about...

In 1617 licenses were required if the tavern allowed bowls or croquet to be played, and later the same applied to music and dancing.

Not far behind it came the first taxes on brewing ale.

Then came further rules empowering Justices of the Peace to obtain sureties for good behaviour from the landlords. The precise wording of so-called Victuallers' Recognisances as they applied to Worcester ale-house and innkeepers a century or so later is the chapter that follows, but from this time on, every landlord was required to furnish two guarantors to ensure the strict observance of a growing number of conditions, on forfeiture of a not insignificant amount of money in the event of non compliance.

Similarly, the justices also retained the ability to close erring alehouses as well as to control the increasing proliferation of new ones.

Just ahead of the Civil War it's estimated that the number of ale-houses, taverns and inns now numbered more than fifteen thousand – and growing. Similarly, the tradition

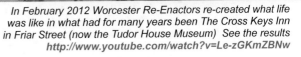

In February 2012 Worcester Re-Enactors re-created what life was like in what had for many years been The Cross Keys Inn in Friar Street (now the Tudor House Museum) See the results http://www.youtube.com/watch?v=Le-zGKmZBNw

of the English drunkard was by now well established while at the same time the innkeepers were also becoming increasingly commercially aware, the honest ones gaining business acumen and finely-tuned professionalism in their craft, the dishonest ones finding a ready market in which to fleece their often fuzzy-headed clientele.

Around this time too, the political situation was also bearing down on the industry and, in a move calculated to hit the old enemy France, if not to ban, at least to curtail the sale of an increasingly popular commodity, wine.

The 1700s

he greatest change by the beginning of the 1700s was a marked switch away from foaming ale or beer towards spirits – notably, the product of fermented grain mash flavoured with juniper berries, the resulting concoction taking its name from the French 'genèvre, the Dutch jenever, and Italian ginepro *(juniper)*.

This was gin, and its increased production had been actively encouraged by the Government as a lucrative way of utilising surplus grain and thus increasing income into the collective kitty. As the saying of the time went: 'drunk for a penny, dead-drunk for tuppence'.

Every small town had its own distillery; Worcester had several, and it's reckoned that by the early 1730s, distilleries in London alone were producing 11 million gallons of gin a year – enough to supply every man, woman and child in the capital with a pint of gin a week. Duties on spirits were largely exempt and the resulting orgy of over-indulgence has been grittily catalogued in William Hogarth's acidic look at the Big City of his day.

It came at a heavy price though, and while 'Gin Lane' specifically lampooned the capital, the indictment of rampant excess could equally be levelled at every town in England and Wales at the time. Not for nothing did gin acquire its 'Mother's Ruin' reputation, nor was drunkenness limited to the poorer classes.

Encouraged by lower duties on gin, the gin houses or 'Gin Palaces' had spread from London to most cities and towns in Britain, with most of the new establishments illegal and unlicensed.

The Condition of this Obligation is such that Whereas
the several Victuallers hereinafter mentioned
are this day licenced to keep a Common Ale
House or Victualling House in the City aforesaid
for the Term of one whole year or until the
next General time of Licencing for the
City aforesaid If these for the said several
Victuallers shall keep good Order and
Government and suffer no Disorders to be
committed or unlawfull Games used in
their said Houses Yards Gardens or Backsides
thereto belonging during the Continuance
of their said Licences then their several
Recognizances to be void or else to remain
in full force,

19th century engraving of Worcester
(CCMH and CFOW)

...and the drunkenness and lawlessness created by gin was seen to lead to ruination and degradation. Accordingly, The Gin Act 1736 imposed high taxes on retailers – though it led to riots in the streets. The prohibitive duty was gradually reduced and finally abolished in 1742 though the Gin Act 1751 was more successful in curbing the previous few decades' excesses by forcing distillers to sell only to licensed retailers and bringing in gin shops under the jurisdiction of local magistrates.

Soon, in the wake of a rapid succession of 'Gin Acts' accompanied by increased duties and a strengthening of the powers of the justices, the nation's love affair with gin rapidly declined and beer resumed its rightful place as the Brits' preferred tipple.

By now, renewal of the licence to sell alcohol had become annual, demanding the would-be licence-holder's presence at annual Brewster Sessions regulated by Corporations, presided over by magistrates, monitored by locally-appointed constables and traditionally held in September *(though this was later, as in the case of Worcester, switched to February)*.

The 1800s

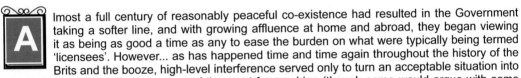

lmost a full century of reasonably peaceful co-existence had resulted in the Government taking a softer line, and with growing affluence at home and abroad, they began viewing it as being as good a time as any to ease the burden on what were typically being termed 'licensees'. However... as has happened time and time again throughout the history of the Brits and the booze, high-level interference served only to turn an acceptable situation into a complete debacle. 1830 saw one of the most far-reaching (though some would argue with some justification 'short-sighted') decisions ever made... as things appeared to be going so well, they abolished beer tax in 1830 and opened up the field so as to allow any ratepayer to sell beer *without a licence*.

The impact was not only immediate, it was also explosive – opening up the floodgates for the greatest proliferation of beer outlets ever known anywhere else in the world.

In effect, the move created a brand new lowest-level tier of outlet, the *beerhouse* and for 2gns *(£2.10p)* any householder who paid rates could apply to sell beer or cider in his home and even to brew his own on his premises.

The resulting explosion of beerhouses – in most cases rarely little more than the kitchen of someone's humble abode – captured the spirit *(no pun intended as under the terms of the Act, the sale of spirits and even fortified wines like port were not allowed)* of the nation.

The Government's thinking was that by encouraging the consumption beer, a repeat of the worst excesses of the gin years would be avoided: instead, it led to a near-repeat situation, this time as 'the beer years'.

It was here that the rumour that Worcester could offer one pub for every day of the year started – a misconception then, as now, but at least a mark of the respect Worcester folk held for their now mushrooming drinking establishments. *(More on this particular topic in 'Civitas in beero and pubbii fidelis' following this chapter.*

Unhappily for many that shelled-out their 2 guineas, not all survived the first few years of this glut of what by now were becoming known for the first time as 'public houses' but as time went by and the survivors had begun strengthening their positions – many, it should be pointed out, in the tender care of the distaff side as later pages clearly demonstrate – so the concept of the modern pub began to take shape.

It was the creation of the beerhouse that saw the *(private)* living and *(public)* drinking areas assume their own space with the novelty of seating available in the taproom as opposed to standing space only in the bar-room.

Some of the more go-ahead 'licensees' even went so far as to offer the added refinement of a parlour: '...the beer was usually served in jugs or dispensed directly from tapped wooden barrels on a table in the corner of the room. Often profits were so high the owners were able to buy the house next door to live in, turning every room in their former home into bars and lounges for customers' (Wikipedia).

More Beerhouse Acts followed in quick succession: that of 1834 introduced the concept of the 'off-licence' though in 1840 licences were made available only to the occupiers of would-be beerhouses.

And so it continued with even Queen Victoria chipping-in with her own pithy quote as related earlier.

The 1900s

I t's hard to believe in these days of Big Brother that restrictions on how, where and when folk could indulge their taste for ale or cider or spirits at the dawn of the 20th century were largely non-existent.

Opening during the hours of Divine Service – as laid down in the Victuallers Recognisances was a distinct no-go, as was '...keep(ing) open his or her or their premises during late hours of the night or early in the morning for any other purpose than the reception of travellers', but beyond that, pretty much anything else went.

The Brits had taken to the pub with a gusto and for many now it was a daily routine – those in the factories and sweat shops drinking the new lower gravity mild ale throughout the day to replace the water lost in their sweated labour and then, if they could afford it, revisiting during the evening, often until the early hours.

By the time increasing militarism abroad had exploded into the horrors of the Great War and the Government began demanding full production of arms and ordnance with which to stave-off the enemy menace, the originally steadfast Brit was found to be wanting and a further regime of legislation had to be brought in to get him off his now complacent backside.

This was DORA – the Defence of the Realm Act – and for the first time it took an uncharacteristically heavy hand not only to legally enforce new limited opening hours but also to restrict children in the pubs. If the British munitions worker and others required to remain sharp and *compos mentis* in order to maintain maximum ordnance output wouldn't do it of his or her own volition, the Government would have to do it for them.

The steps they took were sweeping, sparking-off nothing short of outrage and fostering protests on the streets – though significantly less so in the press whose duty it was to follow the Government line at a time of national crisis. The new emergency Act slashed prescribed opening hours from a flexible 20 hours-plus a day to a new, closely-monitored time-set: noon to 2.40pm and 6.30pm to 9.30pm.

The draconian move was considered vital not only to curb increasing drunkenness and the impaired output of munitions that had been fatally demonstrated in a high proportion of duds being sent to the Front, but also to preserve grain supplies, and it did not go down well.

But worse was to come...

By the end of what became known as The Great War, the restrictions stayed in place. Not only that, but with only minor tinkerings that eased the pressure on hard-pressed landlords, the measures taken to protect munitions production at a time of national crisis continued to form the pattern for drinking for the next half a century – a period that, significantly, included periods of boom and bust *(as history shows, mostly bust)* and another world war.

Maybe it was the euphoria of victory in the Second World War, or maybe it was the realisation of how close the world had come to Armageddon but it's generally reckoned that the decade and a half immediately post-1945 was the hey-day of British pubs.

Before then, in 1932, Berrows Worcester Journal – a publication I was to edit some 56 years later – claimed that in the County, 140 licensed premises (out of 1,100) had closed in the previous 25 years. In the same period, 60 had closed in the City out of 265.

Then came World War II. It's true there had been a steady decline in the physical number of pubs, but after the crushing of the Axis forces in 1945, it seems everyone wanted to step out of reality for a few hours a week – or in many cases, a day – and the pub was the perfect antidote to the austerity and low spirits that had been the lot of the hard-pressed Brit for too long.

This period, euphoric though it undoubtedly was during those few immediate post-war years, ultimately proved to be the beginning of the end of the pub as we'd come to know it – a process that's still continuing and still has some way to run, but is as incontrovertible and as it's irreversible.

Paradoxically, the moves also then being taken to combat the declining amount of drinks sold, contributed more to the acceleration in their decline than in reversing it and that particularly sorry tale is considered later on in this book.

But maybe now is a good time to take a look at how The Faithful City responded to what was happening elsewhere in Britain and the proliferation of pubs that gave it the reputation of being home to more pubs *(and churches)* than anywhere else in Britain.

Whether either of those claims holds water remains to be seen – but it's fair to say, whether it's yea or nay, we had a bloody good go!

As for the future – and the continuing saga of Worcester Pubs Then and Now, if you've a mind to continue, you can pick up the pieces of where we've left off in the chapter *'...and that's when it all went pear-shaped'* beginning on page 414

1909 Jolly Boys outing from the exotically-named Peep o' Day (see page 142)
(CCMH/CFOW)

You can do it now or later: the choice, like whether you go to the pub or not and if you do, which one, and even further – what, and if you drink once you're there – is yours...

3: Civitas in beero et pubbii

nfinitely-better accounts of the history of Worcester have been written by infinitely better-qualified observers than me, but the fact remains that the history of Worcester's pubs is inseparable from the wider history of Worcester – the converse, of course, being equally true – and it's impossible to divorce the two.

Thus, a look at how Worcester evolved and metamorphosed into The Faithful City of today provides the essential backdrop to the continuing saga of Worcester and its never-ending love affair with its pubs.

Whatever name you want to hang on it – **Caer Guorangon** *(Roman)*, **Vrangon, Wrangon-caester, Wigorna Ceaster** *(Saxon),* **Wircester** *(Norman),* **Wusster, Hooster, Chinatown** *(80s CB-speak)* **Sauce City** *(ditto)* or even **The Woo** currently in favour with the students now laying siege to the City, Worcester once had it all.

Like Terry Molloy *(Marlon Brando)* in 'On the Waterfront', written by Bud Schulberg in 1954:

> ***"I coulda had class. I coulda been a contender. I coulda been somebody, instead of a bum, which is what I am, let's face it..."***

Worcester had class. It was a contender. It was a somewhere. And while it'll never be a bum-town, there's aspects of the City c2013 that Worcester folk of certain age might think of as indicative of The Faithful City no longer being the Worcester they grew up in and, yes, loved.

One element remains constant though – that Worcester folk had, and many still have *(though the trend is, for any number of reasons, decreasing)* a striking fondness for its pubs...

A tale often told is that Worcester was once home to more pubs per head of population than anywhere else in Britain – indeed, that at one time you could visit a different pub every day starting on January 1st and not return to that same pub until the following January 1st – and while both stories are well short of the mark in terms of actual verifiable accuracy, they speak volumes about the pride Worcester folk traditionally take in telling tales of its inns, taverns, ale-houses and sundry other drinking establishments.

The Englishman's essential thirst for a goodly draught of foaming ale aside, perhaps the typical Worcester-ite of the day took the lead from his betters: a daily beer ration for mediaeval monks at the cathedral was a gallon a day. From 1497, constables and the City elders were encouraged to take regular 'perambulations' around the City and were described as 'a fertile source of popular jollification' in which hard drinking and practical joking formed the principal ingredients:

fidelis

'...the exact direction and limits of the City boundary were then pointed out. A boat or barge was hired to carry the party over the Severn and a man with a plank to help them over the ditches... partaking liberally of wine, ale, beef and tobacco at various stages of the route and distributing ale and money to poor women and others at St Mary's Steps in Edgar Street'

– 'Rambler' John Noake ('Worcester in Olden Times')

John Noake also notes that '...one of the great events of the year was the annual procession of the bailiff (equivalent to today's Mayor) to St Johns which is a village divided from the western side of the City by the river Severn. In this ancient pendicle which in spite of the Municipal Reform Act retains even to the present day the esprit de corps derived from the old recollection of its privileges and importance, and revives a shadowy grandeur of the yearly election of officers whom proceedings afford at least profit to the tapsters and fun to the local journals, an annual fair was held on the Friday preceding Palm Sunday and upon that day did the civic dignitaries of Worcester attended by their customary officers, walk in procession through the village, over which, however, notwithstanding the parade, they possessed no authority, it being situated without the limits of their jurisdiction.

'This custom is of a remote origin and is said to have originated in an agreement with the prior and convent and the bailiffs and aldermen that if the latter would not obstruct them in laying and keeping down the pipes in which they brought Henwick water to the cathedral, the Corporation might bear their mace within the bounds of the sanctuary and also of St Johns, which belonged to the convent. The constable having 'cried the fair' the party would adjourn to the Swan or Bell (both noted houses two centuries ago) and there run up a pretty score for the City funds. Not content with this, his Worship and Co would sometimes cause their august bodies to be conveyed thither (a distance of only a few hundred yards) in a vehicle, for in 1732 occurs an item of 9d (for) a turnpike for coach to St Johns fair'. From the before going premises however, it is probable the coach was employed in coming from the fair, the civic party being then unquestionably in a more unfit state to do the locomotive on their own account. The potations were repeated also on arriving in the city for in 1658 is a charge made for 'wine spent at St Johns faire and later the return of Mr. Maior (sic), aldermen and constables therefrom. It was at length deemed advisable to compound with his worship for a fixed annual sum for this purpose and accordingly £5 was granted to him yearly, besides certain charges

for the constables'.

Similarly, in 1723, members of the Corporation *(ie: councillors)* are reported to have spent £1.12s 2d (£1.61p) on beer at the Diglis Pleasure Gardens 'during a perambulation of the City boundary'.

To this day, the Mayor has a very generous drinks allowance and the 'fridge in the Mayor's parlour is re-stocked daily.

I t's not as widely put about as it might have been, but Worcester's 5,000-year past harks back further than any other English cathedral city – and that includes those that have capitalised on their history infinitely more vigorously than Worcester has ever managed to: not least, Canterbury, Durham, Lincoln, York, the old enemy Gloucester.

The City – a good 900 years before earning its royally-bestowed description of 'Faithful' – is said to have had a bishop even before the nation had a King, and contemporary records right up to the mid-19th century stand witness to the fact that Worcester had it all – style, wealth, architecture, mobility, foresight, importance and the very real prospect of up-ending even London as the nation's capital, all gratuitously combined with the ability to carry it off handsomely.

Small wonder King George III selected Worcester to be the Government's and the Royal family's base in the event of Napoleon carrying out his threat to invade England (1805).

Not long earlier, the City's consummate style and elegance is neatly summed-up in a description of the one-time Roman military station that emerged over the centuries into what was then termed a metropolis, thus:

> *'...Worcester is considered one of the most ancient and respectable cities in England; and there are but few reckoned superior to it in extent and population, and a less number in beauty. The streets of the city are handsome and regular.... indeed, for beauty, cleanliness, respectability, and as affording all the comforts of life, unsparingly, no visitor will be disappointed on his arrival at the city of Worcester, and but few will leave it without regret'*

(Pigot's Directory 1842)

As the pay-off to another lofty passage that sang the City's praises out loud, chronicler Valentine Green also wrote at about the same time: 'Ancient Worcester... presents a feature in the national character of past ages not unworthy of minute contemplation... the City will not', he presumed, 'be found destitute of sufficient interest to merit attention'.

A quarter-century later, pamphleteer, farmer and journalist William Cobbett similarly gushed over what he saw, praising Worcester as 'one of the cleanest, neatest, handsomest towns I ever saw' adding that '...everything you see gives you the idea of real, solid wealth'.

That the City was viewed as a national front-runner and stylistic torch-bearer is scarcely surprising given all that appeared to be going for it, but it's especially intriguing to wonder what might have been, considering that its reputation had been won in areas not sounding the least bit familiar these days: needle-making, carpet-weaving, and clothing (*as noted by one scribe 'no town of England at this present time maketh so many cloathes [sic] yearly as this town doth'*).

At the same time, church bells cast in Worcester were renowned for their sweetness of tone. Stout, or porter, was reckoned to be the best available anywhere on account of the pure-water wells in and around the City though most notably at Henwick, and further feathers in Worcester's cap spring-up aplenty – including the distillation of gin, and manufacture of snuff, corsets, carriages, mustard, nails, churchwarden pipes, lace and inland boats, all reputations not only long-lasting, but also by every account, richly deserved.

On more familiar ground, Pigot wrote in his Worcester Directory for 1842 '...the glove trade, likewise, is very extensive here, and, from the beauty and quality of the article, is in great repute at the foreign

market: this manufacture, it is estimated, furnishes employment to between seven and eight thousand persons in the city and its vicinity, besides numbers of the industrious classes in the adjacent parishes'.

He also went on to say 'Worcester is considered the most extensive hop market in the kingdom, and the average of that article sold here annually is 20,000 pockets. A distillery and a rectifying house are establishments of magnitude, as is also one for the manufacture of British wines and vinegar. The coal, corn, malt, timber and slate trades are of considerable importance; and there are iron foundries, tanneries and roperies, and several persons engaged in the currying and leather-dressing business'.

And still that's not all...

To this can also be added the not-inconsiderable fortunes of what were in their day household names, almost up there with the Apples, Microsofts and globalised corporates and multinationals of today: the **Porcelain Works** established in 1735 and awarded Royal status; **Lea & Perrins** whose Worcestershire Sauce still graces kings' kitchens if not their tables; **McKenzie and Holland's** Railway Signals; **Thomas' Pumps; Dents Gloves; Webbs Horsehair; Hill Evans and Co**'s vinegar; **Williamsons** Tin ware, and **Hardy and Padmore**'s cast iron grates.

Worcester, it seems, not only revelled in the most favourable of reputations, but also worked itself hard enough to cling-to and even enhance its seemingly easily-won reputation with each passing decade.

But then it all veered seriously off-course...

To cram ten disastrous years into little more than a sentence, with typical laissez-faire Worcester-ness, the City was pitifully slow off the mark to grasp the vital, not-to-be-missed opportunities being tantalisingly dangled by the new phenomena of the age – the canals and, not far behind, the railway.

Instead, Worcester sat back, shrugged its shoulders, went to the pub and allowed greedier and more ambitiously far-sighted rivals to steal its thunder. Net result, inevitably, was that Worcester's loss proved to be others' gain: Birmingham, Gloucester, Redditch and Kidderminster all come to mind, and for a City whose reputation was founded on transportation – and chiefly, its greatest asset, the mighty Severn which, in the 19th century was the busiest river in Europe – it amounted to a sleepwalk into disaster, leaving a legacy of backwaterdom *(no pun intended)* for successive generations.

Fast-forward to c2013 and the City is still trying to live down the fatal errors its decision-makers opted-for at that time – in all, a bad show for a location once described as *'the most polished city in this part of the Empire'*.

Despite this, Worcester's drinking establishments continued to multiply at a cracking pace – a reflection of both the good trade its more industrious citizens were still forging and the vigour with which the citizens put their backs into earning sufficient wages: even so, the warning signs of impending disaster if the City failed to pull its collective finger out and put right its now glaring shortcomings were becoming obvious.

Now, I should point out here that neither that statement nor earlier comments are intended to convey an image of Worcester as a city of staggering inebriates, tottering topers and hopeless work-shy drunks sleeping it off in doorways: far from it. Every town, street, house and family has its boozer, and drink, as we've established was, is and always will be a major element of the essential British make-up. Indeed, given the number of pubs crammed into so comparatively small an area, the rate of drunkenness and alcoholism in Worcester is, and always was, encouragingly low.

But the signs were there for anyone who took the trouble to read them...

In 1500 Worcester had three inns. Within half a century, according to local historian Bill Gwilliam whose research into Worcester pubs was the most exhaustive up to now, the number of licensed establishments in Worcester was limited and stood at 10: **The Cardinal's Hat, The Talbot, The Bull, The White Hart, The Antelope, Hickock's House, The Bell, The Griffin, The Saracen's Head and The Lion** (sadly, neither Bill, nor his source, 'Rambler' John Noake specified which 'Lion' or where it

was. Indeed, Noake actively bemoaned the lack of information on the subject amounting to 'fragments of the history of this institution of Worcester' as mentioned previously),

There was also at the same time, according to John Noake '44 licensed ale houses' – though where he got his information from is frankly a mystery as details are so sketchy as to be virtually non-existent: hence, again, his 'fragments' observation.

The price of ale was fixed by the Corporations. In Worcester's case, '..every brewer from henceforth do make but one manner of ale and that it be good and wholesome, upon paine of diffrenchessynge *(dis-enfranchising)* after a ratt (rate) of one penny a gallon of the best and three gallons a penny of the other sorte and that no citizen or other do feche no alle at St Johns nor elsewhere above these p'ces'.

Prices were additionally changed and re-fixed by the forerunners of our Council from time to time according to the price of malt, and no brewer was allowed to trade until he had put a sign at his door whereby the official aletasters might know when and where to 'drop in' to receive their drops and fee.

The aletasters, of course, had an important role to play and their sworn oath was that they '...shall resort to every brewer's house in this City on their tunning day and there taste their ale, whether it be good and wholesome for man's body and whether they make it from time to time according to the prices fixed – so help you God'.

> *'The quaint phraseology of the times described these tasters as 'sadde and discreet persons' ordained to see that the ale be good and sweet. The aletasters laid their informations as to any defaults, weekly and the corporation, not being content with the critical acumen of their own officers became tasters themselves and laid heavy penalties on any brewer who sold his ale before the bailiffs, aldermen and cham(ber) had tasted it, seen it, and disposed it to sale after the goodness of it'*

(John Noake – 'Worcester in Olden Times')

In 1650, an item appears in the City's receipts of 12d (5p) paid for cutting down the signs of unlicensed ale-houses: '...also paid Sampson Bourne for three sealed potts (sic) to measure the alehouse keepers' potts 9s 6d (47$^1/_2$p – a huge amount at the time) and in the bye-law book 'it is desired that Mr. Maior *(mayor)* and aldermen will take some care to see the abuse of small measures and the new and evil use of cannes *(hops)* to be reformed'.

Ten years later, a by-now bashed-about post-Civil War Worcester was on its knees for having sided with the King, yet it still managed to increase the number of its drinking establishments. New ones at the time are said to have included **The King's Head** Sidbury, **The Bear** at west side of the (old) bridge, **The Ship** at the Quay, **The Crown** in Sidbury, **The Rose** in Foregate Street, and **The Prince's Arms** in The Cornmarket.

The morals of the more dissolute Worcester citizens were also under scrutiny at this time: a local law was passed forbidding any clothier, while carrying on that trade to take a licence as a victualler '... for that many dishonest work-people purloined wool and cloth from their masters and disposed of it for drink to the victuallers'. Indeed, so alarmed had the corporation become about the rising amount of drunkenness that 'tippling' was punishable by a spell in the stocks, then situated at The Cross. In 1677 a decree went out 'whereas many lazy fellers have, to the ruin of their poore wifes and children spent their time in kettle pinne alleys *(skittles)*, shovellboard tables, and such-like unlawful sports, for the pr'vencion (sic) of so great evil, an order is made on Mr. Mayor and Aldermen to fine alehouse keepers 5 shillings in all such cases'.

The games of 'tenys, bowls, close dyte (dice) and cards' were also prohibited by civic statute – and pressure was also being put on the City Fathers to outlaw bear baiting – though says John Noake 'this was not as easily set aside as some other sports'. In 1697, the City accounts showed payment of 4s 6d (22$^1/_2$p) to John Huntbach ' for a large bull ring and staple at The Cross' and John Noake additionally notes that it had been one of the mayor's duties to make sure that there were plenty of bulls and bears provided for baiting and that sometimes bulls were baited 'before the mayor's door:

> *'...in some cases the bulldogs kept by the butchers for this purpose seem to have been the terror of the town. The brutal sport of baiting, amongst others, was prohibited during the Commonwealth (1653-59) but Mr Macaulay says with much show of truth 'the Puritans hated bear baiting, not because it gave pain to the bear, but because it gave pleasure to the spectators'*

(Worcester in Olden Times')

In the same vein, it was only a few years later that the traditional Worcester sport of cock throwing was denounced...

'This inhuman practice was one of the peculiar sports of Shrove Tuesday and its origin has been attributed to a number of causes: the common tradition is that the crowing of a cock prevented our Saxon ancestors from massacring their conquerors, the Danes, on the morning of a Shrove Tuesday whilst the latter were asleep in their beds – but the more probable explanation is that the cock was originally set up as the type of our Gallic neighbours *(ie the French)* so that each rustic while aiming his stick at the unfortunate bird rejoiced in the notion that if he was not knocking down a Frenchman then it was something very like it'.

 ccording to the custom of the country, Worcester's now-mushrooming legion of landlords at the time traditionally supped with the strangers and passengers '...and if they have daughters they are also of the company to entertain the guests at the table with pleasant conceits where they drink as much as the men... when one drinks the health of any person in the company, the custom of the country does not permit you to drink more than half the cup which is filled up and presented to him or her whose health you have drunk' reports John Noake in his *'Worcester in Olden Times'*.

By 1734, Worcester's top ten inns had been singled out for use as, presumably, polling stations and/ or counting houses. These were **The Stag, The Golden Cross, The Unicorn, The Bell & Unicorn, The Bellman, The Star, The Royal Oak, The Crown, The Crispin and Crispianus, and the White Horse** – and in 1766 came the first real documentary evidence of the unusually-high proliferation of establishments in the now booming City. **The Register of Victuallers' Recognizances** laid down:

> *Esquire Aldermen of the said City and said justices of our said Lord the King assigned to keep the peace within the said City and each and every one of them acknowledged himself to owe (and) to be indebted to said George, Lord the King and his successors the sums of money respective within... if therefore the said victuallers shall keep good order under government and suffer no disorder to be committed or unlawful games used in the said house, yards, garden or backside thereto belonging during the continuance of the said licence, then the several recognisances to be void or also to remain in full force'*

The register shows every 'licensed' house, its licensee and its two guarantors attesting to the pledge of law-abidance. By 1790 these were: **Adam and Eve** (High Street); **Angel** (environs of Angel Street); **Angel de la Trompe** (Sidbury); **Angel** (St. John's); **Antelope** ('Anteloppe' - Broad Street); **Atlas** (Shambles); **Bell** (St Martins Gate); **Bellman** (Cornmarket); **Black Boy** (Leach Street), **Blackamoor's Head**, Foregate Street; **Bull and Sun**, Bull Entry off High Street; **Bush Inn**, Cripplegate; **Cardinal's Hat**, Friar Street; **Coach and Horses**, Edgar Street; **Ye Cocke**, Edgar Street and Sidbury; **Crispin (and Crispianus)**, St Johns; **Cross Keys**, Friar street; **Crown & Sceptre** ('near the Foregate); **Falcon** (Old) Sansom Street; **Fish Inn**, Friar Street; **Fleece *(or Golden Fleece)*** Angel Place; **Globe Vaults**, 1 and 2 Friar Street; **Golden Cross**, High Street; **Green Dragon**, Cornmarket; **Green Dragon**, Foregate Street; **Green Dragon** (corner of Cooken and High Street; **The Griffin**, location unknown; **Hare and Hounds** (then Horse and Groom) College Street; **Hop-Pole Inn and Royal Hotel**, Foregate St; **King's Head**, Sidbury (formerly **The Bell); King of Prussia**, Edgar Street/Frog Lane); **Lion; Mitre** (St Peters Parish) probably Lich Street; **Mitre**, High Street; **Parrot Inn**, Broad Street; **Plough**, Silver Street; **Queens Head**, High Street; **Red Lion**, Newport Street; **Ring o'Bells** (listed as St Peter's 1703); **Rose and Crown**, Foregate Street; **Salutation**, St Johns; **Saracen's Head**, Tything; **Seven Stars**, Palace Street; **Stag; Star & Garter Hotel**, Foregate Street; **Swan** High Street; **Talbot**, Sidbury; **Talbot**, The Cross; **Three Cranes**, Lich Street; **Three Cranes**, High Street; **Three Pyes**, Lich Street; **Trinity Inn; White Hart,** College St; **White Horse**, Silver St, **White Lion**, Cornmarket; **Wool Pack**, Dolday (Doldy)

By 1827 the recognizance had been upped to £30 each licensee with £10 sureties given by two friends or colleagues,

> *'...on the conditions (the victuallers) shall keep the true assize in uttering and selling bread and other victuals, beer, ale and other liquors in his or her or their house and shall not fraudulently dilute or adulterate the same and shall not use in selling thereof any Pots or other measures than as of the full size and shall not willingly or knowingly permit drinking or tippling nor get drunk in his or her or their house or other properties or*

their premises or will suffer any gaming with cards, draughts, dice, bagatelle or any other sedentary games at his, her or other house or any of the outhouses or appurtenancies or tenements thereto belonging by journeymen, labourers, servants or apprentices nor knowingly introduce, permit or suffer any bull, bear or badger baiting, cock fighting, or other such sport or amusement in any part of his her, her or their premises nor shall knowingly or designedly and with a view to harbour and entertain such permit or suffer Men or Women of notoriously bad Fame or dysolute boys and girls to assemble and meet together in his or her or their houses or any of the premises thereto belonging and shall keep open his or her or their house or premises or suffer and drinking or tippling in any part of his or her or their premises during the usual hours of Divine Service on Sundays nor shall keep open his or her or their premises during late hours of the night or early in the morning for any other purpose than the reception of travellers but do keep good rule and order therein according to the purport of a licence granted for selling ale, beer and other (by?) refusal in the said House and Premises for a whole year occurring on the 4th day of October next then that recognizance to be void or else to remain in full force'

Within just a few years, the City's population ('as taken by Mr. Young') amounted to 11,001. With around 126 licensed drinking establishments, the ratio per head of population equated to one to 87.3 men, women and children. At that time, Worcester gazetteer, Grundy adds the following to the list earlier published by Pigot:

Angel, Silver street; **Bell Inn**, Angel Street; **Bell Hotel** Broad Street; **Bell Inn**, St. John's; **Black Swan**, Quay street; **Bleeding Heart** Sanfom Street; **Brewers Arms** 12 Crofs; **Bridge Inn**, Bridge street; **Britannia**, Doldy; **Bull's Head**, High street; **Bush Tavern; Carpenter's Arms** 4 Doldy; **City Arms**, Church street; **Coach & Horses**, Shambles; **Coach & Horses**, Tything; **Coach and Mares** 50 Doldy; **Cock**, Copenhagen street; **Cock**, Cripplegate; **Cock & Cross** St Johns; **Cross Keys**, Sidbury; **Cross Keys**, Trinity; **Crown Inn**, Broad street; **Crown** 'Wich Road (Droitwich Road); **Crown**, Pump street; **Crown** St Johns; **Crown and Anchor,** Henwick; **Crown & Anchor,** Silver street; **Dog and Duck**, Henwick Hill; **Dolphin**, Queen Street; **Dolphin**, Copenhagen Street; **Dragoon**, Birdport; **Dun Cow** All Hallows Well; **Ewe and Lamb**, Angel st.; **Fish**, High Timber street; **George Inn,** The Tything; **Golden Lion,** High street; **Green Dragon**, Newport street; **Green Man and Still,** Tything; **Greyhound; Hand and Sheers,** Fish Street; **Hen and Chickens,** Merry Vale; **Holly Bush**, Foregate; **Horn Tavern,** Angel St.; **Horse and Jockey**, Quay street; **Horse and Jockey**, Pump Street; **King's Head**, St. John's; **Kings Head**, High Street; **Lamb**, Birdport; **Leopard**, Broad street; **Marquis of Granby**, Cooken Street; **Mason's Arms**, Frog Lane; **Merry Fellow; Mugg (or Mugg) House**, Hylton St.; **Pack Horse**, Garden Market (St Nicholas Street); **Peacock** Trinity; **Pewterer's Arms; Pheasant,** New street; **Plume of Feathers,** Sansom Street; **Punch Bowl**, College St.; **Queen's Head**, Tything; **Red Lion**, Sidbury; **Rein-deer Inn**, Mealcheapen street; **Rising Sun**, Cripplegate; **Rising Sun** Powick's Lane; **Rodney**, Cornmarket; **Seven Stars**, New Street; **Severn Galley**, Newport Street; **Severn Trow**, Hylton St.; **Shakespeare (Shakespear)** Angel street; **Ship (fhip)** Cooken Street; **Spread Eagle** Dolday; **Swan,** New Street (Swan with Two Necks/Nicks); **Swan** Powick's Lane; **Swan**, St. John's; **Talbot**, Tything; **Unicorn Inn**, Broad street; *Wheat Sheaf,* Corn Market; *Wheat Sheaf,* Henwick; *Wheat Sheaf,* Sidbury; *White Horse* Cripplegate.

(Note: spelling and the use of capitals to denote proper names were both very much hit-and-miss affairs *at the time and relied on the whims of the ledger clerk so if a word appears mis-spelled or 'Street' is uncapitalised that is how it appeared in the register)*

In 1835 new 'wards' were created to cope with monitoring and overseeing the rapidly-expanding City – which, by 1843 had taken on a familiar look:

Saint Helens: *(a newly-created ward emerging from what had been High ward and part of St Andrews):* Bulls Head, Golden Lion, Mouth of the Nile, Duke of York, Old Mitre, Crown, Plumbers Arms, Horse and Jockey, Old Crown, Coach and Horses, Cross Keys, Archangel

Saint Swithin: Butchers Arms, Sun Tavern, City Arms, New Inn, Rising Sun, Bakers Arms.

All Saints: Crown, Union, Bell, Leopard, Falcon, Hen and Chickens, Hole in the Wall, Old Farriers Arms, Bridge, Boars Head, Green Dragon, Britannia, Plasterers Arms, Sow and Pigs, Woolpack, Duke of York, Hope and Anchor, Herefordshire House, Ten Bells, Well Sinkers Arms.

Saint Andrew: Dolphin, Ship, Glo'ster Arms, Plume of Feathers, Cock, Queen Caroline, Wherry, Glovers Arms, Lord Nelson, Painters Arms, Duke of Wellington, Old Severn Trow

St Clement: Severn Trow, Bear, Apple Tree, Rising Sun, Cock, Dog & Duck, Porto Bello, Mug House, Wheat Sheaf, Bush

St Martin: Rein Deer, Wheatsheaf, Angel, White Horse, Boat, Black Horse, Navigation, Swan, Pheasant, Old Greyhound, New Greyhound, Fish, Crown & Anchor, Union, Shades, New Inn

Extraparochial: Union, Royal Oak

Saint Nicholas: Bird in Hand, Ewe and Lamb, Shakespear (sic), Fountain, Waggon & Horses, Farriers Arms, Three Tuns, Horn & Trumpet, Star & Garter, Hop Market, Dog & Duck, Golden Heart, Pack Horse.

St Peter the Great: Waterloo, Angel, Kings Head, Red Lion, Masons Arms, Chequers, Shades, Bowling Green, Albion, Coventry Arms, Barley Mow, Wheatsheaf, Fountain, Fish

St John in Bedwardine: Angel, Bell, Kings Head, Swan, Star

St Michael in Bedwardine: Punchbowl, Hare & Hounds, White Hart, Talbot, Black Boy

Claines: Grandstand, Talbot, White Lion,

Tything of Whitstones: Coach & Horses, Lamb & Flag, Green Man, George & Dragon, Saracens head, Queens Head, York House.

And then in just a few remarkably explosive years following the relaxation in the rules dictating just who could open an ale-house and where – essentially, anybody who could lay their hand on 2 guineas (£2.10p), the tally had risen to include:

The Globe and **Market Tavern** (St. Helens ward); **New Market Inn** and **Berkeley Arms** (Saint Swithin); **Ewe & Lamb, Red Lion, Queens Arms** (Saint Andrews); **Boat House and Royal George** (Saint Clement); **Ram, Railway Hotel, Railway Express, Park Tavern, Beauchamp Arms, Alma** (Saint Martin); **Five Ways, Paul Pry and Yorkshire House** (Saint Martins); **Waterloo, King William, Park Street Tavern** (Saint Peter the Great): **Herefordshire House** (St John in Bedwardine); **Railway**

19th century engraving of Worcester (CCMH/CFOW)

Refreshment Rooms (Foregate Street), **Elephant & Castle, Rainbow and Swan** (Claines); **Carpenters Arms, Moors Ketch** (Tything of Whitstones); **Navigation, Beehive, Crown, and Crispin** (Saint Martin).

The result is that by now there was some 200 pubs serving a population of around 20,000 – one per hundred head of population: small wonder rumours began to circulate about Worcester's fondness for its pubs, and already a clearly recognised pattern had emerged.

What's more, some of those named above are still around today.

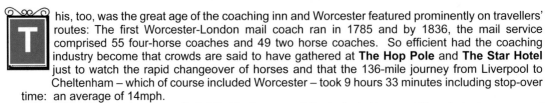 his, too, was the great age of the coaching inn and Worcester featured prominently on travellers' routes: The first Worcester-London mail coach ran in 1785 and by 1836, the mail service comprised 55 four-horse coaches and 49 two horse coaches. So efficient had the coaching industry become that crowds are said to have gathered at **The Hop Pole** and **The Star Hotel** just to watch the rapid changeover of horses and that the 136-mile journey from Liverpool to Cheltenham – which of course included Worcester – took 9 hours 33 minutes including stop-over time: an average of 14mph.

In 1839, a Worcester wag called J.R. Martin penned the ballads Four and Twenty Innkeepers and Four and Twenty Beer Houses, the first of which is printed on the inside covers of this book.

Four and twenty beer houses all in a row

There's the new Lamb and Flag by Griffin Beaufy White
Whose Cock and Hen club is held every Monday night
And Williams at The Moors Ketch, I dare say
He wishes he could 'ketch' more every single day.

Then in the Butts you'll see The Fleece
And close by The Paul Pry
Where you'll get some home-brewed
Just step in and you'll not intrude

If you go to The Market Tavern you'll have no cause to murmur
For mine host is Richard Matthews, the turner.
At The King William there's Thomas Nash
Some say he's saved up lots of cash

Then there's the Blackbird and The Blue Bell
And The Red Cow and The White Lion
And The Red Lion and The Rose and Crown
And a little hundred more somewhere in the town

In-and-out, round-about, up-and-down below
These are the Worcester beer houses
So drink, sing and be merry

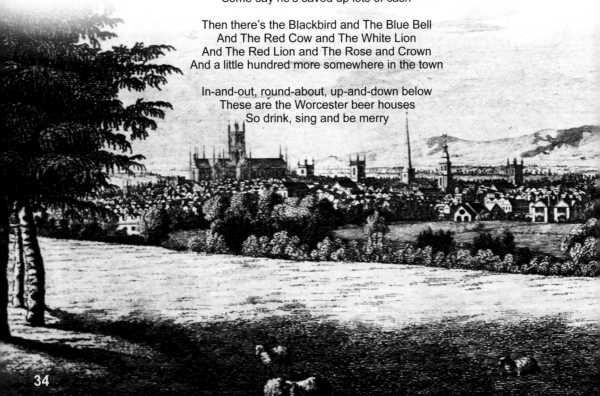

Worcester's population virtually tripled over the next century: from 13,000 in 1799 to 46,000 in 1900. To gauge the acute impact of this explosive amount of growth, it's interesting to note that the following half century (1900-1950) saw virtually no change in the population. It is also perhaps a reflection of Worcester's underlying economic fragility that while the city sported many of the trappings associated with the prosperity of the period, its size at the beginning of the 19th century was more or less the same as it had been 400 years before yet with a vastly bigger population living in increasingly squalid conditions.

Indeed, contemporary reports paint a less-than-flattering picture of the true state of apparently genteel and well-heeled Worcester. In fact, its health and well-being left much to be desired:

...by the end of the 18th century, population growth was starting to become a problem for public health as space was taken up by slums. People came to (Worcester) to find work and often worked in unhealthy factories and lived in unsanitary conditions. Housing conditions were poor and cramped, and this only worsened during (the next century). Worcester, in common with most other locations in the mid 1800s had been hit by cholera outbreaks – the worst being the densely populated areas around St Andrews and the so-called 'Pinch' off Tybridge Street so called on account of its triangular or 'pinched' shape... the awful conditions people were living in, with open cess pools and overcrowded graveyards resulting in decaying remains seeping through the walls of housing, with the fumes reported to have tarnished candlesticks! Each house would have been shared by several different families, who would have taken their water from the nearby River Severn. The rest of Worcester's poor lived in housing conditions that were little better. They lived in courts containing five to twenty houses, which had no efficient drainage, two privies the contents of which were received into a large open cesspool. The courts were also surrounded by stables and pigsties, much to the complaint of the authorities. This then included over 2000 houses, 769 privies and 406 open cesspools. In Worcester, the mortality rate was so high (26.5 deaths per 1000, the average was about 15 per 1000) that the local authorities were forced to act.

(Worcester Cico Parks Movement.
More: http://www.worcester.gov.uk/index.php?id=1907)

The great perception of the period – certainly among the more genteel classes – was that the increasing proliferation of lower class alehouses was the root cause of all the nation's evils: Godlessness, gambling, and rampant promiscuity, aside from the more obvious effects of drinking in establishments largely untrammelled by recognised opening hours.

Throughout the City, opening time was entirely at the whim of the licensee and his customers, and could be anything up to, and even in excess of, 20 hours a day.

The question all this raises, of course, is did this unusually high numbers of alehouses, taverns and inns come about *as a result of* Worcester's affluence at the time, or was it the high numbers of alehouses, taverns and inns that created the air of affluence *in the first place*?

Engraving of the City from the north east
(CCMH/CFOW)

Similarly, it stands the asking: was it the sheer number and attraction of the alehouses, taverns and inns that created what's still viewed as the typical Worcester character – laid-back, laissez-faire, largely easy-going and more than a little complacent, an attitude attested by the comparatively few 'greats' that the City has produced despite its size, wealth and importance – or was it the character that created the demand for the sheer number and bonhomie of the alehouses, taverns and inns?

They're both arguments that are eminently worth pursuing – though perhaps at a later stage: suffice to say, Worcester and pubs were pretty much made for each other and when you talk of one, talk of the other isn't far behind.

It's not for nothing either, that poet, playwright, actor, impresario, theatre owner, teacher, lawyer, bard and keen boozer William Shakespeare – who would almost certainly have had dealings in Worcester, would undoubtedly have been a visitor to some of the previously-named inns, and whose marriage certificate still rests here – memorably scribed: '...a quart of ale is a dish for a king' (A Winter's Tale').

As in most towns and cities, cock- and to a lesser degree, dog-fighting were not uncommon events until they were rightly outlawed, and after 1766 Worcester publicans had to sign an undertaking on penalty of disbarment that they would not indulge in bull, bear or badger baiting or cock fighting on their premises.

The move must have hit premises such as **The Pheasant** in New Street particularly hard because cock-fighting had long been a popular pastime here, hosting 'a main of cocks': on one memorable occasion a four-day match took place here between the gentlemen of Worcestershire and the gentlemen of Gloucestershire involving 41 cock fights with a purse of £10 per fight and 200 guineas (£224) waged on the prime contenders. It's not recorded who won, but the implication is that it would have been the gentlemen of Worcestershire because a re-match not long after was held at **The Masons Arms** in Frog Lane (Severn Street) where a cock-fighting ring had been specially set up *(the thinking being that the miffed gentlemen of Goucestershire wold have demanded a re-match and the wily Worcestershire gents would in return have demanded it was on home turf – or so I'd like to think.)*

That the City was a blood-thirsty place is also attested-to by contemporary newspaper reports telling of at least two 'winner takes all' prize fights between a lion and, on both occasions, six mastiffs at £100 a time. Held on Talbot Meadow, behind **The Talbot** in The Tything – the customary pitch of travelling wild-beast shows, especially that of Wombwell's Menagerie – it's said the lion won on both occasions.

It's reported that hundreds of apparently genteel Worcester folk flocked to watch the gory spectacle on both occasions...

ut what were the pubs of the time actually like?

The City is fortunate in still having some pubs around that have played their part in history, and a look inside **The Cardinal's Hat** or **The Swan with Two Nicks** or **The Pheasant** or the recently re-born **King Charles** provides a fair illustration even today.

Probably short of something better to do, on 22nd May this year (2013) I less than half-seriously *(a lot less than half!)* described City archaeologists as 'all of a tizz' over a document found that very morning outlining some scribe's *(unnamed, but few were in any doubts whose)* visit to six of the remaining ancient hostelries, starting off along this historic stretch...

22nd of ye Merrie monthe of May: Yea verily didst venture into six fayre hostelries of ye olde citie this verie day and partooke of seven pyntes of ye foaming ayle much favoured by ye citizens faithful. Atte 1.45 of ye clocke in ye afterlunch, didst first looke inne at Ye Cardinals Hat in Ye streete of ye Friar, latterly much trumpeted in ye presse. Therein, ye serving wench, tho' comely, didst prove harde worke, but atte last didst pull for me a pinte of Farmers Dark Ale seeming from ye brewerie callest Attwoods from ye distant kingdome of Hartlebury. Atte £3.10 didst think itte a bitte steep but notte as steepe as some beeres from ye far-off land of ye spaniels atte £4.50 nowe lesse. Methinks bloodye notte! Onelie one other customer atte ye same tyme and he a cheerless varlet with ne'er a smile for ye tireless scrybe. Ten and five minutes after ye clocke didst chime ye hour of two, entereth Ye Pheasant inne ye streete callest Newe tho dost looke olde and runneth-down to mee thees dayes. Therein, didst chatte to ye landlord Master David of ye family Ranford (late of Countie Halle) and serving wench Mistresse Amy over a pynte of Blonde Bombshell brewed by ye master Snaith in ye northerlie kingdom of ye White Rose. Atte £2.95 twas barely a snippe, butte twas kwite tastie and ye companie didst prove mirthful. Half o' ye hour later, didst then pass ye shoppe of ye newe-fangled harpsichords, dulcimers and string-ed lutes to Ye Swan with Two Nicks, wherein didst parlaye long to ye bar Master (methinks he didst quote 'manager', butte I knowe notte of this worde) Andie, a sounde sidekicke methought.

Whilst therein, a beere callest Kaleidoscope from ye brewerie of St George in Callowe Ende didst catch myne eye that twinkleth atte the sounde of £1.85 – I kiddest thou notte, £1.85 yea verily! Ande Andie sayeth that all ye reele ayles doth command ye pryce of £1.85 alle ye daye, alle ye days of ye weeke wich your merry scrybe didst finde muche to his liking – notte leaste as they dost include Ye Malvern Hills Black Pear ande moore from ye breweries Saint George ande Beowulf. For sure, wouldst venture therein agayne – nexte tyme to fille mine bootes noe lesse! 3.35 of ye clocke, didst then fynde your scrybe – bye nowe feeling'st inne fine fettle – atte ye syne of King Charles, latterly a house that didst serve ye vittles of ye finest qualitie, butte be'est nowe transform-ed into a bar serving ye reele ayles sutch as Sadlers and a newe one onne mee, Craddocks (Craddock beingst ye name of ye landlords, brothers twain bye all accountes). Forsooth, ye beere calledst Hop Bomb be'est a goodly brewe that didst tickle myne olde tastebuddes nowe end. Atte 4 of ye clocke didst seemingly take leeve of mine senses ande stepp-ed into another centurie whenne didst venture into Ye Postal Order of ye Wetherspoon fayme cause did'st by thenne need to fynde a privy like bloodie quick! There didst partake of a pynte of Woods Shropshire Hills Beauty, notte atte alle a bad pynte with taystes of hoppes and ye fruits, ande notte a badde pryce neether: £2.15. Indeede, was even talked into another by Celtish Chris – hee of ye whyte hayre from ye Isle that callest itself Emerald, forsooth! Then didst putte behind me the sites and soundes of ye faithful Citie and didst venture – nay, atte tymes, didst stagger – to Ye Olde Talbot in Ye Cythinge. Ande so atte five and twenty minutes after the hour of five did'st order a pynte of Tim Taylors Landlord beere, a bitte steepe at £2.99 methought ande served by an oafish ladde who smilesdst notte and didst notte even utter 'thank thou' after trousering mine ackers. Thus itte was that your merrie scrybe (for by thenne hee was, and passt caring forsooth) tottereth home, kwite happy with ye proceedings of ye afterlunch. Ande it came to pass that Ye Mistress Backenforth – for she it was that greeteth your cheersome scrybe atte fifteen minutes after the hour of six when atte laste he reached his humble abode on Ye Blanquettes – sayeth 'whatte bloodie tyme dost thou calle this?' with a look that withereth the strongest of men. Ande so, the ende to a perfeckte day!

In more sober frame of mind...

Most would have been a single room, sparsely furnished, often at the front of an otherwise unremarkable house in which the family lived upstairs. Light was by smoking candle or tallow, ambient (room) heat would have been supplemented by a log fire, and the only facilities would have been a bar, perhaps a few tables and the minimum seating arrangements as most drinkers, hardier than today's, would have been expected to stand.

They would also have been very smelly: stabling for horses may have been provided and many publicans also had their own piggeries in the yard. Beer was brewed on the premises – adding to what must have been a powerfully pungent whiff already – out in the backyard *(or backside as legal documents of the time indicate)* often in an out-house or for the better-off, a purpose-built brew house. The family dogs and cats – vital for keeping down the number of rats inevitably attracted to such pungent locations – would have been free to roam. The beer and the ale was served by gravity dispense – the simple device of holding a jug or pot under the tap of a cask and letting the beer flow out, and with few exceptions, it's an art that's lost – not least as the cask, and the beer in it, is at constant room temperature which causes it to go off quicker than if it's slightly chilled. The beer engine, allowing beer to be pumped up what would originally have been brass tubes didn't become a regular feature of pubs until the late 1880s. There'd also have been spittoons of course, and sawdust on the floor - perhaps to mop-up the outpourings of the less experienced spitters who'd missed their target.

And there was smoke – lots of it: aside from the smoke from the fire and the candles and tallows that would have stained the walls and ceilings with an all-over dingy tan film, tobacco was also par for the course for all who could afford it and Worcester women are said to have taken to the weed every bit as much as the men.

Drinking vessels would have been pewter or porcelain 'cups' and even until comparatively recently the Worcestershire habit of referring to even a modern-day glass mug as 'cup' was common.

Then – less so now with a marked shift in drinking patterns, old habits died hard in the old inns: regulars had their own seat in which they'd grow old. It was then passed on to the sons. Fathers and sons stuck to the same brew and would generally frequent only those houses where it was sold. On entry, every regular would immediately be presented with his own tankard and pipe, both kept religiously behind the bar for his own exclusive use. In later years, Worcester was on the north-south dividing line whereby those north of the line preferred the straight-sided 'schooner' (later 'sleever' as it resembled the starched over-cuffs favoured by clerks to keep their sleeves clean during long hours of ledger-scribing) while those south of the line preferred the barrel-shaped handled mugs considered sissy by the hardened northerners.

Even up to the mid 1960s Worcester drinkers were evenly divided in their preference of drinking vessel until the breweries played their hand and generally opted for the cheaper, more easily replaced straight-sided glasses.

It was after the Defence of the Realm Act of 1916 that the ritual of putting pubs' clocks forward 10 minutes and also placing a towel over beer taps –alongside, perhaps, the installation of a brass bell to signify 'Time Gentlemen Please' came about.

Then there was the vast number of different games you could have played in any one of a hundreds of pubs. Al fresco games like bowls and croquet were well also catered for and later the same games you'd find elsewhere – darts, skittles and card games were all part of the scene, although there were some games that Worcester took to more so than many of its neighbours and thus adopted its own variations of the same which were sometimes at odds with other towns. Crib was always a great favourite – but played in Worcester with five cards instead of six which is cribbage, and there's the difference.

Quoits, the art of throwing a rubber ring over a metal spike, was a more prevalent pub game here than anywhere else and was a particularly hotly-contested sport in Worcester bars: even up to the 1970s, **The Vauxhall** had a masterful quoits team *(but then all their teams were masterful)* and even as recently as the late 1980s you'd see a quoit board gathering dust in a pub corner somewhere but rarely with any takers: **The Barbourne** in New Bank Street still had its quoit board in the bar up to the mid 1990s. The City even had a three-times English Quoits Champion and eight times national team player locally born Walter Jones, who was also an international bowls player, representing England in the side that toured South Africa in 1938. Later licensee of **The New Inn** in George Street and **The Berwick Arms**, he was also instrumental in setting up Worcester Bowling Club.

Tip-it, a variation of spoof was another Worcester favourite involving a coin, usually a halfpenny, and played by teams of two or three... 'Whoever was in the middle was 'the worker', all the teams' hands would be under the table and the worker would tap the table with the coin then place into one of the hands and say 'up' when he was ready. All hands would then be on the table and the opposing team would have to guess which hand. If you touched a hand and said tip it straightaway it was worth 2 points. If you took the hands away one at a time and guessed correctly it was worth one point. If you dropped the coin on the floor the first team to shout 'piece' claimed the coin!' *(quoted by Wayne Frost on the Worcester Pubs Then and Now website. https://www.facebook.com/groups/worcesterpubsthenandnow)*

"It was a great game with lots of cheating" he said and it was a common feature in any one of several hundred Worcester pubs.

Many another pub featured table skittles – the art of swinging a tethered wooden ball at a formation of pegs. Shove ha'ppeny was another sport Worcester folk excelled in, tapping a ha'penny or similar disc (note the spelling, unlike the current Yankified 'disk') with the fleshy part of the hand to slide it up a smooth board marked with graduating lines: the first to 'clear' all twenty rows by sliding his ha'penny within each number's row without touching the demarcation lines was declared the winner. Another impromptu variation thereof was of throwing a coin or flicking a beer mat or cigarette card (in the 1920s and 30s many brands gave away cards depicting dog breeds, cars or film and sports stars as part of their early marketing strategies) underarm at the fireplace, the winner being the one whose coin/mat/ cigarette card landed nearest the hearth. As such, he collected all: '...so the more that played the more the winnings and the better you were at it, the bigger the value of the coin you tossed to tempt the others to try and win more' *(Ian Maysey on the Worcester Pubs Then and Now website)*

Even until the mid1970s Worcester had several Phat leagues and the City was recognised as a heartland for the game, teams regularly competing in hotly-contested leagues long after its popularity had fizzled out elsewhere. A trick-taking partnership card game similar to whist but with Worcester variations, its aim was '...to score points by winning tricks containing valuable cards which may give an immediate score to the team that wins the trick. Further points are pegged after the end of the play by the team that has collected more than half of the 'muck' in their tricks. There are 88 points in each deal – 80 phat plus 8 for the muck' *(Wikipedia)*

Still, as we've already established, every pub is different, each one's essential spirit was conclusively shaped by the character of those that ran it and those that frequented it. Thus, sadly, there's no way of knowing for sure precisely what **The Cardinals Hat** was actually like on September 2nd 1651 when an army of Scots was camped just out of town *(actually on Pitchcroft)* and King Charles II and his merry band of Roundheads were in town knowing they were going to have the scrap of their lifetimes the next morning. Or what the mood was like in **The Golden Cross** or the nearby **Golden Lion** the day Wellington gave Napoleon the what-for at Waterloo. There's unlikely to be anyone around who could tell you how the conversation went in **The Royal Exchange** or **The Nelson** on Armistice Day 1918, though a few souls will be able to describe the no doubt delirious goings-on in **The Star Tap** or The **Shakespeare** on VE Night. On the other hand, search in the right quarters and you will definitely come across a few who can recall **The Pheasant** or **The Berwick** or **The Old Greyhound** or **The Swan with two Nicks** say, or either of the **Talbots** on that wet June Coronation night in 1953. And possibly you yourself might recall slotting a threepenny joey into the jukebox in **The Eagle Vaults, The Horn and Trumpet, The Ewe and Lamb** or even the brand new **Glovers Needle** or **Punchbowl** to hear the latest tinny musical sensation '*She Loves You Yeah Yeah Yeah-h-h-h-h*'.

it wouldn't take much by way of imagination to picture any of the above events by visiting the actual locations. Many of them are still there: try it – you'll find it a hugely rewarding experience: fashions might have changed out of all recognition but pubs simply didn't change that much, a comment that holds true right up to the final quarter of the 20th century when market forces – not all of them to the better good of the pub, the publican or the pub-going public – paved the way ahead for all manner of changes **(See '...and that's when it all went pear-shaped' starting on page 414)**

 arking back to the 'contend-uh' references made earlier in this chapter *(by which, of course, no offence is intended by the comment '...instead of just a bum'. I'd like to point out that Worcester is my town and I'm fiercely proud of it and of being a true born-and-bred Worcesterite. Thus, if I say it, it's OK, but if some foreigner says it, that's a different issue altogether, and tantamount to blasphemy).*

So what of the tales and legends that have grown up about Worcester's pubs over the centuries – and how much credence can be placed on them?

So far as I can tell, the biggest one of all is a non-starter and the nearest I can get to the magic 'pub-for-each-day-of-the-year' is 238 pubs between 1875 and 1925 – a not unimpressive tally by any stretch of the imagination but not cutting the mustard by a long chalk *(note: mixed metaphors, Bob. B-minus).*

On the most sobering note of all, you might just care to reflect on the fact that today it can just about stretch to 100 with the inclusion of 'distant' locations such as Fernhill Heath, Rushwick and Kempsey. As is evidenced throughout this book, the number of active pubs in Worcester today (2013) is roughly the same as it was in 1775 – and that's the most sobering thought of all, *not least as the population of Worcester is seven times more now than then.*

So while it's pretty much established beyond a reasonable doubt that Worcester has never at any one time had the distinction – or luxury, come to that – of a pub for every day of the year, there's no questioning that the City is right up there with the Big Hitters when it comes to having more pubs per head of population than anywhere else.

It's interesting to note that Beeston in Nottinghamshire currently views itself as a front-runner in that particular category – which, of course, includes minors under the legal drinking age: its total is 1:1167 people. *(Source: Pubs.org.uk).* Typically, Worcester is under-selling itself yet again as the tally today indicates around 100,000 people for 1000 pubs. 1:1000

It's my belief that those charged with promoting the City to a waiting world at large would do well to consider focusing on Worcester's rich legacy of still-extant pubs as a tourist attraction in its own right. That said, I maintain Worcester continues to do itself a dis-service both by those tasked with promoting the City signally failing to do their bit in promoting the pubs in terms of history, quality and quantity and also on the part of the publicans and breweries supporting the tourist promoters' endeavours.

Even as far back as September 1987, I wrote **(The Trumpet)**

'...there's growing concern that the County's push to attract more tourists will fizzle-out without a whimper. As other tourist attractions go to town wooing visitors, real fears have been expressed that the City will find itself cold-shouldered because of lack of pubs in shopping and tourist areas – and an unwelcoming attitude in many remaining hostelries. Tourist chiefs are getting jumpy over the prospect of winning tourists through high-interest attractions like the Commandery, Porcelain and cathedral, only to lose them again through not offering traditional English pie and a pint lunches. It's

a view shared by City leaders: as Leader George Randall put it this week 'I'm worried we're losing so many pubs. Don't fool yourself into thinking that tourists will still come – they won't, especially if – when – word gets around that you can't get a drink or pub lunch in Worcester. If we're not careful, we're going to find ourselves in a wanting situation'. And warning bells have also been sounded in several quarters over the City centre's vanishing pubs, with not one pub now open in the tourist centres of High Street, Shambles, Bridge Street and The Foregate. Twenty four pubs closed down in the City's tourist-orientated heart between 1930 and 1965 when some 49 pubs called 'time' for the last time, and the last few years have seen the graveyard grow for many more City centre pubs: Hollybush (to be a restaurant); Pack Horse (steak bar); Golden Lion (due to be shops and wine bar); Western Bar (entertainment arcade); Ewe and Lamb (chip shop); Old Chapel (derelict); and Reindeer (empty – awaiting a plan to open up the courtyard into a shopping mall). Meanwhile, the Long Stop is also threatened in the Centro shake-up costing £2 million but with no provision for a pub, and the Old Greyhound is also reckoned to be near its end'.

Another area the City triumphs in – and thus might seriously consider a concerted tourism push – is in the number of 'haunted' pubs. As a journalist both locally and nationally as well as tame scribe for at least three breweries, it was always easy to invent a ghost when in doubt. I confess to having done so on many an occasion and even cobbled together trick photographs in both pre- and post-Photoshop days for which I'm still haunted *(no pun intended – oh, I don't know though)* by the memory of it.

In a blog I wrote in April 2012 on some of the City's classic ghosts: I referred to one that apparently spooked innocents next door to **The Vulcan**:

> '...it's a little known fact that the City is home to some classic ghosts. I mentioned that fact to old Sam in **The Exchange** the other day when I pointed out that I'd been doing some research into the subject. "Oooh, Bobby, you goo careful now" he shot back, his eyes darting all around as though somebody was about to creep up behind him and yell 'boo!' in his ear'ole. " 'Ee doan wanna goo a-messin' round along o' them spirits. Anyfink can 'aaappen an prob'ly ull". I tried not to laugh but it wasn't easy. Clearly concerned for my future existence and well-being, he advised me to leave well alone and write 'summink else'. It was then he told me that as a lad growing up in The Blockhouse – 'close by th'old Vulcan-as-wuz' as he put it – the people next door had been so troubled by a ghost that they'd called on the vicar of St Pauls just over the road to conduct a special ceremony… "Our dad banged on 'is door an' told 'im, 'padre, we wants you ter come round at the crack o' midnight and circumcise that poltergeist afore 'ee kills some bugger". I nearly choked on me beer'.

http://newsmagbobsblog.wordpress.com/2012/04/page/2)

Even so, and despite more than dollop of scepticism, there are just too many spectral coincidences to dismiss the entire concept as out-of-hand and just too fanciful for words...

No, I've never seen a ghost and the closest experience to ever having done so was in the bar of the **Great Western Hotel** when one Boxing Night I watched a glass move completely independently a good foot across a table: nor was I the only one to witness this extraordinary occurrence. I also had a strange experience in **The Coach and Horses in the Tything** when I'm sure somebody, or something was trying to attract my attention by knocking the wall next to me even though not a soul was there. For all that, tales of Fred at the **Barley Mow**, Sid at the Five Ways; the girl with her hair on fire at the **Cardinal's Hat**; the misogynistic being that haunts the **White Hart** (now the **Hand in Glove**); the unfortunate young barman at **The Vine**; the friendly cavalier at The **Kings Head**; unexplained goings-on at the **Welcome Inn** *(formerly the Garibaldi)*; Chris Watts' recollections of the **Albion** and others at locations including **The Old Talbot** (inevitably); **The Firefly, The Imperial, The Paul Pry, The Ketch, The Cricketers, The Slug'n'Lettuce, The King Charles** and even the locations of former pubs such as **The Coach and Horses** in the Shambles. Odd though, so far as I can tell, the only pub on the west side of the river laying claim to a ghost is **The Bell** – but that when a troop of scouts spent the night there trying to flush him or her out, he or she went all coy and failed to materialise.

Another title that Worcester could very easily romp home with is – or at least *would have been* – 'The City with the Highest Number of Pubs Standing Next Door to Each Other'. You've only got to look at **The King Charles/Swan with Two Nicks (New Street); Royal Exchange/Bar12 Cornmarket);** and previously **Cardinals Hat/Globe** (Friar Street); **Old/New Greyhound** (New Street); **Ship/Gloster Arms** (Copenhagen St) and many more in Newport Street, Dolday and the historic thoroughfares around Lich Street and Cooken (Copenhagen) Street.

Now while we as a City appreciate the worth of our pubs, it has to be said that we native Worcester-ites also tend to be hyper-critical of what's on our own doorstep. Curiously, it's also a sobering observation that 'outsiders' would appear to appreciate Worcester's pubs more than Worcester folk do. These are comments I make from my own experience of a) visiting hundreds of other English towns and cities over several decades as a newspaperman and b) welcoming others of like mind to my town – *and every time that happened they pointed out something about one or another Worcester pub that I hadn't really appreciated until then!*

The same principle can equally be applied to the cathedral and to the nearby Malvern Hills, both objects of joy and wonderment to visitors, yet we all know people who have lived in Worcester all their lives and never visited either.

Another accolade that's indisputable is that the City has always had *(and still enjoys)* the reputation of being the scene of some the best pub crawls in the Midlands: indeed, anywhere....

The 'hard' evidence that Worcester's now-dwindling crop of pubs is the envy of outsiders is attested-to by the number of visiting pub-crawlers, some of which will travel 130 miles for the privilege *(of which more in a minute)* and hen- and stag-night revellers from all points north south, east and west, and as I said earlier, those charged with promoting the City to a waiting world at large would do well to consider focusing on Worcester's rich legacy of still-extant pubs as a tourist 'draw' in its own right.

In the 1930s, the great test of many a young man's manhood was the famous Cross to Shrub Hill run about which it was said that if you could drink half a pint in every pub you passed and were still sufficiently lucid to be able to ask for your ticket (destination unspecified but it's unlikely to be material anyway) then you could indeed call yourself one of the lads.

The route would have taken you into *(in order)*: **The Hollybush (1), The Packhorse (2), The Dog and Duck (3), The Imperial (4), The Old Yorkshire House (5), The Old Falcon (6) The Union (7), The Crown and Anchor (8), The Boat (9), Express (10), The Black Horse (11), The Alma (12), The Turks Head (13), The Swan (14), The Navigation (15), Lansdowne (16), The West Midlands Arms (17)** then a small chance to clear your head, not to mention to cling to Heenan and Froude's factory

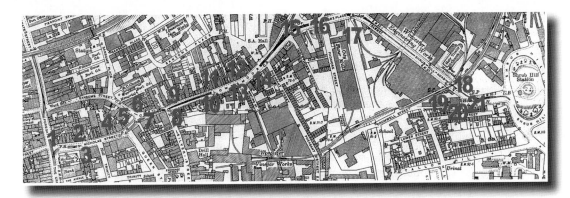

walls, clear to the station where you were faced with a rash of pubs all within a few yards of each other: **Great Western (18), Railway (19), Ram (20) and The Prince of Wales** – total of 21 pubs, volume drunk? $11^{1}/_{2}$ pints.

Sobering to note that today you could perform that self-same feat along the same route by car and still not be too far adrift of being the right side of the drink-drive laws.

A recent trawl on the internet also threw-up *(under the circumstances, no apologies for the use of that particular phrase)* a former Worcester lad called Gus whose memories of Blockhouse pub crawls of little over half a century ago paint an illuminating scene of the area.

One such took place on February 23rd 1958 and the running order was:

Liverpool Vaults, Shambles *(Spreckleys)*; **Freemasons Arms**, Carden Street *(Atkinsons)*; **Oddfellows Arms**, Carden Street *(Spreckleys)*; **Bricklayers Arms**, Park Street *(Banks's)*; **Park Tavern**, Little Park Street *(Flowers)*; **King William**, St Pauls Street *(Hunt Edmunds)*; **Vulcan**, St Pauls Street *(Banks's)*; **Potters Arms**, St Pauls Street *(Atkinsons)*; **New Inn**, George Street *(Banks's)*

In an aside, he notes '...**The Potters Arms** was next door to the **Vulcan**, on the **King William** side. We'd been well warned about it - so we went to the Vulcan first, before borrowing glasses from there to have our quick one in The Potters, where their own glasses weren't washed, but merely wiped with a damp dishcloth... even so, it wasn't the squalidest pub in Worcester at the time – that dubious honour

Nags Head	Croft	New Inn	Great Western	Four Ways	Oddfellows	Lame Dog
Canon	Locomotive	Crown	Ram	King William	Freemasons	Bricklayers
Horn+Trumpet	Carpenters	Crowle House	Prince of	Waterloo	Royal Oak	
Rovers Arms	Arms	Beehive	Wales	Roebuck	Beehive	
Old England	Telegraph		Railway	Vulcan		
			Shrub Hill	Potters Arms		

The Blockhouse laid bare in the early 1970s (CCMH/CFOW) but the map shows the great proliferation of pubs the area had been renowned for. See the Blockhouse section starting on page 286

went to the **Duke of Wellington** on Birdport, close by the Police Station'.

I like the sound of Gus. What's more, he adds that the evening's entertainment was so successful that they – he doesn't list his friends sadly, but like him, they sound like a merry bunch – decided to make it an annual event, and on 15 March 1959 a new and revised route ran: **Royal Exchange**, Cornmarket *(Mitchells & Butlers)*; **Plough**, Cornmarket *(Marstons)*; **Old England**, Providence Street *(Cheltenham & Hereford, later Whitbread)*; **King William**, St Pauls Street *(Hunt Edmunds)*; **Waterloo**, Waterloo Street *(Cheltenham & Hereford later Whitbread)*; **Croft Inn**, James Street *(Marstons)*; **New Inn**, George Street *(Banks's)*; **Potters Arms** *(Atkinsons)*; **Vulcan** *(Banks's)*.

He also notes: '**The Potters** had changed hands - or else it seemed a good idea at the time... The one thing that now strikes me as odd about those two evenings is that on both occasions we walked past the same pub without going in - **The Locomotive** in George Street. I can only assume it was because it was an Ansells house – a brewery conspicuously absent from the above lists, although we caught up with it a couple of months later on the 25-pub All-Dayer to celebrate taking my Intermediate Exam'.

More recently, an organised annual pub crawl by a crowd of non-locals – this cheery crew appear to come from the environs of Manchester, itself no slouch when it comes to possessing the necessary attributes for a successful carouse from pub-to-pub – is the annual 12-pint Worcester Wassail, one of four regular pub crawls in their annual calendar that also includes Didsbury Dozen, the Rail Ale Crawl (when the carousers take the train to Batley and take if from there) and the Craven Crawl. However, it's **The Worcester Wassail** that appears to be gaining national status among dedicated pub-crawlers with its own blog, printed itinerary and website *(http://www.stevemorgan.me.uk/the-worcester-wassail-viii-a-splash-of-worcestershire-sauce)*.

Last year's (2012) was the eighth and it took place on December 21st starting – chief organiser, IT expert Steve Morgan logs – 'at 9:26 am'.'...to drink twelve pints of ale because that's just what we do every year. A twelve-pint pub-crawl known as 'The Worcester Wassail'. If nothing else, you can say we're consistent'. It's also interesting to see ourselves as 'foreigners' see us...

This is their itinerary and description of each pub as well as the obligatory toast they made at each pub on the route:

Location #1: The Cap 'n' Gown ('...established in 1849 and, up until a few years ago, little had changed except hopefully the odd barrel) then it had a dodgy do-up and was full of faux wood panelling with a strange L-shaped layout. The good news is they've worked on the old girl since, put in some new furniture and have produced a cosy boozer. Don't get too cosy though – even if two foot of snow does fall again outside whilst we're here – we're only just getting started. There, the toast is *"Civitas in Bello et Pace Fidelis – The City faithful in war and in peace".*

Location #2: The Lamb and Flag which Steve describes as '...a reminder of what pubs should be like and one of the reasons we drive 108 miles each year. A proper old man's pub that's as famous for its impeccably kept Guinness as it is for its staring locals, forgive them they probably haven't seen a new face in here in a few years... so old fashioned that the place still exercises lunch and evening openings *(never mind 24-hour drinking this place can't manage 12 hours)* and you won't want to miss out on this gem'. The toast here is: *"Filled with mingled cream and amber I will drain that glass again. Such hilarious visions clamber Through the chambers of my brain. Quaintest thoughts, queerest fancies Come to life and fade away. Who cares how time advances? I am drinking ale today".*

Location #3: The Dragon Inn ('...a 1750s, Grade II listed, CAMRA pub that you won't need to be dragonned inn-to). See the blackboard for today's specials – these are not your meal specials but rather a list of banned conversation topics. Exercise care as one of the banned topics is actually 'the banned topics' – so this guide is probably banned just by virtue of its discussion of the banned topics. This board is the obvious result of nobody actually wanting to directly tell some boring bastard that he/she were boring everybody. Tied to a Sheffield micro-brewery there are some interesting, but occasionally very strong, brews in here. *The toast: 'Champagne for my real friends, real pain for my sham friends'*

Location: #4. The Saracen's Head ('...an old coaching house, now run by a friendly South African landlord – friendly, but who doesn't like the f****** rude language – so mind your c****** mouth! So there we have it, we HAVE met a nice South African. Phil and Steve hold the world record for the world's longest and shittiest game of darts in here risking the timing and success of the Wassail and much endangering Russ's eyes in the process. *The toast: "I only drink to make other people seem interesting'.*

Location #5. The Pig & Drum: ('...this is supposedly the 'dodgy' end of Worcester. Apparently someone dropped some litter once, or maybe someone raised their voice; I forget now, and in the correct proportion there is only 400ft of it. Lowesmoor features probably the best chip shop in the West Midlands'). *The toast here is: 'There are only two times when I drink beer, when I'm alone and when I'm with someone else'.*

Location #6. The Fire Fly – described as 'a controversial stop on the Wassail as it's a bar rather than a pub but it links the Wassail up nicely and it's been on since the start and we don't like change. In the bar's defence they usually have two or three guest ales on of reasonable quaffing quality and dodgy olives are available for the poncey amongst us, Peruvian marching powder for the rest. *The toast: 'Pretty women make us BUY beer. Ugly women make us DRINK beer'.*

Location #7. The Swan With Two Nicks ('...a nice looking pub but they do insist on blaring music through a wholly inadequate, knackered PA. I wouldn't bother sticking money into the video jukebox – if you do, expect to wait two hours to hear your selection and, as we'll probably be behind schedule at this point, you won't make yourself too popular. Upstairs is the Lunar (sic) bar where the décor is akin to a cross between a tart's boudoir and a scene from the third rate film Austin Powers!
The toast: "You can't be a real country unless you have a beer and an airline – it helps if you have some kind of a football team, or some nuclear weapons, but at the very least you need a beer" - Frank Zappa).

Location #8. Eagle Vaults: ('...the old man pub of yesteryear and this one sometimes has ace rockabilly bands on. Clad in traditional Victorian tiles on the outside – the vomit just wipes off them

– the Victorians really did think of everything except how to catch Jack the Ripper and how to not die of TB. *The toast: "Beauty lies in the hands of the beer holder".*

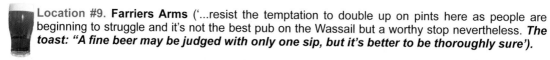

Location #9. **Farriers Arms** ('...resist the temptation to double up on pints here as people are beginning to struggle and it's not the best pub on the Wassail but a worthy stop nevertheless. *The toast: "A fine beer may be judged with only one sip, but it's better to be thoroughly sure').*

Location #10. **The Plough** ('...the Worcester CAMRA pub of the year 2009. New to the Wassail in 2010 due to the sad (?) temporary demise of the **Pig & Drum** and now one of the firm favourites. It's a bit pokey but very friendly so you might want to quietly slope out of the Farriers when nobody is looking to secure your pint and ownership of the pub quiz trivia books! *The toast: "Here's to alcohol, the rose coloured glasses of life". F. Scott Fitzgerald, The Beautiful and Damned)*

Location #11. **Ye Olde Talbot:** ('...go straight over the roundabout or head clockwise around it to have your photo taken with old Teddy Elgar's statue – we don't see so much of him nowadays due to the new £20 note not featuring him but is my stock University Challenge classical music answer. Follow the path on the left hand side and you'll find this boozer on the corner of Sidbury and Friar Street. It's a bit of a carvery style place and you'll need to carve through the crowds to get a pint as it's always rammed for reasons that are not entirely clear *(is anything clear at this point?)*. Try not to knock over work group's table of drinks as Bob did one year – it takes a lot of explaining from a lot of people – with "...but I've just drank 10 pints" apparently not a suitable excuse for ruining a works' Christmas dinner'. *The toast: "Alcohol: because no great story ever started with someone eating salad")*

Location #12. **Heroes:** (...continue up Friar Street and on the left, keep your blurry eyes peeled for a free-standing sign for Heroes – there is a small door way with a set of stairs you can fall down later. Watch your head and projectile Jae R. Moggs' vomit stains as you enter. This place has its fair share of nooks and grannies and seems popular with the Worcestershire yoof. Steve smooth talked his way out of being thrown out twice last year despite only being guilty of standing next to an abusive drunk, ironic really as he'd spent all day with a large group of them. Once you've drunk your giant bottle of ale it's on to a club or for Steve to fall over in the street clutching a Chicken Burger. Names have been changed to protect the guilty party's career prospects. *The toast (reprise) 'Civitas in Bello et Pace Fidelis – The City faithful in war and in peace'*

(Thanks to Steve Morgan http://www.stevemorgan.me.uk for permission to quote from the Worcester Wassail website)

Oh, and talking of toasts, here's one of my own:

'To Worcester pubs: God bless 'em and all who (was)sail in 'em'

The following pages give you the chance to recall every Worcester pub yet known. If you're planning to raise a glass to each, I'd recommend a handy chair nearby – or better still a very large bed. There's 516 of them – 656 if you count the different names some pubs have been blessed with over the years!

So cheers... see you at the other end.

The maps

and what the symbols mean

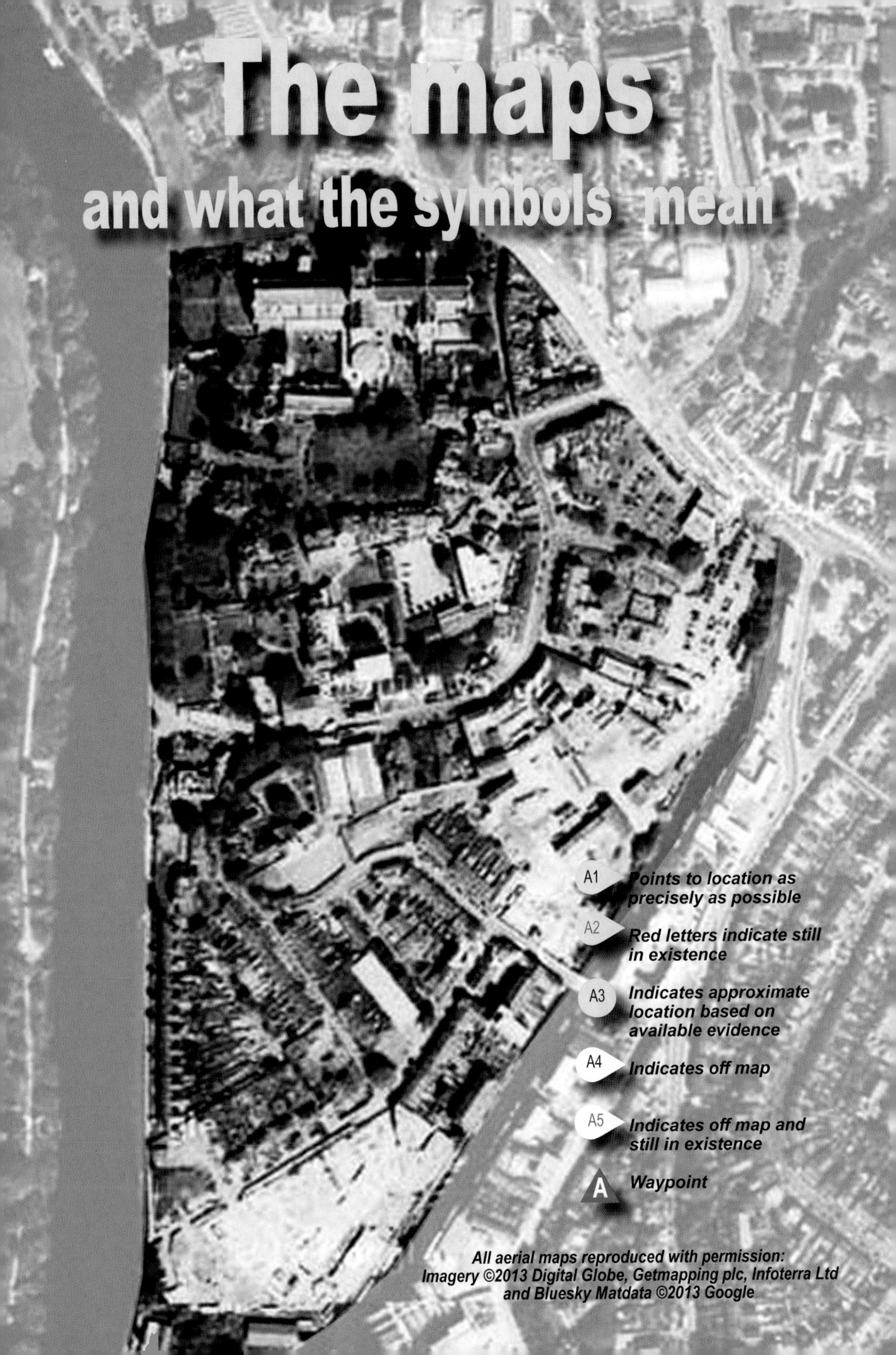
A1 Points to location as precisely as possible
A2 Red letters indicate still in existence
A3 Indicates approximate location based on available evidence
A4 Indicates off map
A5 Indicates off map and still in existence
A Waypoint

*All aerial maps reproduced with permission:
Imagery ©2013 Digital Globe, Getmapping plc, Infoterra Ltd
and Bluesky Matdata ©2013 Google*

North of the railway
p. 113-156

City 1
p. 201-244

City 4
p. 345-378

St Johns and west of the river
p. 65-112

City 2
p. 245-290

City 3
p. 291-344

East of the canal
p. 157 - 200

City 5
p. 379-394

St Johns

W1 City Arms
W2 Angel
W3 Brewers Arms
W4 Garibaldi
W5 Bedwardine
W6 Drakes Drum
W7 Mayflower
W8 Coppertops
W9 Crispin and Crispianu
W10 Cock and Cross

The Railway

County Grou

Bromwich Road

and west of the river

Pages 65-112

A The bridge

B St Johns church

C Bromyard Road

D Bransford Road

E Malvern Road

F Tybridge Street

G Railway bridge

H Hallow Road

Imagery ©2013 Digital Globe, Getmapping plc, Infoterra Ltd and Bluesky Mapdata ©2013 Google
Mapping: © Bob Blandford and The Whole Picture Publishing Company

A Foregate St Stn
B Castle Street
C Pitchcroft and
   The Moors
D The Tything
E Arboretum
F Toll House
G Ombersley Road
H Droitwich Road

N1   Cheshire
     Cheese
N2   Postal Order
N3   Monroes
     Cellar Bar
N4   Green Dragon
N5   Foley Arms
N6   Queen's Head
N7   Three Tuns
N8   Grandstand - 1
N9   Grandstand - 2
N10 Rose & Crown
N11 Carpenters Arms
N12 Prince of Wales
N13 Moors Ketch

North of the Great Western railway

Pages 113-156

Blackpole

E39

E38

Warndon

E37

E36

Warndon Villages

E34

E40

Tolladine

M5

Ronkswood

E29

Originally due to be called 'The Great Tolladine Inn' - The Barn Owl (E39), Berkeley Way

Typical 50s-60s estate pub architecture. Left - Punchbowl Ronkswood (1958). Below Prince of Wales (1963)

A Bath Road

B Sidbury

C Red Hill

D Wylds Lane

E George Street

F Newtown Road

G Rainbow Hill

H Tolladine Road

I Warndon

Imagery ©2013 Digital Globe, Getmapping plc, Infoterra Ltd and Bluesky
Mapdata ©2013 Google
Mapping: © Bob Blandford and The Whole Picture Publishing Company

of the canal

Pages 157-200

Pages 202-244

City Centre 1

C1/48
C1/55
C1/47
C1/54
C1/53
C1/46
C1 51
C1/52
C1/45
C1/44
C1 50
C1 40
C1 34
C1/35
C1/43
C1 38
C1 39
C1/36
C1/37
C1 33
C1/42
C1/32
C1/31
C1/41
C1/30
C1 29
C1 28
C1/26
C1 25
C1 27
C1 13
C1 15
C1 12
C1/16
C1/17
C1/18
C1/19
C1 14
C1/20
C1/22
C1/21
C1/23
C1 24
C1 10

A	The bridge
B	Newport Street
C	Dolday
D	All Saints
E	Angel Place
F	Angel Street
G	The Cross
H	Foregate Street
I	Five Ways
J	The Butts

C2/1: Golden Cross
C2/2: Talbot
C2/3: Bushwackers
C2/4: Slug'n'Lettuce
C2/5: Hop Market Inn
C2/6: Crown & Sceptre
C2/7: Railway Refresh
    -ment Rooms
C2/8: Toby's Tavern
C2/9: Plume of Feathers
C2/10: Golden Hart
C2/11: Old Falcon
C2/12: Holly Bush
C2/13: Pack Horse
C2/14: Dog & Duck
C2/15: Long Sow Cutter
C2/16: McBride's Mug
    House
C2/17: Old Ewe and Lamb
C2/18: Gentlemen and
    Porter
C2/19: Three Tuns
C2/20: Drum
C2/21: Masons Arms
C2/22: O'Neills
C2/23: Imperial/Metro
C2/24: Dolphin
C2/25: Peacock
C2/26: Cross Keys
C2/27: Holy Lamb
C2/28: White Lyon
C2/29: Wheatsheaf
C2/30: White Horse
C2/31: Commercial
C2/32: George
C2/33: Falstaff
C2/34: Pheasant
C2/35: Cross
C2/36: King Charles II

C2/37: Royal Exchange
    Prince's Arms
    Rodney
C2/38: Stag
C2/39: Shades
C2/40: Plough
C2/41: Railway Bell
C2/42: Union
C2/43: Crown & Anchor
C2/44: Boat
C2/45: Express
C2/46: Dove
C2/47: Black Horse
C2/48: Elephant & Castle
C2/49: White Lion
C2/50: Alma (Pig'n'Drum)
C2/51: Turk's Head
    (Brewery Tap)
C2/52: Apple Tree
C2/53: Swan
C2/54: Navigation

C2/55: Lansdowne Hotel
C2/56: Eagle
C2/57: Pheasant
C2/58: Cock and Magpie
C2/59: Sun Tavern
C2/60: Bridge 1
C2/61: Bridge 2
C2/62: Railway (Rainbow
C2/63: West Midland
Arms
C2/64: Ship
C2/65: Carpenters Arms
C2/66: Telegraph
C2/67: New Inn
C2/68: Railway Express

A The Cross
B St Nicholas Street
C Sansome Street
D Lowesmoor

E St Martins Gate
F George Street
G Pheasant Street

City Centre 2

Pages
245-290

C2/62

C2/61

C2/60

C2/49

C2/59

C2/48

C2/55

C1/64

C2/63

C2/54

C1/56

C2/50

C2/46

C2/53

C2/44

C2/52

C2/47

C2/51

D

C2/45

C1/57

C2/43

C1/58

G

C2/40

C2/41

C2/27-35

C2/67

C2/68

C2/65

C2/66

E

F

C3/1:	City Arms	C3/42:	Swan
C3/2:	Bellman	C3/43:	Crown
C3/3:	Queens Arms	C3/44:	Market Tavern
C3/4:	Stag	C3/45:	New Inn
C3/5:	Emperor of Russia	C3/46:	Market Hall Vaults
C3/6:	Sedan Chair	C3/47:	Butchers Arms
C3/7:	Glove	C3/48:	Coach & Horses
C3/8:	Royal Oak (1)	C3/49:	Liverpool Vaults
C3/9:	Royal Oak (2)	C3/50:	Seven Stars
C3/10:	Kings Head	C3/51:	Old Chappelle
C3/11:	Guildhall Tavern	C3/52:	Travellers Inn
C3/12:	Golden Lion	C3/53:	New Greyhound
C3/13:	Luna Restaurant	C3/54:	Old Greyhound
C3/14:	Adam and Eve	C3/55:	Plough
C3/15:	Swan	C3/56:	Pheasant
C3/16:	Swan (2)	C3/57:	Swan with Two Nicks
C3/17:	Three Cranes	C3/58:	King Charles
C3/18:	Three Crosses	C3/59:	Green Dragon
C3/19:	Three Pyes	C3/60:	Reindeer
C3/21:	Old Punch Bowl	C3/61:	Fleece
C3/22:	New Punch Bowl	C3/62:	Union
C3/23:	Black Boy	C3/63:	Oddfellows Arms
C3/24:	Chequers	C3/64:	Freemasons Arms
C3/25:	Duke of York	C3/65:	Royal Oak
C3/26:	Kings Arms	C3/66:	Beehive
C3/27:	Mitre	C3/67:	Lame Dog
C3/28:	Cathedral Vaults	C3/68:	Nag's Head
C3/29:	Ye Olde Talbot	C3/69:	Cannon
C3/30:	Kings Head	C3/70:	Old England
C3/31:	Globe Vaults	C3/71:	Horn & Trumpet
C3/32:	Cardinals Hat	C3/72:	Rovers Arms
C3/33:	Parrot	C3/73:	Four Ways/Thistle
C3/34:	Cross Keys	C3/74:	King William Vaults
C3/35:	Woolpack	C3/75:	Waterloo
C3/36:	Conservatory	C3/76:	Roebuck
C3/37:	Old Crown	C3/77:	Vulcan
C3/38:	Old Oak	C3/78:	Potters Arms
C3/39:	Eagle Vaults	C3/79:	Croft
C3/40:	Fish	C3/80:	Locomotive
C3/41:	Horse & Jockey		

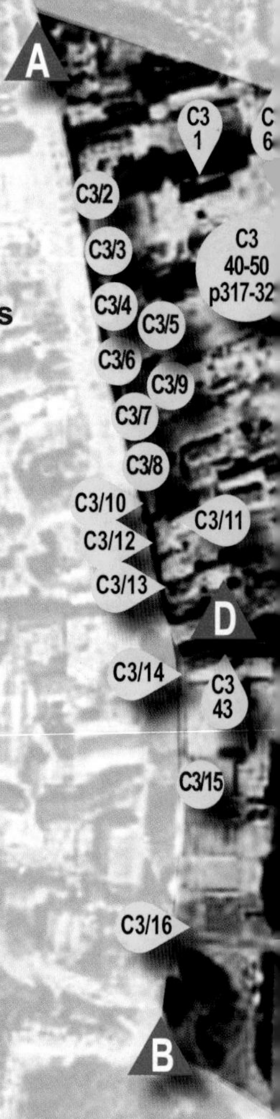

A

C3 1

C 6

C3/2

C3 40-50 p317-32

C3/3

C3/4

C3/5

C3/6

C3/9

C3/7

C3/8

C3/10

C3/11

C3/12

C3/13

D

C3/14

C3 43

C3/15

C3/16

B

City Centre 3
Pages 291-344

H

C3/59

C3/60

C3/58

C3/57

F

C3/56

E

C3/54

C3/55

C3/53

C3/52

C3/51

C3/50

C3/39

C3/40

C3/41

C3/38

C3/37

C3/36

C3/62

C3/35

C3/34

C3/33

C3/32

C3 17-29 p300-305

C3/31

C

C3/29

C3/80

C3/79

C3/78

C3/77

C3/76

C3/69

C3/68

C3/70

C3/75

C3/74

C3/71

C3/72

G

C3/73

C3/64

C3/65

C3/63

C3/66

C3/67

A High Street (East side)

B College Street

C Friar Street

D Pump Street

E The Shambles

F New Street

G Blockhouse

H George Street

City Centre 4
Pages
345-378

C4/7
C4 5
C4 6
C4/10
C4 4
C4 12
C4/11
C4 3
B
C4/57
C4 55
C4 2
C4/56
C4 52
C4 17
C4 15
C4/13
C4 51
C4 18
C4 14
C4/54
C4 16
C4 1
C4/53
E
C4/49
C4/64
C4/50
C4/48
C4/63
C4/47
C4/62
C4/46
C4/45
C4 61
C4/60
C4 65-76
C4/43
C4/44
C4/59
C4/58
C4 40
C4 32
C4 30
C4 29
C4 28
I
C4 31
C4/26
C4 27
C4/39

A The bridge
B All Hallows/All Saints
C The Cross
D Bank Street and Powick('s) Lane
E Chapel Walk
F Copenhagen Street
G Fish Street
H Elgar statue
I South Quay

Imagery ©2013 Digital Globe, Getmapping plc, Infoterra Ltd and Bluesky
Mapdata ©2013 Google
Mapping: © Bob Blandford and The Whole Picture Publishing Company

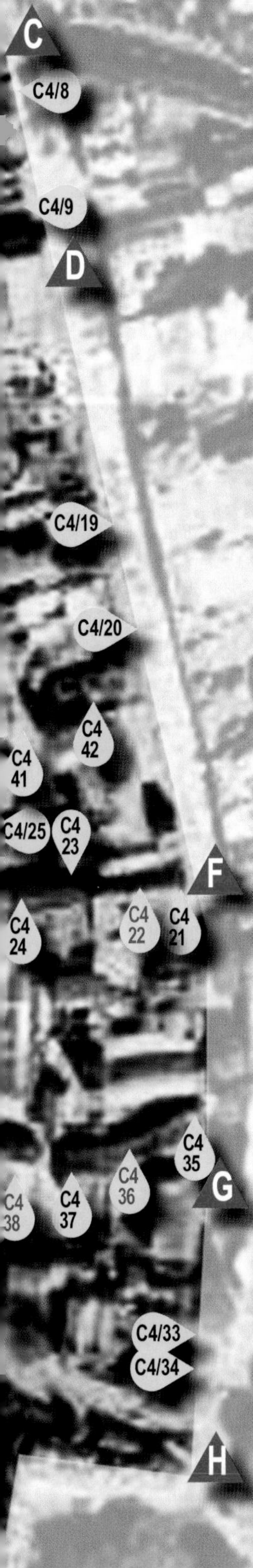

C4/1: Bridge
C4/2: London Wine & Spirit Vaults
C4/3: Dun Cow (Hen&Chickens)
C4/4: Beauchamp (Leopard)
C4/5: Unicorn
C4/6: Arcadia/Long Stop
C4/7: Parrot
C4/8: Vintorne
C4/9: Globe
C4/10: Fountain
C4/11: Bay Horse
C4/12: Berkeley Arms (Swan)
C4/13: Rising Sun
C4/14: George
C4/15: Silver Grayling
C4/16: Painter's Arms
C4/17: Queen's Arms
C4/18: Glover's Arms
C4/19: Angel Arch
C4/20: Admiral Vernon
C4/21: Green Dragon
C4/22: Mouth of the Nile
C4/23: Dolphin
C4/24: Porter Stores
C4/25: Marquis of Granby
C4/26: Ship
C4/27: Glo'ster Arms
C4/28: Merry Fellow
C4/29: Cock (and Old Cock)
C4/30: Plume of Feathers
C4/31: Horse and Jockey
C4/32: Wherry
C4/33: Mitre (also Stationers Arms)
C4/34: Swan
C4/35: General Hill
C4/36: Farriers Arms
C4/37: Oddfellows Arms
C4/38: Plough
C4/39: Seven Stars
C4/40: Red Cow
C4/41: Bull and Sun

C4/42: Victoria
C4/43: Duke of Wellington
C4/44: Prince Blücher
C4/45: Prince Regent
C4/46: Fourteen Stars
C4/47: Leather Dressers Arms
C4/48: Lamb
C4/49: Dragoon (also Jolly Sailor)
C4/50: Woolpack
C4/51: Nelson
C4/52: Pewterers Arms
C4/53: Quiet Woman
C4/54: Hole in the Wall
C4/55: Farmers Arms
C4/56: Press
C4/57: Malt Shovel
C4/58: Bottle in Hand
C4/59: Queen Caroline
C4/60: Severn Trow (and Pheasant)
C4/61: Severn Swan (Black Swan)
C4/62: Farmers Arms
C4/63: Fountain
C4/64: Farriers Arms (and Old Farriers Arms)

C4/65-76: *Also existed but precise locations unknown:*

Shoemakers Arms
Barley Mow
Salt Scales
Crown and Canton
Black Hussar
Laurence's Mug House
Kings Arms
Kings Head (also King David)
Bricklayers Arms
Crispin
Well Sinkers Arms

City Centre 5

C5/1
C5 2
C5 8
C5/3
C5/9
C5/4
C5/22
C5/5
C5/10
C5/23
C5/7
C5/6
C5/13
C5/11
C5/12
C5 14
C5 16
C5 17
C5 18
C5/19
C5 20
C5 21

Pages 379-394

It's a little known fact – but true nonetheless – that a pub once existed in the square building butting up to historic Edgar Tower" this was the Coach and Horses (C5/8) – one of three Worcester pubs so named.
See page 386

CIVITAS · IN · BEERO · ET · PVBBI · FIDELIS

The following 329 pages list every known pub in Worcester from the 1400s onwards. Inevitably, any researcher that delves so far back into the depths of time is going be left floundering in the dark from time to time – and this researcher is no exception!

So while every care has been taken to record the facts with all due faith, the only certainty is that there will be errors and omissions: both, hopefully at the barest minimum. Curiously, research into the 1770s was sometimes easier and more productive than into the 2000s – and I refer here particularly to the legions of pub tenants and managers that came and went with alarming regularity during what's being recognised as a particularly tough period for all pubs. If I missed out you, or one of your relatives or favourite gaffers of the time, please feel free to inform me of that fact: the omission was not deliberate – and anyway, it's to be hoped that the record can be put straight in Volume II of which I'm sure there will be one!

As regards attribution to the copyright owners of photographs, where the rightful owner is known, names have been listed and where requested, dues paid. If for some unintentional reason due reference has not been made, I would again appreciate you alerting me to that fact so that the record may be put straight. Nowhere throughout the preparation of this work has there been a deliberate attempt to include any information or image to which I had no right.

By way of explanation, pubs existing prior to 1850 are denoted by a tankard

Those later than 1850 are shown with a modern 'sleever'

5: St Johns and West of the river

Map: 48-9

(Map reproduced from 1886 Ordnance Survey map with permission of the Ordnance Survey)

taking in: Tybridge Street, Bull Ring, Bransford Road, Bromyard Road and Malvern Road, with a few surprises along the way!

Even to this day, Worcester folk from the east side of the river refer to the City's western reaches including St Johns as 'the dark side', and several other things might also surprise you about the area west of the Severn – the green and fertile area that, it will come as no surprise whatsoever, draws its name from St John the Baptist.

Two in particular, however, might colour your perception of what's also known in friendlier fashion as 'the village in the City'....

One, that the Severn was tidal up to and beyond the City up to the 1830s – with the result that the low-lying land that's now Tybridge Street as far west as today's Bromyard Road/Bull Ring roundabout seethed under river water twice a day.

And two, the hark-back of which is revealed in its persisting strong sense of regional pride and a remoteness that locals deny but is easily detected by those from, presumably given the earlier comment, 'the bright side', is that the area west of the Severn was an independent township even up to 1837 when it was first incorporated into the City of Worcester.

Up to then it had rejoiced in the name of 'The Township of St John' revelling in the privilege of being able to stage its own annual fayre on the Friday preceding Palm Sunday and legislate from its own courts, free of the ties and restrictions of the burgeoning City rapidly to-ing and fro-ing and generally getting on with the serious business of expansion on the other side of the river.

'Rambler' John Noake's charming description of the traditional annual procession of the bailiff *(or mayor)* to St Johns – which he describes as 'one of the grand events of the year' paints a colourful picture of the civic procession to the 'village divided from the western side of the City by the river Severn'. Despite the City's big-wigs having no authority there *('it being situated without the limits of their jurisdiction')* it appears to have been an ancient custom that was religiously undertaken for about two hundred years.

> *The constable having 'cried the fair' the party would adjourn to the Swan or Bell*
> *(both noted houses two centuries ago) and there run up a pretty score for the City*
> *funds. Not content with this, his Worship and Co would sometimes cause their*
> *august bodies to be conveyed thither (a distance of only a few hundred yards), in*
> *a vehicle for in 1732 occurs an item of '9d (4p) turnpike for coach to St Johns fair'.*
> *From the before going premises however, it is probable the coach was employed in*
> *coming from the fair, the civic party being them unquestionably in a more unfit state*
> *to do the locomotive on their own account.*

(John Noake – 'Worcester in Olden Times')

(CCMH/CFOW)

36

Late 1800s shot of St Johns with the toll-house – and lurking toll-keeper! (CCMH/FOW)

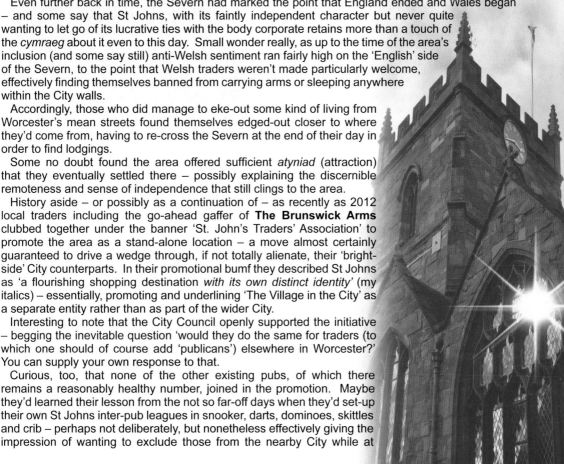

Even further back in time, the Severn had marked the point that England ended and Wales began – and some say that St Johns, with its faintly independent character but never quite wanting to let go of its lucrative ties with the body corporate retains more than a touch of the *cymraeg* about it even to this day. Small wonder really, as up to the time of the area's inclusion (and some say still) anti-Welsh sentiment ran fairly high on the 'English' side of the Severn, to the point that Welsh traders weren't made particularly welcome, effectively finding themselves banned from carrying arms or sleeping anywhere within the City walls.

Accordingly, those who did manage to eke-out some kind of living from Worcester's mean streets found themselves edged-out closer to where they'd come from, having to re-cross the Severn at the end of their day in order to find lodgings.

Some no doubt found the area offered sufficient *atyniad* (attraction) that they eventually settled there – possibly explaining the discernible remoteness and sense of independence that still clings to the area.

History aside – or possibly as a continuation of – as recently as 2012 local traders including the go-ahead gaffer of **The Brunswick Arms** clubbed together under the banner 'St. John's Traders' Association' to promote the area as a stand-alone location – a move almost certainly guaranteed to drive a wedge through, if not totally alienate, their 'bright-side' City counterparts. In their promotional bumf they described St Johns as 'a flourishing shopping destination *with its own distinct identity'* (my italics) – essentially, promoting and underlining 'The Village in the City' as a separate entity rather than as part of the wider City.

Interesting to note that the City Council openly supported the initiative – begging the inevitable question 'would they do the same for traders (to which one should of course add 'publicans') elsewhere in Worcester?' You can supply your own response to that.

Curious, too, that none of the other existing pubs, of which there remains a reasonably healthy number, joined in the promotion. Maybe they'd learned their lesson from the not so far-off days when they'd set-up their own St Johns inter-pub leagues in snooker, darts, dominoes, skittles and crib – perhaps not deliberately, but nonetheless effectively giving the impression of wanting to exclude those from the nearby City while at

New Road c1910
(CCMH/CFOW)

2013 (BB)

the same time welcoming those from the far western reaches of the County.

No doubt the economic climate and the threats to the continued existence of pubs had some influencing role, but sometimes it still appears that a hard core of St Johns folks continues to hanker after independence. That said, according to Wikipedia, '... it seems that there is no plan to regain independent status' - which comes as something of a relief, as the area west of the City was, and still is, home to some cracking little, and large, pubs.

Though somewhat decimated over the past half century, we're fortunate to have seen several public houses survive to a good old age, along with a higher proportion of new pubs than anywhere else in the City – notably the two 70s additions in Lower Wick, **Manor Farm and The Maple Leaf,** two 50s additions in Dines Green, **The Mayflower** and **The Drakes Drum** *(both of which have since foundered, leaving one of the City's biggest estates pub-less)* and **The Coppertops**, now standing virtually alone where there was once if not a plethora of drinking houses, at least a fair choice.

Even so, an evening spent savouring the atmosphere of a small town by visiting those still active within what's still a comparatively compact area, generally proves to be a satisfying one.

According to the archaeologists, the basic framework of roads through St John's was established well over a thousand years ago. Bromyard Road leading west from the north side of the churchyard appears as a *strete* in 963, and Bransford Road, also leading west, with the long St John's Green on its south side, appears as 'suth street'.

In common with many a township, St John's, like Worcester itself, owes its entire existence to its proximity to a major river crossing, assuming the mantle of importance as the meeting place of roads converging on the only cross-Severn route up- or downstream for miles.

Even from mediaeval times, a ford – or at least, a raised causeway and eventually a bridge – spanned the Severn linking east and west via Newport Street and Tybridge Street both of which were the M4 of their day, thereby explaining the proliferation of old pubs clustered around what would have been the old bridge. *(A secondary, though historically far less important factor than the river, was the opening of the railway line to Hereford, completed in 1860, resulting in not one but two stations serving the increasingly affluent Westside: Henwick Halt and Boughton Halt).*

Thus it was that with the coming of new bridge – ten years under construction and not completed until

1792 – the old highway into and out of the City found itself overshadowed with the building of the raised 'new' road. Curious that this name still persists more than 220 years on (though perhaps not so curious as the 'New' prefix still sticking to several Worcester pubs even though their present appearance shows they're anything but!).

Even so, it's this still-spacious and leafy New Road that gives most travellers their first glimpse of the townships on either side.

Unlike the original prime route into the City with its tight cluster of pubs on both sides of the river at Cripplegate *(west)* and Newport Street *(east)*, but for one exception both the new gentrified Bridge Street and New Road remained pub-free.

An interesting old Worcester superstition is that when crossing the bridge, whether new or old, and in either direction, a wink at the cathedral brought good luck – all of which was fine except when a whole bus- (or cart-) load did it leaving those not in the know wondering if the entire city wasn't affected by some grave form of ocular affliction.

For years, New Road itself only added to the remoteness and sense of independence still evident in St Johns by creating the next best thing to a sense of country separating the two townships. Tree-lined and still airy, despite the County Ground since becoming enclosed and townified with the construction of the ultra-modern new hotel complex, the Kings School Ground to the left and Cripplegate Park to the right conspire to create the impression that you've already left the City and are entering an entirely new village. New Road was two-way until early 1969 when the three-lane highway that takes its name from the narrow street it cut a swathe through – Tybridge Street, running across the sites of some noted old pubs – opened. Up to then too, north and west-bound traffic could turn right at the bridge into Tybridge Street which was itself two-way.

A to B: from the bridge to St Johns Church

As with most areas, the parish church remains the area's focal point. St John-in-Bedwardine can trace its origins to around 1165 though the red sandstone tower dates from around 300 years later. A squat, though easily-recognised landmark, the church was severely bashed-about in the Civil War by Cromwell's troops who not only fired their muskets into – and sharpened their pikes on – the wall, leaving scars that are still visible 360-odd years on, but also, perhaps deliberately rather than accidentally, shot off the church's 'lofty leaden steeple'. The deed poses serious questions about the motives of the Government's agents' actions, a sentiment that occurs again and again in any history of the City and inevitable loss of pubs therein.

For the present we'll concentrate on the eastern approach to St Johns Church: the Bull Ring – so named for the simple reason that one *(a bull ring, that is)* had been located here for the purpose of 'enraging' cattle before being slaughtered – a practice believed to

St Johns 2013 (BB)

St Johns c1910 (CCMH/CFOW)

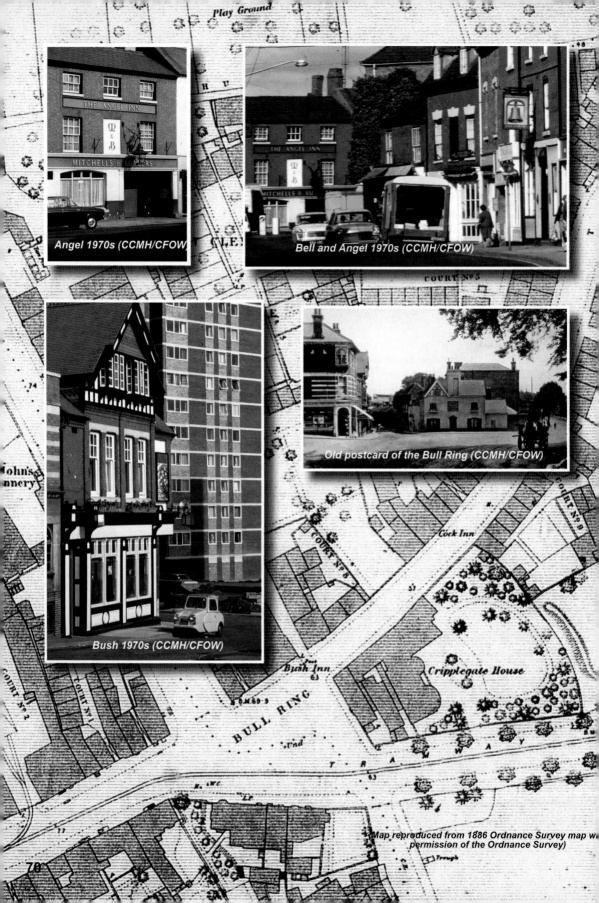

Angel 1970s (CCMH/CFOW)

Bell and Angel 1970s (CCMH/CFOW)

Old postcard of the Bull Ring (CCMH/CFOW)

Bush 1970s (CCMH/CFOW)

Cock Inn

Cripplegate House

Bush Inn

BULL RING

(Map reproduced from 1886 Ordnance Survey map with permission of the Ordnance Survey)

70

improve the subsequent quality of the resulting meat. One of the duties of mayor had traditionally been to ensure a regular supply of bulls for the citizens' consumption, while butchers who slaughtered unbaited ones found themselves hauled up before the authorities charged with a punishable offence: interesting to note, though, that the City fathers preferred this dirty work to be conducted outside the city walls on the 'dark' side. What was now known as 'the Bull Ring' was described as 'a natural piazza', and when construction work began to reduce the incline   '...the base of the post used for bull-baiting was discovered' *(Source: Bill Gwilliam – Old Worcester People and Places)*

Before incorporation into the City in 1837, records relating to the parish of St John in Bedwardine had not been particularly well kept – the legacy today being only a sketchy image of what had been a considerable number of pubs in and around the church and The Bull Ring so while we know they existed, plotting actual locations is nigh-on impossible and all too often, all we have to go on is the location 'Cripplegate'. This one is typical...

City Arms
Location: Cripplegate
Years active: 1760 – 1870s
Location unknown except for 'Cripplegate', but clearly an inn with a long history as it's listed in Victuallers Recognizances in 1766 and also referred-to by Noake in his Worcestershire Relics 1877 – 111 years later. Almost certainly on the site of what was the City's first supermarket, Burton's built 1956.

Toll-house and site of the City Arms (CCMH/CFOW)

Licensees: *Francis Evans (1766); Penelope Yates (1835). Several other licensees by name of Yates (or Yeats) also appear in the St Johns area – notably Samuel Yates and Robert Yates (Crown & Anchor 1885 and 1905 respectively), and Samuel and Joseph Yeates and George Yates at The Chequers between 1872 and1900 so it's possible Penelope may have been related. But as neither of these pubs could be described as 'Cripplegate' the precise location of The City Arms remains a mystery and its position here can only be described as approximate.*

Of the pubs known to have clustered on what can be whittled-down to The Bull Ring, only one remains – though of late it's been suffering from open/close syndrome to the point that no-one at present (2013) can be sure if it's still a going concern or not. This is The Bush but as it's now set back off the main drag and effectively forms part of a chain of pubs along Tybridge Street, we'll return to **The Bush** in a while, by which time it might have opened (or closed) again.

The Angel
Location: St. John's
Years active: 1660s (rebuilt 1830s) – 1985
Sadly no longer in business as such, though the building remains, as does a perpetual reminder of its former use in the form of its name **'The Angel Inn'** still emblazoned above the first floor, looking a bit sad and sorry for itself but leaving you in no doubts of what it had been when it was great, which I can readily confirm it once was...

Mentioned as early as 1670 when it's thought to have been in existence for at least 10 years and listed in Universal British Directory 1791 under the heading 'Principal Inhabitants of St John's in Bedwardine (sic) as under stewardship of John Owen, the building is today St Johns Carpets warehouse with flats above. It had also been a fruit and veg shop after it

Angel, St Johns 1965 (JAS)

closed in the mid-1980s. The present building dates from around 1830-40 though with later additions and alterations. It is, according to St Johns Conservators '...brick and stucco under slate roof; dentilled eaves... dog-legged in plan with through vehicular access to right. 3 storeys and cellar. 3 first-floor windows. Stucco detailing includes sills and whole of ground-floor with pilasters, fascia and cornice/ first-floor sill-band; below second-floor sills is a long recessed rectangular panel with moulded surround bearing the name 'The Angel Inn'. Hmmmm....impressive.

The Angel was also listed in the first known trades directory for Worcester, Grundy's Royal Directory for 1792, under Angel Hotel and Angel Inn.

It was also occasionally used for inquests. On 5th October 1826, the inquest was held here into the death of Samuel Turnbull who 'fell from a wagon and died'. The Angel had clearly been an important pub in the St Johns community – even enjoying the attraction of a bowling alley and quoit ground in 1908 – and an insight into the glories that had been is still evident with the ornate glazed metal lantern on its wrought-iron bracket, still visible despite having been re-sited out of the way of the interminable traffic that constantly chokes what would otherwise be a delightful area.

On 21st October 1914, then licensee Joseph Thomas Chadd was convicted at Worcester Magistrates Court for 'unlawfully permitting Frank Oliver Bomford to pay wages to his workmen on his licensed premises' and was fined 10/- (50p) with 9/- costs or 14 days imprisonment.

An M&B house until its demise, The Angel was long a favourite with parents bringing their children and leaving them to their crisps and Vimto in what would once have been a coaching yard and is still fondly remembered by those generations.

Just a few weeks after the Royal wedding in 1981 when Di and Bob Rickard were tenants I wrote: '...(Bob) ekes out a further living by selling 'things' – anything – over the counter and at market prices. As a result, the bar's a bit like a Calcutta bazaar with everything from Rubiks' cubes to Charles and Di salvers, walkie-talkies to cassette tapes. It's only a little pub but it's big-hearted, big on friendliness and big on ideas. The bar's tiny, *(it was just the length of the frontage and not very wide at that)* cramped, hard-nosed and given over to working men's' business of sinking beer and setting the world to right... short on niceties, short on space, short on comfort – no poseurs' pub this – but big on everything else'.

Other facilities, I noted, included 'a smoke room doubling as a children's room, and upstairs function room (still with the Christmas decorations up in July!) that's used by rifle teams, with a back yard and a garden'. My overall comment was that The Angel was not the prettiest of pubs – in fact I described it as downright ugly – '...but at least it's alive. Long may it remain so'.

Sadly I never got my wish: it closed four years later.

Licensees: W. Barnes (listed as Angel Inn St Johns when St Johns is in a separate section to Worcester which has its own section) 1790; Samuel Smith (1820, 1829, 1835); Joseph Collins (1842 and 1850); Clement Downes (1873); Maria Sayce Downes (1879-1886); John Hodges (1886); Arthur Trott (1890); Thomas Marlow (1891); George Farley (1892); Benjamin Henry Spencer (1897); Archer Thomas Broad (1900); John Andrews (1901); John Rodway (1901– died); John Perks (1902); Frank Walter Heaven (1905– died); Mabel Ellen Heaven (1906); John Appleton (1908- c1915); Joseph Thomas Chadd (1915); Cyril Leonard Blunt (1926); John Parkes (Feb-Sept 1951); Albert George Burford (1951); Graham Joseph Moore (1953); Albert Ronald Smith (1957); Des Burden (1961); Ivor Firth Richardson (1966); Margaret Ann Blick (1970); Peter Blick (1971); David 'Chick' Smith (1971); Robert Bettles (1972); Alan Miller (1975); George Jones (1978); Bob and Di Rickard (1979); Keith Connor (1982); Peter Wood (1985)

from St Johns Church along Bromyard Road and beyond

Keeping St John's Church to your left and heading westwards along what's now Bromyard Road, it's quite a way to the next pub – though there's an interesting diversion that's well worth the effort despite being past its best, architecturally at least. Turn into Comer Road and there you'll find...

W3 **Brewer's Arms**
Location: 5, Comer Road
Years active: 1900 - present

In existence since around 1900 – 15 years after St Johns came into the Worcester City licensing area – The Brewer's Arms is still in fine fettle, though showing its age. Lovely old photographs of the pub in its youth, with horses and bikes since having given way to the inevitable rise of the motor car, demonstrate the Brewers' appeal when it was fulfilling the purpose it had been built for: serving a predominantly local trade with good ales (initially Ind Coope and Allsopp, based in Burton-upon-

Brewers Arms 1912 (CCMH/CFOW)

...and 101 years on! (BB)

Trent, who by August 1954 had been swallowed up by Aston-based Atkinsons and thus, by osmosis into Mitchells and Butlers).

113 years on, and it's still doing just that – the point that there's a large element of a time warp about it – not that there's anything wrong with that. Orignal windws and doors remain and the fine ornate lamp that's more than evident in a 1902 picture is still there. At least The Brewers is still going. Another one with a great reputation for a goodly pint, **The Brewer's Arms** has been listed variously as 5 and 2 Comer Road. In 1982 when it was under the stewardship of Tom (and Joyce) Ewins, who'd earlier also been tenants at **The Eagle Vaults** on the corner of Friar Street and Pump Street, I remarked on the very St Johns-ness of the pub, as noted earlier. Quoting then gaffer Tom I wrote: '...being local they *(the customers)* are naturally close-knit. We know who to expect and can set our watches by 'em'. Visits since then have confirmed that not much has changed. I even described **The Brewers Arms** then – as I would even today – as '...just a boozer (with) no frills, no extras, not a lot of finesse yet so big on cosiness you can't be certain you haven't walked into somebody's parlour by mistake' *(the latter a handy phrase I was to use in various similar formats describing several Worcester pubs in the 1980s).*

I concluded: '...Tom's a real old stager and this is something of a old stagers' pub' (an observation I maintain to be largely true still) ...nice if you like a good pint and are not too concerned with the niceties. Then a one room pub, *(it still is)* I asked the landlord if he saw it as a lounge or bar. 'It's a lounge bar' came the reply. Stupid question really' (see, I was self-effacing even then!). I went on: '... no carpet which is no great shakes but narrow seats all along the room ending in a little railway compartment that you could happily curl up and sleep in. Plus big garden 'enough for 100' reckons Tom'. It's still there.

Licensees: *William Cook (1885-1887 when he died); Thomas Roberts (1897-1901 when he died . It was then taken over by his widow Jennietta Roberts); Edward Thomas Mitchell (1902-1911); Fred Short (1915-42 when he died when it was taken over by his widow Matilda Short); Francis Eugene Hector Horlick (1948-1950); George Rowe (1950-1953); Henry James Gallent (1953-1955); Edward George Rowarth (1955-1957); Reginald Frederick Reeve (1957-1970); Joan Blanche Reeve (1970-1978); Thomas Ewins (1978-1984); Robert Turner (1984); Diane Jones (1985); David Jones (1990); Victor Thomas (2000). Current licensee (2013); Deborah Louise Daniels. Worcester City Licence no: 1338*

Returning to the main A44 Bromyard Road, on the next corner is another survivor from the time of the great westwards expansion and population growth of 'The Village in the City' precipitated in many ways with the coming of the railway in 1860...

The Garibaldi
Location: 80 Bromyard Road
Years active: 1900 - present

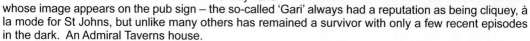

(BB)

Listed at 80 Bromyard Road and still open some 80 years after making its debut, The Garibaldi was for many years a Marstons House (originally Lewis Clarke's of Angel Place) drawing, like most in the City's westside, a dedicated trade predominantly from the expanding new residential properties that surrounded it.

The less notorious of two Worcester pubs named after 1860s Italian freedom fighter Giuseppe Garibaldi – described as 'the Che Guevara of his day' and whose image appears on the pub sign – the so-called 'Gari' always had a reputation as being cliquey, à la mode for St Johns, but unlike many others has remained a survivor with only a few recent episodes in the dark. An Admiral Taverns house.

Licensees: *Henry Baker (1898-1902); Joseph Lightwood (1902); Wm. T. Crockett (1902-1913); Francis E. Crockett (1913-16); Percy Amyes (1916); Bertha Amyes (1917-1922); Arthur Johnson (1922-1929); Will Curnock (1929-1934); Percy Hiron (1937-1939); Albert Francis Haynes (1939-1941 when he died); May Kate Haynes (1941-42); Herbert Williams (1942); Alice Myra Williams (1942–1957); Herbert John Booth (from 2nd September 1957-1963); Alf Willcox (1963-1971); Charles Freeman (1971-1976); Richard Powell (1976-1979); Dennis Hardeman (1979-1981); Edward Thompson (1981-1983); John Edmands (1987); Roy Ingram (1988); Bryan J. and Lorraine James (2000). Current licensee (2013); Mrs Helen Allen. Worcester City Licence no: 1071*

Vying for position less than 150 yards westwards and on the same side is a big old pub that belies its years and has been a firm favourite for generations though now appears to be skipping out of favour as young managers and tenants take over, pandering to the growing student – for which read, 'occasionally out of control' – population:

The Bedwardine
Also known as: The Sandpits
Location: Bromyard Road
Years active: 1870 - present

(BB)

Bedwardine 3rd April 1962 (RHS)

Originally The Sandpits, and dating from around 1870 – which means it was in existence even before St Johns was included in the City Licensing area (1885) – The Bedwardine is still going though its future at present appears to rest more with the karaoke-warbling and pool-playing cultures, much to the disgust of local residents who were much more comfortable in the days when it was a large family-oriented pub with a big garden.

The original **Sandpits**, dating from around 1870 takes its name from the rich mineral finds including sand and gravel that were suddenly in huge demand at the start of the great expansion in construction from around ten years earlier: the income thus generated contributing greatly to the site owners' wealth. To them it was, in fact, a 'happy land' – as nearby streets, probably built using much the same materials that ended up above-ground that had not long before been underground, stand witness.

The boom times of that golden era also resulted in an expansion in industrial projects with nearby factories including Mining and Engineering Company (Meco), heavy engineers Alley & MacLellan, shoemakers Willis' Cinderella Works, glovemakers Frank Bryant, the busy BRS (British Road Services) depot a stone's throw across the road, and in latter years several Kays depots and departments – all their workers contributing to the fortunes of the large red brick pub that most seemed to favour.

First listed in Littlebury's Directory of Worcestershire 1873 at 128, Bromyard Road and consistently ever since, on 26th February 1920, Arthur Cecil Scott (possibly Snr-Snr) had bought the then Sandpits for £2,900. 38 years later, on 21st February 1958, John Davenport and Sons Ltd (Davenports Brewery) of Bath Row, Birmingham bought the premises for £18,000. **The Sandpits** inexplicably changed its name to **The Bedwardine** on 3rd August 1960.

Twenty one years on, the Bedwardine was the second of two pubs listed in the very first Bob Backenforth Beer guide (along with **The Barbourne**). Then a Davenports pub under the managership of Ron (and Marilyn) Hemming, locals and local employees still accounted for the majority of its trade, though sports teams – not least skittlers attracted by what many considered to be the best skittle alley in Worcester, reputed to be polished at least once a week alongside a growing reputation for simple but appetising grub – expanded its customer-base.

'The local element counts for a lot' Ron admitted in 1981 with the rider 'but there's always a welcome for everybody'. A big sporting pub even then, it had a reputation for cleanliness with a lovingly-furnished lounge – now like so many, incorporated into one barn-like multi-purpose room. The Bedwardine of late appears to have been taken over by the students from University of Worcester, with reports of some noisy and occasionally unsavoury, if little more than student high-jinks, goings-on. It is currently a Star Pubs & Bars Ltd house, registered in Edinburgh.

Licensees: *William Morris (1885-1886); Julia Murphy and Alexander Parry (1886); Alexander Parry, John Irzon, Frederick Porter, June Clarke (1887); Harriet Ball (1890-1893); Edward Thorp (1893-1895); William Thomas (1895-1896); George Lewis (1896-97); Edwin Salt (1897-99 when he died); Hannah Salt (1899-1908); Arthur E. Smith (1908-1920); Arthur Cecil Scott (1920-1946); Arthur Cecil Scott Jnr. (1946-1958); Arthur William Ellard (1958-1959); Frank Edward Sheldon (1959-64); George Boycott (1964-1965); Albert Haines (1965-1969); William Lester (1969-1976); Ronald Hemming (1976-1982); Stephen Cummins (1982-1984); Alfred Lingen (1984-1986); Kenneth Wright (1986); Chris Osborne (1990); Barry Hampton (2000); Jenny Watkins (2001-2009). Current licensee (2013); Ms Hannah Batchelor. Worcester City Licence no: 1237*

Drakes Drum 1970s (CCMH/CFOW)

Continuing westwards, turn into the Dines Green estate to the point of coming almost full circle, the two 1950s estate pubs The Drakes Drum and The Mayflower both reflecting the names of new estate's Tudor theme, are both now sadly gone – not just change of use, but flattened and houses/flats hastily, some say obscenely so, constructed on their sites. The move has left one of the City's biggest social housing (ie Council) estates little more than an arid desert in the pubs sense. Formerly farming land, Dines Green was built in the late 1950s by building contractor Spicers to house mostly working class families 'at the lower end of the social scale' (Wikipedia). The 450-home estate consisted of a mix of semi-detached homes mostly built using pre-cast concrete, and large blocks of flats. At the time, Dines Green was typical of the bright new world then developing in Prime Minister Harold Macmillan's 'never had it so good' era – even though contemporary records show that the estate's tenancy profile was centred mostly on unskilled positions and tradesmen.

Clearly, an estate pub was just what the doctor ordered to keep the masses calm, satisfied and well served for ale, and Dines Green surpassed even that: it got two within the space of just a little over a year! The first to open was:

Drakes Drum site 2013 (BB)

Drakes Drum 1960s (JAS)

W6 Drakes Drum
Location: Tudor Way
Years active: 1958-2008

'The Drum' was a big typical Ansells estate pub with distinct bar and lounge in 'plastic and formica' décor considered up-to-the-minute and avant garde at the time, though rapidly descending into the twee. The pub's official 'Final Order to Operate' was granted by Worcester's magistrates on 9th December 1958. On June 21st 1967 licensee John Rayner was convicted for allowing betting transaction on the premises and was fined £25 with £9.18s (£9.90p) costs. On Jan 27th 1981 licensee John Harris was convicted for allowing liquor to be sold to a person under 18 years. He was fined £25.

Cliff Adams commented (on Worcester Pubs Then and Now FB Friends Group page: ***https://www.facebook.com/groups/worcesterpubsthenandnow)*** '...my mate Ron Cook ran the roughest pubs in Birmingham and thought he would take a pub in Worcester for a peaceful life so he took the Drakes Drum *(see list of licensees below)*. He reckons more riots and punch-ups took place there in the first 12 months than any pub he ran in his time as a landlord'.

Nothing now remains of **The Drakes Drum**, always considered the more volatile of the two Dines Green pubs where the inevitable rivalry between it and its slightly snootier neighbour further up the estate wasn't always of the friendly variety. The once lively – in all senses of the word – pub closed in 2008 after exactly half a century, and is now the site of a new Worcester Community Housing 23-apartment development.

Interesting to note that during the course of demolition, a pool that was home to the protected Great Crested Newt was discovered in what had been the back lawn: the reference to newts was not lost on locals who'd been alarmed about the rising amount of disturbance from the pub for several years before it closed.

Licensees: *Eric Harold Williams (1958-1959); Stanley David Howells (1959-1960); Albert George Kettingham (May-November 1960); Fred Layton (1961-63); George Weston (1963-1965); John Rayner (1965-1967); Gwilyn Humphreys (1967-1969); Anthony Stewart (1969-1970); Derek Dimmock (1970-1972); Charles Rushton (1972- 1975); Ronald Cook (1975-1977); John Anthony Harris (1977-1982); Raymond Lewis (1982-1986); Derek Debens (1986); Michael Moore (1986); Alan and Georgina Darby (1990); Peter Stokes (1997); Sean, Finbarr, Daryll Ferguson (2000).*

Around the same time that the Drakes Drum made its debut on the bright new Dines Green estate, rival brewery M&B wasn't far behind in vying for the locals' demand for an alternative local. This turned out to be:

The Mayflower
Location: Grenville (and Gresham) Road
Years active 1960 - 2010

Mayflower 2012 above, and a year later 2013 (BB)

The estate's second - and many considered superior, pub opened on 1st December 1960. Its first licence had been granted by magistrates to Vincent Luther Dishman on 7th December 1959 replacing the licence originally held by John Ernest Sussex of the soon-to-be-demolished **Freemasons Arms** in Carden Street . While the new Mayflower was considered to be better designed and fitted than its rougher counterpart not half a mile away - as well as attracting what some saw as a slightly better class of clientele - there wasn't a lot to distinguish between the two with similarly spacious bar and lounge areas and, by contemporary standards, more car parking than would ever possibly be considered necessary. On July 4th 1967 licensee Patrick McGee was fined £25 plus £21 costs for allowing the premises to be used for betting transactions.

Fast forward to 2010 and **The Mayflower** - then attracting a £250,000 price tag - went the same route as its Dines Green forerunner in calling orders for the last time: landlady Adele Price saying she wasn't leaving through choice. And in common with its rival with which it had shared a mutual 50-year love/hate relationship, Worcester Community Housing was again swift to move in and remove all traces of the pub. Licence still surprisingly live in 2013; license holders Aqueo Investments of Malvern (no 1183)

Licensees: *Vincent Luther Dishman (licence granted 7th December 1959); Thomas Sidney Harris (1960-62); Patrick McGee (1963-1967); Derrick Langston (1967-68); Ronald Rickets (1968-1975); Arthur Stephens (1975-1976); Michael David Simms (1978-1985); Mary Walsh (1985); Mike and Pam Stevens (1985-1990); Thomas and Carol Bethell (2000); Adele Price*

I should say that this Dines Green section has given me no pleasure whatsoever to write, so let's move hastily on. Luckily, while we're at the City's westernmost reaches, we don't have too far to go - and this one's very much alive and kicking....

The Coppertops
Location: Laugherne Road
Years active: c1970 - present

Mitchells and Butler's house once popular with chicken in a basket crowd and Saturday night cabarets which also hosted some surprisingly big names early on in their careers, and in some cases, others on their way back down; legendary Status Quo is said to have once played here as did some of the top comedians of the day. Downstairs restaurant also added to the appeal of a pub viewed as an extension to the Dines Green estate, though successive gaffers tried to distance themselves from their often rowdy neighbours. It had been open perhaps ten or eleven years when, in 1981, I reviewed it for the Good Beer Guide. I must've been in mischievous mood that day as I wrote: 'The scene: Bar. Coppertops. Tuesday. Half one-ish. Action: thirsty reporter walks in. Total silence. The gaffer blinks. 'Yes' he gestures, shaken, not stirred. Reporter: 'Pint of mild please'. End of action. Curtain. Slow hand clap. If it's drama you're after watch the clock going round'. Ouch! I don't doubt I didn't go back there for about 20

Coppertops 2012 (BB)

years. I confessed – barely necessarily given the intro – that I was not ever so taken with what had been 'a posey estate pub done to death with copper tops everywhere and the olé olé, hacienda-style, bullfighting and sombrero español look' that characterised the late 1960s: the Lounge was actually called the Matador Lounge, with Topaz Room and Orlando's Bar - the restaurant that was run as a separate entity and I described it as 'absolutely incredible: tastefully done, smart to a tee and in a class of its own'. The Coppertops was then, I noted, a posey estate pub made worse on account of the old copper tops getting tarnished and no doubt having being thrown out. I found the place dark, cold and unwelcoming where the beer (M&B, 47p) was 'flat, cold, fizzy and empty' and the place 'cold enough to freeze the whass'names off a whass'name – though I admitted that the Saturday night cabarets at £1.25 a throw, added a welcome sparkle but that the real draw was the restaurant. Recently re-opened after a long spell in the dark with new, young owners that I hope can make a go of it. A Punch Taverns house

Licensees: *Joseph Edmunds (1980); Anne and Brian Abbott (1990). Current licensee (2013); Mark Wild.*

Worcester City Licence no: 1303

from St Johns Church to St Johns Green

St Johns Green 2013 (BB)

St Johns Green 1930s (CCMH/CFOW)

In 1958, the Worcester Directory listed three pubs with a 'St Johns' address: The Angel at no 24, The Bell (Hotel) at no 35 and The Swan at no 81, so let's look at those next.... The Angel we've already discussed, so let's consider the proliferation of pubs that many associate most with the 'Village in the City': St Johns to what was known for years as 'St Johns Green' and along the surprisingly well-serviced, pub-wise, Bransford Road. Somewhere around here (details sketchy) once stood...

W9 Crispin, and Crispin and Crispianus
Location: St Johns
Years active: 1600s-1780
Precise location unclear, but mentioned retrospectively by Noake (1877) as one of a number of 'ancient' City inns, some of which were probably not much less ancient than the eighteenth or even 17th century, possibly also on the same site as...

W10 Cock & Cross
Also known as The Cross
Location: St Johns
Years active: 1780 - 1800
Seemingly short-lived inn listed only as 'St Clement ward', later more accurately as St Johns, though precise location unknown. First mentioned in Victuallers Recognizances in 1766 ('Croff') under licensee Thomas Smith; in 1790 under H. Baker and two years later by Grundy as in the ownership of 'Mrs Brown'. Evidently in close proximity to the church and possibly an earlier name for another inn – an outside chance it could even have been the forerunner of what was, still is, and on present reckoning always likely to remain, the suburb's most enduring and popular pub...

Bell 2013 (BB)

W11 The Bell Inn
Location: 35, St Johns
Years active: existing pre-1820 to present
Facing the church, to which it owes its existence and with a history that goes back almost as far, The Bell was, according to Worcester chronicler Hubert Leicester originally the Church House, playing an important part in the social life of the parishioners by baking the bread and brewing the ale for those who were not able to bake and brew in their own homes.

'The profits of these houses were devoted to parish purposes. Many afterwards became licensed public houses and this accounts for so many inns being close to churches **The Mug House** at Claines and **The Bell** in St Johns may be quoted as cases in point' (*'Worcester Remembered' - 1935*).

The Bell was also the historic site of the Court of Pied Poudre – set up to adjudicate in all cases arising during the annual fair traditionally held on St Johns Green on the Friday before Palm Sunday and which, the law demanded, had to be settled before the dust ('poudre') of the fair was off the foot ('pied') or more correctly feet

Bell 1964 (JAS)

of the litigants. The cellars were also used as cells for offenders. Mind, more than one licensee here found himself hauled up before the powers-that-be... On February 1st 1875 licensee Robert Williams was convicted for refusing to admit a police constable here and was fined £1 including costs. Five years later, his successor Richard Rowberry was convicted (Jan 5th 1880) for allowing gaming and was fined 16/- (80p) plus costs. On November 26th 1883 Ann Rowberry was convicted for permitting drunkenness and was fined 10/6d (521/2p) plus 9/- (45p) costs. Long-term licensee Arthur Michael (1947-71) had been a professional footballer playing with Crystal Palace, Kidderminster Harriers and Worcester City – where he was also coach and trainer for 30 years. 'The old pub cloakroom was a courtroom years ago. People were tried there and then taken down to be hung on the Bull Ring. All the cells were still there in the cellars and the beams down there came from old sailing ships. When we moved in, it was what I would call a 'spit and sawdust' pub. The floor was stone slabbed with rough wooden seats and tables. We changed all that and had a parquet block floor put down and proper leather seats put in. The bar at the back, what we used to call the smoke-room has got a bay window that looks onto the passage. That's got a preservation order on it... The passage with the bar on the left – there used to be little shops on the other side at one period. The smoke room and the 'spit and sawdust' room were totally apart. The latter was terrible really, old tables with scuffed tops, a dirty old fireplace as black as night. Most of the customers were cider drinkers but they soon went. It was the rough old cider that was served. The first thing I saw when I got there was five mice playing... so grandpa when down to the City ground where he was a trainer and brought a cat back – and I had a cat in the pub for 21 years! It was a popular pub. If you didn't get in at the weekend before eight pm you didn't get a seat. Beer was 10d (4$\frac{1}{2}$p) for a pint of mild and if we didn't take £100 on a Saturday, I thought I was doing poor business' *(Pip and Tom Michael, 'Memories of St Johns' edited and compiled by Philip M. Adams).*

The current 3-storey red-brick building, still with some of its timber framing exposed, dates from 1780-1800 and the M&B pub (originally Hitchman's of Banbury 1914-1936 and then Hunt Edmunds and Co. of Banbury 1936-1966), remains a favourite with the local CAMRA on account of its support of local real ale breweries, still has a thriving social social side with brewery visits, team contests and a lively music and entertainments scene in the back functions room. The public bar and two side bars to the right as you enter still retain something of the 'olde' pub as was. As befits a pub with such a long history, The Bell also lays claim to its own ghost who's noted for clinking bottles and glasses though he/she failed to materialise some 30 years ago when a troop of 12 scouts made an all-night vigil in the cellars hoping for a glimpse of the mischievous (and obviously shy) spectre. Listed variously as Bell, Bell Inn and Bell Hotel at addresses 52 and 35 St Johns and with an entry in Universal British Directory 1791 under the heading 'Principal Inhabitants of St John's in Bedwardine (sic) as under stewardship of William Munn and the following year in Grundy's Directory, its licensees have been: *Wm Mann or Munn (1792); Thomas Spilsbury (1820 and 1829); William Spilsbury (1835); Wm Hancock (1842 and 1850); Robert Williams (1872-1876); Richard Rowberry (1876-1882); Herbert Cresswell (1887); Mary Jauncey (1888); George Woodyatt (1890-1891 when he was declared bankrupt); Thomas Walker (1891-94); Thomas Yarnold (1894); Thomas Hopwood (1896-99); Ellen Hopwood (1899-1922); Waldegrave Ingram (1922-1927); William Webster (1927-1929); George Albert Jenkins (1929-1932); Walter Slater (1932-1943); Gertrude Ellen Phelps (1943-1947); Arthur Thomas Henry Michael (1947-1971); John Ruff (1971-1977); David 'Chick' Smith (1977-1981); Reginald Wilson (1977-1981); William J. Clarke (1981-2001). Current licensee (2013); Guy Philip Stephenson.* Worcester City Licence no: 1216

Another pub in this location though precise records provide little by way of 'hard' evidence is....

W12 **Salutation**
Location: St Johns
Years active: 1700 - 1750
Precise location unclear, but mentioned by Noake (1877) as one of a number of 'ancient' City inns, some of which are probably not much less ancient than the eighteenth or even 17th century.

On the same side, less than a hundred yards south - past the present day shops that includes an almost intact mediaeval building side-by-side with a Chinese takeaway and others – is the old St Johns Cinema, later ZigZag nightclub and even more recently, though actually more than thirty years ago, Tanya's. It's now (2013) a much vandalised and derelict eyesore of a site, but here once stood a pub called:

The King's Head
Location: St Johns (site of former cinema and nightclub)
Years active: 1790 - 1911

The King's Head, built in the reign of George III who demonstrated a particular affection for the City though at the time St Johns was still considered a township in its own right, dates from around the time of the rebuilding of the nearby Bell and was active for around 110 years, closing on December 29th 1911. In March 1903, licensee Walter Muddell was fined £1 with £2/10/6 (£2.52^1/$_2$p) costs or one month in prison for three offences in quick succession - all three for allowing gaming on the premises: January 24th 1903, February 21st and February 28th. Four years later it had given way to a bright new palace to the new phenomenon of the age, the cinema, becoming St Johns Cinema and also for a time a music hall – though that too had slipped into 'Bug-house' territory and by the 1950s was reduced to showing iffy French ciné and titillating art (ie nudist) films. Prior to that, The King's Head had been listed in Universal British Directory 1791 under the heading 'Principal Inhabitants of St John's in Bedwardine' (sic) as under the stewardship of John Harding and again the following year in Grundy Royal Directory 1792.

Licensees: *Gabriel Bristow ('King's head st johns' 1790); John Glover (1820); Ann Matthews (1829 and 1835); Joshua Bridges (1842-1870s); Charles Hughes (1872-1881); William Hughes (1881-1883); John Turner (1883-1894 when he died); Mary Turner (1895-1897); James Whitehouse (1897-1900); Thomas Watkins (1900-1902); Walter Muddell (1902-1909); George Edward Jones (1909)*

Just two doors away, stood – indeed, still stands though looking exceedingly sorry for itself and just begging for the bulldozer to come and finish it off:

The Swan (later The Smoke Stack)
Location: 83, St.Johns
Years active: 1750 (rebuilt 1930s) - 1990

The original Swan dates from the 1700s but this final incarnation is a much later building, probably 1930s and devoid of any character. Described by 'Rambler' John Noake 1877 as 'probably not much less ancient than some of the City's ancient inns', the original Swan is also listed in Universal British Directory 1791 under the heading 'Principal Inhabitants of St John's in Bedwardine (sic) as under stewardship of Francis Bevan' and in Grundy Royal Directory 1792 as 'Thos Crow fwan inn widowwer'.

It was also occasionally used for inquests. On 29th July 1824, the inquest was held here 'into the body of a new-born male child' and on 4th October 1827 that of Isaac Jones who'd fallen into the river from a trow and drowned, aged 42. On January 12th 1916, long-term licensee Edward Coombs who ran the Swan from around 1915 to 1946 was fined £2 for unlawfully supplying to William Stuart Handley (a name that often occurs in such cases implying that he was 'plant' or snoop for the licensing authorities), a measure of intoxicating liquor for which he asked an amount exceeding that measure' a clumsily-worded allusion to overcharging. Despite today's listed status, the former Ansells-owned site (formerly owned by Rushtons Brewery Ltd) has been run-down, boarded-up and little more than an eyesore since its closure in 1990 and is surely soon due for a rendezvous with a bulldozer.

Licensees: *Francis Bevan (1792); Thos Crow ('fwan inn widowwer); Joseph Matthews (1820); Thomas Price (1829); Thomas Frances (1835); Joseph Watkins (1842-c1860s); Frank Hodges (1872-1876); William Hendley (1876-1881); Francis Morton (1881-1888 when he died); Fanny Morton (1888-1894); Edward Brown (1894-1897); Thomas Birbeck (1897-1900); George Coombs (1900); Edmund Coombs (1900-1912); Lily Coombs (1916-1923); Edmund Coombs (1923-1945 when he died); Lily May Coombs (1945-46); Florence Emily Pengelly (27th May 1946 - 1st November 1948); George Warman (1948-1954, transferred to Stanley David Howells and transferred again to John Arthur Meadows (1955-56); transferred to George Kenneth Webb July 1955 and then to William Frederick Ypres Rumsey 6th February 1956); Michael Kevan Regan (1960-61); Albert Canvington (1961-62); Thomas Davies (1963); Ernest Gardner (1963-1968); Edward Fisher (1968-1976); Derek Thomas (1976)*

Star, now Ruby Restaurant 2013 (BB)

Star, 1970s (CCMH/CFOW)

Bransford Road

...could rightly be considered a one-time pubs paradise given the long line of pubs that once stretched ribbon-like along its length: the area is still not badly served, given the present times, but remains a shadow of its former self when it boasted a string of thriving pubs stretching almost as far as Rushwick, starting with:

W15 The Star
Location: Bransford Road
Years active: 1820-1990

Now Star Chinese Restaurant, but in a building that is still recognisable as the pub it had been, The Star first saw light of day around 1820, enjoying a respectable 170-year life-span before yielding to economic pressures. On April 3rd 1903, licensee Edward Brown was fined £1 (or 14 days in prison) by Worcester magistrates for unlawfully allowing a person to deliver intoxicating liquor in an unsealed vessel to an under-age boy. A Robert Allen Brewery house (later Hanson's), The Star – for which records exist showing an application for a bay window in March 1893 – was highly popular in its day, particularly as a sporty pub games venue big on league sports crib, darts and dominoes, with a well documented list of licensees. Listed variously as St Johns, St Johns Square (1835), Bransford Road, 99 Bransford Road, 98 and 99 Bransford Road, and 38 Bransford Road, the list includes *Samuel Webb (1820); Susannah Webb; (1829); Frances (also listed as Francis) Hill (1842-c1860s); Joseph Barnett (1872- 1884 this was taken over by Amelia Barnett his widow in 1884-1891); John Underwood (1891); Emily Baker (1891); William Lightwood (1892-1897); Edward Brown (1897-1914); Charles Walker (1915-1918); William Surman (1918-1922); Reginald Harold Taylor (1922-1942); Florence Taylor (1942-1946); Reginald Taylor (1946); Howard Griffin (1946-1952); Albert Victor Cooper (1952-1961); David John Humphries (1961-65;) Eric Every (1965); William Barton (1965-1967); John Hopkins (1967-68); Bruce Whitney (1968-1970); Anna Rawlings (1970-1972); Albert Fisher (1972-74); Brian Dike (1974-76); Raymond Dayus (1976-79); Raymond Jones (1979-1983); Colin Mills (1983-84); Anthony Ratcliffe (1984); John Lynch (1984-85); George Smith (1985); Roger Marsh (1990).*

Two little-remembered pubs existed on the other (ie south) side of the road

W16 The Royal Oak
Location: 49 Bransford Road
Years active: c1820 and 1885-6

Few records exist of this pub, save a record of its address, from which we can gauge its approximate location: 49 Bransford Road.

Licensees: *Joseph Gwillam (1872-1881); Herbert Powell (1881-1892); Thomas Wilkinson (1882-83); Charles Powell (1883); Frederick Miles (1883); Emma Garland (1884)*

Bransford Road 2013 (BB)

Bransford Road c 1908 (CCMH/CFOW)

It's possible that the Royal Oak's life and that of the following pub, were shortened as the direct result of being sandwiched between two apparently larger and, history would suggest, far more popular pubs, The Star and The Crown. Filling the void left by the demise of the Royal Oak, 30 years later saw the creation of another pub – though it too was seemingly short-lived– right opposite and just a few doors away from the longer-established Star. This was:

 W17

The Express (Tavern)
Location: 38 Bransford Road
Years active:1900 - 1922
   Comparatively short-lived, The Express closed January 31st 1932 and became a plumber's premises.
Licensees: *James Brooks (1872-1888 when he died); Susanna Brooks (1888-1903 when she died); Mrs Mary A, Duesbury 90 Bromyard Road (1903-1911 when she died); Charles Duesbury (1911); George Perkins (listed as 'beer retailer' 1911-1918 when he died. The pub was then taken by his widow Maria Perkins 1918).*

Possibly the site of the Royal Oak 2013 (BB)

   Akin to the ill-fated Royal Oak, it's similarly likely that this pub's life was shortened through being sandwiched between its larger rivals. Just across the road still stands:

W18

The Crown
Location: 178a Bransford Road
Years active: 1790 - present
   The Crown, still a pleasant-looking little pub despite its years – and still looking as though it belongs on some sort of village green which, is probably once did – appears to have enjoyed a healthy life from around its first listing, Universal British Directory 1791 under the heading 'Principal Inhabitants of St John's in Bedwardine (sic) as under stewardship of William Tustain and also a year

later as David Powell with address given simply as St Johns (1790).

On 27th August 1897 licensee Arthur Rowe was convicted by Worcester magistrates of unlawfully selling intoxicating liquor here without a licence. He was fined 5/- (25p) with £2/6/0 (£2.30) costs. On 5th February 1959 Goldsmith Riley died while still the licensee of the Crown: the license was transferred to William Thomas Barker on 2nd May 1960. Licensee Ron Hale (1967-1969) was known as 'The Duke of Lowesmoor' after running **The Alma** Lowesmoor following a stint as a bookie with his father Jack. He claimed to be the only Worcester publican who was also a tic-tac man!

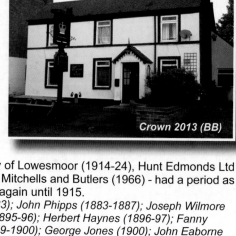
Crown 2013 (BB)

It's possible that The Crown - originally owned by G H Browne Brewers London (1888-1898) and then by Albion Brewery (1898-1903) later by Harpers Hitchman Brewery of Lowesmoor (1914-24), Hunt Edmonds Ltd registered at Bridge Street Banbury (1966) and thence to Mitchells and Butlers (1966) - had a period as a private residence as it appears not to have been listed again until 1915.

Licensees: *David Powell (1790); Richard Rees (1872-1883); John Phipps (1883-1887); Joseph Wilmore (1887-1894); George Badham (1894-95); Sampson Brian (1895-96); Herbert Haynes (1896-97); Fanny Holder (1898-99); Arthur Rowe (1897-98); Charles Link (1899-1900); George Jones (1900); John Eaborne (1900-03); Albert Roberts (1903-1908); John O'Connor (1908-10); Thomas Challoner (1910-14); Benj Westwood (1914) but then continues with Mrs Mary Westwood (1914-29); Flora Westwood (1931-34); Walter George Phillips (1934-39); Chas. or Goldsmith Riley, (address then changed to Crown Inn 66 Bransford Road (1939-1960); William Thomas Barker (1960-63); Harold Jauncey (1963-66); Ron Hale (1966-1970); Brian and Marilyn Hunt (1972-82); Maurice Hannay (1983); John Mitchell (1990); Colin Robinson (2000); Current licensee (2013); Peter Christopher Styles (dps Ms Rosie Melville) Worcester City Licence no: 1178*

A diversion now - but a welcome one... In School Road on the right hand (ie western) side stands another pub that had an unassailable reputation for several generations - though its light, like several others, has somewhat dimmed in recent years. This is:

The Berkeley Arms
Location 4, School Road
Years active: c1870 – present

The Berkeley – generally pronounced as Berkley rather than the Bar-kley as applied to other pubs taking their name from the Worcestershire family – is a popular late-Victorian local that's always been big on games. It's always been – and never really seemed much bothered about being anything other than – just a friendly local pub with a reputation for good ale (Hanson's), good company, and good pub games.

On 9th June 1873, its licensee Samuel Haynes was convicted by City magistrates of unlawfully permitting drunkenness at the pub for which he was fined £1 with

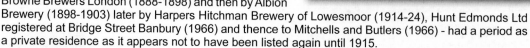
Berkeley Arms 2013 (BB)

11/- (55p) costs. In more recent years *(like, 1981)* then licensee – former plumber Barrie Dixon who'd been a regular at The Berkeley long before becoming its manager – said '...the only attraction here is the beer. There's nothing else, so we aim to keep a good pint' (mild, I noted, was at the time 44p in the bar and 45p in the lounge, bitter 46p and 47p).

The Berkeley also seems to be one of just a few that managed to shrug-off the traditional St John's cliqueyness: talking about the beer Barrie said at the time: '...it's for that reason we're pretty much packed out every night of the week – and not all by locals either. Some regulars come here from over the river and if that's not a good recommendation, tell me what is!". I believe I failed: as I confessed, 'I really can't improve very much on that... My, but the beer's a delight and beyond that there's ... well, there's... let's face it, not very much at all' I wrote, adding: '...the 'cosy, workmanlike, strictly functional bar does a fair impression of a sardine tin most nights of the week'. There was, I noted, four topics of conversation: 'football and dominoes, and dominoes and football!'

Licensees: *Samuel Haynes (1872-1891); Thomas Tomkinson (1891-97); Edgar Wells (1897-1898); Joseph Churchill (1898-1900); Rueben James (1899-00); George Carter (1900-01); Henry and Lavinia Howell (1901); Frederick Baker (1902-3); Albert Barnfield (1903-04); Reginald Winn (1904-06); Thomas Gardner (1906-08); Edwin T. Rea (1908-10); Charles Moore (1910-1911); George Woodhouse (1911); Flora Clements (1911-12); George Baker (1912-15); Harry Bancroft (1915-16); Alice Bancroft (1916-17); William Whitley (1917-1920); Harriett Pountney (1920-26); Alfred Curnie (1926-28); William Wood (1928-1932); Silas Stewart (1932-36); George Edward Knight (1936-37); Frank W. Knott (1937-1950); Alfred Smith (1950-1959); Nellie Edith Filler (1959-68); June Stephens (1968-72); Abel Tolley (1972-4) John Shepherd (1974-79); George Smith (1979-80); Barrie Dixon (1980-2); John Higgins (1982-83); Peter Smith (1983); Trevor Sandall (1983-84); William Rutter (1984-86); Alfred Thomas (1986); Paul Lane (1990); John Reeks (2000); Gordon and Pat Taylor (2001-2005). Current licensee (2013); Richard John Kenwrick. Worcester City Licence no: 1333*

Returning to the main road and still headed westwards in the direction of Bransford, you could almost be forgiven for missing the next pub which is...

W21

The Herefordshire House
Location: 99, Bransford Road
Years active: 1859 - present

Another St Johns pub with a pedigree that stretches back longer than most would give it credit for – over 150 years.

First listed in Victuallers Recognizances in 1859 and later Littlebury's Directory of Worcestershire 1873, it's tucked away off-road so passers-by could be forgiven for not knowing it's there. Listed variously as Bransford Road and 99 Bransford Road, 'The Herry' closed briefly in 2012 but has since re-opened.

It's another popular local M&B pub that I remarked on in a recent blog *(http://bobbackenforth.wordpress.com* October 2nd 2012: '... saddened too by the rumour – and I stress, so far it is just a rumour but it comes from a postman, so he should know – of yet another good old house shutting up for good: The Herefordshire House in Bransford Road, where I must admit I haven't set foot in since the day I got embarrassingly brushed while playing darts for the old Sketchley's Club. That was 1976 and I haven't had the brass whass'names to call in again on account of I blush very easily. Wish I had now...' It would appear my fears were ungrounded as I made a visit as recently as June 2013 when while not packed to overcrowding on a Sunday lunchtime, it had a fair smattering of friendly punters that again made me wish I hadn't taken so long to become re-acquainted with it.

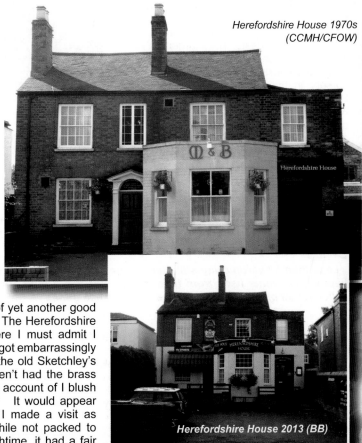

Herefordshire House 1970s (CCMH/CFOW)

Herefordshire House 2013 (BB)

Licensees: *Henry Farr (1859); John Roberts (1872-75); ? Hundley (1875-79); Penney (1879-1881); James Ashcroft (1881-1883); Robert Martin (1883-4); William Moore (1884-5); Mary Bedford (1885-9); Ernest Morris (1889-90); Emma Baker (1890-92); Allen Underwood (1892-3); Thomas Brooks (1893-6); William Taylor (1896-7); Matthew Henry Bissell (1897-1901); William Walker (1901-05); Thomas Kay (1905-*

7); *Thomas Arthur Pearson (1907-1927 when he died); Arthur. Beasant (1924); Joseph Henry Richards, Herefordshire House, 99 Bransford Road (1935-1949); Douglas Smith (1949-50); Leslie Francis Seymour Austin (1950-1953); Reginald Alfred Yeale (1953-1954); Lawrence Owen Grogan (1954-1958); Henry Gould (1958-1959); William Laurie Stark (1959-1973); Elsie Stark (1973-74); Peter (and Jeannette) Bodily (1974-1981); Carol O'Meara (1981-85); Peter Wood (1985); Michael Hill (1990); James Wainwright (2000). Current licensee (2013); Gary and Lorraine Key Wainwright. Worcester City Licence no: 1007*

Two long-forgotten rarities follow...

(W20) The Half Moon
Location: Bransford Road
Years active: 1870 - 1880?
Barely remembered pub – or more likely off-licence on site of Silplas builders merchants and BCP Motor Services. Owned by R Hyde of Rushwick. Closed in 1873 with only one licensee recorded: James Horsley (1872)

Site of the Half Moon (BB)

(W22) The Gardeners Arms
Location: 1, Little Boughton Street, roughly where Smiths Ave now stands
Years active: 1872 -1911
As its name suggests, The Gardeners Arms was created specifically for workers at what was once considered the biggest and best nursery in the UK. Certainly, at one time Smith's Nurseries stretched from Bransford Road to Malvern Road and Lower Wick,

Site of the Gardeners Arms (BB)

covering 180 acres, supplying florists throughout the region and employing hundreds of groundsmen and others - all of whom no doubt thirsted for a good pint or two of foaming ale after the working day. The nursery's wily gaffers, cottoning-on to the fact that their workmens' wages were being spent in nearby hostelries hastily jumped on the bandwagon and created a pub – as like as not with the intention of clawing back the cash they'd just handed out. Active as a pub between 1872 until December 29th 1911.

Licensees: *John Lyons (1872-1879); Edward Sheriff (1879-1888); George Webb (1888-1891); John Robins (1891-1896); Harry Jones (1896-7); Rueben Jones (1897-1898 when he died); Harry Jones (1898-1899); Thomas Ogree (1899 when he died); Ada Costello (1901-1909); Eliza King (1901-1909)*

Less than 50 yards away still stands one of St Johns' most enduring and popular pubs that happily re-invents itself from time to time but has a long and unbroken history as well as a collection of photographs from years long since gone...

(W23) The Portobello (originally, Porto Bello)
Location: Bransford Road
Years active: 1820 to present (rebuilt 1984)
Like many on what was one of the main drovers' routes into Herefordshire, The 'Port' has been in existence since around 1820.
First listed in Pigot's Worcestershire Directory 1829 and a strong contender for the title 'the biggest angler's pub in Worcester' the 'Port' can call on a long and but for a short spell for reconstruction, unbroken history even up to the present. The original building was transformed out of all recognition when it was tarted-up and extended into the brand new Portobello which opened 1984 though its spruce new facelift also saw the emphasis switch from the beer it sold (Banks's, originally Robert Allen and Co Ltd) in favour of food - which was a shame as I gave it the max 3 stars when I reviewed the (old) Portobello in 1981, then under the managership of Ron and Flo Brown. As Brummie Ron put it: "...this is a drinking mon's pub, ah doh know worrelse yo' can say abaht it – 'cept as we seem ter attract a lot of elbow-nutters – them as 'as to be standin' elbow-ter-elbow 'fore they can enjoy theerselves".
As I noted: '...it's get-it-down-your-neck time all the time where if you want your braces dangling it's alright, where if you're the shy and retiring type you're unlikely to get noticed and where conversation

Portobello 1900 (CCMH/CFOW)

Portobello 1972 (CCMH/CFOW)

Portobello 1910 (CCMH/CFOW)

(Map reproduced from 1936 Ordnance Survey map with permission of the Ordnance Survey)

isn't compulsory though if it centres on fishing, football or skittles and comes over loud and chucklesome, you're probably in!'. I described decoration as 'this year's in-colour: tobacco-stain amber'. At the time it boasted eight skittles teams and men's and ladies' darts and crib teams while the previous month's spirits order was just... *three bottles!*

With the creation of the 'new' and very much scrubbed and sterilised Portobello three years later, the emphasis switched dramatically, catering for couples and workers from the then-active businesses seemingly flourishing nearby and re-creating itself as a foodies' heaven with exposed fake beams, pretty brickwork, books bought by the yard, and a mock Tudor feel. While it maintained a public bar, the two sides never quite saw eye-to-eye and the Port paid the price of cutting off its core drinkers' trade – particularly feeling the pinch when Kays closed its Bransford Road branch and then, a few years later, its massive Bromyard Road warehouse, combined with the demise of former Willis' Cinderella shoe factory and virtually all of the one-time thriving engineering concerns on its doorstep, all of which had till then furnished a large proportion of its customers. Now a Marstons house.

Licensees: *Elizabeth Lloyd (initially listed as Porto Bello, but thereafter 'Portobello' 1829); John Griffin (1872-1879); Susannah Griffin (1879-1880); John Griffin (1880-1883); George Cartwright (1883); William Osser (1883-4); James Priest (1884-6); William Daw (1886-1899); Arthur Allen (1899-1903); James Hunt (listed as Portobello Inn, Bransford Road, St Johns 1903-4); Walter J. Blake (1904-9); Frederick Mills (1909-1915); Alfred Hawkes (1915-31); Henry Evans (1931-1942); Patience Berry (1943-1952); Leslie Gordon Dobson (1952); James Bartlett (1952-1955); Albert Parker (1955-1960); Bruce William Whitney (1960-1963); Lilian Fellows (1963-4); Basil Owen (1964-1971); Gerald Robinson (1971-75); Robert Bettles (1975-6); Ray Brookes (1976-7); Graham Smith (1977-78); Michael Moore (1978-81); Ron Brown (1981-1983); Martin Mulhearn (1983); John Bonehill (1983-4); Stephen Jackson (1984-85); Richard Wallace (1985-1989); Peter Smith (1989); Chris Gore (2000); Royce Hasbury (2001). Current licensee (2013) Marston's, dps Edward William Joseph Salmon. Worcester City Licence no: 1094*

Finally, on the road to Bransford...

W24

The White Hall
Location: Rushwick
Years active: 1840-present

Whitehall 2012 (BB)

Rushwick was not strictly within Worcester City boundary limits, nor was it listed in the Worcester City Police Register of Intoxicating Liquor Licenses to 1961, though the Whitehall's history stretches back sufficiently far to make it interesting and worth a visit.

Listed variously as Bransford Road (1844); White Hall, Upper Wick (1873) and Whitehall Rushwick, St Johns (1900), its (incomplete) list of licensees includes: *Thomas Davis (listed as White Hall (1842-180s); Thos. Symmonds (1873); Fredk. Summers (1900); Mrs Sophia Hook (1902); Ben Holt (1908); Joseph B. Heath (1910); J. Calder (1915); Jsph. S. Potter (1930-1940s)*

from St Johns Church along Malvern Road

In direct contrast to the swathe of pubs along Bransford Road – many springing-up along the route of the drovers who herded their cattle towards the Bull Ring for slaughter and thence wearily back again, presumably laden with cash and without their beasts in tow – the long and leafy Malvern Road offers just one pub, with another tucked away and almost lost in the straight lines of housing dating from the late 1800s.

We're now at a point south of what had been St Johns Green – site of the Mop Fayre, and the former turnpike, close to what's now the Citroën garage, opposite the **Swan** and former **Smoke Stack** standing just two doors away from the old **Kings Head** demolished in 1915 to make way for St Johns Cinema.

Headed southwards, towards Malvern, you can't help but notice...

W25

Brunswick Arms
Location 500 Malvern Road
Years active: around 1900 - present

The Brunswick - 'Brunny' to those more intimate with it than me – is a mean, solid-looking pub, situated on the Malvern Road/Great House Road junction: as such it tends to cater mostly for St Johns' locals, and the sporty ones at that. It's now a huge-games passionate one-roomer that's a bit brash in a lights-flashing computer gizmos kind of way while on its lively website

'The Brunny' – Brunswick Arms 1950s (right) (CCMH/CFOW) and in 2011 when it seems it had two famous guests! (below BB). Gaffer Chris Hankins reckons the pub offers 'the largest collection of traditional pub games anywhere. "You are welcome to learn, play and enjoy all of these games and free tuition is available at most times"

(http://www.brunswickarms.co.uk) gaffer Chris Hankins reckons the pub offers 'the largest collection of traditional pub games anywhere. "You are welcome to learn, play and enjoy all of these games and free tuition is available at most times. Games include: crockinole, shove ha'penny, bagatelle. quoits, sjoelbak, Irish rings, darts, crib, dominoes, and more". All of which is a million miles from what it had once been. Describing the pub when it was kept by her aunt and uncle Violet and William Smith (1912-31)

Mrs D Gravenall recalled in 'Memories of St Johns' edited and compiled by Philip M. Adams: "... there was no Christopher Whitehead school then, just a big open meadow. I remember a gravel sweep in front of the pub and steps up to the front door. There were railings up each flight and on top of these was a shelf. These were for people who rode on horses to the pub: they could rest their drinks on the shelves whilst remaining 'in the saddle'. The smoke room was for the more upper-class drinkers... it was a lovely room, polished furniture with green leather upholstery and brass fittings – including the spittoons. One (Thursday afternoon) the men had a bet that one of them could drink a whole crate of stout. The pot man brought up the crate and this man set to and drank the lot. The next morning there was a knocking at the back door. It was the man's granddaughter asking if we could get a doctor 'as granddad 'as been took bad'. Unfortunately he died – probably as the result of 24 bottles of stout. Beer was brewed at the pub. The brewhouse was in an outbuilding and I remember there being a great big vat I there where all the ingredients for the beer were put in, boiled up and stirred around. A man from Customs and Excise always came to test the specific gravity of the beer. He used to have a little leather attaché case with 'H. M. Service' on the side and inside lying on red velvet were the brass measuring instruments'. (Memories of St Johns' edited and compiled by Philip M. Adams).

In 1981 then gaffer Cliff Dale with his arm around wife Pat said about The Brunswick '...there's nothing I'd like to change and nothing I'd dare change. I'm proud of my little pub'. I couldn't say for sure if the same rings true 30-odd years on, though I suspect he'd no doubt wriggle in his grave if he could see it now. Then, it probably hadn't changed one jot since it had opened some 80 years before: it had a lounge and a bar and a functions room and a garden. Today it has a bar and garden. Of the lounge, I said 'it's not unlike your favourite auntie's sitting room with all her best friends round for drinkipoos' (I'd noticed about 30 women sat round chatting and that was a lunchtime). It was, I noted 'an absolute pearl' and a few years earlier, The Brunswick had additionally scooped the Sunday Mercury Pub Food Award. Today it's all-in-one where the large girls' tattoos outshine their blokes' and TV sports take precedence.

Originally operated by Hitchman and Co of Chipping Norton, later Hunt Edmunds and Co of 26 Bridge Street Banbury (later M&B) the pub unfortunately earned a reputation of a St Johns rough-house – an unusual accolade – in the later 80s.

Licensees: William Bedford (1872-1881); Susan Bedford (1881-89); Francis Osbourne (1889-1897); Thomas Tomkins (1897-1909, but listed as Thomas Tomkinson in 1908); Walter Blake (1909-12); William Smith (1912-31); Arthur Walter Tunkiss (1931-39 when he died); Arthur Henry Wilcock (1943-1947); Gertrude Ellen Phelps (1947-1966); Harold Jauncey (1966-75): Cliff Dale (1976-86); Patricia Davies (1986); Sean Condon (1990); Stephen Gayden (2000); Maura Ellis (2001). Current licensee (2013); Christopher Walter Hankins. Worcester City Licence no: 1174

The next pub is hidden from sight as if it's too shy to make its presence felt except when it's dark. It's also very red. I don't doubt, then, it's called...

W26

The Fox
Location: 19 Pitmaston Road
Years active: 1898 - present

Pitmaston Road 1910. The Fox can be seen half way down on the right hand side (CCMH/CFOW) And above, 2013 (BB)

The Fox is a purpose-built Edwardian Ansells (originally Rushdons Brewery) pub dating from around 1900 and catering for the (then rapidly) growing population of St Johns.

On January 13th 1916, licensee Matthew John Tolley was found guilty by City magistrates that he did '...unlawfully supply William Stuart Hundley *(that name again)* as the measure of intoxicating liquor for which he asked, an amount exceeding that measure'. Hard to see what the crime was - ie by the sound of it he gave his customer too much. Seems the police sergeant had put the comma in the wrong place, thereby completely changing the meaning *(try it!)* Essentially, he'd charged his snooping customer too much and was fined £2 for having done so.

More recently The Fox is one that St. Johns folk tend to keep for themselves – with the exception of visiting crib-players who found themselves bemused for more than two decades by two elderly women players (one of which was the captain I recall) who won virtually every game they ever played despite most seasoned players calling them the worst (and certainly least conventional) crib players they'd ever encountered!

Licensees: *Margaret Williams (1898-99); Emily Fern (1899-1902); Clarence Russell (1902-7); Arthur Johnson (1907-14); Matthew John Tolley (also listed as Jn Matthew Tolley, though possibly father and son, 1914-1941); Westall (1941-2); Irene Deakin (1942-4); Reginald Fawdry (1944); George Worman (1944-8) Cyril James Bartlett (1948-1950); Archie Llewellyn Tyler (1950-1956); Raymond Thomas Brown (1956); James Frederick Ashdown (1956-58); William Stephen Buckley (1958); Henry Grosvenor (1958-1960); Dorothy Allerton (1960); Joseph Powell (1960); Winifred Jauncey (1960-1963); Cyril Diment (1963-6); Charles Rushton (1966-72); Harold Turvey (1972-83); Arthur Bryan (1983-4); Kenneth Lamb (1984-2001). Current licensee (2013); Kenneth Lamb. Worcester City Licence no: 1275*

Fox 2013 (BB)

Hard right at the Bromwich and Malvern Roads roundabout (the Lower Wick garage) and along the spine road of the estate built on former orchards and originally intended for Army families is...

W27 The Maple Leaf
Location: 49 Canada Way
Years active: 1970 - present

The Maple Leaf remains one of the better-designed and better preserved of the St Johns pubs, still looking like what it's always been: a sprawling late 60s estate pub - though, thank the Lord, it has resisted the temptation, like many of similar pedigree, of seeing its inside hammered-about into a huge multi-purpose lounge-cum-bar-cum-playroom. Instead, The Maple Leaf – so named on account of the predominantly Canadian theme the 77-home former orchard estate goes by – happily retains a distinct bar/lounge which also doubles up as carvery restaurant, still operating with distinction, much to its credit. At initial glance, The Maple Leaf appears to be ageing well. An Admiral Taverns house.

Licensees: *Ronald Perks (1980); Eric Richards (1990); Steve Gravener (2000). Current licensee (2013); Ms Heidi Kirkham. Worcester City Licence no: 1246*

Maple Leaf and sign 1972 (CCMH/CFOW)

A mere stone's throw away across the now scarily-busy A449 which even half a century ago retained something of the country lane feel about it despite being a main A-road, you'll find...

W28 — Manor Farm
Location: Lower Wick (site of Bennett's Dairies)
Years active: 1990 - present

You're walking on history when you visit Manor farm: the location, the former Bennett's Dairy processing and distribution plant that took the place of the Blue Calf Club from the early 90s is the historical site of the former church of Wick Episcopi and it's also thought to have played a role in the Civil War. Winston Churchill also stayed at dairyman John Bennett's house nearby when he was made a Freeman of the City in 1951. Today, the big sprawling pub - well, bar and restaurant really, 'pub' being a misnomer on account of the strong emphasis on food - remains an impressive looking building inside and out. Not always happy experiences of eating here, though. A Harvester roadside eating house operating under the style 'Manor Farm Crown Carveries') it belongs to the same group (M&B Leisure Retail Ltd) as **O'Neill's, Lyppard Grange, The Ketch and The Timberdine.** (The Ketch operates under the style Toby Taverns and The Timberdine under Harvester but they all belong to the same chain). Current licensee/dps (2013); Michael Anthony Wilton. Worcester City Licence no: 1321

From a couple of pubs that are too young to have witnessed a lot of history, let's now gorge ourselves on some of the City's most historic westside inns and taverns. This is the tight cluster of pubs that grew up with the increase of traffic – wheeled, as well as on two legs and four – into the burgeoning City along the main east-west route. It means a return to The Bull Ring, but then when the traffic behaves, that's rarely an unpleasant experience. But first a small diversion... Back to B, pass The Angel and the modern supermarket that took the place of the old tram depot, pass the chippie and the pawn shop with its discarded Fender guitar copies and cast-off bits of machinery of indeterminate use, and turn to Henwick Road. 150 yards in front it just looms up in front of you....

W29 — Grosvenor Inn (and Arms)
Location: 21 Henwick Road
Years active: 1870 - present

Robert Allen (later Hansons pub first listed Littlebury's Directory of Worcestershire 1873 as Grosvenor Inn, Henwick Road and thereafter as 21 Henwick Road. Known as 'The Crackers' and noted for the quality of its beer (Hanson's) throughout latter half of 20th century, it remains surprisingly unchanged, with distinct lounge and bar, equally attractive with still recognisable original features and attracting regular and dedicated customers to suit. Long-term Grosvenor licensee Frank Moss (1930-65) had been a favourite Aston Villa player who'd captained the Villa in the Cup Final and the following Saturday captained England. Both his sons Frank Jnr and Amos were pro footballers too. 'It was a good pub and it had its characters. One of them, and our best customer, was 'Wingy' Holland who'd lost one of his arms in the First World War. One Saturday I got the crib board out and stuck a match in for every drink he had. We opened at 10 and by 1 o'clock he'd drunk 16 pints – and he'd carry on drinking till closing time. On Sunday mornings, nearly all the customers wore a button-hole and mum used to lay out food on the bar, things like squares of cheese, shallots, pickled walnuts and crusty bread. You always knew when someone wasn't having Sunday lunch because they'd get stuck into the food' *(D Moss, quoted from 'Memories of St Johns' edited and compiled by Philip M. Adams).* Once popular, The Grosvenor has now somewhat fallen from grace - due in no small part to lack of a car park. Garden is a hidden gem though. Recently gained some local notoriety when its gaffer who often talked of his exploits in the Parachute Regiment, was visited by some real Paras who'd called in to see if they recognised him as one of their own – and didn't. They weren't best pleased. Now a Marstons house.

Licensees: *Charles Sidney Jones (1872-1880); Charlotte Parker (1880-7); William Perks (1887-1889); Charles Williams (1889-1899); Frederick Robert James (1899-1900); Alice James (1900-02); William J. Hunt (1902-1908); John Henry Luffman (1908-1917); James Randle (1917-1926 when he died); Mrs Betty Randle (1926-30); Frank Moss (1930-1965); Katie Moss (1965-6); Hilda Willis (1966); Clifford Willis (1966); Russell Potter (1966-8); John Hopkins (1968-74); Anthony Wilson (1974-75); Wilfred H. Stokes (1975-*

View of St Johns from St Ckements church (1960s) The Grosvenor is bottom right (CCMH/CFOW)

80); George Smith 1980-3); Ronald Brown (1983-6); William Rutter (1986-90); Ray Jones (1990-2000). Current licensee (2013); William Dailly. Worcester City Licence no: 1116

(right) The Grosvenor in 1886 from the OS map of that year, reproduced with permission Ordnance Survey

Henwick Road c1910 (CCMH/CFOW) and 2013 (BB) showing that not much has changed in the last century - even wonky telegraph poles! A short-lived pub called The Wrens Nest was somewhere around here but like the creature it was named after, it's proving shy and elusive!

W30 **The Wrens Nest**
Location: Henwick Road
Years active:

Barely known pub, specific location unclear though possibly one of the properties in this 1900 photograph (below) the only reference is an application to the City planning department made by a 'Mr Lewis' and dated 22 Nov 1897 for the construction of a water closet. Address given simply as 'The Wrens Nest' Henwick Road. Interesting to note the similarities in the two photographs below despite 113 years separating them!

St Johns Church to Tybridge Street

Back now to The Bull Ring - and here's where we came in (to use an old cinema-going phrase, now rarely uttered). Here you'll find an undoubted pearl of a pub, architecturally, aesthetically, alcoholically, gastronomically and pretty much any other 'ly' you'd care to throw at it. Assuming it's still open (no guarantees) this is...

W31 The Bush (Inn)
Location: Bull Ring
Years active: 1780 (rebuilt 1879) to 2010

The Bush 1964 (JAS) and 2013 (BB)

The Bush is a once fine 18th century inn included by Noake (1877) as one of a number of City inns, some of which are 'probably not much less ancient than 1500' (or thereabouts) and also described in Baylis, Lewis Almanack 1885-8 *(printed 5 New Street, price 1$^1/_2$d)* as 'one among the ancient hostelries (which) were **The Bush, The Rein-Deer, The White Horse, The Talbot** *(Sidbury).* **Lion, Bull, The Bear** *(Hylton Street)*, **Saracen's Head, Trinity Inn, The Talbot** *(The Cross),* **The Globe, The Woolpack, The White Hart, The Cardinal's Hat, The White Lion** *(Cornmarket)* **The Griffin, The Bell, The Antelopp and The Swan** *(High Street).*

On a corner location listed variously as Cripplegate, St Clements, Bull Ring and Clement Street, the Bush's reputation for good company, good beer *(its mild particularly)* and colourful characters (and barmen) was legion up to a sudden and inexplicable falling from grace about 10 years ago. The census of 1841 lists then licensee John Webb as being aged 60 and living here with his wife Honor, 40.

Just a look at the inside *(assuming it's open which is not always the case)* and you'll see The Bush positively reeks of history, charm and character – one of which, no doubt was former licensee James Morgan who, on April 28th 1946, was cautioned by the Chief Constable no less as to his future conduct after persons were found on the premises after permitted hours, the scamps!

Latterly owned by Showells Brewery originally of Oldbury, later Burton-upon-Trent, then Ind Coope and Allsopp (1925-47) before being transferred by conveyance on 9th August 1954 to Atkinsons (later Bass) Brewery of Queen's Road Aston. In *'Memories of St Johns'* edited and compiled by Philip M. Adams and available at the Hive, Les and Helen Jackson-Jones who ran the Bush for 33 years described their first day at the pub in May 1960: '...it was run down. The fabric of the building wasn't too bad but the worst thing we had to contend with was the bad name the pub had. Right up to the time we left, there were some people who would not come into the Bush because they still remember what it had been like. They had called it, jokingly, 'The Tatters Arms". At the end of their first week, takings were £17 when it was 11d (4$^1/_2$ p) for mild 1/1 (5$^1/_2$ p) for bitter. On the day they took over – May 2nd – Atkinsons Brewery amalgamated with M&B. "I always said it was us who kept the pub (afloat) for the first five years" reckoned Helen who'd previously been the licensee of the Pear Tree at Smite. During their time there, Johnny Dankworth and Cleo Laine played as did The Hellions including Dave Mason and Jim Capaldi. So did The Skeeters. "We rarely had any trouble at all because Les had a way with him – he always took the leader out. If anyone got their ticket it was for life – no coming back in a few weeks even. It was all rather sad when we left. We didn't really make enough money to buy the pub and we were too old to go into mortgages and things like that so we decided to get out" *(Memories of St Johns'*

1964: The Bush (far left) just before its surroundings were about to undergo massive changes. And the scale of those changes (left) 2013 (BB)

edited and compiled by Philip M. Adams). The Bush is now owned by Enterprise Inns.

Not surprisingly, up to its demise The Bush had won high praise from no less august a body than the **National Inventory of Historic Pub Interiors** who described it as:

'A lovely, small corner site pub dating from 1879 with two separate rooms and some good fittings. The public bar was originally divided into three with a jug and bottle compartment and also a partition across the middle of the remainder *(you can spot the scars on the counter where the partitions met it)*. It has an excellent bar-back with a prominent pedimented feature, mosaic type mirrors and a clock stating 'Yates & Greenways, Bar Fitters, Birmingham' - the reason why this is one of Britain's Real Heritage pubs... At the back of the pub is the small smoke room, originally the living room, which retains its bell-pushes. Note how the fixed seating is cut away so it is possible to stand at the hatch to the back of the servery. A real curiosity is that as well as having a jug and bottle section there was also an outdoor department (with service through another hatch) - in other words two places where you could go and order take-home supplies (such a dual arrangement is very rare). The jug and bottle was a separate compartment as mentioned while the outdoor involved a hatch to the servery from the tiled corridor. The side entrance has a further corridor with another hatch to the servery. A front window has been replaced with one in the style of the other etched windows, but with the notation 'The Bush Inn'. On the first floor are three function rooms - the largest, now the restaurant, has 'Billiards' etched into the windows and presumably, was used for that purpose' *(Source: National Inventory of Historic Pub Interiors)*

Not much more to be said really - except that, as stated earlier, The Bush has been suffering from open/close syndrome of late with a number of short-lived tenants/licensees coming and going, sometimes at a day's notice, creating confusion and a reluctance to visit in case it's shuttered and barred. And that's a tragedy because when it was good, it was great as The Bush had a great reputation for serving a cracking pint.

Licensees: *John Pardoe (1820); John Webb (1829 and 1835); Thomas Reeves (1842-c1870 listed as Reenes in 1850); Thomas Epps (1872-1875); William Joyner (1875-1896); Frederick James (1898); Albert & Mary Douglas (1898-1900); George Price (1901-02); Thomas Piper (1902-3); James Aston (1903-4); George Wheldon (1904-05); James Aston (1905-09); Joseph Frank Millington (1909-10); William Durham (1910-13); Matthew Tolley (1913-14); Charles H. Bains (1914-21); Thomas Jones (1921-24); Stephen Oates (1924-26); Nugent Foort (1926-27); Caleb White (1927-8); Peter Pavely (1928-31); John Arthur Chadwick (1931-36); John Grady (1936-9); Albert Lewis (1939-41); Norman Gibbins (1941-45); Arthur James Morgan (1945-1953); Edith Anne Morgan (1953-1954); John Ernest Franklin (1954-1956); Eric Ernest Ballinger (1956-1960); James Edward Leslie Jackson-Jones (1960 -1993): John O. Bury (2001). Though currently closed, its licence remains in force (2013); designated premises supervisor Ms Tracy Wagstaff. Worcester City Licence no: 1085*

It was just about here that the original Cripple's Gate - or more likely a toll-house used to collect the fee for using Tybridge Street - once stood. A short stub of road fronting The Bush is all that now remains of the former Cripplegate/Tybridge Street thoroughfare - the major highway into and out of the City in its day. Once home to a sizeable Welsh community (for reasons outlined earlier) who spoke their own language: Torcae - an earlier name for Tybridge Street has a distinctly Celtish ring to it. The area was noted as the location for the manufacture of nails, tobacco pipes and the rope used by bowhauliers on the Severn. 'At the bridgehead on the south side was Williams Distillery which made spirits: their gin was said to be unsurpassed in England... Like all dock areas it contained many pubs and squalid houses. All around were crowded courts of hovels, the most notorious and unsanitary known as The Pinch where the first case of cholera appeared, (sparking off) the 1832 epidemic (Source: Bill Gwilliam - Old Worcester People and Places).

The route led to the river bank and thus directly across to Newport Street, its counterpart on the eastern bank which was similarly awash with pubs, as we shall soon see.... Let's start at the top (Bull Ring) and work down towards the river. Here, though as is the case with many ancient pubs on the westside, details are so sketchy as to be non-existent save name and general location, stood:

W32 White Horse
Location: Cripplegate
Years active: 1780 - 1810

Location not precisely known, but listed Grundy Royal Directory 1790 under stewardship of John Powell - white horfe Cripplegate. Beyond that, nothing else is known.

The Cock 1964 (JAS)
Two years later it was flattened

W33 The Cock
Location: 106, Tybridge Street (also described as Cripplegate)
Years active: 1790 to 1966

Small, but long-lifespan pub on the main route into the City from the west. A 'Cock' is listed in Victuallers Recognizances in 1766 and 1814 as St Clements ward though other entries for **Cock & Cross** list different landlords so they are unlikely to be one and the same.

The Cock is also listed thereafter variously as Cripplegate, Cripplegate St Johns, Clement Street (1842) St Clement Street (1850) 47 Tybridge Street (1900) and 106 Tybridge Street (1940) and is one of four on same side of Tybridge Street listed in 1915: **Cock (no 106), Lamp Tavern (no 84), Apple Tree (no 20)** and **Bear (no 2)**. Latterly owned by Hitchman and Co Ltd, brewers of Banbury, the company that like others found itself eventually swallowed up into the M&B empire, The Cock enjoyed a healthy lifespan though it was run down and looking extremely sorry for itself by the time of its demise on September 29th 1966. 'Mrs White' (presumably, née Evans) whose father ran The Cock from 1919 said 'Dad used to get his beer from Harper and HItchman's in Lowesmoor at the bottom of Rainbow Hill, later on he changed to Hunt Edmunds. The brewers used to bring the beer in hogsheads on horse-drawn drays and let them down to the cellar on ropes – beer was 4d (2p) a pint. During the war a man come round to the pub and said that when any black American soldiers came in we must serve them: we only had a few though because the white ones came in as well and they never mixed. I do remember one night when four black soldiers came in. They were in the smoke room sitting in the alcove when they asked if they could sing. There was a good crowd and these soldiers sang some spirituals: it was lovely. When the pub was going to be demolished I remember seeing the old piano still there: it seemed such a shame that no-one had given it away to a club or something. It was a sad time really'. *('Memories of St Johns' edited and compiled by Philip M. Adams).*

Licensees: *Ann Hawkins (1790); Edward Hawkins (1766); Mrs Holloway (described as 'vict. cock Cripplegate - 1792); William Martin (1814-20s); Jno. Glover (1827); Ezekiel Gummery (c 1840-1870); Charles Higgs (1872-93); Richard M.Giles (1893-1903); Charles Denley (1903-10); Edwin Rea (1910-13); Harry Smith (1913-14); Ellen Clara Skinner (1914-19); Augustus Evans (or Albert Augustus Evans 1919-1946); Alice Evans (1946-1951); Thomas William James Hine (1951-1960); Constance Mary Barker (5th September 1960- close 1966.*

Glovers Arms
Location: Turkey (Tybridge Street)
Years active: 1820s

W34

Seemingly short-lived hostelry listed only in Worcester Lewis Directory 1820 with no listings thereafter. John Morgan listed as 'vict and glove manuf'

Rising Sun
Location: Cripplegate
Years active: 1780 - 1865

W35

Famous in its day and no doubt quite a substantial property, it takes its name from the badge of Edward III. Listed as being in Clement Street and appears to have enjoyed a healthy life span between 1790 (and probably some time before) to around 1865 with just three known licensees: T. Cosnett (1790); F. Cosnight (probably different spellings of the same family name) listed as 'vict. rifing fun Cripplegate' (1792); and William Evans (1814-c1855) who had earlier been tenant of **The Severn Trow** (1812). A handbill and sales particulars exists in the WRO archives in the The Hive dated 23rd May 1859 when it was sold at auction 'at six in the evening'. For lease at £89.6s per annum, it's described as 'old established and well-frequented inn in St Clements Street with yard and appurtenances' (that included a tenement adjoining leased to Maria Farrington and adjoining piggeries). The handbill gives other details but no number – so the inn was clearly important enough to be known simply by its name. It appears to have had, with the tenement adjoining, a frontage of 29 feet and was in the possession of Henry Evans 'aged about 56' and John Clements 'aged about 50'. It's possible the Rising Sun was demolished and in its place rose....

Lamp Tavern
Location: 84, Tybridge Street
Years active: 1898-1965

W36

A better known 'Lamp Tavern' than its Moor Street namesake with a longer and better catalogued history, this former Ansells house once had a butcher's shop attached and was listed variously as 36 Tybridge (1908) and 84 Tybridge Street (1940). In 1915 it was one of four on same side of Tybridge Street as listed above. Closed May 1965 and is still remembered by many. Bert Shepherd's parents had owned **The Green Dragon** in Newport Street, and pubs in Birmingham and Gloucester, and his granddad owned **The Sandpits** (*later The Bedwardine*). In '*Memories of St Johns'* edited and compiled by Philip M. Adams, he recalls that the family lived at The Lamp and also owned the butcher's shop

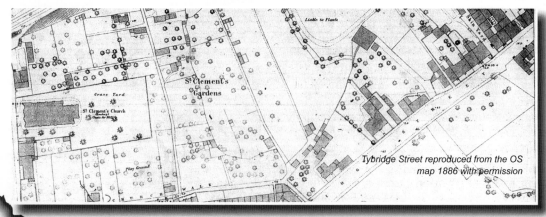

Tybridge Street reproduced from the OS map 1886 with permission

The surprisingly long-lived Lamp Tavern
5th September 1958 (RHS)
And the same site today (BB)

next door. 'The Lamp was a home brew pub. Dad did the brewing in the cellar and the outhouses at the back. The barrels of beer were always cold because there was a stream running through it and as soon as the river came up, so did the stream. The barrels used to float up to the ceiling. There was a smoke-room and a bar at the pub with a little outdoor window where people would come to have their jugs filled up. Upstairs were the living quarters – two bedrooms, bathroom and living room. Along with the family, old Granny Shepherd lived there as well. There were never any fights at the old man's pub. It was a different story though down at **The Bear and The Royal George.** The black marias would drive up and every weekend you could hear it. There were some hard nuts down there, there's no denying it. We used to get a lot of Welsh people up for the races... and one of them smashed the serving window. By sheer luck, police sergeant 'Taffy' Herbert was coming up the street. Anyway some of the people from the pub were holding this bloke when Taffy walked up. He asked Dad 'what's this going to cost to put right?'. Dad told him and he said to the man 'cough up then'. Then he got hold of him and booted him up the backside and out into the street. Instant punishment, end of story – that was it' *(Memories of St Johns' edited and compiled by Philip M. Adams).*

Licensees:: *John Moses Jones (1898-1920); John Denning (1920-22); Bert Shepherd (abode 1, MacIntyre Road 1922-1956); Irene Kathleen Clay (3rd December 1956-3rd February 1957); Beatrice Rail (1957); Freda Turner (1957-58); Rose Beatrice Beauchamp (1958-1959); Winifred Jauncey (1959-60); Doris Gregory (1960-62); Ena Shepherd (1962-63); Florence Groves (1963); Patricia Davis (1963).*

Hand and Heart
Location: Clement Street (Tybridge Street)
Years active: 1850 - 1870

One entry only: Billings Directory of Worcestershire 1855 listing licensee as: J. Leek ('beer retailer - 1855)

Pavilion in the Park
Location: Tybridge Street
Years active: 2012 - present

New venture dating from 2012 and though not really a pub, it's open during all licensed hours for drinks as well as food – so earns its place here. Quoted on its website *(http://www.thepavilioninthepark.co.uk/index.html)* thus: '...the unique Pavilion in the Park offers a completely new and exciting concept for the city of Worcester combining food, drinks, music, sport and live events and entertainment, and has certainly attracted a lot of attention already with such a great mix of ingredients. Located in Cripple Gate Park *(The Old Breeze Night Club)*, it's had a contemporary makeover by the new owners and now offers a warm welcome for people of all ages. Take the family along for a bite to eat in a great location or head there with friends in the evening to see live entertainment in a relaxed atmosphere. There's something for everyone on the menu, from a great grill selection to fish dishes, salads and sides to a menu section dedicated purely to children's dishes. Live bands every Saturday after 9:30pm so you can enjoy your food then dance the night away'. Registered at Thorneloe House, (Ground Floor) 25 Barbourne Road, current licensee (2013); Robert Neal Thompson. Worcester City Licence no: 1018

Pavilion in the Park 2013 (BB

The Ordnance Survey map for 1886 shows all the Tybridge Street pubs packed into a small area teeming with run-down houses and courts all of which would have been flooded several times a year – a common enough experience as those that were around pre-1830s would have been in the tidal flood plain. Even so, the harsh conditions didn't stop people from living there.

W39 Apple Tree
Also known as: Old Apple Tree
Location: 20 Tybridge Street (Turkey St)
Years active: 1760 - 1926

Described as being sited '...at 20 Tybridge Street on North side, 10 doors up from Hylton Road, next to number 3 Court' The Apple Tree – also listed 'Old Apple Tree' in 1900 – a fitting title as it appears in the Victuallers Recognizances of 1766 and so would have been 134 years old even then! Older than originally thought, it's also listed in Pigot's

Worcestershire Directory 1829 as Apple Tree, Turkey, Turkey Street, Clement Street, St Clement Street and Tybridge Street. One of four on same side of Tybridge Street listed in 1915: **Cock** (no 106), **Lamp Tavern** (no 84), **Apple Tree** (no 20) and **Bear** (no 2), the Apple Tree ceased to be a public house at the end of 1926. The Hive houses a fascinating bundle of original documents relating to ownership of the Apple Tree from 1854 when it was bought at auction for £400 plus interest by Alfred Rea. On his death it passed to his son James Portman Rea – described as 'maltster', who over the next twenty years set about buying up property in the City including six more pubs: **Ram Inn** in 'New Town Road' later Regent Street, **Swan with Two Necks** (sic), **White Hart, Red Cow** beerhouse, **Hen & Chickens** and **Rising Sun**. It was then conveyed to Edwin Gardner and Henry Butt Roan, described as maltsters and corn merchants, then to Worthington and Co Ltd of Burton-upon-Trent who sold it in 1899 to John Joseph Lewis of Astwood Worcester. On 21st July 1901 it was conveyed to Hitchman and Co of Chipping Norton, Ox. for £1,250. That company was itself taken over by Hunt Edmunds & Co Ltd of Banbury in 1924 and they in turn were taken over in 1965 by what was to become the massive Bass & Mitchell & Butlers Ltd empire.

  Licensees: *William Pugh (1766); Thomas Joynes (1814); James Bridges (1827); John Lane (1835); John Wm Lewis (1842); Nicholas Hill (1850); Richard Smith (1850); James Porter (1855); William Ranford (1872-75); John Kelsey (1875-76); William Foxall (1876-1877); James Linton (1877-1879); Charles Griffin (1879-81); George Hughes (1881); William Jones (1881-85); William Hinks (1885); John Martin (1885-90); Henry Leach (1890-97); Francis Smith (1897-8); Alfred Hayes (1898); Charles Daniel (1898-1900); George Smith (1900); Fred Bedford (1901-1904); James Lightfoot (1904-5); John Bishop (1905-9); Henry Farley (1909-11); Arthur Thomas (1911-14); James Digger (1914-15); Charles Davies (1915-16);Joseph Williams (1916-20); Ernest Bird (1920); George Hyatt (1920-6 when he died); Mary Hyatt (1926)*

  Next, just 9 doors down stood another important location in the City's pub annals, still remembered by a dwindling number (me included) to this day....

Below: The Bear (1920s) (CCMH/CFOW) and
(inset above) same scene 2013 (BB)

W40

Bear Inn
Also known as: Sawyers
Location: Hylton Road (Turkey, Turkey Street, Clement Street, St Clements Street, Tybridge Street). Now site of McDonalds
Years active: 1710 - 1967

The Bear's lifespan could easily stretch from early 1700s to 1970s with several re-builds in its long and illustrious history. Sited at the key junction of Tybridge Street and Hylton Road, its corner location is now home to MacDonalds after being Worcester Carsales whose showrooms were demolished to make way for the modern concept that was (short-lived) **Sawyers**, and dovetails neatly with the burger chain's architectural standards.

The Bear with its famous oak panelled interior was one of the City's most famous inns and it's still fondly remembered at first-hand as it was still operating as an Ansells pub up to the late-ish 60s.

Listed in Victuallers Recognizances in 1784 under licensee Matthew Noddyins (?) and still a century on in Baylis, Lewis Almanack (1885-8, printed 5 New Street price 1½d) as 'one among the ancient hostelries, The Bear was also mentioned by Noake (1877) as one of a number of 'ancient' City inns. The corner-site pub was the last stop before the river, crossing directly over to Newport Street on the west bank. It was also an important venue for County carriers in the 19th century with carriers to and from Broadwas, Castle Hill Shelsley Beauchamp and Whitbourne operating from The Bear. In the 1841 census licensee Skinner Caswell (45) was living here with his wife Ann (30) and two servants, John and Ann Lee.

Originally at the heart of a densely populated area, it was regularly flooded, (at one time tidal) and is listed variously as Turkey (1792), Turkey Street (1829), Clement Street (1842); and not Tybridge Street until 1900 and then listed as no 1 (1910) and no 2 (1940). Even so, The Bear proved one of the great survivors. On 16th February 1922, then licensee William Edward Philpott was found guilty of being drunk on his own premises and fined 10/- (50p). When re-opened as Sawyers 1987, the starkly-designed building that replaced The Bear was dubbed 'Madonnas Boobs' on account of the conical (some said comical) structures projecting from the roof (they're still there). It's now a McDonalds

Licensees:: Matthew Noddyins (1784); Samuel Carr (described as 'innholder' 1790); W. Barnes (1792); Charles Strange (1814-1820s); Skinner Coswell (1827) amended to Skinner Caswell (1835,1842 and 1850); John Fortey (1855); Samuel Booth (1872-77); Sarah Booth (1877-79); William Thomas (1879-97); George Farley (1897-1898); Edward Haigh (1898); Richard Foster (1898-99); William Daw (1899-1904); William Arthur Pitt (1904-20); William Edward Philpott (1920-22); Mrs Elizabeth Rose Stanton (1922-1938 when she died); Ernest Dickinson (1938-9); Frederick Charles Mackenzie (1939-1952); Frederick Stanley Bowkett (1952-1954); Ellen Bowkett (1st November 1954-4th July 1955); Leslie Field (1955-1957); Norman Charles Wadmore Leyshon (1957-1959); Leslie Symonds (1959-1960); Douglas Payne (1960); Ethel Griffin (1960-1) Thomas Henry Davies (1961-1962); Cyril Diment (1962-3); Pamela Snook (1963); Glyndwr Jones (1963-4); Charles Rushton (1964-66); Michael Malloy (1966-7); Edward Harris (1967); John Renshaw (1967).

H-A: from Hylton Road to the bridge

*Roughly at point **H** stood the Portobello Tea Gardens – one of several locations popular with promenading Worcester folk in the 18th and 19th centuries where couples would pay 1/6d (7½p) per person to cover expenses for 4 o'clock refreshment and music provided by a band. Dr Pat Hughes in her 'The Story of Worcester' (ISBN 978 1 906663 57 5) says:*

> *'...another popular resort was William Bird's Tea Rooms, later The Portobello on Henwick Hill. Sir John Byng visiting in the summer of 1781 called it 'a bread and butter manufactory' and noted that regular public events were held advertised as tea drinking for the price of 1s (5p) per person. The usual approach seems to have been by ferry and it must have been a pleasant venue with the best view in town and the adjacent country'*

(Dr Pat Hughes and Annette Leech – The Story of Worcester).

1800s view of Worcester from The Porto Bello Tea Gardens
CCMH/CFOW

The (North) View of the **CITY of WORCESTER** *from the Porto-Bello-Henwick-Hill.*

'There was a fine view from the 18th century house to the cathedral and it was a very popular place with the young bloods of the City' *(Source: Bill Gwilliam)*.

In Regency times the gardens were famous and an enthusiastic contemporary writer described them as superior to the London tea gardens – though they are said to have been forced into closure not long after following the (unspecified) spread of 'maliciously spread rumours of evil reports'. He described the scene: '... for the beauty of the views of the vale of the Severn towards the City enlivened by its lofty spires, graced with its bridge and backed by the sublime towers and pinnacles of the cathedral surpasses anything that London can boast of'.

This was the site of...

W41 Porto Bello
Location: Henwick
Years active: 1790-1860

Originally Porto Bello Tea Gardens, it evidently became an inn around 1790 and was the fore-runner of a longer-lasting and more accessible Portobello - though only by about 10 years - to be built in Bransford Road. The 1841 census shows licensee Ann Lloyd then 50 living here with her son Thomas D. aged 15 described as 'gardener'. It's thought that what's now the lodge of The Cedars was the actual old Portobello as reminders of paths and walls are still said to be found in the undergrowth

Licensees: *William Walker (Porto Bello Tea Gardens) - 1790); William Simpson (listed as Porto Bello, Henwick Hill-1820); Ann Lloyd (1835); Thomas Brookes, (listed as 'Portobello, Henwick' 1842-1850); George Lock (1850)*

W42 Dog and Duck
Location: Henwick Hill
Years active: 1780s to 1840

The better part of three quarters of a mile from The Bear, it's thought the Dog and Duck ferry – crossing the Severn from Ferry Bank to the north side of Pitchcroft and considered the busiest of several Worcester ferries on account of not only transporting people across the Severn, but also cargoes to and from the City from the Martley area – took its name from the inn the ferrymen used, rather than vice-versa. Similarly, it's thought the inn, active between late 1780s and 1840 after which it became the private residence of successive ferrymen, took its name from the one-time 'sport' whereby

Dog and Duck Ferry
(CCMH/CFOW)

(CCMH/CFOW)

punters would bet on the likely winner of a choice of dogs paddling out to a point mid-way across the river to catch 'sitting' ducks who'd had their tendons cut and could only sit and wait to become some fired-up hound's Sunday lunch. Not unnaturally, the sport was outlawed by the church – not least as it was usually conducted on the Sabbath – about the same time the pub became unfashionable. Despite that, the ferry remained in operation up to as recently as the early 1950s though beyond that, not much more is known about the inn.

Licensees: *John Bevan (1790); Ross James (listed Grundy Royal Directory 1792 as 'dog & duck Henwick'; Abraham Nott (1820); Wm Spilsbury (1842). No further listings*

W43 Wheat Sheaf (more commonly, Wheatsheaf)
Also known as Roman Indian, Queen Elizabeth
Location: Henwick (Henwick Road)
Years active: 1780 - present

Still popular (though these days largely, though by no means exclusively, with students from the newly-enlarged University of Worcester), 'The Wheatie' is a one-time wayside inn, now surrounded by houses of varying pedigree. Thought to have been built on the site of two earlier inns, **The Roman Indian** and **The Queen Elizabeth** – about which, nothing is known of either. An earlier 'Wheatsheaf' is also thought to have been sited roughly where Hylton and Henwick Roads converge near the entrance to the University. Dating back to late 1700s, the address 'Wheatsheaf Henwick' (or Wheat Sheaf Henwick - 1829) singled it out as somewhere special, later Henwick Road (1900) and latterly 192 Henwick

Road.

It was occasionally used for inquests. On 17th August 1815, the inquest into the death of Joseph Silcock who'd been head gardener at Witley Court for 7 years was held here. The Wheatsheaf was first listed Grundy Royal Directory 1792 and still retains something of an old world feel to it - albeit a bit topsy-turvy as it's built on the edge of a steep slope reaching all the way down to the river, which means, of course, splendid views. Without a doubt, planners and elf'n'safety bods would have something to say about the preposterously steep stairway leading to the toilets - not, of course that the customers, who seem to care more passionately about The Wheatie than most others on the City's westside, actually care a jot. It's theirs, it has a

Wheatsheaf 2012 (BB)

dedicated and passionate crowd of regulars not all of whom are prepared to share it with outsiders, but it's well worth the try.

For seventeen years from December 16th 1969, it was run by former Marstons free trade rep and house inspector Ray Freeman and his wife Janet who'd been born in the Bell at Broadheath, run by her father for 40 years. "The pub was 'on the floor' with hardly any trade at all. One thing we didn't notice before moving in is that the pub had – inside and out – 180 steps. There were darts and crib teams at the pub when we arrived but that created too much hassle and rows amongst customers so we dropped the lot, apart from having friendlies. It didn't so us any harm. We spent 17 hard working but very happy years at The Wheatsheaf and made so many friends: now we have our memories' *('Memories of St Johns' edited and compiled by Philip M. Adams)*. As I said when I wrote a review of the Wheatie in 1981, it's a place that's so cheery it lifts your spirits the moment you fall down the first step (of which there's lots!): '...the bar with its oak beams and low ceiling... It's old but not dingy-old, low-ceilinged but compensated for in cheery decoration, and the outside patio overlooks the river right across to the cathedral. Beautiful!'

I've been back many a time since – not least on July 25th 2012 when I made a video of a walk from The Camp House at Grimley along the river bank and into Worcester via The Wheatsheaf and The Saracens Head

http://www.youtube.com/watch?v=g3gXlTrSKAc

– and each time, nothing's changed, except some of the faces. Oh yes, and the prices: in 1981 Marstons Burton Bitter (the Wheatsheaf had been a former Lewis Clarkes house, Lewis Clarke's brewery was in Angel Place) cost me all of 49p. Would that it still did!

Licensees: *John Fluck (listed as 'Wheatsheaf Henwick' 1790); William Fluke (1820); Samuel Weaver (1835); William Turvey (1842); William Moore (1872-76); Hannah Moore (1876-7); Ann Moore (1877-1883); James Bateman (1883-87); William Morley (1887-1903); Reuben W. Evans (1903-09 when he died); Mary Jane Evans (1909-10); James Baker (1910-1940); William Taylor (1940-1); Jessie Taylor (1941-1961): William Edward Taylor (6th Feb 1961-1970); Ray and Shirley Freeman (1961-70); Walter Bowley (1986); Simon Bear (2001); Current licensee (2013); Jonathan Guy Beech. Worcester City Licence no: 1327*

A lovely walk back into the City is best afforded by taking the riverside path route via the Wheatie's metal stairs and back garden and thus on to the tow path. But if you do that, you'll miss two other noted inns – one lost in the mists of time, the other ex-Lewis Clarke's (now Marston's) house, whose loss might once have been a shame, but maybe now not so much...

W44 **Severn Trow**
Location: Hylton Road (Street)
Years active: 1790 - 1850
Short-lived pub close to the river, not to be confused with its more recent but longer-lasting and better documented namesake in Quay Street, that apparently masqueraded falsely as 'Old' Severn Trow when this one was signally older. Listed Grundy Royal Directory 1790 and 1792 as Hinton Lane, Hylton Street (1820) and St Johns (1829)

Licensees:: *Thomas Pugh (1790); William Evans 1800-1812; William Bailey (1814); John Harding (1820); William Morris (1827 and 1835); John Yapp (1842-1850s). Not listed after 1850*

*The Old Severn Trow
c1900 (CCMH/CFOW)*

W45

Crown and Anchor
Location: 233 Henwick Road (also Henick Hill, Old Henwick Road and Lower Henwick Road)
Years active: 1790 to present

First listed Worcester Royal Directory 1790 and variously as crown & anchor Henwick' (1792); Henick Hill *(note spelling)* 1829; Old Henwick Road (1842); Lower Henwick Road (1855); and not Hylton Road until as late as 1870s *(and even then as Hylton Road, St Johns)* The Crown & Anchor is another of those that sadly seems to have lost its way after a spell as a big favourite with those from both sides of the river. In 1885, Samuel Yates was convicted for selling beer 'at a place not licensed' and fined £5 with 20/- (£1) costs. Ninety eight years later (1983) Christopher Moseley was convicted on three offences of aiding and abetting consumption of alcohol after hours and fined £10 for each offence. In 2004, then landlord Nick Cassell made a stand against what he termed 'unfair treatment' by the pub's owners Union Pub Company - claiming the pubco was forcing him to pay over-the-odds prices for his drinks leaving him struggling to make a living. "It's an issue that affects every person who goes drinking because I could cut my prices and still make money if I wasn't tied to the brewery". But a public meeting called to thrash out the issue and drum up support for similarly struggling pub tenants had to be re-scheduled as it clashed with a televised England football match. Since then, a succession of often indifferent managers has held the pub back from regaining its potential, though a visit is recommended nonetheless, if only to see how damaging unsympathetic alterations can ultimately prove to be. There's a sadness about the place now that not unnaturally leaves me feeling wistful for the past as I recall cracking quiz nights and mirthful sessions with other journalists from the nearby Berrows 'factory'. Now a Marston's house.

Licensees: *Richard Rickards (also described as 'haulier' 1790); Benjamin Boyce (1820); William Mace (1829); William Thomas (1835); Mary Ann Patrick (1840s to c 1870); William Blundell (1872-76); Andrew Inight (1876-79); Henry Aaron (1879-81); George Everill (1881-84); William Winson (1884); Samuel Yates (1885); John Huskins (1885-7); Thomas James (1887); Thomas Lewis (1897-8); George Edward Jones (1898-9); Oakford Tull (1899-1904); Frank Wardle (1904); Robert Yates (1904-5); Edward Beesley (1905-7); Walter Tombs (1907-8); Ben Bray (1908-1915); ? Pratt (1915-1920); Martha Edkins (1920-22); Lewis Bentley (1922-7); John Horton (1927-30); Ernest Evans (1930-4); George Heaton (or Hector) MacDonald Roberts 'Mac' (1934-1955); William James Steele (1955-56); William Cecil Baker (1956-1970); Barry Cookayne (1970-2); Christopher Baggus (1972-4); Thomas Turberfield (1974-81); Christopher Moseley (1981-4); Richard Jones (1984 5); Jackie and Doug Howells (1985-88); Paul 'Gomez' Baylis (1988-1990); Michael J. Foster (2000); Nick Cassell (2004). Current licensee (2013); James Gavin Lavin. Worcester City Licence no: 1397*

The Crown and Anchor is fast approaching its 250th birthday but doesn't appear to be coping well with the stress of modern times. Seen here in happier days (above) 25th July 1958 (RHS) And (right) Crown and Anchor October 2013 (BB)

Oh... and talking of the Berrows 'factory'....

W46 The Chequers
Location: Hylton Street (also Hylton Road)
Years active: c1820 - 1928

First listed Billings Directory of Worcestershire 1855, The Chequers was sited roughly where the southern corner of Berrows House now stands. Originally a Showells house, the license was transferred to **The New Chequers** at the corner of Astwood and Brickfields Roads, opened 1931.

Licensees: *John Morris - beer retailer (1855); Samuel Yeates (1872-1894); Joseph Yeates (1894-1897 when he died); George Yates (1898-1900); Frederick Bedford (1900-01); Frederick Cook (1901-1904 when he died); Eliza Cook (1904-7); William Richards (1907-11); Sidney Smith (1911-12); Arthur Gardner (1912-15); Arthur E. Yeates (1915-16); Joseph Gould (1916-17); Alfred Banks (1917-1924); John Fletcher (1924)*

Virtually opposite, on the other side of the road stood...

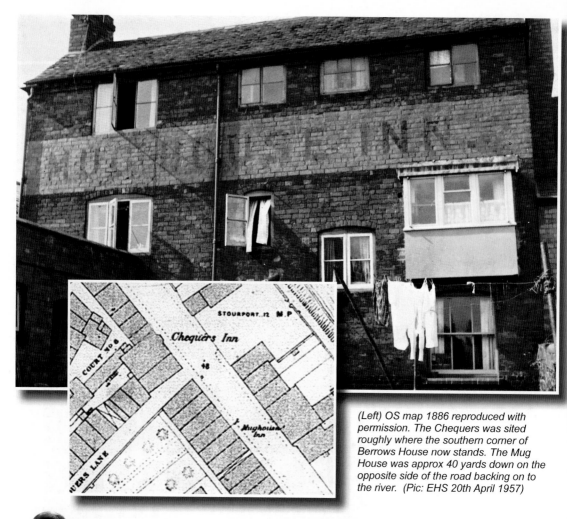

(Left) OS map 1886 reproduced with permission. The Chequers was sited roughly where the southern corner of Berrows House now stands. The Mug House was approx 40 yards down on the opposite side of the road backing on to the river. (Pic: EHS 20th April 1957)

W47 The Mugg (or Mugg) House (also Old Mug House)
Location: Hylton Road
Years active: 1760s - 1912

Older than originally thought, the Mug House first appears in Victuallers Recognizances in 1766 and later in Worcester Lewis Directory 1820. Entered variously as Mug House, Hylton Street, Hylton St (1829) St Clement's (1850) and Hylton Road (from 1910), it was also occasionally used for inquests. On 27th January 1831, the inquest was held here into a colourful character called Cucumber Billy, a waterman who'd fallen into the Severn at Bewdley seven weeks earlier and had just been found. It was, most likely, a deeply unpleasant job. 1841 census shows Joseph Miller (50) as licensee and his wife Elinor (45) but Victuallers Recognizances a year later list Elinor as licensee.

Licensees: *John Holloway (1766); Mrs. Susannah Lloyd (1820-1830s); William Munn (1835); Joseph Miller (1838-42); Eleanor Miller (1842-c 1850s; William Stalworth (1855); Mrs Mary Allen (1872-5); John Cooke (1875-1879); Robert Bryan (1879-1886); John Whittingston (1886-7); Charles Greenway (1887-8); Walter Stinton (1888-9); George Farley (1889-1891); Henry Tredwell (1891-7); Thomas Davis (1897-1903); Charles Cook (1903); Frederick Martin (1903); Alfred Willis (1903-4); James Aston (1904-05); Frederick Bedford (1905-6); (Arthur Yeates (1906-1910); Agnes Walker (1910) then a private house. OS1886*

Next follows a succession of pubs that documentary evidence of their existence provides little more than a name and generic location – in several instances as general as 'St Clements'

W48 **Bull**
Location: Hylton Road
Years active: 1830-50???
Of which nothing more is known

W49 **Boat House**
Location: St Clements?
Years active: 1700- 1800s
Could have been two called by the same name and not much is known about either: one described as being in existence in 1700, but an 1850 directory guide lists licensee as William Spilisbury and the Victuallers Recognizances of 1859 shows John Lydiard as licensee. A William Spilsbury had earlier been licensee of **The Bell** in and around 1830-5)

W50 **Duke of Cumberland**
Location: 'St Clements ward'
Years active: 1760s
Listed in Register of Victuallers' Recognizance of 1766 as in St Clement ward but without a licensee's name but with no further reference so either vanished or was re-named. Precise location unknown and even researching the history of successive Dukes of Cumberland in a bid to throw up some clues to location draws a blank. The title has been in existence since 1664 and the last to hold the title was Ernest Augustus William Adolphus George Frederick (21 September 1845-14 November 1923) who was deprived of his British peerages and honours for having sided with Germany in World War 1 even though he was the senior male-line great-grandson of George III and the eldest child and only son of George V of Hanover and his wife, Marie of Saxe-Altenburg. Even so, to this day, his descendants are in the line of succession to the British throne - none of which helps in the location of this little known pub. The fact is, it could even have been sited on the east side of the river.

W51 **Pleasure Boat**
Location: 'St Clement ward'
Years active: 1760
Seemingly short-lived inn listed only as 'St Clement ward' in Victuallers Recognizances in 1784 but more accurately as Hinton Lane (later Hylton Road) 1790 under licensee Edward Broughton described as 'builder and victualler'. No further listings

W52 **Rose and Jossamine**
Location: 'St Clement ward'
Years active: 1760
Seemingly short-lived inn listed only as 'St Clement ward' first mentioned in Victuallers Recognizances in 1766 (*'Rose and Joffamine'*) under licensee Thomas Herbert with no further listings and other references to Thomas Herbert

W53 **Boar**
Location: 'St Clement ward'
Years active: 1760
Another apparently short-lived inn listed only as 'St Clement ward' in Victuallers Recognizances in 1766 under licensee John Jones with no further listings

W54 **Cherry Tree**
Also known as Bay Horse
Location: St Clements ward
Years active: 1760s:
Listed in Register of Victuallers' Recognizance of 1766 as in 'St Clement ward' under licensee John Williams but not listed after that so either vanished or was re-named. Not thought to have any connections with Cheery Tree Walk on the east side of the river off what's now Farrier Street

Passing under the railway arch in the direction of the bridge - and in an area that despite regular flooding was as densely populated as anywhere else on the other side of the Severn, stood:

W55

The Wheelwrights Arms
Also known as Bay Horse (1879)
Location: 41, Hylton Road
Years active: 1872-1922

Also known as Bay Horse in 1879, this was a short-lived apparently family-run local in an area not short of pubs at the time (1872-1922). At least, this is one that can be positioned with some certainty, being described as 'sited on the west side four doors north from The Bear' and listed as 41 Hylton Road, it closed 1922 and became coal merchants.

Licensees: *Martha Mabels (1872-76); Thomas Price (1876-1891); William Bell (1891-3); William Abbott (1893-1913); Frank Abbott (1913-18); Clara Abbott (1918-19); Frank Abbott (1919-20 when he died); Clara Abbott (1920) listed Littlebury's as 'beer retlr'.*

Crossing the road and passing Madonna's (Bear) Boobs close to what's now the plastic flower-bedecked pumping station, here once stood:

W56

The Red Lion
Location: Tybridge Street)
Years active: 1670 - 1730

The Red Lion was referred to by Noake (p122) and was described as being on the west side of the old Severn bridge 'About two centuries ago' (ie around 1677) an old inn called The Red Lion was immediately at the west end of the bridge (don't forget, this is the point where the old bridge linked Tybridge Street and Newport Street and is 150 yards upstream of the present bridge). The Red Lion, it seems, had been leased to Alderman Cooksey a name among the oldest in the Worcester records and the landlady then was 'the good widow Chance' (c1727)

The Royal George (background) seen from the river (1930s) CCMH/CFOW.

Two favourite pubs in close proximity - The Bear left and the Royal George (right) CCMH/CFOW

...and the same site 2013 (BB)

The Royal George
W57 Location: 2 Hylton Road
Years active: **1767 - 1939**

Dating from around 1767 with first listing as 'St Clement ward' in Victuallers Recognizances under John Singleton and later listed in Worcester Lewis Directory as Tybridge Road (originally Old Bridge Street, also Torcae Street also Turkey) as well as Old Bridge Place (1820), Hylton Street (1829 and 1842), Hylton Slip St Clements (1850); St Clement's (1855), Hylton Road (1873) and latterly as 2 Hylton Road (1910) when the old pub – later a Rushtons Brewery house before becoming Ansells – was about to expire it gave its name to a newer **Royal George** set to be built in faraway Tunnel Hill Road in the 1940s. This, original, Royal George was also occasionally used for inquests. On 28th January 1828, the inquest was held here into Ann Meredith aged 7 who'd fallen from Upper Quay into the Severn and drowned. In January 1873 licensee John Maund was convicted for refusing to admit a police constable and was fined 10/- (50p) plus 10/- costs. In 1902, licensee John Wheeler was convicted for selling rum to a drunken person and fined £1 with £1/4/- (1.20p) costs

Licensees: *John Singleton (1767); Mrs Lloyd - described as 'wherry owner' (1790); Joseph Lloyd (1814-c1830s); William Hooper (1835); John Lane (1842); Anne Lane (1850); Charles Royston (1850); John Green (1859); John Maund (1872-74); Nathaniel Williams (1874-1883); Joseph Heath (1888-1898); Edward Gill (1898-1901 when he died); Thomas Hailes (1901-2): George H. Wheeler (1902-07); John Bean (1907-08); Mark Oldershaw (1908-09); John McCann (1909); William Chamberlain (1909-10); Harry Gregory (1910-14); William Tildesley (1914); William Cox (1914-15); Thomas Bradley (1915-27 when he died); Gertrude Bradley (1927-31); Frederick Mackenzie (listed as Charles Frederick Mackenzie 1937, 1932-1940s)*

Again, virtually opposite in an area known as The Pinch where tanneries and a gin distillery (OS1886) once stood no doubt making it a very smelly place, stood...

W58 The Farmer's Arms
Location: Bridge Place (Hylton Road)
Years active: 1850s-1909

First listed Billings Directory of Worcestershire 1855 The Farmer's Arms was an Ind Coope public house after 1888. Closed in 1909 it originally occupied the site later taken up as the Power Station (originally Corporation Electricity Installation Works, under Chief Engineer Cyril M. Shaw M.I.E.R., M.I.M.E. The site is now...?

Licensees: *James Fudger (listed as beer retailer 1855); Ann Matthews (1872-1880); Richard Taylor (1880-1883); George Farley (1883-1889); George Hall (1889); James Parsons (1889-90); William Griffiths (1890-93); Henry Evans (1893-94); Allen Underwood (1894 when he died the Arms was taken over by his widow Ann until 1897); William Paddy (1897-1898); Charles Daniels (1898-99); John Cook (1899-1903); George Thornberrow (1903); Mrs Ada Hall (1908)*

W59 Hero
Location: Bridge Place (Hylton Road)
Years active: 1860

Riverside inn, only apparent reference in a document of 1860 describing it as 'on the west side of the old Severn bridge, bounded on the west by the road running to Hinton Lane (Hylton Road), on the east by a towing path, north by The Royal George.

Below: Hylton Road and The Pinch 1910 The Farmers Arms is sited left of the white building. (CCMH/ CFOW)
Inset (left) 2013 BB

6: North of the GWR

Map: pages 50-51

bounded by Worcester-Birmingham canal to the east, GWR to the south and the Severn to the west, and taking in the main routes out of the City – Tything, and Barbourne, Ombersley and Droitwich Roads – with deviations to include forgotten gems in Severn Terrace, The Moors, Lansdowne and the Arboretum

After the Battle of Worcester, Cromwell ordered every building outside the then City wall, the northern limit at that time being The Foregate, to be destroyed – and that created a chance to re-plan and start again.

It was an opportunity not altogether missed by the more affluent of Worcester's citizens who rose to the challenge by creating as fine an entrance to the City as anywhere else in the land, unhindered by petty obstructions like churches, squires' homes, and sundry other less grandiose structures like 'ancient' inns – a feature that makes tracing their precise locations 363 years on something of a doddle compared to some of the following *(and more especially, the previous)* chapters!

It also means there are no 'ancient inns' in this area – virtually (though by no means exclusively) all, even those long since closed, post-dating 1750.

It took the better part of a century but by 1750, Foregate Street was firmly established and looking not unlike the way it does today. Hubert Leicester in his 'Forgotten Worcester (1935) said '...at the Restoration a set of modern houses were built, all furnished with stables and coach houses with gardens at the back, and this street became the home of the richer citizens and professional men'.

Then, as now, the most imposing of all was the Shirehall built in 1835 for the Worcestershire Authorities for holding their Assizes and Sessions and other administrative and legislative business. The marble statue of Queen Victoria was carved by Worcester-born Thomas Brock in 1887: interesting to note that when councillors in Birmingham wanted something of the same imposing and majestic quality to stand outside their town hall they enviously eyed the Worcester statue and had it copied in 1951, siting version #2 at the top of New Street where it stands today. It'd be interesting to see what Thomas Brock'd have to say if he was around today and how the copyright laws would stack up!

High-jinks in the war years resulted in Worcester's original statue being walloped-over in green paint – for which two local lads received strokes of the birch for their efforts, though some reckon it was the work of American GIs stationed locally.

An interesting comparison of the site then and now is viewable on YouTube

Foregate Street ic 1800 (CCMH/CFOW)

originally made to show how much Worcester has changed, but actually showing how much it's remained the same!

A - B: **Foregate Street to Castle Street**

This is the area that also includes the former library, art gallery and museum and the elegant former private homes of Worcester luminaries Dr Wall – founder of Worcester Porcelain, John Dent – founder of 'the great mercantile house' (Leicester) Dent, Allcroft and Co., and Sir Charles Hastings – founder of the British Medical Association.

The section of Foregate Street from the railway bridge (erected 1853) to Salt Lane, now Castle Street, was also the site of some famous old City inns – not one of which now survives.

One of the most famous of these, mostly because its name is perpetuated as a narrow short-cut between Foregate Street and Farrier Street was:

Cheshire Cheese
Location: Foregate Street, probably where the Odeon now stands
Years active: 1750s - 1820

Pre-1792, and referred to by John Noake in his Worcestershire Relics (printed March 1877, price 5/-). Suggesting it stood close by the side entry to the Museum or Athenaeum *(when the museum stood, literally on the Odeon site)* he said ... '(the) Entry (was) formerly and is still known as Cheshire-Cheese-entry, but I know not the origin of the name; probably there was an inn of that name there and a tradition remains that the first coach which plied from Worcester to London from the Cheshire Cheese yard (a large open space before the museum was built on a part of the site). This seems to confirm the idea of an inn having being there'. Which sounds logical enough to me!

Below:
Foregate
Street 1890
(CCMH/
CFOW) and
right the
same view
today (BB)

Foregate Street 2013 (BB)

Foregate Street 1930s with the Post Office where the Postal Order now stands (CCMH/CFOW)

N2 Postal Order
Location: corner of Foregate Street and Pierpoint Street
Years active 1997 – present

A huge barn – some have called it 'cathedral'-like, typical J.D. Wetherspoon's pub constructed within the shell of the former telephone exchange (1950s). You either love or hate Wetherspoon's pubs – The Postal Order is typically typical though it has earned a reputation is some quarters as 'Bassetts' on account of attracting a clientele of All Sorts, and worse: 'Scumbag Palace' is just one of its other alter-egos. Accordingly, comments on the merits and de-merits of so large a pub with difficult-to-access toilets and marked cross-section of customers are evenly divided.

This comment, fairly typical of the antis, saying it all: '...as a student I frequented (the Postal Order) often, because of the cheap drink. Now I work here, I have to say that, while I appreciate the cheap drinks will attract 'diverse' customers, it can attract some extremely difficult customers and they are not a particularly employee-friendly chain. Their pubs have no personality, and while working there I feel like I am working for the company rather than the pub. Full of old alcoholic men and tanked-up chavs. Am currently looking for a new job' *(source: www.bestpubs.co.uk)*. It has to be said though, that the food, while fairly bland, generally represents good value while the chain also appears to support the growing number of small local breweries and is rightly represented in CAMRA guides.

The beer certainly is comparatively inexpensive and often surprisingly good, but I should point out too that I have been ticketed *(barred – not the only similarity I share with William Shakespeare)* from there on three separate occasions – each time for remonstrating with lackadaisical staff for serving others out of turn and with pushy customers who are happy to let it happen. Despite all that, I confess to being a regular there for breakfasts – though I notice a distinct falling-off in quality of late – as well as to sample some of the newer ales, its location, virtually opposite a bus top and taxi rank making it ideal as a last stop before traipsing off home. Bob (Backenforth)'s blog *(http://bobbackenforth.wordpress.com)* makes frequent references. A J. D. Wetherspoon pub registered in Watford. Current dps (2013); Robert Edward Deeming. Worcester City Licence no: 1118

Monroes Cellar Bar
Also known as: Monroes, MS Monroes, Grapeshot, Cellar Bar
Location: 43 Foregate Street
Years active: 1980s - present

Originally The Grapeshot, then Ms Monroes with a plaster image of Marilyn herself greeting you at the entrance and now Monroes Cellar Bar, it's established in cellars dating from the great 1700s re-construction – so don't let them tell you it was part of the reputed tunnel system stretching from Whiteladies to the cathedral: it isn't! What it is, is a cellar bar featuring regular live music, quiz nights and drinks promos as well as DJs and club nights all aimed at a predominantly young and nighttime culture audience. It no doubt has a fascinating history – including a spell as a furniture store – but not as a pub/bar. Current licensee (2013); Glenn Conway. Worcester City Licence no: 1155

John Wall's and Dr.Hastings' former house.
Monroes is in the cellar. 1972 (CCMH/CFOW)

N4

Green Dragon
Location: Foregate Street
Years active: 1670s – 1750

The Green Dragon – of which there were three in Worcester – was an ancient inn referred to by Noake in his Worcestershire Relics (1877) and thought to have been sited opposite where the Shirehall now stands: '...one inn of this name (existed) in Foregate Street where Mr Mayor Shewring and the Corporation comforted themselves while James II was at Mass in the Catholic chapel 1687. And this was a great house for the parish authorities on processioning days. (He also commented that there was also a Green Dragon in the Cornmarket '...kept by one Suthal 1720; and a third Green Dragon in the house earlier known as the Earl's Post, at the corner of Cooken (Copenhagen) Street and High Street.

B-C: Castle Street

H ubert Leicester in his 'Forgotten Worcester (1930) described Castle Street, originally known as Salt Lane, thus: '...the street called Castle Street but for long years known as 'Salt Lane'. The conveyance of salt from Droitwich to Worcester had been carried on over a period dating back to pre-Christian days (when) the merchants, in order to avoid the toll payable if the salt entered the City, made a road across the fields leading to the Severn, where salt was loaded on to the barges for exportation'. Then, in 1930, he said that the street was notable for two buildings – The Infirmary and the Castle – from which the later thoroughfare derived its name.

When the old infirmary *(still standing in what was Silver Street but is now looking sad and sorry for itself overshadowed by the brash new plastic and glass buildings alongside City Walls Road)* became overcrowded, a site was sought for a replacement – and an artichoke field here was chosen as the very site in 1765. Work began on the new Infirmary in 1767 and the first patients were admitted in 1772 *(Pat Hughes – 'The Story of Worcester')*. Over the road, the prison, located in the castle that gives its name to the street was built in 1809 for the incarceration of all prisoners from the County of Worcestershire and completed in 1813. 'The new county gaol is a large erection, and is situate just without the boundaries of the city, near the race course; the interior arrangements are judicious and commodious; it cost £19,000 building' *(Pigot 1842)*.

It's said only one prisoner ever escaped – and when he got home to his wife, she packed him off and sent him straight back where he'd come from – presumably having to knock hard and ask permission to be let back in! Despite the castle's looming presence, the street it gave its name to was also notable as the location of several seemingly popular pubs. At the top, on The Tything, was

Queens Head, The Tything c1880 (CCMH/CFOW)

Queen's Head, Tything
Location: corner of Salt Lane (now Castle Street) and The Tything
Years active: 1790 – 1877

Evidently a pub with some history, first listed Grundy Royal Directory 1792 and reported as both Foregate Street (Pigot's Worcestershire Directory 1829) and Tything (uncharacteristically 'Tyhing' in Hunt & Co's Commercial Directory for Gloucester, Hereford and Worcester 1842), The Queen's Head stood on the north side at the top of Salt Lane (Castle Street) was owned by The Corporation of Worcester from 1876–77 though lost in the widening of Castle Street in 1880. The census of 1851 lists then licensee James Davies described as 'innkeeper 38 as living here with his wife Charlotte 45.

Licensees: Mary Kettle (described as ' Queen's head Tything' (1792); Joseph Tipping (1820); Jas. Tippins (1829); Jonathan Tippins (1835)'; Ann Davis (1842); James Davies (1850-c 1857); Henry John Kettle (1872 - 1876).

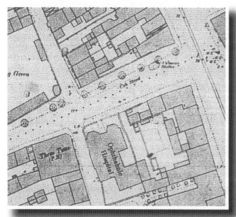

Foley Arms
Location: Salt Lane (Castle Street)
Years active: 1850 – 1876

One, or possibly two properties down on the same side of the road stood The Foley Arms, listed Billings Directory of Worcestershire 1855 but also demolished at the same time as its neighbour to make way for the widening of Castle Street (1880) It stood opposite the old Eye (or Ophthalmic as it's shown on the 1886 OS map, right) Hospital, next down Castle Street where The Queen's Head stood at the top).

Licensees: John Stinton ('beer retailer – 1855'); Thomas William Sankey (1872-6)

Ordnance Survey map 1886 reproduced with permission

Three Tuns (and Hotel)
Location: Salt Lane (Castle Street). Also described as 'Back of Foregate St'
1851
Years active: 1820 - 1958

The Three Tuns was a solid and imposing-looking inn and hotel later with sombre grey concrete cladding – no doubt echoing the castle and County Gaol further down the same road – post-dating the castle by just a few years in the early 1820s. Despite its appearance, it remained a survivor right up to the early 1960s when it too went the way of its neighbours in being demolished for another period of widening of Castle Street – this one also taking in Farrier Street which, up to that time (1960) had been little more than a narrow back lane about half the width of the current street. With the address 3, Castle Street, and listed in the census of 1851 as 'back of Foregate Street', the Three Tuns was later a Julia Hanson and Sons (later Banks's) house registered at the brewery's office in Tower Street Dudley and was entered under 'hotels' rather than 'inns and alehouses'. Today it all looks very different – the site is now Esso Service Station.

Licensees: William Ward (1829); Richard Heming (1835); Joseph Price (Three Tuns, still listed as Salt Lane 1842 – c1870s); John Woodward (1872-80); Charles Morton (1880-97); Thomas Ridge ('Three Tuns Inn, Castle Street' 1897-99); Charles Stokes 'Three Tuns Hotel, Castle Street' 1899–1910); John Wilkins (1910-12); Albert E. Probert (1912-5); Catherine Probert (1915-22); Martha Edkins (1922); John Hogg (1922-4); Joseph Warton (1924-5 when he died); Ernest Leach (1925-7); Frank Deeley (1927-9); George Frederick Dean (1933-48); Alfred Day (1948-55); Wilfred Ralph Taylor (1956-58). It closed the following year.

Three landmark features now gone: ThreeTuns, Christ Church and the County Gaol. In their place Esso garage police station and a carpet warehouse (formerly H.A. Saunders (CCMH/CFOW)

Pitchcroft – reckoned to be one of the oldest racecourses in the country and the site of the great Spring v Langan Prize Fight (1824) in which Herefordshire-born Tom Spring emerged the eventual winner after 80 bruising rounds of bare-knuckle fighting in front of a 50,000 crowd – was the site of two noted old establishments, both called...

The glory that was the Grandstand
and later, showing various stages
of demolition 1972

(CCMH/CFOW)

Grandstand
Location: Pitchcroft (east side)
Years active: 1824 – 1901

It's thought the existing Grandstand is either the third or even fourth of the same name built on Pitchcroft. This original Grandstand was on the east *(ie Castle Street)* side of Pitchcroft after which, subsequent incarnations were sited westwards on the banks of the Severn, overlooking the river. In fact, images exist showing what's thought was the Spring v Langan scrap with The Grandstand in the background. It was built in 1824 and demolished 1901. In 1868 it was kept by Francis T.H. Ellis and listed in Hunt & Co's Commercial Directory for Gloucester, Hereford and Worcester (1842) at address either Pitchcroft or Pitchcroft The Moors. It was also occasionally used for inquests. On 30th April 1829, the inquest was held here on Henry Joyner aged 1, 'killed by a waggon'. The following year two inquests were held here: 29th April on Edward Haywood who 'fell from the rigging of a barge and drowned in the Severn' and Henry Bolland aged 5 who also fell in the river – which seems to be a regular, and tragically fatal, occurrence at the time.

Licensees: Robert Dallow (1842); William Poyner (1843); Amelia Dallow (1855); Charles Higgs (1859); Edward Skyrme 1875-92 who also kept **The Bird in Hand** *on the Cross at the same time.*

Grandstand
Location: Pitchcroft (west side)
Years active: 1901 – 1968

The second Grandstand, built in 1901 and demolished in 1976, was a huge, ornate red sandstone building owned by 'The Mayor, Aldermen and Citizens of the City of Worcester'. The licensee of the former Grandstand, Edward Skyrme had his licence transferred to the new building, being listed as '*E. Skyrm' 1900 as Grand Stand inn, Pitchcroft, The Moors'; Edward F. Skyrme (until 1892 when he died); Emily Skyrm (note spelling, 1892-1894 when she died); Edward Frederick Skyrme (1895-1928 when he died – it was then run by Sophia his widow until 1929); John Leopold Daniell (1929-45); Reginald Thould (1945); Lewis Page (1930); Percy J. Amyer (Grand Stand Inn - 1940); Frank Monckton 1945-7); Cecil Probert (1947-48); George Herbert Taylor (1948-9); Christina Maclaine Taylor (1950 – 60s); Katherine Lance (1966).*

Severn Terrace, with Detroit's Diner on the corner leads to an important area, rich in pubs: The Moors, originally Moorfields, a set of once enclosed fields east of Pitchcroft, originally made up of attractive dwellings built by successful businessmen who had moved out of the City in order to enjoy the uninterrupted view across Pitchcroft. 'But in the mid 19th century, the area fell up on evil days: mean little houses and tenements crowded into the gardens and a series of courts occupied the land where once there were pleasure gardens overlooking the croft. Today only a few Georgian houses remain, the group facing The Swan Theatre and in Severn Terrace (Source: Bill Gwilliam – Old Worcester People and Places). In this locality – no doubt much to the intense grievance of prisoners incarcerated in the nearby gaol that dominated the area – also stood a number of pubs vying for attention: The Moors running parallel to the Severn was home to two, and Moor Street running roughly west-east linking The Moors with Loves Grove housed five. Then, as now, The County Police had their HQ here: small wonder available records indicate few, if any serious misdemeanors by any of the seven pubs clustered around one small area. First, in a building that's still standing – unlike a solitary one of the others, all of which have been swept away as part of a major redevelopment project in the early 1960s – was...

Engineers on Pitchcroft 1910 with The Grandstand in the background (CCMH/CFOW)

*The old Rose and Crown, 1970s
later the offices of the Swan Theatre
(CCMH/CFOW)*

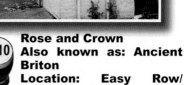

N10 Rose and Crown
Also known as: Ancient Briton
Location: Easy Row/ Severn Terrace
Years active: 1850 - 1913

Mid-Victorian (1850s) inn close by the old prison listed variously as (19) Easy Row (1900), and (20) Severn Terrace (1910). A Burton and Lincoln Brewery public house for some of its lifespan, it closed 1913 and is now a private house (?), formerly props office for the Swan Theatre. Evidence suggests that this could also have been called 'The Ancient Briton' but changed to Rose and Crown about 1900. In 1877, licensee Luke Rubery was convicted for selling in prohibited hours and ordered to pay 5/6d (27$^1/_2$p) costs.

Licensees: Christopher Jennings (listed as 'beer retailer' 1855); Sarah Brown (1872-4); Joseph Teague (1874-5); William Arker (1875-6); Luke Rubery (1876–83); John Frankland (1883); William Windsor (1883-4); Henry Elliott (1884-7); Hannah Baylis (1887); Enos Button (1887-8); William Mortlock (1888-92); Edwin Buston (1892–95 when he died); Edward Thorp (1895-6); Arthur Powell (1896); Eliza Harrison (1896-7); Samuel J. Bromage (1897-1900); Alfred Lock (1900-04); Richard Ball (1904-6); John Sudbury (1906–1912); Arthur Cross (1912-3)

N11 Carpenter's Arms
Location: Spring Gardens, Tything
Years active: c 1840 – 1961

Long-life pub situated immediately across the road from what's now Moor Street Clinic at 25-26 Loves Grove on the corner of Spring Gardens and Loves Grove (left side from Castle Street). 1841 Census shows Hannah Winwood as publican and the census of 1851 lists then licensee, possibly her son Thomas Winwood (50) as living here with his wife Hannah (49) and their three sons, two daughters and servant Mary Coley. Also listed Billings Directory of Worcestershire 1855 as 13 Spring Gardens Tything, Littlebury's Directory of Worcestershire 1873 and 25 Loves Grove (1937). Later a Mitchells and Butlers house.

Licensees: Hannah Winwood (1841); Thomas Winwood (1851); Rd. Baylis - beer retailer (1855); William Winwood (1859-80); Richard Collins (1880-94); Walter Copson (1894-8); Chas. H. Busby (1898 -1901); Arthur Broad (1901); George Farr (1901-3); John Robinson (1903-6); Edward Albert Starling (1906-1918); Emily Starling (1918-19); Edward Starling (1919-33); John Hudson (1933-35); William Thomas Cobley (1935-7); William F. E. Duffill (1937-41); Aulton (1941-44); Thomas Ernest Yates (1944-1946); Donald Wilfred Hands (1946-56); Hilda Lauris Deeley (1956-7); Charles Henry Jeffries (1957-9); Ronald Herbert Eiles (1959-) It closed the following year

*Ordnance Survey map of 1886
reproduced with permission*

N12 Prince of Wales
Location: 27, The Moors
Years active: 1898 - 1939

The Prince of Wales, opened right at the end of the 1800's (so would have been named after the future Edward VII who came to the throne the following year) was sited number 27, just four doors away from the more enduring **Moors Ketch**. It is thought to have been demolished c1941. In 1904, licensee Caroline Mason was fined £1 plus costs for selling beer to a boy under 14 in an unsealed vessel here. In 1916 licensee Laura Moore was fined £1 or 14 days in prison for: i) selling an excess measure and ii) for selling beer to a child under 14 for which she was additionally fined 10/- (50p) or 7 days in prison. Just eight years later she was hauled up before magistrates again, charged with having sugar other than in the sugar store, contrary to Section 7 of Customs & Inland Revenue Act of 1885. She was fined £1 or 14 days in prison. Licensee Charles *(he was better known by his middle name Trevor)* Edmunds had been a First Division footballer in his day and he went on to run **York House,** a matter of less than a hundred yards away, after the Prince's closure in 1939.

Licensees: Miss Caroline. A. Mason (1898-1909 when she died); Beatrice Thompson (1909-11); Mrs Laura Moore, 27 The Moors (1911–c1936); Charles Trevor Edmunds (1936–1939)

N13 Moors Ketch
Location: 35, The Moors (also 56 Moorfields Street)
Years active: 1850 – 1924

The census of 1851 lists then licensee Elijah Clements (34) described as 'vict' and living here with his wife Emma (28) and servant John Summers. First listed as a public house in Billings Directory of Worcestershire 1855 and appears to have existed about 80 years (closed by 1930). Address originally 56 Moorfields Street, later 35 The Moors.

Licensees: Elijah Clements (as 'beer retailer' – 1855); Joseph Lightwood (1859); William Askin (1872-4); William Gambling (1874-5); George Gambling (1875-9); William Sewell (1879-86); Arthur Joseph Crockett (1895-1920); Thomas Downes (1920-22); John (name unclear - 1922)

N15 Brewer's Arms
Location: 23-25 Moor Street
Years active: 1900 - 1960

Pub and off-licence (wine, beer, cider and perry) listed variously as Brewer's Arms Inn at 23 Moor Street and Brewers Arms at 29 Moor Street and as '23-25 Moor Street' in 1957. On 12th January 1916 John Henry Wiggin was fined £2 for 'unlawfully supplying William Stuart Handley (that name again!) a measure of intoxicating liquor for which he asked an amount

Brewers Arms, Moor Street
11th January 1958
(RHS)
and
2013 (BB)

exceeding that measure. A Flowers House, registered at Flowers' Brewery Stratford-on-Avon, it closed on 23rd November 1960 and demolished 1961 to make way for the re-development of Moor Street

Licensees: James Watkins (1872–1876); Selina Watkins (1879-1901); Harry J. Kettle (1901-3); George Henry Wiggin (1903-10); John Wiggin (1910-36); George Worman (1936-7); Cecil George Crump (1937–1952); Fanny Crump (1952-3); Thomas Henry Rone (1940s-60)

N16 Live and Let Live
Location: 29, Moor Street
Years active: 1850s-1860s

Just two properties along from The Brewer's Arms and seemingly failing to live up to its wishful name as it's listed just once: Billings Directory of Worcestershire 1855.

Licensee: William Hooper (listed as 'beer retailer' - 1855)

N14 York House
Location: Moor Street
Years active: 1830s -1965

Once popular, all-purpose local on a sloping plot leading on to Pitchcroft, dating from 1830s when the then-remote area was still known as Moorfields and the location Moorfield Street (1850). A few remnants remain for those who care to take a look, even after being closed more than 50 years and the site left undeveloped.

A Spreckley's house registered at 7 Foregate Street Worcester, it was also noted for its sale of plum jerkum, a largely exclusively-Worcestershire drink like cider but made from plums and known for its potency and often mixed with cider to reduce its strength. 'A Worcestershire man who was brought before magistrates on a charge of drunkenness confessed he had a drop too much (jerkum). Perhaps he took it neat' *(Wikipedia)*. The York House was later transferred to West Country Breweries, 265 High Street Cheltenham and ended its days more peacefully as a Whitbread pub.

Licensees: Michael Noke (Moorfields –1835); Joseph Tovey (1842); Hannah Dugard (1843); Charles Dooley (1850); William Derrett (1855); George Williams (1859-76); Williams Phelps (1876-9); Elisha Clay (1879-81); John Allen (1881-2); Charles Daniels (1882-97); James W. Andrews (by now, The Moors–1897 -1900); Edward Bennett (1900); Thomas Wardale (1900-01); Frank Thomas (1901–1928); Henry Savage (1928-30); George J.A. Fox (1930-6); Cyril Henry Marston (1936-9); Charles T. Edmunds (1939-42); Rex Sidney Clinton Dorrington Baker (1946-1956); Mildred Georgina Holloway (1957-8); Harold Bayliss (1958-59); Harold Thomas Young (1959-62); Elsie Andrews (1962)

York House 1972 (CCMH/CFOW) and (Inset) 2013 (BB)

N17 Lamp Tavern
Location: Moor Street
Years active: 1850-1899

First listed in Billings Directory of Worcestershire 1855 as Moor Street and thereafter as 38 Moor Street (1873) and 16 Moor Street (1900). This Lamp Tavern was a Showell & Co public House for part of its life. There was also a (longer-lasting) Lamp Tavern just across the river in Tybridge Street.

Licensees: John Shaw (listed as 'beer retailer ' 1855); John Protheroe, (1872-1890 when he died); Ann Protheroe ((1890-92 when she died); Emily Hadett (1893); Ernest Charles (1893-95); Arthur Osborne (1895); Walter H. Tyler (1895 - 99):

Return to point B now – the top of Castle Street – and here are some of the City's most enduring inns. As we've established, The Queen's Head stood at the top of what had been Salt Lane (northside). Opposite is (still) one of the great survivors and still an ever-popular pub with all ages though its history has been, shall we say, chequered. This is...

N18 Saracen's Head
Also known as: Blackamoor's Head
Location: Tything
Years active: 1715 (poss 1500s) – present

Hugely popular inn with a long, well-documented history stretching back as far as 1715 when it was originally called **The Blackamoor's Head**, this was a coaching house, for many years sited outside the City boundary and popular with the City's upper and middle classes. Mentioned by Noake (1877) as Blackamoor's Head and Littlebury's Guide to Worcester (1880 p105) by then listed as 'Saracens Head Agricultural and Commercial Inn, 4 Tything, Henry William Dowding Proprietor Livery and Bait Stables. Well Aired Beds. Wines, Sprits, Ales &c , of the best quality'. The pub/inn also appears in Grundy's Royal Directory 1792. Interestingly, next door stood the Temperance Hotel (1930s). Not listed as 'one of (Worcester's) five principal carriers' Inns in Baylis, Lewis Almanack 1885-8 (printed 5 New Street price $1\frac{1}{2}$d) which were **Hop-Pole, Star and Garter** in Foregate Street, and **The Bell, The Crown** and **Unicorn** in Broad Street, but as 'other carriers' inns alongside **The Rein-Deer, Golden Lion, King's Head, Talbot, The Angel** and several others in various parts of the town.

According to Bill Gwilliam in his *'Old Worcester People and Places'* (p137): '...it had a considerable area of land attached to it and its bowling green was for long the favourite recreation ground of the well-to-do citizens from the north of the city. The land next (to it) was a favourite pitch for travelling circuses

The ever-popular Saracens Head. Top 1964 (JAS)
Above and right 1970s CGMH/CFOW

and what were almost certainly circuses of a different kind, travelling preachers'.

He goes on to say that marquees erected for audiences to hear the great travelling preachers of the day held 2,000 people and the Saracens Head hosted notable boxing matches and events such as air balloon ascents when 'up to 250 people availed themselves of the opportunity of a partial ascent *(by the balloon Rainbow)* by taking a bird's eye view of the City'.

The bowling green later became the site of the first Fire station, and it wouldn't take too much imagination to picture the brass helmeted firemen and their flared-nostril steeds pulling the water tender up the passageway en route to tackle some raging blaze. It's also rumoured that the actual original prison records of the old County Gaol in Castle Street were sold to The Saracens Head for the purpose of lighting pipes – with the result that no-one is sure how many felons were hanged or even how many prisoners were incarcerated there – or why!

On 22nd November 1916 then 'Sarries' landlord William Roberts was fined £20 for unlawfully supplying intoxicating liquor during prohibited hours and a further 10/- (50p) for unlawfully supplying spirits to be consumed off the premises. The combined offences proved enough for the Central Control Board (Liquor Traffic) to order the closure of The Saracens Head for the sale and supply of intoxicating liquor on and after 15th January 1915 until 3rd April 1918. Clearly the chastening experience didn't stop him as six years later on 5th February 1924 he was again found guilty of unlawfully selling whisky above the maximum price and fined £2/2/0d (£2.10p) with £1/10/0d (£1.10p) solicitors costs.

Jointly owned from 1934 by brewers Frederick Smith Ltd of Aston Model Brewery Birmingham 6 and Horace William Goodwin Newton – former MP and barrister described as 'gentleman' – of Landale, Strontian Argyllshire, who'd set out early to buy-up plots of land in and around Birmingham which, with the passage time, formed a major part of the M&B portfolio – it was transferred to M&B of Springfield Brewery Wolverhampton on 30th April 1958.

The Sarries, for years a Mitchells house, now a free house, remains a popular pub, sought after by locals and visitors, especially rugby fans attracted by the cosy and often boisterous though generally good-natured atmosphere in the bar and the outside passageway created by current (2013) tenant South African Steve Kitchener whose masterstroke was to create a canopy over the courtyard and install heaters and TVs for now outlawed-smokers.

You can see the result in two videos I produced in 2012 here:
http://www.youtube.com/watch?v=g3gXlTrSKAc   and
http://www.youtube.com/watch?v=H7FPgiEs60k

Licensees: *Robert Raxter (listed as 'Saracen's Head inn Tything' 1790); James Butler (1820); Thomas Butler (1829); Thomas Butler (1835); James Fielders (listed as 'Saracen's Head (commercial) Tything' ; James Fielder (probably the same as previous, but with different spelling -1855); Robert Merrick (1859); Benjamin William Norman (1872-1874); Henry Dowding (1874–1884); Goode (1884–1890); George Epps (1890–1896); William Roberts (1896-1923); Frank Peters (1923–1926); Mary Higgs (1926–29); William Roberts (1929–1932 when he died); Arabella Roberts (1932–34); Tom Patrick Higgins (1934-51); Alfred Potter (1951-52); William Laurie Stark (1952-1958); Patrick Joseph McSharry (1958-60); Howard Binder (1960-1963)'; Charles Harding (1963-5); Fred Layton (1965-80); Alan Whitehead (1980 –83); Geoff Wise (1983-2001); Current licensee (2013) Steven Robert Kitchener. Worcester City Licence no: 1007*

 Dragon Inn
Also known as: George and Dragon. George Inn.
Green Dragon
Location: 51,The Tything
Years active: 1790 - present

One of the oldest pub names first coined in 1344 when the Order of St George created the martyr as patron saint of England. First listing Worcester Royal Directory 1790 and again two years later in Grundy Royal Directory 1792 as 'george inn Tything' (sic) but subsequently (from 1820) as George and Dragon, Tything. Later owned by Mitchells and Butlers of Cape Hill Brewery Birmingham.

Then in the 'new' parish of Tything of Whitstones, the census of 1851 lists long-lasting licensee James Whitaker (1829 to around 1870 having succeeded his father Thomas) as being aged 60 and living here with his wife Sarah 58. In 1873 licensee Eliza Finch was convicted for allowing liquor to be drunk after hours and was fined £1 plus costs.

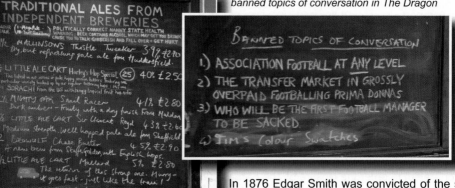

In 1876 Edgar Smith was convicted of the same offence and also fined £1 plus costs. On 12th January 1916, then landlady Alice Scutt 'did by the hands of her servant or agent to wit (sic) one Beatrice Simmonds unlawfully supply to one William Stuart Handley *(see Characters: whether or not he was one remains to be seen, but he appears again and again in police records and was evidently an official snooper placed by the authorities to catch out erring landlords/ladies)* as the measure of intoxicating liquor for which he asked an amount exceeding that measure' (ie overcharging). She was fined £2. On 28th May 1921, she found herself up before the magistrates again answering charges of selling beer to George Carless *(presumably another snooper)* during prohibited hours and unlawfully selling beer to Thomas Rutter – who possibly may also have been a persona non grata. She was fined £2 on each count.

Recent landlord Richard Appleton was reputed, with some justification, to be the rudest landlord in Worcester – possibly the reason he fell out of favour with the local CAMRA after the pub had been voted its 'Pub of the Year' following which, his notice-board states, among banned topics of conversation is 'bloody Protz lot'. He also owns a brewery which he's fond of promoting but is also a keen importer of other real ales. A later visit (August 2013) revealed a delightful beer called Mallard (5% abv). The banned notice board is still there, though with different topics *(see pic)*. The Dragon long held a reputation for good live music, especially blues during the 1990s to mid 2000s and a visit is always and interesting experience that may or may not leave you feeling better about yourself than when you went in. Dedicated and passionate crowd of generally intelligent and coherent *(at least, at first)* followers though – so not all bad! Now a Little Ale Cart Ltd house.

Licensees: William Handy (also described as 'auctioneer' 1790); John Tandy (1792); John Whitaker (1820); Jas (James) Whitaker (1829–c1870); Hannah Smith (1872-1874); Eliza Finch (1874–1876); Edgar Smith (1876-1877); Henry Kettle (1877-80); John Williams (1880-1883); John Blunson (1883); George Payne (1883-4); Edward Bennett (1884-5); Thomas Edgington (1885-6); James Herbert (1886-8); George Skeffington (1888-89 when he died); Charles Osborne (1889-98); Joseph Scutt (1898–1908 when he died); Mrs. Alice Scott (misspelled 1902, corrected to Mrs Alice Scutt (1908-22); Sydney Smith (1922-3); James Farrell (1923-6); Sidney G. Giles (1926-30); Victor Harris (1930-2); George Inett (1932-9); James Henry Albutt (1939-41); Eileen Albutt (1939–41); William Laurie Stark (1944-1952); Reginald Martin (1952); Clement George Beeby (1952-1954); Ernest Coad (1954); Walter Needham (1954–57); William Matchet (1957); Harry Andrews (1957-8); Francis Samuel Addams (1958-59); Edward George Bidwell (1959-1); Arthur John Merrick (1961-62); Bernard Moverley (1962-3); John Brown (1968-70); George Weston (1970); John Taylor (1970); Ian Jones (1973-4); Roger Maskell (1974-8); Geoffrey Wise (1978-83); Cynthia Whitehead (1983-7); Ian Mayhew and Susan Naylor (1987); Richard Appleton (-2012). Current licensee (2013); Mrs Catherine Esther Louise Ottaway.

Worcester City Licence no: 1233

The Green Man and the best pub sign in Worcester 1970s
(CCMH/CFOW)

The Green Man 1964 (JAS)

N20

The Marwood
Also known as: Green Man. Green Man Inn. Green Man and Still
Location: 40, Upper Tything
Years active: 1750-present

An unusually narrow-fronted inn dating from mid-1700s. First listing Grundy Royal Directory 1792 when it was run by '...John Grout fen (senior) who also ran the Crofs keys in what was then called Oxford Road (now London Road)'. The premises, now The Marwood, are owned by St Oswald's Trust – or more correctly The Master of the Hospital of St Oswald.

The Ancient Lodge of Oddfellows met here in 1796 and the inn is also the location where herbalists from Wyre Forest and Teme met and exchanged herbs in the yard behind where there was a copper still for distilling *(hence the original name)*. Joan Laight the 2-year old spared by policeman Herbert Burrows when he murdered her parents Ernie and Doris and baby brother Bobby at **The Garibaldi** in Wylds Lane was brought here to live with her mother's sister Kate Harrison in the immediate aftermath of the tragedy. In 1875 licensee Ellen Stock was convicted for selling alcohol to a drunken person and ordered to pay 7/6 costs. In 1960 landlord Frederick Ernest Brace was fined £5 plus advocate's fee of 1 guinea (£1.05p) on each of four charges of supplying liquor during non-permitted hours. He'd only just taken over the running of The Green Man (he'd previously been landlord of **The Liverpool Vaults** in the Shambles) and when he and his wife Dora retired, the licence was taken over by their daughter Eileen and son-in-law Derek Burton who ran it until 2003 – 43 years in the same family!

In 1981 I wrote of the Green Man, then under the tenancy of Derek (and Eileen) Burton: '...a bit unusual is the Green Man – not in the mould of the majority of Worcester's pubs, oh dear me no!' Landlord Derek was in a rush to get back to work *(he was a butcher by trade, a role he pursued by day, and Eileen was the manageress of a cake shop in St Johns, I noted)*. I described the little bar '... just like walking into your granny's front parlour – provided your granny owns a juke-box! There's the mantelpiece, the coal fire, the clock, the telly, the photographs...'

The original Green Man sign inspired by a 14th century curved stone boss in the cloisters of the cathedral is reckoned by many, me included, to have been among the most eye-catching in the City but though it attracted much attention, it vanished when the pub ill-advisedly changed its name to **The Marwood** around 2007 when it took on more of the character of a bistro – a role it still appears to hanker after, though is prices have proved too steep for a regular following. Many original features remain though, so the place is worth a look. Licence holders, Sectoa Ltd, registered at Houston Renfrewshire.

Licensees: John Higgins, listed as 'victualler greenman Tything (1790); William Hunderhill, Green Man & Still Tything Street 1820- c1830s); John Hope (1835-40s); John Newland (1843); William Morris (now Green Man 1855); Thomas Stock (1859); Mrs Ellen Stock, Green Man (1872-76); George Williams (1876-80); Charlotte Williams (1880-5); William Thomas (1896-1906); Henry C. Thomas (1907-10); Frederick J. Thomas (1910-15 when he died); Austen Schofield (1919); Charles Tolley (1919-21 when he died); Kate Tolley and George Harrison (1921-1944 (Kate died in 1936 and George in 1944); Gertrude Eliza Griffiths (1944-1959); Frederick Ernest Brace (1960-1964); Derek Burton (1979 -2000). Current licensee (2013); Benjamin Richard Marwood Coates. Worcester City Licence no: 1173

N21 Lamb and Flag
Also known as: Lamb and Fleece. Old Lamb and Fleece
Location: Tything
Years active: 1780 – present

Quaint but still popular pub derives its name from the ecclesiastical sign of The Lamb of Christ, and was built on land once owned by St George's Hospital, ownership later transferred to Lewis Clarke's Brewery of Angel Place. The Lamb and Flag, originally Lamb and Fleece *(and inevitably Old Lamb and Fleece)* existed in the 18th century but its first known listing is 1820 Worcester Lewis Directory at addresses variously listed as 30 Tything Street (1842) and 30, Tything (1900).

On 27th February 1920, landlord Arthur Besant was fined £5 plus £2/2s (£2.10p) solicitor's costs for unlawfully selling rum above the maximum price here. In more recent years due to its tenancy being taken over by Irishman Don Clark, the pub won a reputation as an Irish bar, selling Guinness dispensed in the traditional Irish way of drawing from one keg and topping it up from another, using a knife to level off the resulting head. As a result the pub had – and still has, though to a lesser degree under Don's seminary-trained son Gary – a dedicated following, many of whom congregate to drink and chat long into the night in the back yard, much to the annoyance of neighbours. It also had a reputation for quirky sports like conkers and had a thriving cricket team until recently. Still good for lively above-yer-average-intelligence conversation though. Reportedly none-too-pleased at having lost its

Always good for quirky conversation, The Lamb and Flag in 1972 (above - CCMH/CFOW) and 2013 BB

long-standing crown for selling the best Guinness in town to **The Cricketers** – a sharp and salutary lesson in not allowing complacency to gain the upper-hand!

Licensees: S. Vaughan (1820); Jas. Eaton (as 'Old Lamb and Fleece, Tything'–1829); Henry Birt (1835); Sarah Birt (1843); Samuel Beadle, Lamb & Flag 1843-1850s); Thomas Surman (1855); Henry William Birt (1872-79); Herbert Witherington (1879-83); Julius Sladdon (1883-86); John Tombs (1886-9); Arthur Trott (1889-90); George Manning (1890); Frederick Manning (1890-2); Robert Clarke (1892); William Johnson (1892-97); Leonard Johnson (1897-1902); Chris Edwin Wilkins (1902-7); John H. Jones (1907-9); Ernest Edward Price (1909-12); Arthur Besant (1912-1924); Ada Luffman (1924-6); James Brooks (1926-8); George Kingdon (1928); Alfred Harris (1928-34); Alfred Edward Ladd (1934–1946); George Alfred Cullis (1946-51); Tom Patrick Higgins (1951-2); Dorothy May Florence Higgins (1952-70); Raymond Lewis (1970-1); Don Jones (1971-1980); Garry Jones (2000)

D-F: Barbourne Road and The Arboretum

Before continuing along Barbourne Road where more long-lived survivors still exist, let's take-in the three colourful and occasionally lively pubs that existed (note the past tense) in and around The Arboretum when the neighbourhod was also home to four off-licences. St Oswalds Road - originally little more than a footpath through a graveyard – was made in what Hubert Leicester (1930) described as 'a driving road' about 1890.

The extensive Arboretum Pleasure Gardens that stretched from here to the canal is reckoned to be Worcester's first public park, opened in 1859, and looking at the tightly packed rows of cramped houses that now make up the area that takes its name from the well-laid out lawns and arboreal terraces much frequented by 19th century promenaders, it's plain that the only similarity between now and then is the use of the name. This is the grand public park where entertainment took place usually in the evening, including music, dancing masquerades, balloon ascents and fireworks and were very popular with the middle classes. Though a small fee was due, free access was given to Arboretum Gardens on one day a week in order to encourage those less likely to afford the entrance fee – a 'gift' from the City's Corporation who granted the then massive amount of £1,000 in order to encourage more workers to attend these parks. One of the original gatehouses still exists in Sansome Walk. Firework shows, tightrope walking and a horticultural show were all part of the

The Foresters 1972 (below - CCMH/CFOW) and right, 2013 (BB)

attractions on offer but it eventually proved so expensive to run and maintain that the organisation behind it went into liquidation in 1863 and the site divided into land parcels – being sold to build mostly artisans' houses. With the coming of a major new influx of tradesmen and labouring classes, also came the need to build pubs to cater for a growing demand...

Foresters Arms (Hotel)
Location: Sansome (or Chestnut) Walk (no 2)
Years active: 1860 - 1990

Thought to date from around 1860 with the municipalisation of the Arboretum Pleasure Gardens, The Forester's Arms appears in Littlebury's Directory of Worcestershire 1873 as, Foresters Arms, Chestnut Walk and thereafter variously as Foresters' Arms Hotel, 40 Chestnut Walk and Foresters Arms, 2 Chestnut Walk. In 1873, licensee Thomas Price was convicted for selling in prohibited hours here, and fined £1. Three years later Annie Thorne was convicted for allowing gaming and fined 10/- (50p) including costs. She was again convicted in 1879 for failing to admit a police constable and was fined £1 plus costs. Under the tenancy of John Speller Horton (1937–1940s) whose son Martin lived at the pub (later progressing to play cricket for Worcestershire and England before becoming New Zealand's national coach and on his return to the UK, and specifically to his home town, chief cricket coach at WRGS, a post he held until 1996 at the same time as being as Chairman of Worcestershire CCC) the Foresters, still open up to around 1990, had inevitably gained a healthy sporting reputation – including hosting boxing tournaments in an annexe that doubled as a skittle alley. A number of key boxers including Worcester's own championship contender Jack Goodyear and, it's rumoured *(stress, rumoured)* fallen-from-grace champion Randolph Turpin fought here as well as amateur events. A Spreckleys House registered at 7 Foregate Street later West Country Breweries Ltd (forerunner of what was to become Whitbread at 265 Cheltenham) it is now residences for students.

Licensees: Thomas Price (1872-6); Annie Thorne (1876-1880); William Kings (1880-4); Edward Bennett (1884-5); Thomas Stephens (1885); Edwin Jones (1885-8); J Huskins (1888 when he died); William Perks (1889-1891); George Webb (1891-3); Albert E.W. Baddeley (1893-1902 when he died); Thomas Radford (1902-7); Henry Baker (also listed as bowling saloon 1907-11); Aaron Sillitoe (1911– 1914 when he died); Mabel Ross (1914); Amelia Sillitoe (1914-35); John Speller Horton later Mrs Lilian Muriel Horton (1935–1963); John Starkey (1963-74); Anthony Collins (1974); Donald Thomas (1974-84); Henry Staff-Brett (1984); Jeffrey Coopey (1984-6); David Tye (1986-7); Richard Ellis and Ben Scotthorne (1987); Kenneth Rennie (1987-9) Maurice Fenn (1989); Martin Daniel (1989).

Arboretum Inn
Location: 52 and 53 Northfield Street (also listed as 35 East Street)
Years active: 1890s - 2003

Sign of the times – the Arboretum, earmarked for flats:
(Left) in happier days: 1970s (CCMH/CFOW)

An off-licence from 1875 licensed to sell beer, cider and perry off premises, its first listing as an on-licence pub is in Kelly's Directory of Worcestershire 1900 or possibly a little earlier. Originally owned by Hitchman and Co, brewers of 26 Bridge Street Banbury, later Mitchells and Butlers. On 14th May 1912, Arboretum licensee John Price was fined £1 with £2.10.0 (£2.50p) costs, or one calendar month imprisonment, for unlawfully supplying liquor to a police constable when on duty.

For many years 'The Arbo' unofficially doubled up as Labour Party HQ as group (and City Council) leader George Randall, who lived 100 yards away in the same street, adopted the pub as his local – as did former mayor, also Chairman of Environmental Health, Licensing Chairman and prominent Labour Party sidekick Ray Turner who still lives virtually opposite the pub. Current (2013) MP Robin Walker, staunch Tory like his father, ex-MP Peter Walker, also classed it as his local. It's also rumoured all four Beatles wandered into here for a swift pint before curtain up at the Gaumont. If that was true – and it's by no means cast-iron – it would have been their first appearance in the City on May 28th 1963 as by the time of their second appearance on September 4th *(the first house of which I attended, sitting in the fifth row and I still have my original programme from the night)* they'd become so famous chances of being able to wander into a local pub without being mobbed were nil. In 1981 when it was under Chas Sanders' tender care, I wrote '...it's a regulars' pub, mainly for those old enough to remember a long way back. If you live within the Arboretum confines, the pub's almost exclusively your own'. I concluded 'there's quite a lot going on in this pleasant little house'. Charles later became a City traffic warden with the reputation for only booking expensive cars on account of their owners being more likely to afford the fine – but on the Worcester Pubs Then and Now Friends FB page:

(https://www.facebook.com/groups/worcesterpubsthenandnow) his son John claims his father even booked him four times: '...I thought I could get away with it as he was my Dad but he could never remember what my car looked like!' In 1987, later licensee John Allen was convicted for selling outside hours and was fined £50 with £15 costs. In recent years The Arbo, one of the Admiral Taverns group, suffered from lack of a car park and closed in 2003. Earmarked for flats (2013) the original engraved windows are still in place.

Licensees: *Francis G. Farmer (1897-1907): John Price (1907-1913 when he died); Louisa Price and Williams Hill (1913); Albert Edward Dredge (1913-1932 when he died); Nellie Dredge (1932-9); Walter. George Phillips (1939-47): John Henry Willis (1947-69); Bruce Acton (1969-79); Charles Sanders (1979-84); John Allen (1984); Derek and Elizabeth (Betty) Mellors (2000);*

Just around the corner...

Washington (Washington Arms)
Location: Washington Street
Years active: 1900 - 2002

Named after Henry 'The Loyal' Washington who was Royalist Governor of Worcester at the time of the Great Siege of 1646. A slug-it-out Spreckley's, later West Country and Whitbread, pub and off-licence (beer, cider, perry, wines and spirits) near the canal on the edge of the Arboretum, 'The Washie' was once popular but fell out of favour as its reputation for cider – and the effects of – wore

down those living nearby: certainly lack of a car park alongside a swathe of double yellow lines abounding

The Washington looking better 10 years after it closed
(left - BB) than in the 1970s (above CCMH/CFOW)

throughout the densely-packed Arboretum also took its toll. Though now long closed, the building – not unimpressive and listed as 42 Washington Street – still remains, though looking lost and forlorn and in dire need of someone to love it again. In 1981 I wrote: '...darts ride high and quoits is making a reckoning too but the pub's main attraction is two-fold: its position – slap in the middle of the Arboretum (location, not pub!) and the cider, 'jake' to those in the know'. As I noted, the conversation '...tended to revolve around drinking mens' pursuits – beer, birds and belly laughs'. Few, excepting those living nearby, had many of those (belly laughs) when it closed, even though it was well past its best and had gained a bad reputation by then.

Licensees: Arthur Spreckley (1900-01); Herbert Jones (1901-2); Charles Dovey (1902); Charles Pardoe (1902–1919); Henry Pardoe (1919-36); Lionel W. Jakeman (1936–1940); Charles Alfred Wood (1940-1959); Kenneth Herbert Wixon (1959-1968); Frederick Charles (1968-74); John Walker (1974-6); Stanley Jones (1976-80); June and Bob Allen (1980-86); Wilfred Young (1986-98); Roy Gibbs (2000); Michael Raymond (2001)

Return where we left off, Point D

D-G: Barbourne Road to the Old Toll House and east of The Tything

N27

Cap 'n Gown
Also known as: **Plume of Feathers. Feathers**
Location: 45 Upper Tything
Years active: 1898 – present

Drawing its name from the crest of the Prince of Wales first adopted by the Black Prince, son of Edward II, this is the newest (1898) of three inns called **Plume of Feathers** (shortened to 'The Feathers' after about 1936). A former M&B pub and off-licence (beer, cider and perry), originally Showells Brewery then leased by Ind Coope and Allsopp, in 1912 licensee George Price was convicted for permitting drunkenness on the

The Feathers 1964 (JAS) Name changed to Cap,n'Gown

premises and was fined £1 with £2.2s (£2.10p) costs or one month in prison.

Still in operation and now a Hook Norton house with drab, spartan furnishings dominated by massive TV showing sports and attracting like-minded followers, its fortunes have been a bit up and down, largely depending on the punters' reaction to a succession of short-lived gaffers and their tastes in décor. Listed throughout as either 'The Tything and/or 44 (or 45) Upper Tything, 44 and 45 The Tything, three snug bars were bashed-about into a single L-shaped lounge bar in the late 1960s. Ancient name Feathers *(or more correctly Plume of Feathers)* was inexplicably and not very popularly re-named after 80 years as the nonsensical **Cap'n'Gown**, with original signboard showing mortar-boarded WRGS student outside the school *(standing opposite)* even though the school only takes pupils up to University entrance level – thus completing the bizarre-ness of the move. Note: the background of the sign has since been walloped-over in to a solid brown backdrop – now echoing the drab interior. A Hook Norton house registered at Hook Norton Brewery, Banbury. Licence No 1123.

Licensees: *William Trevis (1898-99); Timothy Trahearn (1899-1905); Harry Gregory (1905-6); Alice Clifford (1906-8); Alfred R. Wilkes (1908-11); George Price (1911–13); William Finch (1913-6); John Robinson (1916-17); Walter Whitley (1917-36); James Thomas Potter (1936-8); Albert Henry Richings (1938-40); Elsie Richings (1940-1); Elsie Molly Moreton (1941-47); Ernest Alfred Perry (1947-51); James Parker (1951-3); Joseph Purfield (1953-55); Ernest Camden (1955-64); Dorothy Camden (1964-5); George Weston (1965); Bernard Moverley (1964); Dennis Salisbury (1980); Chris Haynes (2000); Jim McKeever/Anne Brennan (2001); Rachel-Marie Charles-Short (2007-10); Suzanne Poluczanis (2010-present)*

Coach & Horses
N28 **Also known as: now Lloydies Bar)**
Location: The Tything (no 39)
Years active: 1790 to present

Famous old coaching house dating from the 18th century and first listed Grundy's Royal Directory 1792 as coach & horfes tything. Also Coach & Horses, Tything Street (1842); Coach & Horses Up. Tything (1900), Upper Tything.

Latterly owned by Robert Allen & Co brewers and registered at 7 Lovatt Street Wolverhampton,

Coach and Horses 1964 (JAS). Name changed to Lloydie's Bar

forerunner of Banks's – whose ales The Coach had a great reputation for. Only ever two bars – front and back – plus a functions room up a precarious steel staircase at the rear, the Coach has enjoyed a chequered history of late though was even until fairly recently renowned as a great games pub where there'd be several crib and dominoes schools and a long line waiting for their crack at the dart board. As recently as 1996 the brewery is reputed to have spent £100,000 to return it to the way it had been before disastrous 1960s plastic-and-formica re-vamps: as my late father Sidney Thomas Blandford said when I took him in there immediately after the re-fit: "...blimey, they haven't spent much on this place have they? It's exactly the same as the last time I was in here" – *that, it seems had been 1942!* Currently no evident pattern for opening – which appears to be at the licensee's whim – and a reputation for being clique-y and unwelcoming to strangers with regulars feeling they have the right to hog the bar simply on account of being regulars, it's expensive and not particularly welcoming for passers-by and 'irregulars'. I once had a strange experience in there though: when standing people-watching and minding me own business in the north-west corner – which would have been the original yard into the stables at the back – I heard a distinct and insistent knocking immediately behind me – not once but several times. Further research reveals that there is nothing behind that wall which is also inaccessible from the other side: as I noted in a blog: oooo-er!

Licensees: William Clark Jnr 1790: J. Clarke (1792); Edward Kettle (1820–c 1840); Chas. Bowyear 1842 -c1858); Elijah Clements (1859-79); George Payne (1879-81); James Shaw (1881-97); John Gardner (1897-1909); Mrs Jane Copson (Coach & Horses, 39 Upper Tything, 1909–1910); (though 1915 Littlebury's lists James Powell as licensee); Harry Lawson (1910-14); James Powell (1914-33); Arthur Henry Vale (1933–1958); Herbert Thomas Smith (jnr and snr–1958-1970); James Trimm (1970-1); Alice Trimm (1971-4); Roderick Griffin (1974); Cyril Misters (1974-7); Ray Brookes (1977-83); John Arnold (1983-9); Dick and Sandra Wallace (1989-1995); Royce Hasbury (1996 - 2000); Michelle Windsor (2001): Current licensee (2013); David Wilson-Lloyd. Worcester City Licence no: 1398

In this area too, would have stood two inns that records prove to have existed, though precise locations are difficult to establish. These are:

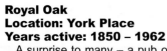

Round of Beef
Location: The Tything (precise location unknown)
Years active: poss 1880s
Referred-to by Bill Gwilliam who says that a card exists in Worcester Public Library advertising the house – which was apparently renowned for its free Sunday lunches – though no further information has yet come to light and it's not shown on the OS map for 1886 or in Worcester City Police Register of Intoxicating Liquor Licenses.

Three Blackbirds
Location: Tything (precise location unknown)
Years active: 1840 - 1870
Single listing (Billings Directory of Worcestershire 1855) and none thereafter. Precise location unknown and not shown in the Ordnance Survey map of 1886 so presumed to have gone by then. One licensee listed: Joseph Warmington - listed as 'beer retailer'

A slight detour next to find a little-remembered pub that's not where you'd expect a pub to be, and might surprise those living nearby today – even though it only closed as recently as the early 60s. In the heart of a densely packed residential area off the decidedly up-market Britannia Square, stood (still stands though no longer as a pub)...

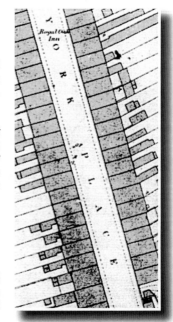

Royal Oak
Location: York Place
Years active: 1850 – 1962
A surprise to many – a pub operated from within a terraced house in the even-then up-market area around Britannia Square. Sited on the east side and listed variously as 45 and

45-6 York Place. Though gutted by fire (Nov 1885) it was re-fitted and continued to operate until the 1960s – the same landlord, William Henry George Wall gaffering there for its final 20 years. First listed Billings Directory of Worcestershire 1855 and still standing, seemingly now indistinguishable from its neighbours, The Royal Oak features in both the 1886 and 1936 OS maps of the area. A Spreckleys Brewery house (the brewery stood a matter of maybe a hundred yards away in Barbourne). It was later taken over by West Country Breweries and thence by Whitbreads. Licensee George Brighton went on to run **The West Midland Arms**

Licensees: Richard Allen (as 'beer retailer'–1855); Jno (Jonathan) Jordan (1872-77); Lewis Barnes (1877-79); Frederick Jordan (1879-84); John Jordan (1884-6) Thomas Pritchard (1886-94); Robert Chittleboro (1894–6 when he died); Mary Chittleboro (1896-7); Thomas Love (1897-9); James Hope (1899-1900); George Brighton (1900-05); Benjamin Robinson (1905-19); Miriam Cross (1919-21); Leonard Wright (1921-9); Agnes Drake (1929-31); Percy Hiron (1931-4); William George Henry Wall (1934-1962) note: the Worcester City Police Register of Intoxicating Liquor Licences lists him as William Henry George Wall – more likely to be correct!

Back to The Tything and here's a major survivor with amazing longevity..

N30 Talbot
Location: Tything
Years active: 1750 - present

Listed as 'tything' (sic), Paradise Row Tything, Barbourne Road (1900) and 8 Barbourne Road (1913 – present), The Talbot is named after a breed of hunting dog, and though originally well outside the City boundary has a long history of being a courthouse used by magistrates and coroners as well as a concert venue and commercial hotel popular with visiting theatricals.

In the 17th century magistrates regularly adjourned to the Talbot for the more comfortable discharge of their functions and amid the potations of sack and beer and the fumes of tobacco, when many a prisoner was sentenced to the pillory, the stocks and the whipping post. Coroners also held their courts here: it was here that the inquest was held on the skeleton of John Hemming murderer and victim of the Oddingley murders, and on 15th November 1832, the coroner acting here *(then listed as Claines)* delivered his verdict on Joseph Cox, killed when a quantity of earth fell on him during the lowering of the road at Rainbow Hill.

Behind the inn up to the second half of the 19th century was The Talbot Meadow, the customary pitch of travelling wild-beast shows, especially that of Wombwell's Menagerie and

The Talbot 1964 (JAS) and 2013 (Inset - BB)

contemporary newspaper reports tell of at least two 'winner takes all' prize fights between a lion and, on both occasions, six mastiffs. Purse was £100 each time, and it's said the lion won on both occasions having seen off twelve fighting dogs. The Talbot was also used, after the sale of the old Worcester Castle, for the nominations for the County elections – when, for a fortnight or so it formed the focal point of political Worcestershire.

Licensee Frank Higham (1937-9) had been a First Division footballer in his day. On 28th May 1958 licensee Kitson Rudd was fined £5 with advocate's fee of £3gns (£3.15p) for supplying intoxicating liquor during non-permitted hours.

In the 1960s the upstairs functions room proved to be a popular venue for intimate concerts by some notable names and was also popular with stars and performers at the Theatre Royal and later Swan Theatre: as such, it also had a brief reputation as something of an extroverts' (for which also read 'gay') bar. A Kelsey house, registered at Radford Hall Brewery Leamington, its original oak panelling in what was for years a first class lounge but is now a dark corner of an all-in-one pub, still exists with later renovations attempting with only limited success, to copy its obvious style. In 1982 under Ray Cross' tenancy with Courage's, I wrote: '...you'll either love it or hate it... when I was there so was a circuit judge (honest, your honour), a jockey, a marine engineer, a town planner or two, a brace of teachers and a fistful of others of indeterminate ilk, some obviously travellers – commercial and private, new to the town and wondering what to make of us all. Edges a bit on the hoity-toity' I noted.

The Talbot has suffered badly of late through loss of the intimacy created by a series of small bars that not only incorporated the old bar and lounge areas, but also a former dining room, reception area, ground floor toilets *(that once had exceptionally fine ceramic tiling)* bottle store and the one-time vehicular passageway into the Tything, into what's essentially now a great big all-purpose bar/lounge/dining/pool room, albeit all with small dividers. The Talbot has also suffered from being run by a series of young, unsuitable managers that have turned it into a gross under-achiever that actually deserves to do much better than it appears to. From what had been an up-market hotel with a clientele to match, the emphasis is now clearly on cheap'n'cheerful food for those who can't be bothered to cook for themselves, sports fans shouting at the telly, and a few who don't know when they've had enough.

That said, it has to be said it does represent fair value for money. A Barras chain/Spirit Pub (Services) Ltd house, registered in Burton-upon-Trent.

Licensees: *Stephen Smith (1790); Thomas Nanfan (listed as 'Talbot inn tything' (1792); Thomas Severn (1820); Anne Stanton (1842); Charles Webb (1855); Edward Higgs (1872-4); Benjamin Niblet (1874-5); Edward Higgs (1875-99); Eliza Shepherd (1899-1901); Walter Noake (1901- 9); William Andrews (1909 when he died); Leah Andrews (1909-18); Frank Dunford (1918-30); Ernest Harding (1930-7); Austin John Schofield (1937); Frank Higham (1937-9); John. Moreton (1939-40); Herbert Williams (1940-5); David Henry Ebonall (1945 -1948); Thomas Richard Ronald Jones (1948-51); Ralph Edward Davies (1951-55); Joseph Alexander Burgmans (1955-57); Kitson Rudd (1957-60); Roger Moran, transferred to Florence Joan Moran (1960- 62); Frank Sinnett (1962-3); Ernest Brown (1963-5); William Millichap (1965-8); Thomas Wright (1968); Ray Cross (1980- c2000); Alan and Linda Bloomer (2001). Current (2013) licensee: Ms Rachel Elizabeth Lunnon. Worcester City Licence no: 1441*

(N31) **Britannia attached to Britannia Brewery (later Spreckleys)**
Location: Barbourne Road
Years active: 1930s-c1962
Less than 100 yards north of The Talbot on the opposite side once stood Spreckleys Brewery. This was the City's first large scale brewery, originally known as Britannia Brewery, built in 1850. It was started in early Victorian times by a Mr Joseph though the City, it seems, did not take to large-scale brewing, being content with home-brewed ale. But times were changing and breweries began buying up public houses which became tied houses and the Britannia Brewery was the first of its kind in Worcester, later taken over by the Spreckley brothers who came from London. Brewers and wine merchants, their descendants operated the brewery – a looming, severe-looking Satanic Mills-style complex where the former Brewery Service Station is now – right up to the early 1960s, its remaining buildings standing out as something of an eyesore for some years: the malting house still survives in Brewery Walk though far more interesting is the gin house that housed the horse engine used for pumping water up to the top of the tower from which it went through the brewing process by gravity. The rare, apex-roofed circular building *(so designed to permit optimum use of space for the circular route the work-horse would have traipsed several hundred times a day)* also survives – though some waggish graffiti-ist had sprayed the tale 'do not bend' on the curving front wall, I noted recently. The brewery that operated a number of pubs in the City before being swallowed-up into the West Country Breweries, then Whitbread chain, was forced

to take drastic action in 1900 after a number of people had been taken severely ill after drinking beer produced by a competitor in Manchester. Tests showed the Salford brew to contain arsenic – thought to be the result of chemical reaction by cheap sugar substitutes – with the result that the brewery had been forced to tip thousands of gallons of tainted ale into the sewers. Rocked by the fall-out from the affair, the City's two main breweries at the time – Lewis, Clarke's in Angel Street and Spreckleys here in The Tything – took out prominent advertisements in the local press attesting to the purity of their products. Under the headline 'Pure Beer', Spreckleys' notice in Berrows Journal read: '...we state that our beers are brewed from malt and hops only'. But at least there was one positive upshot arising out of the national scare: it led Worcestershire County Council to pass a resolution calling on all Worcestershire's MPs to do their best to induce the Government to pass an Act prohibiting 'the use of ingredients other than malted barley in the manufacture of beer, unless otherwise labelled'.

"Dark Satanic mills' Spreckleys Brewery (1940s Worcester Record Office) and 2013 BB)

During extensive renovation work in 1938 skeletons were found under the floor of the old Britannia Inn and so far as is known, no explanation as to who, why or how they were found there has ever been forthcoming. Aside from the brewery, attached to it was an off-licence, also bearing the name 'Britannia' and still active up to around 1962. Bill Gwilliam describes it as a pub (ie full on- and off-license), but according to the Worcester City Police Register of Intoxicating Liquor Licences, it had only ever been granted an off-licence, and then only on the conditions that it would be surrendered once the brewery ceased producing its own beer, and that bottled beer (was) sold in pursuance of the company's business. The licence had been issued to the Spreckley family (Herbert William up to 1950 then Walter Freer Spreckley up to the brewery's demise c1962). The brewery also had an off-licence outlet at 7 Foregate Street at the same time.

Next, let's step into the backstreets – where we'll discover four in the Lansdowne area, all within a stone's throw of The Talbot (and of each other)

Whey Tavern
Location: corner of Lansdowne Road and Flagge Meadow Walk
Years active: 1820s - 40s

Short-lived alternative to the 'sophistication' of **The Talbot**, this was a 'popular port of call for the citizens until about 1840 when houses began to encroach on the area and the rural retreat became less so. The Tavern was also popular for selling 'whey', that part of the milk that remains liquid when the rest has curdled – then regarded as being good for health and complexion. (*Source: Bill Gwilliam Old Worcester People and Places*). Very possibly on the same site and postdating it by about 30 years, was...

Chestnut Tree
Location: Lansdowne Road (no 17)
Years active: 1870 - present

Late 19th century pub, address 17 Lansdowne Road (1900) originally in rural setting but with artisan houses since built all around. Chequered history of late, with first decade of 21st century marked with very patchy open/closing arrangements but now (2013) seems to have met a like-minded pair in joint licensees Dann Rush and Colin 'Mad Pierre' Robinson – the nickname comes from the Legionnaire chef in the cartoon strip in the Daily Star – who appear to be wanting to do the right thing by The Chestnut Tree. Already its music nights (and Sunday afternoons) are very well attended. Originally a Harpers Hitchmans house, registered at Lowesmoor brewery, it became a Mitchells house. In 1878, licensee Frank Morris was convicted for allowing gaming here and was fined £2 plus costs then later the same year was again hauled up before the justices and fined 20/- (£1) costs for selling in unlawful hours. Not as big inside as it looks from the outside, it must have been cramped into disbelief until it had swallowed up a cottage that had existed side by side up the mid 1970s. Its two bars – one of which I described in 1981 as 'bland, open-faced and red-necked' and the other as 'crushingly uninteresting' have since been knocked into one and there's a large garden for days when the sun

shines. The Chestnut Tree was in the same family – father and son, Thomas and John Hine running it for nearly 40 years, and I noted it was no longer the 'embarrassingly successful ruckus of a cider house' it had once been. Now an Enterprise Inn with a growing following.

Licensees: Maria Davis (1872-4); Frank Morris (1874-9); Frances Osborne (1879–80); Samuel Bayley (1880-4); Arthur Radford (1884-9); James Turvey (1889-99 when he died); Eliza Turvey (1899-1904); Ernest Harry Hopper (also listed as Harper, 1904-21): Florence Crockett (1921-22); Austin John Schofield (1922-33); Albert Henry Richings (1934-7); Geoffrey Dan Thomas (1937–1954); Cyril Costello (1953-1960); Thomas William James Hine (1960-66); John Henry Hine (1966-7); Mabel Hine (1967-73); John and Carole Hine (1973–1990s); Arthur Wells (2000); Adrian Birch (2006 – 2010); Current licensee (2013); Colin Sidney Robinson aka Mad Pierre. Worcester City Licence no: 1244

N34

Lansdowne Inn
Location: Lansdowne Street
Years active: 1900 - present

Turn of the century local (c1900) on corner of White Ladies Walk listed as Lansdowne Inn at 19/20 Lansdowne Street. Some years ago, 92-year old Alfred Wilkes recalled the Lansdowne in 1907 in the (then) *Worcester Evening News:* '...the rooms were lit by gas lamps, stone floors were covered in sawdust and spitoons lined the bar. It was not unusual to put a drop of gravy browning in the beer to make it look better'. He said his father had installed a ladies' room at the pub and that local women would call in for their groceries and have a drink. "It was my mother's idea really because she liked a natter with the

The Lansdowne 2013 (BB)

women and my father agreed as the men preferred the women out of the way'. He also describes the 'Sick and Dividend Club' run at 'The Lannie' in which regulars chipped in 1/- a week (5p) towards health care in the pre-National Health days.

One-time Julia Hanson off-licence (wine beer, cider and perry) and general stores purchased by conveyance 2nd July 1928 for £2000, in July 2013 it was advertised by owners Admiral Taverns as '...a terrific starter pub with all the facilities that any pub could want. Trade accommodation: open plan trading area/public bar/ pool & sports area and function room. There is a kitchen without catering equipment which will have to be supplied and installed which should provide another income stream. The Beer garden is terraced and in good order. It is the ideal location for BBQ's in the summer with the games room in a separate room off this area. The private accommodation is in good order and consists of 3 bedrooms, a private kitchen, bathroom and office so would be ideal for a family. Estimated ingoing required: £3,500. Starting rent: £5,200. Fixtures and fittings: £2,000 on IPA. Funding options available for the right tenant'. Over the years, 'the Lannie' has proved popular with WRGS lads of questionably appropriate age, and postmen who'd finished their rounds but were unwilling, for some reason I never quite fathomed out, to return to work... A noted regular too, was Barbara Evans the dream dancer in Tony Hancock's TV episode 'The Ladies' Man' (first broadcast 15th April 1960) though I once had to take her to task on account of her annoyingly snappy little Yorkie that I threatened with a boot up its pert little arse. A Bob Backenforth beer guide from around January 1982, when it was under the managership of Fred Stevens *(who later jacked it in to become a window cleaner)* was written but, so far as I can tell, no longer exists. It would have been good though as 'The Lannie' under Fred as well as former National Association of Licensed House Managers (NALHM) representative Pete Richardson – who was convicted in 1983 for selling after hours and fined £25 – and all-round good 'un Pete Barker, was then my kind of pub (Banks's): funsome, gamey and with a great reputation for good beer and good conversation.

Licensees: Margaret Sleator (1872-6); George Adams (1876-83); Margaret Adams (1883-96 when she died); William Oakley (1897-1900); William Davieson (1900-02); Catherine Hunt (1902-3); Joseph Richardson (listed as licensee and grocer (1903-1907); Alfred Robinson Wilkes (1907- 28 - listed as grocer and beer retailer); Frank Short (1928-32); William Martin Bird (1932-7); Christopher Spicer (1937-9); Herbert Rea (1939); James Davis Lansdowne Inn (1939-59); George Cooke (1959 – 63); George W. Morris (1963-78); Fred Stevens (1978-83); Pete Richardson (1983); Pete Barker (2000); Michael Creese (2001); Kevin Meggeson (2012)

Jolly boys' outing from The Peep o' Day 1909 (CCMH/CFOW). The Peep today

At the other end of the row of huddled artisans' cottages for whom The Lansdowne was created, still stands what was once rejoiced in the utterly splendid name of...

N35 Peep o' Day
Location: 23, Cumberland Street
Years active: 1870 - 1968

Little-remembered corner pub (even though it was still thriving within living memory and survived all-but a century, closing c1973) in the largely artisan-residential Lansdowne area. Still standing and now premises of Industrial Trading Co Ltd. A Spreckley's house, later West Country (and Whitbread) house a lovely photograph exists showing a day trip – all male, you'll notice – from here, thought to be from about 1909.

Licensees: Henry Cook (1872-80); Elizabeth Kettle (1880-1); Daniel Harwood (1881-4); Edward Bennett (1884-5); Samuel Cheese (1885-1901); James Probert (1901-2); John Wall (1902-3); William Appleton (1903-4); Mrs Eliza Turvey (1904-12); Walter Grove (1912-14); Edward Brown (1914-24 when he died); Arthur Hirons (1924–1933); Tom Sefton (1933-34 when he died); Winifred Sefton (1934-6); Amos Fisher (listed as 'Peep-o-day' (1936–1946); Henry Savage (1946 when he died); John Starkey (1947–63); Thomas Johnson (1963-64); John Richards (1954-5); Charles Eouse (1965 – close)

Take a right at St George's Lane and 150 yards away, a surprise awaits.... This is (was):

N36 Perseverance
Location: St Georges Lane North (53)
Years active: 1900 - 1930

Little-remembered turn-of-the-century pub, though more likely off-licence, situated at 4, later 53 St Georges Lane North, on the corner of St George's Walk (between Henry Street and St George's Walk). It's now occupied by a pair of semis

Licensees: Herbert Ricketts (1902–c1915); George Wiggall (1915); George Cooper (1930 . Became an off-licence by 1930.

You'll never again be guided by the cheers of the crowds, but here is historic turf: it's where lowly Southern Leaguers Worcester City FC beat the mighty Liverpool (then Div 2) on January 15th 1959 after it had been delayed a few days because of frost. Butting close up to it was originally St George's Tavern, reincarnated 1968 as...

The Cavalier (previously St Georges Tavern, rebuilt 1968
Location: St Georges Lane North
Years active: 1910 – present

Awash with blue and white on home game days, St Georges Tavern was a Charrington's, then Flowers house, later Whitbreads, alongside the nearby Worcester City FC Supporters Club and spiritual home for Worcester City Football Club fans. Its busiest day must surely have been January 15th 1959 – dubbed 'the day 10,000 Worcester grandmothers were buried' on account of the number of supporters asking for time off work to see Southern Leaguers and part-timers Worcester City humiliate the mighty Liverpool. It's reckoned 15,111 crammed into the ground, 14,000 of them City fans. On 29th December 1924, a charge of unlawfully allowing a child under 14 in the bar was dismissed against licensee James Thomas Potter on payment of 4/- (20p) costs and £1.10/- (£1.50p) advocate's fee. Replaced in 1968 by the modern 'Cavalier' that was being built while the old Tavern was still in operation, the newer incarnation featured skittle alley and was popular with narrow-boat cruisers in the summer, though few football fans took to it, and it has subsequently tried re-inventing itself as a pseudo pub/ restaurant under several well-intentioned tenants/managers none of whom ever quite made a go if it. In 2012, its licensee came under fire when hygiene and health inspectors found the pub's kitchen facilities to be below the standards expected under the Environmental Health regulations. A Punch Tavern, registered in Burton-upon-Trent.

Licensees: (as St Georges Tavern: Henry Holloway Pardoe (1911-17); John Ulatt (1917-22);

St Georges Tavern (CCMH/CFQW)

St Georges Tavern about to be demolished. 1967

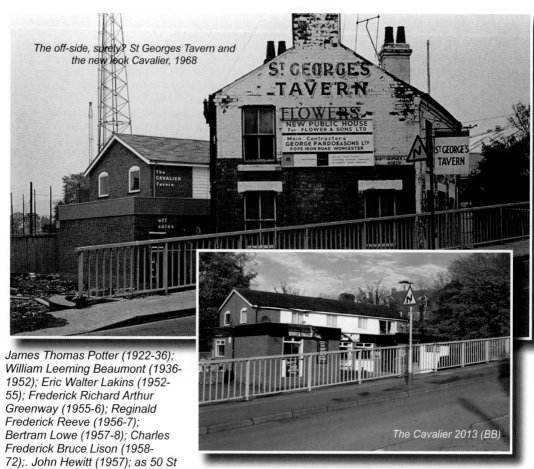

The off-side, surely? St Georges Tavern and the new look Cavalier, 1968

The Cavalier 2013 (BB)

James Thomas Potter (1922-36); William Leeming Beaumont (1936-1952); Eric Walter Lakins (1952-55); Frederick Richard Arthur Greenway (1955-6); Reginald Frederick Reeve (1956-7); Bertram Lowe (1957-8); Charles Frederick Bruce Lison (1958-72);. John Hewitt (1957); as 50 St Georges Lane and 107 St George's Lane north. As Cavalier: Alan Nash (1972-84); David Morrison (1984); Chris and Eileen Baggus; Stephen & Kathleen Keen (with others - 2001); Current licensee (2013); Mark Wild. Worcester City Licence no: 1295

Return now to Barbourne Road. Barbourne Brook formed the City boundary when Barbourne was annexed to the City in 1837 and for half a century afterwards, it formed The Rubicon – marking the end of civilisation and the start of the great rural wilderness: sadly, it proved no barrier to the speculative builder... Barbourne bridge was a mere footbridge almost at water level with a ford for vehicles beside it. At the south side of the bridge stood...

N38

Swan
Location: Barbourne Road
Years active: 1850 - present

Ancient inn – almost certainly at one time a pleasant little house in the country with a brook running close by and looking not unlike John Constable's famous 'Haywain' with horses at the stream and waggoners sitting on the benches outside, enjoying the host's home brewed ale. Before the coming of the railway it's reckoned some 20 stagecoaches a day stopped here either bound for, or headed from, Birmingham. Rebuilt with all modern facilities, it's still going (2013) after more than 150 years serving customers from the Barbourne area as well as travellers along what up to mid 1960s was the UK's main route to the South West *(equivalent to today's M5).* A popular Lewis Clarke's, later Marstons house in its day, it's now a sporting one-roomer dominated by a pool table in place of what had been distinctly cosy lounge and bar. ***(Note to pub architects, accountants and managers: when, oh when, are you going to see that while the move looks good on paper and/or spreadsheets, and may maximize potential profits generated per square metre, the move does nothing to assist the*** character of the pub, serving only to destroy the essential ambience and intimacy previously generated by a combination of several bars? Please desist. BB). In 1985 newly appointed landlord Phil Blake and his family were reported to be living in a caravan in the car park while a former tenant refused to leave the premises despite an eviction order: the issue was only resolved after several weeks following intervention by the LVA with the blame for the 'farcical situation' leveled at both the brewers (Marstons) and the City Council's enforcement team. Now an Admiral Taverns house.

Licensees: John Downes (listed as 'beer retailer' 1855); William Henry Wall (1872-83); Thomas Lewis (1883); Enos Button (1883-7); Robert Clarke (1887); James Cooke (1887-92); Hannah Dixon (1892-3); George Webb (1893-98); John Sylvester Mayman (1898-1914 when he died); Mrs Lucy Ann Mayman (1914–1941); Herbert George Davis (1941-51); Gladys Davis (1951-2); Edgar Whiteley (1952-3); Arthur James Newbrook (1953-1964); Leslie Newbrook (1964-5); David Newbrook (1983-4); Michael Jones (1984-5); Phil Blake (1985 -) Current licensee (2013); Rebecca Louse Fahy. Worcester City Licence no: 1072

The Swan,
Barbourne 1972
(CCMH/CFOW) and
right 2013 (BB)

N39 Pope Iron
Location: Waterworks Road
Years active: 1750s? – 1870

of which few records exist today except to record its appearance as 'a half-timbered inn at the waterside slip at the end of the lane now called Waterworks Road' pinpointing its location as, or at least close by, where the cottages fronting the Severn now stand. Its name has been a source of conjecture for centuries – opinion divided between whether it refers to a famous old inn named 'Pope Joan' (that is, of Arc) or the Pope's crook or, as is considered the most likely of the three, a grappling hook used by boatmen and so-called on account of its similarity to the ecclesiastical staff. Historian Bill Gwilliam also offers a fourth, and frankly more logical suggestion: that it is derived from the 17th century ironworks on Barbourne Brook, owned by Bromwich Pope. Extensions to the waterworks around 1880 hastened the original Pope Iron's demise and it was replaced by....

N39 The New Pope Iron (now The Winning Post)
Location: 6, Pope Iron Road
Years active: 1873 – present

First appearing in Littlebury's Directory of Worcestershire 1873 as replacement for the earlier **Pope Iron Inn**, the 'new' Pope Iron is shown on the Ordnance Survey map 1886. A Spreckleys, later West County (and Whitbread pub) the name was changed to 'The Winning Post' by former Bell/Cavalier/Feathers horse-racing fanatic Irish gaffer Jim MacKeever (*earlier responsible for the inexplicable name change of* **The Feathers** *to* **The Cap'n'Gown**). Continuing the tradition of being a big sporting pub – which it still is, now more so than ever under The MacKeevers – it's another that has gone the single barn-like bar route though this time with reasonably satisfying results that have transformed the former run-down and frankly rough-looking Pope Iron into today's gleaming and spotlessly clean Winning Post. In 1981 when it was run by tenants Norah and *(part-timer, doubling up as a lorry driver)* John Bishop I wrote: '...it's tucked away in a cobwebby corner of town where even The Law has been known to stop and ask for directions as to where it is. But if there's a place with a great one-hundred-and-eighty carat reputation for darts *(darts... 180... geddit?)* then this is it. It's darts and crib and darts and darts every night of the week and the whole place bows down to the double (and triple-) throwing darters. *(At the time I noted there was twenty seven 180Club certificates on the wall – several won by John Bishop himself)*. I also noted 'it's a real plain Jane of a pub' that had taken on a garish appearance, shimmering under the weight of 1200 beer mats stuck to the wall. *(They've since been replaced by what appears to be a similar number of jugs hanging on hooks: bloody hundreds of 'em!)*. As I wrote: 'I could say unflattering things about the Pope all night long, but I'd still end up somehow liking the place'. It consisted, I noted, of 'one room that looks like two and a (then) outside loo (since rectified). As I said, it was 'a bit dreary, but the welcome from behind the bar is warm and ever so genuine. The Pope really is two Bishops and praise be to them, brother'. By way of contrast, the present (2013) landlord has been known to put more than a few backs up and he's not known as the most welcoming landlord – he virtually banned everybody who drank cider when he first took over the pub, though I can safely state with the benefit of first-hand experience, he's well respected by those that stick with the Winning Post, and even liked by a few. He has also recently completed a course and is an S.I.A registered door supervisor.

Licensees: Eliza James (1872-8); Lizzie Harrison (1878-80); Elizabeth Dancocks

The 'new' Pope Iron, successor to an ancient river-side inn sited 100 yards away. Both now superceded by 'The Winning Post'

Above: 1972 (CCMH/CFOW) and left 2nd March 1958 (RHS)

146

(1880-1); Louisa Davison (1881-5); Thomas G. Pardoe (1885 -1922); Arthur Rushton (1922-4); William Inight (1924-30); William Harry Price (1930-67); Victor Whittaker (1967–70); Arthur Sherwood (1970-6); John and Norma Bishop (1976-85); Donald Hall (1985-1990); Stephen White (1990); Linda Rhead (2000). Current licensee (2013); James Joseph McKeever. Worcester City Licence no: 1237

G-H: **Old Toll House and Ombersley Road**

Vine
Location: **Corner Ombersley Road and Vine Street**
Years active: 1870 – present

Popular Davenports, later Greene King, now Punch Taverns pub on the City's northside, the Vine was the terminus of the Ombersley Road trams until they ceased running in 1928. Listed as Northwick ter {ie Terrace} (1873), Ombersley Road (from 1900) and 131 Ombersley Road (1910) it's a solid-looking once-cherished pub originally owned by brewers Samuel White and Son of Winson Green Birmingham (later Davenports) that was popular with rookie Canadian and Australian pilots from Perdiswell Aerodrome in WWII. Enjoyed a healthy spell as

The Vine - in need of some tlc 2013 (BB)

a lively and entertaining pub with Saturday and Sunday night entertainment and sing-alongs run by ex-Gurkha jock Bob Cummings and his predecessor Alan Hughes, the once-loved Vine is now much run-down and sorry-looking of late and was temporarily closed for several weeks up to October 2013. In 1981 I quoted then gaffer Walsall-bred Alan Hughes: "... it's one o' them as yo' con never tell. One day it's packed ter bostin' and the same toime next wik yo'm talking ter the dog!" I described The Vine as 'a smile-a-minute, anything goes, good natured funny-house of the top-most order that's got me annoyed at not having discovered it sooner *(I quickly made up for lost time)*. Distinctly non-flashy, I added that '...it's one of those that doesn't have to try too hard to score, and another where they probably couldn't care one jot whether you like it over-much or not because everyone else that's there is loving it and that's all there to be said. The smoky, noisy workingmens' bar, I noted, was '...full of cheery chappies and mild head-cases' – typically, Reg 'Happy' Starkey who'd hang himself up on a hanger on a coat rail and sing a more than passing selection from Jesus Christ Superstar, then for afters bash a tray over his head until it was shapeless sheet of mangled tin while hollering out a hysterical version of 'Mule Train Yee-Haa' much to the delight, surprise, and concern, of onlookers. Lounge then populated by 'nicely dressed-up young and youngish couples out to gaze into each others' eyes or to get a load of the free, hugely entertaining knees-ups and sing-alongs on Saturdays and Sundays. Either way...' I said, '...you can't help but feel yourself hugely taken in'. The description contrasts sharply with its later years as a sports TV-dominated bar and little used lounge, reserved exclusively for the horse punters and pool ball-bashers given over to the curious pastime of shouting at the telly – theatre-sized and overpowering at that. A recent book *'Haunted Pubs and Hotels in and around Worcestershire – Hunt End Books)* relates the tale of the ghost of a young barman said to have collapsed in the cellar and died here – returning on regular occasions to make his presence felt by tampering with the gas taps and dispensing equipment.

Licensees: *Francis Thomas (1873); Robert Price (1885-1908); Francis Harwood (1908-19); George Barnes (1919-27); Samuel. White (also listed as 'brewer' 1927–1952); William Henry Hill (1952); John Smith (1952-56); Jack Hirons (1956-58); Kenneth William Grewcock (1958-60); John Horton (1960); Peter Richard Bright 1960-2); Ronald Wood (1962-9); Albert Haines (1969-74); Joseph Cox (1974-7); William Scott (1977-9); Ralph Lewis (1979-80); Alan Hughes (1980-1984); Sylvia Dunbar (1984-6); Kenneth Wright (1986); Robert H. Cummings (1986-90); Toni and Charlie Sanders (2000). Current licensee (2013); Mrs Lyn Hughes – awaiting new tenants. Worcester City Licence no: 1106*

A short diversion eastwards to the top of Vine Street and here's...

N41 Northwick Arms
Loacation 29, Vine Street
Years active: 1890 – 2010 (re-opened 2013)

Comparatively recent newcomer (1885 when it first came into the City's newly-extended Licensing Area) it's first listed in Kelly's Directory of Worcestershire at 18 Vine Street (1900) and thereafter as 29 Vine Street (from 1910). Thought also to have been a general store at some stage in the 1930s then returned to being an inn owned and served by Flowers, later Whitbread. Consistently up-and-down in fortunes, the Northwick closed in 2010 with talk of demolition and replacement with flats, but is now (2013) re-opened after planners turned down the original application and allowed two new properties to be built in what had been the car park. Re-opened August 2013 under new former tenants of **The Deers Leap.**

Licensees: Catherine Baylis (1885-90 when she died); William Henry Goodman (1890-99 when he died); Sarah Goodman (1900-07); Henry J. Winwood (1907–1910); Mrs Jane Copson (1910-15); Lester Hughes (1915-29); Ralph Goostrey (1929-30); Thomas Chip (1931); William Edward Banks (1932-40); Albert Dredge (1940-1); Edna May Dredge (1941-47); Albert Harry Dredge (1947-61, deceased 6th February 1961 and the licence taken over again by Edna May Dredge before transfer to Alfred Morris (1961-1974); Ronald Courtney (1971-5); Paul Nightingale (1975-6); Alan Boorn and Eric King (1976); Martin Rudd (1976-81); Francis Lamb (1982-4); Shelagh Moseley (1984-6); Nicholas Eames (1986-7); Ian C. Lockyear (1987-90); Gail Monaghan and Michael Swift (2000). Current licensee (2013); Michael Anthony Horkan. Worcester City Licence no: 1038

Northwick Arms, re-opened 2013 (BB)

Return to the main A449 Ombersley Road and here's...

N43 New Inn
Location: Ombersley Road
Years active: pre-1870 – present

Dating pre-1870s and first listed in Littlebury's Directory of Worcestershire 1873. Built on land that had been in deep countryside only a few years earlier, and still considered a country pub in the village of North Claines right up to boundary changes in 1951. On August 15th 1898, the New Inn came up for sale at Griffiths and Millington's Auction Mart at Pierpoint Street (at 6 for 7 o'clock). As Lot 3, it was described as 'A Fully-Licensed Home-Brewing Roadside Inn' featuring large garden, paddocks, bowling green, Tea Gardens etc is a very old-established and well recognised place of call being the most important full-license Public-House between Ombersley and Worcester, situated as it is within 5 minutes walk of the Tramway terminus and having service of omnibuses passing the door it is a very favourite and popular resort of Worcester residents, who find it a most charming and attractive rendezvous. Internal arrangements of the House, which is double-fronted are Bar and private sitting room combined with spirit cupboard under the stars, very pleasant and commodious smoke room with bay window having most attractive front outlook, unusually large kitchen or taproom fitted with old fashioned and fitted fireplace

*The New Inn 1900 - with Ombersley Road left and Whinfield Road right (Copyright unk)
Below the same today (BB)*

and also having a bay window commanding pleasant views, and a spacious dining room... outside brew house (which is) most conveniently arranged and fitted with a very complete plant, the property of the tenant. Also large yard part-paved and part-turfed, substantially-built stable for 5 or 6 horses, a portion of which has been boarded-off for use as a coalhouse, two lofts over the same, and a Larder, a wood erection of a coach-house with spare roof and sliding doors, two brick-built piggeries and usual out offices'. All this had up to then been let to Mr Adam Cross 'who has been at the property $5^{1}/_{2}$ years, renting at the very modest rate of £45 per annum'.

Eighty-three years on (1981) my description wasn't anywhere near so flowery... Then under managers John and Janet Trevor, seems I was pretty much ambivalent about the New Inn, reckoning at the time that it couldn't quite make up its mind which direction it wanted to go in – describing it as '...wanting to go working class but seeing itself as more than a shade hoity-toity and up-market for that...

'The New Inn is B-I-G. the split-level bar (it still is) is pretty basic stuff where it's working clothes and 30-plus'. Not really a pub with a competitive edge, I noted it had taken John two years to raise a crib team and darts was proving a slow starter too: '...but it's the lounge that's the puller, old beams (still there and probably fake), red velour, cosy corners and shady nooks. Couples' corner is this: somebody out with somebody else's wife and a few out with their own (I can't believe I wrote that – must've been for some good reason!). Today, and still a managed house with a wacky Scouser in charge (Keith Newby Esq) the bar/lounge divide has been swept away and the New Inn has doubled in size to take in what had been gardens (and no doubt the original piggeries) while its emphasis has switched from a good local boozer to one that attracts eaters-out on account of its cheap, but I can vouch for first-hand, cheerful fayre. Sorry, list of licensees incomplete for the reasons listed in the first sentence.... A Marstons house

Licensees: *Thos. Carruthers (1873); G.A. Hiron (1900); Arthur Hirons (1908 - 1915); Sabrea Louisa Goodman, later Hunt (1937-1958); Arthur Frederick King (1958-64); Martyn Wood (1980); Craig Simon (1990); Alan Nash (2000); Peter Strickland (2001). Current licensee (2013); Keith George Newby. Worcester City Licence no: 1103*

E-G: Old Toll House along Droitwich Road

Let's now re-trace to point F and take the Droitwich Road. Hard right at the Old Toll House lights, take Turrall Street – named after Thomas George Turrall of the 10th Battalion Worcestershire Regiment who was awarded the Victoria Cross for conspicuous gallantry and devotion to duty in the field on the 3rd July 1916 when he held a position single-handed and saved an officer's life while under heavy fire – dog-leg round past the 'new' bank (after which the road is appropriately named) and here is (sadly, was)

Barbourne Inn:
Location: 18, New Bank Street
Years active: c1900 – 2010

Once part of Robert Allen's Brewery, later Corona Works sited next door (north-side) incorporated into the City licensing area September 30th 1885 and made up of two former artisan cottages knocked into one to form a cosy but often lively local that many still fondly remember and miss with a huge sense of loss. Address 18, New Bank Street on account of 'new' bank at southern end. Still (2013) standing and licence still in force, but unlikely ever to open again.

First reference Kelly's Directory of Worcestershire 1900   Robert Allen & Son, New Bank St & Northcote Street (1900) and called Robert Allen's Brewery 1908. Noted landlord Will Curnock

Much-lamented Barbourne: in 2010 (BB) and below, just visible half-way up on the left-hand side 1965 (JAS)

(licensee 1938-44 when he died while still tenant here), had been an expert conjuror before becoming a licensee and regularly entertained his customers with apparently amazing sleights-of-hand. Later a training pub for managers as it was always said the wide range of customers there would prepare them for anything. Though managers tended to stay a maximum of nine months while undergoing their training, The Barbourne always enjoyed a reputation for a good cellar. First pub in Bob Backenforth's weekly 'Source' beer guide when under the managership of Richard (Dick, and Sandra) Wallace, I explored the possibility of something new for Worcester – a pub or good beer guide. Not knowing whether or not the idea might take off, future events showed I needn't have fretted. I quoted Dick: "...it's the beer. That's why they come, the beer". I could have ended it there as it said all I needed to say. Even so, I expanded: '...it's very much a local's pub – abut 98% I'd say are long-term regulars' *(of which I was one. I also recall my first ever visit, a wedding reception in 1963)*. As I wrote eighteen years later: 'I've never seen so many so-called experts on so many different topics – horse-racing especially, but also football, darts, fishing, dominoes and crib (the next year and for the following three I was to captain the Barbourne crib team, and very well we did too). They'll even have a go at (The Sun) crosswords too!' I noted. Facilities I described as spartan '...but it all adds up to the traditional, untouched, almost Victorian charm of the old place that still looked as if it could easily slip back into what it had previously been – two artisans cottages knocked into one'. A great self-policing pub, I recall one troublesome and unwelcome customer being thumped so hard outside the Barbourne he ended up in the garden over the road and was still there by the time the pub opened the next morning when his well-intentioned assailant returned for a lunchtime livener, picked him up, brushed him off and took him back inside where he duly bought him a pint! A great Worcester pub full of great Worcester characters, rough-edged but essentially gentlemanly, and sadly missed. Despite closing in April 2010, its licence (no 1249) issued to L.T.Management Services Ltd of Attleborough (2013) remains in force, leaving hopes that it might be resurrected, but its sad and sorry state and lack of parking would suggest it's a forlorn hope. September 2013 earmarked for flats.

Licensees: Henry J. Hope (1902); Robert Allen (1898-1911 when he died); Ernest Hughes (1911-13); James Smith (1913); John Taylor (1913-14); Abraham Smith (1914-15); John Taylor (1913-14); Abraham Smith (1914-15); William Chamberlain (1915-20); John Rowe (1920-9); Horace J. Bentley (1929); Albert Barnes (1930-1); Walter Edward Frederick Lilley (1931-5); Joseph Ralph Hollis (1935-8); William Frederick Curnock (1938-44 when he died); Elsie May Curnock (1944-63); Bruce Whitney (1963-4); Annie Shelving (1964-74); Raymond Brookes (1974-6); Graham Smith (1976-7); Peter Richardson (1977-8); Maurice Colbourne (1980): Richard and Sandra Wallace (1980-2): John Adams (1982); Gordon and Pat Taylor (1982-3); Anthony Ratcliffe (1983-4); John Bonehill (1984-5); Jim and Diane Thomas (1985-6); Ian and Hazel Emery (1986); Roger A. Hill (1990 - 2001); Alan Bloomer; Kate Chris Webb; Graham 'Grizz' Philips (2008-10).

Crown
Rebuilt as: The Deer's Leap (aka 'The Jump')
Location: 'Wich Road (Droitwich) Road
Years active: 1780s to 1979 (rebuilt). Deer's Leap 1980 to 2010

Characterful roadside pub lasting 1780s to 1979, tirn down and replaced characterless, soulless The Deers Leap (1980), itself demolished 2011, now the site of a doctor's surgery.

The original Crown (at 42 Droitwich Road) was a popular if ramshackle M&B local with higgledy-piggledy floors following different phases of construction/extension on different levels, and frontage right up to the pavement. In what would have been a rural setting when first built, c1780s, it was also occasionally used for inquests. On 18th September 1817, the inquest was held here into the death of John More, labourer 50, and a year later into Thomas Knapp who 'accidentally fell into the river'. In 1826, an inquest was also held into Thomas Evans who, it seems, had died from excessive drinking'. In 1827 **The Crown** and **The New Inn** in Ombersley Road were chosen for the inquests on the same day (29th March) into the deaths of two men, Henry Simonds and William Carter, who'd both drowned in the sinking of a canal boat. Famous for its M&B mild, The Crown was demolished 1980 and replaced with the much more modern and go-ahead 'Deers Leap' – aka **The Jump** – that proved to be a considerably more rowdy and raucous affair attracting teenagers and young people drawn by the often live music on offer throughout the week and at weekends. Its name and sign considered to be a romantic rendering of the love-struck stag crossing a chasm to reach the object of his affections, the reality is somewhat starker: it was simply the M&B trade mark. Though mourned by some locals

Originally The Crown, later the Deers Leap (right)1979 (CCMH/CFOW), now dispensing medicine of a different kind, Barbourne Health Centre 2013 above (BB)

who drew up a petition to save it from demolition and replacement with a doctor's surgery in 2010, the aggressive wording of the petition back-fired on its originators and the City Council opted in favour of the development when they might otherwise have been persuaded to throw it out. Despite trying ever so hard, The Deers Leap never became particularly popular for the quality of its beers or the food it began offering.

A video of its demolition here: *http://www.youtube.com/watch?v=Msjqurzbf K4*

Licensees: S. Barnes (1792); also Robert Chamberlain jun, listed as 'vict Crown 'Wich Road'; Thomas Danby (1829 and 1835); James Little (1850); (not listed 1842 to 1855); Mrs. E. Little – by now listed as Droitwich Road (1873); Edwin Yeates (1885-1909 when he died); Mrs Mary A. Yeates (1909-11); Alice Duffett (1911); Henry Baker (1911-22); Norman Milford Cragg (listed as brewer 1922-44); Harry Norman Bott (1944-48 when he died); Harvey Wilfred Dinsdale (1948-55); Raymond Francis Wood (1955-56); Francis Patrick Joseph Correy (1956-57); Reginald Morris (1957-8); Nevlle Kendrick (1958-59); James Henry Talbot (1959-63); Laurence Harper (1963-6); Gordon Putton (1966-9); Roger Rae (1969-73); Alan Harris (1973-6); Alan Harris and Peter Quinn (1976-7); Peter Quinn (1977). Mandy Louise Smith (2010). Licence no 2914 surrendered.

As Deers Leap: John Hughes (1980); Brian and Delia Heeks (1990); Nigel Roscoe (2000); Martin O'Boyle (2010)

N46 Alma
Location: Droitwich Road
Years active: c1864 to present

Listed variously as Alma 1864–1940 and Alma Inn (to present) at 74 Droitwich Road and named after joint British and French victory of the Battle of Alma that took place on the 20th September 1854 on the river of that name in Crimea, now part of the Ukraine. Until recently a large frieze celebrating the famous victory was sited in the bar:

You loyal Britons pray draw near,
Unto the news I've brought you here,
With joy each British heart does cheer
For the victory gained at Alma.

It was in September, the 18th day,
In spite of the salt sea's dashing spray,
We landed safe in the Crimes,
Upon our route for Alma.

A lovely picture of a ladies' outing from 1900 is also re-printed below, showing a very emaciated horse that today would have the RSPCA crashing down on the owner who'd run a good chance of being locked-up for the crime, and rightly so too. A short while earlier, according to the pub's website, the Alma played host to Worcester's most famous son, Sir Edward Elgar, who 'enjoyed a drink at the bar whilst his mother worked behind it'. I can go along with the former comment *(just)* but would seriously doubt the latter (Elgar's mother Anne Greening was the daughter of the licensee of **The Shades** in Mealcheapen Street where it's said she met her future husband and father of her famous son, Dover-born William. Mind, Wikipedia gets it wrong too: it lists the future Mrs Elgar as daughter of a farm worker. In the late 50s-60s boxing tournaments were held here, with future champ Jack Bodell once boxing in the upstairs room. Originally Holts Brewery, later Ansells house. Then with a distinct lounge (front) and bar (side, now just one L-shaped room) I wrote of the Alma in 1981, at the time under flamboyant and supremely confident *(for which read 'annoyingly cocky')* Welshman David Howells '... personally I found this pub a bit back-to-front; while the bar's only used by a handful, the lounge is overflowing' I wrote, describing it as 'low-ceilinged, dark, cork-lined and choked with a lot of tables and chairs, while the bar relied heavily on all things Crimean – to the point, I noted, that I expected the Charge of The Light Brigade to come half-a-league, half-a-league, half-a-leaguing onwards at closing time'. Mild (at 47p and 49p in the bar and lounge) and bitter (at 48p and 50p in the lounge) wasn't all it had been – but was, as I recalled it, pleasant and inoffensive enough if unlikely to bring back the lost legions (this was after a disastrous draymen's strike).

Ladies outing from The Alma 1912 (CCMH/CFOW)

...and 1980s (CCMH/CFOW)

Alma 1964 (JAS)

The Better Beer

Marred of late (2013) by a landlady whose attitude prevents many – me included – from venturing in there. A Punch Taverns inn.

Licensees: Josiah Rice (1885-98 when he died); Mrs Martha Rice (1899-1907); Francis Harwood (1907-8); Frank J. Rice (1908-20); Francis Harwood (1920-25); Edward Price (1925-7); Frederick R. Stevenson (1927-9 when he died); Leah Stephenson (1929-30); Albert Victor Lloyd (1930-4); John Joplin (1934-6); Arthur Hale (1936); Frank Wright (1936-8); Frank Deakin; (1938-40 when he died); Elizabeth Deakin (1940-2); Charles Phipps (1942-3); Phillip Scott (1943-4); Mrs Irene Annie Deakins (1944-1946); Alfred Wilcox (1946-52); Emily Elizabeth Pengelly (1952-58); Dorothy Smedley (1958-59); Albert John Keteingham (1959-60); Stanley Howells (1960); James Dobson (1960-2); Philip Gregory (1962-6); Cyril Diment (1966-7); Thomas Tether (1967-72); Alice Tether (1972-8); John Evans (1978-9) David Howells (1979-80s); Henry Fussell (1990); Les Clutterbuck (2000). Current (2013) licensee/dps: Steven Mark Fereday. Worcester City licence 1119

N47 Bell
Location 45, Droitwich Road
Years active: c1900-2000

Address 49 Droitwich Road. Still standing, though ceased to be a pub 2000, later insurance office, taxi office and presently being turned into students flats. On 17th January 1908, Bell licensee Benjamin James Burford was fined 10/- (50p) with £1.10s. 6d (£1.52$^1/_2$p) costs for 'unlawfully suffering gaming' here. Originally a Tom Allen Brewers of Malvern public house and the Royal Wells Brewery of Malvern before becoming a Flowers establishment, later Whitbread, even later Davenports/ Greenall Whitley house, it's a pub and off-licence (wine, beer, cider and perry) with a long line of theatrical associations, run by Welshman Tom Williams whose brother Emlyn, noted actor, playwright, one of Britain's top film stars (he played Caligula in the   Korda brothers' epic 'I Claudius' along side Charles Laughton who also has reputed Worcester connections (see **Paul Pry**), novelist, autobiographer, director and chronicler of the Moors Murders, as well as author of one of my favourite books 'George', lived here for a while. Tom's son Nigel also took to the boards, appearing in Crossroads and TV ads, often cast as a louche smooth-talking rake. Later, after being run for a

The Bell has always enjoyed great theatrical traditions.
Above 1964 (JAS). Top, long after playing its last act as a pub 2013 (BB)

short time by ex-County cricketer Fred Cooper (1966) it was run by ex-BBC Black and White Minstrels and Players Theatre London members Len Baker and Fred White when it was not unusual to see theatricals and noted variety performers like Ronnie Corbett, Sheila Burnett and Harry H. Corbett (Harold Steptoe)'s ex-wife Sheila Staefel and others propping up the bar or staging impromptu cabarets both in the bar and in the skittle alley. In 1981 I noted '...the first thing that strikes you is the remarkable array of signed photographs from big(-ish) names in the theatrical world, Roy Hudd and The Krankies included. The second thing you notice is the pink, peach and black colour scheme that's likely to stop you in your tracks. And the third is the tree in the lounge that appears to change with the seasons'. It then had two bars and a skittle alley, '...all long, narrow and low ceilinged'. The building has recently been given a face-lift and is appearing to be preparing for a new lease of life since de-licensing around 1998.

Licensees: Elisha Harding (1885-6); Sofia Griffiths (1886-7); Arthur Haycock (1887-9 when he died); Florence Haycox (1900-06); Benjamin James Burford (1906-8); James Randle (1908-11); Jack Rogers (1911-15); George Marchant (1915-16); Charles Roe Underhill (1916-59); Frederick James Orton (1959-62); Tom Williams (1962-66); Fred Cooper (1966); Walter Oldfield (1966-69); Raymond Drinkwater (1969-70); Len Baker and Fred White (1970-86); Ronnie Windsor (1986-90); Jim McKeever (1990s); Nicholas Adams (2000)

N48

Fountain
Location; corner of Checketts Lane and Droitwich Road
Years active: 1940s-52

Long-forgotten full-licence pub on the corner of Checketts Lane and Droitwich Road, until licence lapsed on 8th February 1952. Up to then record exists of only one known licensee (Worcester City Police Register of Intoxicating Liquor Licenses page 138) Albert Edwin Morris

Site of The Fountain (2013 - BB)

N49

Perdiswell House Hotel
Loc'n: 40 Droitwich Rd
Active: 1950s to present

Originally Little Perdiswell House, described by historian Bill Gwilliam as 'a new pub in a Victorian grange' is a large 1950's pub, later one of the first Ansells steak bars and still viewed primarily as an eating house aimed at families with children. Its Provisional licence was granted at adjourned annual licensing meeting

Perdiswell House (2013 - BB)

on 3rd April 1952, confirmed on 1st May and made final on November 3rd with additional Supper Licence granted on 6th February 1953. In 1981, then under the managership of Bob (and Karen) Hazard I asked Bob why people came. He replied: '... because it's friendly. It's a good friendly atmosphere, we've got a good new bitter on and there's always food. Does that answer your question?' It did. Admirably. Outside I described as 'a pretty one with trees and drinks on the lawn' *(which is still the case)*. Inside, lounge and restaurant *(both now combined)*, still pretty, and a neat little bar now also swallowed up in the great big whole that the Perdie has since become. The restaurant was a 55-seater (I celebrated my 21st birthday party here {success} and also my first wedding anniversary {failure}) and I described the bitter as 'amicable enough: '...I mean it ain't going to get you jumping up and down in unbounded delight, but it certainly is pleasant enough, hand-drawn in the bar (47p) and electrically pumped in the lounge (51p). Now with a very likeable landlord, but given over to families, with wacky warehouse area and strong emphasis on kids, quiz nights and food. An Orchid Pubs & Dining Ltd house, registered in St Albans. A recent visit (2013) improved no end by a cracking couple of pints of 'Spitfire'. *Licensees: John Harley Wilson (1952); Hilda Muriel Heath (1952-56); Reginald Frank Jeynes (1956-63); Philip Keen (1963-7); John Escott (1967-70); Roger Wise (1970); Michael James Cowley (1970-9); Jonathan Dowse (1979-80); Robert Hazard (1980-2); Robert Dickson (1982-3); Nicholas Steggles (1983-6); Anthony O'Connell (1986); Tony Johnstone (1990); Sharron Harding (2000); David Baker. Current licensee (2013); David Albert Baker. Worcester City Licence no: 1440*

Raven (and Raven Inn)
Location: Droitwich Road
Years active: 1820 – present

Raven (2013 - BB)

A raven appears on the coat of arms of Queen Mary I as well as all properties associated with 'Salt King' John Corbett after whom this popular pub takes its name. Described as being in 'Holy Claines' ward, the Raven was a noted stop- and pick-up point for stage-coaches leaving and entering the City.   For this reason wooden benches were put up 'beneath the immemorial elms' as chronicler William Corbett put it: '...in my youth when strolling in Claines in the 1860s I also rested on the Raven's benches and sampled its tap' . So, apparently did one of the Oddingley murderers Richard Heming who'd been hoping to make his escape to Bristol by stage coach from here. Not strictly a Worcester pub, being well outside the City boundaries almost all of its life, the Raven is sufficiently popular and well-known to merit a place here – not least as being outside the City licensing area until comparatively recently, it enjoyed an extra half hour's drinking time in the morning session, calling time at 2.30pm while City pubs had to close at 2pm. The difference meant a steady stream of drinkers crossing the styx to the Raven for a final 30 minutes' swill. A Mitchells house and popular roadside inn, the Raven was first listed in Pigot's Worcestershire Directory 1829, though it may have existed earlier. Since extended, then extended again, it's now a massive eating house and carvery offering cheap and cheerful carvery food with nothing to attract the casual drinker – who in its hey day frequented the Raven in droves, attracted exclusively by the beer as well as a succession of very friendly landlords and barmaids. Nothing can compare, though, to the cold beef rolls in a basket that the Raven was legendary for during the 60s and 70s. Some original features including the leaded windows showing the sign of the Raven – ie Salt King John Corbet's trade mark – are a poor substitute for the great Raven as was, and presence of kids' ruckus room, while a godsend for some is an annoyance for others and detracts from the appeal for many. Licensee list incomplete as The Raven was officially outside the City boundary until comparatively recently. Registered in Alcester as The Raven Carvery Limited

Licensees: James Smith (1829); James Smith (1835); John Tapp (1850); W. Evans (listed as Raven, Droitwich Road, North Claines – 1900); listed, no name (1910 ?); Mrs S Nicholas (1915); Mrs Mary E. Lane (1932); Rupert Baker (1940s); Neville and Mary Key (1964); Robert Dowling (1990); Alan Sinnott (2001). Current licensee (2013); Adrian Paul Harland. Worcester City Licence no: 1126

N51

Mug House
Location: Claines
Years active: 1600 - present

Mug House (2013 - BB)

Thought to be the only pub in a churchyard anywhere in the UK, and for many years the Village House where parish meetings were held prior to the Parish Councils Act, The Mug House has a massive history stretching back some 650 years though was also outside the City boundary up to comparatively recently. Ghost sightings include a Royalist soldier believed to have been cornered in the churchyard and murdered there, and a little girl joyfully singing 'Half a pound of twopenny rice' while she sits on a swing. The organ in the church is also reputed to be heard being played even though the building is locked and barred and no-one is inside! Incomplete list of landlords that inlcudes Ann Mansell, John Minton, Jn Trow, Wm Blissett, George Hobbs 1915 and the legendary Walter Trow (to 1984)

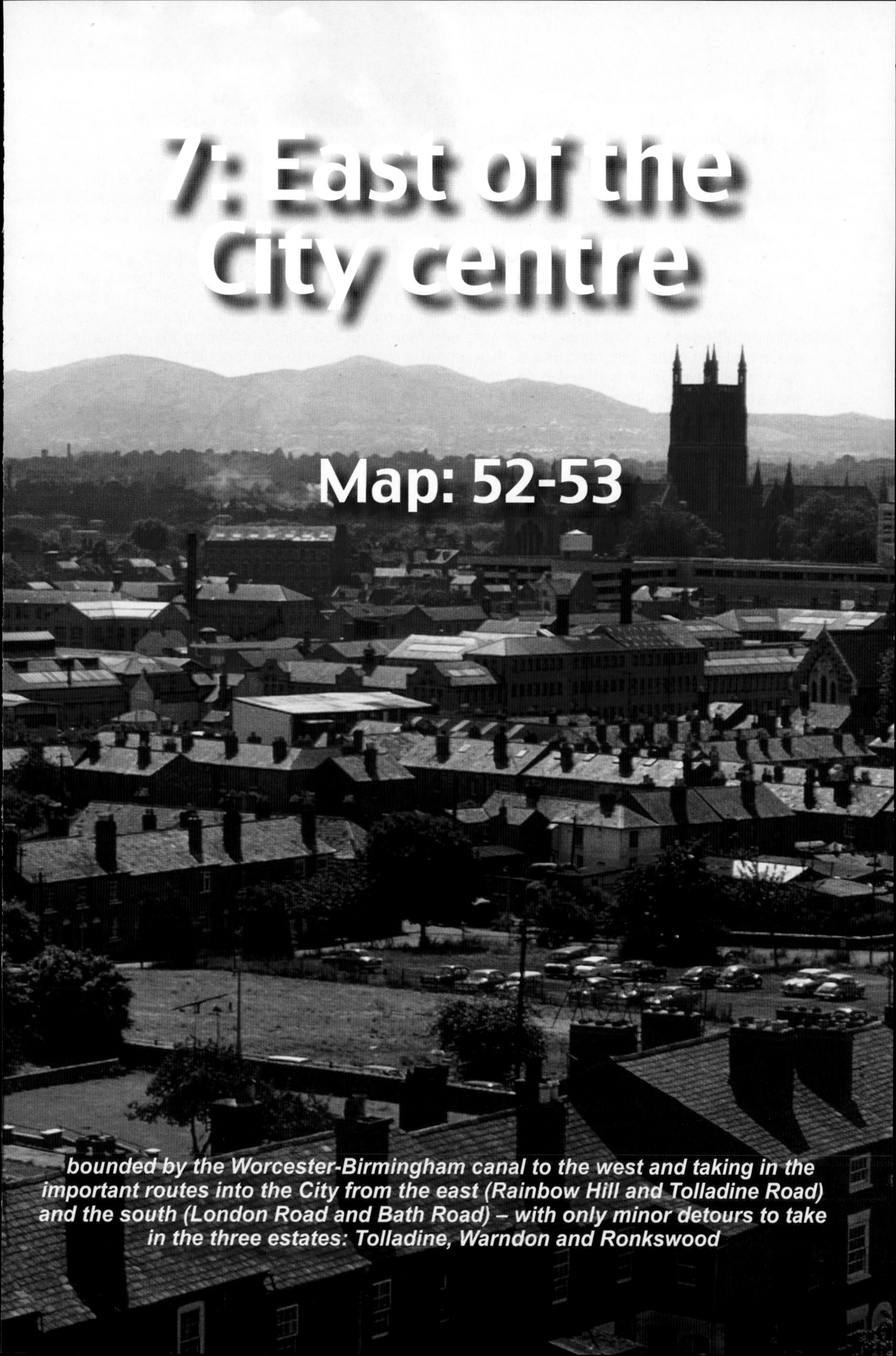

7: East of the City centre

Map: 52-53

bounded by the Worcester-Birmingham canal to the west and taking in the important routes into the City from the east (Rainbow Hill and Tolladine Road) and the south (London Road and Bath Road) – with only minor detours to take in the three estates: Tolladine, Warndon and Ronkswood

Very little existed east of the City wall up to around 1840 and then a rapid eastwards expansion almost doubled the size of the City over a surprisingly short period. The reason? Virtually exclusively, the coming of the canal.

Up to then, as outlined earlier, Worcester had enjoyed major prosperity as a manufacturing town, as a spa, as a cultural centre, and as the capital of a flourishing county of Worcestershire, and the City had earlier been viewed as the fifth largest and the third most important in England – with writers, gazetteers and noted observers heaping praise on its looks, its character, its attitude and its success.

At the head of the tidal section of the River Severn, the City had achieved high status as a major trans-shipment centre, particularly in the transport of coal from the Midlands and salt from Droitwich, and the canal was to revolutionise all that. Even so, in typical Worcester fashion, heels were dragged at a time that speed was of the essence and its coming was dogged with problems – not least, widespread rejection from local landowners and fears over the effects of losing the pleasant open space that had been Sansome Fields. But progress was inevitable and though the revolution came years after other cities had welcomed the canal concept with open arms, official approval for the Worcester to Birmingham 'cut' brought a period of rejoicing to the City:

Come now begin delving, the Bill is obtain'd
The conquest was hard but a conquest is gain'd
Let no time be lost, let business be done
Set thousands to work, that work down the sun

With pearmains and pippins 'twill gladden the throng
Full loaded the boats to see floating along
And fruit that is fine and good hops for our ale
Like Wednesbury pit-coal, will always find sale

The long awaited opening of the Worcester and Birmingham Canal in 1815 had been far from smooth. Not only that, but the canal itself also proved cripplingly expensive... it's reckoned that every mile cost the then staggering amount of £20,333 – at least £4,000 a mile more than any other canal built between 1760 and 1840 and £10,000 a mile more than most *(Source: Bill Gwilliam – Old Worcester People and Places)*. It also took much longer to build than others. Even so – and despite finally arriving forty years later than other more go ahead companies had managed, only preceding the coming of the railways by a mere fifteen years – the resulting industrial growth that came in its wake nonetheless breathed new life into the eastern aspect of the City in general, and two till-then wholly undeveloped areas, Lowesmoor and Diglis, in particular.

Accordingly, with the new-found prosperity the canal brought came an up-swing in new commercial activity and with it, the call for new housing – as well as, fortunately for us, pubs to serve the workers needed to toil and labour at the new-found sweat-shops and factories that had sprung up along the hand-dug waterway. Thus, as the new iron and metal foundries and factories set up in its wake began to prosper, so the City's till-then pretty face took on a different look as development began to show a rapid expansion eastwards.

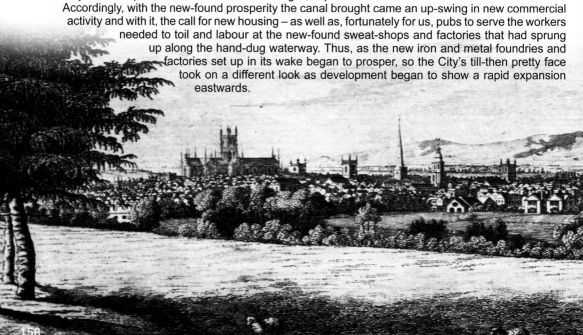

The impact of the canal and hard on its heels, the coming of the railway, sparked-off a half-century of growth and expansion unparalleled in scale even up to the burgeoning new estates of the 1930s and 1940s *(Tolladine and Brickfields)* and 1950s and 60s: *Ronkswood, Dines Green and Warndon* – particularly the latter, at its inception considered the biggest public housing project in Europe.

An insightful study of the transportation situation facing the City, 'Worcester's fight for a railway and its consequences for the urban, commercial and industrial development of the city in the early Victorian period' by David J Cannings-Bushell, BA(Hons), tells the tale, warts'n'all:

'The arrival of the canal initiated a burst of industrial growth. After 1815, businesses such as Thomas & Son Wind Pumps, Elt's Footwear, Larkworthy's Agricultural Machinery; Russell & Dorrell, Dent Allcroft, Nicholson & Sons, organ builders; Chamberlain's Porcelain, Willis's Cinderella Shoe Factory and the Vulcan Iron Foundry were all started, the majority in Lowesmoor. Webb's Horsehair Carpet Factory which started in 1835 rapidly expanded until, by the 1850s, one of their special lines was horsehair carpet foot rugs for the OW&WR and other railways in Britain. Hill Evans Vinegar works of 1830 grew to become the largest in the world. McNaught's Carriage Works became one of the most famous of 19th century coachbuilders. In 1837, Lea & Perrins began production of its famous Worcestershire Sauce. For none of these industries did the absence of a railway seem a problem although, in later years, firms like Hill Evans had their own private connection'

For David Cannings-Bushell's excellent and fascinating description of this critical period in the City's history, visit http://www.canbush.com/at308-tma061.htm

Suffice to say, with the joint influence of first the canal and then, after an even more difficult birth, the railway, the landscape of Worcester had taken on a vastly different hue from the 1830s onwards, and for the next half century and more, the City presented a vibrant, if compared to its Regency hey-days, rather grimier face. Speculative schemes of mean back-to-back housing suddenly sprung-up and as if from nowhere, creating a series of new working class suburbs. In their wake rapidly followed a corresponding number of equally mean alehouses, commercial hotels, missions, chapels and music halls – all, for the most part, built between the old City wall and the open land stretching as far as the new canal and then even further beyond.

For a while, all appeared well with the world and Worcester was once more showing its muscle as a production centre. But with the passage of time and the onset of successive dark periods of financial and economic crises to which the City has always been particularly susceptible, the legacy of empty warehouses, deserted industrial sites, even meaner and more depressing terraced houses and pubs with questionable reputations still haunts us – scarcely lifted by even later developments carrying with them a clear sense of déjà-vu...

A: South of the cathedral

From Sidbury along Commandery Road to Bath Road, it's hard to miss the imposing-looking pub that almost immediately looms up in front of you. This is...

19th century view of Worcester from the north (CCMH/CFOW)

The Albion - with a prime place in my personal history! Picture: WRO

...revisited 2013 (BB)

E1

The Albion
Location: Bath Road (No 48)
Years active: c1826 to present

Once highly regarded local, now looking a bit sorry for itself as though it's waiting for someone to switch a light on, The Albion, built around 1826 and first listed in Victuallers' Recognizances for 1827, remains one of the City's most recognisable landmarks with its distinctive curved front. 'Albion' was one of several names the Romans applied to Britain – taken from their first sight of the white *(ie: alba, Latin white)* cliffs at Dover. Mythical Albion is often seen being guarded over by helmeted and tridented female warrior Britannia – who also features on this Albion's pub sign and rightly so, too.

The Albion was an M&B house registered at Cape Hill Brewery Birmingham, listed variously as The Albion (1842-1900); Albion Hotel (1910); and Albion Inn (from 1940) official address 48 Bath Road.

It was also occasionally used for inquests: on 6th November 1828 an inquest into an unknown man found drowned in the Severn was held here and a year later a double inquest: John Henry Perks who'd fallen from a boat into the Severn, as well as Mary George, wife of the porter of Edgar Tower who'd taken arsenic and died. More recently, a former landlady is also reputed to have fallen into a fire and burned her hand off. In 1989, then landlord Chris Watts - who also claims the presence of a ghost walking the premises – forced open a locked first floor door and found a store room untouched for over 50 years: piled-up in there was a treasure trove of undisturbed magazines, newspapers, posters, handbills and pub receipts dating from the 1920s. Closed for almost a year before re-opening in January 2013 The Albion was, I wrote in a blog about the time it re-opened 'the first pub I ever went in and the first I was carried out of':

'...the re-opening of any good old Worcester pub that's been closed for too long is always going to be good news, but I must confess the re-opening of this particular good old Worcester pub gives me special cause for joy on account of the fact that The Albion was, I believe I can state with some degree of certainty, not only the first pub I ever went in, but also the first pub I was carried out of...' One of my favourite pubs in the 60s and 70s, I still have fond memories, though it's an entirely different proposition now – particularly since Chris Watts' departure (2012) and his wife Geri's (Gel's) untimely death not long after. Shame. An Enterprise Inn, it remained closed for the better part of a year after Chris Watts left and re-opened January 2013 under licensee Jamie Sherlock.

Below: The Albion photographed 27th February 1960 (RHS)

Above: The Albion just visible off centre right behind the left of the chimney stacks in this 1880s photograph of a long forgotten Worcester

(CCMH/CFOW)

Licensees: *William Smith (1827); John Sanders (1835); Thomas Everton (to 1850); Thomas Chandler (1855); William Parker (1872-79); John Impey (1879-85); Thomas Epps (1885-7 when he died); Jane Epps (1887-91); Thomas Epps (1891-7); John Robinson (1897-8); James Wheeler (1898–1902); Charles Woolfries (1902-4); Edgar Wells (1904-06); George Morroll (1906-7); John Luffman (1907-08); Waldegrave Ingram (1908-15); Charles Cox (1915-26); Mrs Mary A. Harris (1926-31); Ernest William Smith (1931-2); Ernest Luther (1932-6); Ralph Bevan (1936–1940); Percy George Jones (1940-1954); Victor Norcott (1954-69); Arnold Young (1969); Albert Hammond (1969-72); Brian Hill (1972-4); Howard Roberts (1974-83); Philip Robert Wise (1983-5); Leslie Clutterbuck (1985-6); Tony Ratcliffe (1986); Chris (and Geraldine) Watts – (1997-2011). Current licensee (2013); Jamie Sherlock. Worcester City Licence no: 1083*

> *A 'hard' right over the canal bridge would take you to two lost gems in Mill Street The Alma and The Unicorn, so for the moment take the first left down Diglis Road. There on a bend is a pub that's long held a special place in Worcester drinkers' hearts – and still does, mine included...*

The Anchor
Location: 54 Diglis Road, also Diglis (also 'Diglis Wharf ' 1842)
Years active: 1840s – present

Still standing, and looking as though it'll always be there, the Anchor has been listed variously as Anchor and Anchor Inn at Diglis Wharf (1842); Lower Bath Road (1910) and Diglis Road (1940).

A Banks's pub originally owned by Robert Allen and Co registered at 7 Lovatt Street Wolverhampton, the Anchor has always been held in the highly regard by its regulars and visitors alike – for the quality of its home brewed ales (19th century), the inestimable efficiency and effortless bar skills of its long-running gaffer Ken Beard who'd remember pints left 'in' from months before (1960s – 1990s) and more recently for its heart-attack breakfasts put by some as nudging 3,000 calories. *(At time of writing, the present gaffer has had a spat with the brewery on account of selling more food than beer and so is temporarily*

Diglis Road with The Anchor in
the distance.
(Above) 1970, (CCMH/CFOW)
Left - a landscaping showpiece
2013 (BB)

closed). The Anchor was also home to the longest-running crib game in the world – a continuous game that lasted unbroken from 1958 (Easter Monday was the first day) to around 1990, and featured at least two of the original four players six nights of the week, 5.30pm-6.30pm, year-in year-out for more than three decades. The same table was used – the veneer on the four corners and the centre worn almost white through continuous use. No money changed hands but tallies were recorded at the end of each session, and the score-sheet kept on a special shelf behind the radio that Ken Beard turned on as a variation of ringing the bell to call 'time'. The 32-year old game only finished when the original players including legendary motor trade dealer and repairer Doug Tansell *(whose sons still run Airora Garage in the same corrugated tin premises Diglis Road)* could no longer make their way to The Anchor for their night's recreation that only stopped for Sundays and Christmas Day.

The Anchor was also home to 'Dead Man's Chair' – a welcoming wooden carver's chair cosily sited next to the permanently roaring log fire: regulars shunned it on account of three of their number who adopted it as their own having died in quick succession – in two cases the result of tragic accidents, within a few months of each other. A chance cleaning of a picture recently also revealed on its reverse a long-lost photograph of The Anchor in 1902 and what's thought to be the daunting Miss Hannah Mason, licensee and coal dealer from the turn of the century and well into the 1920s. Described in Banks's blurb in 1985 as 'steady as a rock despite the changing tides of time' the Anchor firmly clung to the 'unspoiled by progress' tagline of its Banks's masters. About the same time, Ken Beard *(pictured above)* told me that the first time he ever saw The Anchor as a lad of twelve, it was a true fisherman's retreat – and that not much had changed since. For all that, Ken always remained unhurried, unfazed, laid-back and perpetually unruffled: "Me? I've seen 'em all in here from TV stars and millionaires down – and they all get the same treatment" he chuckled. Especially noted for its ales, the Anchor's bar has been slightly extended of late to take in what had once been the living quarters, but its essential character remains. A Marstons house.

Licensees: *Richd. Jones (1842 and 1850), William Marston (1855); Edward Marston (1873); Sarah Marston (1885-91); William Marston (1891); Edward Marston (1873); Miss Hannah Mason (1900, listed as licensee and coal dealer 1902 and 1920s, as Mrs Hannah Mason (1915); Silas Stewart (1927-30); William Hill (1930-32); Walter and Annie Beard (1932-63); Ken Beard (1971-86); Ronald Brown (1986-89) Martin Deeley (1989); Norma Kettley (2000). Current licensee/dps (2013); Paul Watton. Worcester City Licence no: 1136*

Returning to the Bath Road heading south, a solid looking (and at time of writing very rundown and neglected) structure on the right hand side opposite where the original old Co-op and a modern convenience store now stand is...

E3 The Berwick Arms (Inn)
Also known as: Barrel and Organ
Location: 250 Bath Road
Years active: from 1900. Closed 2008, still standing

Owned by Spreckley Bros and registered at 7 Foregate Street, later West Country Breweries (Whitbread) and named after the Berwick estate whose chequered coat-of-arms features on the pub's (still standing) sign, The Berwick Arms is listed as Cherry Orchard (1873) and 250 Bath Road. Big and lumbering, it sits on a corner plot once with large garden where its forlorn-looking car park now stands. A noted licensee here (1913-31) was three-times English Quoits Champion and eight times national team player locally born Walter Jones, who was also an international bowls player, representing England in the side that toured South Africa in 1938. Former licensee of **The New Inn** in George Street he was also instrumental in setting up Worcester Bowling Club.

Suffering badly from a reputation as being a bit of a rough-house in its day, successive attempts at cleaning it up and moving up-market met with varying degrees of success throughout the 60 and 70s – to the point that in the late 1960s The Berwick had weeded-out the Barneshall bovver boys and openly welcomed families and couples, but new blood allowed it to lapse before committing the unforgiveable sin of knocking distinct lounge and bar into one. In an attempt to woo a younger clientele it changed its name to **'The Barrel and Organ'** for a while before scrapping that notion and reverting, rightly so, to its original name. Always a pub you could count on for games and sports, The Berwick suffered from being bashed about and knocked into one soulless big room. Though now (2103) closed for several years, the licence issued to Peter Christopher Styles of Bromyard Road remains in force, though much trumpeted plans to re-open

The Berwick- about to become a 4-bed house (BB)

the pub in have fizzled out and the Berwick is now pegged to be turned into a 4-bedroom private house.

Licensees: *William (illegible) Cherry Orchard, Bath Road (1873); Charles Hayler (1885-93); Francis Howe (1893-1913 when he died); Seraphine Howe (1913); Walter H. Jones (1913-31); Frederick William Stafford (1931–1945); Charles William Farmer (1940-1956); David Thomas Torbett (1956–68); George Llewellyn (1975-6); Thomas Goddard (1976); Philip Taylor (1976-80); Guy Goodwin (1980-81); Michael Lamb (1981-83); David Radburn (1983); Barry Cockayne (1983-85); Jamine Boston and Anthea Massingham (1985-6); Anthony Taylor (1986-88); John Sewell (1988)* **As Barrel and Organ:** *Thomas Allen (2000); Robert Douglas (2001)*

Continuing along Bath Road up past the new estates left and right to the traffic island in what even as recently as fifty years ago was largely open country, the next destination of note is:

The Timberdine
Location:
Broomhall, Bath Road
Years active: 1986 - present

Fashioned out of a breathtakingly attractive black and white former farm- and manor house, and still with what appears to be original timbers though the form of the building is marred by the addition of new extensions, The Timberdine is now a bustling Harvester (ie M&B) roadside eating house. Only operating as a pub and restaurant since comparatively recently – mid 1980s – it looks as though it should have been home to some wicked highway robber and could tell some tales of dastardly deeds and bodice-ripping lust and romance, but sadly doesn't. Steaks aren't bad though, and a huge garden and car park makes it ideal for families. Current licensee or dps (2013) Stuart Matthew Band. Worcester City Licence no: 1145

Back to the main road and just before you hit the murderously busy Ketch Island stands to your right a historic old once-wayside inn: The Ketch – which, incidentally, while it gives the impression of being in direct competition to The Timberdine and that the two glower at each other in deadly rivalry over the Bath Road, the facts might surprise you...

The Ketch
Also known as: New Inn, Toby Carvery
Location: Bath Road
Years active: 1600 – present

Though first mention is in Littlebury's Directory of Worcestershire 1873, the Ketch Inn has a history stretching back well before The Battle of Worcester 1651. An ancient wayside inn of the 17th century, it's where Cromwell's troops are said to have drunk its ale and Samuel Butler wrote the satirical mock heroic poem Hudibras concerning the various factions involved in the Civil War, published in three parts between 1663 and 1678. Just below The Ketch is the point where Cromwell ordered his men to build the famous 'bridge of boats' to allow them entry into Worcester via the back door, and the Ketch still has one of the best views from a pub window anywhere in Britain, though now marred by the recent addition of Carrington Bridge. The Ketch pleasure gardens were highly popular in the 19th century and are said to have been *'...laid out in elaborate imitation of the famous gardens with alcoves, fountains and dancing greens (while) pleasure boats carried passengers from Worcester bridge to the pleasure gardens'.* This, same as several popular inns within walking distance of the Cross, is where Worcester folk made a beeline for on bright summery days – and what better than a pleasant walk, ride or cruise to

The Ketch goes back to before the Civil War - and it was here Cromwell ordered his troops to build the famous 'Bridge of Boats' in 1651

Main pic WRO
Lower pic CCMH/CFOW
Above" today (BB)

a sweet country inn in order to partake of its goodly ales and perhaps a game of skittles in the Ketch alley, to be followed by a supper of ham and eggs in the parlour (1873). Listed variously as Ketch and Ketch Inn at Kempsey Road and later Bath Road, the kitchen was described as 'spotless, and the company of its kindly hostess Mrs (Hannah) Clarke and her jovial son Ned who was brewer, ostler and tapster completed evenings of delight' (Source: Bill Gwilliam) In 1981 I described The Ketch as 'bar that's workmanlike with plenty of blacked beams, studded seats and not unpleasantly yellowed walls, plush lounge/restaurant with little cocktail-style bar that looks clear across to the Malverns, skittle alley that looks tatty on the outside but is pleasantly cosy inside, and bed and breakfast facilities for seven people. Outside pretty, neat and trim, inside trim, pretty and neat'. Then, aside from coach parties, food was lunchtimes only and included what I described as 'things in a basket' for around £1.60 and T-bone steak I noted with some alarm, at the eye-wateringly high price of £4.50. Fast forward to 2013.... it's now a popular though much extended carvery under the style of Toby Carvery – a very different proposition to the facilities I described in 1981 – and is almost exclusively given over to eating, though the fayre on offer is plain, homely and not at all poor value for money. In fact, a full carvery roast today will cost you roughly what a steak would have cost you 30 years ago! Interesting to note that The Ketch is operated as a Toby Carvery while the Timberdine over the road is a Harvester: don't be fooled – both come under the Mitchells and Butlers umbrella!

Images of The Ketch from the collection of Clive and Malcolm Haines, and below 2013 (BB)

Licensees: Mrs Hannah Clarke (1873); Samuel Thomas Stinton (1900); F Partridge (1908-c1913); Ernest Roberts (1915); Charles Poucher (1903); (unknown – and unregistered in the Worcester City Police register of intoxicating liquor licenses as it lay outside City police boundaries) In 1981, Bert Hamnett (1980). Current licensee or dps (2013); Kristy Alison Walters. Worcester City Licence no: 1176

Let's re-trace our steps back to B Sidbury, and head eastwards along London Road.

By any stretch, this is a notable length of road, steeped in history – and well served with pubs.

E6 **The Red Lion ('Red Lyon')**
Location: Sidbury
Years active: 1760 to 1990
The Red Lion – generally held to be the most popular pub name in Britain of which there were 759 in 2007 (reduced to 724 by 2012 and no doubt reduced even further by now) – this one stood on the corner of Wylds Lane in what's now Thai Time Asian restaurant.

First listed as 'Red Lyon' in Victuallers Recognizances in 1766 under Thomas Savage later Grundy Royal Directory 1792 at 2 Sidbury, and variously thereafter as 1 Sidbury (1900) and 109 Sidbury (1940), it's a former Lewis Clarke's house registered at the brewery in Angel Place and later Marstons. Licensee Frank Keetley (1937-60s) had been a First Division footballer in his day and in 1981 I wrote: '...must confess to a sneaking regard for this pub – not least as it reminds me of how pubs used to be: low ceiling, small windows, long and narrow bar and a good old-fashioned gaffer (Martin Underhill) who knows what he's on about. Besides, the kids and the serious drinkers are segregated so that the bar remains traditionally decorated and the lounge – Lion's Den – just right for late-teens/early twenties with loud Space Invaders, even louder juke box and cosy secluded corners... toilets could do with a bit of tarting-up though' I noted – adding that '...being an old listed building doesn't help'. It's been an Asian restaurant since it sadly closed as a pub in 1990.

Licensees: Thomas Savage (1766); William Tomlins (listed as 'red lion 2 Sidbury – 1790 and 1792); John Worthington (1814-20s); Thomas Worthington (1827); George Bowker (1835); Jno. Flemming (1842); Thomas Dance (1850); George Hartwright (1855); Henry Roberts (1872-1885); Arthur Culpin (1885-1902); Charles Richard Stallard (1902-6); John Albert Hodges (1906-11); Robert Price (1911-12); James and Ellen Hope (1912-22); Mrs Maria Perkins (1922-28); Mrs Elizabeth Ellen and Walter Lilley (1928-35); Frank and Nellie Keetley (1935–1968); Martin Underhill (1968-1988); Arthur Wells (1988)

(Right) Red Lion 1964. (JAS) and above 2013 - Thai Time (BB).
A friend asked me recently 'ere Bob, what do they serve in them thigh restaurants?'
I didn't know what to tell him!

Cross over Wylds Lane and you pass the still impressive...

The Barley Mow
E7 Location: Sidbury
Years active: c1820 – 2006

Fine, red-brick, architecturally rich sandstone building still standing and dating from early 1800s when the area would still have been quite rural. Listed as Barley Mow London Road (1842), Barley Mow Hotel 1910 and Barley Mow 115 Sidbury (1932), it was also occasionally used for inquests. On 20th July 1815, the inquest was held here into Joseph, eldest son of Joseph Ford, baker, aged 'about 16'; on 22nd September 1825 into Elizabeth Sergeant who 'fell into a sluice and drowned' and two years later Caroline Keir who'd also fallen into the canal basin and drowned.

Local author Anne Bradford in her *'Haunted Worcestershire'* reports of regular sightings of ghost 'Fred'. In the book, former landlady Angie Barratt's daughter Michelle records '...when my parents first moved there we had a club room on the first floor. This is where our ghost lived. He was a friendly entity and I think he was attracted to people because he liked to make his presence known'. She records footsteps 'like someone walking on lino', mysterious openings and closings of the club room door, bottles rattling violently for no reason, gas in the cellar inexplicably being turned off, doors being locked without a key and once a whirlwind in the back yard which sent everything flying around. "My husband was showing someone out late at night and they were the only two people there. Suddenly the visitor said 'there's somebody behind you!' adding that the ghost appeared to be going down steps behind the bar. But there are no steps. He said the ghost looked like a long-haired yobbo but we have assumed that he was cavalier because of Worcester's association with the Royalists' (Angie Barrett)

Another landlord, Andy Mapp said that when he was gaffer: '...a roundhead used to walk through the bar, pause, then disappear through the wall. A hand would often be felt on my shoulder or someone brushing past the bar staff or myself. Spooky!'

Paul Moore lived in a flat three doors up from Barley Mow and worked in his uncle's antique shop next door to The Loch Ryan Hotel in what was originally used as stables for the horses that pulled the boats along the canal. "I used to hear strange noises in the back but never saw anything".

A once thriving boozer, it closed down in 2006 and at time of writing is said to still include a host of original features like Victorian radiators.

After being wrecked by flooding and languishing on the city council's 'at risk' register because of its poor condition, in June 2013 City planners gave the OK to turn the Grade II listed building into six apartments: the top two floors are set to become flats, while the site's owner, Mr Shah who owns Sidbury Spice and Caspian pizza takeaway opposite is also considering opening the ground floor as a restaurant.

Originally a 'Kelsey's noted ales' house – in 1930, the pub was licensed to a Benjamin Kelsey – the premises was registered at Radford Hall Brewery Leamington.

Licensees: Robert Spooner 1829 to 1850); George Hallard (1855); Jane Harding (1859); Fredrick Hughes (1872-1876); Edward Jones (1876-1879); Charles Clerk (1878-9); Herbert Haynes (1879-86); George Chance (1886-7); Edward Sherriff (1887-8); Eliza Hornidge (1888-95); Daniel Dibble (1895-7); Henry Corrall (1897-8); Alfred Hayes (1898-1900); Absalom Trigg (1900-02); James Phillips (1902-3); George A. Price (1903); Mrs Clara Mason (1903-08); Arthur H. Collins (1909-13): Daniel Francis (1913-14); Albert E. Turbill (1914-20); Robert Jones (1920-22); Robert Mitchell (1922-23); Samuel Bowler (1923-4); William Briscoe (1924-9); Frederick Dallaway (1929); Charles Hughes (1929-36); John F. Clark (1936-7); James Albert O'Mahoney (1937-9); Frank

M. Pettitt (1939-41); William Mortimore (1941); William James Price (1943-49 then transferred to Thomas Edward Hodgetts and back to William James Price to 1951); Horace Charles Seabourne March 1951-May 1952); Frederick Tomlinson (1952); Sidney Davies (1952-3); John Evans (1953); Charles Corley (1953-4): Charles Edward Stanier (1954-57); Thomas George Hughes (1957-8); Harry Bosely (1958-60); Joseph Powell (1960-1); Jean Lynette Latham (1961); Sidney Jones (1961-2); Joan Young (1962-3); Hubert Peet (1963-5); Morris Jeffs (1965-6); Nadina Gardnier (1966-7); Kenneth Dixon (1967); Ralph Revill (1967-70); Kenneth Eustace (1970-1); George Barrett (1971-1988); Angela Barrett (1988); Adam Gregg (2000).

 Loch Ryan Hotel
Location: Sidbury
(listed as 'Loch Ryan Hotel 119 Sidbury. Tel 372111'

 Cross Keys
Location: London Road
Years   active: 1870s-1960s

The Cross keys was also here, closing c 1963. Scant information about this one and new-build flats now occupy the site of otherwise still original buildings. When built, Sidbury still known as Oxford Road. Original licensee John Grout Senior also 'Green Man and Still' Listed variously as Oxford Road, London Road, Sidbury Place, 111 London Road (1900); 110 London Road (1910) and 7 London Road (1915)

Licensees: As Cross Keys:
Richard Ricketts (1766); John Grout fen (senior). Listed as 'Crofs keys and green man and still inn, Oxford Road 1792); John Allcroft, (vict – 1820); William Otley (1829); George Wormington (1835); Robt. Gell (by now London Rd – 1842, and Sidbury Place (1850); Henry J. Mason (1855); Mrs Sarah Hale

1970s photograph (top) remarkable for showing the sites of four licensed houses, where now there are none: Red Lion, Barley Mow, Loch Ryan and Cross Keys. 1972 (CCMH/ CFOW).

Below. Loch Ryan and site of the Cross Keys 1965 (JAS)

(1872-4); James Beavan (1874-6); Margaret Peacey (1887); John Irzon (1887); Thomas Harber (1888); George Cullis (1888-90); John Cullis (1890-2); Francis Osborne (1892); Thomas Harwood (1892-98); Thomas Joyner (1898-1903); Mary Culpin (1903-8); Albert Davis (1908-10); Frederick Harris (1910-24); Arthur Rushton (1924); Arthur Owens (1924-6); James Farrell (1926-7); Charles Ricketts (1927-9); Charles Surman (1929-30); Percival Laxton (1930)

Right: site of Cross Keys 2013 (BB)

Fort Royal in Ansells livery left of centre 1972 (CCMH/CFOW)

E9 Fort Royal Inn
Also known as: Ale and Porter Stores. London Vaults. Clock Tavern (also Old Clock Tavern). Luckys. Little Sauce Factory
Location: Fort Royal, London Rd
Years active: 1870s - 2007

Fort Royal 2013 - The Carpet Factory (BB)

Once popular corner site pub and beer and spirit stores dating from around 1870 with more alternative names than a serial fraudster as successive landlords juggle with trying to get the right mix – none of which have succeeded with the possible exception of Colm ('Mad') O'Rourke who made a go of the old Ansells-owned Fort Royal in the 1990s – largely through its Desperate Dan Cow Pies complete with pastry horns. At 55 London Road, it had been owned by Royal Wells Brewery Malvern and Gregg and Brettell Ltd, who sold the property on 5th May 1941 to Aston Brewery Birmingham 6 (later Ansells) for £2750. Still standing but no longer operating as a pub, recent years have seen The Fort Royal Tavern re-invent itself in a number of other guises including **'Little Sauce Factory'**, **Clock and Clock Tavern** (1983-4) and **Luckys** (1986-9), but lack of parking save a tiny rear car park hindered its continued success as a pub though a series of licensees came and went aiming to turn it into an up-market English and French, later, Asian, restaurant. It is now (2013) The Carpet Factory

Licensees: **As Ale and Porter Stores**: *George Probert (1870-76); Mary Stewart (1876-78); Walter Cullis (1878-1906 when he died); Henry Hayes (1907-8); William Sewell (1914); Reuben Smith (1914-26 as Ale and Porter Stores, 55 London Road); Albert Bryan 1926-8); William Bowcott (1928-36 when he died);* **As Fort Royal:** *Mrs Ada Bowcott (Listed as 'Fort Royal Inn' 1936-41); Sydney Rowe (1941-5); James Frederick Ashdown (1945-1956); Wilfred Haywood (1956-7); Frederick Charles Trafford (1957-9); George Albert Beauchamp (1959-1961); Stanley Bury (1961-3); Ena Shepherd (1963-6); Neville Binnie (1966-7); Thomas Penmen (1967); Maureen Taylor (1967-9); John Sprawson (1969); Eunice Polylase (1969-75); Derek Edwarderson (1975-6); June McGee (1976-7); Nigel (and Neena) Martin (1977-83); James Robinson (1983-6); Mark Lucky and Martin Westwood (1986); Christine Spate (**as Little Sauce Factory** 2000); John and Philip Skett (2001)*

Turn into Fort Royal Hill, follow it a short way – 50 yards or so – and on the corner of Upper Park Street (right) you'll come across a prettily-renovated private house that had once been a popular, if tucked-away pub run by another former footballer...

Above, Park Tavern 1964 (JAS)
Left today a beautifully kept private house (BB)

E10 Park Tavern
Location: Park Place (2 Upper Park Street)
Years active: 1870 – 1990

Now a well preserved an attractive private house, the Park Tavern goes back to mid-Victorian growth in the City, listed Billings Directory of Worcestershire 1855 and later variously as Fort Royal hl (1873); 4 Fort Royal hl. (1900); 2 Park Street (1910) and 2, Upper Park Street (1915). Lewis Clarkes owned, registered to the brewery in Angel Place. In 1880, Edward Francis Waldron was convicted for permitting drunkenness here and was fined 20/- with 21/- costs. Two years later, licensee William Bunn was convicted for allowing gaming and was fined 10/- (50p) and 12/- (60p) costs. On 24th July 1912, licensee Mrs Clara Kenwrick was fined 10/- (50p) for unlawfully selling beer in a vessel not corked or sealed to a person under 14 years of age. It was later run by former football pro (Blackpool) John Rogerson from 1972 up to the early 80s who said in 1981: '...this ain't a bad dump though how we've stuck up with a little place like this I'll never know – we must be doing something right". But as I recalled, he wasn't 'the old misery guts that that little selection from The Bob Backenforth Book of Boozy Bloomers might have you believe'. I reported him as saying 'Gawd knows what you're going to say about my little pub but I'll tell you something for nothing, you can't beat my kind of customers and that's a fact!' As I reported 'the li'l ol' corner cottage with the creaking sign at the top of the hill ain't really a li'l ol' corner cottage but is actually some rare pearl of a boozer'. Architecturally, I noted, it's 'a real funny house' – though I added that it was also the sort of place you could get anything you want... 'a wall built maybe, chimney swept, freshly caught salmon or something out of a well-tended garden'. Safe to say, I was well taken! Still operating up to 1990.

Licensees: Josiah Baylis (listed as beer retailer 1855-76); Edward Waldon (1876-1880); William Bunn (1880-85); Sarah Bunn (1880-85); George Dance (1885); Alfred Sandford (1885-1891 when he died); Mary Sandford (1891-4); Sarah Chance 1894-7); Thomas Lewis (1897-1905); Margaret Mooney (1905-6); Edward Alexander (1906-7); Robert Harvey Kenwrick (1907-9); Mrs Clara Kenwrick (1909–1921 when she died); John Kenwrick (1921-30); Albert George Meredith (1930–1944); Hugh Ethelbert George Barber (1944-1967); Dennis McDonald (1967-72); John Rogerson (1972-86); Stephen Benton (1986); John and Patricia Richardson (1986-7); Thomas Gilbert and Nora Walsh (1987)

Re-trace back on to the main London Road (A44) and head east. Tucked away not so far off is:

Mount Pleasant (Inn)
Location: 80, London Road
Years   active: 1870 – present

First   mentioned Littlebury's Directory of Worcestershire   1873 (when it would have been well outside the toll gates leading   into   Worcester and thus in open country) and listed variously as 39 London Road (1900); and 80 London Road (1915). Originally owned by Flower and Sons and registered at Stratford on Avon (later Whitbread) it was noted for its home brew which in 1873 was advertised at per gallon: X 8d (4p); XX 1/- (5p); XXX 1/4d (7p).

Mount Pleasant 1972 (CCMH/ CFOW)

Only just taken over by Andrew and Chris Baylis in September 1981 (Andrew had been up to then manager of Bottles wine bar in Friar Street) the brothers had just spent some considerable £££s in dragging The Mount Pleasant kicking and screaming into the 20th century. As I noted: '...it's only two rooms and they look so much like your granny's front parlour it'd be the most natural thing in the world to kip down in front of the fire – except Genesis was coming over loud and strong on the p.a. and I don't think your granny'd go a bundle on Genesis somehow'. It then had two rooms – a main bar and a little side parlour: '...it's no hairy-armed boozer I noted, but is instead 'a nice, pleasant enough (apt given the name), easy-going little charmer'. Seems to keep itself to itself and appears quite happy doing just that, but has a dedicated and enthusiastic following, apparently well-deserved. A Whitbread house

Licensees: Frederick Hunt (1870-6); George Griffiths (1876-79); Alfred Guise (1879–83); John Summers (1883); Frank Evans (1883); Henry Vickery (1897); Charles Burrows (1897-98); William Moseley (1898-99); John Andrews (1899); James Aston (1899- 1902); Thomas Epps (1902-6); Thomas Prosser (1906-7); Jonathan Barlow (1907-10); Clara Allan (1910-12); William Silk (1912-13 when he died); Thomas Evans (1913-14); Charles Cox (1914-15); Thomas Rutter (1915-6); Edward Bliss (1916-17); Harry Howell (1917-21); Jonathan D. Barlow (1910); John Calder (1921-35 when he died); Frank Juggins (1935-7); Marjorie Humphreys (1937); William J. Roberts (1937-1946); William Albert Wickett (1947-54); Arnold Herbert Cressall Smith (1954-62); Douglas McQueen (1965); William John Roberts also listed as 'proprietor tel 3685 in 1964; Edward Roberts (1965-81); Gord Wile (1981); Andrew and Chris Baylis (1981-??) Richard Dyer and Michael Morris (2000). Current licensee (2013); Michael Morris. Worcester City Licence no: 1100

On the same side of the road, 200 yards further up London Road is

Sebright Arms
Also known as: Seabright Arms
Location: London Road
Years active: 1834 - 2011

Set in fine Georgian 3-storey building first listed 1835 Pigot and Co's Worcester Directory as London Road, Upper London Road, and 158 London Road when the pub would have been deep in rural countryside more than half a mile from the toll gate which was situated at the top of the hill, . Named after the Sebright family of noted politicians and peers, it was originally owned by Lewis Clarkes, and registered at the brewery, Angel Place. Licensee Arthur Ives who took over the Sebright Arms in 1956 after nearly twenty years at **The Old Chapel** in New Street had also been a First Division footballer in his day. Now a Marstons house, registered in Wolverhampton but marred with long periods in the dark, it was once a series of higgledy-piggledy little snugs and bars but became one large room and never quite seems to want to come out of hiding. It's currently (2013) closed again. I recall writing in the beer guide about The Sebright in 1981 when it was a hugely popular, if slightly rough-edged boozer and remember that the write-up was rather good because I adopted the pub as one of my regulars for some time afterwards, but I no longer appear to have a copy. Pity 'cos when it was good, it had been exceptional.

Licensees: Jno Curnock (1835); Wm Hayes, Sebright Arms, London Road (1842–c1860s); George Payne (1873); Emily Williams (1885-97); Alfd. Jn. Goodyere (1900); Mrs Sarah Goodyere (1900-1905); Thomas Nock (1905-6); John Bird (1906-8); John G. Quartermain (1908–1916); Arthur Radford (1916); James Aston (1916-27); Albert Gardener (1927-9); Ernest John Peace (1929-39); Percy Holloway Hiron (1939-1955); Arthur Ives (1955-69); William Burrett (1969-76); Charles Freeman (1976-83); Eric Blakemore (1983); Michael Ellis (2000). Current licensee or dps (2013); Miss Donna Bird. Worcester City Licence no: 2863

(Right) Sebright Arms 2012 (BB)

Below, 100 years earlier (CCMH/ CFOW)

Despite the presence of two pubs, both popular in their day – though their lights have dimmed somewhat in recent years – this is an area that's still particularly well-served for off-licences: Eversleigh Villas at 5 Stanley Road; Albert Road off-licence; Alexandra House off licence at 2, Cannon Street, what had been known as The Carpenters Arms at 21 Cannon Street, but was never more than an off-licence and the more recent (April 5th 1955) Nunnery Stores off-licence. On the brow of the hill at the Whittington/Spetchley Road junction it's impossible to miss...

Oak Apple
Location: London Road/Whittington Road/Spetchley Road junction
Years active: 1984 - present

Rambling, modern Marston's (Banks's) pub located, according to its own website 'on the Spetchley Road (A44) into Worcester, The Oak Apple is a modern community pub (c1984) with a relaxed atmosphere. All are welcome to come and try our excellent quality and value for money pub food, we're sure you won't be disappointed!'
(http://www.oakapplepub.co.uk)
Big on quizzes,   machines and sometimes noisy games it's a rambling, modern L-shaped lounge/bar with a big car park and limited outside seating area largely given over to youngsters from the nearby Sixth Form College. Big on formulaic food dished up in a 70s style formica, it does its level best to appear olde-worlde but doesn't quite pull it off as the exposed brick and plush alcoved lounge-bar illuminated by flashing machines and strobe-like TVs is a dead give-away. Current manager (2013): Dave Foreman

Not strictly within the City boundary, but a little-known pub called The Star once existed beyond this point at Swenchard – later Swinesherd.

Star
Location: Swenchard (Swinesherd?)
Years active: unknown
A single reference appears in Billings Directory of Worcestershire 1855: one entry only, under John Woodward. Beyond that, nothing more is known

Re-trace to point D and get ready for some interesting pubs steeped in real – and often notorious – history

B-D: Wylds Lane

A short way up on the right stand the solid looking, not always welcoming

Plumbers Arms
Location: Wylds Lane
Years active: 1870 - present
Still in business almost 150 years after its debut (circa 1870s according to Littlebury's Directory of Worcestershire 1873) with a tendency to cater for a passing variety of groups including Italian and West Indian communities in the 1960s, music-loving youngsters (1980s) and others as the whim takes it, The Plumbers has been listed variously as 8, Wylds lane (1850s) and 76 Wylds Lane (1910). On the corner with Cole Hill in the heart of what in recent years has become a huge Asian community, it had once been the cornerstone of solid working-class families that had migrated to Worcester attracted by the wages offered by burgeoning industry in the mid-late Victorian industrial hey-day. A Mitchells

House, registered at Cape Hill Brewery and for many years decked-out in typical M&B livery and house style (conker brown, pillar-box red and white) The Plumbers hasn't changed an awful lot since the time it first saw light of day and always appears to me to look as though it's sulking – or at best having an off day! Notable for the longevity of one licensee Mrs Annie Varley who ran The Plumbers from 1920 to 1956, today it's one of the Admiral Taverns chain.

Licensees: *George Tudge (1872-6); Harriett Tudge (1876-99); Stephen Morris Overall (1899); Reuben Smith (1899-1900); Thomas Lewis (1900-03); John Clay (1903–1915 when he died); Horace Clements (1915-16); Maria Clements (1916-20); Miss Annie Varley (1920–1956); Phyllis Howard (1956-1959); John Picken (1959-61); Charles Wootton (1962-73); Alan Harris (1973); Michael Garrison (1973-4); Kenneth Draper (1974-6); Dorothy Merrett (1976-7); Brian Pheysey (1978-81); Maureen Love (1982-3); Evans Love (1982-3); Alison MacDonald (1983); Andrew MacDonald (1983-6); Roger Smith (1986-8); Andrew Burns (1988-9); Donald and Kathleen Bradbury (1989); Alf (and Kay) Spencer (1990s); Richard E. Scott (2001). Current licensee (2013); Mrs Christine Wiliams. Worcester City Licence no: 1172*

Cross the road now and you're in for a slice of Worcester's most infamous history...

E16 Garibaldi (Tavern)
Also kown as: The Lamplighter. Welcome Inn
Location: Wylds Lane
Years active: 1870 – 1986

Built by industrialist Richard Padmore c1870 specifically for the men at his iron foundry and run by his son Thomas, the 'Gari' was named after the popular Italian folk hero and freedom fighter likened to Che Guevara in his day (1860s): small wonder it proved popular with Italian immigrants who'd come over before and after the Second World War to work at factories in Worcester, particularly Metal Box, additionally supplemented by Italian prisoners of war who'd been housed on Perdiswell up to their repatriation in 1945. Some, especially those who'd formed liaisons with local girls *(the authorities must have been very lax at the time)* decided to stay and you can still smell the wild garlic they'd planted in Perry Wood – though only a select handful can tell you precisely where the plants are.

Listed in Littlebury's Directory of Worcestershire 1873 as Wyld's Lane and thereafter as Wyld's Lane; 49 Wyld's Lane (1900); and 75 Wylds Lane (1910) its original sign is said to have been painted not by one of the Royal Porcelain artists who were always on the lookout for a 'foreigner' to eke out only a modest wage, but by a one-armed local artist named Albert – and was not considered to be of the highest artistic merit. Nonetheless, the wily Padmores left it on display for many years as they reckoned it attracted people who, though they'd come to snigger at the naïve artwork, still stopped to sample the beer! On 9th June 1873 licensee Thomas Padmore, whose father Richard was responsible for much of the street furniture in the City and elsewhere as well as Foregate Street bridge and the fountain now gracing Cripplegate park, and whose ironworks was ranked among the biggest and most productive in Europe, was fined £1 plus 9/- (45p) costs for unlawfully refusing to admit a police constable. Shame a later landlord, former barber Ernie Laight didn't do the same thing on the night of Friday the 27th November 1925...

That's when 23-year old probationary constable Herbert Burrows, serving with Worcester Police out of the station in Copenhagen Street, stayed on after closing time and shot, using a service revolver he'd acquired from his time as a naval rating, 31-year old Ernie Laight and his 30-year old wife Doris who'd come down into the cellar to see what the commotion was all about: he then went upstairs where he bludgeoned 2-year old Robert (Bobby) in an upstairs bedroom, though he left 6-year old Joan who presumably had slept through it all. Stealing the night's takings of around £60 he'd gone home to his lodgings just over the road before clocking on for duty next morning. Set to relieve PC Percy Devey on traffic directing duties on the Cross the following morning, in a moment of madness (he was later said to have been suffering from tertiary syphilis) he remarked on the previous night's shocking affair at The

Garibaldi: unknown to him, however, nothing had by
then been reported to the police. The bodies were
actually discovered by the pub's char and cleaner
who lived behind the pub in Dent Road. When
police raided Burrows' lodgings they found the cash
and the revolver as well as a mounted sovereign
known to have been worn by the ex-barber *(whose
barber's shop had been in the Shambles according
to Littlebury's Directory of 1915)* turned landlord,
and, faced with such damning evidence, he had little
choice but to confess. He was hanged just 91 days
later, at eight o'clock on Wednesday morning the
17th of February by Thomas Pierrepoint, assisted
by Robert Baxter in the execution chamber of HM
Prison Gloucester.

In a letter sent from Gloucester Prison two days before his
execution, Burrows wrote to Mrs Harrison, mother of Mrs Laight '...
for yours and Joan's sake I wish to deny the rumour that has been
circulated through Worcester, and elsewhere, to the effect that there
was any intimacy between Mrs Laight and me. She was a good and
respectable woman and was respected by myself as well as others
who knew her. There is absolutely no truth whatever in the rumour
and in my opinion it was circulated by people who had nothing

better to do. If you wish to publish this denial, please do so. If you can, forgive me, for I am sorry'.

Former Worcestershire Regimental Sergeant Major Henry Farley had the unenviable task of running the Garibaldi in the immediate wake of the triple murder and when he left in 1930 regulars clubbed together to buy him a permanent memento of his time there, now in the possession of grandson Jim Farley.

Another tragic Garibaldi death, according to Paul Cooksey *(who also described the Gari as 'another one that sank after a name change')* was a brown parrot kept in a cage by an extractor fan at the end of the bar about the time the pub was lurching towards its final demise.. 'It had a bad cough and eventually died of lung cancer' he reckons.

The original building had been owned by Spreckleys Bros, registered at 7 Foregate Street, later West Country Breweries, registered at 265 High Street Cheltenham (Whitbread) but it was re-built around 1950. The former Garibaldi you see today – also **The Lamplighter** in the 1980s and **The Welcome Inn** a little later – is now shared between and Indian take-away and a taxi firm.

Licensees: Thomas Padmore (1872-1882); Mary Annn Hibbons (1882-97); Edward G. Dorrell (1898-1905); Albert Douglas (1905-8); Mrs Ann Rowberry (1908-10); Samuel Ball (1910-25): Ernest George Elton Laight (1925); Henry Farley (1926-30); Henry Savage (1930–1945); William Henry Goodwin (1945–1958); Austin Howard James Howells (1958-63); James Talbot (1963-9); Harold Palmer (1969-70); Robert Brown (1970-3); Irene Brown (1973-7); Charles Rhodes (1977-8); Alfred Spencer (1978-86); Patrick Cremin (1986)

In the now heavily-built up area between the rear of the Garibaldi and the canal, a clutch of once favoured pubs – of which none now remain nor, but for one exception neither do any present-day reminders...   These were (not necessarily in order of popularity...)

Park Street Tavern
Location: Park Street Tavern,
Little Park Street (no 18)
Years active: 1850 – 1961

Listed variously as 8 Lit. Park St (1900) and 18 Little Park Street (1940), in 1876, licensee Ann Ballinger was convicted for selling in prohibited hours here and fined 10/- (50p) including costs. Originally Flowers Brewery registered Stratford (Whitbread). Little Park Street still exists, but looking better now than then!

Little Park Street today - site of the Park Street Tavern

Licensees: Charles Ballinger (listed as beer retailer, 1855–1874); Ann Ballinger (1874-74); Henry Warman (1876-80);
George Cartwight (1880-81); Ann Ballinger (1881-96); William Adams (1896-98); Henry Blake (1898-1909); Joseph James (1909-10 when he died); Sarah James (1910); Elizabeth Blake (1910-11); Albert Tolley (1911-17); Mrs Leah Blake (1917-44); William Bertie Blake (1937); Francis Sutton Vale (1944-1955); Frederick Vale (1955-8th July 1958 when his licence was suspended, transferred to Francis Edwin Overbury 6th February 1961)

Bricklayers Arms
Also known as: Foundry Tavern. Bridge Commercial (1873)
Location: 16 (and also listed as 7) Park Street
Years active: c1873 to c1985

No-frills, proudly working-class pub and off-licence and fondly remembered long-term classic owned by Robert Allen Breweries, later Banks's – and still standing though it's now a private house.

Big on sports and still spoken of in the most glowing terms, I described The Brickies in 1982 as 'poky as a broom cupboard demanding the services of a shoe horn to get you in – either that or sharp elbows 'cos it's only a little one-roomer of teensiest proportions. And talking of rumours (neat switch there didn't you think?) I've heard tell from a few as this 'un could be the very best in town. Like, top-holiest numero uno'. I described it as 'a rare oasis where the facilities and decoration are currently good for a laugh but my, the supreme niceness just sidles over and says 'hiya pal, where ya been?" As I said, the pub itself

The much-lamented Bricklayers Arms today (BB) and on 15th September 1957 (RHS)

wasn't much to write home (or even in Worcester Source) about – and if you did, you could get it all on the back of the stamp and save yourself the cost of an envelope'! I added that it was putting up a brave fight against itself, throwing in for good measure that 'as for the beer (Banks's mild then 47p) if I was to fill this whole line with stars, maybe you might then get the drift'. I had to content myself with max: just three! Still spoken of with fond affection and greatly missed by those who liked their pint served up in 1930s surroundings even as late as the mid-1980s as there was always something of the time warp about it!

Licensees: John Baker (1872-81); James Berry (1881-82); Mary Davis (1882-85); Alfred Baylis (1885-96); Clara Bissell (1896-1900); Mrs Nellie West (1900-04); Laura Waldron (1904-5); Reuben Smith (1905-7); Francis William Perkins (1907-1910); George Webb (1910); George Morroll (1910-22); Elizabeth Morroll (1922-6); Alfred Foakes (1926-32 when he died); Edna Rose Foakes (1937-became Mrs Edna Rose Gould 1932-1939); Horace Gould (1939-74); Cyril Misters (1977-81); Raymond Hyett (1981-3); Brenda Goodman (1983-5); George Goodman (1985).

E19 Black Lion
Location: Dent Street
Years active: 1850s 1930s

On the edge of The Blockhouse, address given as 3 Dent Street and dating from the big expansion of workers to the City in the mid-Victorian (1860s-70s) influx. Little more is known and no trace now exists.

Site of the former Black Lion, Dent Street

Licensees: John Craven (listed as 'beer retailer' Billings Directory of Worcestershire 1855); Elizabeth Wakeman (1872-6); Frederick Hunt (1876-80); Sarah Holton (1880-81); Benjamin Cambridge (1881-3); Christopher Waddington (1883); William Digger (1883-5); Amos Inns (1885-7); James Connolly (1887-8); Francis Hodges (1888-91); Henry Wills (1891-4); John Greenway (1894-7); Eliza King (1897-8); William Walker (1898-1901); James Hope (1901-03); Edgar Inight (1903-4); John Jaynes (1904-14); John Bennett (1914-16); John Ratcliffe (1916-25); Mrs Beatrice Ratcliffe (1925-31); Gertrude Bradley (1931-2); Frederick Wall (1932-4); Frederick Holt (1934)

We're edging now to golden quarter when it comes to pubs – the like, and density of which we'll never see again. It's certainly true that you had your pick of the crop if you lived here in the days long since past. Sadly for some, and a vast visual as well as environmental improvement for others, it's all since been swept away and the area given over to soulless big-commerce retail superstores and warehousing – to the point that where classic old Worcester pubs once stood their place has been taken over by a pizza parlour, a phone warehouse, builders merchants, pet supplies outlet and carpet suppliers... (sighs)

E-F: George Street to Newtown Road

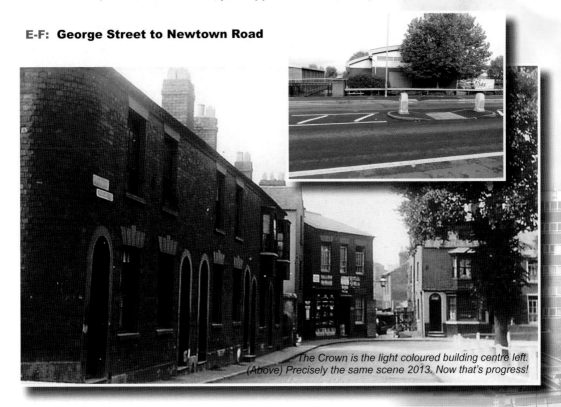

The Crown is the light coloured building centre left.
(Above) Precisely the same scene 2013. Now that's progress!

Crown
E20 Location: Tallow (also listed as Tallow's) Hill (No 8)
Years active: c1850 to c 1943

Just beyond the notorious *(and, on many occasions, fatal)* bend in the road that was the blind dog-leg over the canal bridge, stood the Crown. In the census of 1851, new licensee of what was then a new pub, Thomas Fosters originally from Tipton lived here with his wife Hannah. Twenty years later, 42-year old James Haden was licensee here, living with his wife Margaret (41) and children Ellen (18) and Agnes (16). Local man Bob (nicknamed Bingo) Whiting went to live with his Aunt Daisy there just after the pub had failed in the war years and the premises turned into a private house (no8). It was, he said 'a brilliant and vibrant place with a great community spirit'. "We kept five pigs and 30 odd fowls at 8 Tallow Hill where, from its days as a pub, there was a large yard and white-tiled outside lavatories which were ideal for housing the pigs" he said.

(Source: http://www.worcesternews.co.uk/archive/2003/06/21/
Worcestershire+Archive/7629072.Telling_tales_of_Tallow_Hill)

Licensees: Thomas Fosters (1850-55); George Collins (listed Billings Directory of Worcestershire as bee*r retailer 1855; Frederick Herrington (1859); James Haden (1871-2); Mrs Emily Williams (1872-9); James Hudson (1879-98); James Shaw (1898-1900); Louis Hudson (1900-02); Herbert Jones (1902-5); George Webb (1905); James Badgery (1905-12 when he died); Mrs Sarah Badgery (1912-19 when she died); William Rodway (1919-23); Christopher A. Rookes (1926-30); Henrietta Rookes (1930-32); John Bailey (1932-33); George Kenwrick (1933-4); Albert Wheeler (1934-5); Goldsmith Riley (1935);*

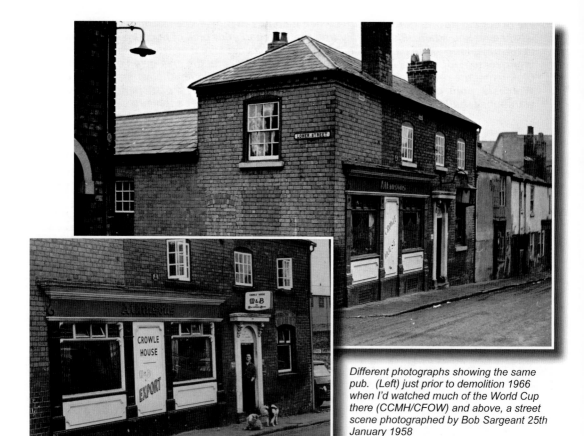

Different photographs showing the same pub. (Left) just prior to demolition 1966 when I'd watched much of the World Cup there (CCMH/CFOW) and above, a street scene photographed by Bob Sargeant 25th January 1958

E21

Crowle House
Location: Lower Street/Hill Street, Tallow Hill
Years active: 1850 - 1966

Mid Victorian (1850) canalside pub and off-licence (beer, cider and perry for consumption off the premises) – official address (1940) 6 Hill Street - tucked away and not particularly well frequented by any others than locals in the densely-packed Tallow Hill area. The 1851 census shows Susan Smith (66) living here as head of the household (describing herself as 'beerhouse keeper') with house-servant Harriet Stringer. Originally Showells Brewery, registered at 120 Station Street, Burton on Trent, leased to Ind Coope and Allsopp, later Atkinsons Brewery and transferred to Ansells on 9th August 1954. Popular mostly with die-hard boozers unimpressed by flashy furniture or anything more high-tech than a TV (I actually watched much of the coverage of the 1966 World Cup campaign in there) it was demolished in 1968 when it was already past its best, as part of development of the area into a trading centre, itself since demolished and replaced with an even swisher, grander one. Such is progress.

Licensees: Thomas Powell (listed as beer retailer 1855); George Cormick (1872-1880); William Wright (1880-81);William Taylor (1881-2); Peter Yapp (1884); Richard Merry (1883-4); Mary Yapp (1884); William Carless (1884-7); James Davies (1887-8); William Haynes (1888); Thomas Harwood (1888-90); Edwin Jones (1890-4); William Daw (1894-6); Thomas Cox (1896-7); Alfred Daw (1897); James Kington (1897-98); Robert Lee (1898-1911); Christopher Rookes (listed as beer retailer – 1911-23); Frederick Chaplin (1923-5); William Oliver (1925); Alice Bruton (1925-6); Fred Kinchin (1926-7); Thomas Bailey (1927-9); Frederick Doodey (1929-34); Robert Sneed (1934); Doris Sneed (1934-5); William Morris (1935-54); Leslie William Rencher (1954-64); Frank Jones (1964)

Next, another all-time classic spoken only in hushed tones and with a nostalgic tear just beginning to well up in many an eye...

Tranquil street scene of Tallow Hill showing The Beehive (bow window half way down) and former Crown (white building at bottom (CCMH/ CFOW). (Above) It's all a bit different today! (BB)

E22 The Beehive
Location: Tallow (also Tallow's) Hill
Years active: 1860s to c1998

Demolished to make way for widening of Tallow Hill and Tallow Hill Trading estate, the location of The Beehive is now the forecourt of Shrub Hill Trading Estate (seee pic on following page) Affectionately remembered red-brick M&B house, owned by the brewery and registered at Cape Hill, The Beehive, in common with most of the pubs and workers' cottages in and around the area dates from the time of the Victorian (c1850s) housing boom to cater for the growing masses attracted by the engineering firms then springing up and subsequently thriving on the rapidly industrialised eastside between the canal and the railway. The name specifically refers to the sign of co-operative activity popular in mid-Victorian years rather than any reference to apiculture or honey. In the 1851 census, its first licensee Edwin Andrews was 53 and lived here with his wife Hephzibah aged 51 and originally from Burslem. Just one of The Beehive's (many) claims to fame is that it was run for more than four decades up to the 1950s by two generations of the Prothero (or Protheroe) family including a husband and wife. On 20th October 1959, licensee Valentine Johnson was fined £25 with advocate's fee of £3.3s (£3.15p) for permitting the house to be used for betting – but if only the authorities had even an inkling into what went on there in later years they'd have had a field day... As I said in 1981 when it was under the gaffership of 'Honest' Barrie Ward: '...just as every beehive is full of workers, so's this one. Take a pint of mild with a head like a priest's collar, add an earthy bunch of fun-loving, chucklesome blokes, stir-in an atmosphere so cosy you could curl up and kip down there, mix-in the genuine all-but untouched, slightly seedy flavour of the 'thirties and serve to suit preferably once or twice a day. That's my recipe for the good life and the Beehive is the perfect place to try it out'. I continued: '...niceties-wise there just ain't none, but what it lacks there it more than makes amends for in serving an A1 top-hole spiffo pint of the grandest, highest order and allows you some of the best down-to-earth company in town'. I

Same site 2013 (BB)

The fondly-remembered Beehive and neighbouring houses, 1972 (CCMH/CFOW)

could have said criminal, damaged, strange, hard-case, take-no-crap, comical, larger-than-life or characterful – but no, I said 'best', and that's precisely what I meant. One of the City's most celebrated hard-men Johnny Stenson used it as his HQ and once taking exception to something I'd written, let it be known that I was being summoned into his presence and that I'd better not disappoint him – or bloody else! I duly arrived, received an almighty and steely-eyed bollocking for not having asked his permission first, followed by a slap on the back that left me seeing stars for a week, an order not to make the same mistake again, and then a wink followed by a pint of mild handed over in a fist that made the glass look like a miniature. Following a difficult period with young and sometimes unsuitable landlords after Barrie paid the price for falling foul of the powers-that-be, The Beehive closed around 1999 and its loss regarded as a black day. We'll never see its like again.

Licensees: Edwin Andrews (listed as 'beer retailer', 1855); H(enr)y Crompton (1859 - 80); Richard Tyler (1880-5); William Crockett (1885-94); Herbert Edwin Jones (1894-1900); William Ketteringham (1900-03); William Evans (1903-7); William Preece (1907-9 when he died); Eliza Preece (1909); William Hinkley Protheroe (1909-38); Mrs Lilian Protheroe (1938-57); Donald Edward Winter (1957-1958): Valentine Johnson (1958–61); William John Marshall (1961-62); John Taylor (1962-7); Ronald Ricketts (1967-8); George Tombs (1968-70); Brian Smith (1970-5); David Smith (1975-7); Reginald Wilson and David Smith (1977-8); Reginald Wilson (1978-81); 'Honest' Barry Ward (1981-1986); Gordon Condon and others...

E23

Ram (Tavern)
Location: Regent Street (Shrub Hill)
Years active: 1843 – c1935

First listed Victuallers Recognizances 1842 as Regent Street and thereafter variously Shrub Hill (1910) and Shrub Hill Road (1915), this was a Worthington pub and then Spreckley Brothers until its closure. With a rear entrance from Regent Street that now runs alongside the Great Western Hotel and leads to the rear entrance of the modern warehouses fronting Tallow Hill. The

Ram proved to be another survivor lasting almost a century up to its closure in the mass clearance projects of the 50s and 60s. Probably the same Ram *(listed as 'New Town Road')* in James Portman Rea's will of 17th March 1847 as one of seven pubs he owned in the City: **Swan with Two Necks (sic), White Hart, Ram, Apple Tree, Red Cow beerhouse, Hen & Chickens and Rising Sun**.

Licensees: James Evans (1835); Edward Andrews (1850); Walter Jones (1855); William Day (1872-1897); William Churns (1897); Mrs Louisa Dawes (1897–1908); Harry D. Price (1908-1929); Amos Fisher (1929 – 35)

E24 Great Western Hotel
Also known as Great Western Vaults. Maximillian's. Cromwells
Location: Shrub Hill Road (no8)
Years active: 1850 - 2004

Built in 1850 when the railway came to Worcester, and originally owned by Lewis Clarke's, registered at the brewery at Angel Place, the imposing building faced the station whose architectural style and detailing with matching grey bricks and stone dressings it copied, dwarfed and dominated all its neighbours. Listed as Great Western Family and Commercial Hotel and Vaults (1915) it was considered very swish and up-market for travellers visiting the City for the water cures and other attractions in its hey-day: the 1871 census shows Daniel Nash (30) as head of the household, living here with his wife Alice (31) children Alice (6), James (5), Maud (3) and Ethel (1) and 'servants' Mary Chambers (25), Emily Roberts (27), Mabel James (21) Fanny Pratt (23), Emma Stoneman (cook 34), Ann Walton (chambermaid 38), Mary Morse (waitress 25), Beeta Crutchley (nurse 19), James Wickham boots 25); Emily Herbert (kitchenmaid 15) and Mary Bradley (kitchenmaid 18) but it sank over recent years as its glory faded and mean low quality housing encroached on its doorstep. In 1905, Thomas S. Burch went bankrupt while licensee here. Running a hotel seems fraught with all manner of problems considering the long list of Great Western licensees brought before magistrates: on 26th August 1892, Henry Pratt

Built to serve - and look like - the nearby Shrub Hill Station: The Great Western Hotel.

Above 1980s (CCMH/CFOW) and right 1960s (JAS)

The Great Western is all that's left of what was densely packed housing and pubs - their sites ready for large-scale re-development.1964 (JAS) And 2013 (BB)

was fined £1 plus costs for 'unlawfully opening during non-permitted hours'; Ada Marguerite Blunt faced three charges on 3rd September 1920: i) unlawfully selling gin and rum above maximum permitted price. £10 fine plus £1.1s (£1.05p) solicitors fee: ii) unlawfully failing to mark on receptacle maximum price and strength of spirits sold (fined £5), and c) unlawfully failing to exhibit in public bar notice stating beer prices (fined £5). Between November 1957 and September 1958, licensee Bernard George Payne was fined £5 for driving a motor car without due care and attention, alongside charges of permitting drunkenness on licensed premises (fine 10/- (50p)) and quitting a motor car without setting brakes (£5 with 15/- (75p)) costs. On 7th May 1959 he was also fined £30 with advocates fee of 3 gns (£3.15p) and disqualified for being drunk in charge of a motor car. On 20th May 1961 John Ernest Payne was cautioned by Chief Inspector Paterson for supplying intoxicants and permitting consumption after permitted hours. While still a comparatively up-market hotel, its two bars – left and right of the entrance – were also popular with non-residents, many of whom took advantage of its hotel status to drink into the night. In 1985, new owner Brian Dyde unveiled a £100,000 facelift plan to restore the Great Western to its former glories including re-vamp of the hotel's 18 first-floor bedrooms and plans to double the size of the dining area to cater for 100 people. His plans also included the development of a large new downstairs bar called **Maximilians,** later **Cromwells,** accessed via Cromwell Street – both of which drew a keen clientele for a while, including some strong pub games teams, though subsequently suffered from its distance from the City's bright lights. Now (2013) closed and has been for some years, its licence remains in force (no 1286 issued to John Glacken who'd previously set up a telephone preference IT business in a unit nearby), suggesting its days may not yet be over, though unlikely ever to re-open either as a pub or a hotel.

Licensees: Daniel Nash (1860s-73?); Charles Haines (1873-1877); Henry Haines (1877-9); Daniel Nash (1879-83); John Bridges (1883); Alfred Perkins (1883-89); Henry Pratt (1889-96); Fanny Hare (1896-98); Thomas S. Burch (1898-1905 when he became bankrupt); Thomas Martin (1905); Annie Burrow (1905-8); Leonard Blunt 1908–17 when he died); Ada Marguerite Blunt (1917-22); Gladys Pearson (1922-4); Ada Blunt (1924-5); Richard Talbot Lovell (1925-31); Geoffrey Dobson (1931); Trina MacDonell (1931-3); Marjorie McDonnell (1933-45); George Duncan Wallace (1945-46); Leslie Edward Reynolds (1946-53); John Edward Hadley (1953-4); Bernard George Payne (1954-60); John Ernest Payne (1960-65); Elsie Payne (1965-9); Michael Payne (1969-71); Derek Price (1971-3); Peter Ovenden (1973-85); Brian Dyde (1985);

Maximilian's Bar: Brian Dyde, Salim Dabbour (2001)

E25 Railway
Also known as: Railway Arms, Railway Tavern, also Railway Hotel
Location: Shrub Hill Road
Years active: 1850 - 1964

Opened early 1850s as part of the expansion of Worcester following the introduction of the railway, and listed at 14 Shrub Hill Road, The Railway Arms, also known as Railway Tavern proved to be one of the survivors, still existing more than a century later though admittedly not much longer. With a rear entrance from Regent Street, it closed c1964. The census of 1851 shows head of the household to be Sarah Davis aged 26 living here with 'servant' Ann Perry and lodger John Gordon. Later owned by Grigg and Bettell Ltd registered at Holt Street Birmingham later Aston Brewery (Ansells). On 3rd September 1920, Thomas Curnock was fined £10 with £1/10s (£1.50) solicitors fee for unlawfully selling rum above maximum price.

Licensees: Sarah Davis (1851); Edward Davis (as Railway Hotel 1855–1874); Mary Davies (1874-6); David Pyrah (1876-9); Charles Smith (1879-1883); William Woodrow (1883); Walter Dyson (1883-4); Clara Pratt (1884-7); George Clarke (1887-8); Mary Ketteringham (1888-9); John Cartridge (1889-90); William Kellaway (1890-93); William Hunt (1893-1902); Lister Hughes, Railway Arms, Shrub Hill Road 1902-1915); Thomas Curnock (1915-32); Ivor John Griffiths (1932-1934); Alfred Hancox (1934-5); Ernest Green (1935-6); William Abrook (1936-7); James Abraham (1937 –1939); Frank Ramsey (1939-1952); Lily Mary Bamsey (1952-61); Evelyn Blake (1961-2); Maud Gardner (1962-3); Glyndwr Jones (1963); Barry Nock (1963)

The Prince of Wales 13th April 1963 front and rear views (RHS). And above right, the same view today (BB)

Prince of Wales
Location: Shrub Hill Road
Years active: 1850 - 1963

Still spoken of with fond affection by those who remember the last great days of Worcester's pubs – though it must be said, with a large degree of rose-tinted nostalgia – the Prince of Wales was already a century old by the 1950s, appearing run-down and ailing in all existing photographs. Rear entrance from Regent Street, it closed c1963. Originally owned by Julia Hanson and Co (later Banks's). On 2nd June 1893 and 27th April 1894, licensee Susan Smith was fined 5/- (25p) with costs for unlawfully permitting drunkenness for the first offence, and £3 plus £1.14s (£3.70p costs for the second. On 29 August 1914 William Tolley was fined £2 with £1.12s (£1.60p) costs for selling brandy below the required standard. Licensee Jerry Sheveling had been a First Division footballer in his day and the pub was run by his widow and presumably his daughter after his death.

Licensees: Henry Knott (listed as 'beer retailer–1855); Major Philips (1873-1886); Robert Hooley (1886-1891 when he died); Emma Baker (1891-2); Henry Baker (1892-3); Susan Smith (1893-4);

William H. Crockett (1894-1904 when he died); Elizabeth Crockett (1905-6); Robert Jones (1906); William Tolley (1906–1915); James Randle (1915-17); Albert Henry Holloway (1917 –1948); George Frederick Dean (1948-54); Gerald Francis Sheveling (1954-56); Ann Sheveling (1956-61); Anne Louisa Sheveling (1961-63)

1920s view of Shrub Hill Station (CCMH/CFOW)

and the same view today (BB)

E27

Shrub Hill Station Railway Refreshment Rooms 'Up' and 'Down' platforms
Location: Shrub Hill Station
Years active: from 1850 – 1960s

In any book on pubs and licensed houses, it's easy to forget that many local stations also had licensed Refreshment Rooms – and Shrub Hill and Foregate Street are no exception. In addition to listing under 'Inns and Taverns' in Billings Directory of Worcestershire 1855 under licensee Thomas Watton, the Worcester City Police Register of Intoxicating Liquor Licenses shows that full on-sale liquor licenses were issued for the 'up' and 'down' platforms at Shrub Hill Station, owned by the Great Western Railway Company and registered at Paddington Station, London W2 (later British Transport Commission at 55 Broadway, Westminster London W1 then 222 Marylebone Road) and were licensed for the sale of all intoxicating liquors and subject to the same opening and closing hours as well as other restrictions as laid down by the City's Licensing Department. For an image of what all British Rail refreshment rooms (though I confess, I never saw anyone looking particularly refreshed coming out of one) looked like, Noël Coward's and David Lean's **'Brief Encounter'** is as good a start as any! Milford Junction could easily pass for Shrub Hill Station in the 1940s and 50s.

*   **Licensees**: Graham Royde Smith (listed Secretary of the London, Midland and Scottish Railway Company (-1949); William Henry Johnson (1949-51); Thomas Henry Barker, Secretary of British Transport Hotels Executive, registered at St Pancras Chambers London NW1*

The road design in front of Shrub Hill Station changed dramatically in 1967 from a notable 90° bend to a much gentler-angled layout with the building of what was originally designed to be GWR's HQ – square, angular, imposing and downright ugly Elgar House. Disliked by railway staff who favoured Gloucester for their regional HQ, a carbon-copy replica was built there and still stands there today – another loss for Worcester in line with its sorry history of all things rail-related. The out-of-favour building was then leased to Kays for its merchandising and advertising (ie catalogue production) sections, opening on January 1st 1968. Forty years on and the eyesore of a building that frankly should never have got past the planners' garret, is now earmarked for long overdue demolition as part of an ambitious £mega-million regeneration scheme for the area, unveiled in 2012.

Pass the angular 60s block where I spent 18 months writing priceless prose for Kays catalogue (often nipping into The Beehive or the Great Western when people weren't looking) hard left at the traffic lights, under the railway arch and 250 yards on the left is:

E28 Gun Tavern (Gun)
Location: Newtown (New Town) Road (no 39)
Years active: 1850 – 1936 (re-built) 1936 - 2007 (re-opened 2013)

Older than many expect given the predominantly rural nature of the area up to the coming of the railways (c1850) The Gun Tavern, is still standing and recently (2013) re-opened after closing in 2010 – another chapter in a chequered and not always illustrious history. The existing 1930s building is the second of that name built on the site, originally listed Hunt & Co's Commercial Directory for Gloucester, Hereford and Worcester (1842). According to Bill Gwilliam, The Volunteers – presumably, forerunners of the Territorals – had a rifle range in the fields nearby, hence the name. A Spreckleys house registered at 7 Foregate Street, later West Country Breweries (Whitbreads), a noted licensee was John – better known as Jack – Whittle (1937-58) who was also a leading First Division football referee. In 1981 and under the managership of Gerry (and Marie) Fensome for just a month, his first ever customer is reputed to have asked him "'Ere, what's wrong with this beer mate? There's no tadpoles swimming about in it!" – which, said Gerry, sums up what the pub had come to. I even joked at the time that previous gaffers' attempts at food had stretched as far as plain, beef or salmonella-flavoured crisps a remark that'd have me hauled up before some main-chance solicitor today. With '...a lick of paint here, bulbs replaced there, weeds turfed out of the car park, carpets – sorry, carpet – cleaned, chairs de-grimed and pipes cleaned out (Gerry reckoned 24 times before a single pint crossed the counter), I described it as 'a big all-in brown bar that looks like it means serious business of the boozing kind, contrasted with a select little lounge that borders on the pretty and actually smells of fresh flowers. Plus games/functions room that brings together skittles, pool and loud juke box sounds. And car park that nobody knows how to make the best of'. The latter comment still rings true – though frankly, that comment could be as easily applied to the rest of the pub. Re-opened July 2013 after several years out of ammo and I've yet to renew my acquaintance.

The Gun 1964 (JAS). Still recognisable 2013 even after several years out of ammo. Recently re-opened

Grand old image of the original Gun Tavern 1900s (CCMH/CFOW)

Licensees: Chas. Harding, Gun, New town (1842–c1860s); Henry Perks (Gun Tavern, New Town 1873-91); Thomas Vaughan (1891-2 when he died); Susan Vaughan (1893-6); George Potter (Gun tavern New Town Road and 39 Newtown Road 1896 -1927 when he died); Mrs Ada Potter (1927-34); John Henry Whittle Gun Tavern 39 New Town Road (1934– 1959); Cyril Turberfield (1959-1968); Byron Cockrell (1968-9); Alistair Wrightson (1969-70); Harold Palmer (1970-73); Peter Askew (1973-5); William Telling (1975-81); Frederick Rust (1982-83); William Knight (1983); Philip Butcher (1983-4); Peter Hodson (1984); John Malin (1984-6); Bridy Malin (1986); Gerry Fensome (1981-); Michael Reynolds (2000). Current licensee or dps (2013); Jennifer Louise Gunnell. Worcester City Licence no: 1317

Way, way up Newtown Road and deep inside Ronkswood now, where all its road names are taken from cathedrals: Exeter, Liverpool, Lichfield, Ripon, Carlisle etc. Curious that concept didn't also apply to the estate's sole pub (still surviving – though the contemporary church standing immediately opposite is earmarked for demolition). Instead it took on the name of a noted City inn, fittingly in the shadow of our own cathedral, that had just passed on....

E29 Punchbowl
Location: Lichfield Avenue, Ronkswood
Years active: 1958 to present

Sprawling – occasionally brawling – estate pub built to serve the growing population of Ronkswood and for a time, fiercely territorial with occasional forays to tackle its Warndon, Tolladine and Dines Green counterparts who responded with due vigour and pride. Provisional licence granted 8th February 1957 and confirmed 15th April 1957 with Final Order to Operate granted 19th December 1958, the city's third Punchbowl opened on December 1st 1958, taking its name from the (then) recently defunct **Punch Bowl** in College Street, sacrificed in the same name of progress that had criminally wiped England's last remaining mediaeval lich-gate off the face of the earth (so yes, unlike most Banks's pubs, definitely spoiled by progress). The Punchbowl is typically 50s new-build Banks's (originally owned by Robert Allen and Co., now Marston's) it's described as 'a rare example of a barely altered 1950s pub with four rooms and off sales (no longer in use). The front left entrance leads to a lobby with original tiled walls (the toilets here are also unchanged. The

bar on the right with a quarry-tiled floor retains its original bar counter, bar back, brick fireplace and fixed seating. There's a rather odd arrangement in the far right corner where a long recess accommodates the dartboard and the seating curves round to protect it, but we reckon that's the way it's always been. Smoke room on the left has original counter, bar back, classic 1950/early 60s tiled fireplace and fixed seating. Just beyond that is the former off-sales which is essentially intact with its tiled dado, bar counter and bar back fitting but the front door on the left hand side of the building has been blocked up and the room is now an office and can only be viewed by request to the licensee. To the right of the bar is a small pool room, formerly known as the 'blue room' and which again has its original bar fittings and seating though there is new floor tiling next to the counter. Toilets in this area are also unchanged apart from modern wall tiles. The big function room at the back has seen the most change. The bar counter has a new top and new panelling but the originals survive underneath. The bar back shelving looks less than convincing but is the same as in the off-sales so must be presumed to be kosher. At the rear is a skittle alley, accessed from the function room, which was added 20/30 years ago and this necessitated blocking up of a window. It can be carpeted over and used as a second or extension to the function room. As you'd expect, all the fittings are utilitarian and entirely redolent of the period. The intactness of both these fittings and the plan form make this a precious survivor, especially as it still fulfils its function as a social centre for the estate which surrounds it'.

(Source: http://www.heritagepubs.org.uk/pubs/national-inventory-entry.asp?pubid=10129)

For reasons I don't recall at the time, Bob Backenforth didn't include **The Punchbowl** in the Good Beer Guide – despite being the only pub whose gaffer actually requested it. He even offered the services of 'minders' all the time I was there – of which I shall say no more!

Licensees: *Ernest Raymond Fisher (1957-59); Roland Archibald Hilary Charles (1959-60); Albert Parker 5th February to 5th September 1960); Horace Arthur Reynolds (1961-?); Pete and Ann Richardson (1980); Wayne Johnston (2000). Current licensee (2013); Susan Tracey Smith. Worcester City Licence no: 1335*

G: Rainbow Hill

E30

The Vauxhall
Location: Astwood Road (no 37)
Years active: 1870 - 2005

Older than its looks imply *(it's currently an Asian restaurant called Balti Mahal)* dating to the 1870s at the time of the City's population growth in all directions. Listed variously as 17 (1900) and 37 (1910) Astwood Road, it saw its days out as a Spreckleys house, registered at 7 Foregate Street later West Country (Whitbread). The Vauxhall – named after the London Pleasure Gardens that the City is said to have been able to beat the capital at its own game – gained a certain notoriety in 1973 as the pub David McGreavy drank in before murdering the three Ralph children in nearby Gillam Street. A Whitbread house with a great reputation for sports until its demise c2005 after which it lay empty for the

Vauxhall (right) 1964 JAS) and below 1972 (CCMH/CFOW)

next four years. In 1981, under the tenancy of Ron and Di Turberfield *(Di was later to play a large role in the running of the LVA)* I remarked on the tough time Whitbread gaffers had been having around then, but noted 'the Vauxhall's got something special going for it: it's a sporting pub where the conversation revolves around sport, where the teams – drawn from all over the City – are very, very good, and which players in all games talk about with due and well-deserved reverence'. Aside from participation in every league – its teams often walking away with all the trophies, free after-match helpings of rabbit stew gave the Vauxhall an added attraction *(source: David Finch)*. Despite that, it was not, I remarked '...anything like Charing Cross Station' on the lunchtime I'd ventured in there. I described it as 'a monster of a pub' with what's likely the biggest bar in town '...and everywhere it's sports trophies – 24 no less, for quoits, darts, crib, pool, 7-a-side cricket and fishing *(What-t-t-t-t, I noted, no hang gliding, commenting that the bar's certainly big enough!)* It was a great big bar that I described, only half-seriously, as '...where you can only see the other side on a clear day and where if it was closing time at one end, it was probably still opening hours at the other'. I also only half-jokingly remarked that home teams had a distinct advantage over visitors on account of the light gleaming off all the silver in the trophies cabinets, thereby rendering visiting teams half-blind and dazzled. Closed c2005 and I don't think particularly missed after Di Turberfield's departure – though I could be wrong.

    Licensees: *John Sanders (1873-1885); James Thomas (1885-89); Edward Bennett (1889); John Smith Vauxhall Inn (1889–1923 when he died); Alice Smith (1924); Charles Walker (1924–1938); Percy Cecil Groves (1938-49: died 27/4/49); Donald George Slack (1949-1953); Henry Thomas Nicholls (1953-56); Anthony Gerald Nicholls (1956-67); Ron Turberfield (1969-87); Diane Turberfield (1987); Martin Habbith (2000); Michael Bemm, Ryan McGaffin (2001)*

This is another area seemingly well served with off licences: Astwood Road of licence stands opposite, and nearby stood Vauxhall Street off licence and the noted Albert Stores, occasionally called Albert Inn though never anything more than an off-licence, run by Gilbert John Winkle, a larger-than-life, roly-poly red-faced man only ever seen in outsize trousers and cardigan and often the target of cruel taunts and name-calling by children.

The Goodrest
Location: Barker Street
Years active: 1930s - present

Large, cheerful 1930s estate pub originally owned by Robert Allen and Co, registered at 7 Lovatt Street, Wolverhampton (later Banks's, now Marstons) built to serve the growing population on the City's eastside, much given to sports and inevitably attracting a sportsy fan base, and replete with a popular bowling alley – though of chequered history of late. First listed Kelly's Directory of Worcestershire 1940 and shown on 1936 OS map its reputation is for hard-drinking at a large slug-it-out bar as well as a sharply-contrasting spacious and comfortable lounge. It was also one of the last to have a 'Men Only' bar. In 1981, manager Barrie Dixon, previously of **The Berkeley Arms** in School Road fame, described it as being 'on the Saturday night circuit so the pub's reputation spreads across the city as a result'. It struck me as being like two different pubs: '... take somebody out of the bar, blindfold him, drive round the block and bring him into the lounge and he'd swear he was in a different pub' I noted. I also described it as '...a great, solid, brick ship-house *(spell-checked, OK)* of an estate pub, a veritable Cunard liner of a boozer where what was once six bars have been knocked abut into two massive rooms where the contrast could scarcely be greater, plus ever-popular skittle alley-cum-functions room: big, bustling and (then) positively bursting at the seams. Bar's been known to be a bit unstable at times, though'. These days just looks big and lonely and for some reason puts me in mind of Shrek.

Licensees: Percy Turner (1937); William Inight (1938-50); Frederick Arthur Philips (1951-54); Frank Gilbert (1954-61); Charles Walter Morris (1961-63); Anthony Bradley (1963-8); Derek Jones (1968-82); Barry Dixon (1982-3); Gordon Taylor (1983-90); Michael Forward (2000). Current licensee or dps (2013); Edward William Joseph Salmon. Worcester City Licence no: 1164.

The New Chequers (New Chequers Inn)
Location: junction Astwood Road/Brickfields Road
Years active: 1932 - present

Large 1930s corner-site pub (originally Showells Brewery, registered in Burton on Trent, leased to Ind Coope and Allsopp, M & B granted annual tenancy from 1st October 1959). First listed in Kelly's Directory of Worcestershire 1932 at 222 Astwood Road and later (1940) at 226 Astwood Road. Named in recognition of a more famous City centre inn, **The Chequers** and despite several bouts of tarting-up *(the latest completed as recently as April 2013)* many of the original features and fittings still remain. On 25th July 1947, licensee Thomas Frederick Brookes was fined £10 when he 'did suffer Thomas Kenwick to use a room in licensed premises for purpose of betting with persons resorting thereto'. I remember too one Friday evening in 1974 being approached in the bar by a dapper little man with black curly hair and a ruddy complexion *(he also had on a light blue suit that I reckoned to be at odds with his rough appearance)* who sidled over and with a smile said his missis and her mate had been watching me, and did I want to split 'em with him? Already late and fearing something of a domestic

The New Chequers
1964 (JAS) and largely
unchanged 2013 (BB)

showdown after a long day's scribing (plus an after-work session with some journalist mates in Birmingham and above all of those, being married with two daughters – I declined and made my excuses. Good job... events later showed that this was Fred and Rose West whose 'mate' – new found as it happened, having been chatted up in the bus stop over the road and invited into the pub was the seventh of 11 victims Shirley Hubbard. The New Chequers, one of the Punch Taverns chain, has somehow not benefitted from almost continuously being knocked about in the name of improvement, only for the same thing to happen again yet always managing to look the same. Its saving grace appears to be mourners from the crematorium over the road.

Licensees: Jn Henry Fletcher (1932); Harold Troman (1937); Geo. Lockett (1940); Thomas Frederick Brookes (1942-1948); Howard Henry Dovell (1948-54); Reginald William Ford (1954-59); Philip Henry Martin (1959-60); Lottie and Valentine Johnson (1960-64); Arthur and Pam Stephens (1980); Douglas MacMillan (1990); Wayne Burton (2000); Current licensee (2013); Craig Douglas Davis. Worcester City Licence no: 1324

H and I: the new estate pubs at Tolladine, Tunnel Hill, Blackpole, Warndon and Warndon Villages

E33 The Farmer's Boy
Location: Tolladine Road
Years active: 1957 - present

Built 1956-7, opened 1957 on site of Deppards Farm. Modern estate pub (M&B, registered at Cape Hill Brewery, Birmingham) with not too savoury a reputation throughout its life. Dave Finch who lived opposite on Tolladine Road (the corner house) tells of regular Saturday night fights, often involving women who'd strip to their underwear for the set-to – either that or having their finery ripped-off in the ensuing melée. It was, he

The Farmers Boy - now shared with a balti house (BB)

said, the best show in town for a lad growing up. Prior to that, he says his mam used to send him over to the building site with tea, cakes and biscuits for the builders in return for scraps of wood for the fire. Initial licence granted 8th February 1946 to Frank Harold Taberner as replacement of **Crown and Anchor** Lowesmoor, renewed annually up to 6th July 1953. First landlord was Walter (Wally) Needham who refused to have cider on the place until early 60s. Marred with an unassailable and wholly justified reputation as the Tolladine rough-house, it now seems to have shaken off its fighting stance and is sharing its once generous site with a well-respected balti house under licensee to Mohammed Altaf (licence no 1187)

Licensees: Walter Needham 8th February 1957 – 1964?); Current dps (Designated Premises Supervisor - 2013); Mrs Gina Wells.

The Virgin 1972 (CCMH/CFOW) and 2013 (BB)

E34 **(Ye) Virgin**
Also known as: Virgin('s) Tavern
Location: 331, Tolladine Road
Years active: 1840 – present

With origins earlier than many would credit, The Virgin, also Ye Virgin and Virgin's Tavern and thought to be the only one so-named anywhere in the UK, was first listed in Hunt & Co's Commercial Directory for Gloucester, Hereford and Worcester (1842) at 'Ronkswood' and also as Virgin's Tavern Road before settling on Tolladine Road. Probably on the site of an earlier wayside tavern frequented by nuns on pilgrimage (hence the name – not in memory of The Virgin Queen as subsequent signs outside have suggested) it would have stood in open countryside for several decades, pre-dating Tolladine estate and nearby housing development by a significant margin. Lewis Clarke's house registered at Angel Place, later Marstons. On 6th October 1958, licensee Ernest Hodgetts was fined £15 with 15/- (75p) costs and advocate's fee of 3gns (£3.15p) for receiving 2 crates of beer, and again on 3rd August 1960 for permitting licensed premises to be used for betting – being fined £25 and ordered to pay 15/- (75p) costs and 2gns (£2.10p) advocate's fee. Its large car park – it's been many a year since it could be described as full – was once a bowling green with a shed-like shelter in front, popular with courting couples, and in the 1970s, The Virgin is recalled as being home to 'a poodle that smelt and a cat that would attack you for no reason'. In 1981 under John and Audrey Powell, the gaffer explained the name and remarked that not many nuns went in here then – or for that matter, virgins. As I said, '...leave your airs and graces outside, undo your shirt buttons and get set for a good 'un'. I noted that at the same time as I was there,

so were the gaffers of **The Garibaldi, The Alma Diglis, The New Inn and The Worcester Steamer Company** as well as assorted other locals and good natured regulars. 15 well-polished trophies in the bar stood witness to the locals' 'amazing skills' in dominoes, darts and crib. It was then a small bar, since extended to include what had been outside toilets, and then new, 'surprisingly pretty' split-level lounge offering Marston's Trad bitter which, I noted, was 'quite exceptional' 50p (1981). The Virgin was seriously damaged in an arson attack by the then tenant (2010) but has since re-opened following a make-over but its glory days appear to be over. A Marstons house.

Licensees: *Thomas Dance, (listed as 'Virgin's Tavern, Ronkswood' 1842 – c 1870s), Mrs Frances Dance (1873); Joseph Hughes (1885-91); Robert Clarke (1891-2); William McKay (1892); Ann McKay (1892-3); Martin Curnock (1893-7); William Goodman Crofts (listed as Ye Virgin Tavern 1897-1902 when he died); Mrs E. Goodman Crofts (1902-3); Henry Marshall (1903-4); William Evans (1904); Eliza Andrews (1904-5); Jessie Harper (1905-7); Mrs Harriett Carr (1907-10); Harry Heath (1910-13); John H Walker (1913-16); Mrs Gertrude Walker (1916-19); John Walker (1919-23 when he died); Gertrude Walker (1923-34); Garnet Fred Edwards (1934-8); George Edmund Knight (1938-1951); Ernest Hodgetts (1951-64); Cyril Mellor (1964-66); Barry Payne (1966-8); Norah Fisher (1968-80); Richard Powell (1980-3); Stephen Copestake (1983-4); Barry Drysdale (1984); Geoffrey Haydock (1984-6); Wayne Astbury (1986); Terence Mesheffrey (1986-88); Malcolm Loftus (1988). Current licensee (2013); James Grimsley. Worcester City Licence no: 1251*

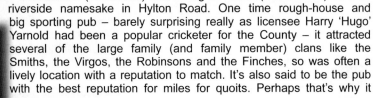

The Royal George
Also known as: Jolly Sportsman
Location: Tunnel Hill
Years active: 1930 - 1990

Originally Spreckleys house registered at 7 Foregate Street, later transferred to West Country Ales at 265 High Street Cheltenham (Whitbread) and taking its name (and licence) from its riverside namesake in Hylton Road. One time rough-house and big sporting pub – barely surprising really as licensee Harry 'Hugo' Yarnold had been a popular cricketer for the County – it attracted several of the large family (and family member) clans like the Smiths, the Virgos, the Robinsons and the Finches, so was often a lively location with a reputation to match. It's also said to be the pub with the best reputation for miles for quoits. Perhaps that's why it

changed its name from the fighting ship of that name (with a sign to match) to The Jolly Sportsman in April 1987. It's still standing but to its credit has since been lovingly restored as private apartments – like an exiled war criminal, living in comfortable anonymity, well respected and giving nothing away about its wicked past.

Licensees: *Arthur Kimberley (1938-9); George Inett (1939-42); Henry Thomas Nicholls (1942-1953); Ernest Ronald Hobday (1953-55); Henry Yarnold (1955-59); Cecil Charles Connelly (1959-60); Roy Newcombe (1960); Arthur William Morrison (1960-67); Anthony Addis (1967-9); Philip Elson (1969-70); Robert Bettington (1970); Dennis Martin (1970-71); William Lowe (1971-3); Brian Reed (1973-4); William Telling (1974-5); Alan Cornock (1975-77); Robert Booth (1977); David Simpson (1977-8); Brian Sunter (1978); Alan Boorn (1978-9); Sydney Harris (1979-83); John Palmer (1983-4); David Gibson (1984-7); Derek Pearle (1987); Frances and John Rogers (1990)*

It was on September 2nd 1952 that the City's Housing Committee first agreed the planning layout for a new 203-acre housing scheme on the City's north-eastern quarter that was to become Warndon. A population of between 5,000 and 6,000 was envisaged as well as provision for two small shopping areas with sites for public houses, four primary schools, allotments and childrens playgrounds.

On March 8th 1955, the Housing Committee reported that tenders had been invited for the construction of roads and sewers for Phase 1 and the tender from Ballasts Ltd amounting to £115,490.16s. 6d was accepted and work started in October 1955. In September 1961, a site was earmarked at the corner of Cranham and Windermere Drives for the erection of a petrol filling station and tenders were also put out at the same time for the three proposed estate pubs. They were duly won by Ansells (The Lakes), Wolverhampton and Dudley Breweries (Prince of Wales) and West Country Breweries (Glovers Needle).

When Warndon was just green fields: evocative shot of the brand new estate, 20th February 1960 by Harry Sargeant (See section on contributors starting on p.462)

E36 The Lakes
Location: Ambleside Drive (no 29)
Years active: 1963 – present

The first of three Warndon pubs listed here – and the second to open, c1963. Big, bustling two-roomer with once separate off-licence, the Lakes which, as per the rest of the estate particularly in this part of Warndon, derives its road names from areas of outstanding natural beauty in and around the Lake District *(Windermere, Langdale, Rydal, Derwent, Ambleside etc)* admirably fulfilled its role as estate pub with rivalry with its near neighbours nowhere near so marked as on Dines Green. Ansells house

The Lakes - scene of famous bands' early appearances, and wedding receptions! Brand new in 1964 (JAS) And below, 2013 (BB)

that, as all estate pubs are wont to be, was always capable of spilling out into hassle but was largely self-policing. Perhaps most famous as the location where many local groups got their chance to perform in front of a tough, though generally fair and often appreciative audience. My group The Skeeters played there on a particularly unmemorable night, Steve Brett and The Mavericks featuring a pre-Slade Noddy Holder came down from Birmingham and a yet-to-be-discovered hard-case brickie called Tom Jones from Pontypridd also played there as Tom Jones and The Squires to, I would venture to say, a far more appreciative audience who would probably have paid the same amount for admission as for the local bands. Later, the location for my own wedding reception June 28th 1969). Closed 2013 but a recent planning application (August) suggests plans to re-open as something bigger and better. A Punch Taverns house.

Licensees: Eric Williams (1962-4); Barry Nock (1964-5); George Newman (1965-6); William Wintle (1966-71); Edward and Sheila Neary (1971-80); Barry Taylor (1980-4); Derek Boyn (1984-5); William Aston (1985). Licensee (2013); Ms Debbie Bradley. Worcester City Licence no: 1231

The Prince of Wales
Location: Windermere Drive
Years active: 1963 - present
    The newest in a succession of pubs named after three heirs to the throne: this one built 1963 (and named in honour of Prince Charles the longest king-in-waiting in history). Banks's,

Prince of Wales 1970s (CCMH/CFOW) and below, 2013 (BB)

now Marston's house, more prone to lawlessness and police raids than either of its near neighbours, its reputation was consequently as the 'hardest' of the three Warndon pubs which some of its clients often proved too keen to perpetuate. The curious fact is that so long as you stayed in line, it was probably also the friendliest – and also had a bigger choice of alternative rooms, all contrastingly well carpeted and decorated and the scene of some memorable quiz nights and music events as well as a skittle alley of some renown. A quieter proposition now than in its hey-day though still with a bad, if currently undeserved reputation, it's actually quite a delight inside – though perhaps a tattoo or two will stand you in good stead.

Licensees: Ernest Fisher (1964); Bruce Whitney (1964-8); Ernest Bradley (1968-75); Anthony Wilson (1975-80); Peter Richardson (1980-3); George Smith (1983-4); Raymond Jones (1984); Vic Pritchard (1980); Anthony J. Wilson; Thomas Turner (2000); Kevin Mooney (2001). Current licensee (2013); Andrew John Lippitt. Worcester City Licence no: 1334

E38

The Glover's Needle
Location: Windermere Drive
Years active: 1962 – present

The first of the 'new' Warndon estate pubs built to serve the growing population of what was, at its concept, the biggest social (ie Council) housing development in Europe. Originally Whitbread house (more recently Greene King of Bury St Edmunds making it a 'sister' to the City's oldest pub **The Talbot** in Sidbury – which is where any similarity ends) opened late 1962 with Bill Reynolds as its first licensee and reputed to have large beer tanks installed underground. Still the same shell, it originally housed a separate off-licence that has since been incorporated into the main lounge area. The Glover's Needle also originally had a 30-foot illuminated spire on a concrete plinth sited outside where the present, less imaginative, sign now stands, but it was blown down in a gale in 1966 and never replaced. Oddly-shaped, with clear, 3-step level difference between the bar and the lounge when it first opened it changed its character in the mid 70s when it was

The Glovers Needle – re-styled 2013 as a Hungry Horse

bashed into one huge multipurpose single-level barn of a lounge bar with later addition skittle alley doubling as functions/concerts room. In March 1984, regular Brian Sawyer of nearby Brookthorpe Close sunk 21 pints in a session to raise funds for Rose Hill Special School and 'King of the Trenchermen' world record breaker Peter Dowdeswell *(see Characters and other Worcester legends)* also broke the world $3\frac{1}{2}$ pint yard of ale record here on the same day: 7.91 seconds! Under the stewardship of very likeable original licensee Bill Reynolds and later his widow Iris for almost all its colourful life, the Glovers remains perhaps the most enduring and popular of the Warndon pubs, possibly on account of always being marginally more family-friendly than the others.

Re-opened May 2013 as Hungry Horse (Greene King) outlet offering all manner of outrageous eating challenges though still welcoming drinkers who at time of writing don't seem to be at all put out that families are now happily eating where hardened boozers once happily boozed. Even so, it has to be said that the drinks side is coming off a very poor second to the food.

Licensees; Bill Reynolds; Iris Reynolds Smith (1980); Edward C. West (2000). Current licensee or dps (2013); Rebecca Whiley. Worcester City Licence no: 1160

E39 Barn Owl
Also known as: Cornucopia. Poachers Pocket. The Great Tolladine Inn)
Location: Berkeley Way, Warndon
Years active: 1984-present

Twice re-named, predominantly food house constructed out of what had been outbuildings and barns for Great Tolladine Farm that up to then stood alone in open country. Contrast to now! Opened May 1985 as The Cornucopia, its original concept had been to create a distinctly up-market restaurant.

'The Cornucopia Restaurant development is a private venture which involves converting three derelict 17th century barns into a luxuriously-appointed restaurant, public house and functions room. It will also feature a wine loft, cocktail bar and diners' gallery. International cuisine with the emphasis on classical French cooking will be provided in the 70-cover restaurant while the Great Tolladine Inn will serve traditional Banks's beers and hot and cold food at lunchtimes and early evenings. The Warndon Suite will be available for conferences, weddings and private functions' I wrote in a report heralding the new venture in 1985. Now a Marstons house with a considerably lower standard of food than the original cordon bleu concept, there's plenty of space for diners inside and out and the large garden is often packed to capacity with families on summer evenings. *Current licensee/dps* (2013); Ms Amanda Loraine Hook. Worcester City Licence no: 1225

Lyppard Grange
Location: **The Lyppards (Ankerage Green)**
Years active: c1990 - present

Built to serve the expanding Warndon Villages scheme begun in the 1990s and now extending from the M5 to the outer reaches of Ronskwood and Newtown, Lyppard – a trendy, twee rendering of Leopard Grange, is constructed out of the remains of '...a rectangular brick house of two stories and an attic built in 1705, with a later 18th century addition on the north and a modern single storey wing

Lyppard Grange - once someone's house and still looking like it (BB)

on the east. *(Source: British History Online Parishes: St Martin', A History of the County of Worcester: volume 3 -1913)*. Opened c1990 this is another that aims itself at those who can't be bothered to cook for themselves *(and why should they when food this good is so cheap?)* unlike many, it also welcomes those who just want a quiet pint or two – which is just what you'll get, provided the diners are controlling their kids, which isn't always the case. References to the original Grange, little of which now remains and where a young lad was killed during demolition to create the pub, include a keystone on an upper floor window bearing the date 1705 and the salvaged oak staircase with moulded handrail and twisted balusters. Once thought to have had its own encircling moat, what now remains of several once well-stocked ponds is protected as being home to great crested newts (some say inside too). A sneaking liking for this one though – not least for its large garden, highly popular with families on summer evenings and for cheap and cheerful sizzling steaks. Alongside **O'Neills, Ketch, Timberdine, Manor Farm** and others, another member of the Mitchells and Butlers stable.
  Current licensee (2013); Ms Joanna Carole Jennings. Worcester City Licence no: 1141

The Blackpole
Location: Blackpole Road
Years active: 1980 - present
New pub opened Blackpole Road

Typical large, roomy, neatly-planned 80s Banks's (Hanson's, now Marstons) estate pub that benefits from being close to housing estates as well as burgeoning industrial and commercial sites. Another one that's derived little benefit from being bashed about into one huge multi-purpose lounge bar when it was getting along just fine as two entirely distinct entities with skittle alley attached and pleasant garden in front. Also a managed house with gaffers ranging in quality from the exceptional to the downright misplaced

The Blackpole 2013 (BB)

and useless – and attracting customers a) to suit and b) that they deserve. One of the better couples was former **Barbourne Inn** managers Dick and Sandra Wallace, of whom I wrote in 1982: 'Says Dick, "There's a world of difference between a place like this and The Barbourne. I like to know every one of my customers by name and stop and chat, but the sheer size of the place knocks that 'un on the head for a start'. As I said then: 'Gawd, but it's a big 'un. It rambles on and on and then rambles on a bit more – so much so that it takes 23 part-timers to run it'. I commented that the gaffer ought to hire out opera glasses so's you could see who's in. Due to its location, I noted: '...it cops for all sorts – them stepping out for a pint after work, them as is out of work and them as'll never need to *(shocking grammar)*! I added: 'despite the still new freshness of the place, it's good to be served the minute you walk in by one of the twenty three, smiling, waiting, glass at the ready – and that's still my experience, 31 years on which says something about some of the gaffers and their staff, I guess. Of facilities, I said: 'gi-normous Jacobean lounge that's open-faced bricks, antique-y beams, little snug snoggin' alcoves, white plaster, red carpet and little wall lights, plus similar sized bar that's so heavy on the brickwork you could be forgiven for thinking it was inside out'. It's still a favourite that I visit at least once a week though I confess the everlasting sports TV channels on three TVs get a bit much if, like me, you posses neither the time nor the inclination for sport and little patience with those that dress up in their team's shirts with – God help us – somebody else' name on the back: I saw three Ronaldos and two Giggses (whoever he is) in there recently. Oh yes, and to the previous statement, I could also add 'energy'. A few years ago, I also learned three new words in there by eavesdropping on three Blackpole barmaids describing their night on the town the previous evening. Appears to lead the field in wanting to get the 'Book early for Christmas' message across. This year (2013) posters and displays went up in July – as I noted in a resulting blog (August 5th): '...what are they thinking of up there…? Christmas. I kid you not – bloody Christmas already! I feel meself turning into Ray Davies with his Autumn Almanyack and the memorable line 'cos the summer's all gorn'. I swear I even sensed the unmistakable whiff of sprouts on the go already… (sighs)...

Licensees: *(incomplete but it's a lot!)* Stephen Bond (1980); Richard and Sandra Wallace (1982); Peter E. Gore (2000); Dave Baker 2008-11 when he left to re-manage **The Perdiswell)**; Current licensee or dps (2013); Christopher Madin. Worcester City Licence no: 1095

The Barn Owl deserted after the rain but a lively and popular eaterie for familes in the sunshine! (BB)

8: City Centre 1

Map: 54-55

bounded by the GWR (Great Western) Railway) to the north, Foregate Street to the east, north side of Broad Street and Bridge Street to the south, and the Severn to the west, and taking in North Quay, Newport Street, the notorious Dolday, The Butts, Angel Street, Angel Place and the west sides of High Street and Foregate Street.

Edward Prince of Wales formally opens the 'new' bridge 1932. Diana Ogilvy was mayor (right) and Samuel Southall town clerk (centre left) CCMH/CFOW

The present river bridge is the fourth, officially opened on October 28th 1932 by Edward, Prince of Wales – who would have been crowned Edward VIII, but chose instead to give it all up some months before his planned Coronation. *(**Interesting fact:** immediately facing **The Vine** on the opposite corner of Vine Street is a postbox cast with the legend Edward VIII who was never formally crowned. It dates the box pretty accurately as late 1936).*

We're looking now at the important location that has always been, and still remains, the gateway to the City as well as to all points north, south, east and west.

It has to be said that the view to the south with the cathedral and St Andrews spire (the Glover's Needle) reflected in the river is one of the prettiest and most photographed views of any of the English cathedrals, and local superstition had it that a wink in the direction of the cathedral brought good luck – though there was a downside to this – as outlined in the chapter on pubs on the City's westside.

This area of the City shared a clear distinction from the location directly across the Severn on the west bank: unlike the 'dark' *(ie west)* side which up to the 1830s flooded twice daily with the ebb and flow of the tides, an effective barrier prevented flooding here on the, presumably, 'light' side. This was the mediaeval City wall and it seems to have been pretty effective in doing its job of keeping out a) undesirables and b) stinking Severn water.

Worcester's first bridge was constructed in wood and was destroyed by fire in 1299. A bridge of stone that included fortified towers for the purposes of defence was completed by 1313 and was still standing 468 years on: indeed, so well had it been constructed by the mediaeval masons, its demolition in 1781 demanded the use of explosives. Interesting too that some of the material from that bridge was also used to create the original quay walls.

Work on the 'new' bridge sited 150 yards downstream of the original crossing had begun began in 1771, was completed in 1780 and opened to the public in 1781 *(H. A. Leicester – Forgotten Worcester 1930):* '...to make a driving way to it, a row of houses extending from Newport Street to the top of Quay Street was pulled down and Bridge Street made. John Gwynne was the architect and the total cost of the bridge including 'the new road' was £29,843'.

Until 1809 a toll was charged for passing over the bridge, marshalled by two toll houses at the New Road end, one of which survived up to the 1930s. It's rumoured that the first and last tolls were paid by the same man: William Broughton. The opening of the 'new' bridge was captured on film – as was the Prince's planting of a black pear tree in Cripplegate Park: the ivory-handled silver trowel he used for the ceremony subsequently engraved and still on display in the Mayor's parlour at the Guildhall.

Note the caption to this 1932 postcard (CCMH/CFOW)

NEW BRIDGE, WORCESTER.(15)

Until 1960 the main cross-river route for all traffic into the city from then still 2-way New Road was over the bridge, through Bridge Street and thus into Broad Street and the Cross, but chronically increasing traffic and regular congestion in Bridge Street – the same width today as it had been in the 1750s – created the desperate need for an alternative route: it was then made one-way *(westerly)* with the alternative easterly route dog-legging along North Quay and The Butts.

As is to be expected, the eastern bridgehead, akin to its western counterpart around The Pinch and Tybridge Street was rich in pubs, among them some of the oldest and best remembered though not all for the most savoury of reasons – all catering for travellers into and out of the City.

Eight pubs all listed as 'Newport Street' and stretching for little more than 100 yards, would have presented the traveller with a bewildering choice: it's a remarkable abundance of pubs, even by Worcester standards – of which not one remains. The first pub in this section, however, is a survivor on the northern bridgehead. This is...

A - B: The bridge to Newport Street

Old Rectifying House
Also known as: The Flamingo
Location: N. Parade
Years active: 1870s to present
Eye-catching, attractive-looking pub in a building originally owned by Williams Distillery said to make gin 'unsurpassed in England', and later The Corporation of Worcester, 'The Old Rec' is one of the City's most visible pubs, viewable from Tybridge Street on the western approach to the City and apparently unchanged externally since the earliest photographs dating from around 1870s. One-time gin distillery – 'rectifying' is one of the processes involved in distilling spirits – it was regularly subjected to floods and even until fairly recently, the Rec's northern wall facing the Severn had several 18th and 19th century metal plaques denoting flood levels: now only one remains and that's been inexplicably painted over.

North Quay and the brand new (soon to be Old) Rectifying House 1889 (CCMH/CFOW)

Note how the river wall has been raised since the picture (top) was taken. 2013 (BB)

The original plans as presented to the City's planners in 1873 still exist in The Hive, and a comparison between the drawing and the actual building is a revealing exercise. The 'Rec' originally had an open passageway running right through the middle and out to the back yard, with bars on either side. When it flooded, licensees had to raise beer barrels out of the reach of floodwater; they also placed empty barrels or crates along the passage for customers to walk along in order to make their way to the upstairs room that came into its own at such times, and I have a clear recollection of newspaper seller Johnny O'Shea toppling over one of the crates one beery lunchtime, and splashing about in several feet of flood water (1960). A few days earlier a WRGS friend *(John 'Tinker' Bell, son of the licensee Tom Bell who was to spark a minor scandal by running off with barmaid Maisie)* and I were filmed for TV news being lifted off the verandah into a waiting boat after the river had suddenly risen. The pub suffered from a reputation as a bit of a rough-house and set-tos with gipsies, hop-pickers and country-dwellers out on a day's jaunt and for a whom a rough-and-tumble completed a typical day out. In the 1980s 'The Old Rec' underwent a major change re-styling itself as The Flamingo featuring carpets with pink flamingos woven in a blue background and described as 'very cocktail', mostly by then concentrating on food and aiming for a younger audience with live music. I wrote in May 1987 'aside from already being a popular haunt with bright young things on the razzle, The Flamingo's restaurant is already demonstrating winning ways – chef Brad clearly knowing his craft though, like all top chefs, inclined to be temperamental... slots into the gap between yer common-or-garden steak house and the top price ritzy restaurants'. An advert (May 1985) says 'as we are new in Worcester we would like to bring to your attention the facilities that the Flamingo Bar and Restaurant has to offer. We have carried out improvements to the Old Rectifying House and are very proud to boast one of the nicest Restaurants (sic) overlooking the river. We have bar snacks every lunch time between 12.15 and 2.15 our a la carte Restaurant is open between 7.15 and 10.30pm every evening. Our Restaurant which seats 70 people is open for business lunches and conferences with or without bar and food facilities'. Recent reports (2013) suggest that the Old Rec is continuing along similar lines and it's been visited by female beer blogger Barchick who described it as 'one of Barchick's most important boozing spots, so in a way the history lives on.

When the Old Rectifying House was brand new: thought to be landlady Alice Priday (1900-01 in the centre) (CCMH/CFOW)

'On the ground floor you'll find a spacious yet comforting bar and restaurant. Exposed bricks, an aesthetically pleasing island bar, mismatched chairs and low light cast a mood that's more Hoxton than Worcester, a feat that's not easy to achieve we're sure. Upstairs is more of the same plus natural light that spills through the French windows. It's important to know that the beer garden can be accessed from both floors, it's one of our favourites and the high performance patio heaters mean you can fag and booze it up all year round: result! The cocktail list is by far the most experimental and advanced in town, it'd more than hold its own in any capital city. We started with a Pecan Old Fashioned (Woodford Reserve over their own homemade pecan and vanilla syrup) and a Popcorn (popcorn infused Jack Daniel's, brown sugar, bitters and maple syrup foam) and continued along the same lines until BarChick's poor date had to stagger to work, bless...'

Barchick re Old Rec (http://barchick.com/find-a-bar/worcester/the-old-rectifying-house)

Licensees: *Frederick Walker (1873 - 91); Frederick Hunt (1891); John Hanwell (1891-7); Robert Clarke (1897-9); Charles Priday (also listed as Bridge Street, 1898-1900 when he died); Alice Priday (1900-01); Alice Roberts (1901-3); Charles Bramham (1903); Catherine Bramham(1903-4); Harry Farr (1904); Percy Lobb (1904-5); Miss Clare Clissold (1905–1914); Frank Ward (1914-17); Sidney Preece (1917-18); Nellie Preece (1918-19); Albert Hill (1919-22); Archibald Deveraux (1922-28); John Wilks (1928-9); Arthur P. Wilkin (1929-30); Ernest Roberts (1930-6); Frederick Clarke (1936-46); George Rowbottom (listed as 31 Broad Street 1937 – 1946-9); George Rowbotham (1946-49); Eric Walter Lakins (1949-51); Frederick Ramon Fawdry (1951-54); Hiram Cutler (1954-56); Jack Bernard Waldron (5th November 1956–6th May 1957); Harold Edgar Rumsey (6th May 1957-58); John Ralph Dunn (3rd Nov 1958-7th December 1959); Thomas Bell (1959-61); Ralph Llewellyn Davies (1961-63); Thomas Davies (1963); Donald Pearce (1963-4); Kathleen Lance (1964-6); Nellie Thornton (1966-7); Michael Malloy (1967); Betty Smith (1967-9); Edward Digham (1969-70); John Derbyshire (1970-3); Vera Perkins (1972); Robert Stevens (1972-3); Timothy Norfolk & Robert Shaw (1973-4); R. Shaw & Duncan Amos (1974-6); Peter Martin & Christopher Smith(1976-7); P. Martin & Thomas Shimmell (1977-8); Thomas Shimmell and Stephen Lunan (1978-79); Trevor Buckley (1981); Neil Smith (1981-2); Peter Matthews (1982-3); Charles Harding (1983); Duncan Spandler (1983-4); Arthur Jacobs & Rowland Williams (1984); Joe Kuomi (1984- ?); Paul Starkey (2001). Current licensee (2013); Matthew Denwood. Worcester City Licence no: 1051*

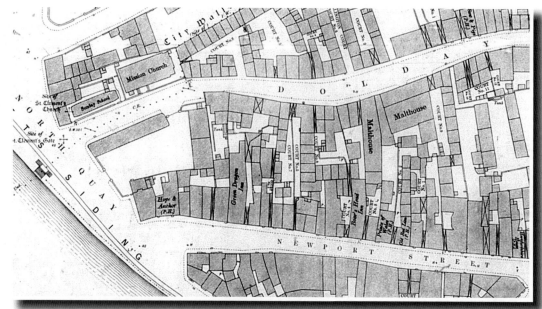

*Ordnance Survey map of Worcester 1886 showing the proliferation of pubs in Newport Street and Dolday. Today (2013) the sole survivor is **The Hope and Anchor**, since extended to take in the property to the west and now known as **Severn View Hotel** after also being called **The Steam Packet Tavern**.*
Map reproduced courtesy Ordnance Survey

B-C: Newport Street to All Saints

Newport Street emerged out of the Roman road leading into the City from the original Severn ford and later, the first bridge,

According to John Noake in his Worcestershire Relics (March 1877) '...the top of Bridge Street and bottom of Broad Street was the beast market from which an alley called Rush Alley ran down to the river in the same direction as the present Bridge Street. Here, the poor rush sellers held their little market from time immemorial until the spring of 1876 when they were ruthlessly driven away by the police... this was one of the oldest market places in the City as in the middle ages rushes were in great demand to straw the floors both of our churches and private dwellings before the application of wood or stone for that purpose'.

Newport Street itself was originally called Eport, Eweport, Euport or Eyeport *('eye' signifying water, hence denoting a port or quay where vessels carrying commodities in and out of the city)*. Around 1677, Newport seems to have become the generally adopted name, although 'Maddocks Slip' is also listed as leading from that street to the river – through a water gate built into the old City wall.

John Noake wrote that '...as late as 1773 'you met with the city wall parallel with the Severn. In that wall was the water gate and a little to the right St Clements Church. A church existed here in the 1600s and was seriously damaged by Cromwell's troops after the Battle of Worcester in 1651: a later version also existed up to 1838 but cessation of the tidal conditions at Worcester allowed the church to be re-sited over the river in St Johns where it still stands' *(it now rejoices in the name 'the ugliest building in Worcester)*. The old water works (of which the pumping station still remains) were on an island in the river between the old and new bridges. In his description of **The Red Lion Inn** that once stood here, John Noake added a footnote of the corresponding area on the eastern side of the river: '...on the Worcester side (sic) William Astley a shoemaker, lived in a tenement described as being 'six and a halfe taylors' yards wide and twelve and a half long'. In 1751 a tobacconist Henry Hill occupied the house adjoining the Worcester side of the bridge. Houses were described as being 'on the wall' near the bridge – implying they had been built into the wall, as part of St Clements church seems to have been'.

The old Roman road evolved into Newport Street and it was to be the home of more pubs crammed to the linear foot than anywhere else in the City. It was also the site of Meredith and Williams noted gin distillery. First in this remarkable run of ale-houses and pubs along what's still called Newport Street is:

The Severn View Hotel
Also known as: Hope and Anchor. Steam Packet Tavern
Location: Newport Street
Years active: 1832-present

C1/2

On the site of the old **Hope and Anchor** and later, **Steam Packet Tavern** that had emerged from the mass clearance of courts (ie slums), the present building was constructed in 1832 and later re-styled with its present name, making its first appearance in Pigot's Worcestershire Directory (1835) and listed as 25 Newport Street and later 54, Newport Street. **The Severn View Hotel** – a name it adopted in 1932 – was noted for its quality home brewed ales as a hand-painted advertising sign prominently adorned its walls for many years. Achieved some notoriety on October 4th 1905 when William Yarnold murdered his estranged wife Annie ('Tippity-Toe Nance') who'd been living with another man, George Miles. They met briefly here before he stabbed her in the back on her doorstep in the nearby Moors. He was duly hanged at Worcester County Gaol just two months later. Listed in Kelly's Directory of Worcestershire 1932, it's named variously as **Severn View** and **Severn View Hotel**, originally owned by The Holt Brewery and later transferred to Aston Brewery in turn to become Ansells. This is another pub that suffered from a bad reputation throughout much of its life as a haunt for gipsies and travellers, and was considered largely no-go, especially at weekends, until major refurbishment in 1970s when its reputation had been one where a pint of mild cost '1/6d and a black eye' (Bob Backenforth). By then a free house, in 1981 I wrote: '...what's there now is a carpeted monster of a lounge, all for-real stucco plaster, black beams and red velour seats, pool room (without pool table, I noted) and one of the prettiest skittle alleys in town' – though I described it as '...sadly something of a sham edging ever-so-slightly towards the crabby what with its horse brasses, toby jugs and fake-o weaponry, bed warmer, tropical plants, too-popular prints and fake log fire'. I also noted that when I was there '...a noisy bunch of pimply kids were boppin' away to piped Genesis'. (Interesting to note they might even be grandparents now!). I concluded: '...there was a goodly mix of folks and if you were wondering where your daughter was last night there's a good chance she was here'. The pub '...didn't win me over, and being a passers-by kind of pub it's unlikely to generate a great locals trade. Room for improvement in the beer' I noted. A look-in today reveals some of the original leaded windows though inside, not much remains of the old place, a victim of unsympathetic '70s re-styling. In 2012, the pub was owned and run by Worcester's first Asian licensee.

Licensees: *Charles Goodman (1835); Jos. Bateman (as Hope & Anchor Inn & Steam Packet Tavern, Newport Street 1842); Joseph Bateman (1850); John Woodward (as Hope and Anchor, Newport Street 1855); Elizabeth Parker (1873-6); Henry Bickerton (1876-82); James Gibbons (1882-5); John Bennett (1885-94); Miss Jane Clarke (1894–1911); Jesse Harper (1911-13); Walter Sturgeon (1913-16); Jane Clarke (1916-22); Herbert Jaynes (1922-4); Percy Amyes (1924-55); James Frederick Ashdown (1925-29); Thomas Lane (1929-39); Archibald Deveraux (1939); James Ashdown (1939-45); Philip Edward Everett (1945-48); Alfred Ernest Victor Brookes (1948-50); Harold George Thomas (1950-53); Geoffrey Gordon Wigley (1953-55); Aubrey Wilfred Lyle Ashton (1955-6);*

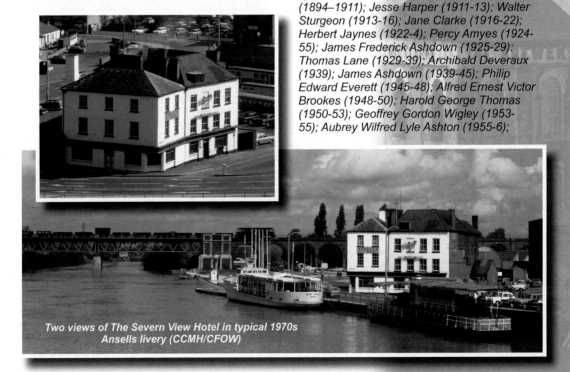

Two views of The Severn View Hotel in typical 1970s Ansells livery (CCMH/CFOW)

Newport Street - the M4 of its day and the main gateway into England from the west. Nine pubs clustered around this one street alone... (CCMH/ CFOW)

Stafford Festubert Rail (5th November 1956-4th March 1957); Peter Clay (1957-59); William Morgan Davies (1959-60); Douglas McClure Payne (1960-3); William Sherwood (1963); John McGroarty (1963-4); Gordon Jones (1964-6); Haydon Furness (1966-7); Anthony Steward (1967-9); Robert Brown (1969-70); William Clarke (1970-1); Leonard Instone (1971-3); George Jessey (1973-6); Roland Butt (1976 – 79); Malcolm Burke (1979); Wally and Val Groves (managed by Tony Hallam (1979-82) and more. Current (2013) licensee and dps: Mehrdad Noobakhsh. Worcester City licence 1455

...and the same scene 2013 (BB)

The Green Dragon
Location: Newport Street
Years active: 1780s – 1940s

Existing in 18th century and with a remarkably long life, with cellars reputed to be 'very fine, with mediaeval stone vaulting'. It had featured large stabling accommodation from the time when Newport Street had been the main exit from the City leading to the (old) bridge. Referred to in Grundy Royal Directory 1792 and variously listed as green dragon inn 21 Newport ftreet (1792) Green Dragon, Newport Street (1842), Green Dragon, 44 Newport Street (1910). Henry Pratt was convicted in 1902 for opening during prohibited hours and was fined 1/- plus costs.

Ada Blunt was convicted in 1920 for selling rum and gin here above the maximum price and was fined £10 plus £1/1/- costs. She was also fined £5 for failing to mark on the receptacle the price and strength of spirits sold and fined a further £5 for not showing notice in public bar the beer prices.

Licensees: James Glover (1792); Richard Butler (1820–c1830s); Joseph Trow (1830s–1850s); Robert Thomas (1855); J. McSweeney (1873);Charles Haines (1872-77); Henry Haines (1877-79); Daniel Nash (1879-1883); John Bridges (1883); Alfred Perkins (1883-9); Henry Pratt (1889-96); Fanny Hare (1896-8); Thomas Burch (1898-1905); Annie Burrow (1905-8); Leonard Brunt (1908-17 when he died); Ada Brunt (1917-22); Gladys Pearson (1922-4); Ada Blunt (1917-22); Richard Lovell (1925-31); Geoffrey Dobson (1931); Trina MacDonell (1931-33); Marjorie MacDonald (1933-45); George Wallace (1945-6)

Severn Galley
Location: Newport Street
Years active: 1760 - 1800

Listed in Register of Victuallers' Recognizance of 1766 and 1784 under ownership of Joseph Crump, later (1792), listed as 'Richard Buck jnr. vict severn galley 13 Newport Street' . Later (1814) became known as...

Boar's Head

C1/5
Location: Newport street
Years active: 1800-1906

Dating from around 1800, the Boar's Head was first listed as 14 Newport Street in Lewis' Worcester Directory 1820 but had become a shop by 1920. Its end was no doubt speeded-up in the wake of a report into the state of Worcester's pubs in 1906 by the Chief Constable who noted of The Boar's Head: '...'the premises are very old and accommodation rather poorer than the rest (there were, he'd earlier noted, five licensed premises in the street a tally he considered 'too many') though the house was well conducted. The landlord, Harry Evans has been there 18 years and is 80 years old, and if he was put out he would have to go on the parish' he said. The pub was only granted a provisional licence as a result – though Old Harry (or Henry as he's also named elsewhere) appears to have carried on for another 9 years, by which time he'd have been 89!

Licensees: As Severn Galley: Joseph Crump (1766). As Boars Head: John Lockley (1814); Samuel Kempson (1820); Mary Kempson (1829-c1840); George Kempson (1842–c1870s); Elizabeth Cahill (1872-90); Michael Lee (1890-1); Edward Bennett (1891); William Wiltshire (1891-4); Henry Evans (1894-1906)

Prince of Wales
C1/6
Location: Newport Street
Years active: 1870 – 1893

First listed in Littlebury's Directory of Worcestershire 1873, the Prince of Wales was one of a clutch of 9 inns along a 100 yard stretch of what had traditionally been the main west-east route into and out of the City, It also appears to have been one of the more lawless as police records show one of only four known licensees Humphrey Bowen was fined 20s (£1) for having his house open during closing hours and for permitting prostitutes to assemble for which he was fined £2 plus costs.

Licensees: Humphrey Bowen (1872-77); Richard Price (1877-81); Joseph Mather (1881-83); Richard Taylor (1883-93).

New Red Lion
C1/7
Also known as: Old Red Lion
Location: Newport Street
Years active: 1850 - 1952

Long-life pub in a terrace awash with pubs. Listed as 18, Newport Street (1900) First listed Billings Directory of Worcestershire 1855 and still around a century later. Owned and run by Sefton

The New (also Old) Red Lion in Newport Street in 1964 (Jim Sargeant). Left same scene 2013 (BB)

family dynasty throughout the first half of the 20th century Transferred to Ansells (and Holt Brewery). On 9th June 1873 licensee Henry Walker was fined £1 with 12/- (60p) costs for harbouring prostitutes here – as was his near neighbour Humphrey Bowen at **The Prince of Wales.**

Licensees: Francis Bubb (described as 'beer retailer 1855); John Morris; Henry Walker (1872-1898); Thomas Sefton (1898-1905 when he died); Harriet Sefton (1905-9); George W. Sefton (1909-13 when he died); Mrs Bessie Sefton (also listed as brewer 1913–1944 with Miss Bessie Sefton junior); William Percy Thompson (1944 - 7th November 1952. Licence surrendered the same year)

Star
C1/8
Location: Newport Street
Years active: 1780-1790

Single listing in Worcester Royal Directory (1790) under licensee James McLaughling but not in the directory two years later and no further references either to the pub or to the licensee, so assumed very short lived.

Distillers Arms
C1/9
Also known as: The Swan
Location: Newport Street
Years active:

Listed in Register of Victuallers' Recognizance of 1784 when reference is made to 'Distillers Arms, formerly The Swan, Newport Street'. Doesn't appear to be particularly long-lived as either, and no licensees are listed

Herefordshire House
C1/10
Also known as Herefordshire Tavern
Location: Newport Street
Years active: 1784-1965

By no means certain, but likely to be a successor of The Herefordshire Tavern, listed as 'All Saints' in Register of Victuallers' Recognizance of 1784 under licensee Thomas Bulford and so dating from not long after the reconstruction of the 'new' bridge and Bridge Street – hence the Herefordshire connection. Later appears in Hunt & Co's Commercial Directory for Gloucester, Hereford and Worcester (1842) and listed as an important venue for County carriers in the 19th century, carriers to and from Broadheath and Broadwas operating from here. Listed variously as Newport Street, 4 Newport Street and 3 Newport Street, it was later owned by Showells Brewery of Burton-upon-Trent, leased to Ind Coope and Allsopp Ltd, and Atkinsons Brewery at Aston Park Brewery Birmingham). Still operating until 1965, the pub with its distinctive gold lettering denoting 'Atkinsons' is still fondly remembered.

Licensees: Mary Caldwell (1842–c1853); John Hill (1855); Mrs Spilsbury (1853-74); John Poick (1874-6); John Collins (1876-9); Mary Collins (1879-1900); John Tainton (1900-01); Benjamin Westwood (1901-13); William Inight (1913-16); John Rose (1916-17); John Rose (1916-17); Edwin Rea (1917-8); Harry Gregory (1918-20); Herbert Tredwell (1920); Charles Walker (1920-22); Philip Pembridge (1923-4); Frederick Kind (1924-4); William Arthurs (1924-28); Frederick Ooks (1928-9); Harold Price (1929-31); Percival Dennis Laxton (1931 -1950); Richard Alfred Thomas Shortridge (1950-1); Ernest Neville Key (1951-63); Fred Layton (1963-65);

TheHerefordshire House and 'Mother'James café (right) (CCMH/CFOW)

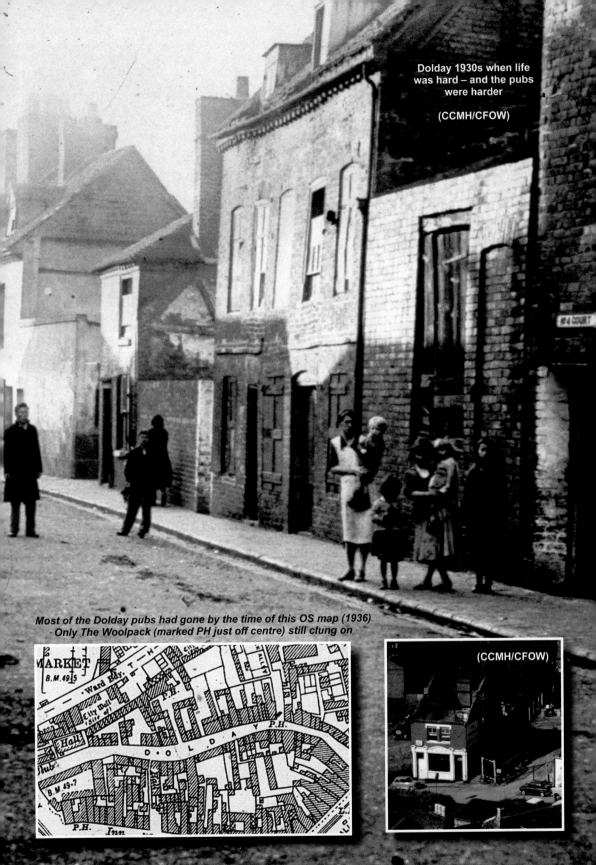

Dolday 1930s when life was hard – and the pubs were harder

(CCMH/CFOW)

Most of the Dolday pubs had gone by the time of this OS map (1936) Only The Woolpack (marked PH just off centre) still clung on

(CCMH/CFOW)

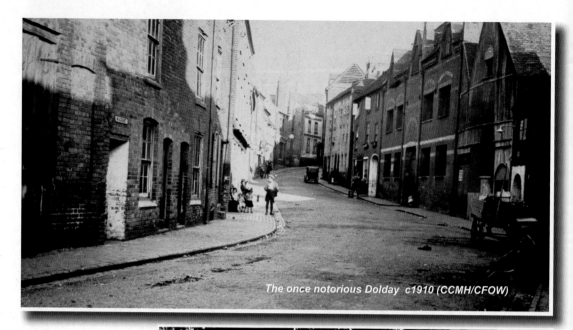

The once notorious Dolday c1910 (CCMH/CFOW)

The road layout has changed more than a little since the late 1950s when The Herefordshire House was still recognisably in Newport Street – the building that's now The Mediterranean Fish Bar is more correctly described as Bridge Street. Now at point **C**, the narrow road you'd take to enter Blackfriars car park is the rump of the once-notorious...

...and rather more sedate in 2013 (BB)

C: Dolday

...home to thieves, ruffians, pimps, prostitutes and all manner of ne'er-do-wells, a street reckoned to be so rough and dangerous that even as late as the 1930's feisty young lads would dare each other to run down its length. Originally Doldale or Dowldall this is the notoriously poor and deprived area where the monks of nearby Blackfriars dispensed doles to the poor. Let's start from the bottom at a point roughly the southern corner of Blackfriars multi-storey car park. Here once stood:

Coach and Mares
Location: Dolday
Years active: 1790 - 1800
    Listed 1790 under George Ward and 1792 (as coach and mares as 50 Doldy) under John Ward with no further listings.

212

Britannia
C1/12
Location: Dolday ('Doldy')
Years active: 1750 - 1880
Probably mid 1700s, first listed in Register of Victuallers' Recognizance of 1766 under licensee Elizabeth Powell (widow) and again in 1784 listed in Grundy Royal Directory 1792, location 37 Doldy. The census of 1851 lists then licensee Thomas Farr (46) as living here with his wife Rosina (26) described as 'landlady'. Not shown on the 1886 OS map, so presumably gone by around 1880.
Licensees: Elizabeth Powell (widow – 1766); William Walton Jr. (1790); Edward Morris (1814-c1830); EdwardJarratt (1835); Thomas Farr (1842); Richard Reynolds (1855); Charles Goodyear (1873)

C1/13
Sow and Pigs
Also known as: The King William (1814) and (possibly) Don Cossack 1814-1830s
Location: Doldy (Dolday – number 34)
Years active: 1784 - 1909
Constructed at a time that Doldy, or Doldy Street – later Dolday – was the most notorious street in Worcester, The Sow and to have re-christened twice more (first to **King William III** then **Don Cossack** before returning to its original name. Sited in the thick of the degradation that was Dolday, it was positioned two doors below the infamous Rack Alley and two down from **The Woolpack**. It was thus a tough landlord that managed to survive – though one in particular (though it's more than likely given the time-span we're talking, two or even three different generations of Thomas

Harmless enough now, but a century ago this was the site of some notoriously 'hard' pubs. (BB)

Nash, 1829 to possibly as late as turn of the century) seems to have come through it all comparatively unscathed. Listed in Register of Victuallers' Recognizance of 1784 under John Lloyd but had changed its name to **The King William** by 1814 then appears to have quickly gone back to its original, as later listings indicate. In 1881 licensee John Fryer was convicted for permitting drunkenness on the premises and was fined 10/- (50p) and 9/- (45p) costs.
Licensees: John Lloyd (1784); John Skinner (1814); James Gummery (1827); Thomas Nash (1829); Robert Groves (1835); James Gummery; Thos. Nash (listed Hunt & Co's Commercial Directory for Gloucester, Hereford and Worcester (1842); Slater's Worcester Directory (1850); Billings Directory of Worcestershire 1855 and Littlebury's Directory of Worcestershire 1873); William Price (1874-1880); John Fryer (1880-81); Henry Evans (1881-5); Thomas Thomas (1885-6); William Abbott (1886-90); John Izon (1890-5); Oliver Drewer (1895-1905 when he died); Mrs Emma Drewer (1905 – 1909).

C1/14
Ten Bells
Location: 'Doldy' (Dolday)
Years active: 1830 – 1928
A Showells Brewery-owned house later in its life. According to the Chief Constable who produced a detailed report on the state of Worcester's pubs following concerns over rising levels of drunkenness in 1906 '...this house does a good trade and there has been no convictions for 30 years'. Even so, the justices only granted the pub a provisional licence – no doubt speeding-up its end as a result.
Shown on OS map 1886 as at 9 Dolday on the south side opposite Rack Alley. Closed c 1928
Licensees: William Bristow (1835); Robert Groves (1850); Charles Hughes (1872-6); Henry Garfield (1876-1880); William Price (1880-90 when he died); Elizabeth Smith (1890-96); David Rowland (1896-8); James Greaves (1898-99); Benn Westwood (1899-1901); John Bagley (1901-10); William Roberts (1910-11); William Harris (1911-25); Fred Lee (1925-6); Frederick Fooks (1926-8)

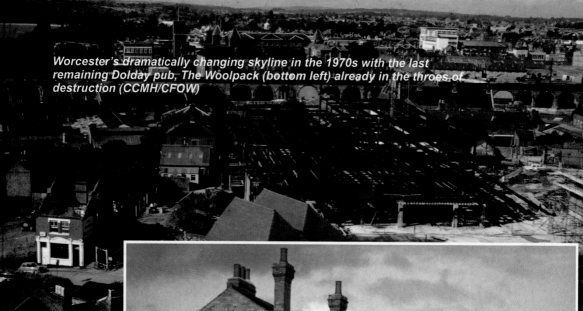

Worcester's dramatically changing skyline in the 1970s with the last remaining Dolday pub, The Woolpack (bottom left) already in the throes of destruction (CCMH/CFOW)

The Woolpack in happier times - early 1960s

(Jim Sargeant)

C1/15 Woolpack
Also known as: Wool Pack
Location: Dolday (Doldy)
Years active: c1810 - 1968

First listed in Victuallers Recognizances in 1814 under licensee John Williams. At 26 Dolday, mentioned by Noake (1877) as one of a number of 'ancient' City inns, some of which are 'probably not much less ancient than... the eighteenth or even 17th century' the Woolpack had a reputation as a rough-house for all its 160-year life – extending right up to 1968. It was also occasionally used for inquests. On 23rd September 1819, the inquest was held here on William Morris of Bewdley who died 'by visitation from God'. A Kelsey house, it was owned by Kelsey Brewery at Radford Hall, Brewery Leamington. In 1874, licensee John Andrews was convicted for selling liquor in prohibited hours – notably 10 a.m. on a Sunday and was fined 10/- (50p) plus costs. He appears not to have learned his lesson (10/- was then about a week's wages) was fined again two years later (17th March 1876) for the same offence – this time attracting a £5 penalty plus 9/- (45p) costs. But even that wasn't enough to stop him: in 1877 he was convicted of permitting riotous conduct on the premises and fined £4/5/- (£4.25p) plus 15/- (75p) costs. On 12th January 1916, John Sudbury 'did by the hands of his servant or agent, to wit May Sudbury unlawfully supply to William Stuart Handley as the licensee intoxicating liquor for which he asked an amount exceeding that measure'. He was fined £2. A survivor of a pub that I recall visiting after 1950s summertime chara trips to Weston-super-Mare from the nearby Newport Street bus station and also on the occasional lunchtime before returning to school (WRGS) for the afternoon's (hic!) lessons during the 'A' level years! (A clue: the second was same year as England won the World Cup)!

Licensees: *John Williams (1814); John Goodman (1820); Thomas Croucher (1827); John Underwood 1827-35); Ann Hall (1835); Daniel Mason (1842–c1860s); William Lee (1873); John Andrews (1874-6); Chris Hughes (1876-83 when he died); Mary Hughes (1883-98); Alfred Hayes (1898-99); John Price (1899-1902); George Belwood (1902-11); James Hope (1911 –1912); John Sudbury (1912-21); George Harborne (1921); Arthur Lockett (1921-3); Samuel Clarke (1923-4); Michael Bensom Richmond (1924-1936); Henry Amos Edwards (1936-9); William W. Hundley (1939-41); James Davis (1941-2); William Albert Thompson (1942-47); James Vernall (1947-53); Albert George Ketteringham (1953-55); James Brown (1955-61); Charles Corps (1961); Brenda Ward (1961-2); William Scrine (1962); Norman Bassett (1962-4); Cyril Mellor (1964); James Hudson (1964-66); James Trimm (1966-8)*

Woodman
Location: Doldy
Years active: 1850 - 1860
Another Dolday tavern that seems to have had a short-lived lifespan, listed just twice: under William Hadley (1850) and Billings Directory of Worcestershire 1855 under stewardship of James Browning, listed as 'beer retailer'

Plaisterer's Arms
Also known as: Plasterers Arms
Location: Doldy (now Dolday)
Years active: 1810 - c1850
Listed Worcester Lewis Directory 1820
Licensees: *James Overbury (1820 and later as Plasterer's Arms, Doldy St 1829 – 1840s); Wm Little (1842)*

Carpenter's Arms
Location: Dolday
Years active: 1750-c1820
Listed in Register of Victuallers' Recognizance of 1784 under William Pearcey, later (1790) as Wm Piercey and two years later (1792) as William Perry – an unfortunate series of transcription errors) – at carpenter's arms at 4 Doldy (sic) and what looks like *(handwriting illegible)* Ann Presley, described as 'widow', but as like as not another unfortunate transcription error in those pre-biro and/or MS Word days, 1814. Not there by 1835 *(Pigot)*

Bush Tavern
Location: 14 Dolday
Years active: 1790s
Thomas Arden victualler bush tavern 14 Dolday. Not there by 1835 *(Pigot)*

Spread Eagle
Also known as Eagle and Serpent (1784). Royal Oak (1814)
Location: Dolday
Years active: 1780 – c1820s
Another Dolday pub, possibly older than the others listed in Register of Victuallers' Recognizance of 1784 and in Grundy Royal Directory 1792 both under James Prosser *'fpread eagle 13 Dolday'* but changed name to Royal Oak by 1814 under licensee Thomas Roberts.

Drum
Location: Dolday
Years active: 1760-c1790
Listed in Register of Victuallers' Recognizance of 1766 as under licensee John Handley and in 1784 under Thomas Reeve but not listed after then, so assumed closed.

Unicorn
Location: Dolday
Years active: 1760 - 1784

Listed in Register of Victuallers' Recognizance of 1766 as 'All Saints ward' and 1784 as 'Unicorn in Dolday' under licensee John Shingleton but not listed after 1784, so assumed closed. Considered to be different to the nearby Unicorn *(later Arcadia and Long Stop)* in neighbouring Broad Street as different licensees are listed from 1766.

Prince Regent
Location: Dolday
Years active: 1811-30

Probably the same as **Prince Regent** in neighbouring Birdport: so 'Dolday' is most likely a transcription error.

Falcon
Also known as: Falcon Vaults. Castle & Falcon
Location: Broad Street and Blackfriars
Years active: c1760 - 1906

Taking its name from the crest of Queen Elizabeth 1, it was called **Castle and Falcon** in the 18th century. Situated at the southern end of Dolday and corner of Broad Street and referred to in Register of Victuallers' Recognizance of 1766 and later Pigot's Worcester Directory (1835) and Hunt & Co's Commercial Directory for Gloucester, Hereford and Worcester (1842). On the corner of Broad Street (No 28) and Blackfriars Entry, licensee Thomas Smith was convicted in 1896 for permitting drunkenness here and was fined £2 plus 11/- costs. Daniel Perry was convicted in 1901 for allowing drunkenness on the premises and was fined 10/- plus £14/6 (72$\frac{1}{2}$p) costs.

The site and its adjoining properties was swept away in 1910 to create the new open-space of what would become Angel Place in 1927. Its end was no doubt speeded-up in the wake of a report into the state of Worcester's pubs in 1906 by the Chief Constable who noted **The Falcon's** proximity to **The Ten Bells** in Dolday and that 'within 240 yards there is 33 pubs'; as a result it was only granted a provisional licence thereafter, no doubt speeding up its end about four years later when it became Worcester Dairy Company. Up to then, The Falcon had been renowned for its Sunday joint.

Licensees: Robert Burton (1766); Richard Cope (1814); Frances Lewis (1835); Thomos (sic) Jones (1842–c1860); John Lascelles Lacon (1873-89); John Keeting (1889-91); Thomas Pritchard (1891-3); Alice Weston (1893- 6); Thomas Smith (1896-8); Joseph Ordish (1898); Kathleen Ordish (1899); Charles Henry Townsend (1899- 1901); Daniel Perry (1901-2); Benjamin Ford (1902-05); George Knight (1905-06)

We're now back in Broad Street at a point between D and E on the map. It's still a fine-looking thoroughfare with most of its Regency buildings largely intact, though with vastly different frontages. From here to what's now Angel Place – of which more later – stood the southern boundary of the Black Friary (H. A. Leicester, 'Forgotten Worcester – 1930).

E - F: Crowngate to The Cross

The Dolphin
Location: Broad Street
Years active: 1790s

Little is known of the first Dolphin – including its location which is unlikely to be the same as the much later inn of the same name *(see below)* which is known to have been built on the site of one of Worcester's once great inns, **The Antelope**. Even so, it's likely to have been very close to the same spot – though the only reference, in Worcester Royal Directory 1790 provides nothing more than the name of its licensee (William Bibb) and street name.

The Dolphin
Also known as: Dingles. Dingle, Son and Edwards, Wine and Spirit Vaults. The Vaults. Beards Stores. Now Boston Tea Party.
Location: Broad Street (also listed as 1 Little Angel Street)
Years active: 1927 – 2009

The second of two Dolphins listed as 'Angel Street'. This second and much later **Dolphin** is now a

The Dolphin at different times of its long life: early 1960s (Jim Sargeant), surrounded by development and progress, 1970s (CCMH/ CFOW) and a sedate coffee house The Boston Tea Party 2013 **(BB)**

coffee house and bistro-style café bar and in its day was a not-unimpressive-looking pub on the corner of Broad Street (originally Brodestrete or Broodestreet) and Angel Street, having also served as noted wine and spirit merchants, wine stores and bistro and whose impressive gable end wall has been used for some remarkable artwork over the years. Constructed out of the mass clearance of old properties to make way for the newly-constructed Angel Place around 1927, it's on the site of one of the City's most famous 'ancient inns – the often-quoted **The Anteloppe** or **Antelope** (1500s – 1600s) referred to by Noake in 1877 as '**The Antheloppe**' and describing it thus: '...the house now occupied by Mr. Carter saddler Broad Street as one of a number of City inns, some of which are 'probably not much less ancient than the early 1500s'. Once a popular City centre pub, it was originally Beards Stores before transforming into Dingle, Son and Edwards, Wine and Spirit Vaults, next door was Allen, Mumford and Co Ltd wine and spirit store and immediately facing it on Broad Street was the original Farmers' Club. Later, as **The Dolphin**, it was bought by J and G Oldfield by conveyance for £20,000 on 4th August 1955 and operated on a 6-day licence up to 1960. Licensee Arthur Edward Sage was a flamboyant character and City councillor with white mutton-chop whiskers, a neat line in smart suits and a ready smile – the perfect profile for a pub landlord. He later went on to run the **King Charles (aka Barrels, Tubs and now Bar12)** in the Cornmarket. He was succeeded by former Div 1 footballer John Rogerson (Blackpool) who went on to run **The Park Tavern**. Now known as **Boston Tea Party**, specialising in coffees and light teas, registered in Bristol.

Licensees: Dolphin 1: William Bibb (1790). Francis Dingles (1872-1907); Charles Edwards (1907-50); Dolphin 2: Charles Edwards (a director of Charles Edwards Worcester Ltd (to 1946); Frank Lofthouse (1950-61); Arthur Edward Sage (1961- 8);John Rogerson (1968-9); John Guise (1969-73); Roy Lawrence & Graham Hallam (1973-6); Michael Farndon (1976-7); Malcolm Stark (1977-8); Jonathan Dowse (1978-9); Philip Savage (1978-81); John Remington (1981-7); Steven Edington (1987). Current (2013) licensee,dps: Suzanne Marie Lowe

The Bell was demolished in 1912 to create the opening to what's now Angel Place (CCMH/ CFOW)

Bell Inn
Also known as: Bell Hotel. Bell Inn. Bell Posting House and Hotel
Location: Angel Street (also 17 Broad Street)
Years active: 1750s - 1912

Listed as 'one of (Worcester's) five principal carriers' Inns in Baylis, Lewis Almanack 1885-8 alongside **Hop-Pole, Star and Garter** in Foregate Street and **The Crown** and **The Unicorn** in Broad Street. (The other carriers' inns are: **Saracen's Head, Rein-Deer, Golden Lion, King's Head, Talbot, and Angel)**. It was demolished c1912 to make way for the creation of Angel Place and had been described as 'a spacious yard that overflowed with farmers' carts and gigs *(Bill Gwilliam)*. Earlier it had been a favourite with political parties and in 1836 had been the scene of a political riot when a decanter was thrown from an upstairs window into a dissenting crowd – who then stormed the building and broke every window and all the fittings said to have been in reach. Listed in Register of Victuallers' Recognizance of 1766 and 1784 under Edward Wellings and in 1784 under William Webb.

Licensees: Edward Wellings (1766); William Webb (1784); Samuel Hudson (1790); S. Care or Cave (1792); Edward Lovesey (1814); Edward Howell (1820); William Web (1842 - 1855); Samuel Hurdman bell inn Angel ftreet , James Sommers (Bell Inn, 17 Broad Street) William Essington Webb (1873); Thomas Pinkett (1874-1882); Thomas Harrison (1882-7); Thomas Morris (1887-8); Henry Frank Williams (1888-1903); Elizabeth Telling (1903); Caroline Anderson (1903-4); Thomas Stanley D'aeth (1904-12)

Crown Inn (and Posting House)
Also known as: Lloyds No1
Location: Broad Street
Years active: 1660s to present

Still standing and operating as Lloyds no1, one of the Wetherspoon chain, this is a famous old coaching house – described in 1669 as 'Inne by the Signe of The Crowne'. With its cobbled courtyard still intact, this is the site of one of the last 'Men Only' bars in the City, and the original window where travellers purchased tram tickets up to the cessation of the trams in 1928 still remains in place with, to J.D.Wetherspoons' credit, a plaque nearby describing its significance. The Crown could also lay claim

Lloyds No 1 - 2013 (BB)

to fame as being the precise location that rounded-off Sir Edward Elgar's musical education. It's said that he was recruited as a 9-year old to join the second violins of the Glee Club orchestra that regularly met here for smoking concerts. Recruited by his teacher, who was also leader of the Glee Club Orchestra, to join the musical fraternity, he rose through the ranks to become teacher and accompanist of soloists who performed here. In 1929, Philip Leicester, son of Elgar's friend and former mayor Hubert Aloysius Leicester whose descriptions of Worcester about the same time are extensively referred-to throughout this book, described the room used by the Glee Club thus:

> '...we pass under the archway of an ancient hotel, go down a cobbled yard and climb a dark and narrow staircase. At the top we find ourselves in a long and narrow room. Huge fires roar a cheery welcome. Round the walls and at numerous candle-lit tables are seated perhaps a hundred men of all ages and conditions from prosperous City fathers to young clerks. Half a dozen buxom wenches flit about with trays of tankards and glasses and the air is heavy with smoke'.

A much older Elgar is said to have attended one of the Glee Club's last meetings here as late as December 1932. For many years his chair lovingly remained in its original location – now serving as the gents' upstairs toilet – though it's said to have been destroyed in a fire at an upholsterers where it had been sent for repair in 1966. But at least the famous old lamps outside have been preserved. Also a hotel popular with visiting pop stars in the 60s, it's been listed variously as inn, hotel-com and family (1842), family and commercial hotel and posting house (1855), commercial hotel and posting house and residential hotel. Listed in Register of Victuallers' Recognizance of 1766 and in 1784.

Advertised as 'one of (Worcester's) five principal carriers' Inns in Baylis, Lewis Almanack 1885-8 (printed 5 New Street price 1$\frac{1}{2}$d) alongside **Hop-Pole, Star and Garter** in the Foregate Street and **The Bell,** and **The Unicorn** which stood almost directly opposite, the building was owned by and operated

as The Crown Hotel (Worcester) Ltd.

On 5th February 1920 licensee Flora Godfrey was fined £5 with £2.2s (£2.10p) costs for unlawfully selling beer *(noted by the magistrates with what appears to me to be more than passing interest as Bass)* above maximum price.

Licensees: William Taylor (1766); William Maule (1790); Thomas Wells crown inn 10 Broad Street (1792); John Hooper (1814); Ann Hooper (1820); James Sayer (and business partner Barnett, possibly Alfred 1827); Alfred Barnett (1855); Thomas George Fuggle (1873-81); Charles Wooton (1881-3); Pearce Hadley (1883-7); Arthur Hassall (1887); Anne Knapp (1887-98); (A.M and L. M. Halbeard (proprietresses 1819-1919); Flora Godfrey (1919-38); Mrs May Elizabeth Hudson (1938-48); Rosina White (1948); Natalie Elizabeth Skinner (1948-55); George Hector McDonald (1955); Francis Albert Sharnock (1955-56); Archibold Parry (1956-7); Herbert John Booth (1957); David William Hunt (1957-58); Cyril Jones (1958-61); Ronald Gannon (1961); Sydney Smyth (1961-2); John Ellison (1962-73); The licence was surrendered in 1973 but regranted to John Clark (1987); Robin Taylor (1978-83); Andrew Medhurst (1983) Current (2013) licensee or dps: Claire Alice Heitzman. Worcester City licence 1131

E - H: Angel Place to Five Ways

The demolition of old properties to create what's now Angel Place started in the early 1920s and took with it a number of ancient inns while creating largely unremarkable new ones. The 1886 OS map of the area showing the location pre-reconstruction demonstrates a huge difference to its 1936 successor by when the new-look Angel Place, still recognisable as what's there today, had been in existence for almost a decade. Interesting to note that the building that now houses Angel Chef is the only structure ever built on that site – and that was well into the 20th century, less than 100 years ago. Strange? Not really... throughout history this was the orchard of the Dominican Friary until it was bought by the City Corporation in 1624. Thirteen years later it became the site of the communal grave of perhaps a quarter of the City's then population – all struck down by the plague that lasted between June 3rd 1635 and April 19th 1638. As an observer of the time put it: 'the new cemetery at Angel Lane is gorged with corpses'. It's reckoned that as many as 1600 victims could be buried on the site and for three centuries up to 1920 it lay undisturbed and undeveloped through fear that disruption of the tainted soil 'might reactivate the deadly pestilence'. But in 1920 and made of sterner stuff than previous administrations, the City Corporation appropriated the site for the sale of sheep, erecting the shell as it stands today as the

Sheepmarket. In the 1970s Ray Reardon Ltd wanted to pull down the old sheepmarket to build a snooker hall in its place, but the scheme never progressed. It became Angel Mall in the mid-1980s and is now Angel Chef.

C1/29 Old England
Location: Little Angel Street
Years active: 1850-1860

One entry only – in Billings Directory of Worcestershire 1855 – under stewardship of Joseph Clark, listed as 'beer retailer'. The census of 1851 shows him as being 54 and described as 'beerhouse keeper' and living here with his wife Charlotte (53) and sons Thomas (30) and Joseph (16).

C1/30 Fleece
Also known as: Golden Fleece
Location: Angel Street
Years active: 1600s to 1860s

Precise location unclear, but described as 'near Blackfriars' and mentioned by Noake (1877) as one of a number of 'ancient' City inns, probably not much less ancient than the eighteenth or even 17th century. Listed as 'in the occupation of T. Stirrop clothier (1684) and one Morgan (1733) it's listed in Register of Victuallers' Recognizance of 1766 under licensee John Walker; William Lloyd (1790); later transferred to Lucy Phillips - described as head and widow aged 52 in the census of 1851 and as beer retailer (1855). No further references.

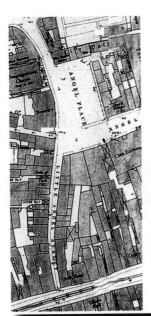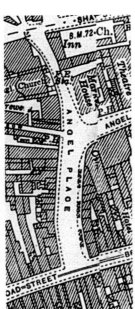

The same view – Broad Street and Angel Place OS 1886, OS 1936 and Google maps (with permission)

C1/31 Duke of York
Location: Angel Place (Little Angel Street, also Little Newport Street)
Years active: c1810 to 1965

First appeared in Victuallers Recognizances in 1814 under licensee Edward Southerne and later Worcester Lewis Directory 1820 and Pigot's Worcestershire Directory 1829 and listed variously as Little Angel Street, 17 Little Angel Street, and Angel Place (1940). Still open up to late 1960s, this was the scene of the great election scandal of 1906 when grave irregularities were noted in the selection of Worcester's prospective MP. It was also occasionally used for inquests. On 16th November 1820, the inquest was held here into the death of Robert Galloway aged 'about 58'. He'd been the driver of the True Blue Birmingham coach and had died, according to the coroner operating from here, as the result of a rupture of a blood vessel. On 13th September 1910 licensee Sarah Ann King was fined £1 with £2.16s (£2.80p) costs for unlawfully selling beer to a drunken person. Owned by Flower and Sons Ltd of Stratford on Avon later Whitbread, the Duke of York had

Haunt of pugilists and hard-cases – the grand old Duke of York. (Jim Sargeant)

And the same view today (BB)

a reputation as a boxing pub from its days under the tenancy of very handy boxer John – better known as Jack – Horton, with bouts being staged in the rear functions room for many years afterwards. Later it had earned a well-deserved reputation as a rough-house and I recall my band playing there in 1964 with the clear warning that if a fight breaks out, 'whatever you do, don't stop playing – else they'll turn on you'! It looked very shabby and run down by the time of its demise (1965).

Licensees: Edward Southerne (1814); John Clapham (1820); Benjamin Alcock (1827); Frederick Prosser (1835); James Turner (184 -c1850); Mary Turner (1855); T. Gough (1873-90 when he died); Louisa Gough (1890-5); John T. Turner (1895-1902); Francis J. Clarkson (1902-3 when he died); Rose Clarkson (1903-4); Walter King (1904-6); Mrs. Sarah Ann King (1906-1910); Thomas Green (1910-13); William Henry Bridgwood (1913-5); Charles Parsons (1915-19); Edward Price (1919-25); John Horton (1925-7); James J. Wooding (1927-30); George Pittaway (1930); John Speller Horton (1930-35); George Price (1935–1944); William Albert Wickett (1944-46); Charles Prew (1946-52); Ernest John Surman (1952-53); Lance Kelvin Jasper (1953-56); Bertram Lionel Lowe (1956-57); Albert Henry Smith (1957 – 62); George Lovejoy (1963-5); Christopher Hammond (1965-6); Thomas Overbury (1966)

C1/32

Dive Bar
Also known as: Horseshoe Bar. Bobby McGees
Location: Blackfriars

In-vogue trendy 'dive' bar – ie downstairs – built in the cellars of the concrete and glass Blackfriars Market opened by Ken Dodd in 1969. Plastic and formica typical 60s style with a trendy horseshoe-shaped bar aimed at a young (and often underaged) market. Named 'Bobby McGees' after a country hit of the time 'Me and Bobby McGee' written by Kris Kristofferson and recorded

Blackfriars Market 1972. The oval sign (below right) reads 'Bobby McGees' (CCMH/CFOW)

And the same view today (BB)

by Roger Miller on May 16th 1969. Often subjected to police raids and a favourite location for the strange contemporary phenomenon of streaking, usually male!

 C1/33

Angel Vaults
Also known as: The Vaults
Location: Angel Place
Years active: 1900-1966

Best remembered as The Angel Vaults and listed as Angel and Vaults Hotel. First listed in Worcester Trades Directory 1910 at 21 Little Angel Street (now Angel Place) this outlet was attached to and operated by Lewis Clarkes Brewery, later Marstons who also owned the property and operated it as a pub on a 6-day licence. On 3rd September 1920 licensee Alfred Ayres was fined £5 with £1.1s (£1.05p) costs for unlawfully selling rum above maximum price. Lewis Clarke's Brewery (off licence) was next door at 23 (also 17and 19) Angel Place, attached to the brewery and licensed for beer, cider and wine, run separately by the brewery managers including Ernest Olwen Pearson (described as 'Brewers' Manager'). It's thought that the young lady in the doorway of the Vaults shown here is Clare Clissold the clue is the name that appears in huge letters just below the first floor windows! If it is, it would date the photograph as 1903-4.

Licensees: Thomas West (1877-82); Edward West (1882-98); Samuel Newell (1898-1900); Thomas Crook (1900); William Luker (1900-01); Thomas Burchfield (1901); Frank Crockett (Vaults Hotel – 1901-03); Clare Clissold (1903-4); Edwin Turner (1904-07); Thomas Prosser (1907-1920); Alfred Ayres (1920- 27 when he died); Alfred Ayres (1927-36); Harry Alfred V. Hatfield, (1936-49); John Hale (1949-53); Mr and Mrs Charles Allan Sier, Vaults (The) 21 Angel Place, residential (1953 - tel 6075); 1953-58}; Benniett John Davies (1958- 62); Gordon Marler (1962-5); David Jones (1965-66); Walter Ablett (1966)

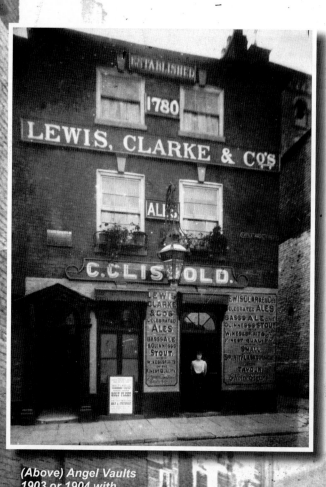

ESTABLISHED
1780
LEWIS, CLARKE & CO'S
ALE'S
C. CLISSOLD.

LEWIS CLARKE & CO'S CELEBRATED ALES BASS ALE & GUINNESS STOUT. WINES & SPIRITS OF THE FINEST QUALITY

LEWIS & CLARKE & CO'S CELEBRATED ALES BASS ALE and GUINNESS STOUT WINES & SPIRITS of FINEST QUALITY SMALL SPIRIT FLASKS 1 PINT TAVOURI

(Above) Angel Vaults 1903 or 1904 with Miss Claire Clissold in the doorway Note the lamp in both photographs

(CCMH/CFOW)

This is Little Angel Street before being widened into what's now Angel Place. The photograph would have been taken from the corner of The Vaults (CCMH/CFOW)

224

*The same scene
2013 (BB)*

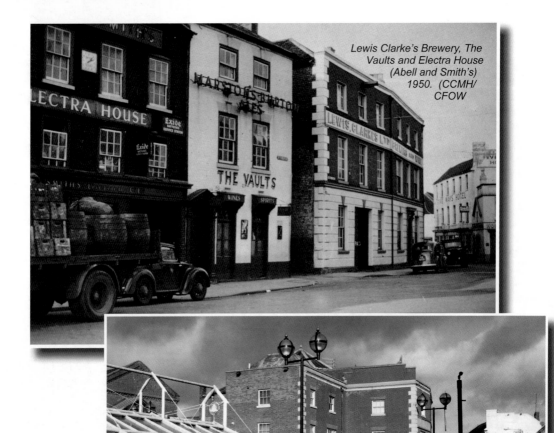

Lewis Clarke's Brewery, The
Vaults and Electra House
(Abell and Smith's)
1950. (CCMH/
CFOW

...and the same view
2013 (BB)

C1/34

Mode Lounge Bar and Club
Location: Angel Row
Years active: c1994-present

All-day open lounge bar and club in what had been Lewis Clarke's Brewery and run by the owners of Tramps Nightclub *(listed 2013 as premises licence holders with dps Dean James Hill)*. Not strictly a pub, but all day drinks licence merits its place here – not least on account of its association with one of Worcester's two great breweries. Describes itself in its website ***http://www. night-clubber.com/mode*** as 'the official pre-club bar for Tramps Nightclub. It hosts Play at Mode every Wednesday, the best student sport social night in town!' and proclaims '...fantastic drink offers every night, accompanied by our quality DJ's playing the latest chart tracks to get you in the mood for your night out. Mode also proudly boasts the largest bar garden in the city centre. You will always find something to do in Mode with live sport showing every night, great entertainment machines, pool tables, Wii games and an xbox area that is on the way very soon! So drop in and enjoy our venue and grab your pre-paid ticket for Tramps Nightclub from our bar staff.   Mode... Getting you in the mood'   Nuff said

Brewery Walk 1970s
(CCMH/CFOW)

...and the same view
2013 - now plus Mode (BB)

At the bottom of what's now Angel Place is:

Angel Street

Lewis Clarke's Brewery pre-Blackfriars car park and shopping mall (1960s (CCMH/CFOW)

...renowned for the quantity and quality of its pubs and other commercial concerns over the years, if currently looking a bit tired. With, at the bottom *(ie west end)*, Lewis Clarkes Brewery, later swallowed up into the Marstons empire facing the ever-popular Fruit Market and with the new Corn Exchange *(later Habitat and more recently Italian restaurant Ask, both now also closed)* and with the Theatre Royal halfway along its length (now the Co-Operative supermarket) Angel Street had been a bustling, beating commercial heart with a run of attractions. Now, aside from two pubs with lasting appeal, possibly the remaining vestiges of what had once been Shakeey's remains as a noted, if dubious, focal point. Interesting to note the site of the old Theatre Royal and what had been the **Oyster Bar** originally separating **The Ewe and Lamb** and **The Fountain** are set well back from the line of the existing buildings: this had been in preparation for a proposed new super-highway slashing right through the City from Shrub Hill and Lowesmoor straight down Angel Street and thus to the river – and presumably a new bridge. Everything in its way would, like so much before it, have been swept away. The idea was never taken up: take a while to look and ponder on what would have been lost..

Five live pubs viewable in this 1970s shot: Horn and Trumpet, Ewe and Lamb, Fountain, Shakespears and Holly Bush (CCMH/CFOW)

'The Blower' 1964 (Jim Sargeant)

C1/35
Horn and Trumpet
Also known as: Horn Tavern
Location: Angel Street
Years active: 1760s-present

First appears Listed in Register of Victuallers' Recognizance of 1766 and later Grundy Royal Directory 1792 and in continuous use ever since. Listed variously 'horn tavern 7 Angel St' (1792); Old Horn and Trumpet (1820) and 12 Angel Street (1850s) this was an important venue for County carriers in the 19th century, carriers to and from Abberley, Ombersley, Stourport and Little and Great Witley operating from here. The outside brick shell now covers the original 16th century timber-framed building. Originally, possibly still, owned by The Corporation of Worcester, it was leased to Ansells Brewery 25th August 1943 for £850 a year. Listed 57-8 Worcester Directory as 12 Angel Street. Tel 2132

Tales of a lurid past abound around the popularly-monickered 'Blower' – not least its existence as an alleged whorehouse popular with GIs during the war and all-comers after it, and raucous nights with visiting rugby teams and subsequent wheel-barrow races *(sometimes naked)* around Angel Place! In 1981 licensee Chris Baggus who'd already been there eight years after gaffering **The Crown & Anchor** said '...it's been eight years trying to shift the place's dreadful, awful reputation and I still get cards addressed to 'The Horn and Crumpet' and that's exactly what I've been fighting against'. He said that in his first week he'd kicked out 157 what he termed 'undesirables' and that if any of 'em came back – which he doubted they would – they wouldn't recognise the place 'in a million years'. The Blower that lunchtime, I noted, was doing an admirable impersonation of Paddington Station in the rush hour. What had up to then been five 'distinctly tatty bars with a not quaite naice' feel had emerged two super up-market lounges – the so-called Big Lounge and Small Lounges – indicating, I noted with more than a degree of mischief, that the old Horn & Trumpet appeared to have rolled over, laid on its back and allowed the architects and the builders to have their wicked way with it. The Blower has even since then been massively extended to the rear and now features what's almost certainly the longest bar in the City centre at least. Sad to note that just seven years after my Bob Backenforth review, Chris and his missis Eileen jacked-in the licence to their lovingly restored pub and quit the trade *(as it happened only temporarily)* due to the escalating amount of violence in the City Centre. As I wrote in the Berrows Worcester Journal of which I was then Associate Editor: '...the tenanted licensee of the Horn and Trumpet sank all his savings into the Angel Street pub 15 years ago, but he says he's become sickened by the pitched-battle gang fights involving knives, bottles, sharpened coins and glass... the vicious abuse and late night disturbances that constantly flare-up as spoiling-for-a-fight youngsters mill around Angel Place after pubs and clubs have thrown out. "I can't take any more. I've had enough" he said'. Shame: Chris Baggus had been a model landlord. Sadly, the passage of 23 years has not seen that much change. The pub, however, remains a remarkable survivor and is well worth a visit – not least during the Worcester Music Festival when it hosts some good bands. A Marstons house.

Licensees: James Clark (1784 listed as 'mufician horn tavern 7 Angel St' 1792); Edward Fidoe (listed as Horn Tavern 1814); Old Horn and Trumpet 1820); Richard Ricketts (Old Horn and Trumpet c.1820 – c 1840); Thos. Boden, Horn & Trumpet (1842 – 1850s); James Surman (1855); Mrs. E. Humphreys (1873-76); Charles Keatley (1876-79); William Daws (1879-81); Edward Thomas (1881-89 when he died); Herbert Witherington (1889-91 when he died); Mary Witherington (1891-2); Maria Cobham (1892-95 when she died); Alice Churchill (1896- 8); Thomas Smith (1898-1902); Thomas Mills (1902 - 1916); John Clark (1916-18); James Ashdown (1918-21); Ernest Peace (1921-29); Arthur Johnson (1929 – 1943); Mary Johnson (1943-4); Harry Davis (1944-54); Edward Simms (1954-5); Cedric Walls (1955-65); Peter Walls (1965); Eric Pitt (1965-66); John Jenkins (1966-71); Sidney Roberts (1971-4); Christopher Baggus (1974-88); Peter Holland (2000); Paul Warren (2001). Current (2013) licensee or dps: Miss Donna Bird. Worcester City licence 1191

Waggon (or Wagon) & Horses
Location: Angel Street (also listed as Dolday)
Years active: 1790 - 1850

Not much known about this one save that it was listed as Dolday in 1790 under Thomas Arding (Worcester Royal Directory) and Angel Street in Victuallers Recognizances 1827 and

1900: Horn and Trumpet (left) and The rear of The Crown, now Lloyds No1 (right) CCMH/CFOW

later Pigot's Worcestershire Directory 1829... precise location and other details unknown other than that it stood roughly where the 'new' Cornmarket now stands

Licensees: *Thomas Arding (1790); Edward Fidoe (1827-1835): Mary Fidoe (1835-40s); Matthew Cook, Waggon & Horses (1842). No further listings*

C1/37 Curriers' Arms
Location: Angel St.
Years active: 1814 – 1840

Listed in Register of Victuallers' Recognizance of 1814 under licensee Richard Baylis and later (1820) in Worcester Lewis Directory

Licensees: *Richard Baylis (1814- 1820s); Letitia Lowe (1827); James Hazelton Collett (1835). No further listings*

C1/38 Fountain
Also known as: Bottoms Up
Location: Angel Street   Years active: 1840s – 1983

1983: The Fountain in its short-lived 'Bottoms Up' days

(CCMH/CFOW)

Long-life City centre favourite listed at variously as 6 and 11 Angel Street. Appears in Hunt & Co's Commercial Directory for Gloucester, Hereford and Worcester (1842) and Victuallers Recognizances 1843 and has continuous occupancy up to its closure c1983. William Willis was convicted in 1879 for permitting gaming here and was fined 1/6 and 9/- costs. Originally owned by Frederick Smith brewers of Aston Model Brewery Birmingham and mortgaged to Horace William Newton Goodwin of Strontian Argyllshire it was later bought by W. Butler and Co Limited brewers of Springfield Brewery Wolverhampton (M&B) on 30th September 1958. Worcestershire and England cricketer Ted Arnold lived here for many years with his daughter Vera (wife of licensee Francis Oger 1937-52). A welcoming though occasionally hot-tempered pub that was often known to spill out into real hassle, it tried to re-invent itself in 1983 under licensee Mark Lucky as 'Bottoms Up' with everything upside down and topsy-turvy in a bid to attract a younger trendier clientele – including upside down cat, roof, sky, rose box, lamp post and street sign – but the move probably only hastened its demise and it failed not long after. It's now Ayaan's curry house.

Licensees: *John Hill (1843-1850s); Fanny Allsop (1873); Thomas Aldington (1874-75); William Willis (1875-92 when he died); Mary Willis (1892-96); Alfred Henry Willis (at 6 Angel Street – 18d 96-1901); Edith Willis (1901-2); Edward Price (at 11 Angel Street – 1902-1914); Albert Bird (1914-27 when he died); Mrs Sarah Bird (1927-34); William Mears (1934); Francis Oger (1934 -1952); Hiram Cutler (1952-54); Thomas Edgar Hughes (1954-56); William Roy Cadman (1956-57); George James Barker (1957-59); Leslie Ephraim Burton (1959-60 when he died); Arnold Hemming (1960-3); George Colley (1963-66); Alfred Cooper (1966-8); Arthur Cooke (1968-9); Douglas Williams (1969); Victor Mead (1969-70); Robert Hall (1970-72); Jerwerth Roberts (1972-3); Gerald Batchelor (1973-4); Leonard Warrender (1974-6); William Wimpenny (1976-9); Sandra Connor (1979-83); Mark Lucky (1983)*

Fountain and Ewe and Lamb. next-door-but-one neighbours. Note the traffic flow (and propensity) in Angel Street 1965 (Jim Sargeant)

Today both fine old Worcester pubs are Asian food houses and the Oyster Bar a bookie's

One property separated The Fountain and the following pub, The Ewe and Lamb, and this had been the highly popular Oyster Bar occupying 7 and 9 Angel Street and considered exotic for Worcester when it opened on 23rd March 1953. It was licensed to sell wine for consumption on the premises under the loving care of Photios Constantinou described as 'restaurant house keeper'. A reference also appears to a waiter at the bar (see Characters and other Worcester legends). Note how the building that took its place was originally set back from the frontages of neighbouring properties: this was because of an ill-fated plan to smash a major route right through the heart of Worcester taking a swathe of buildings with it – a scheme that would have been as criminal as the so-called Rape of Worcester that did the same to the historic Lich Street. Now a bookmaker's it has reclaimed its lost space

C1/39 Ewe and Lamb, (Ewe and Lamb Vaults)
Also known as: Gaiety Bar
Location: Angel St.
Years active: 1750 - 1990

Separated from its M&B rival by the 'in' 50s venue **The Oyster Bar,** (also licensed) was the Ansells alternative to The Fountain, The Ewe and Lamb. Possibly dating from the mid 1700s, the inn was first mentioned in the Register of Victuallers' Recognizance of 1766 Grundy Royal Directory 1792 and listed variously as '12 Angel freet' (1792); 3 Angel Street (1900) 5 Angel St (1910). A popular pub in its day, a noted licensee was Thomas Lawson *(1899–1914)* former actor and theatre critic who also welcomed touring actors from the Theatre Royal by opening up a tab 'for when the ghost walked' - thesp-speak for 'wait till pay-day'. Both pubs on this side of Angel Street suffered from reputations as potential trouble hot-spots though **The Ewe and Lamb** managed to cling to life up to around 1990 outliving its next-door-but-one neighbour by a respectable 7 years. Like **The Fountain**, this one also tried to do trendy things to lift it out of the mid-Victorian slug-it-out boozer mould it had been happy to go along with for most of its life, re-inventing itself in the 1970s as **The Gaiety Bar** aimed at a younger and trendier audience. Recent renovation by later Asian owners Sheik (Shakeey) Altaf Latif revealed some of the original hand-painted music hall artwork from the Gaiety Bar days. It's now Efes Chicken Kebab Burger and Pizza House

Licensees: *Richard Holt (1766); Francis Davis ('ewe & lamb 12 Angel freet' 1792); Philip Dance (1793–c1827); Mary Dance (1827-1840s); John Morris, (1842–79); Arthur Norwebb (1879- 1881); Joseph O'Shea (1881-83); Robert Rofe (1883-89); John Turner (1889-95); Edwin Turner (1889-95); Thomas Lawson (1899–1914); Harry Lawson (1914-17); Ellen Lawson (1917-28); John Sandbrook (1928-29); Gilbert A. Smith (1929-31); Arthur Dennis Glover (1931-5); Harold Whitehouse (1935-6); John Arthur Chadwick (also listed as John Arthur, 1936–1941); Martin Marti (1941-44); Alfred Ernest Victor Brookes (1944-1948); Archie Llewellyn Tyler (1948-50); Cyril James Bartlett (1950-52); Stanley David Howells (1952-54); Aubrey Wilfred Lyle Ashton (1954-55); John Meadows (1955); Alfred Willcox (1955-63); Edna Page (1963-5); Colin York (1965-66); William Wintle (1966); Maurice Blunt (1966-7); Patrick Kelly (1967-70); Derek Dimmock (1969-70); Patrick Barnard (1970-2); Peter Bedlow (1972-4); John Sanderson (1974); George Jones (1975-77); Thomas Martin (1977-9); Robert Gower (1979-80); John Wilkinson (1980-3); John Brelsforth (1983-4); Brian Tyler (1984-5); Pauline Tyler (1985); Robert Gower (1990)*

Across the road, another remarkable survivor with a long life and fascinating history....

Shakespeare (now The Cricketers)
C1/40 Also known as: Shakespear. Shakespeare's Tavern
Location: 6 Angel Street:
Years active: 1780 – present

For two centuries known and renowned as 'The Shakespeare' on account of its ties with various Theatres Royal next door, 'The Shake' inexplicably – some might say criminally – had its name changed under then licensee Graham Williams in the 1990s to **The Cricketers,** complete with rubbishy

Angel Street.1972 (CCMH/CFOW)

cricket-related paraphernalia replacing original old theatre handbills and posters on the walls and substituting its famous old 'Midsummer Night's Dream' sign outside with a bland fake-o coat of arms showing cricket bat and balls: owzat for naff? Though the old Theatre Royal pulled the curtain down for the final time in 1959, tales of some of the great names in British theatre calling into the Shake via a secret doorway leading from the performers' dressing rooms to an upstairs bar that still exists but is now rarely used, still abound. For years, a bell was rung in 'The Shake' to inform customers using it during the interval that the show was about to resume. After a pleasant lunchtime in there during 2013 I noted: '...reflected today on an article I wrote way, way back about the old Theatre Royal – which, as readers of certain age and those with a historical bent will recall, stood right next door: it's now a soulless 60s supermarket. Of course, in those far-off days – indeed, right up to the early 80s – the pub rejoiced in the name of The Shakespeare, no doubt on account of the fact that it would have been heavily patronised by the legions of thesps, tumblers, hoofers, clowns, warblers, jugglers, terpsichoreans and prestidigitators *(foxed? Look 'em up in the dictionary!)* panto dames, chorus girls, dog acts and varied variety artistes that appeared there twice nightly for a century or more. Old programmes also reveal that the Midlands' contingent of the Fred Karno Troupe also appeared at the theatre just before its two star performers, Stan Laurel and Charlie Chaplin historically went off to find filmic fame and fortune in the colonies. Ipso facto, it's a pound to a bag o' sh... sugar the two comedic pals would have ventured into the (then) Shake for a quart or two while waiting for the curtain to rise. Delighted to see that a hundred years on, it's still home to the clowns and the spectacular fallers-over...'

A new ghost also seems to have made an appearance: present (2013) landlady Alison Tabberer said that one night while sleeping downstairs during extensive renovations earlier in the year, she spotted her husband Adrian standing at the bar. Trouble was, he was also sleeping beside her...

Listed variously as Tavern, Inn, Hotel and Hotel (Comm) and first listed in Grundy Royal Directory 1792 it's likely the Shakespeare existed well before that. Originally owned by Hitchman and Co Ltd, brewers of 26 Bridge Street Banbury, later swallowed into the M&B group. Its history is as colourful as the customers it once (some say still) attracted: on 27th June 1917, Henry Neville Blake was fined £2 for failing to keep a register in the form prescribed by the Food Controller (Public Meals Order 1917). The Cricketers, with centuries of history still evident in its cellars and back rooms underwent extensive renovation in 2012 and now rightly enjoys a growing reputation for good bar food – with the possibility of reverting to its original name and theme décor. Shook the City's Guinness drinking population to the core in July 2013 when its 'blackstuff' was judged the best in town after other pubs rarely even bothered to compete against romping-home consistent title-taker **The Lamb and Flag**. Now a Punch Taverns house.

...and the same 40 years on (BB)

Licensees: *Robert Hurdman (listed as 'Shakefpear's tavern 4 angel ftreet – 1792); Henry Harrison also listed as Henry Harrington (Shakespear Tavern, Angel Street' 1820–1840s); John Humphreys (Shakespeare Inn (commer.) Angel Street' -1842); Timothy Mason (1855); John Skett (1873-5); Jane Skett (1875-6); Sarah Skett (1876-84); Edmund Slater (1884-9); Arthur Radford (1889-98); William Watkins (1898-1906); Thomas Nicholson (1906); James Harlow (1906-12 when he died); Winifred Harlow (1912-13); Henry Neville Blake (proprietor – 1913-1918); David Harper (1918-29); Henry Sharp (1929-30); Horace W. Mansfield (1930-2); John Hewer (1932-3); William Morrison (1933); Haydn Morris (1933-5); William Reginald Walker (1935-7); Robert Clow (1937-42); George Ridgeway Thorne (1942 -1957 when he died); Edith Susan Thorne (1958-60); William James Burrett (1960-63); Richard Gibbons (1963-66); Peter Rogers (1966-73); Richard Woosnam (1973-4); Brian Hill (1974-82); Shiela Hill (1982-83); Graham Williams (1983-2001). Current (2013) licensee/dps: Alison Kate Tabberer. Worcester City licence 1198*

Let's now re-trace our steps to The Cross (Point G) and head northwards. It's now something of a pubs wasteland – despite being a continuation of the High Street – but that wasn't always the case....

G-H: The Cross to Foregate

C1/41 **Bird in the Bush**
Location: St Nicholas ward, probably High Street
Years active: 1760s – 1790s

Not the same as **The Bird in the Hand** – as some observers seem to think – but listed separately and simultaneously in Register of Victuallers' Recognizance of 1766 with licensee given as Thomas Jones, indicating they were two different and with no further listings unlikely to reveal its position. Thus, all that can be said is that this was either an ancient inn on its last legs or just short-lived.

C1/42 **Brewers Arms**
Location: The Cross
Years active: 1700s

Little-known City centre pub of which the only record appears to be Samuel Lockstone listed as brewer's arms inn, 12 Crofs.

C1/43 **Bird in Hand**
Location: The Cross
Years active: 1600s - 1934

Formerly The Bird in Hand

A house on the Cross called **'The Bird in the Bush'** is mentioned in a document dated 1609 for some time it was thought likely it referred to the Bird in Hand – though recent research show they had different licensees and that for some time they ran contemporaneously. Unlike the largely unknown **Bird in Bush**, the long-established and better known Bird in Hand is still standing though evidently regularly re-built and long since de-licensed: it's the narrow-fronted black and white building that's dwarfed between a bookies and an employment agency abd is now a hair extension boutique. Listed in Register of Victuallers' Recognizance of 1766 under Thomas Andrews and later variously listed as 20 The Cross, 21 The Cross and 21a The Cross, the census of 1851 lists then licensee London-born Lucy Evans as widow 43, and living here with a daughter, son and servant Thomas Rastall (also described as lodger). It's thought to have ceased operations at a very respectable age in the 1930s – when interestingly, it had earlier been kept by one Elizabeth Bird!

Licensees: *Thomas Andrews (1766); John Mayfield*

(1814-27); Mary Kempson (1827-9); Richard Evans (1827 - 40); Lucy Evans (1842 - c1860); Edward Skyrme The Cross (see advt 1873-1892 when he died); Charles T. Morton (1892-1908); James Cubberley (1908-12); Percy A. Watson (1912-18 when he died); Beatrice Watson (1918-19); Rose Dangerfield (1919-20); Thomas Lane (1920-9); Mrs Elizabeth Bird (1929-32); Tom Higgins (1932-4); William Roberts (1934)

Rose and Crown
C1/44
Location: Foregate Street
Years active: 1660 - 1780
    Ancient inn deriving its name from the union of the red rose factions in the Wars of the Roses with the white rose under Henry VII, sited, according to John Noake, 'on the west side of Foregate Street'. In existence 1662 and in Register of Victuallers' Recognizance of 1766 where it's located in 'High ward' sometimes just called '**The Rose**'. On or near the site of Mr Barkley, dentist. Recorded as still being in existence 1778, but not listed in Grundy Royal Directory 1792, so presumably closed
    Licensees: *Thomas Mascall (1662); John Daniel (1679); Charles Peachey (1766)*

Queens Head
C1/45
Location: High Street (1715)
Years active: 1700 - 1800
    Precise location unclear other than 'High Street' or Foregate Street, but mentioned by Noake (1877) as one of a number of 'ancient' City inns, some of which are probably not much less ancient than the eighteenth or even 17th century, Kept by 'Trustram' 1715. Listed as Foregate Street in Worcester Royal Directory 1790 under licensee Amy Kettle.

Cross Angel Street and right ahead on the corner of Shaw Street, the building that's now estate agents Your Move was once the City's foremost hotel with a guest list including the future Queen Victoria and Lord Nelson. This was....

Once Worcester's finest hotel

Hop-Pole Inn and Royal Hotel
C1/46
Location: Foregate Street
Years active: 1700- 1865
    Built on the site of the first Poor house in Worcester *(W. A. Leicester)* The Hop Pole Inn and Royal Hotel was Worcester's premier hotel up to around 1850. Apparently, part of the assembly room still exists and the once fine and highly-favoured hotel was first mentioned in 1742, according to John Noake who wrote in 1877 that the hotel had been rebuilt about 1750 '...newly erected on a site where previously stood three tenements and a garden'. Mercers (ie clothiers) are described as living north and south the inn. By 1810 its reputation had spread far and wide and a report by Lord William Pitt Lennox, great cataloguer of the coaching inns says: '...three travellers arrived here by coach

and stayed overnight. Their meals and the bill were as follows: brace of boiled tench 6/- (30p) after which which was neck of mutton 7/- (35p), vegetables and butter 7¹/₂p), a tart 1/- (5p), bread and cheese 1/6 (7¹/₂p). For dessert a goodly supply of oranges and apples 3/- (15p), beer 1/4d (7p), perry 1/6d drunk during the meal (7¹/₂p), later Madeira wine 1 Guinea (probably a bottle each £1.05p). Their three beds cost 1/6 (7¹/₂p)) each, fire and lights 2/- (10p) and rush lights 3d (1¹/₂p). Breakfast cost 1/6 (7¹/₂p) each, plus 3/- (15p) for ham and eggs. With small sundries the bill came to £2/18/10d (£2.95)'.

Queen Victoria also lunched here in 1830 when she visited Worcester as Princess Victoria and the crowds flocking to see their future queen almost caused a riot. H.A.Leicester in his 'Worcester Remembered' (1935) wrote 'an incident in Foregate Street in the early days of 19th century which ended nearly in a tragedy, might have had an important effect on the history of England (and) could have altered course of history. The mother of the Princess Victoria (afterwards Queen) brought her daughter to Worcester to view the cathedral and arranged to take lunch at the Hop Pole Hotel. The number of loyal citizens anxious to see their future queen formed a big crowd at the hotel entrance. On the arrival of the Princess, a free fight ensued, there being no police, and with great difficulty, the Princess was saved from being killed'. Horatio, Lord Nelson also stayed here in 1802 but is said to have been furious with Worcester's 'damned glover women' who he claimed, perhaps with some justification, had snubbed Lady Hamilton. Listed as 'one of (Worcester's) five principal carriers' Inns in Baylis, Lewis Almanack 1885-8 (printed 5 New Street) The Hop-Pole became a high class shop called Victoria House after its one-time royal guest lists. It changed to Scott and Oram and later became Fearis' general stores where for generations, the Shaw Street wall on the other side of which was the bakery oven, formed a convenient place on which to warm hands – and other chilled body parts.

Licensees: Mr. G. Woodcock (1742); Thomas Yardley (Listed in Register of Victuallers' Recognizance of 1766); Christopher Wilkins (1790); Thomas Weaver (listed as 'hop-pole inn 61 Foregate St' 1792); Benjamin Fieldhouse (1814); Isaac Jones (1820-7)

Gorgeous 1920s postcard showing The Star Hotel

(CCMH/CFOW)

C1/47 Star & Garter Hotel
Also known as: Star Bar. The Star. Whitehouse. County Bar
Location: Foregate Street
Years active: 1740 – present

An establishment of some sort is believed to have existed on this site since 1588 – the same year as the Spanish Armada and at the beginning of the 17th century Miles Chandler is said to have held the lease at an annual rent of 'one red rose flower'. Even to this day, parts of the site are leased for 2,000 years at an annual rent of '12 pennies'. First mentioned as an inn in 1748 as having been built 'where was previously a very old house belonging to Walter Wakeman' and listed in Register of Victuallers' Recognizance

The Star Hotel, High Ball Chinese Restaurant and Meesons sweet shop 1960s (Jim Sargeant)

of 1766 under licensee Thomas Ashton, throughout most of the 20th century **The Star,** a famous coaching inn once with vast stabling accommodation at the rear was the premier hotel in Worcester, hosting hunt balls, and celebrations for Three Choirs Festivals, County Assizes and the High Sherriff who traditionally entertained there. "During Mr Spurr's proprietorship (see below 1897-1928) he received princes and potentates, judges and bishops, writers and musicians' (Bill Gwilliam - Old Worcester People and Places) and famous people known to have been entertained here include Ernest Shackleton, Beerbohm Tree, Bonar Law, Cedric Hardwicke, Vesta Tilley, Rafael Sabatini and Dame Clara Butt and tourist cricket teams also traditionally stayed here. It was also popular with high-ranking GIs in the war and later visiting pop stars appearing at the Gaumont including Buddy Holly and The Beatles.

Listed as 'one of (Worcester's) five principal carriers' Inns in Baylis, Lewis Almanack 1885-8 (printed 5 New Street price $1^1/_2$) alongside **The Hop-Pole, The Bell, The Crown and The Unicorn** in Broad Street, this was the venue for County carriers in the 19th century to and from Clifton-on-Teme operating on Saturdays at 4.00p from the Star Hotel Stables. In 1915, a classified ad in Littlebury's Directory described the Star as '...Hotel (County, Family and Commercial) Foregate Street. Every accommodation for Motoring Parties. Ladies' Drawing Room. Special Terms and attention to Business Men. Stock Rooms. Smoking and Reading Rooms. Table d'Hote Luncheons and Din. Grill Room. Posting in all branches. Motor Garage open day and night (Cars for Hire) Headquarters Principal Motor and Motor Cycle Associations'. Later (1990s) noted for its County Bar, once lively and popular with a great cross-section including visiting sports and music celebs mingling with cheerful Worcester drinkers: the same room is now a forlorn conference room, while today's **Star Bar** is a big, brash plastic parody of what it had been. On 3rd September 1920, licensee George Edwin Spurr was fined £5 with £1.10s (£1.50) solicitors costs for unlawfully selling two half imperial pint bottles of beer above maximum price. The property was bought by legendary sportsman and racehorse owner Billy Parrish for £33,000 in 1928, later running it himself (See Worcester Characters and other legends). Afterwards owned by Wolverhampton and Dudley Breweries, it's now operated as The Star Bar within the Whitehouse Hotel complex, part of the Whitehouse Hotels (205) chain registered at West Drayton, Middx.

Licensees: As Star and Garter: Mr. W Dyer (1748); Thos. Aston (1766); Jofeph Davis ('ftar & garter inn 60 Foregate Street – 1792); B. Fieldhouse (1793); John Jones (1814-1840s); Geo. Chamberlain (Star and Garter Hotel and Posting House'1842 – c 1860 (as 61 and 62 Foregate Street under 'The Star Hotel Company Limited, Proprietor Miss E. Dixon manageress 1873-87); James Davis (1887-97); George Edwin Spurr (proprietor – 1897-1928); Sydney Airey (1928-9); Hilda Grey (1929-30); Marie Jarman (1930); Hilda Gray (1930-1); Winifred Jones (1931-33); William Parrish (1933-6); William Gustavus Fisher (1936-52); Enest Raymond Fisher (1952-61); Robert Harborough Brookfield (1961); Frank Nicholson Hobbs (1961-72); Geoffrey Hanson (1972-73); Edwin Bennett (1973). Current (2013) licensee or dps: Beverley Elizabeth Sanders. Worcester City licence 1228

Dudfields Bar
Also known as: Oscars. The Western Bar
Location: 58 Foregate Street
Years active: 1850s to 1980s

Fondly-remembered 2-roomer with lively lounge fronting Foregate Street opposite what was the GPO *(now Tesco Express)* and rougher-edged back bar accessed down a passage.

Listed in 1846 as Bottle Ale and porter merchant and in 1915 listed in Littlebury's Directory at 56 Foregate Street, as Chas Dudfield, bottle ale and porter merchant, alongside (at the same address) R. T. Smith and Co carting agents for GWR Co Ltd., - E.R. Lowe manager, and Luke Wheeler, horsekeeper. (Incidentally, next door at 57, in the direction of

Dudfields Bar 1964 (Jim Sargeant)

City centre is listed Marks and Spencer, penny bazaar, and at 58, Dudfield Charles, restaurant, and in Kelly's Guide the following year as 'Dudfields Restaurant 58 Foregate Street, bed and breakfast, snack bar, Ansells noted ales. C.L.Clewer manager, Phone 2654'. On 9th March 1900, Henry Prior was fined 10/- (50p) with £2.0s.6d (£2.2$\frac{1}{2}$p) costs for unlawfully selling intoxicating liquor to a drunken person. On 2nd February 1916, Charles Dudfield Senior was fined a total of £2 for unlawfully supplying beer during prohibited hours and 'for unlawfully supplying to one Frederick Stock beer which had not been ordered and paid for by him'. On 29th June 1917 Charles Dudfield Junior was fined £2 in that he 'did not keep a register in the form prescribed by the Food Controller'. 'Duddies' took off in the 1960s for the new 'in' drink Newcastle Brown (1/9d [9p]) served in bottles, same as today, sparking-off a penchant for swigging, in direct contrast to the essentially gentlemanly nature of the (front) lounge though perhaps not quite so at odds with the rougher (back) bar. Later, c1974, became **The Western Bar** with wild west theme including swing doors, mounted guns and holsters and fake saddles for seats, then **Oscars** reputed to be so-named on account of pet piranha Oscar that's rumoured to have been regularly fed on goldfish from the other tanks in the bar. Originally very gentlemanly with a thriving Saturday morning crowd of gentlemen drinkers, it was later owned and run by DJ Tony Nugent and had by then (1970s) become more raucous and livelier than its forerunners – to the point of being among the first to call on the services of bouncers and doormen to maintain the peace. It's now Shipleys Amusement Arcade

Licensees: Chas Dudfield (1902– c1930); Mrs Violet Dudfield (1930); John James McCabe (1946-48); Des Barmby; (1964); Peter Homer (Western Bar) (1980)

J-I: The Butts and Farrier Street

The Butts takes its name from being the street *abutting* the City wall – though there's an alternative theory, thought less likely, that the name is derived from the old water butts set up there as targets for archery practise. Long run-down and not particularly attractive, the street has since been dramatically revived – not to mention considerably lightened-up – by the creation of the arch-controversial gold-plated library and City/County Council Hub, The Hive, opened by the Queen on June 11th 2012. Other notable structures including the old City Council depot, Carmichael's garage and other dilapidated buildings have also been swept away to create accommodation for the burgeoning student population. But for the traffic – all through-traffic now channelled up the 2-lane Butts, a street signally uncomfortable with such an unwelcome imposition – the view it presents is certainly a pleasanter aspect today than probably at any time in its life. Where the Cattle Market now stands, stood... you guessed it: the cattle market, and on Mondays it was a thriving bustling scene with the conveniently-situated abattoir adjoining it in a yard open so that the slaughtermen's gory activities could easily be seen – and a most unedifying sight it was too. Also there to serve the farmers and slaughtermen was...

C1/49

Ewe and Lamb
Location: The Butts
Years active: 1850 - 1972

Built adjoining the Cattle Market to cater for its trade and with an extended hours licence on Mondays, it closed c1970, some years after the market had ceased to operate. Listed variously as 23 The Butts (1908) and 19 The Butts (1940) its telephone number was 3148 (1957). Owned by Lewis Clarkes brewers of Angel Place it saw its days out as a Marstons house. The census of 1851 lists then licensee Benjamin Powell (48) as living here with his wife Ann (40) described as 'landlady'. On 6th January 1898, Henry Walker was fined 5/- (25p) with costs for unlawfully selling intoxicating liquor to a drunken person. Charles Allen Sier was twice up before City magistrates,

given a conditional discharge on 21st January 1959 for allowing children in the bar during permitted hours, and on 27th June 1960 he was given a 15-month prison sentence with 15 months concurrent for receiving 2 cases of stolen cigarettes. The shell of the old building remained in a sorry state for some years till it was demolished to make way for the new City Council car park that perpetuates the name of the site's original use, still being termed Cattle Market.

Licensees: *Ann Bushell (1850); Benjamin Powell (1851); Thomas Maynard (1872-1879); Henry Walker (1879-1897); William Maund (1897-98); Tracey W. Preece (1898-99); Archer Seymour (1899-1900); Robert Hunt (1900-01 when he died); Catherine Hunt (1901-02); John Lancaster Bird (1902-06); Frank Peters (1906-12); John W Cragg (1912-27); Edward Whiteley (also listed as Edgar Whiteley 1927-1952); Joseph Norman Gillman (1952-58); Charles Allen Sier (1958-60); Ivor Pritchard (1960-2); Henry Cresswell (1962-3); Albert Young (1963-5); Edwin Hughes (1965-6); Eric Willis (1966-7); Brian Hawthorn (1967-8); John Hammond (1968-9); Charles Sherratt (1969); John Thompson (1969)*

Horse and Jockey
C1/50
Location: The Butts
Years active: 1850-1860

The census of 1851 lists then licensee James Carpenter described as 'coachman and vict' living here with only one other reference: Billings Directory of Worcestershire 1855, licensee listed as John Brown 'beer retailer'

Paul Pry
C1/51
Location: 8, The Butts
Years active: 1850 - 2006 (rebuilt 1901) Re-opened 2013

Thought to date from mid 1850s (Billings Directory of Worcestershire 1855) and one of several pubs of the same name derived either from: an 1825 English play written by John Poole; one of the voyeurs who peeped out on Lady Godiva as she rode naked through the streets of Coventry; an old English newspaper; The Adventures of Paul Pry, nine stories by author Erle Stanley Gardner; or even less plausibly, the pseudonym of artist William Heath. No wonder it's confused about its future.

Owned by Robert Allen and Co Ltd of 7 Lovett Street Wolverhampton the original building was re-built c1901 and is still renowned for its high quality Edwardian craftsmanship in ceramic wall and floor tiles. It was described by West Midlands Inventory of Historic Pub Interiors as 'one of Britain's Real Heritage Pubs' – the result of CAMRA's pioneering effort to identify and help protect and promote the most important historic pub interiors in the country:

http://www.heritagepubs.org.uk/pubs/real-heritage-pub-entry.asp?pubid=193

More rumours circulate about the Paul Pry than any other City pub – some are even true!

Traffic clogged in 1963 (JAS) but still an architectural gem in 2013 (BB)

240

They said: 'Built 1901 by architect Frederick Hughes for Messrs R Allen & Son Brewers, and similar in style to many Birmingham Victorian pubs. A wedge-shaped two-storey building of red brick and stone with Art Nouveau detailing, three oriel windows on the first floor and a stone frieze. The front door on The Butts leads into a vestibule entrance and through double doors with etched glass panels is an impressive entrance hall with a terrazzo floor and floor-to-ceiling decorative tiles in panels throughout. A short passage to the right leads to the public bar. Note the old off-sales with two-part sliding hatch in the partition wall towards the bar. Through the door with a 'Bar' etched panel and a decorative fanlight is a virtually intact room with terrazzo floor (now covered by a carpet), original curved mahogany bar counter with panelled front and consoles, an elaborate five-bay mirrored bar back and a clock in pedimented centrepiece and a balustrade, a panelled dado with benches attached, a Victorian tiled and cast-iron fireplace, a lincrusta moulded ceiling, and a deep frieze. The former smoke room on the left, now a restaurant room, retains its Victorian tiled and cast-iron fireplace and a lincrusta frieze and embossed ceiling, but has lost its fixed benches around the room and baffles by the doors in recent years (they were in place in 2003). Service to the smoke room was via a hatch/door to the back of the servery. There was a Club Room on the first floor above the smoke room that also has a decorative cornice and frieze. Apart from the loss of the fixed seating in the smoke room, the only other important change is the removal of the vestibule entrance from the Infirmary Walk entrance and short passage beyond which was converted into the ladies toilet in 1993 by Banks's but it is still possible to see another off sales hatch on the servery side. Although there were two doors into

Edwardian architectural detailing of the highest order: 1901 (BB)

the public bar the plans do not indicate any divisions/partitions. Also, the gents has been modernised. It closed as a pub in 2008 and when it reopened in 2010 it traded as a Bistro and restaurant with no alcohol, but in early 2011 alcohol returned to the Paul Pry and it is possible to visit the pub 'just for a drink'.

Naturally, the pub is reputed to have its own ghost, fond of opening doors, moving furniture and going walkabout in the night. A commonly told tale is that a prostitute brought here is reputed to have been killed in the cellar and that farmers who passed the story down have said that she was not the only one – some even implying that an excavation of the cellar will provide some grisly answers. Another of the City's most enduring myths is that actor Charles Laughton was born here – the simple fact is, he wasn't (he was born in Scarborough) though that doesn't stop some from perpetuating the tale. With a chequered history of late including being a tandoori restaurant and a Polish pub with no beer run by chef Jaroslaw Karczewski, today The Paul Pry is another that suffers from 'now you see it now you don't' syndrome, but is now open and is well worth a visit. In 1982, I wrote that an upstairs functions room as well as a downstairs bar had just re-opened. The gaffer John Harris (though he's listed elsewhere as Edward) admitted that its former reputation as a rowdy-house had been well justified but, I noted that the clientele at the time was now 'the further side of middle-aged and ever-ready to break into a smile'. Big sporting pub with, throughout much of its life, several dartboards on the go, and always with a big reputation for its beer, landlord Cyril Pearce was charged with manslaughter in 1950 after felling his brother-in-law George Breakwell with a single punch in the bar.. He was subsequently acquitted after a post-mortem report revealed the hapless victim had 'an egg-shell skull'. A sight of the Grade II listed interior ceramic work is a must if you get the chance. Now run as part of the same locally-based group that also includes **The Plough** in Deansway and **The Dragon** in The Tything, all with the same licence holder.

Licensees: John Edwards (listed as 'painter and beer-seller in the census of 1851 and as 'beer retailer' in 1855); Frederick Davis (1859); William Davis (1873-1893 when he died); Selina Davis (1893-5); James Arthur Davis (1895-1900); Arthur Allen (1900-01); Percy Groves (1901-25 when he died);William Allen (1929); John Robinson (1929–1934); Cyril Pearce (1934–1952); Frederick Steer (1952); Thomas Hardwick (1952-57); Fanny Hardwick (1957-70); Barbara Powell (1970-2); Arthur Bryan (1972-5); Victor Bird (1975); Arthur Swingell (1975-7); Royston Gallier (1977-8); Gorge Wilcox (1978 - 1979); Olive Harris (1979-82); Ronald Smith (1982-4); John Merry (1984-7); James Crighton (1987); Chris and June Salisbury (2000). Current (2013) licensee or dps: Catherine Esther Louise Ottaway. Worcester City licence 1373

C1/52 Five Ways
Also known as: Angel
Location The Butts/Angel Street
Years active: 1760s – 2012

Initially The Angel described as 'environs of Angel Street' the original Angel is believed to have been the one that gave its name to Angel Street. First Listed in Register of Victuallers' Recognizance of 1767 under licensee Richard Gyles and in Grundy's Royal Directory for 1792, the precise history, location and licensees of this particularly historic public house are largely unknown – which is unusual and a pity for a hostelry believed by 'The Rambler' John Noake in 1877 to have given its name to Angel Street (though he admits, 'by what authority I know not) and is thought its grounds could have extended all the way through to Broad Street A much newer incarnation on the same site is believed to have been re-named **The Five Ways** around 1870 on account of being at or near the junctions of The Butts, Angel Street, Farrier Street (originally Little Butts) and Infirmary Walk) also going by the name of **Five Ways Inn** (1900) and **Five Ways Hotel** (1957). First appearance as '**Five Ways**' was in Littlebury's Directory of Worcestershire 1873. Owned by Hitchman and Co Brewers of 26 Bridge Street

Five Ways from The Paul Pry 1964 (Jim Sargeant). Above: not much has changed 2013 (BB)

The sad-eyed but sometimes volatile ghost of Five Ways makes an appearance in 1985

(BB)

Banbury. On 7th August 1960, licensee Frederick Albert Luff was cautioned by Inspector George Lewis for permitting gaming on his premises after permitted hours. It's believed too that a barman called Sid hung himself here in the 1930s and that his spirit still haunts the place. Former licensee Trevor Soames reckoned that when sad Sid was really angry, he was capable of throwing metal objects around the room as if they were paper. He said he once threw a brass model aeroplane at him for no reason. He said he's seen him several times always dressed up in baggy shirt with the sleeves rolled up and baggy trousers. "I think he means well but he seems to have a nasty streak about him sometimes. He has the saddest eyes" said gaffer's wife Lynne in a 1985 article. Currently closed (2013) its licence No 1062 issued to L.T.Management Services of Attleborough, remains active and awaiting a new tenant.

Licensees: Richard Gyles (1767); William Wainwright (1859); Chas Ulmschneider (1873-95 when he died); John Millington (1895-6); Thomas Prosser (1896-8); Thomas Hopwood (1898-1921); Ada Cook (1921-9); Archie Glover (1929-30); Walter H Scott (1930-6); Lorenzo and Gladys Kelly (1936-8); Rex Herbert (1938-44); Harold Hunt (1944-1955); Kate Evelyn Hunt (1955-59); Frederick Albert Luff (1959-63); David Collins (1967-9); Anthony Thorne (1969-70); George Patston (1970); Stuart Michael (1970-5); Malcolm Morris (1975-78); Michael Stevens (1978-9); Stephen Wilding (1979-83); Trevor Soames (1984); Rosaleen Wilson (1985-6); Patrick White (1986-9); Pamela Collins (2001); Hannah Batchelor (2013).

Into Farrier Street and opposite the soulless edifice that's now City Council HQ Orchard House, on the open space now forming the back entrance to Whitehouse Hotel once stood...

Farmer's Arms
Location: Farrier Street (originally, Little Butts)
Years active: 1850s
Little-remembered pub with one listing only: Billings Directory of Worcestershire 1855
Licensee: Henry Evans

Virtually opposite, on the barely-recognisable site now occupied by the City Council's HQ Orchard House stood:

Star Vaults
Also known as: The Tap. Star Hotel Tap
Location: **Farrier Street**
Years active: 1840 - 1959
At the rear of *(and traditionally managed by the manager of)* **The Star Hotel** and originally

1972: Farrier Street: the Farriers Arms has gone, The Star Vaults (white-faced building centre right) is clinging to life - just - and Orchard House has yet to make an appearance (CCMH/CFOW)

geared to cater for ostlers, grooms and coachmen in the hotel's coaching days, its address was 2 Farrier Street. This is where the drivers and drovers drank while their masters stayed and caroused at the hotel in whose shadow it sat. Given its clientele, it's barely surprising 'The Tap' was the scene of a fatal fracas on 25th July 1841 between Mr Maiden of **The Shakespeare Inn** and an ostler who clashed, resulting in the ostler being stabbed to death. Maiden was found guilty of manslaughter and sentenced to one month's imprisonment – though notably without hard labour. **The Tap** survived up to the late 1950s as a small, some said 'poky' public house in its own right. A noted landlord was colourful character William Parrish who'd risen from nothing to become owner and manager of the Star Hotel and also owned at different stages in his life **The Hop Pole** and **British Camp Hotel**. *(See Worcester characters and other legends)*

Licensees: Charles Edward Franklin (1910-1915 listed as 'manager'); William Parrish (1930); Laurence Leonard Adames (1937);

Next, a still-fondly remembered Ansells pub...

Farriers' Arms
C1/55 **Location: Farrier Street**
Years active: 1820-1964

Listed Worcester Lewis Directory 1820 as the Butts, also as Upper Butts (1850), Farrier Street (1910), and 3, Farrier Street (1915), at one time this long-remembered favourite had a butcher's shop attached to it. An Ansells house run by a succession of Wheldon family members for almost 40 years, Fred Wheldon (licensee 1910-1932) had been an all-round sportsman who'd played cricket for the County and football for the Aston Villa side that took both FA Cup and League titles in 1896-7. His three sons – Ted, Norris and Jim – were also sportsmen of repute and his grandson John Spilsbury was a Worcester City stalwart until a broken leg ended his career. Worcester City Police inspector George Lewis recalls them as 'a wonderful family'. The Farriers closed in 1964.

Ron Jones of Whinfield Road was then a City weights and measures (forerunner of the present Environmental Health Dept) officer and he recently told me that he was sent in to inspect it the day after it closed and reckoned he'd never seen such a clean place. The copper sparkled, he said, and everything else in the old pub he described as immaculate "...as if the last licensees had scrubbed it from top to bottom even though it was about to be demolished. I took the cards and darts and crib board and all that stuff to The Grubber (workhouse) at Hillborough (now St Pauls)" he told me in 2013.

Licensees: Michael Allen (1820); John Jenkins (1827); James Jones (1829); Henry Evans (1832-1870s); T. Aldington (1873-76); William Clough (1876-80); John Marrioyy (1880-82); George Payne (1882-84); Edward Bennett (1884-6); George Clissold (1886-94); William Stanbridge (1894- 98); George Stallard (1898-1902); George H. Hughes (1902–1908 when he died); Florence Cullis (1908); Frederick Wheldon (1908–1924); Mrs Ann L. E. Wheldon (1924-37); Jack Edward Wheldon (1937); Mrs. L. E. Wheldon (1940); Archdale Bond Osborn (1940-48); Freda Spilsbury (1948-56); Daisy Madeleine Jones (1956- 61); Neil Duncan Watt (1961) temporary transfer granted to Raymond Barnes 12th December 1961)

The popular Farriers Arms was demolished in the widening of Farrier Street 1964 (JAS). Inset today (BB)

9: City Centre 2

Map: 56-57

Bounded by: GWR to the north;
Worcester-Birmingham canal to the
east; Lowesmoor to the South; and
Foregate Street to the west, and
including Sansome Street, St Martins
Gate, George Street, and the
western extremes of Rainbow
Hill and Shrub Hill Road.

SPRECKLEY'S
ALES

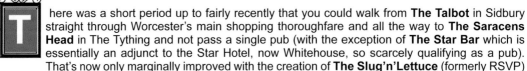

There was a short period up to fairly recently that you could walk from **The Talbot** in Sidbury straight through Worcester's main shopping thoroughfare and all the way to **The Saracens Head** in The Tything and not pass a single pub (with the exception of **The Star Bar** which is essentially an adjunct to the Star Hotel, now Whitehouse, so scarcely qualifying as a pub).

That's now only marginally improved with the creation of **The Slug'n'Lettuce** (formerly RSVP) in what had once been the consecrated nave of St Nicholas Church – but the point is nonetheless made: over recent years, the City has never been able to claim a particularly great proliferation of pubs along its main drag, though there are some gems among those that did exist.

The western side of this sector of the City – and particularly the section C-E which would have been within the City wall – is history-rich, while the remainder is comparatively recent, mostly post-1830s. Even so, both are home to some significant hostelries.

Looking at the last remains of the old City wall along... *where else*? City Walls Road, the scale of the mediaeval building project is staggering and it's a tribute to the masons that sections of the wall not only remain pretty much intact, but still look as if nothing will ever shift them! At no point, apparently, was the City wall lower than 50 feet and, says Hubert Leicester in his 'Forgotten Worcester '(1930): '*... in some places considerably higher and bordered by a deep ditch'.*

Starting from the Fore Gate, the wall continued down Sansome Street *(formerly Town Ditch, point C in the map)* following the same line as the present buildings on the south side to its junction with St Nicholas Street *(formerly Gaol Lane or Garden Market)*, then along Queen Street with Water Course Alley on the left up to what's now Silver Street, at the end of which stood the second, or St Martin's Gate. The wall continued along the east side of New Street *(originally Glovers' Street)* to the bottom of Union Street. Here there was a small Postern Gate, thence along the east of Friar Street and Sidbury to the canal bridge where the great South Gate or Sidbury gate stood. The course of the wall then followed the

The Cross 1920s - and The Golden Cross (left) (CCMH/CFOW)

south side of St Peter Street to the river at the bottom of Severn Street *(formerly Frog Lane or Frog Mill Lane)* where the Water Gate stood. From this point the wall was not continuous – the river being considered a sufficient defence. From the bridge, however, the wall was continuous with a gate *(St Clements Gate)* at the bottom of The Butts, facing north. To complete the circuit of the City, the wall continued on the south side of the Butts to the Fore Gate: The Butts and Shaw Street *(formerly Gardeners Lane)* forming the trench or ditch outside the wall'.

The mighty structure that was **The Fore Gate** stood between what's now The Hop Market and Berkeley Almshouses – once a hospital, erected and funded by Robert Berkeley of Spetchley under the terms of his will dated 1692 and whose name is also perpetuated in two City pubs as well as several more outside the City. Fore Gate was, by all accounts a major fort-like structure built, like the other Worcester gates, not necessarily for military and defence purposes but more so for keeping out traders until they had paid their tolls and also, says Leicester, for '...*preventing the export of articles required for the use of Citizens'.* It's in the direction of this point we'll make a start...

A - B: **The Cross (east side) to St. Nicholas Street**

C2/1

Golden Cross
Location: The Cross
Years active: 1600s– 1830s

A story persists that William Guide, an informer who disclosed details of a Parliamentarian night attack on Royalists in the City in 1651 – precipitating a disaster for Cromwell's men – was hung from the sign post of **The Golden Cross** which was clearly a forerunner of the inn mentioned by Noake (1877) as one of a number of 'ancient' City inns and listed in 1734 as one of 23 Worcester inns where qualifying voters could cast their ballot. Once particularly noted, **The Golden Cross** is thought to have gone by the 1830s and while pondering on the likely location of

The Cross 1920s and The Golden Cross (right) with the ever-present bobby (CCMH/CFOW)

this one over a Wetherspoon's breakfast in **The Postal Order** recently, I looked up at the enlarged and framed photograph of The Cross around 1910 on the wall above the alcove I was occupying. and there it was.... a solid, respectable looking building if by then no longer pristine, marked quite clearly **'Golden Cross'** Ooo-er! Serendipity or what? Referred to by Noake in Worcestershire Relics (printed March 1877 price 5/-) 'There was an inn at the Cross called '**The Golden Cross Inn**, still commemorated by the name of Mr. Allen's outfitting establishment; and also another inn called **The Talbot** celebrated for some of the venison feasts for the Corporation'. Not much more is known of either, though from Noake's comment it's possible this was also the actual, or at least adjoining, the site of...

Talbot
Location: The Cross
Years active: 1740 - 1850

Included by Noake (1877) as one of a number of City inns, some of which are 'probably not much less ancient than... 1517'. In 1930 Hubert Leicester wrote *(Forgotten Worcester):* 'retreating down the Trinity leads us back to The Cross and at the corner is The Union Club. This fine fronted house (another of Thomas White's works) was formerly a bank celebrated by Mrs Henry Wood in 'The Shadow of Ashlydyat' as the bank of Godolphin, Cross and Godolphin. Previously there also stood at this site a celebrated inn known as **The Talbot.** This was the rendezvous of the '48' a body forming part of the Corporation. The '24' (another body) met at **The Globe** in Powick Lane (Note: the '24' and '48' refer to the inner and outer sections of the Corporation, not unlike today's inner Cabinet and the rest of the City's councillors). The same site is also the later location of The International Stores (off-licence) great, bustling magnificent old-style general stores selling all kinds of produce and whose smells of exotic teas, coffee, cheeses and freshly-killed hares, rabbits and other meats strung up on hooks will never go away once experienced. Undoubtedly one of – some might say the best and still fondest-remembered – the City's premier grocer's and general stores licensed to sell beers wines and spirits for consumption off the premises, its licensee was Frank Ernest Hawkins, secretary of The International Tea Company Stores Ltd, and owned by The Trustees of the Worcester Consolidated Municipal Charities Worcester (clerk: Mr J. Lionel Wood, solicitor, Worcester)

It's just a matter of yards north, and here's The Avenue said to have been the site of the first lay school in Worcester, established by members of the order of Trinitarians who came here, it's said, in the 12th century to serve the chantry in St Nicholas Church '...and to assist the incumbent in his administrations, the number of people then attending that church being more than one priest could attend to'. They also built their huge Trinity Hall here, afterwards used by the various trade guilds for their meetings and on at least one occasion, the Assizes. It seems the hall was sold for £185 in 1796 and converted into a furniture warehouse, but the name still refers to this still attractive section of the City.
But for the number of cars that always appear to me to be well at odds with the neat architecture of its still fine Regency buildings, The Avenue probably hasn't changed a great deal in more than two centuries. At the bottom is:

Bushwackers
Location:
Years active. c1990 - present

Trendy, not at all unpleasant eaterie and bar in what was the City Council Health Department with entrance both from The Trinity and The Avenue. One of three similar in the Bushwacker Limited chain *(alongside Birmingham and Swindon)* run by the locally-based Pinches brothers Craig and Darren who, it appears, have dealings in most pub trade affairs in the City including spearheading the Late Night Initiative (and very professionally too, it has to be said), 'Wackers' is noted for good food and attracts a predominantly young crowd who don't object to burly no-nonsense bouncers on the doors or standing shoulder to shoulder while having their ear 'oles savagely assaulted by loud music. A pleasant enough meeting place that once offered free food from 5pm to 7pm, a dizzying video with bland, breathless voice-over is viewable here:
http://www.bushwackers.co.uk/worcester/index.html

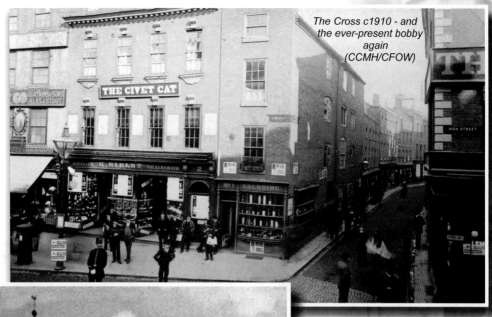

The Cross c1910 - and the ever-present bobby again (CCMH/CFOW)

(Left) The Cross c1912 - (CCMH/CFOW) and today (BB)

Licensees: *Current (2013) licensee and dps: Darren Pinches. Worcester City licence 1325*

B-C: Foregate Street (east side) and St Nicholas Street to Sansome Street

Today's St Nicholas Street was also known as Union Lane and Garden Market before taking on 'Nicholas' Street and only comparatively recently adding 'Saint'. Even so, this is an important area for pubs and similar hostelries and was also the start of the famous Station Run of the 1930s, when it's said that the true test of a boy's progression into manhood was by drinking a half pint in every pub he passed from here to Shrub Hill Station. If he was still capable of asking for a ticket – destination immaterial – he'd proved himself as undisputedly one of the lads by sheer dint of having 11$^{1}/_{2}$ pints under his belt. Now let them tell you binge drinking is a

St Nicholas Church - bedecked for the Prince of Wales

(CCMH/ CFOW)

- and almost a century on, put to imaginative use by a pub chain! 2013 (BB)

modern phenomenon! Try it today and you could probably drive your car and still be within the drink driving regulations. The first in this section could also qualify as being the pub (more accurately restaurant/bar) in the most unusual setting of any in Worcester today...

C2/4

Slug'n'Lettuce
Location: The Cross in what was formerly St Nicholas Church
Years active: 2004 - present

Probably the City's most unusual location for a pub – the former St Andrews Church, built on the site of a 12th century temple, remains of which remain in the crypt and basement walls, now de-commissioned though many original features of the 1732 church remain. Primarily a food bar run by the The Stonegate Pub Co of Luton, who operate the nationwide Slug'n'Lettuce chain, it's popular with day-time eaters even extending to trendy little bistro-style tables and chairs for the al fresco experience. Originally RSVP, the location and setting is remarkable and it also rejoices in tales of its own ghost – that of 'Mrs Mitchell', sister-in-law of a City Alderman who had her remains bricked-up in the church tower in 1761. Her remains are still there,and her spirit is thought to be behind a run of strange occurrences reported in the church since its de-commissioning in 1989. Another tale told of the old church is that of Mrs Glover who'd lived next to the church and whose two children had died from smallpox. 'The grief so unhinged her that her husband had to take her away from home whenever a funeral took place at the church. But a year to the day after the tragedy, the door to the crypt was left open and she was discovered dead on the coffins of her children' *(Valentine Green – re-quoted in Bill Gwilliam's 'Old Worcester People and Places').*

The Slug was forced to close in 2012 following a fall of plaster from the ceiling. Repairs were completed quickly though the pub lost several days' trading while safety checks were made on the fabric of the building. It's one of several unexplained incidents logged by staff of the one-time church – built at the then staggering cost of £3,345.

***Current (2013) licensee/dps*: Emma Woodhouse. Worcester City licence 1104**

Immediately facing it was The Holly Bush which for some time had an entrance from High

Street though its address was always listed St Nicholas Street. The corner site was at one time the City's Benefits and Welfare Office, later Lennards Shoe shop (best Beatle boots in town, 29/11d (£1.49p) later a lighting shop and now a hairdressers

B - C: Foregate Street (east side)

C2/5

Hop Market Inn
Also known as: Hop Market Hotel
Location: Hop Market, Foregate Street
Years active: 1750s - 1964

Listed 1820, Worcester Lewis Directory though dates back further – possibly mid 1700s though the present building dates from 1900 when it was built as part of a road widening scheme, replacing the historic **Hopmarket Inn** and **Hopmarket Hotel** that had previously stood on the site for 150 years and was an important venue for County carriers in the 19th century: carriers to and from Earl's Croome, Ripple, Severn Stoke and Upton on Severn (all Wednesdays and Saturdays 4pm) operated from here. According to Berrows Worcester Journal in 1900: '...the unanimous opinion is that the new structure will be a credit not only to the architects and builders but also to the county which is proud of its hop trade and hop market. To mark the completion of the building, Mr. Charles Pipe, Governor of the Hop Market, laid an engraved stone in the cupola crowning the edifice'. Originally owned by the Corporation of Worcester, later held on 21-year lease by Ansells Brewery at £850 a year from 28th August 1943. William Parrish a rags-to-riches entrepreneur who later owned The **Star Hotel and Tap** and **British Camp Hotel** in Malvern was also owner and licensee here 1930-33). A distinctly up-market bar attracting after-work traders, solicitors, car dealers and hop merchants, the impressive red terracotta building was a popular draw right up to the mid-1960s when, after its demise, it was taken over by Individual Tailoring who are still there, their slightly warped but still impressive framed print of Giovanni Battista Moroni's The Tailor ('Il Tagliapanni' – original in the National Gallery) still occupying pride of place just as it has for the better part of fifty years since the bar closed.

Licensees: Joseph Evans 1820; Edward Perrins (1827 – 40s); George Morgan, Hop Market Inn (commercial), Foregate (1842); John Humphreys (Hop Market family and commercial hotel (1855); Mrs Mary Anne Nicholas (1872-84); Mary Bird (1884-98); William G. Lee ('Family and Commercial Hotel, proprietor'. Tel 56. 1898–1930); Wm Parrish, Edward Dands (1930-33); Trina MacDonnell (1933); Dorothy Bowerman Bulley (1933-42); Charles Moffatt (1942-3); Reginald Thould (1943-4); William Thomas Edward Lawson (1944–1947); John Gunn (1947-8); Arthur Percy Wright (1948-49); Henry Arthur Leslie Freerson (1949-51); David Henry Eborall (1951); John McFarlane Dickson (1951-2); Trina Beatrice McDonald (1952-3); John Wilson (1953); William Thomas Edward Lawson (1953-5); Cyril Thomas Lewis (1955-7); Raymond William Brookes (1957); William Buckley (1957-8); Herbert William Penstone Sparrow (1958); Eric Harold Williams (1958-64);

C2/6 Crown & Sceptre
Location: ('near the Foregate)
Years active: 1700- 1800s

Precise location unknown as are years of existence, but mentioned by Noake (1877) as one of a number of 'ancient' City inns, some of which are 'probably not much less ancient than...' the eighteenth or even 17th century. Listed in Register of Victuallers' Recognizance of 1766 as 'St Nicholas ward' under licensee Thomas Huxley and Thomas Burton by 1784. In 1814 it was licensed to Joseph Evans. A Joseph Evans was also licensee of **The Hop Market Inn** four years later.   It's thus likely they could be on the same site

C2/7 Railway Refreshment Rooms
Location: Foregate Street Station

In addition to listing under 'Inns and Taverns' in Billings Directory of Worcestershire 1855 under licensee Thomas Watton, The Worcester City Police Register of Intoxicating Liquor Licenses shows that full on-sale liquor licenses were issued for the 'up' and 'down' platforms at Foregate Street Station, owned by the Great Western Railway Company and registered at Paddington Station, London W2 (later British Transport Commission at 55 Broadway, Westminster London W1 then 222 Marylebone Road) and were licensed for the sale of all intoxicating liquors and subject to the same opening and closing hours as well as other restrictions as laid down by the City's Licensing Department. For an image of what all British Rail refreshment rooms (though I confess, I never saw anyone looking particularly refreshed coming out of one) looked like, David Lean's 'Brief Encounter' is as good a start as any! Milford Junction could easily pass for Foregate Street Station in the 1940s and 50s.

Licensees: Thomas Watton (1859). NO further details up to Graham Royde Smith (listed Secretary of the London, Midland and Scottish Railway Company (-1949); William Henry Johnson (1949-51);

Thomas Henry Barker, Secretary of British Transport Hotels Executive, registered at St Pancras Chambers London NW1

Let's stay within, or at least close to, the line of the City Wall, down...

C-D: **Sansome, originally Sansom, Street**

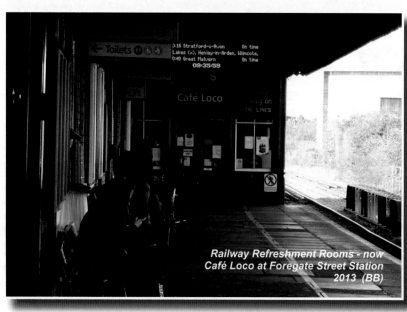

Railway Refreshment Rooms - now Café Loco at Foregate Street Station 2013 (BB)

Toby's Tavern
Also known as: Hoppers
Location: 9, Sansome Street
Years active: 1990 - 2007

Long, single roomer with skittle alley that doubled-up as an extension to the bar, opened up and run exclusively by much-respected one-off LVA chairman Mike Stevens until being bought out by Middle Eastern landlords who, it was stated at the time, (2007) planned to turn it into accommodation. The City's planners had different ideas and so the owners 'gifted' the former pub and night-scene to a homeless charity – since when it seems there's been no takers and the building has remained empty and forlorn. As **Toby's Tavern** (and run by the Chairman of the LVA) it was noted for 'flexible' opening hours, as well as for being home to what's generally regarded as some of the City's most outrageous characters and, it has to be said, many from the wrong side of the tracks – essentially, a polite version of 'wrong 'uns'. Also big on horse racing, cricket and illicit deals on all commodities – with the exception of drugs so far as is known but far from guaranteed – it remained popular and friendly, even with visiting police who usually had a fair idea where they'd find their man (or woman) when called for. Changed name from **Hoppers** – taken from the charming carved frieze over the adjoining property that might once have belonged to **The Hop Pole Hotel** opposite – to Toby's Tavern 1992, and not to be confused with the M&B operated Toby's Tavern chain that (still) operates The Ketch. **Licensees**: Mike Stevens (1992 - 2006) *pictured right*

Mike Stevens

Above: Sansome Sreet showing The Golden Hart (left) and a space waiting for Hoppers, later Toby's Tavern (CCMH/CFOW)

Right: same today (BB)

C2/9 Plume of Feathers
Location: Sansom Street
Years active: 1780 - 1800

Possibly the oldest but least catalogued of four inns named: **Plume of Feathers**. Two listings only – Register of Victuallers' Recognizance of 1784 under licensee Thomas Barnes and Grundy Royal Directory 1792, licensee listed as 'Richard Storer plume of feathers 19 sanfom ftreet.

C2/10 Golden Hart.   Also known as: Golden Heart. Bleeding Heart
Location: Sanfom, later Sansom (Sansome) St.
Years active: c1750s-1972

First listed in Register of Victuallers' Recognizance of 1766 and later Worcester Lewis Directory 1820, and listed variously as 'Hart' and 'Heart' often at the ledger clerk's whim – though with a few diversions the pattern appears to be **Golden Heart** (1750s), **Bleeding Heart** (1780-90s) thereafter **Golden Hart**. Also listed as **Hart** in 1827, but **Heart** in 1835. This was the scene of a murder when the innkeeper Henry Powell was poisoned by his wife and her lover, a man called Keatley in 1888. Both were found guilty of manslaughter and sentenced to 12 years. On 16th December 1892, licensee Henry Kirk was fined £5 with costs for unlawfully permitting gaming on the premises. 76 years on, William Edwards was convicted in 1968 for allowing drunkenness, he was fined £5 plus £15/15/- costs plus two charges of allowing drinking under age which carried a fine of £10 for each offence.

The Golden Hart 1974 - closed two years and still on the market (CCMH/ CFOW)

A Spreckley Brothers house registered at 7, Foregate Street, it was later transferred to West Country Breweries of which a valuable ceramic plaque still existed on the wall up to just a few years ago, while other evidence of its former glory days is still visible (pic)   Now what????

Licensees: As Golden Heart: Rebecca Smith (widow – 1766); As Bleeding Heart: John Thrupp, bleeding heart 2 Sanfom Street (1790); As Golden Hart: Robert Mears (1814); William Turvey (1820–c1830s); Samuel Wooley (1835); John Peel (now Golden Heart, Sansom Street 1842); William Cale (1850); James Wankling listed again as Golden Hart 1855); Henry Gibbons, Golden Heart (1873-79); George Hughes (1879-84); Henry Powell (1884-88 when he died); Charles Fildes (1888-92); Henry Kirk (1892-3); James Peebles (1893-4); William Wiltshire (1894-1902); George S. Baylis (1902-05); George Duggan (1905); Thomas Shaw (1905-1910); Walter S. King (1910-31 when he died); Mrs. Louisa M. King (1930-5); William Roberts (1935-7); Ernest A. Harding (1937-40); Thomas Ranford (1940-1961); Victor Thewlis (1961-3); Mary Thewlis (1963); Anthony Davey (1963-66); William Edwards (1966)

C2/11 Old Falcon
Also known as: Falcon
Location: Sansome Street
Years active: c1810 – 1969

Corner pub in prominent position at the corner of Sansome Street and Lowesmoor variously listed as 17 Sansome Street (1900) and 35 Sansome Street (1915) originally Lewis Clarkes, later Marstons house. First appears in Register of Victuallers' Recognizance of 1814 under licensee Matthew Mason.

The Old Falcon 1972 and (below) its final demise to make way for the planned new City Walls Road (CCMH/ CFOW)

Mentioned by Noake (1877) as one of a number of 'ancient' City inns, some of which are 'probably not much less ancient than...' the eighteenth or even 17th century. Listed in Pigot's Worcestershire Directory 1829 as Falcon, Sansom Street, also as Falcon (Old), Sansom Street, Old Falcon Tavern, Sansome Street, Old Falcon, 35 Sansome Street, it derives its name from the crest of Queen Elizaabeth I. Demolished c1968 to make way for widening of Sansome Street and creation of City Walls Road. On 18th May 1903, licensee William Stephens was fined £2 with £1.14s (£1.70p) costs for unlawfully selling intoxicating liquor during prohibited hours. After it closed for the final time, one-time licensee Tony Fellowes rescued the original leaded glass window frame from over the door (see pic opposite) and even forty years later would bring it out to lovingly show to friends who demonstrated even the vaguest interest.

Licensees: *Matthew Mason (1814); Richard Newland (1827); John Newland (1840s -1876); David Wall (1876-1885 when he died); Ellen Wall (1885-7); James Bateman (1887-9); Thomas Weston (1889-90 when he died); Alice Weston (1890); George Manning (1890-1); Alice Weston (1891-3); Joseph Osborn (1899-1901); Charles Stephens (1901-03); William Stephens (1903-5); Benjamin Robinson (1905); Henry Bluett (1905-07); George Knight (1907-10); Thomas George (1910-14); Minnie Lane (1914-17); Wlliam Finch (1917-23); Sidney Brown (1923-1934 when he died); Alice Brown (1934-5); George Cooper (1935-7); Percy Robinson (1937-49); William Biddle (1949 when he died); Doris Hilda Biddle (1950); Reginald Joseph Bulllock (1950-53); Harold Bryan (1953-4); William Frederick Kirkham (1954); Anthony Edward William Fellowes (1954-1964); Thomas Cassell (1964); James Williams (1964-7); Alfred Sutcliffe (1967-9); John Foster (1969)*

C2/12 **Holly Bush**
Also known as: Old Holly Bush
Location: Nicholas Street, St Nicholas Street, also Foregate
Years active: 1734 - 1986

First appears in Register of Victuallers' Recognizance of 1766 under Joseph Nicholls who a few years later had moved virtually next door and is then (1784) running **The Pack Horse.**

Later listed in Grundy Royal Directory 1792 though earlier references go back to the great Foregate Street reconstruction project of the 1730s. Believed to have operated as a pub since 1734, it's a one-time popular town centre venue with a reputation for being where the City's best darts players used to hang out and the best beer in town. A Marston's house, originally Lewis Clarkes whose brewery was about 100 yards away at the bottom of Angel Street which it faced, it was also the start of the famous Station Run in the 1930s - of which, more in a previous chapter.

Listed variously as 21 Garden Market, Nicholas Street and 1 St Nicholas Street and referred to as '**Old Holly Bush**' in Pigot (1835). It's also one of four listed in the Worcester Directory for 1958-9 with a St Nicholas Street address: **Holly Bush** (no1); **Pack Horse** (11); **Imperial** (37); **British Legion Club** (39). On September 3rd 1920 licensee William Downes was fined £10 with £1.1s (£1.05p) solicitor's fee for unlawfully selling rum above maximum

price. Closed as a pub c1986 and until recently the location of Little Venice Italian restaurant *(also since closed).* In 1981 I wrote: '...if you're of a mind to go drinking at ten in the morning, this one's for you 'cos John (Goodband (who'd done a cheeky New Years Eve 'streak' for the benefit, or disgust, of his customers just a few weeks earlier) is open every hour that's allowed by the powers that be. "The hours are there to be used, so I use 'em all" he said – though he added that he'd oppose 2.30 closing *(at the time it was 2pm in Worcester).* He described his primary trade as 'the oldsters' pointing out 'it's not really one for the kids – though I noted it was a good mixers' pub. It was then a

80 years separate these two images of the corner of Foregate Street and St Nicholas Street but the Holly Bush (right) still survives as a building if not as a pub (CCMH/CFOW)

The Holly Bush (centre right) became Little Venice until it too closed in 2013

2-roomer: Bush Bar where I noted 'main business of the day – getting it down yer neck – is pursued with vigour', and Phoenix Lounge that it struck me at the time attracted more women than men. "We're still a drinkers' pub rather than an eaters' pub" reckoned his missis, Anne. It closed 1986 and became a pizza bar, later Italian restaurant Little Venice, now also closed (2013)

Licensees: Joseph Nicholls (1766); Philip Prosser (listed as 'holly bush 21 Garden Market' 1790); John Hobro (1814); Edward Turner (1827); Thomas Turner (1835); Charles Williams (1842–c1870); William Prosser (1872-1878); Jas Humphreys (1878-82); Elizabeth Humphries (1882-85); James Hooper (1885-7); George Knight (1887-1901); Charles H. Townsend (1901-1908); Eliza Phipps (1908-12); Frank Peters (1912-18); William Downes (1918-24 when he died); Elizabeth Downes (1924); Bertie Witherford (1924–1951); Adelina Witherford (1951); Philip Smyth (1951-52); Winifred Waldron (1952-57); Thomas Lennon (1957-71); Peter Holdsworth (1971-2); Patrick Woolman (1972-9); Stuart McEwan (1979-80); John Goodband (1980-3); Anthony Williams (1983-4); Michael Guest (1984-5); Howard Morris (1985)

C2/13 Pack Horse
Also known as: The Courtyard
Location: Garden Market (St Nicholas Street, Nicholas Street)
Years active: 1700 to present

A renowned carriers inn first referred to in Register of Victuallers' Recognizance of 1766 under licensee Thomas Jolly and later Grundy Royal Directory 1792 ('James Wilfon pack-horfe inn 16 Garden Market') but almost certainly pre-dating both by many years. Listed as Garden Market up to the 1840s – then Nicholas Street and later (1870) St Nicholas Street. The census of 1851 shows then licensee Richard Heming living here, described as 'innkeeper' aged 72. Licensee George Thomas was convicted in 1876 for harboring prostitutes here and was fined £10/- plus costs. Later, licensee Joshua Elcox was convicted (1905) for permitting drunkenness here and was fined 20/- plus 32/- costs. Joseph Coombe was convicted in 1916 for permitting drunkenness and fined 40/-. Meanwhile, 25th November 1948 was a bad day for then licensee Frank Beecher Mountjoy: he was fined £30 with £3.3s (£3.15p) costs in total for three counts of selling intoxicating liquor during non-permitted hours to William Knox, Peter West and James Nesbit Long. A Julia Hanson house (later Banks's, now Marstons) it was granted a supper licence, allowing extended drinking hours provided drinks accompanied a meal, on 6th April 1936. In 1961 The Pack Horse first gained fame as an early Berni Inn – a popular and well frequented chicken *(or steak for the better-off)* house where even as late as 1966 a 3-course meal consisting of juice or soup starter, chicken roasted on a spit with chips, peas and half a tomato followed by ice cream sweet'd set you back as much as 6/6d ($32^1/_2$p).

Undergoing constant change over the years, its range of bars has included downstairs Schooner Bar done out like the galley of a sailing ship (but also perhaps referring to the sherry it sold in 'schooner' glasses), rear 'Stable Bar' at the top of the cobbled courtyard, converted to look like a stable (which, in all fairness at one time it probably had been) complete with bales of straw, horses collars and all manner of horsey impedimenta, as well as ever-changing upstairs, ground level and upper level restaurants and bars, plus back rooms and several other little first floor, ground or cellar bars appearing then disappearing. Oh yes... and the famous spit, roasting chickens on a rotisserie in the window and attracting drooling passers-by: for a short time (1967-8) it also operated as a roasted chicken take-away, a whole chicken served in a foil-lined paper bag for 7/6d (37$\frac{1}{2}$p).

Unaccountably changed to **'The Courtyard'** c 2000 after probably 250 years as 'The Packhorse' and one of the City's great meeting-places and favourite multi-bar town centre pubs for generations. For all its changes though, **The Pack Horse, aka The Courtyard,** remains an enduring favourite and a great boy-meets-girl venue – now especially so as evidenced by scantily-dressed young women on the razz with a habit of spilling

The Pack Horse photographed 21st September 1961 (RHS)

out into the road most late evenings and in all weathers. Usual comment on passing by 'look at the state of 'er, she'll catch 'er death'! (and/ or – a comment on the state of déshabille "...you can see what she's had for breakfast!" A Marstons house.

Licensees: Thomas Jolly (1766); Joseph Nichols (1784); James Wilfon (Wilson–1790); Edward Wilson (1814-1840s); Richard Heming (1842–1850s); John Neat (as Pack Horse, commercial inn Nicholas Street' 1855); George Thomas (1872-86); John Perks (1886-1901); Peter Deakin (1901-2); Joshua Elcox (1902-6); Walter

Watkins (1906-8); Mrs. E. Watton (1908-10); Joseph Coombs (1910- 1935); Frank Ferriday (1935-6); Herbert George Stevens (1936-41); Marjorie May Stevens (1941–1946); Frank Beecher Mountjoy (1946-1949); Victor Charles Terry (1949-54); Harold Scott (1954-5); Tudor Gwyn Williams (1955-56); George Warburton (1956-58); Eric Francis Child (1958-61); Michael Tushingham (1961-2); Gerald Webb (1962-4); Hector Bricknell (1964-5); Arthur Crane (1965-6); Hugh McCoy (1966); Stanley Blower (1966- 69); Basil Hacker (1969-70); Frank Brooks (1970-72); Stanley Blower (1972-4); William Marsh (1974-6); James Pegg (1976-7); Windsor Jones (1977-83); Duncan Spandler (1983-85); Robert Jones (1985-6); Peter Matthews (1986-7); Roy Timmins (1987); Current (2013) licensee or dps: Vagorakis Monoyos. Worcester City licence 1084

A run of pubs is also known to have existed around here, but without known locations save 'St Nicholas ward'. As we're at the heart of the ward – St Nicholas church – this seems to be the appropriate place to list them...

Three Tuns
Location: 'St Nicholas ward'
Years active: c1810 - 1830?

Listed in Register of Victuallers' Recognizance of 1814 under Benjamin White and 1827 *(as Three Tunns)* under Richard Hemming. It's possible this is another short-lived name for **The Pack Horse** as Richard Heming is also listed as its licensee 1842-50s. The census of 1851 also lists a Richard Hemming as licensee and innkeeper aged 72 without specifying the specific public house. No further listings and no indication of precise location, though a short-lived incarnation of **The Pack Horse** seems favourite

Dog and Duck
Also known as: Old Dog and Duck
Location: Garden Market (now St Nicholas Street)
Years active: 1820 - 1850

Appears to be short-lived hostelry in Garden Market and Nicholas Street (later St Nicholas Street) dating from around 1810 but not listed after 1855

Licensees: James Taylor (1814); John Taylor (1820); Sarah Bunn (1835 – 1842); Thos. Evans (**now Old Dog and Duck** – 1842 to c1850s); Martha Evans (1855)

Long Sow Cutter
Location: St Nicholas Street
Years active: 1820s – 1840s?

Great name for an inn, thought to be derived from one of the implements used by glovers that once worked in a dozen attics and garrets around here – but that, sadly, appears to be the full extent of the available information.

McBride's Mug House
Location: 'St Nicholas ward'
Years active: 1784-?

Listed in Register of Victuallers' Recognizance of 1784 as in St Nicholas ward under licensee William McBride but

not listed after that so either vanished or was re-named. At the time 'Mug House' was a popular name with at least six so-called in the City *(not including the still open version in Claines which didn't come into the City boundary until the 20th century)* all around the same time.

Old Ewe and Lamb
Location: 'St Nicholas ward'
Years active: 1760s-80s?

Clearly a different house to the much longer lived – and by its name, much younger version listed in Register of Victuallers' Recognizance of 1766 under what appears to be *(but probably isn't, though this is as accurate as I can get given the illegible handwriting)* the fabulously named Protty Mann. No further references so this could be a very old inn now on its last legs, or just particularly short-lived.

Gentlemen and Porter
Location: St Nicholas ward
Years active: 1780-90

Curiously-named one-off inn listed only as 'St Nicholas ward' with no further details save the name of only known licensee William Wright (Register of Victuallers' Recognizance of 1784)

Drum
Location: St Nicholas ward
Years active: 1760s

Location unknown but listed as 'St Nicholas ward' in Register of Victuallers' Recognizance of 1766 under Robert Shinton but no further listings.

Mason's Arms
Location: St Nicholas ward
Years active: 1780s

Location unknown but listed as 'St Nicholas ward' in Register of Victuallers' Recognizance of 1784 under Joseph Stephens Snr, but no further listings, so either an ancient inn on its last legs or just short-lived.

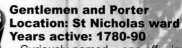

C2/22

O'Neills
Loc: St Nicholas Street
Years active c1990-present

Irish-themed managed bar as noted for its food as for its drink in what was originally Co-op store and butchers, built 1880, and later a variety of other shops including Radio Shack throughout the 70s and 80s. Now seems to have settled on O'Neill's – *slogan Céad míle fáilte (a hundred thousand welcomes)* – since around 1990. But don't be fooled: it's as Irish as Cape Hill in Birmingham and is one of the O'Neills/Reflex chain that's another of the guises of the ubiquitous M&B group that also includes **The Ketch, the Timberdine and Manor Farm)** marketing itself on 'the craic' with a succession of young managers promoting occasional music and games though dominated by sports TV. *Current (2013) licensee* or dps: Kirsty Danielle Gray. Worcester City licence 1159

Imperial (Hotel) also Metro Bar, now Woo Bar
C2/23 Also known as: Brewers Arms, Brewer's Tavern, Yorkshire House, Tap and Spile
Location: 35 (St) Nicholas Street
Years active: 1760-present

Often re-built and re-named inn still in existence and with a colourful history. First listed as Brewer's Arms under licensee James Wilson in the 1784 Register of Victuallers' Recognizance *(four years later he was licensee of the nearby Pack Horse)* and later Jas. Cole, described as 'beer retailer'. 1859 Recognizances reference to name change to **Yorkshire Hous**e. Former Kelsey's house registered at Radford Hall Brewery, Leamington – later Courage's. On 26th April 1895, licensee Richard Tyler was fined £2 with £2.10s (£2.50) costs for harbouring prostitutes here. A favourite squaddies' bar throughout the war years and even into the late 1960s when The Royal Inniskilling Fusiliers, later Royal Irish Rangers, were stationed at Norton Barracks. As a result, the Imperial has always had a reputation for kicking off at the drop of a beret with a past *(and occasional present)* history of violence and affray. For years, many wondered how it was the famous Georgian (1829) mirror that graced the entrance until comparatively recently had managed to survive its turbulent past. Now they just wonder where it's gone. In 1981 I wrote: '...my, oh my, what a surprise! The Imperial as I knew it was just plain not nice at all: the bar's still overshadowed by the original 1820s fittings but the rest is so clean it sparkles'. The Imperial by then had public bar populated with not one but two Space Invaders, fruit machine and overloud juke box I noted, with 'lovely, quiet, beautifully-done lounge plus pool room and five-rooms accommodation. It was then run by Barrie Herbert and Lester Booth who are still fondly recalled more than 30 years on. During refurbishment

1995 workmen reckoned to have disturbed a long-sleeping ghost who mischievously moved tools around and a plumber refused to go back into the cellar after seeing the apparition of a young lad – thought to have been the ghost of a stable boy who died here after being kicked by a horse. Recently (c2000) re-emerged as **Metro Bar** showing sports on a series of

Lowesmoor and St Nicholas Street 1972 - notable for showing three 'live' pubs:
Imperial (left), Old Falcon (centre) and Union ('Flowers' - right. CCMH/CFOW)

The Imperial has rejoiced in a number of names over the years - but none so trendy as the current student influenced 'Woo Bar' (2013 BB)

oversized TVs and attracts a similarly-minded audience with a tendency still (2012) to recreate its dark days as a rough-house. Suffering from a chequered recent history of erstwhile landlords, owners Punch Taverns is currently (2013) on the lookout for a tenant with £20,600 to spare in order to revive the old Imperial's glory days. The Metro is, they say, '...a pub conveniently located in the centre of Worcester. Its exceptional central location brings in good amounts of foot-fall all year round. It is well-known in the community as a destination to watch live televised sports, football in particular. And it is also a popular late-night venue with dancing thanks to regular DJ sets. Inside is quite a large trading area with good spaces for evening and weekend entertainment. Generally, an excellent choice for those with experience in running city pubs. For the future operator of Metro, experience in arranging and staging live entertainment is important, as it's one of the key things it's known for. Along with that, knowledge of marketing and promotion will also be required. The city centre of Worcester is a vibrant location, with a stellar mix of young professionals and students looking for a good night out. All of this provides an excellent foundation on which to build on the pubs existing successes'. Asking price? Damn near £30,000 a year to run... Changed to **Woo Bar** *(oh dear!)* 2013

Licensees: As Brewers Arms: James Wilson (1784); Jas Cole (1855). *As Yorkshire House:* George Henry Hughes (1873). *As Imperial Hotel:* Richard Tyler (1895-); Thomas Birbeck (1902); Arthur J, Radford (1908); William Piff (proprietor –1915); Albert William Jew (1932 -1951); Roy Graham Millingham (1952-3); Thomas Lennon (1953-58); Bertram Lionel Lowe (1958-60); John Dunn (1960-61); Norman Beard (1961-4); Barry Herbert and John Lester Booth (1980s –1990s). **As Metro:** Lucy Grimmett (2000); Alex J. Moody and Joseph Peasgood (2001) Current (2013) licensee or dps: Miss Zoe Anne Atkinson. Worcester City licence 1409

Queen Street and The Trinity (see notes at the opening of this chapter) present a very different outlook to the same view of only a few years ago. At the corner of what's now the car park once stood Gardners Bakery, famous for its dripping cakes, and the rest of the street was always lively – not least late evenings the early 1960s to 1980s when the buses for Ronkswood, Tolladine and Warndon all operated from here and round the corner in The Trinity. 10.30pm any night of the week was the best free amateur boxing – for which read 'free-for-all' – in town.

Dolphin
Location: Queen Street
Years active: 1766-1800

Listed in Register of Victuallers' Recognizance of 1766 under licensee William Davis and under 'Mrs Alfo' in Grundy Royal Directory 1792 described as 'victualler dolphin 5, Queen Street' but no further listings so presumed to have closed not long after.

Peacock Also known as: Old Peacock from 1820
Location: Trinity/Queen Street
Years active: 1760s - 1912

First listed in Listed in Register of Victuallers' Recognizance of 1766 under Ann Bagshaw, widow, and later Grundy Royal Directory 1792 as 1 Trinity and thereafter as Queen Street with a well-catalogued list of licensees. According to H. A. Leicester: 'several inns in the neighourhood also had large storing warehouses, notably **Plough** *('where 19 New Street now is')* **Greyhound, Pheasant, Archangel** *now **The Plough*** in Silver Street, **White Horse** in Silver Street *'on the site of the present lawn adjoining the Public Hall'*, **Peacock** In Queen Street'. It was also occasionally used for inquests. On 12th April 1832, the inquest was held here on Samuel Jones, 22, who, it appears, died of 'a visitation from God'. The census of 1851 shows widowed Lucy Hammond (63 and originally from Eastnor, Herefordshire) as living here apparently alone. Closed c1912 and now the site of former City Council Housing Offices and Weights and Measures depot (a weighbridge stood in the middle of the road here for many years). Now Swinton Insurance and formerly golf equipment shop.

Licensees: Ann Bagshaw (widow–1766); William Baker (1784); John Bullock (described as 'vict {victualler} Peacock' - 1792); Simon Page (1814); William Jenkins (1820); William Teague (1827-35); William Hammond or Hammonds (1835); Lucy Hammond (1842–1850s); James Collins (1855); Thomas Brighton (1872-74); William Baker (1874-6); Thomas Gravenhall (1876-87 when he died); Rhoda Gravenhall (1887-97); Charles W. Evans (1897-99); Walter Willis (1899); Eliz Willis (1899-1903); Mark Hill (1903); William Stokes (1903-5); Thomas Nickisson (1905-6); Harry Yoxall (1906-8); Henry A. Willis (1908).

Site of a long-lived pub called 'The Peacock (later Old Peacock) 1760-1912

Cross Keys
Location: Trinity
Years active: 1760s – 1830

Listed in Register of Victuallers' Recognizance of 1766 under William March but in the same register of 1784, it had been crossed out – so presumably the inn was closed for a short time. Later appears under licensee Henry Knight (Crofs Keys, Trinity - 1795); William Butler (1814 and 1820) but nothing after, so presumed to have closed, though was mentioned by Noake (1877) as one of a number of 'ancient' City inns and could well have been sited in what's now Trinity (or Queen Elizabeth's) house.

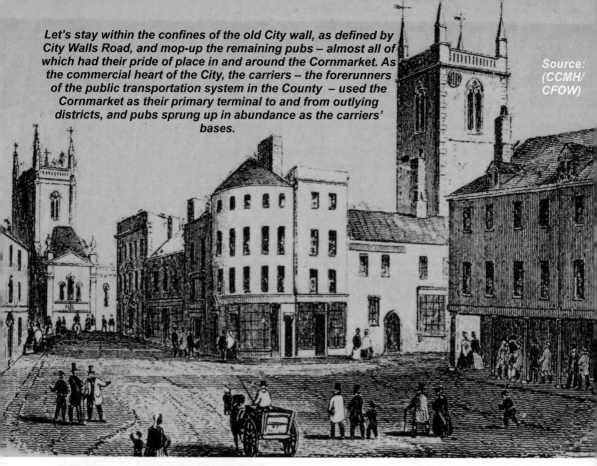

Let's stay within the confines of the old City wall, as defined by City Walls Road, and mop-up the remaining pubs – almost all of which had their pride of place in and around the Cornmarket. As the commercial heart of the City, the carriers – the forerunners of the public transportation system in the County – used the Cornmarket as their primary terminal to and from outlying districts, and pubs sprung up in abundance as the carriers' bases.

As a result, each assumed an agricultural theme as farmers and growers from all over the County converged on the City to sell their produce, and frequented the pubs into which the wagons serving their village came and went on an almost almost daily basis. With the Royal Exchange the centre of corn bartering, all the pubs in the immediate area assumed a partisan stance, and pitched battles by lusty lads from neighbouring villages were not uncommon. Favourites in the area were the King Charles, Fleece, George (Silver Street), Wheatsheaf, Reindeer, New Greyhound, Old Greyhound, Shades, Plough Shades, Queens Head, Old Pheasant, Swan with Two Nicks Royal Exchange and Railway Bell – and not more than 50 yards separating them all! The old stocks for the chastisement of erring citizens was also sited here.

E: The Cornmarket (north side)

C2/27 Holy Lamb
Location: St Martins ward (possibly Cornmarket)
Years active: 1760s
Listed in Register of Victuallers' Recognizance of 1766 under John Band but not subsequently – suggesting it was an ancient inn coming to its end, or that it had its name changed. Not much more is known.

C2/28 White Lyon
Location: St Nicholas ward (probably Cornmarket)
Years active: 1760s-1770s?
Listed in Register of Victuallers' Recognizance of 1766 under John Collins but not subsequently – suggesting it was an ancient inn coming to its end, or that it had its name changed. Not much more is known.

Wheat Sheaf
Location: Corn Market
Years active: 1790 – 1840s

Not much known about this one but with a place in history and a prominent position – as shown in a painting of this historic trading centre of the old City. Listed in Register of Victuallers' Recognizance of 1766 under William Crane.

Licensees: William Crane (1766); John Smith (listed 1792 as 'wheat fheaf inn 12 cornmarket' – to 1820s); Jas. Matthews (1827 and 1835); Esther Matthews (1842) with no listings thereafter implying it had been demolished by then.

White Horse (Inn)
Location: Silver St.
Years active: 1766 - 1880

Included by Noake (1877) as one of a number of City inns, some of which are 'probably not much less ancient than...' 1517. Listed in the Register of Victuallers' Recognizance of 1766 under Ann Barnett (described as 'widow') later (1814) James Chesterton.

Hubert Leicester wrote that: 'several inns in the neighourhood also had large storing warehouses, notably **Plough** (where 19 New Street now is) **Greyhound, Pheasant, Archangel** now **The Plough** in Silver Street, **White Horse** in Silver Street on the site of the present lawn adjoining the Public Hall, **Peacock** In Queen Street'. The White Horse which vanished around 1880 had enjoyed a brief period of fame in 1824 when Irishman Jack Langon who had challenged the then Champion Prize Fighter of England (Herefordshire born Tom Spring, real name Summers, though some say Winter) made **The White Horse** his HQ ahead of the championship bare-knuckle prize fight that's reputed to have attracted 40,000 spectators on Pitchcroft. It's said that Worcester was chosen as the location as it was the half-way point between Spring's home in London and Langon's disembarkation at Liverpool. 'Spring fought two bloody fights against the Irish fighter Jack Langan. The two boxers had very different styles: Spring was light on his feet and fast, while Langan was slower and heavier and Spring was victorious on both occasions'. *(Wikipedia)*. Says Hubert Leicester in 'Worcester Remembered': '...the fight was with bare fists and extended over eighty rounds, until Langan was carried off by force, struggling to continue. It seems several spectators' stands collapsed during the fight, 'injuring over a hundred persons'. The census of 1851 shows then licensee William Probert (30) living here with his wife Mary (34).

Licensees: Ann Barnett (1766); Jonathan Chesterton – listed as 'white horfe inn 26 Silver Street' 1790); James Chesterton (1814–c1826) James Clarke (1827-30s); Jeremy John (listed as 'White Horse Inn, Silver Street (Post House)' 1842); William Probert (1851); Allard William Thomas ('White Horse railway and commercial inn, Silver Street' 1855); Charles Bowell (1872-74); William Bedford (1874-6) Thought to have closed not long after.

Commercial
Location: 5 Silver Street
Years active: 1780s

Little known inn save an oblique 1780s reference in Victuallers Recognizances.

George
Location: Silver Street
Years active: 1850-60

Only known reference Billings Directory of Worcestershire 1855 under licensee William Iles - listed as 'beer retailer'

Falstaff
Location: Silver Street
Years active 1790s

Only one reference Worcester Royal Direcctory 1790 under Mary Hankins. Precise location and further details unknown

Pheasant
Location: Silver Street
Years active:

Listed in Register of Victuallers' Recognizance of 1766 under John (name illegible) but not subsequently. It's believed that this original **Pheasant** was coming to the end of its life and that in 1787 then licensee, Mrs Eleanor Morris, moved from here to set up a new **Pheasant** in New Street: that one is still in existence.

As I wrote in an article in December 1987, 'in any other City, Mealcheapen Street would have been lauded, feted and looked on as... a rare gem of a thoroughfare'. That said, it remains as one of the better examples of conservation working to preserve something architecturally worthwhile... the former home of civic dignitaries, prominent and well-heeled citizens, the City's first post office, prime coaching inn and several pubs. Mealcheapen Street was for centuries the market for meal traders, leading to the City's real commercial heart, The Cornmarket.

The Cross
C2/35 **Location: Cornmarket**
Years active:1600s?

Several references have been made to The Cross, reputed to have stood in The Cornmarket, but information is sketchy and few details are known

King Charles II
C2/36 **Also known as: Slug and Lettuce. King Charles (from 1970). Tubs. Barrels. Bar 12.**
Location: 12, Cornmarket
Years active: 1850s - present

One of several Worcester pubs that shares a wall with another pub – in this case **The Royal Exchange** – the often-re-christened **King Charles II,** now **Bar 12** but possibly something else by the end of next week, had been a popular draw in its earlier incarnations but now opens evenings and weekends appearing to cater mostly for a younger night-time disco and live music audience. In its days when it rejoiced in being, as I recall, four or even five cosy little snugs, a whole suit of armour stood in one of the bars when flamboyant landlord, generously-moustachioed City councilor and mayor Arthur Sage ran it during the mid-60s. A former coaching inn it was also noted for wooden seats made out of former beer barrels (hence the name) as well as 'big black doors and cobbles up the middle' *(Source: Andrea McGrath whose uncle Derek Hancocks ran it with his wife Joyce in the 1970s).* In 1981 and by then bashed about to become '...just one great big crazy mixed-up bar full of great big crazy mixed-up kids' though redeeming itself with a vestige of some of the neat little alcoves, padded seats and carpets it had earlier rejoiced in, I described then licensee and self-confessed nut-case Ray Lewis as a fast-talking, fast-quipping Brummie who admitted: '...we're a kids' pub and there's nothing wrong with that, because the kids treat it with respect. On the other hand, if you can't bring your wife and mother-in-law in, there's something wrong. You *can* bring 'em in – it's noisy, but you can bring 'em in!' He went on to greet one middle-aged lady punter with 'Mornin'

1965: Source: Jim Sargeant

CHARLES EDWARDS. LTD

The King Charles

2013 (BB)

The Public Hall and the King Charles, Cornmarket Source: (CCMH/CFOW)

Source: (CCMH/CFOW)

flower, welcome home. How was prison?' a comment that today'd have the authorities crashing down on him. I noted that in true King Charles tradition, and not for the first time, it had taken on the character of its gaffer – with the inevitable result that you'd either love it or detest it. By then an Ansells house selling only keg beer (*'over-pressurised, over-chilled and over-priced' I wrote*). It was then 52p for mild and 55p for bitter. Ray Lewis later took over **The Drakes Drum** after which he's believed to have returned to the construction industry. In its latest incarnation, **Bar12**, it now describes itself as '...nestled in the Cornmarket of Worcester's city centre, this is one stylish destination venue you won't want to miss!' Calling itself 'the city's most perfect choice for a perfect night out' on its website *(http://www.bartwelve.co.uk/)* and offering music on a Friday evening, opening times are: Mon & Tues – available for exclusive hire, Weds & Thurs 6pm until 2am, Friday 4pm until 2am, Saturday 12pm until 2am, closed Sunday (except Bank Holidays). Now a Punch Taverns inn, registered at Burton-upon-Trent.

Licensees: Francis Dingle (1872-1904); Sarah Pitt (1904-7); William Edwards (1907- 32); Henry Probert (1932-8); Granville Tudge (1938-45); William Smith (1945-52); Arthur Sage (1952-4); Frank Eden (1954-6); George Roberts (1956-67); Arthur Wild (1967-8); Arthur Sage (1968-74); Janet Partington (1975); David Partington (1975); Derek Hancocks (1975-9); Frederick Brown (1979); Ray Lewis (1979-82); Ian McIlroy (1982-3); Derek Boylin (1983-4); Hugh Corbett (1984-5); David Cappendell (1985); Robert Hulme (1985) As Slug and Lettuce: Ken Powell (2000). Current (2013) licensee or dps: Darren Eden. Worcester City licence 1175

C2/37 Royal Exchange (Wine and Spirit) Vaults
Location: Corn Market/Mealcheapen Street
Years active: 1870 – present

Well-documented M&B house in prime position (listed as 13 Mealcheapen Street and also as 14 Corn Market and Cornmarket) that had also been the site of two earlier pubs: **The Rodney** and before that **The Prince's Arms**. The Exchange as you see it today proudly held a once grand reputation and it's long-term favourite with generations of Worcester folk and especially visiting servicemen. (*My Auntie Dot and 'Para' Uncle Bill met here in 1942, and four decades on they pointed*

The names of the shops have changed - but not a lot else!

(Source: CCMH/ CFOW)

Worcester. Mealcheapen Street. Ama Series 532.

out to me the very spot). Ceramic tiles and sand-blasted windows still survive as lasting tribute to Victorian craftsmanship. Dates from 1870s to present day, and still in operation seemingly largely unchanged since its 1940s-50s hey-day – though lately emblazoned with national teams' flags and much given over to over-sized TVs showing endless sport and large tattooed men shouting at the telly.

Licensees: *William Henry Bennett; G. Morrell (1872-80); Joseph Pratt (1880-1); William Belwood (1881-86 when he died); Penelope Belwood (1881); E. Bennet (1887); Louisa Daws (1887-97); Stephen Overall (1897-99); George Morroll (1899-1906); James Wooding (1906-9); Seymour John Melhuish 1909-1933); Philip Henry Penney (1934-57 when he died); listed as Royal Exchange Hotel 13 Cornmarket'; Edwin Percy Bennett (1958-59): Kenneth Edward Cleveley (1959-60); Godfrey Johnson (1960-1); Denis Lancaster (1961); John Stevens (1961-2); Douglas Slater (1962-4); Roy Noble (1964-5); Albert Morrison (1965-7); Peter Griffiths (1967-71); Colin Smith (1971-4); Francis Poole (1974-6); Alan Harris (1976—8); Steve Calder (1978-9); Paul Stanyard (1979-83); Douglas MacMillan (1983-6); Ronald Rainbow (1986); Richard Baker (1986); Ray Brierley (2000) Adrian Birch*

C2/37 **The Prince's Arms** once stood on the same site – one of several built in the post Civil War years at the end of the 17th century (new ones at the time are said to have included **The King's Head** Sidbury, **The Bear** at west side of the bridge, **The Ship** at the Quay, **The Crown** in Sidbury, and **The Rose** in Foregate Street) This later gave way to:

C2/37
The Rodney
Location: Cornmarket
Years active: 1780 - 1800

Little known inn listed only in Grundy Royal Directory 1792 under stewardship of Thomas Hyde – described as 'vict' (victualler), Rodney 14 Cornmarket. George Brydges Rodney, 1st Baron Rodney, KB (bap. 13 February 1718 – 24 May 1792) was a British naval officer best known for his commands in the American War of Independence, particularly his victory over the French at the Battle of the Saintes in 1782. It is often claimed that he was the commander to have pioneered the tactic of "breaking the line". The use of Rodney as a first name originates with the admiral. It became a popular name for boys at the end of the eighteenth century *(Wikipedia)*

unk
Bellman
Also known as: Three Crowns
Location: precise location unclear although it could instead be in the High Street)
Years active: 1700s – 1870

Mentioned by Noake (1877) as one of a number of 'ancient' City inns, some of which are probably not much less ancient than the eighteenth or even 17th century.. Listed 1734 as one of 23 Worcester inns where qualifying voters could cast their ballot. Also known as **The Three Crowns**, it was described in Berrows Journal (1813) as '...well accustomed and conveniently built for a public house or private family with a good brew-house and chambers separate from the dwelling house and a good stable, backside and other conveniences. Enquire of the widow Mason or Mr. Andrew, attorney in Worcester'. *Note: also listed in C3 High Street*

unk
Lion
Location: unclear. Cornmarket or poss High Street
Years active: 1600s

Location unclear, but possibly here or in the High Street, mentioned by Noake (1877) as one of a number of 'ancient' City inns, some of which are 'probably not much less ancient than the eighteenth or even 17th century'. Alternatively, it could also possibly refer to other 'Lions' in the City including The White Lion off Lowesmoor and another of the same name said to have been sited in the Cornmarket.

C2/38   **The Stag Inn** at Worcester is also mentioned at the time of Charles II by M. Jorevin (Antiq. Rep ii 59) and it's suggested its location was around here, but there's no certainty of that.

C2/39
Shades (and Shades Tavern)
Also known as: Piaf's Wine Bar
Location: Mealcheapen Street
Years active: 1820 - 1970

One of Worcester's most celebrated inns, once a fine Georgian house in one of the City's main commercial areas that has at various times also served as private home to the Russell family (described as 'one of the principal families in St Martins parish'), one of Worcester's foremost banks, a coffee house, a hotel and the City's main post office. First listed Worcester Lewis Directory 1820 shown variously as **Shades Tavern and Hotel** at 16 Mealcheapen Street, in 1831, The Worcester Herald ran an advertisement for letting: the edit ran: '...this house for its dimensions and central position is well calculated either as an inn or residence of a medical man, attorney or any trade requiring room'. The census of 1851 shows then licensee widow Elizabeth Simmonds, aged 39, as 'head', her husband Francis having died not much earlier yet still describing herself as 'innkeeper's wife'.

CRUMBIE'S HOTEL AND RESTAURANT,
MEALCHEAPEN ST., WORCESTER.

Every Accommodation for Visitors, Cyclists, and Commercials.

A GOOD DINNER from 1/-

Wines and Spirits from the Wood.
Of the Highest Quality.

JOHN SUFFIELD.

N.B.—The only Full-Licensed Restaurant in the City.

DINNERS à la Carte (daily): SOUP or Fish, Joint or Poultry, Sweets, Cheese and Salad, 2 -

Also living there was James Neal ('boarder'), Thomas Cook, Amelia Ferrit ('barmaid'), Eliza Garneston ('cook'), Ann Jones ('waiter') and Robert Munro ('boots'). Almost 60 years on, it was noted for being the home of Austin's Noted Tripe Rooms specialising in fresh tripe and ox heels daily with special attention given to the preparation, in Neatsfoot Oil, and tripe suppers under proprietorship of F. E. Austin *(see list of licensees below, 1910).* It's said that it was here that the father of Sir Edward Elgar found

Only the building remains of what was once one of Worcester's most famous inns, The Shades - now a stationer's (BB)

The Shades much to his liking when he first arrived in the City – going on to marry the landlord's sister Anne Greening. Their illustrious son also found the meeting place of his folks much to his liking too and was a frequent visitor. Originally a Kelsey's house registered at Radford Hall Brewery Leamington, it was transferred to Wolverhampton and Dudley Breweries, now Banks's. Popular with high-ranking GIs in the war and the scene of some bloody confrontations between sqaddies, it was still open up to the early 1970s before being turned into a wine bar under the name **Piaf's.** It's now run as a stationers with nothing of the old pub's old interior remaining.

Licensees: *James Glover (1820); Thomas Martin (1835); Francis Simmonds (1842 – 1850); Elizabeth Simmonds (1851 - ??); John Crumbie (1872-84); Ann Crumbie (1884-91 When she died); Jane Crumbie (1892-98); John Suffield (1898-1901); Styles Willis (1901-02); Frederick Edwards (1902-03); Joseph Yarnold (1903-07 when he died); Mrs Ada Yarnold (listed as Shades Restaurant 1907-08); Fred Austin - also listed as Shades Restaurant, 1908-12); Henry Wearing (1912-16 when he died listed as The Shades Restaurant and tripe dresser); Rabina Wearing (1917); Florence Sandland (1917-19); Isabella Sandland (1919-25); George Brookbank (1925-26); Thomas Tomkins (1926-7); William Peckham (1927-31); William Yarnold (1931-3); William Strain (1933-5); John D'Arcy (1935-6); Albert Wilcox (1936-7); Alfred Thomas Homer (1937); John Meller, Shades Tavern (1937-48); William Powell (1948-9); Ernest Hodgetts (1949-51); Anthony Eric Greenaway (1951-2); Regina Walker (1952- 3); John Scolley Thurling (1953-4); William Parton (1954-5); Henry Primmer (1955-56); John Dunne (1956-59); Henry William Herbert Watson (1959-61); Ernest Knowles (1961-3); Clifford Wallis (1963-6); Russell Potter (1966).*

The march of progress - the eastern aspect of The Cornmarket c1910 (Source: CCMH/CFOW)

The two other pubs in Mealcheapen Street – The Reindeer and The Fleece are discussed in Chapter 10. Rejoining the High Street at The Cross, we've now come full circle. Let's now look at two ancient inns that stood side by side on the other side of that great dividing line The City Walls (or in modern-day speak City Walls Road) and thence along a once great location for pubs, the legendary Lowesmoor with its 'Big Boys Station Run'

E - D **Lowesmoor – St Martins Gate**

(1965. Source: Jim Sargeant)

Plough
Also known as: The Archangel Angel
Location: Silver Street
Years active: 1873 - 1971

Almost certainly the same **Plough** mentioned by Noake (1877) as one of a number of 'ancient' City inns, some of which are probably not much less ancient than the eighteenth or even 17th century,

(Source: CCMH/CFOW)

...and the same view today (BB)

this was originally **The Archangel** with its location described as 'in or near The Cornmarket'. Later, from around 1790 to 1860, it became **The Angel** before re-emerging as **The Plough**. According to Hubert Leicester: 'several inns in the neighourhood also had large storing warehouses, notably **Plough** (where 19 New Street now is) **Greyhound, Pheasant, Archangel** now **The Plough** in Silver Street, **White Horse** in Silver Street *(described as being 'on the site of the present lawn adjoining the Public Hall)* and **Peacock** In Queen Street'. The census of 1851 shows then licensee John Pearse (39) living here with his wife Sarah 32. Listed variously as St Martins Gate (1910); Silver Street and 4, Silver Street (1940), for most of its history the Plough was an important venue for County carriers in the 19th century, carriers to and from Broadheath, Castle Hill, Crowle, Powick, Shrawley, Tibberton and the ancient faraway village of Warndon operating from here. It was also occasionally used for inquests: on 19th May 1827 an inquest was held here on Charles Price 'aged about 5' found drowned in a ditch. The Plough was also popular with American servicemen during the war, and a GI was murdered here in or about 1942 during a knife-fight between two US servicemen. On 6th October 1958, licensee Herbert Walter Morton was fined £15 with 15/- (75p) costs and £1gn (£1.05p) advocate's costs in that he 'did counsel, procure and command Horace Turner to make false entry on a delivery sheet and the same for receiving a crate of beer'. A long-term survivor lasting up to 1970s before falling to the bulldozer to make way for City Walls Road, the building erected in its place was lately the site of Jaguar dealers and is now (2013) The Bed Centre.

Licensees First listed as 'angel inn 1 Silver ftreet' under licensees as John Hay (1792); Richard Hayes (1820); Thomas Earl (1827); George Lock, Angel, Silver st (1842); John Jeremy (1835); Charles Mills (1850); John Pearse (1851); Richard Hawton (1872-79); Josiah Beckley (1879-92 when he died); Mrs Betsy Beckley (1893-1906); Henry Lee (1906-7 when he died); Mrs Florence Edith Lee (1908-1929); Frederick Charles Clarkson (also listed as brewer 1929-1939); Raymond G. Rivett (1939-40); Josephine Rivett (1940-5); Lawson Wilfred Hacker (1944-552); Raymond Thorpe (1952-3); Reginald Walker (1953-54); Reginald Walker (1953-4); Archibold Sinclair (1954); Harold Palmer (1954-6) William Watkins Pritchard (1956-57); Herbert Walter Morton (1957-1964)

Right next door to it (on the south side) stood:

C2/41
Railway Bell
Also known as: The Bell
Location: Clap Gate (St Martin's Gate)
Years active: 1850s – 1912

Mentioned by Noake (1877) as one of a number of 'ancient' City inns, it was described in 1764 as 'adjoining St Martins gate, old Cornmarket'. Listed in Baylis, Lewis Almanack 1885-8 as 'one among the ancient hostelries (which) were **The Bush, the Rein-Deer, The White Horse, The Talbot in Sidbury, the Lion, the Bull, the Bear in Hylton Street, and the Saracen's Head** among others, it's listed as 1 St Martins Gate and was sited next door to **The Plough**. First listed in Billings Directory of Worcestershire 1855 **The Railway Bell** was a popular, some say even renowned, music hall in its day (c1850s – 1912) said to have been a large room over the pub, known as The Club Room with a stage at one end and, just before its demise a plaque proclaiming that the great Worcester-born entertainer (she was best known as a male impersonator) Vesta Tilley had performed there. Clearly highly popular in its day, a recent newspaper report tells of women calling on the landlady not to serve their husbands as they were spending all their wages in the Railway Bell Music Hall and returning home penniless. Law and order was apparently kept by a 20-stone bouncer called 'Nipper Romney'.

Licensees: Charles Coxall (as 'beer retailer' – 1855); (listed, no licensee's name, Littlebury's 1873); Wm Lane (1900); Mrs C. Hunt (1902); George Ambrose Price (1908). No further listings.

D-G: Lowesmoor

C2/42
Union (Inn, Tavern, Hotel)
Location: Lowesmoor
Years active: c1810 – 1971

Long-lasting (c1810s –1960s), well-documented Flowers (latterly a Whitbread) house on the corner of Lowesmoor/Watercourse Alley that had once been the boundary of the old City wall and even up to late 1960's had a ditch *(and watercourse)* running through it, taking its name from the Union with Ireland just a few years before its was built (1801). Listed as Union Tavern in Register of Victuallers' Recognizance of 1814 under licensee Robert Ingram. The census of 1851 shows then licensee Joseph Bromfield (48) living here with his wife Mary (50), with two sons, three daughters

The Union
Lowesmoor, 21st
September 1961
(Source: RHS)

and the same 19,000
days later! (BB)

and a servant. Licensee John Keeping was convicted in 1876 for selling after hours here and was fined £1 plus costs and two years later convicted for being drunk on the premises and fined 1/- plus costs. Popular and sporty, a one-time landlord Frank Meredith is reputed to be a winner of the Croix de Guerre – a distinction he shares with actors Audie Murphy and James Stewart, dancer Josephine Baker and Cher Ami, a homing pigeon.

Licensees: *Robert Ingram (1814); William Ward (1827); Jos. Ward (1829-1840s); Joseph Bromfield (1842 – c1870s); Henry Bromfield (also listed as ' brewer' 1875); John Keeping (1875-90); Samuel Thomas Castle (1890-1900); Alexander French (1900-02); Kate Newey (1902-4); Thomas Reeve (1904-6); George Wheld (1906-8); John Margrett (1908); John Norman (1908-13); Frederick Austin (1913-14); Albert John Hale (1914- 1936); Frederick Meredith (1936-7); Horace Smith (1937-8); Edward Wright (1938-42); Alfred Mayo (1942); Gertrude Victoria Shaw (1942-53); Reginald Joseph Bullock (1953-56); Joseph Thomas Tedale (1956-7); James Waldron (1957-61); Frank Eastwood (1961-5); Anthony Shelley (1965-6); Alfred Evans (1966); Jose Knighton (1966-8); Mrs J Knighton (1968-70); Edward Wilkes (1970)*

C2/43 Crown & Anchor
Location: Lowesmoor/ Silver Street
Years active: 1790 - 1962

Corner site Lewis Clarke's pub (Lowesmoor and Silver Street) first referred to in Grundy Royal Directory 1792 and listed variously as 'crown & anchor 15 Silver ftreet (1792); 50 Silver Street and 36 Lowesmoor (1900); 38 Silver St (1910); 12 Lowesmoor and 38 Silver Street (1940). Licensee Edwin Harmen was convicted in 1878 for selling to a drunken person and fined 20/- plus costs and again convicted of the same offence five years later and fined £1 plus costs. Closed c1962

Licensees: *Joseph Lightburn (1792); Thomas Jackson (1814); John Chandler (1820); Thomas Williams (1927); Wm Cole (1829); Isaac Roberts (1835); Wm Higgs 1842–c1870; Ann Jevons (1872-76); Edwin Harman (1876-1900); George Vivian (1900-03); Albert Woskett (1903-05); James*

The Crown and Anchor survived to the good old age of 192 but finally fell to the bulldozer in 1970 after lying empty for 8 sad years

Source CCMH/ CFOW

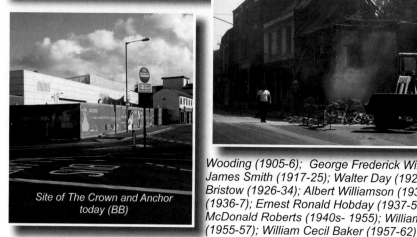

Site of The Crown and Anchor today (BB)

Wooding (1905-6); George Frederick Williams (1906-1917); James Smith (1917-25); Walter Day (1925-6); John Harold Bristow (1926-34); Albert Williamson (1934-6); Alfred Evans (1936-7); Ernest Ronald Hobday (1937-53); George Hector McDonald Roberts (1940s- 1955); William James Steele (1955-57); William Cecil Baker (1957-62)

C2/44

Boat
Location: 17 Lowesmoor
Years active: c1800 to 1965

Listed as Boat inn 26 Lowesmoor, later 17 Lowesmoor. c1800 to 1965. One of six listed 1957-8 Worcester Directory with Lowesmoor address: **Boat (17), Black Horse (39), Alma (53), Union (2), Crown and Anchor (12), Meco Sports and Social Club (50)**. A noted home brew house, the ale must have been top-notch as on October 15th 1897 licensee George Owins was fined 10/- (50p) with 19/6d (9$\frac{1}{2}$d) costs for being found drunk on his own licensed premises here. A few years earlier, on Nov 3rd 1892, licensee William Watts had been fined 21/- (£1.10p) with £1.17.6 (£1..75p) costs for unlawfully supplying intoxicating liquor to a police constable on duty without authority, and on 8th January 1916, Cecil John Instan did, '...by the hands of his servant or agent supply to William Stuart Hundley as the measure of intoxicating liquor for which he asked an amount exceeding that measure'. He was fined 40/- (£2). The original building was owned by long-term (1930-60) licensee Cecil George Instan (and probably his father Cecil John Instan) then sold to Worcester Co-operative Society for £5,000 on October 3rd 1960. Demolished 1970s, now Co-op Funeral Services

Licensees: *James Featherstone (1820); James Taylor (1827-40s); Wm Thomas (1842); Benjamin Turley (1850); James Hobro (1855); Charles Page (1872-76); Thomas Harris (1876-77); Lucy Harris (1877-8); William Thomas (1878-90); Thomas Wood (1890-2); George Owins (1892-8); William and Mrs Fanny Watts (1898-1915); Cecil John Instan (1915-1934); Annie Instan (1934-6); Cecil George Instan 1930-60); Peggy Elizabeth Mantle (1960-5)*

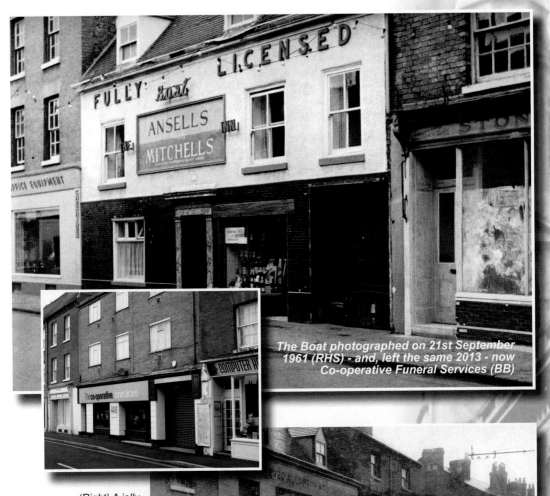

The Boat photographed on 21st September 1961 (RHS) - and, left the same 2013 - now Co-operative Funeral Services (BB)

(Right) A jolly boys' outing from The Boat c1920 then run by Cis Instan. The Boat was also on the famous Station Run of the 1930s

(Source: CCMH/CFOW)

Express (Inn)
Location: Lowesmoor
Years active: 1850 – 1910

First listed in Billings Directory of Worcestershire 1855 Situated at 49 Lowesmoor next to Post Office on east side. Had closed as public house 1911 and became part of Lowesmoor Post Office. This became a refreshment house from 1879 till 89 when it was called **The Volunteer**. It reverted back to being called **The Express** not long after.

Licensees: Edward L. Harrison (1855); Thomas Smith (1873); Thomas O'Neil (1876); Hannah Reece William Dowding (1879-85); Arcade Gandin (1886-7); Mary Geirard (1887-9); Henry Thurston (1889-98); George Houghton (1898-1901); James Davis (1901); Reuben James (1901-2); William Wiltshire (1902-3); James Phillips (1903-7); Walter A. Grove (1907);

C2/45

Dove
C2/46

Location: Lowesmoor

Years active: 1840s to 1870

First referred-to in Billings Directory of Worcestershire 1855 but clearly existed in the decade before then as the census of 1851 shows then licensee John Hartland (listed as 'beer retailer'). Not shown on 1880 OS so closed by then. Just two doors down stood...

Black Horse
C2/47

Location: 39 Lowesmoor

Years active: 1820 (possibly pre-1760s) - 1965

A Black Horse was listed in Register of Victuallers' Recognizance of 1766 under Joseph Dunn, and in 1814 under Alice Morgan (listed as 'widow') but location unknown save for 'St Martins ward' and no further listings – which suggests it was one and the same as its later incarnation or was one situated close by and its name given to a new **Black Horse** in the then undeveloped area of Lower Moor, later Lowesmoor, in or about 1820. A venue for County carriers in the 19th century, carriers to and from Broughton Hackett (Saturdays 4.30pm) operated from here. Listed in Pigot's Worcestershire Directory (1829) and address variously as Lowesmoor, 16 Lowesmoor (1910), 17 Lowesmoor (1900) and 39 Lowesmoor (1940) this was a Robert Allen, later Banks's inn that featured on the Big Boys Station Run with a room at the back that hosted sporting events, boxing being especially popular. On September 20th 1920 licensee Thomas Pulling found himself hauled up before City magistrates on three charges: two counts of unlawfully selling gin above maximum price and a third of unlawfully selling rum otherwise than by measure. He ended up paying fines of £25 and costs of £1.10s (£1.50p) or one month's imprisonment. My group The Skeeters played our very first semi-pro gig here May 1963: fee £5. Closed two years later *(no relationship between the two events)* it became motorbike shop. Still standing, though now a second-hand furniture shop the well-remembered Black Horse gave it name to newly-created alleyway through to 80s housing development in Sansome Place.

The Black Horse on this and the facing page was a highly popular pub for all sorts of reasons.

Source: (left JAS)
Top right 2nd March 1958 (RHS)

**Licensees:
(possibly)**
Joseph Dunn
(1766); Alice
Morgan (1814).
Known: Thomas
Watkins (1820);
Wm. Day (1827);
Thomas Francis
(1835 as Lowes
Moor); George
Mantle, (1842,
1850 and 1855);
Daniel Mason
(1872-84); Henry
Roan (1884-7);
Charles Blackford
(1887-95);
Ernest Styche
(1895-7); George
Skillington (1897);
George Hayward (1897-8); Harry Yoxall (1898-1902); William Everall (1902-3); Edwin Chivers (1903-4); Chas Parsons (1904- 14); Albert Sheldon (1914-16); Thomas Pulling (1916-21); Edward Linnington (1921-7); Charles Gilbert (1927-8 when he died); Mary Gilbert (1928); Harry Silverthorn (1928-9); Richard Harker (1929-30); John Byers (1930-1); William Wood (1931-2); Leighton Maybury (1932–1941 when he died); Muriel Maybury (1941-4); Leighton Maybury (1944-51); Albert James Harris (1951-52); Cecil James Catchpole (1952-55); Christian Altenberg Hansen (1955-58); John Brook Holding Webb (1958-62); Dalcie Webb (1962-9); Edwin Nicholls (1969-70); Blanch Harris (1970). Closed following year.

Let's take a small diversion down Black Horse Walk to recall two pubs that stood close by. At the end of the walk, turn right and the building now facing you was once...

Elephant and Castle
Location: Sansome Place
Years active: 1850 - 1971

Popular bargemens' inn, appears first in Billings Directory of Worcestershire 1855 and listed variously as 'Sansome pl.' (1900); Lowesmoor Wharf (1910) Sansome Lane (1957); 24 Sansome pl' (1958). Named after a popular mispronunciation of the name of successive princesses of Spain – 'Infanta of Castille' – and run by three generations of the same family over a 75-year period. Licensee Thomas Smith was convicted in 1876 for selling out of hours for which he was fined £2 and then in 1880 for permitting drunkenness and he was fined a further £2 plus costs. The building was eventually bought and owned by Sarah Anne Smith, described as 'spinster', who paid £3,550 for the building on 20th January 1944. A Marstons house, it closed c1975 and lay derelict when it became a haven for druggies and drop-outs until the badly decomposed body of a young man, thought to have been a drug addict was discovered there during conversion into flats. The building is now looking very attractive in its new guise, seemingly enjoying a new lease of life.

Licensees: Joseph Green (listed as 'beer retailer 1855); Mary Ann Brown (1872-4); Thomas Middleton (1874-6); Thomas Smith (1876-92); John Smith (1892-3); Fred J.W. Green (1893–1906); John Smith (also listed as brewer 1906-37 when he died); Mrs Sarah Maria Smith (1937–1940s); Sarah Anne and Rose A. Smith (1937);

White Lion
Also known as: The Lion
Location: Lowesmoor Close
Years active: 1842 – 1870s

Listed variously as White Lion, Lowesmoor Close (1842) and White Lion, Lowesmoor Wharf (1855) the inn in what would now be at the head of Lion Walk – hence the name - seems to have been fairly short-lived, with just 3 licensees listed: *William Probert (1842); Charles Beesley (1843); James Cowles (1855). Closed 1870s*

Return to Lowesmoor to pick up from where we left off....

Alma (now, Pig and Drum)
Also known as Toad and Tulip
Location: 53, Lowesmoor
Years active: 1850s to present

The Alma c1964 (Source: JAS) and above right 1970s (CCMH/CFOW)

First listed Victuallers Recognizances 1859 and later Littlebury's Directory of the County of Worcester 1873, the Alma address is given variously as 10 Lowesmoor (1873) and 53 Lowesmoor. The Alma, originally owned by brewers Robert Hitchman and Co of 26 Bridge Street Banbury, later Mitchells and Butlers, was never anything but a modest kind of boozer and has since suffered from a variety of meaningless name changes.

On 8th January 1916, licensee Arthur Edward Hale was fined 40/- (£2) or one calendar month's imprisonment for '...by the hands of his servant or agent did supply to William Stuart Handley the measure of intoxicating liquor for which he asked an amount exceeding that measure'. In 1958-9 it was listed as 'Alma Inn, 53 Lowesmoor; fully licensed, snack bar, E. A. Caterer, proprietor'. Sharp-suited landlord Ron Hale (1955-56) earned the title 'The Duke of Lowesmoor' while running The Alma. He'd earlier been in business as a bookie with his father Jack and claimed to be the only Worcester publican who was also a tic-tac man! For years also the favoured haunt of George 'Honky' Fletcher, famed fish and chip man whose shop was just 50 yards away. On the *Bob Backenforth's Worcester Pubs Then and Now* FB Friends page, Pete Browning said '...I had my first legal pint in the Alma, my Dad and Uncle George took me in. Stood next to Honky Fletcher of fish & chip shop fame and he drank his pint in the time it took me to pick mine up, he drank three more and back to the shop!'.

Noted too as being one of the first pubs run by **Beehive** legend 'Honest' Barrie Ward (1974-81)

In 1981 I wrote of the Alma, then home to its new owners, Cockneys Jim and Glenda Birch, for just five weeks: '...you'd be hard-pushed to find a pub that scores so strong on the tatty stakes yet comes over so strong in the friendly league' I wrote. 'Let's get the record straight, this is tattsville with doors that don't fit any too well, damp patches, crumbling plaster and tiny snugs. And if there was any paper on the walls then I didn't notice it. It's where the loo's up a passageway and outside through a fair representation of a junkyard and looks the kind of place you wipe your feet on the way out. For all that – zing! The magic's there'! I even recorded that 'a twinkly-eyed rogue called Dave who was well-known around town, even bought me a pint (at 48p). I described it as '...smoke room, games room and bar that all look as though they're crumbling at the seams, plus skittle alley that looks as though it already has – horrifying to some, sheer paradise to others'. Later, re-dubbed **The Toad and Tulip**, it is currently **The Pig and Drum** – but now one big *(and still tatty)* room. In 2012 it was at the centre of a well-publicised spat between its outrageously flamboyant licensee Dean Awford and his live-in boyfriend and said to have involved one being hit over the head with some kind of an implement. They have since split up and new tenants installed, though rumour has it some cross-dressers are still known to frequent their old haunt *(comment overheard recently 'it's where they like to eat, drink and be Mary'!)*

Licensees: John Hudson (1859); Alfred Hill (1872-84); Edwin Hiron (1884-93); Frederick Harris (1893-95); Charles Louch (1895-7); Frances E. Crockett (1897-1901); Francis Harwood (1901-2); William Morris (1902-3); Abraham Lamb (1903-8); Arthur Hale (1908-1934); George Brown (1934-5); James Ross Wark (1935-9); Ernest Arthur Caterer (1939-1950); Gerald Edward Bowen (1950-54); Ivor Dennis Jenkins (1954-56); Ronald Frederick Hale (1956-66); Frederick Barker (1966-72); John Merry (1972-4); Barrie Ward (1974-81) John Stevens and Phillip Lewis (1981-2); Jim and Glenda Birch (1982-9); Terence Parsons (1989); Andy Loizou (2000); Andrew R. Ralphs (2001); Dean Awford (2010....). Current (2013) licensee or dps: Robert Ian McCairn. Worcester City licence 1088

Turks Head (now, Brewery Tap)
Also known as: Goodfellows. Blue Oyster. 32 Club. Meco Club. Old Spot.
Location: Lowesmoor
Years active: 1850s to present

Originally **The Turk's Head** and a venue for County carriers in the 19th century, carriers to and from Crowle (Wednesdays and Saturdays 4pm) and Pershore (Saturdays 4pm) operated from here. In 1873, licensee Edward Squires was fined £1 including costs for allowing gaming here. Licensee Jefford James Westwood (1906-22) had been a noted Kidderminster Swifts and Harriers footballer before taking over here: an ad lists him as 'Proprietor'. Later **Meco Club (1950s); Old Spot; Jolly Roger Brewery and outlet Brewery Tap**, run by the Soden brothers, Martin and Paul; later **Oddfellows, Blue Oyster and 32 Club**. Recently (2010) reverted to The Brewery Tap once more openly aiming itself at the gay, lesbian, bi- and tranny set who ask nothing more than to be left alone to do... whatever it is they do. Once reputed to have a ghost, *Worcester Pubs Then and Now* FB page follower Dave Hundley rubbished the idea though he added that he was '... in the Brewery Tap once and someone put the willies up me!' A notable exterior feature was the east-facing wall carrying a 20ft mural of a wooden-legged pirate painted

Brewery Tap with the famous Jolly Roger sign 1986 (CCMH/CFOW)

by eccentric artist Eugene van der Hoog who looked like one of the seven dwarves and lived on a houseboat on the Severn. When first opened as the (straight) Brewery Tap and Jolly Roger Brewery in 1985 I handled much of the publicity for its opening – including TV coverage, with one of its highlights, aside from its home-brews, no less than ten different types of bread, all brewed using beer. Customers initially had to pay a £1 joining fee and £10 a year membership to join

TURK'S HEAD INN,
Lowesmoor, WORCESTER.

☞ *Pure Home-Brewed Ales.*

WINES, SPIRITS & CIGARS OF THE FINEST QUALITY.

☞ Every Accommodation for Cyclists and Motor Cars.

GOOD STABLING.　　LARGE YARD.

Excellent Loose Boxes.　　Green and Quoit Bed.

J. J. WESTWOOD. Proprietor.

(Old Kidderminster Swifts and Harriers).

It had been The Turks Head, then The Meco Club. Now it's The Brewery Tap (BB)

'a private members pub' – the first of its kind in the UK. In the first 10 days of business *(October 1985)* the Tap shifted 360 gallons of ales, and a firkin *(9 gallons)* of Robinsons went in under an hour: between November 1985 and August 1986, they reckoned they sold more than 100,000 pints of home brew and others. 'Going back to the old values is what it's all about' Martin Soden said when **The Brewery Tap and Brewery** opened, selling three Lowesmoor Ales, self-produced in the brewery behind a glass partition so the process was open for viewing at all times – *Quaff* (3.6%), *Severn Bore* (4.6%) and *Old Lowesmoor* (5.6%) and they even planned a Winter Wobbler with an even higher alcohol content.

"Can't help feeling that a lot of the county's pubs have got it all wrong: they're no longer out to give what the customer wants they're giving him what they think he wants and that's something totally different" said Martin at the time. "Somewhere along the line, pubs seem to have lost their direction. Pubs are the very heart of the fabric of English society but sure as sure they're slowly being killed off because people don't want juke-boxes, loud music and beer they can't drink. Britain is pubs, it's beer and we want to resurrect the old English pub as was and elevate it to its true position in Britain's way of life" genial gaffer Paul insisted.

Sadly putting it all into practice proved well-nigh impossible and the pub became a free-for-all that wasn't helped by lads from Brickfields, Warndon, Tolladine and Ronkswood all converging on it on their route into and out of town, though Worcester enjoyed its reputation as being one of the first to host a micro-brewery. It was here too I witnessed legendary trencherman Peter Dowdeswell smash two world drinking records: in March 1986, he sank a $5^{1}/_{2}$ pint yard of ale in just 7.59 seconds and just minutes later, sank a pint of ale standing on his head in 2.39 seconds – and for afters, he even ate the glasses he'd been drinking out of! I'd be willing to bet I watched him drink close to 100 pints that night. More about his drinking records in the chapter on **Worcester characters and other legends**. In August 2013, landlord Lee Winters publicly removed three brands of Russian vodka from behind the bar in what appeared to me to be a fairly pointless protest at Russian intolerance towards gays.

Licensees: As Turks Head: Edward Squires (1873); George Pardoe (1874-5); Edward Squire (1875-90 when he died); Seth Robinson (1890-1905); William Savage (1905-6); Jefford James Westwood (1906-22 when he died also listed James Jeffard 1915); Emma Westwood (1923-7); Ernest Bevington (1927-9); Frank Darke (1929-30 when he died); Annie Darke (1930-1); Samuel Osborne (1931–1938 when he died) As Meco Club (unknown managers); as Brewery Tap: Paul and Martin Soden (1985-1992); As Goodfellows Kathryn Colnon, Susan Clayton (2000); Terence P. Quiddington (2001). As Brewery Tap: current (2013) licensee/dps: Lee Allan Winters. Worcester City licence 1929

Apple Tree (now Firefly)
C2/52 Also known as:. Georgian Bar
Location: 54 Lowesmoor
Years active: 1970s - present

Comparatively recent jazz lounge (also **Georgian Bar** late 1970s), cider house (**Apple Tree** 1980s) and now basic spartan-decorated home-brew house with a growing reputation for live music and the quality of its home brews. Housed in a house originally built as the private home of glover John Lee (c1800) it's the local CAMRA's runner-up Pub of the Year 2011 winner 2012 (much to the miffed-ness of the grumpy landlord of previous winner, **The Dragon**. Anne Bradford in her recent 'Haunted Pubs and Hotels in and around Worcestershire' tells of ghostly goings-on here including noisy instances of furniture being moved about when there's no-one else in the pub.

Licensees: Hamish J. Lothian (2001) Current (2013) licensee/dps: Matthew Bradley Pugh. Worcester City licence 1257

Swan
C2/53 **Location: Lowesmoor**
Years active: 1827 - 1929

Century old but little remembered pub listed variously 53 and 56 Lowesmoor and sited next to Lowesmoor House, 2 doors east of St Martins Street.

First listed Victuallers Recognizances 1827 Billings Directory of Worcestershire 1855, Spreckley Bros public house, licensee Henry Simmonds was convicted in 1911 for selling gin that was adulterated with 10.7% water and fined £2 plus £1/12/6 costs. Thought to have closed c1929

Licensees: Oswell James ('beer retailer' 1855); Robert Stewart (1872-85); Richard Tyler (1885); Henry Smith (1885-96); John Robinson (1896); John Robins (1896-8); William Tolley (1898-1900); Richard Gazzard (1900-10); Robert Stewart (1910); Henry Simmonds (1910-19 when he died); Catherine Simmonds (1919-21 when she died); Henry Coombs (1922); John Jones (1922)

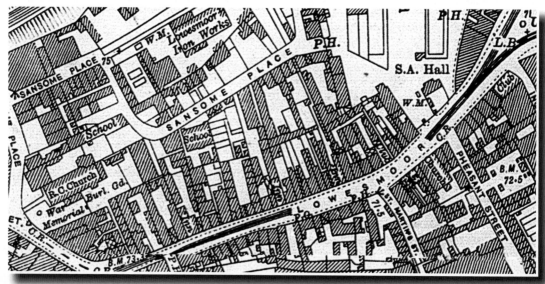

OS1936 map of Lowesmoor, reproduced with permission Ordnance Survey

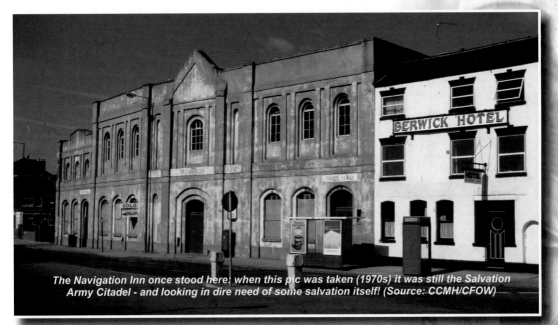

The Navigation Inn once stood here; when this pic was taken (1970s) it was still the Salvation Army Citadel - and looking in dire need of some salvation itself! (Source: CCMH/CFOW)

Navigation Inn
Location: Lowesmoor
Years active: 1820 - 1869

C2/54

First appearing in Victuallers Recognizances 1827 and later Pigot's Worcestershire Directory 1829. Built to accommodate and entertain navvies constructing the canal through Worcester 1810-20s and sited at the gates to Lowesmooor Wharf. In the 1850s John (other records refer to George so they were possibly brothers or likely related in some way) Hill is reported to have kept 'a very popular house with musical entertainment' here. The census of 1851 shows George Hill from Newnham in Gloucestershire as being 54, occupation boatbuilder and publican. In 1869, the inn was demolished by Hill to build a large music hall on the site calling it the New Concert Hall, shaped in the form of a ship's bow and where 'wines and spirits will be served direct from the docks'. It continued under various names including 'The Canterbury' until 1880 and it's believed Vesta Tilley appeared here several times and that Edward Elgar often conducted orchestras here. Now the site of the former Salvation Army citadel and latterly, flatted offices and one-time crafts centre.

Licensees: *John Jeremy King (1829); Thomas Andrews (1835); George Hill (1842-1860s); 'Mr Harris' (1873).*

Lansdowne (Hotel)
Location: Lowesmoor Place
Years active: 1880s -1925

C2/55

Late-Victorian (c 1880s) inn at 79 Lowesmoor next to Salvation Army Barracks (The Citadel). Licensee John Hill – probably the same John Hill who'd built **The Navigation** next door was convicted in 1875 for selling in prohibited hours and fined £2. Howard Hayes was convicted in 1902 for unlawfully selling liquor to a constable on duty and was fined £1/1/- (£1.05p) plus £2/11/4 (£2.57p) plus costs. Closed c1925

Licensees: *Neil Harris (1872-4); Charles Whatmore (1874-5); John Hill (1875-6); Jabez Smallwood (1876-8); Frank Finch (1878-9); John Packer (1881-2); Robert Pringle (1880-1); John Packer (1881-2); Henry Cooper (1882-3); John Kent (1883-4); Thomas Wilkinson (1884); Annie Bennett (1884-6); John Brittain (1886-8); Benjamin Hobbs (1888-9); Elizabeth Phillips (1889); James Aston (1889-99); Henry Pitt (1899-1901: Harold Hayes (1901-7); James Phillips (1907- 1911); Harold Hayes (1911-22); Charles Walker (1922-4); Thomas Hubbard (1924); Charles Gilbert (1924)*

The Lansdowne Hotel,

(Headquarters of the W.C. & C.H.,)

s situated in **LOWESMOOR,** direct
line from **SHRUB HILL
STATION.**

iood accommodation for Cyclists
and Athletes.

VERYTHING SOLD AT THIS ESTABLISHMENT
IS OF THE
VERY BEST QUALITY.

INE ALES, WINES, SPIRITS AND
CIGARS.

Worcester and County Harriers gather at the Lansdowne Hotel 1899

(Source: CCMH/CFOW)

G: Pheasant Street and East to the canal

C2/56 — Eagle

Also known as: Eagle Inn. Golden Eagle (1850s). Spread Eagle (1900 – 1930)
Location: Pheasant Street
Years active: 1850 -1952

Appears in Slater's Worcester Directory 1850 and Billings Directory of Worcestershire 1855 at addresses listed as 21 Pheasant Street though neither the Census of 1851 or the Ordnance Survey map of 1886 or that of 1936 shows any pubs in Pheasant Street. The Eagle is the best remembered of four pubs in the heavily industrialised Pheasant Street (the others are **The Pheasant, Cock and Magpie, and Railway Express** at the junction with St Martins Gate). **The Eagle** appears in Slater's Worcester Directory 1850 and Billings Directory of Worcestershire 1855 at address listed as 21 Pheasant Street. Originally Gregg and Brettell (later M&B) at Holt St, Birmingham. License surrendered 5th December 1952 to take effect from 7th November 1952 Also off-licence for the sale of beer, cider and perry for consumption off the premises.

Licensees: Joseph Munn (listed as 'beer retailer' 1855); Richard Link (1872-76); Mary Hinchcliffe (1876-7); William Digger (1877-83); Mary Pipwell (1883-4); Mary Powell (1884-5); Eliza Holder (1885-6); George Weaver (1886-1911); Archibold Folake (1911); Thomas Philpot (1911-19); Ernest Philpot (1919-28); Henry Richards (1928-38); William Thompson (1938-9); George Worman (1939-44); Archie Tyler (1944-8); Philip Everett (1948)

C2/57 — Pheasant

Location: Pheasant Street
Years active: c1853- c1880

Short-lived pub in the mostly industrialised area of Pheasant Street, not listed as a pub in the census of 1851 or shown on the Ordnance Survey map of 1886 but known to have existed between those dates under licensee *John Ashton (as 'beer retailer'); John Shaw (1872); Noah Dayus (1875-81); James Seymore (1891-89 when he died); Frederick Fulwell (1889)*

C2/58 — Cock and Magpie

Location: Pheasant Street
Years active: 1850 - 1906

Not much known, not listed as a pub in the census of 1851 or shown on the Ordnance Survey map of 1886 but listed in **Billings Directory of Worcestershire 1855 under** licensee James Bromley – described as 'beer retailer' **and** known to have existed at least up to 1906. Its end was no doubt speeded-up in the wake of a report into the state of Worcester's pubs in that year by the Chief Constable who described 'The Cock and Magpie, Pheasant St. as 'accommodation poor, 19 licenced houses within 244 yards.'

Back now to G. Where the road forks, take the Rainbow Hill (ie left-hand) road

Sun Tavern (later known as Sun Beer House)
Location: Lowesmoor Terrace (originally 'St Martins ward')
Years active: 1830s-1850s

Listed in Victuallers Recognizances 1835 under Jon. Baylis (possibly the same John Baylis listed as 'vict.city arms of 4, Church Street' (1792); Jonathan Oseman (1843). Census of 1851 shows licensee Henry Harwood living here with his wife Hannah but no further references. Thought to have become the first of three pubs subsequently called 'The Bridge...

Site of The Sun Tavern - forerunner of The Bridge (BB)

Bridge (1, 2 and 3)
Location: 1 and 2, Lowesmoor Terrace and 30 Lowesmoor (also known as Rainbow Hill Parade 1872-80)
Years active: 1850 present

Three pubs going by the name The Bridge operated close to this location. The first, thought to have been on the site of the former **Sun Tavern** and later Lowesmoor Brewery (see above). The second was sited at 30 Lowesmoor, and was on the opposite side of road – ie southside – to the existing (new) **Bridge.** Built around 1850 with the coming of the railway and the canal, address listed as 1-2 Lowesmoor Terrace. Licensee David Harper was convicted in 1916 for allowing beer to be sold here to a person under the age of 14 and fined 10/- (50p). It closed April 6th 1936, customers moving over the road the following day (April 7th 1936) to the new Bridge **(Bridge #3)** . In 1981 when Mike Stevens had been there 2½ years – and only the Bridge's third gaffer in 35 years – it even gave **The Beehive** a good run for its money as the best M&B house in town. As I wrote: '...it's one of those places – and **The Beehive's** another – where he'll pull you a half, take your cash (mild was 46p, Brew XI 48p) pull the other half, then wait for you to get froth on the end of your nose', Result? I noted: '...so there it is, clean, fresh, slightly gurgling in the glass, head creamy thick and standing a good inch over the rim of the glass. Lift quickly and down slowly: s'magic!' Even with the benefit of a £30,000 face-lift a few months before, I described it as 'a hairy-armed basic boozer of the top-notchiest kind revelling in 'a big, brash, busy, rangy kind of bar and games room that caters for cards, darts and pool, plus skittle alley that caters for parties'. The evidence is still there... *I gave it four stars out of three for the beer!.* The Bridge is still there and has suffered from a reputation as being run down and tired of late: it was even closed for about a year up to recently (2013) but has since re-opened (and possibly since re-closed again). A Marstons house.

The Bridge Lowesmoor - the third of that name

(Source JAS)

Licensees: Henry Harwood - beer retailer (1855); Ann Tyler (1859); William Hicks; David Harper (1872-96); Ben Harper (1896-1910); Alice Harper (1910-11); David Albert Harper (1911-26); William Price (1926-32); Arthur James Checkett (1932-1954); *rebuilt and re-sited on opposite side of road.* William J. Stephens (1955-64); Tim Webster (1980); Mike Stevens (1982); Peter E. Byrne (2000). Current (2013) licensee/dps: Steve Reeves. Worcester City licence 1217

At the canal bridge, turn left down Westbury Street. Here once stood...

A pub called The Rainbow, later The Railway existed just left of the bridge

Same shot 2013 (BB)

Railway
Also known as: The Rainbow
Location: Westbury Street
Years active: 1859 - 1891

Little-known, short-lived twice-named canalside pub sited close to the railway bridge over the canal initially christened after the newly-enlarged road that passed by just a few yards away (Rainbow Hill) then re-named after the latest phenomenon that chugged by countless times a day not 50 yards away, the steam engine. Appears in Victuallers Recognizances 1859 and later in Littlebury's Directory of Worcestershire, and shown on the 1886 OS map. Closed in 1891 when interestingly it converted into a temperance club.

Licensees: *Thomas Evans (1859); Mrs Mary Longley (described as 'Rainbow', Rainbow Hill 1872-6);William Hill (1876-7); Mary Hill (1887-91 when she died)*

Return to the mini island at 'Lowesmoor Triangle'

C2/63 West Midland Arms (also Tavern, and Inn)
Location: 4, Lowesmoor Place
Years active: 1860s - present

Solid-looking survivor of the age of the coming of the railway (built c1860s) that's well past its best, though can look back with pride on some glory days, not least as a pub with a great sporting (especially skittles) background. A keystone over the door shows a rudimentary Bacchus swathed in grapes and vine leaves seemingly inviting customers to enter, drink and be merry. Named after the original operators of the Worcester-Birmingham line, West Midland Railway, the name stuck despite the company being taken over by Great Western Railway just four years after the Tavern was built. A Flowers house, then Whitbread, in 1981 under the new ownership of John and Lillian Woodward and after a massive overhaul – John said they'd thrown out everything from the old West Midland Arms with the exception of three Britannia tables – I described it as being 'spacious, well-scrubbed and airy', adding that I found it hard to relate to what had previously been an out-and-out boozer. As I noted, comparing the new West Midland to its predecessor: 'I almost felt obliged to crook my little finger as I supped... er, sipped'. It was then, as I described it: '...a really good sized bar that's bigger than it looks from the outside, games room that can't be faulted, and cosy skittle alley that doubles as a functions room'. Customers at the time, I reckoned 'consisting of the undecided and the curious'. Today looking run-down and sad and in need of some tlc, it's still surviving, but clusters of smokers skulking about outside tends to deter casual observers from venturing in, leaving it with a small but consistent gaggle of regulars. Shame in some ways, because it's a pub with a long history and some very cheery personal memories.

Gorgeous old photograph of The West Midland Arms. The sign tells us George Brighton was landlord here - dating the pic between 1903 and 1912

(Source: CCMH/ CFOW)

Still chugging on after 150 years – The West Midland Tavern Lowesmoor, named after the railway operators who no doubt once frequented it in their droves (Source: CCMH/CFOW)

And still recognisable today - below (BB)

Licensees: *Mrs Williams (1872-4); Noah Dayus (1874-5); Mary Pollard (1875-9); George Griffiths (1879-86); Martha Hill (1886-97); Edward Tanser (1897-1900); Elizabeth and William Tanser (1900-01); George Herbert Webb (1901-03); George Baker (1903-06); George Brighton (1903–1912); Ernest E. Hughes (1913-26); Walter T. Biddle (1926– 1932); Arthur Candlin (1932–58); George White (1958); Frederick Vale (1958-78); Nellie Vale (1978-9); Robert Brown (1979); Morstan Fryer (1979-80); John (and Lillian Woodward (1980- 5); Mary Field (1985-9); William Hodges (1989); Mike Stevens (1992 - 2006). Current licensee (2013); Mary Elizabeth Jeynes. Worcester City Licence no: 1046.*

C2/64

Ship
Location: Canalside Lowesmoor
Years active: 1850 - 1860

Little known pub at Canalside Lowesmoor springing up with the coming of the canal and probably built to accommodate the navvies, apparently disappearing almost as quickly as it appeared. One listing only: Billings Directory of Worcestershire 1855, under Jas. Badham, described as 'beer retailer'

Carpenters Arms
Location: George Street
Years active: 1870s - 1906

C2/65

Its end was no doubt speeded-up in the wake of a report into the state of Worcester's pubs in 1906 by the Chief Constable who noted of **The Carpenters' Arms**, George St., 'accommodation poor and sanitary conditions inadequate; there were 19 licensed houses within 240 yards.'

Licensees: George Pardoe (1872-1881); Elizabeth Pardoe (1881 – 1883 when she died); George Pardoe Jnr (1883-1900 when he died); Jane Pardoe (1900-01); Alfred Baylis (1901-5); John Smith (1905-6); Hubert Cordwell (1906)

Telegraph (Tavern)
Location: George Street
Years active: 1850 - 1922

C2/66

Situated at 6 George Street, right next to **The Carpenters Arms** (OS1886) Listed in Billings Directory of Worcestershire 1855, closed c1925

Licensees: James Hiron (as 'beer retailer'); Thomas Clarke (1872-4); Tracey Green (1874-96); George Patrick (1896-1902); Reuben Smith (1902-3); Sydney Knight (1903-6); Timothy Trahearn (1906); Arthur Wells (1906-7); Mary A Southall (1907-12); William Turner (1912-17); Lucy Turner (1917)

New Inn
Location: George Street
Years active: 1840 - 1974

C2/67

One of a clutch of mid-Victorian pubs on the edge of the densely-populated Blockhouse area – this one different in being not on a street corner, but clinging precariously on to steeply sloping land nudging the canal bridge facing the mortuary. Later a Spreckleys House registered at 7 Foregate Street (later West Country Breweries Ltd and thence Whitbread) it was first listed in Hunt & Co's Commercial Directory for Gloucester, Hereford and Worcester in 1842 and thereafter as 29 George Street (1900) and was still open early 1970s. A noted licensee here (1895-1913) was three-times English Quoits Champion and eight times national team player, locally-born Walter Jones, who was also an international bowls player, representing England in the side that toured South Africa in

George Street 1974 (Source: CCMH/CFOW) and above, the same view 2013 (BB)

1938. He set up the City Quoits Ground on land opposite the pub (part of the old mortuary) and was also instrumental in setting up Worcester Bowling Club. He later went on to be licensee of **The Berwick Arms** (1913-31) and died in 1955.

Licensees: Geo. Berrow, New Inn, George Street (1842 – mid 1850s); George Burrow (1855); William Clark (1873 – 76); Henry Jones (1876-94 when he died); Mary Jones (1894-5); Walter Hugh Jones (1895 -1913); James Baker (1913-15); Mrs Annie Kendle (1915-30); Henry Evans (1930-1); William V. McClean (also listed as brewer – 1931-2); Gertrude Nellie Bradley (1932-45); Arthur Page (1945-62); Ernest Bradley (1962-3); Basil Owen (1963-4); John Beck (1964-70); Colin Beck (1970-71); Alexander Smith (1971-2); Francis McAuley (1972); Edward Bascombe (1972-4); Peter Murdock (1974)

New Inn George Street, butting up to the canal. The site is unrecognisable today from Bob Sargeant's pic taken 22nd September 1961

Railway Express
Location: Corner of Pheasant Street and St Martins Gate
Years active:
Only known listing Victuallers Recognizances 1859 under John Banner. Corner of Pheasant Street and St Martins Gate

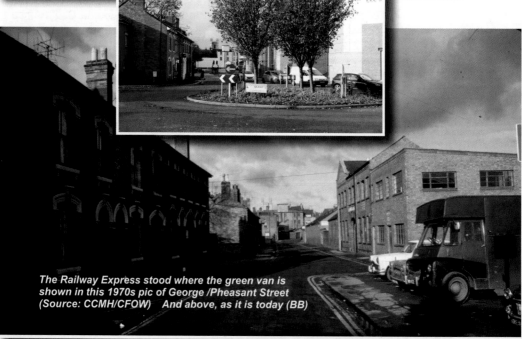

The Railway Express stood where the green van is shown in this 1970s pic of George /Pheasant Street (Source: CCMH/CFOW)   And above, as it is today (BB)

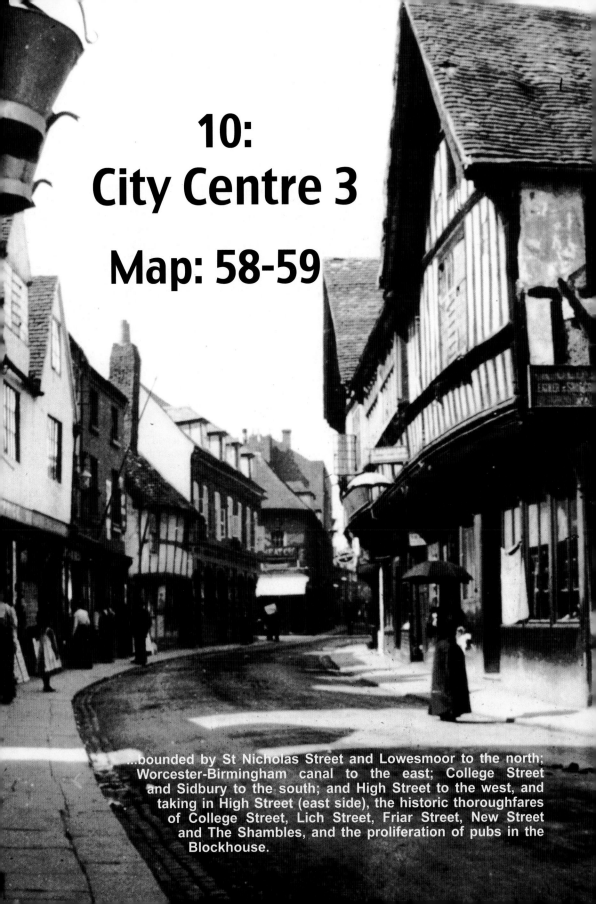

10:
City Centre 3

Map: 58-59

...bounded by St Nicholas Street and Lowesmoor to the north; Worcester-Birmingham canal to the east; College Street and Sidbury to the south; and High Street to the west, and taking in High Street (east side), the historic thoroughfares of College Street, Lich Street, Friar Street, New Street and The Shambles, and the proliferation of pubs in the Blockhouse.

19th century engraving of
the High Street (CCMH/CFOW)

F ew cities, even London, can match the concentration of pubs packed into so small an area as this. It's the biggest single chapter in this book for the simple reason that the area is crammed with history and pubs, and in it is probably everyone's favourite – a viewpoint that would also have rung true two, three four, even five hundred years ago. That said, precise pin-pointing of many ancient inns is virtually impossible. At the time of their pre-postal existence Worcester would have been a much smaller place and all pubs and inns would have been recognised simply by the name: as a result, there are dozens of long-lost inns described simply as being 'in the vicinity of...' though even that's more helpful than a mere ward name.

Still, thankful for small mercies and all that!

I don't doubt that that normally fastidious chronicler of all things Worcester "Rambler' John Noake said even as far back as 1877 '...sorry I am that the fragments of the history of this institution of Worcester are so scanty as to afford little beyond a dry list of names. But slight as this is, I deemed it worth preservation in the hope that some friendly correspondents might be enabled to throw further light upon the ancient Vigornian victualling fraternity'.

A-B: High Street – east side to College Street

In the previous chapter I made the comment that there was a short period up to fairly recently that you could walk along Worcester's High Street all the way from **The Talbot** in Sidbury *(which, incidentally, is significantly included in this key chapter)* to **The Saracens Head** in The Tything and not pass a single pub with the sole exception of a not especially welcoming hotel bar. But that was far from the case earlier in the City's history – and it's here that the loss of once-great pubs is most keenly felt, not least, the tight cluster of four jostling for attention virtually side by side at the point directly opposite the Guildhall. But first a slight, though important diversion...

Church Street was home to a fondly-remembered inn with, for me, the best hand-painted pub sign in town. Beautiful it was – and the cover of this book is in some ways a tribute to whoever painted it. I remember having 'discovered' it as a lad in the 1950s and gazing up at it in wonderment – only to find myself rebuked and warned about the dangers of hanging about outside pubs! This was...

City Arms
C3/1

Location: Church Street
Years active: 1760 - 1961

One of two inns by the name of 'City Arms' – the other is in Cripplegate – this one listed in Victualisers' Recognizances in 1766 simply as 'St Martins ward', later in Grundy Royal Directory 1792. At its end at the respectable age of 201, it was a Lewis Clarke's house (the brewery was in nearby Angel Place) popular with journalists from nearby print works, and denoted by distinctive red, white and black pub sign showing Worcester City's coat of arms. On 14th December 1960, landlord Percival Dennis Laxton was fined £10 for selling adulterated whisky here and Mrs Agnes Laxton £5 for selling adulterated gin. Closed 8th January 1961. Building demolished and replaced by soulless 60's block, now ???

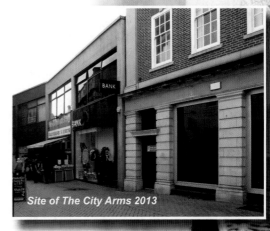

Site of The City Arms 2013

Licensees: Benjamin Gyles/David Bowket (1766); John Evans (1784); John Baylis 'vict.city arms 4, Church Street' (1792); Thomas Wofall (1814-20s); Samuel Wooley (1829); William Harding (1835- ?); Frances Harding (1842–c1860, listed as Frances Reading (1850); James Harding (1872-76); Richard Owers (1876-79); William Payne (1879-81); Thomas Lewis (1886-7); George Westbury (1887-93 when he died); Alfred Link (1893-98 when he died); Mary Link (1898-9); William A. Pointon (1899-1902); John Warden (1902-3); Henry Forbes (1903-4); Elizabeth Noake (1904-6); William A. Brown (1906-1916); Sidney Preece (1916-17); Arthur Redford (1917 when he died); Bertha Radford (1917-8); Joseph Porter (1918-30); Walter Smith (1930–1953); Beatrice Eva Smith (1953); Percival Dennis Laxton (1953-61)

It might be timely at this juncture to include a number of inns of the time, known to have been located around here but whose actual locations, licensees and key facts are proving elusive – though the fact that are known to have existed at all is sufficient to merit their inclusion here: I don't doubt John Noake felt a moan coming on.

The City's first town hall – it wasn't referred-to as Guildhall until the Guilds ceased holding their meetings at Trinity Hall in (where else?) The Trinity in 1796 – was built on the same site as today's Guildhall. The first of that name was described as 'a large structure of timber with a piazza in front and at the end of the piazza a row of shops, the principal entrance to the hall being down a flight of nearly twenty steps. (Hubert Leicester 'Forgotten Worcester – 1930).

It's said that the body of the hall was open to the roof. It was demolished in 1721 just a year or two after Worcester-born architect Thomas White had been commissioned to set about designing and constructing a big, bold new one, which is largely what we still see today – though it not only benefits from a sizeable, and expensive, restoration exercise in 1880, but there's also been ready cash in the public kitty to fund constant renovations and refurbishment – not least of course, bearing in mind that this was for many years the location for Worcester Assizes, and as is still the case, the home of the Council Chamber, mayor's parlour and until only a few years ago, the bulk of the municipal offices. The exotically-named one-time mayor, Hubert Aloysius Leicester, who's thought to have been the first Roman Catholic to hold the role created in 1621, was elected five times in all between 1904 and 5 and from 1913 to 1915 so he's well placed to comment: in his 'Worcester Remembered' he wrote: '...opposite to the Guildhall is The Market Hall erected in 1804. It may be of interest to learn that The Kings Head Inn formerly stood there and that the great actress Mrs (Sarah) Siddons made her first public appearance at a theatre set up in the yard of that inn...' Accordingly, it's well worth recording.

Kings Head
Location: High Street
Years active: 1750 – 1800

Closed early in the 19th century, as stated in the previous paragraph, it's reputed that the great Shakespearean actress and tragedienne Sarah Siddons (1755-1831) gave one of her first public performances here – though reports of her being born in Worcester have since been discounted. Even so, this is the site of the famous Kings Head Theatre in a barn belonging to the inn where Sarah Siddons and some of the greatest 18th century actors performed in what some describe as a nursery or training ground for budding thesps. Its history is illustrious – no doubt stretching back beyond mention in Grundy Royal Directory 1792 and even before that, the Register of Victuallers' Recognizance of 1766.

Licencees: *Hannah Nott (described as 'widow'–1766); George, also listed as Guy Daniel (as King's head inn 30 High Street - 1790 and 1792)*

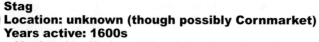

Bellman
Also known as: Three Crowns
Location: precise location unclear although it could instead be in the Cornmarket)
Years active: 1700s – 1870

Mentioned by Noake (1877) as one of a number of 'ancient' City inns, some of which are probably not much less ancient than the eighteenth or even 17th century.. Listed 1734 as one of 23 Worcester inns where qualifying voters could cast their ballot. Also known as **The Three Crowns**, it was described in Berrows Journal (1813) as '...well accustomed and conveniently built for a public house or private family with a good brew-house and chambers separate from the dwelling house and a good stable, backside and other conveniences. Enquire of the widow Mason or Mr. Andrew, attorney in Worcester'. ***Note: also listed in C2 The Cornmarket***

Queen's Arms
Location: The Park
Years active: 1850 – 1860

Very little documentary evidence exists concerning this one except a single listing in Billings Directory of Worcestershire 1855, citing Henry Dunn - listed as 'beer retailer' as licensee A Henry Dunn was also licensee of the Glovers Arms in Merry Vale in 1842

Stag
Location: unknown (though possibly Cornmarket)
Years active: 1600s

Mentioned by Noake p 121 as being in existence '...two centuries ago' but omitting to say where   '... mentioned two centuries ago by M. Jorevin (Antiq. Re ii 59) thus: 'according to the custom of the country, the landlords sup with the strangers and passengers and if they have daughters they are as of the company to entertain the guests at the table with pleasant conceits where they drink as much as the men... when one drinks the health of any person in the company the custom of the country does not permit you to drink more than half the cup which is filled up and presented to him or her whose health you have drunk. He also spoke of tobacco which it seemed the women smoked as much as the men...'

Emperor of Russia
Location: 'St Martins ward'
Years active: c1814

Little known inn listed in Victuallers Recognizances 1814 under licensee John Allcroft but seemingly short-lived and no further entries

Sedan Chair
Location: St Martins ward (precise location unknown)
Years active: c 1760s

Listed in the Register of Victuallers' Recognizance of 1766 under Catherine Barsmore described as 'widow' but not surviving much beyond and no further entries are recorded

1910 photograph of the Guildhall and High Street - and there's that bobby again! (CCMH/CFOW)

...same today - and not a bobby in sight! (BB)

C3/7 Glove
Location: St Martins ward (precise location unknown)
Years active: c1760s

Listed in Register of Victuallers' Recognizance of 1766 under Robert Tomkins but not subsequently, suggesting it was an ancient inn coming to its end, or that it had its name changed. Aside from the general description 'St. Martins ward' not much more is known.

C3/8 Royal Oak – two listed
Location: St Martins ward (precise location unknown)
Years active: c1760s

Two inns by the name of Royal Oak are listed separately in the Register of Victuallers' Recognizance of 1766 and the location of neither is known with any accuracy save 'St Martins ward'. Licensee of the first is listed as Walter James and the second Sarah Allen described as 'widow'. Interestingly, neither establishment survived much longer, suggesting they were both ancient inns coming to their end, or that one or both had its name changed. Nor are Walter James or Sarah Allen listed elsewhere within this section of the City.

C3/11 Guildhall Tavern, also Bulls Head,
Location: 32 High Street
Years active: 1780 – 1931

Not strictly High Street, but at the end of a passageway close to Court No 2, directly opposite the Guildhall and immediately next door (and north of) The Golden Lion. Listed variously as 'bulls head inn 33 High St', Bull's Head, High Street and Bull's Head inn, 32 High Street (incidentally, the Golden Lion was also listed as 32 High Street) and later Duttons after licensee Thomas Dutton (1829-40s) and sited in (then) High ward. Listed in Victualisers' Recognizances in 1776 and shown on Ordnance Survey map of 1886. To coincide with the Three Choirs festival in 1788, attended by King

George, his queen and three daughters, a well-publicised side show held here featured 'The Celebrated Irish Giant O'Brien' reckoned to be Britain's tallest man whose party trick was to remove the tops of lamp standards in order to light his pipe and could sit at a table with his arms resting on the tops of the doors *(his skeleton can still be seen in the museum of the Royal College of Surgeons in Lincoln's Inn Fields)* and 'illusions of ventriloquism' at which, punters were assured, 'a good fire will be kept'.

Licensees: William Evans (1766); David George (1784); T. Corbett (1790 and 1792); Thomas Cahill (1814); William Bowyer (1820); Thomas Dutton (1829-1840s); Charles Knowles (1842); Margaret Knowles (1850); George Wells (1855); George Glover (1872-4); Edward Pardoe (1874-5); Thomas Prosser (1875-8); William Prosser Senior (1878-9); William Woods (1879-80); William Prosser Jnr (1880-98); Louisa Prosser (1898); Thomas Prosser (1898-1902); Louisa Prosser (1902-7); Joseph Coombe (1907–1910); William Chamberlain (1910); Ernest Phillips (1910-14); Alfred G.Wall (1914-6); Annie Wall (1916); Charles Walker (1916-7); John Rowe (1917); Harry Wakefield (1917-19); Frank Pleadon (1919-21); George Fryer (1921-2); Alfred Mills (1922-3); Mary Higgs (1923-5); Alfred Foakes (1925-6); George Townsend (1926); Ernest A. Roberts (1926)

C3/12

Golden Lion
Also known as Golden Lyon (1766) also Duttons (1830-40)
Location: High Street
Years active: 1680-1986

Ever-popular City centre pub The Golden Lion - also known as Dutton's
Source: Top left JAS, other images CCMH/CFOW.
The golden lion figure BB

Appears in Register of Victuallers' Recognizance of 1766 as **Golden Lyon** in High ward under Edward Jones but goes back almost a century before then. Not listed as 'one of (Worcester's) five principal carriers' Inns in Baylis, Lewis Almanack 1885-8 (printed 5 New Street price 1½d) but as 'other carriers' inns' this is a 17th century tavern located at 31 (and 32) High Street – an address it shared with **The Guildhall Tavern** which has led some observers to believe the two are one and the same: police records and long lists of successive landlords however, show that they were in fact distinct from one another). **The Golden Lion** is much renowned for its 19th century literary circle and long association with politics and political associations – not least right up to closure c1984 when, due to being directly opposite Guildhall it was frequently used by councillors and City officials both before, after and very often during Council meetings. Former City Council leader George Randall once told me more important decisions had been made in **The Golden Lion** than in the Council Chamber and it's also reputed that there's a door in the cellar leading underground to the Guildhall, though another *(less likely)* theory is that it was part of the reputed tunnels network from the cathedral to Whiteladies. On 16th December 1892, licensee Henry Kirk was fined £5 with costs for unlawfully permitting gaming on the premises. Originally a Spreckleys house, later West Country and Whitbreads, the final landlords Betty and Dougie Blake (1980-86) opened the pub on Christmas Day for folk living on the streets and gave them a free lunch. It became a men's outfitters after closure (1984) and is now Costa Coffee who to their immense credit had a copy made of the original plaster statue of the lion that stood outside for many years after finding it in an upstairs room, and had it gilded and positioned where the original had gazed down on the City for possibly 200 years. There is also an account of the inn's history on the wall in the shop. The alleyway that also led to **The Bulls Head** *(see previous-but-one listing)* also ran alongside the southern wall of **The Golden Lion**, but that and the reputed death-mask of a man set into the wall are now incorporated into the coffee shop. In 1984, a 400-year old inventory relating to **The Golden Lion** came to light in the St Helens Record Office. The handwritten list measured 13 feet by 6 inches.

First licensee listed as Mrs Porter (1682); followed by Edward Jones (1766); John Doughty 'golden lion 32 High Street' (1790); (not listed 1829); Charles Atkins, Golden Lion, 31 High Street (1842); Henry Preen (1850); Henry William Price (1855); Mrs Elizabeth Price (1872-82); Joseph Andrews (1882-4); George Hughes (1884-95); William Roberts (1895-6); Henry Hayes (1896-1901); Louisa Prosser (1901-2); Henry Kirk (1892); John F. Nash (1902-3); Thomas. H. Smith (1903-21); Albert Bryan (1921-5); Harry Oswald Dale (1925-50); Brian Malcaster (1950); Frederick Fletcher (1950-1); John Evans (1951-3); Mark Clarke (1953-4); Joseph Crutchley (1954-69); Harry Powell (1969); Walter Ablett (1969-71); Joseph Crutchley (1971-7); Douglas Blake (1977-83); Betty Blake (1983-6).

Also likely – though by no means certain – to be to be one and the same as:

C3/12 Lion
Location: unclear. Poss High Street or Cornmarket
Years active: 1600s

Location unclear, but probably **The Golden Lion** or possibly another sited around here or the Cornmarket, mentioned by Noake (1877) as one of a number of 'ancient' City inns, some of which are 'probably not much less ancient than the eighteenth or even 17th century'.

C3/13 Luna Restaurant
Location: High Street

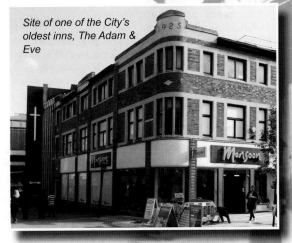

Site of one of the City's oldest inns, The Adam & Eve

Mentioned here only in respect of being Worcester's first Chinese Restaurant licensed for 'on' sales of beer, cider, wines and spirits first granted 6th March 1961, confirmed 20th April 1961. (Not to be confused with Luna Bar – see **Swan with Two Nicks**)

Licensee: Hom Chung Wau

C3/14 Adam and Eve
Location: Corner of Pump Street and High Street
Years active: 1760s - 1840s

A famous old Worcester inn, sited on the south corner of Pump Street and High Street, rebuilt 1925 as Russell and Dorrel's, latterly BT Phone shop, now Monsoon. Adam and Eve was listed in Register of Victuallers' Recognizance of 1766 under John Pocketts and later described by Noake (1877) as 'in the occupation Thomas Gyles in 1778 and subsequently of William Heming, whitesmith' (a whitesmith is a person who works with 'white' or light-coloured metals such as tin and pewter. The term is also applied to metalworkers who do only finishing work such as filing or polishing. Whitesmiths fabricate items such as tin or pewter cups, water pitchers, forks, spoons, and candle holders from cold metal and it was a common occupation in pre-industrial times). While precise years active and closing date are uncertain, this was one of the City's most famed ancient inns, John Noake suggesting that it could rank among the oldest – possibly even late 1600s

104 High Street - site of an ancient inn, The Swan, rebuilt 1898

C3/15

Swan
Location: (104) High Street
Years active: ancient, rebuilt 1898 – 1964

Another mentioned by Noake (1877) as one of a number of 'ancient' City inns, dating from 'the eighteenth or even 17th century'. Licensee Ernest Winter was convicted in 1948 on three charges of selling beer after hours here, and was fined £5 and £2/2/- for the first offence and £5 plus £1/1/- for each of the other two. Ex-Blackpool Div 1 footballer John Rogerson, later of **Dolphin** and **Park Tavern** fame was licensee here in the last years of its life. The licence and name were transferred to a new **Swan across the road** which opened a year later...

...and another Swan, facing it: it closed after being smashed-up by yobs

Licensees: *Edwin Langton (1898-1900); Charlotte du Caun (1900-5); Jane S.Smallwood (1905-9); Francis Beasley (1909-11); Andrew Rogers (1911-13); John Hart (1913-24 when he died); Jane Hart (1924-5); William Barrett (1925 when he died); Florence Barrett (1925-6); Ernest Winter (1926-30); Percy Swain (1930-2); Geoffrey Dobson (1932); Henry Hands (1932-9); Henry Smith (1939); Ernest Winter (1940-1951); William Terence Salmon (1951-4); Harry Sidney Fairburn (1954-57); Horace William Yapp (1957-58); John Rogerson (1958-64)*

C3/16

Swan
Location: High Street
Years active: 1965 – 1969

A short-lived underground 'dive' bar below Russell and Dorrells popular in the mid-60s, though serving only keg beers to a clientele of mostly youngsters, made infamous for having been targeted by a mob of Birmingham bikers who'd mistaken it for their intended target **The Swan with Two Nicks** after one of their members had been beaten up by some Worcester lads and they wanted their revenge. It was apparently so badly smashed-up it never re-opened.

Hubert Leicester who's quoted extensively throughout this book and is rightly viewed as one of the City's great historians, was a great friend of Sir Edward Elgar whose statue, unveiled in 1981 by self-confessed Elgar apassionato Prince Charles stands at this very point B. *From here, directly opposite the cathedral, it's a walk into history...*

B-C: College Street to Friar Street (and including Lich Street)

Referred to by Noake in Worcestershire Relics (printed March 1877 price 5/-) Lich (or Leech) Street '...meant the street of the dead, as corpses were taken through it, passing under the lich gate by **The Punch Bowl Inn** to be buried in the cathedral cemetery. This was the entrance into the City from London before College Street was made and was occupied by respectable tradesmen, like any other street'.

Dating from the early 1500s Lich Gate, which stood a little way down Lich Street was the old entrance to the cathedral cemetery and by the mid-20th century was the only remaining lichgate of a cathedral in the country. Despite this, the whole of Lich Street as well as St Michael's Church and the Lich Gate itself were criminally destroyed in an act of wanton destruction now universally condemned as 'The Rape of Worcester' still regarded as a shocking example of planning gone mad, leaving a scar that Worcester

One of the City's most noted streets snd home to some of its oldest pubs - Lich Street, destroyed in the so-called 'Rape of Worcester' 1960

(CCMH/CFOW)

Hard to credit this is the same view as the contemporary image below right - 100 years apart (CCMH/ CFOW)

The passageway under Travelodge (formerly Giffard Hotel) is roughly where the historic old Lichgate once stood

will long struggle to erase. It was in this historic street – now entirely obliterated – that several once famous old pubs also stood – though their actual locations, save being in this ancient old throughfare, are at best sketchy. Being in such close proximity to the cathedral, it's barely surprising many of the inns and alehouses abounding in this densely packed area have religious names: in Lich Street alone, **The Chequers** and **The Mitre** and not too far afield **The Angel de la Trompe, The Cross Keys, The Adam and Eve and The Seven Stars** among others.

Three Cranes
Location: Lich Street
Years active: 1601 - 1700

According to John Noake in 1877: '...in 1601, an inn so called was described as containing only three small rooms below and three over, with a cellar; belonging to John Honnyett, butcher. In 1690, Anthony Hopkins kept it'. At the same time, he wrote, there was a house called The Three Cranes in High Street and a Three Pyes in Lich Street. Ancient inn, specific location unknown save 'Lich Street' and possibly also known as Three Crosses, Three Cruxxes or Three Pyes (see below)

Three Crosses
Also known as: Three Cruxxes
Location: Lich Street (probably corner of High Street)
Years active: 1500-1600s

Ancient inn, precise location unknown, referred to by Noake (p) 119. Its name a derivation of Cuxxes, thus likely to be one and the same as the inn of that name listed as High Street as well as Lich Street – suggesting it was sited at the junction of both. In her work on the Lich Street and Friar Street Dr. Pat Hughes mentions 'No 17 was probably an inn from early in its history probably Three Cuxxes kept by widow Dicke mentioned in Thomas Allen's will of 1597'.

300

Three Pyes
C3/19
Location: Lich Street
Years active: 1500s - 1600s

A derivation of Three Magpies, ancient inn, precise location unknown save being Lich (or Leech Street), referred to by Noake (p) 119. Possibly one and the same as **Three Crosses** or **Three Cranes**

Punch Bowl
C3/21
Also known as Old Punchbowl, Ye Olde Punch Bowl Inn
Location: 7 College St.
Years active: 1790s - 1958

The Punch Bowl, *(also known as **Old Punchbowl**)* was prominently sited here and despite being older than its newer upstart sited just over the road (see following entry), remains within living memory. A former Robert Allen Brewery house, it gave its name to two descendants: **The New Punch Bowl** sited just across Lich Street and the modern-day, and still extant **'Punchbowl'** that opened in Ronkswood at about the same time as this original Punch Bowl called orders for the last time. Famous for the very nature of its position – College Yard or (7) College Street, its location is notable - right next to the City's former main entrance for centuries, Lich Gate, the last of its kind, criminally demolished in the notorious 'Rape of Worcester' in the late 1950s. Known as *Ye Olde Punch Bowl Inn* 1915, it was also occasionally used for inquests. On 8th May 1817, the inquest was held here into the death of James Wright, 68, 'one of the beadsmen or *eleemosynarii* of the cathedral'. On 19th November 1920, licensee Mrs Lily Osborne was fined £3.3s (£3.15p) with £1.1s (£1.05p) costs on two counts of unlawfully selling whisky above maximum price. A comparatively full list of licensees dating from around 1792 survives...

Licensees: Benjamin Gardiner (listed as 'vict {victualler} punch bowl College Yard (1792); T.H.Wheeler (1793); John Matthews (1820); Edwin Spiers (1829); Benjamin Powell (1835); William Pritchard (1842–1850); Charles Burrows (1850); Joseph Scragg (1855); John Warder (1872-1889); Sarah Runicles (1889-91); Francis Brockington (1891-2); Eustace Armstrong (1892-6); William Appleton (1896); William Marshall (1896-8); Arthur Allen (1898-1901); Joseph Osborne (1901–1914); Mrs Lily Osborne (1914–1936); Charles Howells (1936-40); William Josiah Davis (1940-50); William Inight (1950-2); Frederick Steer (1952); Frederick George Stevens (1952-3); William Henry Smith (1953-55); William George Womersley (1958-58); Wilfred Haywood (1958).

The Old - and through the Lich Gate, the New - Punchbowls (CCMH/CFOW)

New Punchbowl
Location: Lich Street
Years active: 1870s – 1909

C3/22

At 15 Lich Street on the north side, and noted as being opposite the famous Lich Gate (details in account of its much longer-lived namesake above). First listed in Littlebury's Directory of Worcestershire 1873. Licensee John Brooks was convicted in 1875 for selling in prohibited hours and fined 10/- plus costs.

Licensees: John Brooks (1872-80); John Baker (1880-86); Robert Martin (1886 when he died); Sarah Martin (1887-8); Charles Langley (1888-96); Ben Ford (1896-1902); Charles J. Read (1902-3); Francis Rowland (1903); Thomas Clarke (1903-5); George Jones (1905); Alfred Browning (1905-6); Mrs Florence Browning (1906).

Black Boy
Location: Leach or Leech (Lich) Street
Years active: 1700 - 1880

Clearly a popular and long-lived establishment as it's mentioned by Noake as being in existence in 1744 and is still there as late as 1877 – though no images specifically showing the inn have yet come to light. Listed as Leach Street, re-named Lich Street as in Billings Directory of Worcestershire

Licensees: Mrs Wedgeberrow (1790); J. Day (1792); Elizabeth Day (1820); William Wadely (1829); Thomas Corbett (1835); Samuel Shipp (1843-55); John Griffiths (Black Boy, Lich Street - 1855); Anne Page (1859, transferred to Sarah Griffiths).

Chequers
Also known as: Chequer and Squirrel. Chequer
Location: Leach (Lich) Street also High ward, possibly Sidbury
Years active: 1820 - 30

One of two named '**Chequer**' both in the City's High ward, and probably (but by no means certainly as records are vague) originally called **The Chequer and Squirrel**. A **Chequers** also existed in nearby King Street. Listed in Register of Victuallers' Recognizance of 1766 under Edward Moases and later Worcester Lewis Directory 1820

Licensees: Edward Moases (1766); John Baylis (1784); Charles Clarke (1814-20s)
Possibly one and the same as:

Chequer
Location: Sidbury
Years active:

Listed in Register of Victuallers' Recognizance of 1784 and Royal Directory 1790 under licensee Elizabeth Ford

Duke of York
Location: Leach (Lich) Street Lich Street
Years active: 1820 to 1850s

First listed in Victuallers' Recognizances 1827 and Pigot's Worcestershire Directory 1829 (later Pigot 1835 and Hunt & Co's Commercial Directory for Gloucester, Hereford and Worcester, 1842) and thereafter to 1855 with no further reference. Included in the new St Helens ward (from High ward) 1835. A later **Duke of York** also existed in Angel Place.

Licensees: Ezekiel Gummery (c1820s-30s); Thomas Linton (c1830–1840): William Morris (1842–c1860)

King's Arms
Location: Leach (Lich) St.
Years active: 1820-1830

Seemingly short-lived inn in main thoroughfare into the City at the time: 1820 (Worcester Lewis Directory) active at the same time as another **Kings Arms** in the neighbouring St Andrews parish – though diffent lcensees suggest the two are separate entities

Licensee listed as Elisha Powell (1820)

Mitre
Location: (St Peters Parish) probably Lich (originally Leach) Street
Years active: 1660s – 1860s

Ancient inn mentioned by Noake p 121 s being existence in 1664 and listed in Grundy Royal Directory 1792. Noake 1877 'an inn so called in St Peters parish in 1664 and about the same time as another **Mitre** in High Street. Included in the newly-created St Helens ward (from High ward) 1835.

St Michaels Church - and the Cathedral Vaults
- and below, inset, the same site today (CCMH/
CFOW)

C3/28 Cathedral Wine and Spirit Vaults
Location: College Street
Years active: 1873 - 1908

First listing Littlebury's Directory of Worcestershire 1873 at 14 College Street and seemingly short-lived. Shown on 1886 OS map of the City, but not surviving much longer – its end no doubt speeded-up in the wake of a report into the state of Worcester's pubs in 1906 by the Chief Constable who not only noted it had no back yard and that the sanitary conditions were poor, but that its licence had also been transferred three times in the previous two years and that there was 11 licensed houses within 173 yards of the corner of College St. and Sidbury. When it closed about two years later, It became a picture framing shop.

Licensees: Apsley Brett (1873); Thos. Radford, Cathedral Vaults (1900)

C3/29 Old Talbot
Also known as: Ye Old Talbot
Location: Friar Street, Sidbury
Years active: poss pre-1400s to present

Ancient inn, and likeliest contender as the City's oldest *(with **Coventry Arms/Cardinal's Hat** close by in terms of location and lineage)*. Mentioned as far back as any records extend according to John Noake (p118) and probably older than **The Cardinals Hat** on account of being the site of the cathedral monks' brewhouse, later Church House with a largely unbroken history as an ecclesiastical inn, standing in what had been the cathedral churchyard. Prince Rupert is reputed to have entertained his Royalist generals here the night before the Battle of Worcester and no expense was spared for the festivities – but when victorious Roundhead Colonel Essex later attempted the same thing, he was afforded no more than 'a bottle of white wine and sugar'.

According to Hubert Leicester: '...in the boundary wall of the Sanctuary in Sidbury, attention is called to **The Talbot Inn**, originally the Church House of the cathedral, and institution for the convenience of worshippers attending the cathedral from outlying districts. Church Houses in the early days played an important part in the social life of the parishioners and at one time baked the bread and brewed the ale for those who were not able to bake and brew in their own homes. The profits of these houses were devoted to parish purposes. Many of the houses became afterwards licensed public houses and this accounts for so many inns being close to churches **The Mug House** at Claines and **The Bell** in St Johns may be quoted as cases in point'. Not listed as 'one of (Worcester's) five principal carriers' Inns in Baylis, Lewis Almanack 1885-8 but as 'other carriers' inns alongside **Saracen's Head, Rein-Deer, Golden Lion, King's Head, Angel** and others in various parts of the town.

Cited by Noake as 'the inn to which I am inclined to assign the first place both for antiquity and importance' – a view with which I wholly go along with – **The Talbot** or derivations of it has been mentioned for as far back as records extend, existing to the present day without a significantly changed name. In the 17[th]c magistrates regularly adjourned from the Guildhall to here for 'the more comfortable discharge of their functions', and amid the potations of sack and beer and the fumes of tobacco, many a prisoner has there been sentenced to the pillory, the stocks and the whipping post. Sometimes **The Talbot** in the Tything was selected for the same purpose and at a later period **The Star, the Crown and the Hop Pole**. The large State Room used by the Magistrates here is reputed to still exist. Around 1730, **The Talbot** contained stabling for 40 horses and the ground on which it stood was 53 yards long by 21 yards wide out of which was 75 ft by 40 belonging to the Parsonage house of St Michaels. Its neighbours were then G Smith clothier, Catherine Stevens widow, R(ichar)d Parr, barber, Ed Matthews, Jos Chetle saddler, John Snead carpenter. Records also list the five homes adjoining **The Talbot** in 1709: Joseph Hill apothecary, Margery Lock widow, John Leonard, smith, William Hopley hatter and Edward Hayden pin-maker. Fifty years later these were swept away and the same tenements sheltered John Inson (next to Talbot) patten (sic) maker) Richard Charington labourer, John Watton blacksmith, P. Yeates hatter, and G. Lewis huckster (corner house of Lich Street).

About 1790 all these had disappeared and their places taken by Joseph Griffiths huckster, Wm Patten breeches maker, John Green cutler, Morgan a turner, and Charles Allen last maker. In 1688 Jacobite supporters of a French invasion were interrogated and tried here. On 26th April 1895 and again almost exactly a year later, licensee George Smith was fined a total of 15/- (75p) with £2.4s.6d (£2.2$\frac{1}{2}$p) for being drunk on his own licensed premises – the same misdemeanour also committed on two consecutive days, 29th and 30th March 1920 by licensee Thomas Hands who curiously enough got off rather lighter than his predecessor: he was fined a total of 11/- (55$\frac{1}{2}$p) with 18/- (90p) costs.

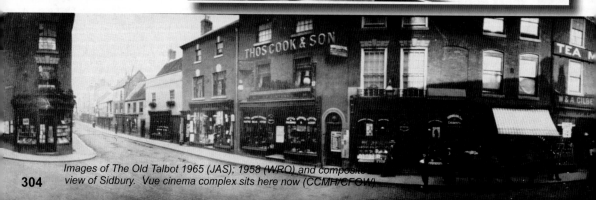

Images of The Old Talbot 1965 (JAS); 1958 (WRO) and composite view of Sidbury. Vue cinema complex sits here now (CCMH/CFOW)

Flowers, later Whitbread house, listed Worcester City Directory 1958-9 under hotels as 'Ye Olde Talbot Inn, Proprietor Mr Vivian Lewis. The oldest licensed house in the City. First Class Commercial Hotel. Bed and Breakfast. AA and RAC. Garage. Mrs L. M. Dawson Proprietress Phone 3573'.

Extensive renovations in 1966 exposed original old beams and excavations unearthed fragments of skeletons and 17th century artefacts such as leather slippers and clay pipes. Now belongs to and run by Olde English Inns (Greene King Brewing and Retailing Ltd registered in Bury St. Edmunds) - the same group that operates the Hungry Horse chain, thus making The Talbot a 'sister' to **The Glovers Needle.**

Licensees: W. Walker (1661); John Surman (1730); H. Blunt (1751); Thomas Williams (listed as 'Talbot inn Sidbury' 1782); Humphrey Handley (1802); Thomas Colston (1829); William Williams (1835); Ann Williams (1842 and 1855, listed as 'Talbot commercial inn'); Edward Pardoe (as 'Talbot, Sidbury and College Street' 1872-4); George Mason (1874-5); Jabez Smallwood (1875-6); Richard Roden (1876-9); Henry Kirk (1879-81); Robert Reed (1881-3); George Sevill (1883-95); George Smith (1895); Eli Edward Griffiths (1896-99); Thomas Hand (1899-1900); Harry Gregory (1900-03); Walter Bolus (1903-5); James Healey (1905-6); Harry Loxley (1906-9); William Miller (1909-15); Ralph E. Goostry (1915-22); Albert Milner (1922-3); Robert Mitchell (1923); Frank Walford (1923-4); Edward Potter (1924-6); Edward Davenport (1926-9); Frank Juggins (1929-35); Sydney Mackay (1935-40); Lily May Dawson (1942-1946); Vivian Thomas Lewis (Proprietress Mrs L. M.Dawson 1946-52); Winifred Ethel Lewis 1952-56); Nena Garnier (1962-6); Clifford Leary (1966-9); Alan Muir (1969-70); Robert Styler (1970-2); Henry Kybett (1972-9); Benito Osonio (1979-81); George Kitchen-Kerr (1981-2); Gerald Davies (1982); Robert Morrell (1982); William Rice (1982-6); Miles Ward and Horst Gritsch (1986); Martin N. Gormley (2001) Current (2013) licensee/dps: Richard Manning. Worcester City licence 1165

Before taking in the history-rich Friar Street, no record of Worcester's pubs could be considered complete without serious attention being given to....

C3/30 King's Head
Also Known as: The Bell
Location: Sidbury
Years active: 1600 – present

Originally **The Bell**, it changed its name to **The Kings Head** at the Restoration of King Charles II in 1660. According to John Noake in Worcestershire Relics, Sidbury Gate and Tower '... extended across Sidbury near the Kings Head inn and so as to include the street which leads to St Peters Church *(St Peters Street, formerly Church-street)*'. He wrote that the first description of this old inn is in 1609 as 'a tenement of the parish of St Peter nere adjoynynge the gate of the said cittie called Sudbury Gate, and hath been knowen and called by the name of **The Bell**, now in the occupation of Roger Folliott'. At the restoration of Charles II (1660) when so many inns assumed the sign of the king's head in memory of 'the martyr' Charles I and in compliment to his reigning son, **The Bell** no doubt followed the example, for in 1678 it was described as being 'formerly the Bell, but then the Kings Head, and in the tenure of Joan Heming at a rental of 20s'.

Built virtually on the site of the old Sidbury gate against which hundreds of Royalist troops were slaughtered as they clamoured to get back into the City following their rout by Cromwell's forces in the Battle of Worcester (1651) only to find the gate locked, small wonder it's home to a well-catalogued and seemingly well-intentioned ghost of a cavalier whose regular sightings as well as mischievious tricks like switching lights on and off, tilting pictures and impishly ringing the bell for 'time' are accompanied with warnings of impending bad news which have an unfortunate habit

Kings Head largely unchanged from this 1964 shot (JAS)

of coming true. Though he's generally reckoned to be harmless and benevolent chap, this particular spectre's presence also seems to enjoy throwing glasses around and turning on taps and lights. In 1982 a Swedish visitor who knew nothing abut the ghost – or much about Worcester's history come to that – was dozing in an upstairs bedroom *(the Kings Head was then residential too and the actual room is now the first floor restaurant, overlooking College Street)* when he says he was woken up by a freezing sensation and shaken violently. He claims he saw the ghost of a cavalier who warned him not to go out that night. He ignored the advice and got himself beaten up by thugs in town, spending a couple of nights in the infirmary.

Not listed as 'one of (Worcester's) five principal carriers' Inns in Baylis, Lewis Almanack 1885-8 but as 'other carriers' inns. On 1st June 1951, licensee Frank Onions was fined £5 for selling beer during non-permitted hours. Robert Allen House, later Banks's, in 1981 I described it as 'working men's bar that borders on the bland, but whatthehell, it's as warm and friendly a spot as you'll find in town, grand old lounge that could have stepped straight out of Blenheim Palace, skittle alley and in summer continental style tables and chairs on the courtyard'. I said then it was 'a grand old pub dating back to1609 with a reputation for beer you'd have found hard to cap in this town' *(sadly in contrast to now)*.

'The bar's an oddly-shaped stand-up and slug it out sort of place that's so friendly it's more like a Northern club than a downtown bar in stuck-up Worcester' (the landlord of seven months then was a Rochdale refugee). One of six pubs listed in Worcester Trades Directory 1957-8 with a Sidbury address: **Kings Head Hotel** at 62, **Red Lion** (109), **Barley Mow** (115), **Loch Ryan** (139 – tel no 372111), **Ye Olde Talbot** (14) **Angel Commercial Hotel** (l36).

Recently taken over and extensively refurbished by the Scoff & Quaff group who also run **The Swan** at Whittington, **The Ewe & Lamb** at Bromsgrove, **The Leopard** at Bishops Tachbrook, **The Tivoli** in Cheltenham, and **The Crown & Sandys**, Ombersley

Licensees: *Roger Folliott (1609); Joan Hemming (1678); Thomas Price (1766); Jos Stephens, jun (1778); George Gorle (listed as 'King's head inn 15 Sidbury' – 1790 and 1792); Thomas Vaughan (listed as vict and coal dealer, Sidbury Wharf (1814-20s); Wm. Featherstone (1827); James Godwin (1832– 1850s); Susannah Godwin (1855); Mrs Anne Grove (1872-87); George Epps (1887-91); Thomas Joyner (1891-93); Charles Stallard (1893-98); George Epps (1898-1906); Charles R. Stallard (1906–1910 when he died); Frederick J. Roberts (1910-18); Walter Levett (1918-20); Edward Brampton (1920-23); Bertram Lee (1923-38 also listed as brewer 1932-1940); Morris Parsons (1938-40 listed as 67 Sidbury 1940); George Russell (1941-6); Norman Edward Jeffrey (1946-1949); Victor*

Edwin MacDonald (1949-50); Frank Onions (1950-4); Gerald Bowen (1954-5); Harold Crosthwaite Scott (1955-56); Richard Puzey Hayden (1956-65); David Humphries (1965-8); Horace Fletcher (1968-74); George Andrews (1974-6); Leonard Cleg (1976-7); George Owen (1977-1980); Colin Mills (1980-1); Ralph Cooper (1981-2); Alan Galloway (1982-4); Peter Gore (1984-6); Peter Childs (1986-7); Michael Lavall (1987); Gordon Taylor; Alfred Thomas. Current (2013) licensee/dps: Stephen Ballard. Worcester City licence 1399.

*Re-trace to point **C** and get ready to be immersed in some serious Worcester history*

C-D: Friar Street to Pump Street

The savage desecration of the historic areas of Friar Street and Lich Street in the 1960s is one of the less edifying chapters in the history of unfathomable decision-making made by people elected to do the right thing by Worcester. This area is so rich in history, every building tells a tale – as Pat Hughes and Nick Molyneaux set out to do in their research into the history of Friar Street. Logging the history of this once eye-catching old street house by house – the unsympathetic addition of modern buildings dramatically marring the overall effect – they describe Friar Street as 'a late arrival on the urban scene being merely a lane giving access to the back properties of the High Street until the foundation of the Franciscan Friary in 1235'. The coming of the Friary 'must have prompted or accelerated the building' of what's now Friar Street.

Moving on to the eighteenth century they write: '...as the street became less pleasant to live in, owners moved out and by the end of the century, most of the buildings were let, sub-let and sometimes let again. Because of this it is often difficult to trace occupants but they seem to be mostly small tradesmen. There was a group of maltsters and bakers, two tailors, three public houses, a dealer in spirituous liquors, a couple of London carriers and a selection of traders and retailers including 'Smith Wm., Translator of Shoes'.

A listing in Worcester Royal Directory for 1790 shows Tho Evett as 'dealer in spirituous liqors' (sic) and an exotically named Amicillus Young as as 'vict' (victualler) without detailing of which premises – though John Young notably set up '**Young's Mug House**' on the corner of Pump Street in 1766, so it's possible the reference is to what's today's **Eagle Vaults**.

C3/31 Globe Vaults
Also known as: Catherine Wheel
Location: 1 and 2 Friar Street (also 33 and 33-35 Friar Street)
Years active: 1780 - 1971

Re-built in the mid 1800s and amalgamated into No 33 when it would have looked much as it does today, the first incarnation here, **The Catherine Wheel** which drew its name from the sign of The Knights of Saint Catherine of Sienna, was originally thought to have been the last (or first) house in Friar Street – hence its original number, No 1. In 1555-6 the Dean and Chapter-owned property was leased to John Cowell: a century on when the house is described as having 'four chambers with two toplofts, with hall, kitchen, bakehouse and shop downstairs' it was under the tenancy of Thomas Jeffreys. Its history as licensed premises dates back to 1775 when it was divided into two tenements occupied by tallow maker John Bedford and baker Henry Sansom who also ran it as a coffee house. By the end of the century it belonged to Thomas Evett 'dealer in spirituous liquors'– a tradition that appears to have continued for nearly two centuries as wine dealers and brewers Joselands occupied the building by 1820 and ran it as a retail spirit shop, a role it reprised when it later closed as a Spreckleys, later Whitbread pub in the 1970s. It changed its name to **The Globe** around 1859 existing for nearly 120 years: it then became a wine and spirits outlet after its closure as a pub. Included by Noake (1877) as one of a number of City inns, some of which are 'probably not much less ancient than...' 1517, also cited as a 'Corporation house' where the '24' and '48' *(effectively the 24 highest-ranking*

Globe (foreground) and Cardinals Hat 1964 (JAS)

Globe (right) and Cardinals Hat
(left) 1972 (CCMH/CFOW)

members of the Council and the 48 members that made up the entire Council) often combined official work with social pleasure here. The building is now Emporio

Licensees: As Catherine Wheel (unknown). **As The Globe:** James Lewis (1859); Henry Gibbons (1872-79); George Hughes (1879-84); Henry Powell (1884-8 when he died); Charles Fildes (1888-92); Henry Kirk (1892-93); James Peebles (1893-94); Anne Osborn (1894-1901); John Robinson (1901-2); John Butcher Lyons (1902-6); Thomas Reeve (1906); Mary Lyons (1906); Henry Harris (1907); Harold P. Hayes (1907-1910); Thomas Shaw (1910-11); John Hodges (1911-12 when he died); Annie Hodges (1912-16); Thomas Lane (1916); Samuel Collier (1916-17); Alice Collier (1917-19); Samuel Collier (1919-23); Albert Bateman (1923-5); William Sutton (1925-8); Frank Pearce (1928–1946); Frederick George Layton (1946-54); Fred Arthur Sherwood (1954-70); Edward Wilkes (1970-1).

Cardinal's Hat
Also known as: Swan and Falcon. Coventry Arms. Austrian Bar
Location: 31, Friar Street
Years active: 1497 - present

A famous ale-house for four centuries at least, it was first mentioned as an inn in 1497. It then changed its name around 1745 to **The Swan and Falcon** and then in 1814 to **The Coventry Arms** after the Earl of Coventry, then Recorder of Worcester and back again to its original religious title in the 1950s. Pat Hughes in her scholarly work on the houses in Friar Street said '...the first reference to **The Cardinal's Hat** goes back to 1497 when the inn was designated by the City Ordnances as being one of the depots for the City's fire hooks. Nicholas Mocock *('mococke of ye cardinals hatte')* ...was involved with the authorities in connection with a brawl at the inn'.

She says that the next tenant, Roger Bury, was landlord of the inn for over thirty years: '...eventful years that saw the Reformation established, overturned and re-established before his death in 1565. In 1555 he was called to give evidence before the bailiffs of the City when one of his customers, Thomas Freeman, accused another, John Palmer, of spreading rumours concerning the death the Queen and the acclamation of Philip of Spain as King – a misdemeanour tantamount to treason.

'...in 1671, John Haynes left the first inventory for the buildings. He had five good, well-furninshed bed chambers, each with one or two beds, the Rose Chamber, the Office Chamber, the Hither and Further Judges' Chambers, and the Great Chamber, all with hearths. Over the kitchen was a more spartan unheated room with four beds, doubtless for the less affluent. Downstairs was a shovel-board (shove a'penny) room, a poorly furnished parlour, an ordinary bed for ye ostler and a kitchen with one long table with chaires, stool'.
(Source: Pat Hughes, Nick Molyneaux)

It was rebuilt in 1765 and it's believed that all that remains of the original building is a single wall – which, if true *(and the source is impeccable)* would make a mockery of subsequent claims of being the City's oldest pub. Nonetheless, its history remains a long and remarkable one. The inn reverted to **The Coventry Arms** in 1814 and underwent an unexplained period of closure between 1817 and 1825. On 29th August 1848, the property came up for auction, described as 'an old established, well-frequented and respectable market inn:

'The house contains Entrance Passage, Tap-room, Bar, Cooking kitchen, front and back Parlours, Club Room, six bedrooms, four attics, Roomy Landing and Staircase, Malt-room, good Cellarage, small Courtyard in the rear leading from House to a capital Brew House. The Stable-yard is approached by a lofty driving way from the Street enclosed by folding doors; the Stabling capable of accommodating nearly forty horses; the Timber-yard may be converted into an excellent Kitchen Garden. In fact the Property is suitable for any purpose requiring space'

Listed variously as **Coventry Arms** or **Cardinals Hat** at Friar Street, 3 Friar Street and 31 Friar Street, Noake refers to it in 1877: **'Cardinal's Hat** (now the **Coventry Arms**, Friar Street) a famous house for more than three centuries at least, and a tenement and garden only divided it from the sign of **The Catherine Wheel,** a rival establishment (later **The Globe**). When this house changed its name I have not discovered. The name **'Cardinals Hat'** has always been contentious on account of its catholic associations, the name **Coventry Arms** being considered more appropriate to Protestant tastes'.

Cardinals Hat (left) - re-opened 2013 after some years in the dark, and the former Globe (now Emporio) (BB)

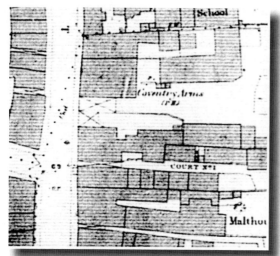

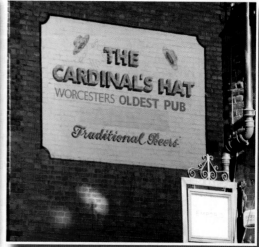

Hubert Leicester later describes it thus: 'Inn under the sign of the Coventry Arms, formerly the Cardinals Hat. Nearly all the inns in the vicinity of the cathedral originally bore ecclesiastical signs **(Angel de Trompe, Cross Keys, Mitre and Seven Stars**'.

On 10th October 1892, licensee Joseph Andrews was fined 10/- (50p) and costs for being found drunk on his own premises here. About 1900 the licensee's daughter or granddaughter was fatally burned in a fire on the first floor – and there have been constant tales of her ghost being seen running across the landing with her hair on fire. On 14th September 1956, licensee Henry Allen was hauled up before the Chief Inspector of Worcester City Police and cautioned as to his future conduct after 'persons were found on the premises after permitted hours'.

Listed Grade II and closed for two years prior to re-opening in 2013 (by which time it had been bought by the same family behind **Bushwackers** and other licensed premises in the City) it had been an important venue for County carriers in the 19th century: carriers to and from Broughton, Broughton Hackett, Comberton, Dormstone, Pershore, North Piddle, Spetchley, Stoulton, Tibberton, Upton Snodsbury, and Whittington operated from here. Previously a Davenports inn listed at Bath Row Birmingham with brewery at the back, taken over 1982-92 by Jolly Roger microbrewery, then later run by controversial Austrian licensees who held out for – and won – the right to sell beer in Continental measures instead of imperial. Andrea Limlei's decision to call it a day after ten years was recorded in 'Pint Taken', Worcs' CAMRA's monthly newsletter who reported: '...for ten years Worcester has been able to claim to have something quite unique. A pub selling Austrian beer by the litre! However, with rising costs, (landlord) Andrea Limlei decided not to renew her lease and now, sadly, the Cardinals Hat is shut. When Andrea and her husband took over running Worcester's oldest pub (sic) and started selling beer in litres they did not realise what they had let themselves in for. They were thrown into a major battle, which made the national papers, with Trading Standards who said the pub could not serve its imported lager in litre measures (but) could be sold only by the pint or half. Trading Standards eventually dropped the case, saying that enforcement of this aspect of weights and measures legislation does not have a high priority'.

Recently described in West Midlands Inventory of Historic Pub Interiors (with not complete accuracy) as 'a good attractive example of an interwar makeover in the 'Olde Englishe' style. Rebuilt in around 1760, the two upper storeys are pinkish-orange brick Georgian style but on the ground floor, in comes a wealth of timberwork from the 1920s or '30s. The interior is really quite small but consists of three separate rooms. The most interesting of them is the 'Panelled bar' at the rear left or room '6' according to the number on the door. It has full-height 16-17th century-style panelling, a Tudor-style stone fireplace, a little stained glass in the windows depicting a cardinal's hat, fixed benches around the walls with bell pushes above and a hatch to the servery. The passage has a panelled dado with lozenge decoration. The two front rooms are rather plainer but both have imitation half-timbering. At the front right is a small snug (with a no. 7 on the door); the left has modern fittings probably dating from a sensitive refurbishment by Banks's brewery in 1996. This latter room has a plaster relief of a cardinal's hat over the fireplace. There are 1930s tiled walls and floors in both the ladies' and gents'. The pub is now known as the 'Austrian Bar' and is dedicated to the sale of Austrian beers in 0.3 litre, half litre and litre sized glasses'.

Re-opened April 2013 under licensee Nigel Smith (also licensee of **The Fleece** at Bretforton) who told Worcester News (April 5th 2013): "I am a sucker for architectural quality and history and this pub seems to be one that needs to be brought back to life and to revive its true English traditions as an ale house. We are hoping to generate business from tourism, but mainly local people. It's all about making customers feel at home when they come in".

In 1981 licensee's wife Mavis Wells told me '...a real talkers' pub is this. We seem to attract a lot of professional people like teachers (Kings School kids, if you want to know where sir is...!), nurses, a lot of cathedral people and even a fair proportion of the Birmingham Symphony Orchestra. And Davenports drivers – their depot's just behind the pub. It's the atmosphere – there's no gimmicks'. I described it as 'so hysterically historical it's a cryin' shame not to have serving wenches, powdered wigs, churchwarden pipes and talk of Bonnie Prince Charlie (the first). If history's your bag try it, after all it's one of the City's oldest pubs and there's a manuscript in the lounge stating that in 1553 it was one of 10 inns and 44 ale houses in the town. I suspect not much has changed since then. Forsooth, pray venture into yon boozer 'ere long'. First pint, I noted was duff – very duff', but visits to the newly re-opened **Cardinals Hat** in June 2013 and subsequently proved a different tale. Historian Pat Hughes reserves a special place for the Cardinal's Hat in her scholarly piece on Friar Street, written in association with Nick Molyneaux.

Licensees: (as Cardinals Hat) *James Banister and his wife Marjery (1544); Roger Bury (1554); James Pritchard (?); John Haynes (-1671); Richard Rogers (listed as 'a carrier' 1684); ? Barrett (1733); ? Gaskell (1769):* **As Coventry Arms:** *Henry Smith (1814); Ann Hooper (1827); Robert Gell (1835); John Gummery (1842); James Phillips (1850); William Phelps (1872-4); Edward Jenkins (1874-80); Elizabteth Hyde (1880-88); George Taylor (1988-91); Joseph Andrews (1891-3 when he died); Mrs. Sophie Phelps (1893-1900); John Haynes (1900-01); Thomas C. Green (1901-10); William Chamberlain (1910-14); George William Taylor (1914-20); Edward Hollies (1920-21); Frederick Walton (1921-30); George Knight (1930-2); Frank Clarke (1932); William H. Such (1932-1948); Wallace Smith (1948-52); Gordon Jackson (1952-4); Charles Henry Smith Millinchip (1954-56); Henry Allen (1956-61); Lawrence Ingram (1961-2);* **(As Cardinals Hat #2):** *Jack Sutherland (1962-4); Albert Haines (1946-5); Leonard Roberts (1965-6); Frederick Wright (1966-7); Wallace Smith (1967-76); Michael Curran (1976-7); Mavis and Fred Wells (1977 – 1990s); Paul Soden (1990-92); Andrea Limlei (1992-2002); Stephen Rogers (2002-3); Susan E. Roberts (and Stephen Rogers 2003-2011); re-opened April 2013. Nigel Smith, managed by Sadie Hughes (2013). Worcester City licence 1124*

Parrot
Location: Friar Street, precise location unclear
Years active: 1600s - 1800

Precise location unclear, but according to Pat Hughes, very likely side-by-side with The Cardinal's Hat – so possibly on the same site as **The Globe** but unclear. Also mentioned by Noake (1877) as one of a number of 'ancient' City inns, some of which are probably not much less ancient than the eighteenth or even 17th century'. Thought to have been kept at one time by John Fuller

Cross Keys
Location: 37-38 Friar Street
Years active: 1660s – 1910

Ancient ecclesiastical inn listed as 37 and 38 Friar Street, thought to have been an inn since about 1660 when it was owned by one George Stock, described as 'a weaver and clothier' who made clothes on a loom at the rear of the premises where he also had a brewhouse with two furnaces. According to Pat Hughes, 'he paid the City for a tavern head and had fourteen vessels of ale and beer in his cellar'. Legend also has it that a secret passage links the former pub with the cathedral and that the spectres of three nuns have a habit of making their ghostly presence felt. The actual building is thought to date back to the thirteenth century, although the timber framework is reckoned to have been installed sometime between 1500-1550. For many years after that, the still-impressive black and white building was divided into separate dwellings, owned and used by different trades people – typically cloth makers, tailors, a baker and a painter, some of whom brewed ale as a side-line culminating in full-time use as **The Cross Keys** which flourished for about 200 years.

However, two events in 1906 and 1907 speeded-up the pub's inevitable demise: first, a damning report into the state of Worcester's pubs in 1906 by the Chief Constable who noted 'this house is greatly decayed, but it has a very large trade and is much used by county people on market day'. At the same time, he noted, there were 30 licensed houses from the corner of Pump St and the Shambles, and the Cross Keys is the worst of the lot.' The second, a year later when a customer called Digger fell into one of the home-brew vats and drowned also bankrupted its then licensee William Walker *(whose brother Harry was licensee of **The Horse and Jockey** in Pump Street at the same time)*. Contemporary accounts reveal that on the day of the tragedy, the usual brewer failed to turn up so Digger volunteered to stir

Not many pubs can match the chequered history of The Coss Keys - here left. Now The Tudor House Museum - and well worth a visit! (CCMH/CFOW)

the beer in the vats. Somehow he fell in – and despite William Walker's attempts to save him, he drowned. Walker – who had previously been licensee at **Crown** (Friar Street), **Black Lion** (Dent Street), **Beehive** (Carden Street) and **Herefordshire House** in Bransford Road and went from here to **The Mug House** in Hylton Road which he ran until it too was forced to close in 1912 – offered to pay Digger's widow £1 a week for life but she demanded a lump sum of £600. The court found in her favour, maintaining that Walker was both drunk and negligent, a verdict that crippled him financially. He died in 1929. The combination of the two factors proved too much for the Cross Keys to survive and it called orders for the last time in 1910 when the building was bought by the Cadbury family who restored it, finding mediaeval features behind centuries of plaster and old ships' timbers as well as a number of Civil War bullets ('Cromwell's Brown Besses') in the stone recesses behind the stone walls of the cellar, before turning it into a confectioners. With a tea room and restaurant upstairs, the building became known as the 'Tudor Coffee House'. In 1921 it was purchased by Worcester

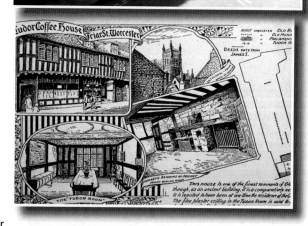

Same scene 2013 (BB)

Corporation for use as a school clinic, and many local people remember coming here as children for inoculations, dental checks and fitness examinations. For a short time during the Second World War, the building was also used as an Air Raid Warden's Post and Billeting Office and is now Tudor House Museum, run by volunteers group Worcester Heritage & Amenity Trust. The museum opened in May 2004 in a bid to keep the building open and available to the public after funding cuts imposed in March the previous year had forced the County Council to mothball the museum. Aside from being a fascinating building with a rich history, its collection showing aspects of Worcester life over the centuries is well worth the visit, with displays of local history, crafts and culture alongside a shop and coffee room serving drinks and cakes.

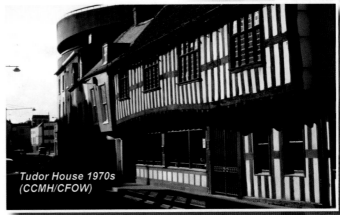

Tudor House 1970s (CCMH/CFOW)

Licensees: *Harry Green (listed as maltster 1690); Alan Malpas (1719); Charles Jones (listed as 'vict Crofs keys 37 Friar Street' (1792); John Mannering (1820); George Wormington (1827-c1840); Edwin Gittings (1842); Joseph Sandford (1855); William Staite (1872-74); William Sandford (1874-94 when he died); William Greaves (1895-7); Harry Jones (1897-1900); Walter Parry (1900-06); William Walker (1906-9); Agnes Walker (1909); Harry A. Jones, address then 38 Friar Street*

C3/35 Woolpack
Location: Friar Street
Years active: 1500s

Another 'lost' inn listed by Noake quoting earlier sources, without the benefit of any further details. Possibly on the site of what became the City Gaol, Laslett's Almhouses, but unclear (the present buildings date from 1912) Even the normally meticulous Pat Hughes dismisses an earlier use for this site as '...Nicholas and James Symonds had the largest property (on this site) and ran it as an inn. They paid the City for a projecting stone window...'

C3/36 Conservatory Café Bar
Location: 34-36 Friar Street)
Years active: 1985 - present

Licensees: *Jason Wells (2000)*

More a café bar than a pub run by the Cropthorne Inns Partnership registered at Vale Business Park Evesham, it remains a popular City centre meeting-place. Previously a motorbike dealers and a pet shop. Current (2013) licensee/dps: Andrew Portlock. Worcester City licence 1270

Crown
Also known as: Old Crown
Location: Friar street
Years active: 1820 – 1938

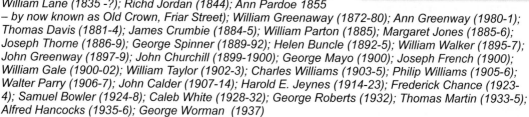

First listed Listed in Register of Victuallers' Recognizance of 1814 as Crown, St Peters under licensee John Smith and later Worcester Lewis Directory 1820 at 29, 22 and 58-59 Friar Street.

In 1884 licensee James Crumbie was convicted for allowing quarrelsome conduct here and was fined 21/- plus costs. And the following year (1885) licensee Thomas (also listed as William) Parton was convicted for being drunk on licenced premises and was fined 10/- plus 16/- costs. He was again fined in the same year for allowing consumption of alcohol in prohibited hours and was fined 21/- plus 11/6d 57$\frac{1}{2}$p) costs

Licensees: John Smith (1814–20); William Bury (1820–c1830) William Lane (1835 -?); Richd Jordan (1844); Ann Pardoe 1855 – by now known as Old Crown, Friar Street); William Greenaway (1872-80); Ann Greenway (1980-1); Thomas Davis (1881-4); James Crumbie (1884-5); William Parton (1885); Margaret Jones (1885-6); Joseph Thorne (1886-9); George Spinner (1889-92); Helen Buncle (1892-5); William Walker (1895-7); John Greenway (1897-9); John Churchill (1899-1900); George Mayo (1900); Joseph French (1900); William Gale (1900-02); William Taylor (1902-3); Charles Williams (1903-5); Philip Williams (1905-6); Walter Parry (1906-7); John Calder (1907-14); Harold E. Jeynes (1914-23); Frederick Chance (1923-4); Samuel Bowler (1924-8); Caleb White (1928-32); George Roberts (1932); Thomas Martin (1933-5); Alfred Hancocks (1935-6); George Worman (1937)

Oak
Location: Friar Street
Years active: 1840s to 1880s

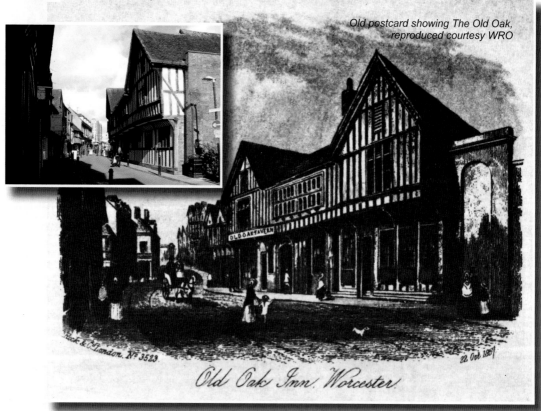

Old postcard showing The Old Oak, reproduced courtesy WRO

Seemingly short-lived pub in Friar Street dating from late 1840s to 1880s, possibly also known as **The Old Oak** and **Old Oak Tavern**. Considered sufficiently important for an unnamed artist to produce an engraving of the inn in 1857, a copy of which is owned by the City and is in the WRO collection in the Hive. Dating from 1840 according to Hunt & Co's Commercial Directory and surviving for about another 40 years under a succession of four short-lived licensees. The census of 1851 shows then licensee John Gummery (66) living here with his wife Ann (64)

Licensees: Samuel Caldwell (1850); Richd. Hughes (1842); John Gummery (1851) George Griffiths (1855); Joseph Ingles (1873)

An evocative description of the southern end of Friar Street appears in local authoress Kathleen Lawrence Smith's delightful and colourful account of growing up in Worcester during the 20s and 30s, **'God Hath Made Me To Laugh'**.

> *'In Friar Street we were at the hub of everything: sights, smells, sensations, the lot – and there were plenty! Our immediate vicinity boasted a butchery, a bakery, a fried fish shop, a large pub, a corn and seed merchants, a granary and an angler's store complete with wriggling livestock so one might truly claim all human life was there – and a bit more too... It may not be your idea of felicity to live directly opposite a pub, but it does add colour to our scene. The clientele of The Eagle Vaults was drawn largely from the tenements and courtyards in our area. Many of them worked – if at all – in nearby factories and had families larger than their incomes. With so many little 'uns occupying the limited space at home, it's not surprising that so many adults sought temporary refuge in the pub. The landlord at the time we arrived on the scene was rather a 'gent' unfitted for the rigours of his trade. But he had had the foresight to marry a woman ideally suited to it. Before her irate figure, Paddy Flynn would go sprawling into the gutter frequently. Arms akimbo she would express her opinion of him in no uncertain terms before turning to re-enter the door over which her husband stood guard'.*

– which is as graphic and entertaining an intro as any to the noted and still eye-catching pub opposite which she'd lived...

Formerly The Old Oak. In the distance (left) The Eagle Vaults (CCMH/CFOW)

Eagle Vaults
Also known as: Young's Mug House. Mug House. Volunteer. Plumbers (or Plummers) Arms. Top Hat.
Location: 2, Friar Street (and 1 Pump Street)
Years active: 1750-present

Initially (1700s) **Young's Mug House** after John Young who'd bought the property and paid for a cellar head and two steps had turned the house into a pub in 1779. When he died in 1786, his widow Amphyllis carried on running the venture though its next owner, Matthew Mason, dropped the name 'Young' but continued to call the place **The Mug House**. From 1814-18 it was briefly and patriotically **The Volunteer** and then settled down to being '**The Plummers Arms**', (sic). In 1829, the name changed again to '**The Eagle Vaults**', which has remained, with a brief and nonsensical variation in the early 1980s when it was called '**The Top Hat**'.

Fine old M&B house registered at Cape Hill Brewery, said to be 'a Victorian tiled front (c1900) on a Charles II house', it makes its first appearance as **Eagle Vaults** in Littlebury's Directory of Worcestershire 1873 ('Eagle Wine and Spirit Vaults, Friar Street') and 1 Pump Street. Addresses listed variously as 19 Friar Street (1910) 2, Friar Street (1940); Eagle Vaults, 16 Pump Street (1957) and simply '**Eagle**, Friar Street' 1959. Described by National Inventory of Historic Pub Interiors as '...built c.1740s and given a colourful glazed tile frontage c.1890s including a fascia of raised lettering 'Wines Mitchells & Butlers Spirits Gold Medal Ales And Stout' and 'Eagle Vaults Spirits'. There is a dado of colourful tiling in the lobby and a mosaic floor which runs through to the back of the pub and which has just been exposed. Originally there were walls either side of the passage, the one on the right which had a hatch for off-sales was removed c.1983, and a wide gap put in the left wall. Both bar to the right and smoke room to the left retain their original fittings almost intact.

The bare-boarded bar has a Victorian counter, fine bar back including gilded glass panels and topped with a clock, fixed seating but the etched windows in this room are replacements. Note that when the wall was removed the left hand curved section of the counter was added which carefully matches the original right hand section, apart from the detail missing on the console bracket. The bare-

Eagle Vaults 23rd March 1958 (RHS)

boarded smoke room retains good original fixed seating in bays with panels above including three plain mirrors on the far left wall and bell pushes all around; original fire surround with bevelled mirror panels in mantelpiece above, and this room retains two splendid original etched and frosted front windows. Good etched panels in the toilet doors. The upstairs function room has no old fittings'.

Once reputed to brew a salty mild ale said to have the second-highest alcohol content of any available elsewhere in England, with typical 1970s flippery and disdain for most things historical, it ridiculously re-styled itself **The Top Hat** for a short time but mercifully reverted to The Eagle Vaults. Now a Marstons house

Licensees: As Young's Mug House: John Young (1766); (poss) Amicillus Young (1790); ***As Volunteer****: Hannah Prosser (1814);* ***As Plumber's (or Plummer's) Arms****: William Masters (1820 – c 1840); Francis Hunt (1842); Elizabeth Masters (1850s).* ***As Eagle Vaults****: Mrs Jane Cullis (1872-4); James Rea (1874-5); Mr Sutton (1875-6); Thomas Brown (1876-7); John Hornidge (1877-9); George Price (1879-80); Sophia Price (1880-3); Evan Davis (1883 when he died); Elizabeth Davis (1883-4); Alfred Wilkinson (1884); Joseph Malpas (1884-6); Henry Kirk (1886-8); Stephen Overall (1888-9); William Morris (1889-1901); William Seymour (1901 – 1934); Harry Percival Hunt (1934 – 1957); Leslie Arthur Sparrrey (1957-8); Thomas William Ewins (1958-78); Graham Owens (1978); Sarah Johnson (1978); Philip Lewis (1979); Michael Stevens (1979); Brian Connor (1979-81); Irene Foster (1984); Steve Foster (1985); Paul A. Shenton (2000). Current (2013) licensee/dps: Anton Peter Barone. Worcester City licence 1219*

Immediately across the road – although some observers believe on the same site as the Eagle Vaults, a view that doesn't really stand up to closer examination, stood...

C3/40 **Fish Inn**
Also known as The Crispin
Location: Friar Street
Years active: 1780 - 1880

Another mentioned by Noake (1877) as one of a number of 'ancient' City inns, some of which are 'probably not much less ancient than...' the eighteenth or even 17th century without the benefit of clear location. Described in 1790 as being 'kept' by Cathedral sexton John Scott and later described as housing bar, parlour, kitchen and back kitchen, four rooms upstairs and a large room over the passage. Outside were two stables and a gig house. Said to have been built in brick, tile and slate and described as 'very old and dilapidated. In Pat Hughes and Nick Molyneaux' microscopic examination of the area she says that licensee Samuel Morris *(see below, listed as licensee 1760 – c1790)* 'paid for a projecting window and two seats on the street front'. Her research reveals she married Penelope Burton, a widow with four children, and in his will of 1776 he left all his estate to her and after her death to her children, and a later landlord, John Summerfield 'left the property with all his furniture, stock of liquors, brewing utensils to his widow Mary for the upkeep of their four children – one of which, Samuel kept it until about 1842. Listed in VIctuallers Recognizances of 1766 under Samuel Morris and later in Grundy Royal Directory 1792 as fifh 19 Friars Street and later 20 Friar Street (1850s). The census of 1851 shows then licensee Charles Hughes (42) living here apparently alone. Thought to have closed c1890 when Charles Street was created and building demolished

Licensees: Samuel Morris (1766); John Scott (also cathedral sexton-1790); William Allen 'innholder' (1790); John Summerfield (1800); Mary Summerfield (c1810–1830s); Samuel Summerfield (1835); Charles Hughes (1842–c1853); Henry Philpott (1854–70s); William Dufty (1873).

From The Eagle Vaults, the left turn into Pump Street – so named on account of the old water pump that was sited here roughly where the Shambles feeds into it. This thoroughfare was home to some memorable now long-gone pubs, one at least in living memory

C3/41 **Horse and Jockey**
Location: Pump Street
Years active: 1785 – 1915

Life must have been confusing for Worcester drinkers in 1792 – with two pubs of this name sited within a short distance of each other (estimated 220 yards). Longer-lived than the Quay Street **Horse and Jockey** (and much longer-lived than the Butts version) this pub first saw light of day around 1785. Listed Grundy Royal Directory 1792) and thought to have closed c1915. Listed variously as 8, Pump Street (1792); 2 Pump Street (1873) and 14 Pump Street (1910) sited next to **Eagle Vaults** and shown on the Ordnance Survey map of 1886). Licensee Henry Walker (1905-7) was the brother of William Walker, licensee of **The Cross Keys** who was bankrupted when a customer fell in to a vat of beer and drowned there in 1907.

Licensees: Wm Evans (listed as 'horfe and jockey 8 pump ftreet' (1792); Joseph Mills (1814); Jas. Williams (1827-42); Elizabeth Whitsey Williams (1842–1850s); Jas. Cook (1855); James Brown (1872-5); Anne Brown (1875-7); William Garland (1877-9); Richard Hunt (1879-88 when he died); Martha Hunt (1888-9); Joseph Thorne (1889-90 when he died); Seraphine Thorne (1891-4); William Sewell (1894-1905); Henry Walker (1905-7); George Carless (1907-1911); David Beauchamp (1911-13); Albert Turbill (1913-14); Edwin Rea (1914-15)

C3/42 Swan
Location: 4 (also 6) Pump Street
Years active: 1870 to 1965

Swan Pump Street 1958 (WRO)

The same 2013 (BB)

Originally a Kelsey's house, dating from around 1870 to c1964, and listed variously as 6 Pump Street (1900) and 4 Pump Street up to its closure, the Swan was an Ansells house at its demise c1965. On 7th April 1899, licensee Ernest Edwards was fined 10/- (50p) with 14/- (70p) costs for being found drunk here on his own premises.

Licensees: William Jones (1872-5); Samuel Redding (1875-6); Charles Philpott (1876-8); William Watts (1880-1898); Ernest Jackson (1898); Ernest Edwards (1898-9); Alfred Hayes (1899); Horace Ross (1899-1900); Eliza Harrison (1900); Robert Breeze (1900-01); Samuel T. Stinton (1901-04); Edgar Inight (1904-08); Henry William Thomas (1908-13); Edgar Inight (1913); Frank Vault (1913-14); Arthur Thomas (1914-17); Albert Evans (1917-19); George Townsend (1919-27); William Seymour (1927-8); William E. Arthurs (1928-36); Vernon Grove (1936-7); William John Smith (1937-40); Aubrey Scriven (1940-1949); Maurice Vernon Davis (1948-50); Jas Hatchett (1950-); Ernest Harding (1950-1); Ernest Camden (1951-2); Reginald Atkinson (1952); Mrs Kathleen White (1952-62); Ivor Pritchard (1962-5); Paul Blamel (1965)

C3/43 Crown
Also known as: Old Crown
Location: Pump Street
Years active: 1760 - 1860

Little known about this one, first listed in the Register of Victuallers Recognizances 1766 under Mary Ashers but probably much older than that. Incuded in the new St Helens ward (from High ward) in 1835 and listed as 4 Pump Street.

Licensees: Mary Ashers (1766); ? Lane (name illegible, listed as vict Crown 4 Pump ftreet (1795); William Bishop (1813); John Smith (1814-20s); Wm Leicester (1827 by now known as Old Crown); William Hyslop (1835); John Wileman (1842–c 1853); John Phillips (1855)

Back now at point D, The Shambles

This noted thoroughfare, originally Baxter (or Bakers) Street was home to butchers, bakers *(and no doubt candlestick makers)* and is correctly regarded as the street of a thousand trades. The Worcester Royal Directory of 1790 shows that the street was home to 1 baker, 17 butchers, 1 glazier, 1 glover, 1 ironmonger, the Servants' Register Office, 1 taylor (sic) and 2 victs (victuallers) – Willliam Grifith, licensee of **The Coach and Horses**, and Martin Holloway whose premises is tantalisingly unspecified and no other reference is made elsewhere to a publican of that name. Always a lively spot, Saturdays even up to the 1950s saw it come alive, often until after closing time and even late into the night as the butchers, many of whom had their own slaughterhouses to the rear of their premises, and greengrocers stayed open well into the night to sell off the last of their produce prior to their one day of rest when street trading *(indeed, all trading including in some cases the sale of liquor)* was strictly prohibited and strongly enforced. Rubbing side by side with busy shoppers, bargain hunters and a host of eccentric, if largely harmless old characters, those frequenting the City's most vibrant and thriving market area were never short of a handy location or two to do a deal or just sit back with something amber, liquid and refreshing in their hand... In 1906 the Chief Constable had his men tot-up the number of inns and other drinking establishments close to here: they discovered 30 licensed houses within 223 yards...

D-E: **Pump Street to The Shambles**

C3/44

Market Tavern
Also known as: New Market Tavern, Inn, Market Fountain
Location: 29, The Shambles
Years active: 1850 - 1908
     Listed in Billings Directory of Worcestershire 1855 and probably the oldest of the four taverns named after their location: the market – **Market Hall Vaults, The Market Tavern, Market Fountain and the New Market Tavern**. Shown on OS map 1886 as **Market Fountain** – probably in recognition of the Padmore fountain placed in here to suppress the stifling heat of the enclosed market Hall. It's the actual fountain that is today to be found in Cripplegate Park. *(I noted a precise copy in the market place in Stavanger in 2013. BB)* Situated on the south side of the market hall, the original **Market**

Beautiful 1910 shot of The Shambles showing The Coach and Horses (left) and the Market Tavern (right) (CCMH/CFOW)

The Shambles, Worcester.

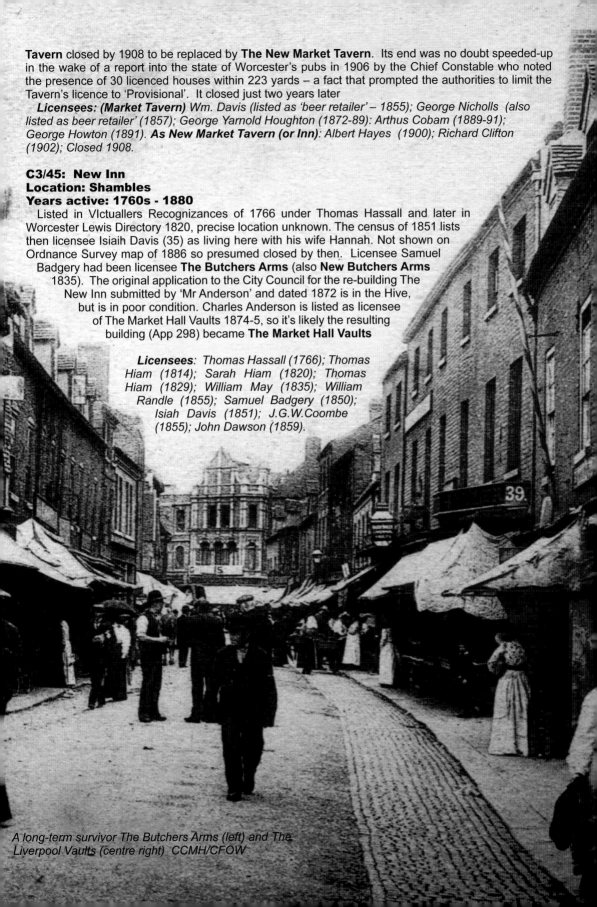

Tavern closed by 1908 to be replaced by **The New Market Tavern**. Its end was no doubt speeded-up in the wake of a report into the state of Worcester's pubs in 1906 by the Chief Constable who noted the presence of 30 licenced houses within 223 yards – a fact that prompted the authorities to limit the Tavern's licence to 'Provisional'. It closed just two years later

   Licensees: (Market Tavern) Wm. Davis (listed as 'beer retailer' – 1855); George Nicholls (also listed as beer retailer' (1857); George Yarnold Houghton (1872-89): Arthus Cobam (1889-91); George Howton (1891). **As New Market Tavern (or Inn)**: Albert Hayes (1900); Richard Clifton (1902); Closed 1908.

C3/45: New Inn
Location: Shambles
Years active: 1760s - 1880

   Listed in VIctuallers Recognizances of 1766 under Thomas Hassall and later in Worcester Lewis Directory 1820, precise location unknown. The census of 1851 lists then licensee Isiaih Davis (35) as living here with his wife Hannah. Not shown on Ordnance Survey map of 1886 so presumed closed by then. Licensee Samuel Badgery had been licensee **The Butchers Arms** (also **New Butchers Arms** 1835). The original application to the City Council for the re-building The New Inn submitted by 'Mr Anderson' and dated 1872 is in the Hive, but is in poor condition. Charles Anderson is listed as licensee of The Market Hall Vaults 1874-5, so it's likely the resulting building (App 298) became **The Market Hall Vaults**

   Licensees: Thomas Hassall (1766); Thomas Hiam (1814); Sarah Hiam (1820); Thomas Hiam (1829); William May (1835); William Randle (1855); Samuel Badgery (1850); Isiah Davis (1851); J.G.W.Coombe (1855); John Dawson (1859).

A long-term survivor The Butchers Arms (left) and The Liverpool Vaults (centre right) CCMH/CFOW

Market Hall (and Market Hall Vaults)
Location: The Shambles
Years active: 1870 - 1896

First appears in Littlebury's Directory of Worcestershire 1873 and seemingly short lived as no records exist beyond 1896 (thought closed). Sited on north side of Market Hall passage

Licensees: Charles Scrivner, Market Hall Shambles (1872-4); Charles Anderson (1874-75); Edward Coombe (1875-6); Isaac Lines (1876-9); Richard Bird (1879-80); John Woodbridge (1880-81); John Richinson (1881-84); Robert Cooper (1884-5); Albert Lovatt (1885-6); Henry Hill (1886-7); George Armson (1887); George Wilding (1887-91); Harry Fletcher (1891-2); Charles Phelps (1892); Joseph Wood (1892-2); Thomas Cavis (1893); John Hughes (1893-6); Thomas Lucy (1896)

Butchers' Arms
Also known as: New Butchers Arms
Location: 16, The Shambles
Years active: c1810 – 1955

At 16 Shambles – incidentally the same address as Pratley's only recently closed – the site is now a chemist's. Noted and popular Mitchells and Butlers house in its day, it was first listed Victuallers Recognizances in 1814 and later Worcester Lewis Directory 1820 – surviving until its licence was surrendered on 7th March 1955 – a most respectable 135 years in existence. On 9th April 1907, licensee Henry William Thomas was fined £2 with £2.14s.6d (£2.72¹/₂) costs for permitting drunkenness on the premises. Peter Cooksey tells a tale of the evening towards its final demise when the Butcher's Arms was jam-packed 'You won't get a seat in there tonight!" ups and proclaims mate A sitting in another lost pub, **The Boat** in Lowesmoor. "I bet you a pound I'll get one. Meet me in there in 'alf an 'our" retorts mate B. The wager duly accepted – and bearing in mind that, as Pete relates it, you'd have got 16 pints for your £ then – mate A plus mates C, D, and E ventured into The Butcher's at the appointed hour to find mate B sitting quite contentedly, enjoying a largely solitary pint. Little did the others know but he was the local rat catcher – or rodent operative as he'd be called today – and he'd tootled off home, collected a cage of rats, put 'em in a bag and just set 'em free in the bar... a lesson in ingenuity and drinks all round, ta ever so!'

Licensees: John Mence (1810-c 1835); Jas. Roberts (1835); Richard Rees (c1838-50); Samuel Badgery 1835 (when listed as 'New Butcher's Arms') James Knott (listed as 'beer retailer' – 1855-1870s); Henry Robinson (1872-5); Edward Thomas (1875-81); Henry Robinson (1881-99); Stephen Morris Overall (1899); William Evans (1899-1903); Henry William Thomas (1903-07); James Stringer (1907-10); Charles Timmins (1910-12); Ernest Harmer (1912-16); Arthur Harris (1916-24); Francis Palmer (1924); Isaiah Weaver (1924-7); Thomas Betteridge (1927-1947); David Baulch (1947-52); Edward Oliver Charles Wills (1952-53): Gordon Victor Beechey (1953-55)

Coach & Horses
Location: 20, The Shambles
Years active: 1780s to 1960

First mentioned in Grundy's Royal Directory 1792. Confusingly listed as 17, Shambles (1792 and 20 The Shambles 1910) and shown in a gorgeous photograph dated 1906. Closed 5th February 1960, the building still exists an alternative medicine shop. On 7th April 1897, licensee Henry Griffin was fined 10/- (50p) with 9/- (45p) costs for being drunk on his own premises. Originally Showells Brewery, leased to Ind Coope & Allsopp, later Mitchells and Butlers and reputed to be haunted. In the 1980s, a shopworker at what was then SuperCigs said that on her first day she saw a figure (quoted verbatim) '...it was upstairs in the stockroom I was counting the sweet boxes when out of the corner of my eye I saw a long black cloak or the coats they wore in those days with a hood, walking up the stairs in the middle of the room. It must have been three floors then because it was walking towards a door which I was told was never used and kept locked I was so scared i just scarpered out of the shop and went home the shortest job i ever had about 2 to 3 hrs long but i didn't get the sack they moved me to super cigs in blackfriers (sic) market but it as been on my mind all these years.... before I saw it a box of sweets fell off the shelf and made me jump but why should i remember it still today and can still see it in my mind surely it would have faded away but I can still remember it'. Now the site of (camping shop??) later sightings have included reports of children running around, and a manager reporting the strong smell of pipe or cigar smoke when he opened up in the mornings.

Licensees: William Griffith (1790 – amended to Griffiths 1792 and described as 'coach & horfes 17 Shambles'); Jonathan Chesterton (1814- c1840); Edward Wild (1842); Isaac Botting (1850); Edward Bowkett (1855); Stephen Latham (1872-4); Hannah Smith (1874-5); Joseph Birbeck (1875-87); Mary Birbeck (1887-93); Henry Griffin (1893-9); Jim Greaves (1899-1900); Harry Wakefield (1900-01);

Thomas Reeve (1901-4); William Pointin (1904-5); Harold Butler (1905); William Hollerton (1905-08); Harry Gregory (1908-10); Thomas Birbeck (1910); Albert Smith (1910-11); Oliver Williams ((1911); George Kenwrick (1911-12); William Ketteringham (1912-13); Sidney Arthur Smith (1913-22); Stanley Webb (1922-4); Robert Mitchell (1924-5); William Oliver (1925-6); William Thomas (1926-7); John Shepherd (1927-9); George Jenkins (1929); John Byers (1929-30); Sydney Smith (1930-41); Renne Rawding (1941-5); Francis Border (1945-6); Thomas George Belcher (1946-1949); Joseph William Roberts (1949); Hiram Cutler (1949-52); Ernest Camden (1952-55); Water James Taylor (1955-57); Clifford Rowell Bobbitt (1957-58); Stanley Saunders (1958); Lillian Rose Fellows (1958-60)

C3/49 Liverpool Vaults
Also known as: Baker's Arms
Location: The Shambles
Years active: 1840 – 1959

Originally **The Bakers Arms** listed in Hunt & Co's Commercial Directory for Gloucester, Hereford and Worcester (1842), Slater's Worcester Directory 1850, and Victuallers Recognizances 1859 up to 1870s and shown as Liverpool Vaults on the Ordnance Survey map of 1886. Spreckleys house legally registered at 7 Foregate Street, and the northernmost of the mid-Victorian Shambles pubs. Re-named after Robert Banks Jenkinson, 2nd Earl of Liverpool, KG, PC (7 June 1770 – 4 December 1828) who was Prime Minister from 1812–27. He was 42 years old when he became premier, which made him younger than all of his successors. As Prime Minister, Liverpool became known for repressive measures introduced to maintain order; but he also steered the country through the period of radicalism and unrest that followed the Napoleonic Wars' *(Wikipedia)*.

On 24th March 1872, licensee George Baylis was fined for unlawfully keeping open his licensed premises during prohibited hours. Appears as **Liverpool Vaults** in Littlebury's Directory of Worcestershire 1873. Closed c1959 when then landlords Fred and Dora Brace took over **The Green Man** (subsequently run by their daughter Eileen and son-in-law Derek Burton until 2003 which means the Tything pub was run by the same family for 43 years)

The Liverpool Vaults photographed 7th September 1958 (RHS)

Licensees: (as Bakers Arms): Thomas Probert (1842); James Knott (1859). **As Liverpool Vaults:** George Baylis (1872-9); Edwin Hirons (1879-84); Joseph Andrews (1884-91); Francis Griffiths (1891-2); Philip Williams (1892-3); George Freeman (1893-4); Harry Jones (1894-99 when he died); Edward Price (1900-02); William Phillpott (1902-3); Henry Baker (1903-7); Harry Waldron (1907-9); Percy Frederick Peters (1909-10); Frederick Roberts (1910-11); Stephen Davies (1911); Seth Robinson (1911-12); Joe Vernon (1912-17); Thomas Green (1917-21 when he died); Charles Worley (1922-39 when he died); Ann Worley (1939); Cyril Henry Marston (1939-1953); Frederick Ernest (and Mrs Dora) Brace (1953-59)

Above: Dora, daughter Doreen and Fred Brace at The Liverpool Vaults 1958 (pic: Becky Ciric)

Atlas
Location: Shambles (1715) Precise location unclear
Years active: c1700 – c1730?

Precise location unclear except for 'Shambles' but mentioned by Noake (1877) as one of a number of 'ancient' City inns, some of which are probably not much less ancient than the eighteenth or even 17th century.

D-F: Pump Street to New Street

Originally, New Street and Friar Street were one single street – the former known as Glover Street (or Glovers') Street on account of the number of craftsmen employed by that trade in and around here, and the latter taking its name from the Franciscan Friars. Bill Gwilliam in Old Worcester People and Places, claims seven glovers were working in New Street in 1820. It's only comparatively recently that Charles Street appeared, slicing between the two and effectively separating them into distinct thoroughfares. A walk along New Street remains a rewarding experience affording another rich sample of what life must have been like for our forebears with many old buildings (and a few pubs) still existing and not looking vastly different to what they'd looked like in Queen Victoria's day. New Street – a street that was also notorious for its tales of cockfighting in the inns dotted along its length – could have justifiably laid claim to being one of the City's best served in terms of public houses, an accolade that would have remained true even up to perhaps two decades ago. Even so, some remarkable survivors are still here...

Seven Stars
Location: 48, New Street
Years active: 1790 - 1800

Listed in Register of Victuallers' Recognizance of 1766 under John Holmes Snr. And later Grundy Royal Directory 1792 listing 'William Ford butcher feven ftars' at 48 New Street, but no further listings suggests it had closed by around 1800

(Ye) Olde Chappelle
Also known as: The Vaults. Old Chapel. Ye Olde Chappelle Hotel
Location: 51 and 52 New Street
Years active: 1870s - 1985

Century-old pub at its demise, originally **The Old Chapel** at 51 and 52 New Street and re-christened **Old Chappelle** during WW1 following the Battle of Neuve Chapelle 1915, it re-invented itself as **The Vaults** during the 1940s before reclaiming its old name in 1959. Had been Lewis Clarkes, later a Marstons House until it closed c1970. On 30th November 1934, licensee Ralph Anison was fined a total of £10 with £4.4s (£4.20p) costs for supplying intoxicating liquor during prohibited hours to five customers: Albert Jevons, Sidney Smith, Elsie Clara Smith, Albert John Clarke and Thomas Brewer.

Licensee Arthur Ives (1937-56) had been a First Division footballer in his day. The building is still standing... it's now Chester's a Mexican restaurant with a justifiably deserved reputation for the hot'n'spicy.

Licensees: *George Morris (1872-79); Edwin Felton (1879-82); Edward West (1882-98); Alfred George Wall (1898-1914); Thomas Charles Green (1914-16); Thomas Rutter (1916); Oliver Williams (1916-18); James Vaughan (1918-23); Wialter Phillips (1923-9); Howard Betteridge (1929-31 when he died): Mrs Nellie Betteridge (1931-3 listed as Old Crappelle 1932); Thomas Watts (1933-4); Ralph Arnison (1934-5); Alfred Elsmore (1935-6); Arthur Ives (1936–1955); Charles Edwin Newbrook (1955-1959); James Crighton (1960-81); Violet Sylvia Crighton (later Cooper 1960-81); Terence Arkell (1981-83); Philip Blake (1983); Michael Kennedy (1983)*

The Old Chapel 1970s
(CCMH/CFOW)

The Old Chapel
1960s (JAS)

Travellers Inn
Location: New Street
Years active: 1820 - 1830
Very little known about this one, save a few oblique references and only one 'concrete' listing from 1822 without reference to any specific licensee or detailed address

C3/52

New Greyhound
Location: 48 New Street
Years active: 1810 – 1965
Barely surprising Worcester drinkers were confused as **The New Greyhound** was sited just just a few yards from the longer established *(and consecutively-numbered)* Greyhound – which inevitably then became known as **The Old Greyhound**. While a greyhound appears on the coat of arms of Henry Tudor (Henry VII), neither of these Greyhounds was actually named after a dog – rather after a famous old coach to London, and the street they both stood in was the location for scores of carriers' coaches to all points. It's reckoned **The New Greyhound** was built to take the pressure off the traffic emerging out of the cobbled back yard of its predecessor but a tale also exists that the original Greyhound (later Old Greyhound, for obvious reasons) licensee John Ranford tired of the inn he'd run with his father William for many years and sold it to a new man, Charles Grove who took it over – but later that same year regretted the move *(or maybe had pulled a bit of a flanker on the unsuspecting Mr Grove)* and opened up a new a new inn right next door, calling it, no doubt much to Mr Groves' intense annoyance, **The New Greyhound.** This newcomer first appears in the Register of Victuallers' Recognizance of 1766 under Caleb Summers Philpott and later Worcester Lewis Directory 1820 as New Street,

C3/53

Site of the New Greyhound

then 48 New Street (from 1900). The census of 1851 shows then licensee Edward Williams (45) described as 'innkeeper' living here with his wife Mary Ann (34), their daughter Margaret (2), brother Frederick described as 'warehouseman', servants Anna Everton, Mary Ann Hyde and Samuel Corbett, and coachman William Filby. Latterly a Spreckleys house, later West Country, then Whitbreads, it's now demolished and the site is the delivery area for Marks and Spencer.

Licensees: *Caleb Summers Philpott (1814); Jane Philpotts (1820); Wm Jenkins (1827–c1850); Abraham Pemberton (1850); Edward Williams (1851); Joseph George Heming (1855–c1900); John Allington (1901-6); Percy D. Tomlinson (1906–1911); Mrs Lucy J. Tredwell (1911–1933); William Harbach Hope (1933-1954); William Webster Smith (1954-56); Leslie Arthur Sparrey (1956-57); Cecil Charles Connely (1957-59); William Charles Stoate (1959 – 62); Clifford Lancett (1962-5)*

Old Greyhound
C3/54
Also known as: Greyhound. Charlstons
Location: 46, New St.
Years active: 1764 – present

Long-life old coaching house, now Charlston's first referred to in Register of Victuallers' Recognizance of 1766 under William Ranford (written as 'Randford') and in Grundy Royal Directory 1792 and subsequently listed variously as Greyhound, old grey-hound inn 38 New ftreet (1793), Old Greyhound 47 New Street (1850), and Old Greyhound, 46 New Street (1910). An 18th century inn thought to date from 1764 when it was bought by William Ranford. *(See the tale above, concerning William's son John and the creation of The New Greyhound).* 1808 James Durnford became the innkeeper, and it was he who rebuilt **The Old Greyhound** as we see it today. It was ranked among the most important of the country carriers' inns in the 19c., carriers to and from Abberley, Aberton, Clifton (via Kempsey), Copcut Elm, Croome D'Abitot, Crowle, Droitwich, Pirton, Powick, Severn Stoke, Stock Green and Witley operated from here. The census of 1851 shows then licensee, James' widow Maria Anne (aged 62) living here with her daughter, also Maria Ann now

The Old Greyhound - a major survivor and still a licensed house though now styled as Charlstons.

1970s photograph CCMH/CFOW and above 2013 (BB)

Weston aged 22, son-in-law Robert Weston (26 and described as 'draper'), grandson William Weston (2), grocer Charles Hack described as 'visitor' and from Cheltenham, Harriet Baylis (servant), ostler John Underwood (48) and his son, also John aged 14 and described as 'servant'.

In 1981, I wrote: '...if you ever saw a greyhound rocket out of its trap and tank down the home straight like a dose of salts, then this is it. Six months at The Old Greyhound and (former Metal Castings Foundry Manager) Arthur and Lorraine (Wells) are romping home to a real winner of a pub. Watch this one – it's my nap as my mate Dennis (Flynn) puts it'. I described it as 'as ramshackle as they come... a rickety-rackety listed building dating back to Lord-knows-when and looks like it: oddly shaped lounge bar that starts off as a snug then becomes something different and soon-to-be-reopened bar, plus car park that if you can get into it, you're a better man than me, kiddo *(this was a reference to the old cobbled entry, now the still-narrow passageway into Reindeer Court, that had been successfully negotiated for centuries by horses and coaches but proved a nightmare for the new-fangled combustion engine)*. I gave it one star for facilities, but max three for the all-important 'Friendly Factor': '...huddled groups moaning about the weather this week – but then who didn't – then suddenly great roars of laughter that'll have you joining in in no time all, chucked-in with some rough-and-ready but ever so cheery faces make it a delight'. Gutted c 2000 and now unrecognisable from the much-loved Old Greyhound of which no visible features now exist, it's a favourite with the coffee-and-snack brigade and no longer a drinking house though still licensed and is proving a popular location with its patrons. That said, **The Old Greyhound** is sadly missed and I swear I still hear the good-natured laughter of good mates long since gone whenever I pop in (not such a regular occurrence these days!) or past (more likely)!

Licensees: William Ranford (1764); John Ranford (1766-90); George Groves old grey-hound inn 38 New ftreet (1792); John Ranford greyhound inn 39 New Street (1793); J. Summerfield; James Durnford (1808–c1830s – listed as 'Dwinford in Pigots 1835); Maria Anne Durnford (1842-1850s); William M. Lacey (1855); George Perry (1872-76); Evan Davis (1876-83 when he died); Elizabeth Davis (1883-4); Henry Baker (1884-7); William Sewell (1887-92); Thomas Croft (1892-5); Reuben James (1895-6); William Daw (1896-8); Herbert Tyler (1898-1902); Robert F. James (1902-4); Ernest Maitland (1904); Arthur Allen (1904); Harry Silverthorn (1904 -1928); Thomas Bowler (1928); Herbert Tyler (1928-36); Alfred Sydney Elsmore (1936-1956); Trevor Wilden (1956-1965); Cyril Berry (1965-81); Arthur (and Lorraine) Wells (1981-88); John Considine (1988) As Charlstons: Stephen Walsh (2000). Current (2013) licensee/dps: Stephen Walsh. Worcester City licence 1412

Plough
C3/55
Location: 19 New Street,
Years active: 1750 - 1798

Listed in Noake 1877 as 'an inn now occupied by Mr Nicholls, broker, New Street, and which was newly built and converted into a private dwelling house about 1791) One of several recorded by Hubert Leicester: '...in the neighbourhood (with) large storing warehouses, notably **Plough** (where 19 New Street now is) **Greyhound, Pheasant, Archangel** now **The Plough** in Silver Street, **White Horse** in Silver Street on the site of the present lawn adjoining the Public Hall, **Peacock** In Queen Street'. Beyond that, not much is known – though a Plough is also listed as being in 'High ward' in Victuallers Recognizances in 1814 under licensee William Foxall, but whether they are one and the same is unclear.

Pheasant
C3/56
Also known as: Old Pheasant. Bishop's Rest (1980s)
Location: New Street
Years active: 1787 to present

Amazingly resilient and long-lasting pub in historical thoroughfare with an illustrious history - including being a favourite with the City Corporation who, according to contemporary reports, had their own personal bowling green at the rear. The bowling green – though long since gone – is still recalled in the names of former surrounding streets (also long since gone): Bowling Green Terrace and Bowling Green Walk. The Pheasant still stops tourists in their tracks and is much photographed. Listed variously as New Street, 15 New Street, 23 New Street and 25 New Street. On 8th May 1908, licensee Alfred Edward Bird was fined £10/- (50p) with £5.13s.6d (£5.66$^{1}/_{2}$p) costs for unlawfully permitting drunkenness on the premises. Formerly a Flowers, later Whitbread, inn it's described on its own website as: 'The Old Pheasant Inn, New Street dates from about 1580. It was built as a house for a prosperous local businessman and consists of three storeys. It became a public house in 1787 when the licensee, Mrs Eleanor Morris, moved from her previous inn, The Pheasant, Silver Street. The Pheasant Inn *(back to New Street now)* was a somewhat superior inn with a bowling green at the back which was reserved for members only. It was the principal inn for cock fighting until the sport was made illegal in 1850.

New Street c1900 (CCMH/ CFOW)

There was accommodation for spectators and it is said that it could hold 80 horses. The Pheasant underwent exterior restoration between 1985 and 1987. It is now a tenanted Enterprise Inns plc pub having reopened on 9th November 2012 after refurbishment and following closure in July 2012'.

In 1981, then tenant, cordon bleu chef and MENSA mastermind Malcolm Staff-Brett who I'd known quite by chance several years earlier when he gaffered **The Bradford Arms** in Castle Bromwich, another favourite while out on the road) said: "...it's just a nice pub, really". I noted a poem on a wall, written by a regular that read: 'food's fab, conversation's pleasant, the beer's the best, at the Old Pheasant' which I noted was 'childish stuff and painfully illustrated but what a nice sentiment'. Facilities at the time consisted of 'charming narrow bar a shade cluttered with tables and chairs I thought, but a real delight in the centuries old, oak panelled, half timbered, leaded windows style, plus skittle alley that converts into a functions room so not normally opened to the hoi polloi of an evening *(it's now where the crash-bang-wallop live bands do their thing)*. Plus two upstairs rooms in wonky lop-sided Tudor manner plus loos that are so well scrubbed and fresh they sparkle'. **The Pheasant** inexplicably changed its name to **The Bishop's Rest** for a short time in the 1980s (including **Blandford Bar** named after former Bishop of Worcester Walter Blandford – and no, so far as I can tell, no relation – not least as he was catholic and thus, as a catholic bishop, celibate). Now reverted to its former name and licensed to ex-County Council Treasurer David Ranford, trading as The Pheasant Worcester Limited, and managed by his daughter-in-law Amy James, it's aiming itself at younger night-time audience with regular live music and sports-event promotions. The same old oak timbers still lend something of the authentic Elizabethan feel about it – although the big TVs and piped music remain a tidge incongruous for my tastes, but then my own love affair with The Pheasant was in the less raucous 1960s Pleasant enough experience and well recommended though.

Licensees: Eleanor Morris (listed as 'pheasant 15 New street) 1790; Jas Whitaker (1793-c1814?); Walter Bowyett (1814); Thomas Trimnell (1820); Mary Trimnell (1835); Wm Daniels (1842– c1853); Edward Kirk (1855); Mrs Ann Godfrey (1872-4); Edward Jones (1874-6); George Perry (1876-9); Raymond Wilson (1879-80); George Seville (1880-83); James Linton (1883-90); Thomas Hamber Senior (1890-4 when he died); Jane Harber (1895-6); Alfred Baylis (1896-99); Henry Griffin (at 23 New Street – 1899-1902); Mrs Emily Griffin (1902-4 took over from her husband when he was put in an asylum); Alfred Edward Bird (at 25 New Street 1904-1923); Elizabeth Bird (1923-6); John Cound (1926-9) **As Old Pheasant:** *Edward James Faulkner (1929–1949); Edward Alfred Gifford (1949-50); Joseph Charles Dixon (1950-54); Edith Annie Ricketts (1954-59); Cyril Edwin Nelmes (1959-72); Dorothy Nelmes (1972-3); Robert Daveridge (197381); Malcolm and June Staff-Brett (1981-4); Brian Hulme (1984-5); Robert Knight (1985-7); Paul Maylott (1987-8); Thomas Hardy and Kevin Lucock (1988-9); Nicola Coker (1989-90); Ian Girmley (1990); Anton Modzarevic (2001); Adrian Birch (-2012).*
Current (2013) licensee/dps: Amy James. Worcester City licence 1715

Swan with Two Nicks
Also known as: Swan. Little Swan. Swan with Two Necks. Luna Bar
Location: New Street
Years active: 1760 - present

One of the City's famous and everlastingly popular pubs with a history stretching back further than initial entry in the Register of Victuallers' Recognizance of 1766 implies (you will find a potted, though well-researched history here:

http://www.theswanwithtwonicks.co.uk/page/building_history)

Thought to date from around the 1550s when it was leased for 21 yrs to Edward Elcox weaver, the first reference to use as licensed premises is in 1764 when Charles Lea paid 6d. (2$\frac{1}{2}$p) to the city fathers for a tavern head. Subsequently listed as **Swan Inn** *('fwan inn')* 1792, **Swan–with-two-Necks (or Swan with Two Necks)**. **Swan with two Nicks** is considered to be at least factually the correct version as it refers to swan marking denoting royal ownership) but also known as **The Swan-with-two-Necks** until comparatively recently when it reverted to its correct form. Located at New Street or 19 New Street up to the turn of the 20th century, but 28 New Street thereafter, it was an important venue for County carriers in the 19th century as carriers to and from Bosbury, Castle Frome, Cradley, Shelsley Beauchamp, Stifford's Bridge, Upton-on-Severn and Welland operated from here. An advert in Berrows Journal referred to the sale of a "good accustomed public house in occupation of William Weaver. In 1821 The Swan was occupied by John Lench, and the premises measured 92 feet from west to east, 36 feet from north to south, (37 feet at the back) described as containing a kitchen and pantry bar, dining room and wash house, passage, back parlour and small parlour. Later (1840s) it was one of seven City pubs owned by maltster James Portman Rea of Sidbury whose property portfolio also included **The Ram Inn** in 'New Town Road' later Regent Street, **White Hart, Red Cow beerhouse, Hen & Chickens, Apple Tree and Rising Sun**.

The census of 1851 shows then licensee, recently widowed Sarah Calder (45) as innkeeper, living here with her son Thomas described as 'dealer in horses', mother-in-law Harriet Calder 78, and servants Philip Inkins, William Day and Sarah Williams. In 1865 The Worcester Herald recorded an anniversary celebration to commemorate the battle of Waterloo, and on 18th June a number of veterans and pensioners gathered together including one veteran of Waterloo itself *('A capital dinner was provided and a pleasant evening spent')*. 1884 the inn was known as **The Little Swan** and the following year licensee David Daniels was convicted for permitting gaming here and was fined 5/- and 15/6 costs. Between

...ditto 1920s (CCMH/CFOW)

NEW STREET, WORCESTER

1912 and 1961 Ernest Watkins and his wife Violet were at the Swan, Mrs. Watkins is still recalled by some today as 'Ma' Watkins, and they were the last landlords to brew their own beer on the premises. Today, cites the website, you might find Ma Watkins on the bar in the form of a specially brewed real ale. She was, by all accounts, a larger-than-life character and if she didn't like the look of you, you could stand all night and not be served. Pickled walnuts were

often on the bar and soldiers from Norton barracks could bring their own jam jars to drink from during the war. To celebrate VE Day the Watkins' brewed a special strong ale which sold for 3d a pint. Even up to the 1950s young Worcester men mandatorily conscripted into the Forces up to 1958 were treated to a free beer on their last night in 'Civvie Street' if they were regulars. **The Swan with Two Nicks** was purchased by Michael Cannon at a cost of £16,000 and it's now run by Linda (née Smith – a former barmaid here in the 1970s) and Colin Griffin who run it as managers and licensees for T.W. Inns (Tropeano & White) shortly after purchasing the property in partnership themselves. They are still here, both members of the Worcester and District Licensed Victuallers Association which Linda chairs, and daughter Lucinda runs the **Luna Lounge** upstairs. Businessman and music promoter and impresario Tony Gibbon is licensee and manager of **Drummonds**, operated as a separate venture at the rear in what had once been (1960s) The Stable Bar. The Swan hit the headlines in December 2007 when mother of three Louise Burkes died after falling from the terrace of Drummonds Bar at the rear and was found the following morning on the footpath alongside the City wall which forms its eastern boundary.

Licensees: *Charles Lea (1766-69); James Crump (1770-71); Charles Lea (1778-79); William Weaver ('fwan inn 19 New Street - 1790; Thomas Bevan (1814); David Jones (1815-20); George Burrow or Burrows (1827); Thomas Calder (1832–1848); Sarah Calder (1848-64); W.H King (1865-68); John Green (1869); James Edward Watton (1872-4); Martha Walford (1874-5); Thomas Price (1875-6); John Holder (1876-82); Thomas Hoskins (1882-4); John Hay (1884); David Daniells 1884-96 (dec'd 1892, subsequently run by his wife Jane until 1896); William Merriman (1896-7); John Smith (1897-8); Albert Allen (1898-99); Leased for l4yrs to Lewis Clark & Co. Brewers of Angel Place; Thomas Mountford (1899-1904); Thomas Marshford (1904-8); George Morrell (1907-10); Ernest Watkins (1910-41 when he died); Violet Watkins (1941-61); Ernest Watkins (1961); Heather Edna Emms (1961), license transferred to Eva Lesley Powley 4th December 1961-3; Lois D'Favell (1963-4); Michael Cannon (1964-8); Edward Cunningham (1968-9); Alan Edwards (1969); Edward Cunningham (1969-70); Martyn Walker (1970-1); David Hogan (1971-2); David Wood and James Murphy (1972-4); John Nicholls (1974-5); Robert Nugent (1975); Stephen Hobbs (1975-6); Colin Griffin (1976); Colin Griffin and Patrick White (1976-8); Colin Griffin and Linda Griffin (1978). Current (2013) licensee/dps: Lucinda Jennifer Griffin and Colin Griffin. Worcester City licence 998.*

King Charles
Location: 29 New Street
Years active 2013 – present

Worcester's newest pub and real-ale bar, opened May 2013 in former King Charles Restaurant, reputedly site of the king's famous escape from the City after crushing defeat at the Battle of Worcester, September 3rd 1651. Co-licensee and owner David Craddock also owns and runs **The Plough and Harrow** and **The Duke William** in Stourbridge. Stocked with real ales from Craddock's Brewery it's jointly owned with his brother and partners Sadlers Brewery, also from Stourbridge and trades as Two Thirsty Brewers Ltd, registered c/o Windsor Castle Brewery in Lye.

Said originally to have been a merchant's house, built probably as outbuildings dated 1577 with front bay rebuilt c1670 as annexe to nos 4 and 5 Cornmarket with jettied upper storey added to both buildings at the same time. Described as 'long and narrow in plan with longitudinal axis at right-angles to street'. Some of the panelling on the ground floor is said to be original 16th or 17th century with later 19th century additions, and elaborately carved chimney-piece depicts various scenes including one of a figure dining and a devil, dated 1635 said to have been removed from Sidbury House, demolished in 1960's. Some of the timbers are almost certainly old ships' timbers. An inscription board attached to No.5 Cornmarket of which it was originally part until a fire c1800 destroyed the middle section, includes the date 1577 as well as the initials WB and RD (for William Blagden and Richard Durant) who in 1577 are recorded as leasing the small triangle of land in Cornmarket. Operating as a top-class restaurant – considered the City's best for the past 40 years up to a tailing-off in favour in the past decade, it was severely damaged by a fire in August 1985 when businesswoman Julie Mercer and her three children Ria, Jarrett and Jolyon aged eight months to eight years reckoned they were lucky to escape alive. Opened as the

new-look **King Charles real ale bar** in April 2013, it's rapidly gaining favour with the real ale set and is now also adding food – especially noted for game pies – to the menu and looks like becoming a winner. It deserves to succeed.

Current (2013) licensee/dps: Christopher John Sadler. Worcester City licence 1379

Turn the corner into The Cornmarket and here's another historical section of the City, rich in former pubs and inns. What's now the exit to the Cornmarket car park was once the porticoed entrance to the Public Hall, since criminally demolished, another example of unfathomable 1960s decision-making, where performers included Charles Dickens, Sir Edward Elgar, Jenny Lind, Gustav Holst and Mendelssohn. It was also the site of the wartime Empire Restaurant and by way of stark contrast in its later years hosted roller-skating as well as Mick McManus, Jackie Pallo, Johnny Two Rivers and their like in the less edifying late 50s-early 60s wrestling bout days. On the corner of the Cornmarket and New Street stood...

Green Dragon
Location: Cornmarket
Years active: 1720 – 1800
    Noake 1877 who wrote: '...there was also a Green Dragon in the Cornmarket kept by one Suthal 1720 (Worcestershire Relics') The corner site (with New Street) site was Oddbins for a while and is now clothing shop Prophecy

On this (south) side of Mealcheapen Street (the north-side pubs were discussed in the previous chapter) is the site – still standing – of one of the City's most famous inns....

Cornmarket/New Street: ancient inn The Green Dragon stood here (BB)

Reindeer

C3/60

Also known as Rein-deer. Reined Deer. Reindeer Inn. Reign Deer. Freemasons Tavern. Yates' Wine Lodge
Location: Mealcheapen Street
Years active: 1673 – 1987

One of the oldest inns in the City with a history stretching back to 1673, **The Reindeer** was an important venue for County carriers in the 19th century, carriers to and from Acton Beauchamp, Alfrick, Bransford, Broadheath, Clifton-on-Teme, Cradley, Orleton, The Shelsleys (Beauchamp and Walsh), Shrawley, Stanford Bridge, Stifford's Bridge, Suckley and Whittington operated from here. Additionally one of the most important of the commercial and political inns of the 18th and 19th centuries this was 'one of the most frequented inns (and) had accommodation for storing vast quantities of corn. It was customary in early days for farmers to bring to the market in the autumn their crops of corn and store them until sold' says Hubert Leicester who also wrote that several other inns in the neighourhood also had large storing warehouses – listing **The Plough** (where 19 New Street now is) **Greyhound, Pheasant, Archangel, White Horse** in Silver Street, and **Peacock** In Queen Street' Listed variously as **'Rein Deer', 'Reindeer' Rein Deer Inn** and **Free-Masons' Tavern and Reindeer** and **Freemasons Tavern and Commercial Hotel,** Mealcheapen Street at 8 Mealcheapen Street (1792), and 9 Mealcheapen Street (1940). Not listed as 'one of (Worcester's) five principal carriers' Inns in Baylis, Lewis Almanack 1885-8 but as 'other carriers' inns alongside **The Saracen's Head, Golden Lion, King's Head, Talbot, Angel** and others in various parts of the town'. On 15th December1905 licensee Thomas Arthur Hill was fined £2 with £2.0.6d (£2.02$\frac{1}{2}$ p) costs for permitting drunkenness on the premises.

Noted as having bars on both sides of the cobbled courtyard – both now shops – the original courtyard is now the main entrance to eponymous Reindeer Court. Owned by Charles Edwards, wine merchants registered at 18 Broad Street (same as Dingles, Edwards and Son) transferred by conveyance 21st March 1952 to J & G Oldfield Ltd, operating from 11 Copenhagen Street with 'no consideration money passed'. In the 1960s The Reindeer was a **Yates' Wine Lodge** – and the standing joke at the time was that it had caught fire and 27 men had been made homeless!

Licensees: Amy Langstone (listed as 'widow' – 1766); John Whitaker ('rein deer inn-1790'); B. Gardner (1793); Edward Burnidge (1814–1850); John Jauncey (1850); Edward Williams (1855); James Turner (1872-9); Richard Riley (1879-83); Charles Hayler (1883); Sarah Crown (1883-4); John Herbert (1884-6); John Larzon (1886-8); Edwin Cull (1888-90); Hannah Cull (1890-3); Robert Wright (1893-4); Arthur Osborne (1894); Henry Harvard (1894); Joseph Mutlow (1894-6); William Marian (1896-7); Walter S. King (1897-1904); Thomas Arthur Hill (1904-6); Arthur Ellam (1906-7); Edgar J. Preece (1907-11); James Phillips (1911-12); Alan Aston (listed as 'proprietor –1912-17); Ada Pit (1917-29); Miss Mabel Pit (1929-40 when she died); Harvey Gresham Hill (1940–1963); John Thurling (1963-66); John Rogerson (1966-8); Russell Potter (1968-72); Arthur Dunkerley (1972-6); Edith Dunkerley (1976-9); Colin James (1979-81); Robert Bullock (1981).

C3/61

Fleece (and Fleece Inn)
Location: 2, Mealcheapen Street
Years active: 1870 – 1929

Appears in Littlebury's Directory of Worcestershire 1873 as 2 Mealcheapen Street and described as 2nd house from Shambles. Closed c 1922, later Price Butchers and now Durrants

Licensees: Elizabeth Phillips (1872-5); Charlotte Phillips (1875-98); Joseph Yarnold (1898-1903); James Faulkner (1903-7 when he died); Mrs Ellen Faulkner (1907-1928 when she died); Edward Faulkner (1928)

Formerly The Fleece (BB)

(Left and inset) Generations of Worcester youngsters enjoyed their Vimto and crisps (even fish and chips) in the courtyard of The Reindeer (1910 - not vastly different to the same scene today)
Main pic CCMH/CFOW, inset BB

G The Blockhouse

The 1970s City Walls Road, faithfully following the line of the mediaeval City walls – the remaining elements of which are still exposed still looking as solid and impregnable as when they were built – still forms an effective barrier between the City and the former wastelands beyond. St Martins Gate stood here – a formidable physical structure preventing any kind of movement in or out except through the closely-watched and monitored gates: the only barrier these days is that the barrier is purely psychological. Up to 1830, the area east of the City wall was raw and dark countryside. After the coming of the canal it remained raw and dark – but of the urbanised and industrialised variety. Thankfully for us, where there's urbanisation and industrialisation on this scale, the demand for victualisation follows not far behind.

The new inhabitants of this rapidly-developed section of the City must have been in need of victualising on a grand scale as what's now The Blockhouse is regarded – with more than a degree of the rose-tinted specs about it – as a drinkers' paradise, where more pubs are reputed to have jostled for attention with their neighbours than anywhere else in the City but which is yet another of those myths about Worcester pubs unsubstantiated by fact. That said, The Blockhouse certainly enjoyed – if that's the right word, which somehow I think it may not be – something of a reputation for all its life....

A report in the Worcester Evening News (10th March 1974) described The Blockhouse as '...synonymous with slums, itinerants, evictions, more evictions, more itinerants and finally massive redevelopment. But back in the misty past this web of narrow streets and back-to-back houses nourished a thriving community of terraced 2-up 1-down into which fitted a family

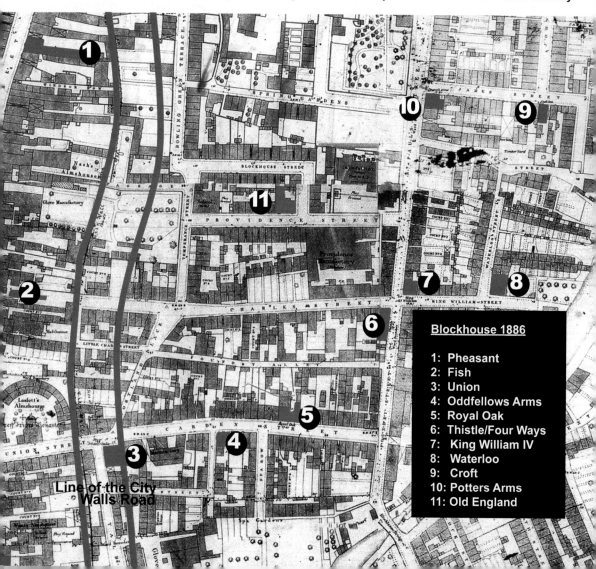

Blockhouse 1886

1: Pheasant
2: Fish
3: Union
4: Oddfellows Arms
5: Royal Oak
6: Thistle/Four Ways
7: King William IV
8: Waterloo
9: Croft
10: Potters Arms
11: Old England

Line of the City Walls Road

of six'. The unnamed reporter painted a picture of homes in Wellington Street with 2/6d a week (12^1/$_2$p) rent when wages at the Vulcan Iron Works were 10/- (50p) a week. In nearby Dent Street at the same time, rent was 6/6d (32^1/$_2$p). Three cigarettes and two matches cost 1d and a skinful of beer 6d (2^1/$_2$p). This was also the home of noted – often notorious characters Nobby Guy, Kempsey Lily and Pint (probably Powick) Nance. See 'Worcester Characters and other legends'

The area chosen as the site of this major expansion was what had been known as Blockhouse Fields, later The Blockhouse and it was transformed from a quiet backwater of ditches and ponds into a smoke-belching, humanity-packed, hard-drinking area of mean streets, teeming courts and terraced homes populated by labouring classes and frequently the scenes of drunkenness, violence and petty *(and not so petty)* crime.

In *'Old Worcester People and Places'*, historian Bill Gwilliam wrote that 'in 1820 a new road called Union Street was constructed from Friar Street to The Blockhouse and it marked a distinct stage in the growth of Worcester on the east – for up to that time the City had been hermetically sealed against ordinary vehicular traffic by the city walls although the old postern gate (1246) gave limited access to the Blockhouse Fields. The district was laid out, according to the times as a garden suburb ...(which) by the 1860s still contained pretty gardens, some quite large and even paddocks, but these gradually fell prey to the speculative builders. The principal street, Carden Street, was named after a venerable member of the corporation, Alderman Thomas Carden, who was mayor in 1790 and whose portrait hangs in the Guildhall' *(Old Worcester People and Places – Bill Gwilliam)*

Built as part of the major housing boom in the late 1830s as Worcestershire country folk stashed their scythes and pitchforks for the last time and headed to the City in search of the new work opportunities created by the burgeoning

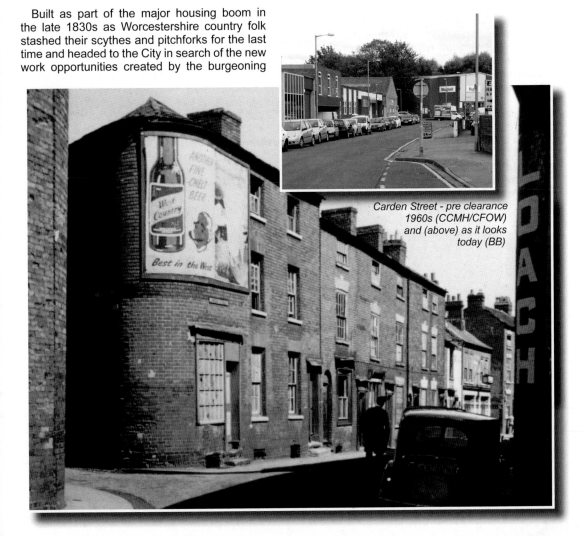

Carden Street - pre clearance 1960s (CCMH/CFOW) and (above) as it looks today (BB)

glove, engineering and porcelain industries,

In a very short time, some 18 pubs were packed into the tight cluster of streets – some of quite remarkable staying power, but not a single one existing beyond the early 1970s and it's with some irony that into the very midst of all this hard drinking and drunkenness, the famous old Temperance Hall (also known as The Hall of Science) was built in the 1860s and was noted for the motto built in bricks calling: *'The Blessing of God Keep Us and Protect Us from All Intoxicating Drinks'*. Despite the letters being 2ft high the fact that they were between the ground and first floors probably meant that most of those for whom the message was intended were probably oblivious to it.

Ex-mayor and long-standing City councillor Jeff Carpenter in his *'Victorian Worcester – a biography'* believes that the Blockhouse licensees of the time 'might have followed the Black Country practice of selling 'wobble – the third 'shut' of the brewing process: '...the ale would be sold by the pailful then taken round to the foundrymen to replace their heavy perspiration'.

Memories of Blockhouse pub crawl still abound, a drinker called Gus posting on the internet details of a regular crawl around the area of which typically on February 23rd 1958 took in a running order of the pubs in and around The Blockhouse *(see 'Civitas in beero et pubbii fidelis')*

Union
Location: Union (or Carden) Street
Years active: 1820 – 1904

First listed in Victuallers Recogizances 1827, this would have been one of the first in what was to become a swathe of pubs in the Blockhouse: most subsequent pubs appeared some 20-30 years later. At the time, it was not assigned to a City ward: along with the nearby **Royal Oak** it was listed as 'Extra-parochial'. Sited on the south side of Union Street next to Sigley's Sweet Factory on the corner with Carden Street as shown in the Ordnance Survey map of 1886, the site later became Bevington's Box Factory c1908. The Google Maps' aerial photograph shows it was sited precisely where City Walls Road now runs: *next time you're driving north towards Lowesmoor, just think you'd be driving right through what would probably have been the bar of the old Union when you pass Union Street!*

Licensees: *Elizabeth Jones (1827); Thomas Green (1835); Wm. Haden (1842–c1860s); Jacob W. Wheeler (1872-4); Charles Philpott (1874-5); Thomas Gerrard (1875-9); Henry Robinson (1879-80); Thomas Collins (1880-7); William Palmer (1887-90); George Halley (1890-2); Albert Harrop (1892); Agnes Harrop (1893); Henry Robinson (1893); Susan Grubb (1893); John Harding (1893-5); Samuel Stiles (1895); Albert Ellis (1895-8); William Brown (1898-1900 when he died); Francis Osborn (1900); Thomas Clarke (1900-02); Arthur P. Lane (1902-4); Frederick Bedford (1904)*

Oddfellows Arms
Location: 52 Carden Street
Years active: 1870 - 1964

Dating from around 1870 and listed variously as Oddfellows Arms (1873) and Odd Fellows' Arms

Oddfellows Arms, corner of Carden Street and South Street 31st May 1960 (RHS)

(1900-1940s) this pub was situated at 52 Carden Street on the corner with South Street, surviving until c1964. One of three in close proximity in Carden Street, separated by six courts and Spa Row: **Freemasons Arms** (10), **Royal Oak** (22), **Oddfellows Arms** (52). A Spreckleys House, later West Country and thence Whitbread, on 7th January 1884 licensee Frederick Glover was fined £4.11s (£4.55p) with 9/- (45p) costs for unlawfully allowing consumption of intoxicating liquor during prohibited hours, and on June 2nd 1893 Eli Edward Griffiths was fined £1 with costs for unlawfully permitting drunkenness on the premises.

Licensees: Edward G. Fowler Odd Fellows' Arms, Carden St (1872-4); William Days (1874-5); Edward Pardoe (1875-6); Frederick Glover (1885-6); Thomas Malpas (1884-5); Alfred Greenway (1885-7); Francis Bellars (1887-8); Elizabeth Phillips (1888); John Birch (1888-90); Albert Harrop (1890-2); Eli Edward Griffiths (1892-4); Elizabeth Spencer (1894-5); Henry Vickery (1895-7); George A. Price (1897-1901): Harry Wakefield (1901-2); William Cofield (1902); John Harrison (1902-4); Joseph Court (1904-8); Thomas Lippitt (1908-9); Alfred Waldron (1909-11); William Kenwrick (1911-14); George W. Lamb (1914-1918); Mary Lamb (1918-19); George Lamb (1919-22); Horace Beard (1922-1957); Percy Turberfield (1957 – died 1961); Percy Turberfield (junior) (1961-4

Two views of the Freemasons Arms. Top CCMH/ CFOW. Below 31st May 1960 (RHS)

Freemason's Arms
Also known as: **Masons Arms**
Location: 10-11 Carden Street
Years active: 1850 - 1959

Listed as 10 Carden Street in Billings Directory of Worcestershire 1855 then as 11 Carden Street (1940), this was one of three in close proximity in densely-populated Carden Street, separated by six courts and Spa Row: **Freemasons Arms** (10), **Royal Oak** (22), **Oddfellows Arms** (52). Originally a Showells House and off-licence (for the consumption of beer, cider and perry off the premises, license confirmed by the licensing authority 1st April 1949) and registered at 120 Station Street Burton upon Trent, later leased to Ind Coope Allsopp and became Atkinsons, it closed 1959.

Licensees: John Morgan (beer retailer – 1855); Lewis Bunn (1898-1900); William T. Miller (1900-05); William L. Jones (1905-9); Oliver Williams (1909-11); Arthur Yeates (1911-15); William T.Miller (1915-20); Ernest Hayes (1920-1); Charles Baines (1921-2); George Mee (1922); John Wood (1922-3); Alfred Robbins (1923-5); Leonard Worrall (1925-7); Frank Hughes (1927-9); Sydney Smith (1929-30); John Sandbrook (1930-1); Ralph Arnison (1931-3); George Morgan (1933-4); Archie Bright (1934-6); Victor Worrall (1936-7); Frederick William Growcott (1937-42); William Johnson (1942-6); William Henry Coley (1946-50); Gwilym Keith Bryan (1950-3); John Ernest Sussex (1953-9)

Carden Street today (BB)

C3/65
Royal Oak
Location: 22 Carden Street
Years active: 1827 - 1937

Among the first of a clutch of pubs to be built in the largely working-class Blockhouse area, listed as 22 Carden Street and dating from 1827 (as listed in Victuallers Recognizances and two years later Pigot's Worcestershire Directory). At the time, it was not assigned to a City ward: along with the nearby Union Inn (not to be confused with **The Union Tavern** in Lowesmoor) it was listed as 'Extraparochial'. In time, one of three in close proximity in densely-populated Carden Street, separated by six courts and Spa Row: **Freemasons Arms** (10), **Royal Oak** (22); **Oddfellows Arms** (52). Licensee Robert Coulter was convicted in 1879 for selling after hours and was fined 10/- plus costs. Licensee John Jaynes was also convicted in 1914 for receiving stolen goods for which he was sentenced to six weeks hard labour. In 1897 a strange case occurred here when licensee Fred Underwood's 25-year old wife Mary Ann was charged with attempting to commit suicide by cutting her throat with a carving knife. Found lying on the floor 'surrounded by a great deal of blood' *(Berrows Worcester Journal)* she said 'I have killed my baby and I think I shall be hung' - yet the couple's 3-year old daughter was found completely unharmed and a doctor reported the landlady to police to be suffering from delirium tremens due to heavy drinking. Worcester magistrates subsequently bound her over to be of good behaviour, recommending she leave the pub business and give up drink altogether. The suggestion appeared to work as the couple seem to have quit the pub not long after.

Licensees: *Matthew Mason (1827); Thomas Mason (1829); Thomas Harris (1835); William Stait or State (1842 – c1860); Robert Evanson (1872-4); Mary Evanson (1874-5); Owen Price (1875-8); Robert Coulton or Coulter (1878-81); Humphrey Clare (1881-90); John Greenway (1890-2); William Trevis (1892-5); Walter Knott (1895-6); Frederick Underwood (1896-7); Acton Roan (1897); Alfred Hayes (1897-99); Thomas Davies (1899); Thomas Waldron (1899-1902 when he died); Mrs Laura Waldron (1902-3); Walter Hubbard (1903-4); William Birchley (1904-5); William Miller (1905-7); Mrs Emily Bird (1907-10); Thomas Reeve (1910-11); Francis Beasley (1911); George Price (1911-12); Charles Kenrick (1912); Arthur Ingles (1912); Charles Wallace (1912-13); Rosamond Ballard (1913-14); John Jaynes (1914); Charles W. Woodhouse (1914–1931); Arthur Candlin (1931-2); Charles Bolland (1932-3); James Bennett (1933-4); Richard Obrey (1934-5); Elizabeth Barker (1935-7)*

C3/66
Bee Hive
Location:
Rovers Arms Carden Street
Years active: 1850s to 1908

Built at the time of the large-scale housing development on the City's eastside, **The Bee Hive** – two words, unlike the similarly-named **Beehive** less than half a mile away and dating from only a few years later. Unusually not shown on the 1886 Ordnance Survey map that clearly shows the other pubs in the area – notably, Union, Oddfellows Arms, and Royal Oak even though documentary evidence proves its existence at the same time. Its end was no doubt speeded-up in the wake of a report into the state of Worcester's pubs in 1906 by the Chief Constable who objected to the granting of a full licence despite a petition signed by 106 residents: it was thereafter only ever granted a provisional licence and is thought to have become a butcher's shop by 1908

Licensees: *Thomas Reynolds (1855) and Joseph Churchill (1902); William Kings (1908);*

338

Blockhouse Lock -
site of The Lame Dog.
It had been closed for
eight years at the time
of this pre-Health and
Safety photograph
(right) 1st September
1958 (RHS)

C3/67 Lame Dog
Location: Blockhouse Lock
Years active: 1870 - 1950

Listed as 'Lame Dog, 6 Canalside Blockhouse Lock' and believed to date from the 1870s a legend inside said "Step in, my friend, and rest a while, and help the lame dog oe'r the stile'. Curiously not featured on the Ordnance Survey map of 1886, it was a mean canalside pub with a none too savoury reputation for cleanliness, alongside a history of volatility and not very good beer. It closed c1950, demolished 1958 and Bob Sargeant's photograph of its demolition (1959) shows it to have been a sad looking building.

Licensees: Mrs Eliza Winters (1902- c 1915); Sidney Alfred Jones (1930–1942)

C3/68 Nag's Head
Location: 1, Blockhouse
Years active: 1900 - 1912

Short-lived pub, owned by Rushton Brewery at 1, Blockhouse, closed c1912

Licensee: Harold Bissell (1908)

C3/69 Cannon
Location: Blockhouse
Years active: 1850-1860s

Listed in Victuallers Recognizances 1859 under Charles Hayes and likely to have been named after the suggested siting of the cannon used by the Parliamentarians to batter the City during the Siege of Worcester in the Civil War. Despite that, precise location and further references are elusive and no other references other than a sole licensee, Charles Hayes, survive.

C3/70 Old England
Location: Providence St
Years active: 1870 - 1964

A grand old long-life Spreckleys, later West Country (Whitbread) pub dating from around 1870 according to Littlebury's Directory of Worcestershire 1873, and still going strong right up to its demise almost a century later. Listed as 13 Providence Street, an application for an extension to the pub made by then licensee William Mayfield and date 1871 is in the Original Archives

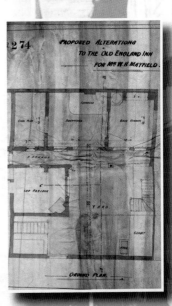

1886 planning application for extensions at The Old England shows it to have been of modest proportions (WRO)

section at the Hive and it shows the pub to have been of quite modest proportions with few comforts. Even so, it lasted right up to 1964.

Licensees: William Henry Mayfield (1872-6); Mrs Mayfield (1876-77); George Thomas (1877-80); George Payne (1880-1); Charles Lea (1881-4); Edward Bennett (1884-5); Thomas Coley (1885-6); Thomas Harber (1886-7); Edward Bennett (1887); James Roberts (1887-8); Charles Joseph Rice, Old England (1888–1908); Miss Fanny Bough (1908-1929); William Wichard (also listed as brewer–1929-1936); Frank Freeman Jones (1936-1951); Alfred Allardyce McNeill (1951-56); Ernest Reginald Thomas (1956-57); Elsie Maud Andrews (1957-62); Austin Lock (1962-4)

Horn and Trumpet
Location: Little Charles Street
Years active: 1850 - 1915

Listed Billings Directory of Worcestershire 1855 Address 23, Charles Street though situated on corner of Temperance Street and New Charles Street. Closed c1915

Licensees: Joseph Ingles (listed as 'beer retailer' 1855); Charles Hancock (1872-99); James Lee (1899-1903); Samuel Fox (1903-4); Elizabeth willis (1904-5); William Cubberley (1905-6); Edward Crump (1906); Alfred Ashwood (1906-7); Alexander French (1907); William Edwin Lamb (1907-13); Charles Hancock (1913-5)

Rovers Arms
Location: Little Charles St.
Years active: 1872 - 1906

Short-lived turn-of-the-century pub active between 1872 and 1906 situated on the corner of Charles St. and Little Charles St.

Four Ways Inn
Also known as: Thistle Vaults
Location: Charles (or Foundry) Street
Years active: 1870s – 1923

First appears Littlebury's Directory of Worcestershire 1873 as Four Ways Foundry Street then variously as Charles Street and 60 (and 64) Charles Street and 2, Foundry Street. On the corner of Charles Street and Foundry Street it was known as **The Four Ways** and **Thistle Vaults** but was no longer in existence after 1923.

Licensees: Thomas Sammons (1872-6); George Marriott (1876-8); John Williams (1878-9); Jane Davis (1879-81); James Abbott (1881-3); William Smith (1883); Hannah Caldicott (1883); Andrew Graham (1883-4); Joseph Brittlebank (1884-97); William Jones (1897-8); James Hope (1898-9); John Greenway (1899-1902); Susannah Mitchell (1902-3); Henry Simmonds (1903-10); Francis Perkins (1910-12); Thomas Shaw (1912-18); Annie Shaw (1918-22); Ralph Goostry (1922-3); William Turner (1923)

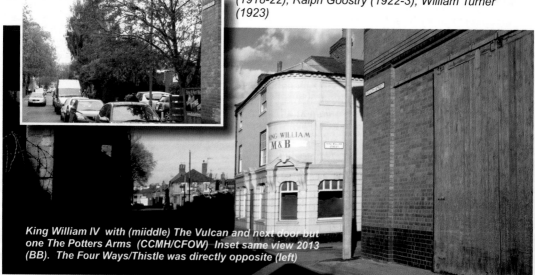

King William IV with (miiddle) The Vulcan and next door but one The Potters Arms (CCMH/CFOW) Inset same view 2013 (BB). The Four Ways/Thistle was directly opposite (left)

C3/74

KingWilliam(IV) Vaults (King Billy)
Location: Foundry/ St Pauls Street (no 91)
Years active: 1859 – 1971

King William IV Vauls aka King Billy (JAS)

The King William IV – 'King Billy' as it was affectionately known even up to (and beyond) its demise in 1971 remains the one folk most recall of all the Blockhouse pubs. First listed in Victuallers Recognizances of 1859 and listed as '**King William**' (the earlier King William [the Third] in Dolday had closed about thirty years earlier) and in Littlebury's Directory of Worcestershire 1873, the King Billy has a complete list of licensees right up to its sad end – several years over a century later – the Drake family: Alfred Arthur, Frederick H. and Alfred Arthur – seemingly licensees for more than a third of its existence. A Harpers Hitchmans house, later Ansells it was registered at 26 Bridge Street Banbury prior to incorporation into the Ansells chain. A great favourite on the Blockhouse pub crawl scene

Licensees: John Davis (1859); William Everton (1872-4); William Henry (1874-6); Henry Coldicott (1876-84); Thomas Nutt (1884-5); James Uncles (1885-88); William Hesketh (1888-9); Joseph Young (1889-90 when he died); Hannah Young (1890); Charles Burgess (1890-1); Henry Kirk (1891); Harry Radford (1891); Ernest Charles (1895-6); George Freeman (1896-7); Jane Higgins (1897-8); Albert Ellis (1899); Alfred Hayes (1899-1901); Walter Carney (1901-2); Albert Ellis (1902-4); John Harrison (1904); Frederick Williams (1904-5); Henry Hope (1905-6); Joseph Churchill (1906–1910); Alice Churchill (1910-11); Frank Sharman Hill (1911-17); Frederick Drake (1917-36 when he died); Alfred Arthur Drake (1937–1960); Charles Andrews (1960-4); Percy Jeynes (1964-71).

C3/75

Waterloo
Also known as: Waterloo Tavern
Location: 2, Waterloo Street (originally Block-house Fields)
Years active: 1820 – 1962

Fondly remembered by those who recall the 30s-50s hey-days of pub crawls in and around the Blockhouse *(see the section on pub crawls in 'Civitas in beero and pubbii fidelis')* and sited on the corner of Waterloo Street and King William Street. This Spreckleys, later West Country (and Whitbread) house actually pre-dates most of the others – and also outlived most of them too, closing as late as 1965. Originally listed as Blockhouse Field (implying outlying territory) before settling into Blockhouse (1829) and finally Waterloo St. (1855), it was also occasionally used for inquests. On 10th November 1825, the inquest was held here into the death of 'a female infant found in a ditch wrapped in rags with a brick attached'. Licensee John Hunt was convicted in 1884 for permitting gaming on the premises and was fined 20/- plus costs. A subsequent licensee Tommy Andrews, here for nearly 30 years (1928-57) had previously been a pro boxer so presumably was able to keep good order.

Licensees: Thomas Dovey (1820–c1830); Sophia Dovey (1835); Herbert Cordle (1842–c1860); George Probert (1872-4); Edward Thomas (1874-5); Henry Robinson (1875-6); John Deeley (1876-7); George Price (1877-9); John Hunt (1879-87); John Smith (1887-92); William Southan (1892-7); James Newell (1897); George H. Hughes (1897-1902); Ernest Charles (1902); Joseph Southall (1903-7 when he died); Lester Henney (1907–1928); Thomas William. Andrews (1928-1957); Laurence Joseph Frost (1957-60); Kenneth Knight (1960-62)

Roebuck
Location: St Paul's Street
Years active: 1872 -1886

C3/76

Listed only in 1873 and not shown on the Ordnance Survey map from 13 years later, it seems to have had a remarkablty fast turn round in licensees with 9 listed over a fourteen year period. Suggest you draw your own conclusions as to why.

Licensees: Edward Thomas (1872-75); Herbert Wheeler (1875-6); Charles Fildes (1876-9); Harriet Baldwin (1879); Thomas Warnford (1879-80); Raymond Wilson (1880-81); James Fudger (1881-4); William Cummins (1884); Joel Francis (1884)

C3/77

Vulcan
Location: 41, St Paul's (and Wellington) Street
Years active: 1900 - 1973

Turn of the century Robert Allen (later Banks's) inn and off-licence opposite St Pauls Church and separated from **The Potters Arms** by one property, owned in 1915 by general dealer George Hudson, who'd have been utterly spoiled for choice as it's also in the same street as **The King William IV** *'King Billy'* at no 91. Though not as long-lived as many in The Blockhouse area, **The Vulcan** was very run down by the time it closed c1973 and several years before it closed was limited to one bar as the floor of the other bar was considered unsafe. A mischievous poltergeist is rumoured to have existed next door.

The Vulcan, St Paul's Street (and next door but one, The Potters Arms) already dilapidated 31st October 1964 (top - EHS). It was to survive another nine years (centre CCMH/CFOW) (bottom) same view 2013 (BB)

Licensees: *Charles Gibbs (1898-99); Edmund Kelsey (1899-1901); George Lock (1901-1910); William Hill (listed as 'beer retailer' 1910 -1936 when he died); William Hill (junior) (1936-1952 when he died); Florence May Matilda Hill (1952-53); Albert Parker (1953-55); Roland Archibald Hilary Charles (1955-59); Alistair Joseph Shearman (1959); Harry Styles (1959); Lillian Rose Fellows (1959-63); Wilfred H. Stokes (1963-1971); Thomas Hodder (1971-3); Roderick Griffin (1973)*

Potters Arms, due for the
bulldozer 1959 (WRO)

C3/78 **Potters Arms Location: 37, St Paul's Street**
Years active: 1870 - 1959

One of a cluster of popular artisan pubs built to serve the rapidly-expanding population of the predominantly working class Blockhouse, **The Potters Arms** was one of two with a St Pauls Street address listed in the Worcester Directory 1957-8: **Potters Arms** (37), **Vulcan** (41). On 19th January 1928, William Henry Martin was fined £5 for selling intoxicating liquor during prohibited hours. Ind Coope, later Atkinson, (Marstons) house, it's first listed in Littlebury's Directory of Worcestershire 1873 as St Paul or more commonly St Paul's Street (at nos. 19 or 37) lasting until c1962.

Licensees: Eliza Brooks (1872-82); John Hudson (1882-8); James Goodwin (1888-9 when he died); Ann Goodwin (1889-95); Arthur Hirons (1895-9); George Hirons (1899-1906); William Rodway (1906-9); William R. Anderson (19 St Paul Street–1909-10); William Wishlade (1910-11); George woodhouse (1911-14); William Richards (1914-23); William Henry Martin (1923-9 when he died); Annetta Martin (1929); Charles Henry Millinchip (1929-30); Charles Edward Millinchip (1930-2); Walter Norman (1932-3); Ernest Morris (1933-4); Edward Boulton (1934-6); Thomas Sandland (1936-40); Sidney Alfred Jones (1940-1959)

C3/79 **Croft Inn**
Also known as: Croft House. Croft Brewery)
Location: 26 James Street
Years active: 1860s - 1974

Dating from mid-1860s, everybody has their favourite story of **The Croft** – the last standing of the multitude of pubs situated in the Blockhouse... mine is of being served cider from a porcelain jug even as late as the end of the 60s. The last survivor of all the Blockhouse inns, it was still standing in the late 70s when it was demolished though it had been closed for some time and was by then sticking out like a

The final survivor, The Croft - on its last legs 1970s
(CCMH/CFOW) Right – site of The Croft (BB)

sore thumb in the midst of new development. Also a brewery in its day though latterly a Marstons House, it's listed variously as Croft Inn (1873) and Croft Brewery (1910) situated at 32 James St (1900) and 26 James Street (1915 onwards).

Licensees: Charles Hayes (1872-76); Louisa Hayes (1876-9); James allen (1879-90 when he died); Sarah Allen (1890-98); Alfred Frederick Hanbury (1898-11); Richard Thompson (1911-21 when he died); Henry Hodges (1921-22); Joe Richards (also listed as brewer 1922-35); Albert Thomas Barker (1935-1956); Albert Thomas Barker (junior) (1956-60); Thomas George Day (1960-2); Sidney A. Jones (1962-9); Sidney G Jones (1969-74)

The Locomotive 1964 (JAS) and centre right 1972 looking towards Hillborough (CCMH/CFOW

Locomotive Inn
Location: George Street
Years active: 1900 – 1972

A later, fondly remembered addition to the growing complement of Blockhouse inns (c1900) at 47 George Street – though with a reasonable longevity approaching three score years and ten: Ansells house and off-licence (beer, cider and perry) closed c1965. On 8th January 1916, licensee Thomas Martin 'did by the hands of his servant or agent, supply to William Stuart Hundley as the measure of intoxicating liquor for which he asked an amount exceeding that measure' (ie overcharged). He was fined £2. Doesn't appear to have enjoyed too strong a reputation – at least in the 1950s when seasoned pub crawler Gus excluded The Locomotive from two memorable (or not, as the case may be) crawls in the late 1950s: '..the one thing that now strikes me as odd about those two evenings is that on both occasions we walked past the same pub without going in - **The Locomotive** in George Street. I can only assume it was because it was an Ansells house – a brewery conspicuously absent from the crawlers' list of favourites – although, he says, they caught up with it a couple of months later on the 25-pub All-Dayer '...to celebrate my having sat my Intermediate Exam'   Seems he failed, surprisingly!

Licensees: Alfred Bryan (1898); William Sier Locomotive Inn (1898- 1900); David Horby (1900); George Allen (1900-1); Ernest Holmes (1901-2); Mrs A.S.Boyce (1902-6); George Chapman (1906-13); Edwin Red (1913); Percy R. Williamson (1913-15); Thomas Martin (1915-27); Tom Hood (1927-30); Will Reading (1930-49); William John Rodway (1949-50); William Bertie Blake (1950-61); Leah Blake (1961-5); Leah Pritchard (1965-8) Ronald Stokes (1968-72)

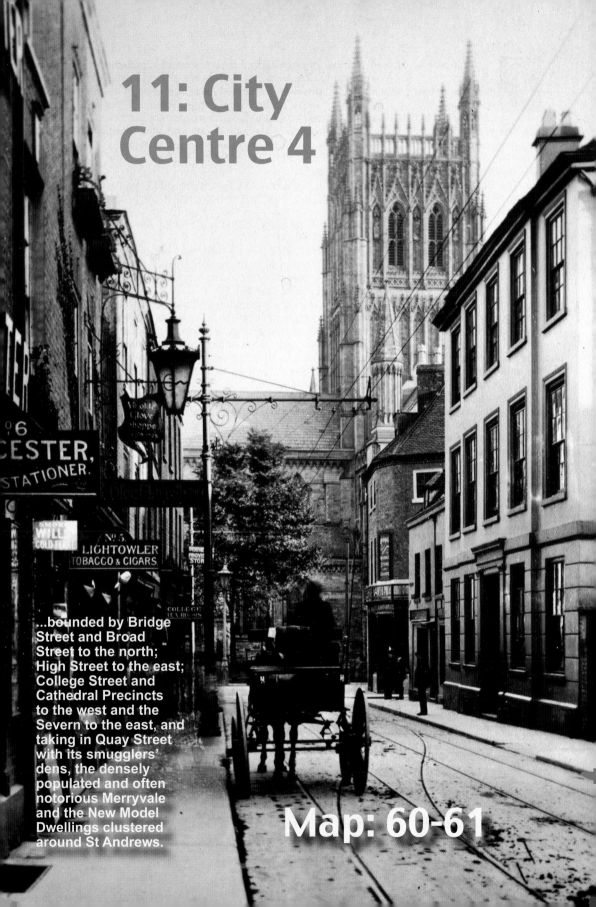

11: City Centre 4

...bounded by Bridge Street and Broad Street to the north; High Street to the east; College Street and Cathedral Precincts to the west and the Severn to the east, and taking in Quay Street with its smugglers' dens, the densely populated and often notorious Merryvale and the New Model Dwellings clustered around St Andrews.

Map: 60-61

n common with all eight sectors of the City in this run-down of Worcester's fine heritage of pubs, this history- and legend-rich area also underwent a large-scale and sometimes savage reconstruction project that not only changed its appearance in the most dramatic form, but also took in its wake a number of ancient and noted hostelries, some of which had already earned their place in Worcester's sometimes murky history.

In **The West** (Chapter 5) it was the construction of the 'new' bridge and New Road in 1780 that left the centuries-old gateway into the City, Tybridge Street, high and dry – in all senses of the phrase.

In **The North** (Chapter 6) it was the 1750s construction of Foregate Street and the later ribbons of development along Droitwich and Ombersley Roads.

In **The East** (Chapter 7) it was the coming of the canal that sliced through what had been bogland, playing fields and pleasure gardens up to 1815 and opened up new areas of high-density housing and satanic mills-style industry.

In **City Centre 1** (Chapter 8) it was the large-scale 1920s re-development that precipitated the creation of the all-new open space of Angel Place.

In **City centre 2** (Chapter 9) it was the mid-Victorian development of Lowesmoor and the first stretch of the City Walls Road that sliced a huge scar right through a major section of historic parts of old Worcester in the final quarter of the twentieth century – an element that's even more visually evident in the previous chapter, **City Centre 3 (Chapter 10)**.

Here too, in **City Centre 4,** the bulldozer swept away everything that stood in its way in the 1930s to create today's Deansway – bisecting two ancient and historic streets particularly notable for their pubs *(Fish Street and Copenhagen Street)* as well as significantly replacing notorious slums, tenements and the otherwise humanity-packed and often no-go areas of Birdport and Merryvale with wide open new vistas that gave Worcester a shiny new face to greet the new Elizabethan Age. In their day, both the latter streets had ranked with Dolday as havens for the City's lawless and low-life, and few save those that had lived there all their lives and knew little different, mourned their loss.

But first, let's start with a street that's been spared any major surgery and still looks much as it did when it was first presented to the world in 1780. This is John Gwynne's Bridge Street. Its own development had seen the destruction of old and run-down buildings but as this was to be the new gateway into and out of the City, it proved a winner in its job of making first impressions count. It looks a bit seedy and run down now, but at 230 years old, who *(or what)* wouldn't?

<u>A-B: **The bridge to All Saints**</u>

From the bridge, crossing the point where castellated towers had once warned outsiders that Worcester was a not a place to mess with...

 Bridge Inn (and Bridge Hotel)
Loc: Bridge St
Active:1790- 1969
First reference appears in 1790 when it must have been virtually brand new: licensee only listed as 'Lycett'. Later entry in 1827 Victuallers' Recognizances shows licensee William Payne paid no surety for his licence (normal charge £30) but that William Payne the Elder had paid £50. He must have been very well-heeled and respected as the rules of the time demand the licensee paid £30 for his license and two guarantors stood £10 bail each. An important venue for County carriers in the 19th century: carriers to and from Broad Green, Broadwas and Suckley operated from here. Later a Spreckleys, subsequently West County Breweries and Whitbread house, it dates from the construction of Bridge Street and the bridge (late 1780s) and was in continuous existence up to its demise in 1965

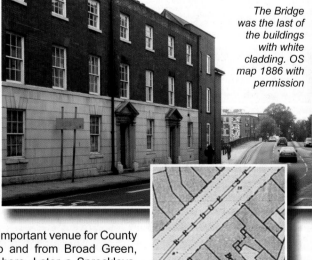

The Bridge was the last of the buildings with white cladding. OS map 1886 with permission

by which time it had inevitably become very run down and out-of-sorts. A favourite with some of Worcester's characters – many of which were jotted-down and recorded by barman Dickie Moon *(see Worcester Characters and other legends)* its address was given variously as 3 Bridge Street and 5 Bridge Street and the building still exists, though now private apartments.

Licensees: Lycett (1790); T. Tipton (1792); William Ford (1814); William Payne (1827); James Baggott (1835); R. Lewis and Jane Lewis (1842 –1875); William Roberts (1875-95); George Rollings (1895-6); George Jones (1896-1908); John Bean (1908-1932); James Coke Whitehead (1932–1953); Timothy Shanley (1953-4); Bertram Jeavons (1954-1963); William Kilminster (1963-5); Brian Richardson (1965-6); Frank Weston (1966); Edward Wilkes (1966-9)

London Wine and Spirit Vaults (CCMH/CFOW)

C4/2 London Wine and Spirit Vaults, also London Vaults
Loc: Broad St
Active: 1870 – 1912

Comparatively short-lived but prominently-sited inn at the corner of Bridge Street with Quay Street, dating from around 1870s though the building dates from the construction of Bridge Street (late 1780s). Listed in Littlebury's Directory of Worcestershire 1873 at 28 Broad Street, considered an important location at the junction of Newport Street, Quay Street and All Hallows and unusually not marked as a pub in the 1886 Ordnance Survey map although licensing records indicate it was very much in existence at the time. Closed aound 1912 and is now?? but has also been ex-England and Worcs CCC bowler Roly Jenkins' sweet shop and Ronald Lewis' music store where many a young Worcester lad with ambitions of being the next Cliff or Hank bought musical instruments upstairs and ventured downstairs into what, presumably, had been the old pub's cellars, to buy the records they hummed, strummed or drummed along to. Almost certainly related to licensee George Clissold, Cissie Clissold was licensee of **The Angel Vaults** nearby in 1906

Licensees: John Lascells Lacon (1873); George Clissold (1902); Thomas Reeve (1908).

Dun Cow
Also known as Hen and Chickens, Old Hen & Chickens
Location: All Hallows Well, Merryvale
Years active: 1780 – 1850s

The term 'well' stems from a cylindrical building housing a well that stood here, and even in living memory the area was still referred to by the same term – though constant 60s, 70s and 80s redevelopment brought about by the need to cater for the ever-multiplying motor car has altered the look and shape of this part of the City more than most. Appears as **Dun Cow** in Register of Victuallers' Recognizance of 1784 under licensee William Watton and later in Grundy Royal Directory 1792. Licensee listed as Edward Perrins at address dun cow 4 All Hallows Well. Changed its name to **Hen and Chickens**, later also known as **Old Hen and Chickens** and listed as Merry Vale in 1792 later demolished to make way for what's now Deansway.

Licensees: as Dun Cow: William Watton (1784); Edward Perrins (1790). **As Hen & Chickens:** *Stephen Strickland hen & chickens 11 Merry Vale (1792); John Thomas (1814); Jon. Bennet (1820); William Butler (also listed, John Groves 1827 and 1835); Joseph Oakes, Hen & Chickens, All Hallows (1842); Joseph Tovey (1850)*

B-C: All Saints to The Cross

Beauchamp (formerly The Leopard)
Also known as Beauchamp Arms (1859)
Location: 42 Broad Street
Years active: 1720 – 1963

A popular and ancient City centre Lewis Clarke's house and hotel – the brewery was only a stone's throw away in Angel Place – it existed as **The Leopard** for two centuries from the early 18th century, first listed in Register of Victuallers' Recognizance of 1766 and later the City's first trades directory, Grundy Royal Directory 1792. An important venue for County carriers in the 19th century, carriers to and from Alfrick, Broadwas, Cotheridge, Crown East and Welland operated from here. On 29th June 1896, licensee Walter Willis was fined £1 with £1.2.6d (£1.12$\frac{1}{2}$d) costs for unlawfully selling intoxicating liquor to a drunken person. Name changed to **The Beauchamp Arms**, also known as **Beauchamp Hotel** 1898. Closed c1963

The Beauchamp (right) and tram c 1910 (CCMH/CFOW) and inset 2013 (BB)

Licensees: As Leopard: Edmund Jones (1766); ? Stone (1790); Elizabeth Lowe (listed as 'leopard 42 Broad street' (1792); John Calder (1814); Mary Calder (1824 –1850s); Betsy Calder (1855). **As Beauchamp Arms (and Hotel):** *Arthur Humphrys (1859); Evan Davis (1872-6); Edward Evans (1876-1885 when he died); Ann Evans (1885-9); William Pike (1889); Frederick Roberts (1889-90); Henry Melhuish (1890-1); Maria Ford (1891-3); Albert Osborne (1893-4); Walter Willis (1894-1900); Henry Hayes (1902-6); August Collins (1906-12); William Smith (1912-13); Charles Lucas (and hotel proprietor – 1913-17).* **As The Beauchamp:** *Alice Lucas (1917-20); Charles Lucas (1920); Walter Smith (1920-3); George Townsend (1923-5); Charles Manton (1925-7); Isiah Weaver (1927-9); Patrick McDermett (1929-30); Archibald Devereaux (1930-8); Ernest Ward (1938-9 when he died); Sarah Ward (1939-40); Francis James Whittaker (1940); Francis Vincent (1940-3); Arthur Ernest Lewis (1943-1949); George Rowbotham (1949-50); Stanley Charles Wallis Lockyer (1950-52); Harry Sagan (1952-3); Thomas Edward Hodgetts (1953-59); Arthur Lloyd (1959-61); Harry William Watson (1961 – transferred to Rose Hannah Watson 6th November 1961-1963)*

The Unicorn (far right) now the passageway to Crowngate shopping mall (CCMH/CFOW)

Inset 2013 (BB)

16 BROAD STREET, WORCES

Unicorn Inn (and Hotel)
Location: Broad Street
Active: 1760s – 1930s

A famous inn and hotel with a long history stretching back to mid 18th century when it was originally **The Unicorn Hote**l occupying imposing premises in Broad Street – still called Unicorn Chambers though the site of the original **Unicorn** entrance is what's now the Broad Street walkway into Crowngate. *(Note: not to be confused with another **Unicorn** nearby (Dolday) which is listed contemporaneously, but with different licensees. Another **Unicorn** existed less than two minutes walk yards away in The Trinity).*

First appears in Register of Victuallers' Recognizance of 1766 under licensee Thomas Williams and later Grundy Royal Directory 1792 as 'unicorn inn 55 Broad Street' and continues as a hotel until c1860s and is shown on the Ordnance Survey First Edition of 1886. Listed as 'one of Worcester's five principal carriers' Inns in Baylis, Lewis Almanack 1885-8 alongside **Hop-Pole, Star and Garter** in Foregate Street and **The Bell** and **The Crown**, and was the staging post for the famous L'Hirondelle Liverpool-Bristol stage coach. It was also occasionally used for inquests. On 19th August 1830, the inquest was held here into the death of Thomas Masefield who was apparently found dead 'on the privy after suffering a fit'. On 20th July 1898 Alberta Archer was fined £2 with 31/- (£1.55p) costs for selling intoxicating liquor without a licence. Later (c1906) became Berrows Printing Works.

Licensees (incomplete): Thomas Williams (1766); James Prosser (1784); Joseph Williams (1790); William Perry (1792); Thomas Wells (1814); John Nichols (1820); Daniel Meek (1842 – c1860, listed as Unicorn Hotel (commercial), Broad Street (1842) and 'Unicorn family and commercial hotel and posting house, Broad Street 1855; Thomas Watton (1873); George Hay (1873-6); Elizabeth Little (1886); Walter Harrison (1886); Benj Stanton (1886-7); James Swinton (1887-8); Hannah Phillips (1888-9); William Matthews (1889-98); Alberta Archer (1898-99); Frederick Jones (1899-1901).

Arcadia
Also known as Arcadia Restaurant. Long Stop
Location: 56, Broad Street
Years active: 1930s - 1985

C4/6

Popular narrow-fronted City centre pub next door to what had been the **Unicorn Hotel** and Berrows printing Works, listed in the Worcester City Police Register of Intoxicating Liquor Licenses throughout the 1940s and 1950s as **Arcadia Restaurant**, owned by Ansells Brewery Ltd registered at 69 Aston Road North, Birmingham. It was also the favoured haunt of legendary foghorn-voiced newspaper seller Johnny O'Shea whose pitch was directly opposite and whose picture hung on a wall in there. **The Arcadia** changed its name to **The Long Stop** late 1970s in the hope of attracting cricket fans en route to the County ground – much as **The Shakespeare *(later The Cricketers)*** was to do a few years later. In the Bob Backenforth Good Beer Guide *(Worcester Source)* of October 1st 1981, I wrote of the then **Long Stop**, run by former police detective sharp-suited Eric Richards who later played a prominent role in the running of the Worcester and District LVA: '...time was, The Long Stop kept the best Ansells hereabouts – legendary it was: sadly not so today. The first pint of bitter (52p) was so soupy you could stand a spoon up in it. It went back'. The comment caused all sorts of ructions – even to the point of me being threatened with repeating the self-same feat in court on penalty of... well, something costly, no doubt. It never got that far, but resentment by the gaffer and miffed customers rolled on for many years, though Eric Richards and I have since been known to smile about the affair. I went on: '... then a pint of Burton Bitter (56p) – at least that's what it said it was – was acceptable, just, but not acceptable enough to set the old taste-buds a-singing out with joy. As for the pub, it ain't the cosy good natured rough 'un I remembered. In its place what's really a rather pleasant L-shaped lounge bar *(a bit too pretty for the*

The Arcadia (later Long Stop) 1964 (JAS) and put to different use 2013 (BB)

lorry drivers and factory workers who once jammed the place for the sheer joy of getting at the Ansells, I noted) with an overloud juke-box. Happy hours and live music had also been introduced to drum-up lost trade. I concluded: 'sorry though, couldn't take to this one at all. One star for facilities, one star for food, one star for beer and two for friendly factor. For some reason, I never went back in and it closed about four years later *(no connection, I'm sure)*. Eric Richards then went on to gaffer the newly opened **Maple Leaf**.

Licensees: Minnie Fowler Barnes (1899-1901); William Potter (1908-9); James Precious (1909-16); Montague Davis (1916-30); Ernest Morris (1930-33); John Joplin (1933-4); Ernest Roberts (1934-5); Frank Wright (1935-6); Arthur Powell (1936-9); Gladys Wilson (1939-50); Stanley David Howells 1950-52); John Robert Kimberley Panting (1952-4); Hubert Blake (1952-4); Samuel Bradford (1954-5); Stafford Rail (1955-6); Albert Ketteringham (1956-8); Ronald George Lakins (1959-60); William Thomas Groves (1960-64); Thomas Swingler (1964). **As Long Stop**: *Eric Richards*

Parrot Inn
C4/7
Location: Broad Street
Years active: 1600s - 1800
Precise location unclear, but mentioned by Noake (1877) as one of a number of 'ancient' City inns, some of which are probably not much less ancient than the eighteenth or even 17th century. Kept by 'one Moore'.

Vintorne
C4/8
Location: Broad Street
Years active: 1670 – 1720
Listed by Noake as being existence 1696 kept by one Cotterill, but no further details exist

D-E: Bank Street to Chapel Walk

It's not for nothing Bank Street changed its name from Powick Lane: for years this ranked with The Cross as the City's prime banking area – as the still fine buildings on the right, looking down towards what's now another Crowngate entrance, still testify. Here's where bankers, the City's top businessmen and members of the corporation gathered for their recreation – and theirs was a broad choice of inns and taverns to meet in too, with at least six inns open in this street alone at the same time around the mid 1800s. It's also typical of the great contrasts Worcester presented – at the top (ie east) end, refined, upper-crust and business-like Bank Street, dog-legging round to the mean courts and tenements of Powick Lane and thus into the dingy streets that made up Merryvale and Birdport at the other (ie west) end. It was in this maze of squalid housing and probably lively pubs that Worcester's VC hero Claines-born Fred Dancox lived with his wife and children (actually in Bull Entry) as a recently unveiled plaque in Chapel Walk records.

(**To read more on Fred Dancox and how he won his VC go to:**
http://www.worcester-online-newsmag.co.uk/issue3/ and navigate to pages 23-24)

Globe
C4/9
Location: The Cross (also listed as Powick Lane)
Years active: 1700s
A noted and in its day quite famous old inn dating from the 1700s and a favourite with the top echelons of The Corporation. According to Hubert Leicester 'The '24' (essentially the top layer of decision-makers at the Guildhall including the Mayor, Aldermen and Town Clerk) used **The Globe** as their rendezvous – described as 'in Powick Lane' though correctly described as 'on the corner with High Street (west side). 'At the top of this lane *(note the wording)* stood the celebrated Globe, referred to as the headquarters of the '24" wrote Hubert Leicester

Fountain
C4/10
Location: Bank Street
Years active: 1820s - 1830
Single appearance in Worcester Lewis Directory 1820 under licensee Thomas Sammons. No further listings

Bay Horse
Location: Bank Street
Years active: 1820-1830s

In the heart of the City's growing commercial centre, the Bay Horse appears to be quite short lived with only ever one licensee listed – Victuallers Recognizances 1827 under Elizabeth Stevens, though a possible transcription error as Pigot's Worcestershire Directory two years later lists her as Elizabeth Evans, although she may have re-married. There appears to be no further listings.

Berkeley Arms (Inn)
Location: 10, Bank Street
Years active: c1840s - 1972

Hitchman and Co-owned (later Mitchells and Butlers) inn with ornate frontage still standing as a facade and looking as it did in its hey-day, but just a front to what was until recently a computer games shop now closed. Address 10, Bank Street. On 3rd May 1916, licensee Arthur Gardiner was fined 40/- (£2) and 20/- (£1) respectively after being found guilty of '...by the hands of his agent Ellen Eliza Maisie unlawfully supply to William Stuart Hundley – clearly a police, or weights and measures snoop as his name appears several times in similar cases involving a number of Worcester landlords – the measure of intoxicating liquor for which he asked an amount exceeding that measure (ie: overcharging). The second charge referred to the same misdemeanour, this time to one William Walley. On 19th April 1971, the Worcester Evening News reported on plans to re-develop the area: '... the impressive façade of the **The Berkeley Arms** is to be carefully preserved and incorporated into an

A great shot of 1970s Worcester from the Haines brothers' collection (note Electricity Works top left) with The Berkeley Arms foreground centre. Inset The Berkeley Arms today, no longer a pub and the shop's empty (BB)

352

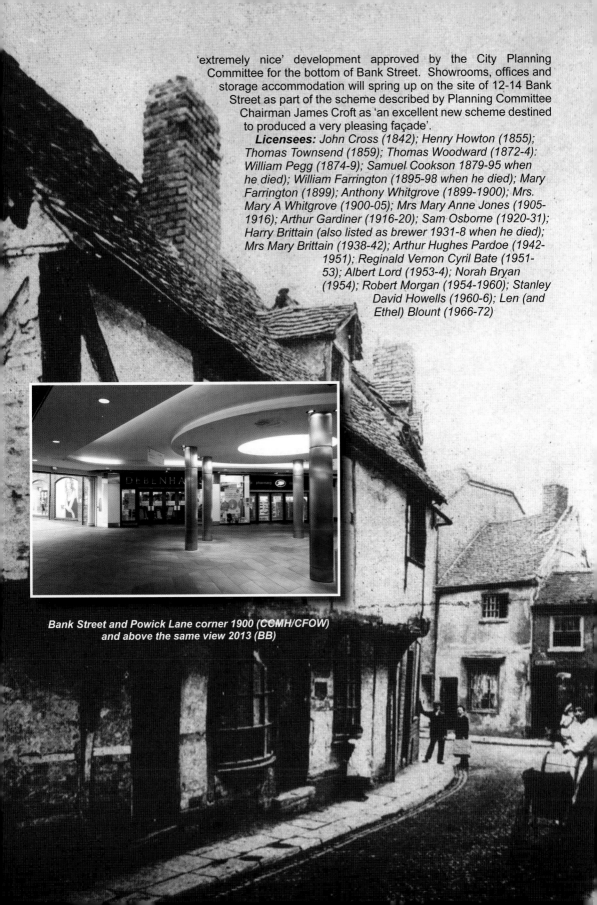

'extremely nice' development approved by the City Planning Committee for the bottom of Bank Street. Showrooms, offices and storage accommodation will spring up on the site of 12-14 Bank Street as part of the scheme described by Planning Committee Chairman James Croft as 'an excellent new scheme destined to produced a very pleasing façade'.

Licensees: John Cross (1842); Henry Howton (1855); Thomas Townsend (1859); Thomas Woodward (1872-4): William Pegg (1874-9); Samuel Cookson 1879-95 when he died); William Farrington (1895-98 when he died); Mary Farrington (1899); Anthony Whitgrove (1899-1900); Mrs. Mary A Whitgrove (1900-05); Mrs Mary Anne Jones (1905-1916); Arthur Gardiner (1916-20); Sam Osborne (1920-31); Harry Brittain (also listed as brewer 1931-8 when he died); Mrs Mary Brittain (1938-42); Arthur Hughes Pardoe (1942-1951); Reginald Vernon Cyril Bate (1951-53); Albert Lord (1953-4); Norah Bryan (1954); Robert Morgan (1954-1960); Stanley David Howells (1960-6); Len (and Ethel) Blount (1966-72)

Bank Street and Powick Lane corner 1900 (CCMH/CFOW) and above the same view 2013 (BB)

This was also the same site as:

Swan
Location: Powick('s) Lane
Years active: 1790 - 1800

Entries in Worcester Royal and Grundy Royal Directory 1790 and 1792) listing ownership of Mrs Manfell (Mansell) Swan, 10 Powick's Lane with no further references

Rising Sun
Location: Powick's Lane (later Bank Street)
Years active: 1760s to 1920

Probably deriving its name from the badge of Edward III, this is an extensively listed pub in the City's thriving Victorian commercial centre variously described as 'St Peters ward', Powick (and Powick's) Lane, and Bank Street (from around 1930) surviving from mid- 1760s to 1930s. The census of 1851 lists then licensee Samuel Hall (42) as living here with his wife Eliza Ann 36. Next to 10, Bank Street???) One of seven City pubs owned by maltster James Portman Rea of Sidbury whose portfolio at his death in 1852 also included the **Ram Inn** in 'New Town Road' later Regent Street, **White Hart, Red Cow beerhouse, Hen & Chickens, Apple Tree and Swan with Two Necks** (sic).

Licensees: James Turner (1766); Mrs Williams (1790); William Watkins (listed as 'rifing fun Powick's Lane' 1792); Richard Maund (1814); Saml (Samuel) Hall (1842 - c1860); Alfred Wilmore (1871); William Jeffries (1872-4); Robert Price (1876-9); William Redding (1879-80); George Williams (1880-3); H. Roan (1883-8); Eli Griffiths (1888-93); William Stanbridge (1893-4); Thomas Clarke (1894-5); George Hughes (1895-8); Alfred Hayes (189-89); Benjamin Henry Spencer (1899-1903); Ada Spencer (1903-8); William Evans (1908-12); William Phillips (1912-13); Ellen Phillips (1913-16); Ellen Hands (1916-17); Frederick Walton (1917-20)

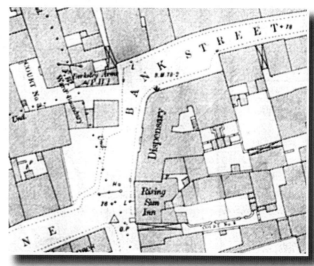

OS map 1886 reproduced with permission Ordnance Survey

George Inn
Location: Powick Lane
Years active: 1600s

Included by Noake (1877) as one of a number of City inns, some of which are 'probably not much less ancient than...' 1517 and listed in Register of Victuallers' Recognizance of 1767 under Ann Tombs (widow) but little else known

Silver Grayling
Location: Powick Lane
Years active: 1850 - 1860

Short-lived inn in Powick Lane, rejoicing in a single listing: Billings Directory of Worcestershire 1855, under John Griffin, described as 'beer retailer'

Painter's Arms
Also known as White Swann
Location: Powick Lane (also Bank Street)
Years active: c1810-1830s

Another seemingly short-lived inn despite two names, dating from around the first half of the 19th c listed in Victuallers Recognizances in 1814 but with no licensee's name - it may have been in a period of transition or temporary closure because in 1827 sureties of £50 were given for 'The White Swann' under licensee Jane Edwards though it re-appears in Pigot's Worcestershire Directory 1829 and 1835 as **The Painters Arms** under licensees Jeremiah Davis (1829) and later, Moses Turner (1835)

Queen's Arms
Location: 15, Powick Lane
Years active: 1840 - 1958

First listed in Slater's Worcester Directory 1850 and no doubt named in honour of Victoria – then on the throne for 13 years – appears to have lasted for almost a century before closing in 1958. Owned by Gregg and Brettell Limited, later Ansells and listed variously as Powick Lane and 15, Powick Lane, the site is now the rear entrance to Boots the Chemist. Licensee Ann Hobro (1859) appears to have come from a long line of licensees: John (1790) and Edward Hobro were also licensees of the nearby **Plume of Feathers**

Licensees: *Thomas Bickerton (1840s–c1850); Thomas Bickerton the Younger ('Yr'– 1850); Charles Williams (1851); Ann Hobro (1859); Thomas Bickerton (1872-92); John Izon (1892); Arthur Summers (1892-3); George Blackford (1893-4); John Izon (1894); John Calder (1894-5); John Calder (1894-5); William Main (1895-6); Albert Douglas (1896); Jane Harber (1896-9); Charles Williams (1899-1903); Francis Crockett (1919-20); Arthur Gardiner (1920-1); John Derning (1921-7); Joseph William Pittock (1927-47 when he died); Cyril Bartlett (1947); Bessie Cooper (1947-54); Stanley David Howells (1954-8)*

What was Powick Lane 2013 (BB)

Glovers' Arms
Location: Merry Vale (also listed as Powick Lane)
Years active: c1810-1920

First appears in listed in Victuallers Recognizances in 1814 under licensee Luke Welles and later Worcester Lewis Directory 1820 and lasted over a century until 1920

Licensees: Luke Welles (1814); John Morgan (listed as 'vict and glove manuf' 1820); Luke Wells (1820-c1830s); Henry Dunn (1842); Frederick Hale (1850, when he died he was then followed by Mrs. Mary A. Hale 1900-1906 when she died, followed by (probably) son Frederick George Hale to 1920 who then moved virtually next door as landlord of the Nelson/Lord Nelson

D-F Return now to the High Street

Angel Arch
Location: High ward, possibly High Street
Years active: 1800-1820

Little known inn with seemingly little recognition, precise location unknown save being in High ward, so probably, but far from definitely sited somewhere in the High Street. Listed in Register of Victuallers' Recognizance of 1814 under John Curnock but not listed after 1814

Fifteen years later (1829) a John Curnock is also listed as licensee of **The Cock** in Copenhagen Street.

Admiral Vernon
Location: High ward, possibly High Street
Years active: 1750 - 1810

Named after famed naval captain and MP, Edward Vernon – nicknamed 'Old Grog' – (12 November 1684 – 30 October 1757) who as vice-admiral in various naval campaigns against the Spanish, including the capture

(Above) Glovers Arms, Merrivale 1890 (WRO). OS map 1886 reproduced with permission Ordnance Survey

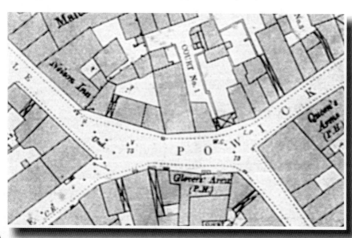

of Porto Bello a name that's also perpetuated in two Worcester pubs adopting that name. 'In an active Parliamentary career Vernon advocated an improvement in naval procedures and he continued to hold an interest in naval affairs until his death in 1757' *(Wikipedia)*. Precise location unknown save being in High ward, so probably somewhere in or near the southern end of the High Street. Listed in Register of Victuallers' Recognizance of 1766 under Charles Peachey but not listed after 1814

F-H: Copenhagen Street to South Quay

Copenhagen Street – its name was changed from Cooken Street in honour of the visit of Lord Nelson, hero of the Battle of Copenhagen 1801 – originally stretched unbroken from the Guildhall which it runs alongside, straight down to Warmstry Slip on the river where the fountains now provide fun for the children. It was no doubt the scene of a different kind of fun when bakers and brewers who sold below-par vittles, as well as nagging wives were strapped into the cuckolds' or cucking stool sited here – and dunked in the river as punishment for their misdemeanours.

'At the top, on the corner of High Street, was the Earl's Post, famous for the last stand made by the Royalists at the Battle of Worcester in 1651. The name suggests a boundary post and it may well have been the limit of the city in Saxon times'

(Bill Gwilliam – Old Worcester People and Places p 45)

It was also well-stocked with pubs and similar outlets. The length of the street – originally perhaps 250 yards from High Street to the river – was severely curtailed with the opening of Deansway in the late 1930s, creating two distinct halves, and like Bank Street and Powick Lane in the previous section, the contrasts between the two extremes of the same street could scarcely have been more marked: at the top fine houses and the homes of the well-to-do – and complemented with, no doubt, fine inns – a the bottom, squalor and deprivation. It was in this second *(ie western)* half that a pioneering new housing project of the 1850s lifted the gloom and depression of the mean courts and slums when the Corporation, no doubt encouraged by philanthropists including Charles Hastings and others concerned at the declining health and reduced lifespan of swathes of the City's population, took a major leap forward in the development of what would later become known as 'social housing'. These were The New Model Dwellings that provided homes and a degree of sanitation for some of the City's poorest and were, as their name suggests, the very 'model' of how public authorities could *(and history shows, later would)* provide publicly-funded homes for the masses whose lives had largely consisted of ill-health, disease and early death, to live in. For the better part of half a century, the barrack-like structures had an impact on extending well-being and life expectancy for thousands who might otherwise have been committed to an early grave, but by the 1930s the by-now not so 'new' model dwellings had become little more than the notorious slums they'd replaced, and were swept away in the large-scale redevelopment of the new wide and forward-looking Deansway.

Green Dragon
Location: corner of Cooken (Copenhagen) and High Street
Years active: 1600-1820s
Seems Green Dragons were great favourites for pub names in the Middle Ages, this is one of four so-called – sited 'in the house earlier known as the Earl's Post, at the corner of Cooken Street and High Street and this last was described as more than 200 years ago as consisting of hall, kitchen, five drinking rooms below stairs, a dining room, three chambers above stairs, a garrett, three

chambers over the stables two large cellars extending in length north and south and other necessary rooms with stables for about eight horses. In 1686 this was in the tenure of Thos Chetle, gent' *(John Noake – Worcestershire Relics)* It's also said that Earl Leofric, and his wife Lady Godiva, lived here for what appears to have been a lengthy period. Listed in Register of Victuallers' Recognizance of 1767 under licensee John (handwriting illegible but looks like Prikeshot).

    Licensees: *John Prikeshot? (1776); Richard Butler (1814)*

Mouth of the Nile
Also known as: Bier Keller. Police Club. Keystones. Now Keystones Cocktail Club
Location: 1, Copenhagen Street
Years active: (as Mouth of the Nile) 1812 - 1929
As later incarnations: 1969 - present

Copenhagen Street 2013 and (right) the newest incarnation of an illustrious inn (BB)

Apparently long-lived establishment, existing for well over a century and with a landlord who also seems to display surprising longevity: Thomas Ellis – possibly more than 40 years. Listed in Victuallers Recognizances in 1814 under licensee John Bennett and later Worcester Lewis Directory at Copenhagen Street (1820s) and 5 Copenhagen St (1910). Already in a street that had changed its name in celebration of Horatio Lord Nelson, this one underlined the City's respect for the much-feted hero-admiral by being named after his victory against the French in the Battle of Aboukir Bay *(more popularly Battle of The Nile)*. Fought on 1-3rd August 1798 in which the French sustained as many as 5,000 casualties with more than 3,000 captured, 2 ships of the line destroyed, 9 ships of the line captured and 2 frigates destroyed against the loss of 218 of Nelson's men with 677 wounded. 22 years on, Nelson-mania was still high and when he and Lady Hamilton visited the City when he was made a freeman, but as the name 'Lord Nelson' had already been claimed by an earlier pub sited in Birdport (**The Lord Nelson *1800-1950***), this imaginative second-reserve name was brought into play. For some years later a shop, then (1969-72) a below-ground German-themed Bier Keller selling the then trendy German biers and lagers in trendy litre and half litre steins as well as a lethal brand of schnapps. Then for many years the police club. Latterly Keystones a dark but popular cellar bar with a reputation for good acoustics favouring live music and one of the prime locations for the Worcester Music Festival. Recently (April 2013) re-opened as Keystones Cocktail Club with a cartoon theme – especially Mack Sennett's Keystone Cops, a clever reference to its former use as the Police Club.

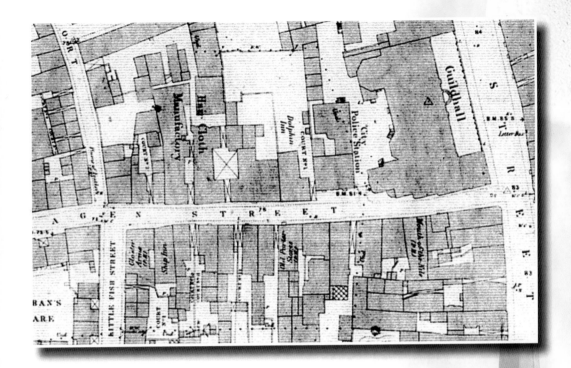

Licensees: John Bennett (1814); John Thornes (1820); William Williams (1829); Thomas Holloway (1835); Thomas Ellis (1842- 1879); Herbert Norman (1879-83); Sarah Pardoe (1883-5); Charles Pardoe (1885-6); Nathan Powell (1865-6); Arthur Wilcock (1892-3); William Thomas (1893-5); Edward Price (1895-9); William Collins, Mouth of the Nile, 48 Copenhagen Street (1899-1900);William John Rodway (1900-01); James Whitehouse (1901-4 when he died); Mary Whitehouse (1904-7); George William Turner, Mouth of the Nile, 5 Copenhagen St (1907 - 17); Florence Turner (1917-29) Closed by 1929.

As Keystones: Current (2013) licensee/dps: John-Paul Batterton. Worcester City licence 1078

C4/23 Dolphin (and Old Dolphin)
Location: Cooken (Copenhagen) Street
Years active: 1780s to 1895

First listed in Register of Victuallers' Recognizance of 1784 under licensee William Bibb and 1792 as 3, Cooken Street, later Worcester Lewis Directory 1820 and 1842 as 4 Copenhagen Street and thought to have closed about 1908 when it was demolished to make way for the new City police station. It stood next door to the old City police station which was spared the bulldozer and was later turned into an adjunct to the Guildhall buildings housing IT and other Council staff, and today (2013) home to Worcester BID and Tourism departments.

Site of The Dolphin (see OS map 1886 above)

Licensees: William Bibb (1784); John Sanders (1814-1840s); Thomas Arden (1842 – c 1855); Edwin Robinson (1855); Henry Warman (1872-4); William Warman (1874-5); Henry Warman (1875-6); John Hudson (1876-82); Elizabeth Pegg (1882-6); William Philpott (1886-90); Edwin Steade (1890 when he died); Ada Steade (1890-1); William Gilbert (1891-4 when he died); Evelyn Gilbert (1894)

Porter Stores (and Old Porter Stores) also Wine and Brandy Vaults
Location: 15 Copenhagen St
Years active: 1820 - c1938

Earlier **The Wine and Brandy Vaults**, listed in Littlebury's Directory of Worcestershire 1873 Closed c1938 to make way for the new Fire Service HQ. Licensee Josiah Stallard (1884) was founder of the great wine merchant tradition and his former shop still open up to the 1980s and the OS map of 1886 suggests this may have been the original **Porter Stores**. The building that later became Waterstones booksellers in High Street was also a Stallard Wines outlet.

Licensees: John Powell (1829); John Allgate (listed as Old Porter Stores, Copnhgn St – 1872-4); Joseph Hodgetts (1874-5); John Algate (1875-81); Josiah Stallard (1884); Herbert Norman (1884-94); George Winwood Porter Stores, Copenhagen Street (1894-1900); William Marshall (1900-01); Agnes Allen (1901-5); Waldegrave Ingram (1905-6); Edward Dorrell (1906-11); Prudence Dorrell (1911-22 when she died); Philip Penney (1922-5); Henry Savage (1925-8); Arthur Edgar Bozward (listed as 'Porter Stores, 15 Copenhagen Street 1928-34); William Money (1934-5); William Inight (1935-8);

The Old Porter Stores - later Josiah Stallards

Guildhall Rear Entrance Disabled and Private Parking Only

Marquis of Granby
Location: 22 Cooken (ie Copenhagen) Street
Years active: 1766 - c1820

Seemingly short-lived pub (c1766-c1820) named after accomplished soldier John Manners (1721–1770) Marquis of Granby who was such a popular figure of his time, his name was adopted by many new pubs being constructed around the mid-late 1700s: towns in Quebec and Massachusetts were also named Granby in his honour . Listed in Register of Victuallers' Recognizance of 1766 under Richard Bedford, later Elizabeth Bedford (listed as 'vict.' - ie victualler) and in 1814 under Samuel Kempson.

Ship (fhip)
Location: Cooken (later Copenhagen) Street
Years active: 1760 - 1906

Historic old pub and one of several sited next door to another pub (in this case **The Glo'ster Arms** as follows). First listed in Register of Victuallers' Recognizance of 1766 under licensee James Price and Grundy Royal Directory 1792 but by 1908 had become a private house – its end no doubt hastened by a report into the state of Worcester's pubs in 1906 by the Chief Constable who noted that the pub was just not needed and the rooms were small and ill-adapted for a public-house, but that it had been well conducted.' It closed about a year later.

Licensees: James Price (1766); John Birbeck (listed as 'vict {victualler} fhip 37 Cooken Street 1792); Sarah Birbeck (described as 'widow – 1814); Elizabeth Bullock (1827-1840); Richard Wilson (1842–c1860s); Sarah Allen (1872-6); John Allen (1876-7); William Newland (1877-9); Federick Evans (1879-83); Joseph Compton (1883-4); Edward Cotterill (1884-7); Joseph Ranford (1887-9); James Hampton (1889-94);Thomas Gardner (1894-1906).

Gloucester (and Glo'ster) Arms
Location: Copenhagen street
Years active: 1820 - 1915

On east corner of Little Fish Street and Copenhagen Street and next door to **The Ship Inn**, first listed Worcester Lewis Directory 1820

Licensees: John Hay (1820); William Hay (1827); John Hembrow (1835); Edw Griffiths (as Gloucester Arms, 36 Copenhagen Street – 1842- c1860); William Frederic Bennett (1872-4); George Adkins (1874-6); Elizabeth Adkins (1876-9); Sarah Booth (1879-80) Joseph Thorne (1880-6); Edwin Cotterell (as Glo'ster Arms – 1886-1904 when he died); Mrs Caroline Cotterell 1904-8 listed as Mrs Caroline Wheeler until 1913 when she died. William Roberts ran the establishment from 1913-15. Closed around 1915 Littlebury's Directory of that year lists the name bracketed with 'void'

Merry Fellow
Location: Copenhagen Street
Years active: 1780 - 1800

Two listings only: Worcester Royal Directory 1790 and Grundy Royal Directory 1792 both under 'T Johnson vict merry fellow 36 Cooken ftreet' 1792. No further listings

Cock
Location: Copenhagen street
Years active: 1760s - c1932

Smugglers' haunt, whose cellar was reputed to have been linked to the nearby Wherry by a secret passageway and thus under St Andrews churchyard to **The Red Cow**, thought to have been the smugglers' HQ and clearing-house in the supply chain for contraband goods to enter the City. First listed in Register of Victuallers' Recognizance of 1766 under James Anthony, but probably re-built c 1870 with a life-span up to c1936 when it was demolished to make way for the new-look Deansway.

Licensees: Joseph Birbeck (1790); Mrs Birbeck (described as 'vict. Cock 7 Birdport' - 1792); William Davies (1814); Thomas Calder (1827); John Curnock (1829); Thomas Calder (1835); Henry Talbot, (1842 and 1850); possible period of re-construction; Robert Baker (1872-80); John Griffin (1880); Edward Evans (1880-1); Robert Baker (1881-97); Richard Hutton (1897-8); Rewben Smith (1898-9); Edward Crump (1899-1901); James Digger (1901-5); Arthur Ingles (1905); Oliver Williams (1905-8); Arthur Thomas (1908-11); John Ratcliffe (1911-15); Frank Roberts (1915-21); Alfred Mason (1921-5); John Yates (1925-6); Cecil Crump (1926)

Above: The Cock 1900 (CCMH/CFOW) and the same view today (BB)

Plume of Feathers
Location: Copenhagen Street (also known as 'Pie Corner' 1790) Later Bridport
Years active: 1760s - 1897

Dating from the time of Copenhagen Street's growing influence as a commercial centre (c1760s) and listed in Register of Victuallers' Recognizance of 1766 under Mary Lacey described as 'widow', this **Plume of Feathers** – one of four so named in the City – appears to have enjoyed a life-span stretching some 150 years. Directory of 1790 indicates location as 'Pie Corner'. Sited on corner of Copenhagen Street and Birdport and listed variously as both thoroughfares, it lay well within the shadow of St Andrews Church, at what's now the corner of Deansway and the rump of Copenhagen Street leading to the Quay Street car park. Would also have been a near neighbour of **The Cock**, nudging up to the notorious New

Model Dwellings, slums swept away in the mass clearance of the early 1930s.

Licensees: Mary Lacey (widow – 1766); Mrs Crump (1790); John Hobro (also 1790); Thomas Chandler (1814); Edward Hobro (1827-40); Mary Little (c1840–1860); Joseph Birbeck senior (1872-9); John Lyons (1879-88 when he died); Eliza Lyons (1888-91); Alfred Hart (1891-3); John Izon (1893-4); Ellen Baker (1894); Archibold Norcott (1894); John Izon (1894-5); William Morgan (1895-6); William Bishop (1896-7); Daniel Workman (1897)

C4/31 Horse and Jockey
Location: Quay street
Years active: 1780 – 1830s

Seemingly short lived pub dating from around 1784 (Register of Victuallers' Recognizance) and listed Grundy Royal Directory 1792. Also listed in Pigot's Worcestershire Directory 1829 but no further entries. Site would have been north-east corner of present College of Technology

Licensees: Stephen Strickland (1784); Mrs Spencer (listed as 'horfe & jockey 38 Cooken Street' (1792); John Burford (1814); Isaac Morris (1820); Thomas Mayberry (1829)

C4/32 Wherry and (Old Wherry)
Location: Quay Street,
Years active: 1860s - 1889

Renowned smugglers inn, and noted haunt of watermen, reputed to be linked to others – notably the nearby **Old Cock** and **Red Cow** – by underground tunnels and passageways, listed in Register of Victuallers' Recognizance of 1766 under licensee John Daniels. One noted landlord was George Rogers, a prominent artist in stained glass and whose work is seen in both Worcester and Gloucester cathedrals as well as local parish churches throughout the County and beyond. It's said that a noted local parson died after leaving **The Wherry** and 'disoriented by the fog' – which may be a polite description out of respect for his calling – fell into the Severn and later died. For all its religious connotations at least two of its licensees fell foul of the law during their time here: John Kemp was convicted in 1877 for selling after hours and was fined £1 plus costs. George Thornberrow was convicted in 1883 for bribing a Police Constable for which he was

(Inset) Old smugglers' inn The Wherry, later put to more sober use as St Andrews Institute and main picture Quay Street 1930s. (CCMH/CFOW) and right - the same view 2013 (BB)

fined 10/6 (52¹/₂p) including costs. Clearly marked on the Ordnance Survey map of 1886 what had been the haunt of smugglers and coarse boatmen **The Wherry** later gained rather more respectability (c1923) as St Andrews Parish Club for men and boys, set up by rector of St Andrews parish, Canon Philpotts as a centre of good conversation and manly rounds of snooker or billiards.

Licensees: John Daniels (1766); Thomas Harbar (1814, also listed 1820 E. Gummery) to 1829; Luke Pyfinch Maybury (1830s–1850s); Emma Rogers (1855); William Hayden (1872-4); James Crockett (1874-5); Samuel Williams (1875-77); John Kemp (1877-8); John Perry (1878-83); George Thornberrow (1883-7); Alfred Cooper (1887-9)

Return to High Street for one very ancient and two comparatively 'modern' establishments...

Mitre
Location: High Street
Years active: 1664 - 1776

Referred to in 1664 and 1732 (Noake p21) Ancient inn mentioned by Noake as being existence in 1664, in Register of Victuallers' Recognizance of 1766 and in Grundy Royal Directory 1792. Noake wrote in 1877 'an inn so called in 1664 about the same time as another **Mitre** (this one most likely in Leach or Lich Street) in St Peter's parish. In 1732 belonged to Mrs Dorothy Price who had as neighbours on one side R. Mence a glover and on the other Richard Hill, gent. In 1766 it was licensed to William Bird with sureties given by David Bowkot and Joseph Nicholas. It seems however the two Mitres in the same see was not acceptable to the Bishop, and so this inn was converted into several tenements and three stables in 1776 and thought to have re-emerged as **The Stationers Arms** a century later

(Right) High Street 1910 (CCMH/CFOW)

Stationers Arms
Location: High Street
Years active: 1870 - 1910

Listed in Littlebury's Directory of Worcestershire 1873 at 102 High Street.

Licensees: *Geo. Hay (1873); Frank Sutton (1900); J. T.Grubb (1908) with no further entries but despite a different number (104) possibly became...*

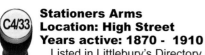 **Swan**
Also known as: Swan Restaurant
Location: 104 High Street

Years active: 1900 – 1950s

Mentioned by Noake (1877) as one of a number of 'ancient' City inns, some of which are 'probably not much less ancient than...' suggesting a much longer background and pedigree and implying this this could even be the final incarnation of **The Mitre** (and later **The Stationers Arms**). A short-lived Swan opened on the opposite side of the road in former cellars of Russell and Dorrells store but suffered a body-blow when it was descended-on by Birmingham bikers mistaking it for **The Swan with Two Nicks**, and never recovered.

Licensees: *Charlotte du Caun (1902); J.S.Smallwood (1908); John Hart (1915); Henry Hands (1937); Ernest Winter (1940)*

G-B: Fish Street to All Saints

Fish Street – originally Corviserstrete – is, like New Street, capable of stopping visitors in their tracks with its black-and-white buildings and particularly fine entrance to St Helens Church reputed to have been built on the site of a one-time Roman temple. It's here that a teenaged Edward Elgar, a catholic, was paid to ring the bell to call the faithful (protestants) to prayer – often arriving late and breathless at St George's Church in Sansome Street where he was also paid to play the organ for (catholic) services. Fish Street, since re-named after the traders that congregated there to sell their wares (well, catch) is also probably the second most photographed street in the City that in its day was never short of pubs either...

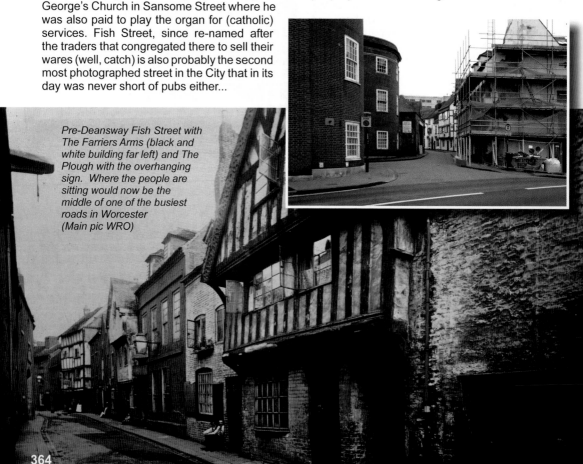

Pre-Deansway Fish Street with The Farriers Arms (black and white building far left) and The Plough with the overhanging sign. Where the people are sitting would now be the middle of one of the busiest roads in Worcester (Main pic WRO)

364

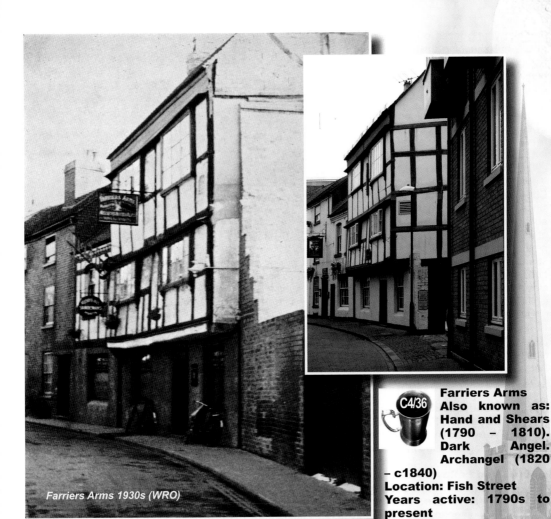

Farriers Arms 1930s (WRO)

Farriers Arms
Also known as:
Hand and Shears
(1790 – 1810).
Dark Angel.
Archangel (1820
– c1840)
Location: Fish Street
Years active: 1790s to
present

Originally **The Hand and Shears**, later **Dark Angel, Archangel** and finally **Farrier's Arms** located at 9, Fish Street and still doing good business with a dedicated crowd of devoted regulars.

The Hand and Shears was a seemingly short-lived under that name (1790-1810) listed only once - Grundy Royal Directory 1792, James Withenbury listed as licensee, address 'hand & sheers 9 Fish Street' then **Archangel** and **Dark Angel** - perhaps a mis-pronunciation of the former or maybe a name that stuck in reference to the character of its customers. It's possible the property reverted to a private dwelling house for a short period until **The Farriers Arms** first appeared in Littlebury's Directory of Worcestershire 1873 at Fish Street and 9, Fish Street. The sign – three upside-down horseshoes –is considered by many to be unlucky though it refers to the days when farriers were more than blacksmiths and shoe-ers of horses, but also served as horse vets. A charming black and white building that still attracts the tourists, recent renovation has not improved its interior looks and layout, and for years it attracted rowdy students from the nearby Technical College. Still, some quaint features remain and the pub is well worth a visit. A Benjamin Kelseys house, registered at Radford Hall Brewery Leamington, it was subsequently a Courage house. It was also occasionally used for inquests. On 10th December 1829, an inquest was held here into the death of an 8-month old infant. Verdict: 'died from a fit'.

In 1981 when it had been run by former **Talbot** licensee and manageress Nona Garnier and her daughter also Nona *(then Pettersen)* for fifteen years, Nona junior said: '...we're just an old-fashioned public house that happens to be pretty busy most of the time. I confessed: 'can't help feeling a bit misty-eyed about this one (as) I knew it way back in far-off 60s WRGS days when with four friends we'd knock back two or even three lunchtime pints before trolling back what seemed miles to school'. As I said then: '...the gang's long since gone, but the Farriers is still pretty much the same and the bar still attracts (largely) young faces out for a bit of a razzle but shunning the bright lights in favour of somewhere that's really pretty basic. But there's still the gorgeous quaintness, a welcome bit o' cramped-ness and a sort of huddle-close-together-in-the-shadows sort of gloominess. It's where 'for real' rules OK, I noted, with carved oak furniture. I described parking around there, even then, as a real pain in the whass'name but urged 'do drop in – even if you have to do it by parachute'. Character-wise not a lot has changed since then though it has been bashed about quite a lot – first by the addition of what had been a small jeweller's shop next door (east side) and then by some

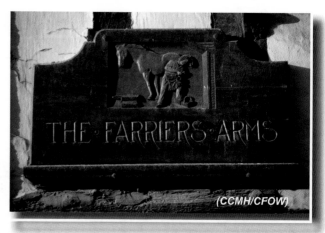

(CCMH/CFOW)

strange re-designing that joined what had been a pretty little lounge to part of what had been the bar and re-jigging the entrance arrangement into left (bar) and right (lounge plus the rump of the bar) and closing off the former separate lounge entrance Weird, and to me out of keeping – but still The Farriers is still worth the effort!

Licensees: (As Archangel) *John Curnock (1820): Thomas Burgess (1829). John (or James) Connor (1835);* **As Farriers Arms:** *Joseph H.Williams (1872-6); Edward Bruntnell (1876-9); Henry Baker (1879-84); Joseph Shipton (1884 – 1925); Percy H. Morgan (1925-30); Archibald Osborn, also listed as Archbld Bond Osborn, brewer 1930-1956); Daisy Madeleine Jones (1956-61); Neil Duncan Watt (1961-62); Raymond Barnes (1962); Howard and Ivy Turpin (1962-7); Nona Garnier (1967-81); Nora Patterson (1981); Robert Thompson (2000).*

General Hill
Location: Fish Street
Years active: 1820-1830

Single listing in Worcester Lewis Directory 1820 under licensee Thomas Burgess

Odd Fellows Arms
Location: Fish Street
Years active: 1840s 1860

Another apparently short-lived pub lasting from 1840s to around 1860 and not shown on OS map of 1886: only one licensee recorded: John Rallings *(Hunt & Co's Commercial Directory for Gloucester, Hereford and Worcester (1842)*, Victaullers Recognizances 1850 and Billings Directory of Worcestershire 1855

Plough
Location: Fish Street
Years active: 1820 - present

Noted pub popular with real ale lovers and CAMRA types who recently voted for it as Worcester's pub of the year, bikers for a while *(not so much now)*, the Labour group on the City Council, cider aficionados, intellectuals, crossword-solvers and a few oddballs some of whom will talk your leg off if you give 'em half a chance and others who just sit and look mysterious, occasionally looking up at you with a questioning glance.   On a busy thoroughfare dating from around 1820s, mercifully spared the bulldozer in the large-scale redevelopment of the 1930s (which explains its oddly-angular shape) and still in business almost 200 years on, it's now in need of some TLC though it remains a favourite with its assorted, if dedicated and occasionally quirky band of regulars. Essentially, this is a thinkers' pub with an intellectual nature and an irresistible charm that draws devotees for miles and ranks high on locals' and visitors' favourite pubs lists due to a potent combination of well-kept ales and ciders, and certain retained olde-worlde charm. (See the **Worcester Wassail** pub crawl on pages 423-4). First listed in Victuallers' Recognizances for 1827, later Pigot's Worcestershire Directory 1829, and switched from High Ward into the newly created St Albans ward in 1835. Still going strong despite a short period of closure in 2011 due, it's reported, to some VAT irregularities. In 1916, licensee's wife Mrs Elizabeth Bearcroft was fined £1 for unlawfully supplying cider here during prohibited hours. A move to turn the upstairs floors into a swish restaurant in the mid 1980s failed fairly quickly and **The**

Plough took off its dinner jacket and returned to its more customary scruffs: jeans, T-shirt and cosy jumper, though for a while under former milkman Phil Wise (whose brother Geoff, originally of the coal merchant family, also ran **The Saracens Head)** it took on the guise of bikers' pub. Phil went on to run **The Albion**.

Licensees: James Cross (1827); Joseph Perkins (1872-6); Jane Lampman (1876-8); Evan Giles (1878-9); Jane Giles (1879-90); John Lewis (1890-2 when he died); Mrs Annie Lewis (1893-7 when she died); John Lewis (1897-1902 when he died); John Good (1902); Albert W. Hartwright (1902-4); Daniel Dibble (1904-5); Thomas Collins (1905-6); Waldegrave Ingram (1906-8); George Bearcroft (1908–1916 when he died); Mrs Eliza Page (1916-30); Arthur James Checketts (1930-2); Henry Israel (1932-3 when he died); Mrs Gladys Israel (1933 – 1961); Philip John Underhill (1961-2); Frank Jones (1962-7); Francis Lamb (1967-9); Frank Anderton (1969-71); John Strode (1971-2); Mike Stevens (1972-9); Phil Wise (1979 - 2000)

Plough Deansway 1964 (JAS) and below undergoing some much needed tlc 2013 (BB)

Of all the divisions of the City, this area is the most difficult to plot actual locations of known pubs: this is for a number of reasons – not least that this is the oldest and most historic quarter for which records, if they were kept at all are at best sketchy, and also because the area was later a maze of courts and tenements that were unsurveyed in any detail right up to the Ordnance Survey map of 1886. The major construction project that was the creation of Deansway also swept away many of the buildings that had once been inns and taverns or, more tellingly, might have provided contemporary observers with clues to their actual locations. Accordingly, there are more circles (ie approximate locations) here than anywhere else in this book – for which, apologies. BB

Former Worcester mayor Hubert Leicester in his Worcester Remembered (1935) painted a grim picture of the scene around here:

'Smugglers found a happy home here for a considerable period and in the course of time they constructed an extensive cave in the neighbourhood of Birdport which they approached through a narrow passage leading from the South Quay, through the grounds of St Andrews Church. By way of Bull Entry an easy entrance was possible into the centre of the City, where their illicit goods could be sold. When some of the old houses were demolished in Birdport (Leicester says around 1905) the cave was discovered extending under several of the buildings and he goes on to imply 'insider knowledge' when he stated that goods landed by night could be in Worcester's shops by the morning 'without coming above ground'

Seven Stars
C4/39
Also known as: Old Seven Stars (1842-60s)
Location: Palace Street (also Quay Street)
Years active: 1700 – 1860

Part of the smugglers' network reputedly linked by underground cellars and tunnels, described by Noake (1877) as Palace Yard, next house but one to the old gates of the Bishop's Palace 1775 and one of a number of 'ancient' City inns, listed Worcester Royal Directory 1790 under Benjamin Smith and two years later in Grundy Royal Directory 1792 as 'Wm Davis feven ftars Palace Street'. Later Victuallers Recognizances 1835 shows licensee as William Jakeman and address as Quay Street). John Crathorne appears as licensee in Hunt & Co's Commercial Directory for Gloucester, Hereford and Worcester 1842 (1842- 1850s) and an entry in Billings Directory of Worcestershire 1855 lists Seven Stars, Quay Street under Martha Crathorne with no further references

Red Cow
C4/40
Location: Birdport
Years active: 1870-1900

Short lifespan, but occasionally notorious pub in the well-served Birdport area of the City reputed to be the centre of Worcester's widespread and nefarious smuggling operations and

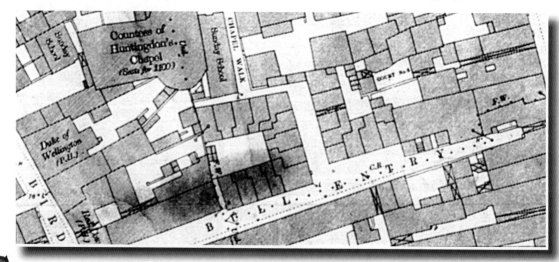

sited at the north-west corner of Bull Entry – a site later used for extension of Webb's horsehair factory and for a small glove factory and, interestingly, located at the north-western corner of what was later the Police HQ and City Magistrates Courts after the construction of Deansway in 1938! Described as 'beerhouse' in the will of owner James Portman Rea of Sidbury who at one time (1840s) also owned six other City pubs: **The Ram Inn** in 'New Town Road' later Regent Street, **White Hart, Hen & Chickens, Apple Tree, Swan with Two Necks (sic)** and **Rising Sun**. Listed Littlebury's Directory of Worcestershire under William Hay (1873) shown on the Ordnance Survey First Edition 1886 and thought to have closed c1900

Bull & Sun (also listed as Sun and Bull, and Sun and Bell – thought erroneously, and Bull and Sunn)
Location: Bull Entry (also Bull Square)
Years active: 1792 - 1838

Confusingly-named (originally Sun and Bull ['fun and bull'] Bull Entry' - Grundy Royal Directory 1792 – but also Bull and Sun and, probably a typo's error, Sun and Bell. Thought to have been part of the smugglers' cellars complex, local historian Bill Gwilliam says the building was demolished 1838, but gave its name to Bull Entry. It was also occasionally used for inquests: that of Susannah Insall who'd died aged 18 months after being scalded by a falling kettle, was held here. Known as **'The Sun'** in 1766 (Victuallers' Recognizes) when it was described as being in High ward, but not listed after 1784.

Licensees: as Sun: Elizabeth Holdship (widow - 1766); 'Sun and Bull': Richard Bubb (1792); William Meysey (1814). **As Bull and Sun:** *Edward Poyser or Prosser (1827); Thomas Horsley (1835)*

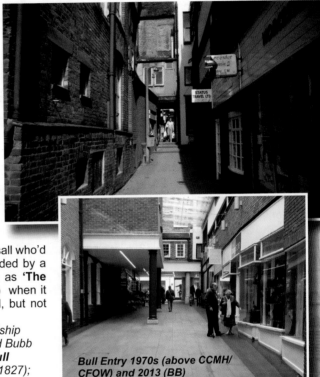

Bull Entry 1970s (above CCMH/CFOW) and 2013 (BB)

Victoria
Location: back of 85 High Street
Years active: 1900 - 1912

This was at the top of Bull Entry on the north side which was Ind, Coope and Co Ltd, brewers. Frederick Arthur Elliot listed as licensee 1908. Gone by 1915

Duke of Wellington
Also known as Marquis Wellington
Location: 14, Birdport (also Birdport Street 1850)
Years active: c1810 – 1967

First reference in Victuallers Recognizances in 1814 as Marquis Wellington later changed to reflect the Iron Duke's progress up the peerage scale *(he was created Duke in 1814, the year before Waterloo and twice served as British Prime Minister).*

Also later listed in Pigot's Worcestershire Directory 1829. Address listed as 14, Birdport (1915). Survivor of the large-scale changes of the late 1930s that saw Birdport and Merrivale transform into Deansway. In the 1930s a Harpers HItchman house registered at Lowesmoor Brewery Worcester and later 26, Bridge Street Worcester. Closed early 1970s and left largely derelict until demolished several years later and said to have been 'the squalidest pub in Worcester' (1959) but survived as a pub up to right up to 1967 though by then derelict and an eyesore. It was only in connection with research into this book – and at a late stage too, just two weeks away from print (October 2013) that I realised a personal connection with this pub... seems my great grandfather Arthur John Blandford lived here, a fact that

The Duke of Wellington gets a top-up (below, centre left) 1970s and later in a sorry state (photographs CCMH/CFOW)

came as a major surprise – though whether or not he was licensee remains uncertain as his occupation is shown as 'carpenter' and other known licensees existed around this time. Even so, the census of 1891 shows he and his family (plus servant Annie Hill aged 19 and single) and four lodgers were the occupants: he is listed as 32-year old head of the household with his wife Agnes Eliza (30), children George William (aged 9 and described as 'scholar'), Arthur Claude (8), Florence Eleanor (5) and Sidney Ernest (later my own grandfather, then aged 3). Also living here were lodgers Edward James Williams (67 and described as widower, occupation painter), William Burrows (single 36 and a ? maker, writing illegible), William George (single, aged 42 and a tailor) and William Simpson, (single aged 20 and a shoemaker). *Licensees: John Hammerton (1814); S. Chandler (1829); Thomas Chandler (1835 –c1853); Wm. Prosser (1855); Joseph Lightwood (1850-76); Clarissa Bennett (1876-8); Annie Bennett (1878-9); Henry Elliott (1879-82); Sophia Bennett (1882-88 when she died); Frederick Garmston (1888); Thomas Harwood (1890-1);* **Arthur Blandford (1891)***; John Bladon (1891-3); Thomas Roberts (1893-7); Charles Perry (1897-1903); Edward Crump (1903-5); Arthur Thomas (1905-7); James Digger (1907–12); William King (1912); William Richards (1912-14); Arthur Cross (1914-17); Alfred Henry Willis Duke of Wellington 14 Birdport (1917–41); Edith Olive Willis (1941-1953); Edith Bird (1953); Alfred William Willis (1953-4); Arthur John Hill (1954-60); James Mobberley (1960-65);Sydney Colloff (1965-6); Christopher Hammond (1966)*

Prince Blücher
Location: Birdport
Years active: 1815 – 1830

Thought to date from around from 1815 (first listed in Worcester Lewis Directory 1820) with only one licensee named - William Mayses - and no entries follow. The name is drawn from Gebhard Leberecht von Blücher, Fürst von Wahlstatt (1742 – 1819), Graf (Count), later elevated to Fürst (Prince) von Wahlstatt, who was a Prussian Generalfeldmarschall (field marshal) who led his army against Napoleon I at the Battle of the Nations at Leipzig in 1813 and at the Battle of Waterloo in 1815 with the Duke of Wellington. He was also known as "Marschall Vorwärts" ("Marshal Forwards") because of his approach to warfare. A popular German idiom, "ran wie Blücher" ("charge like Blücher"), meaning that someone is taking very direct and aggressive action, in war or otherwise, refers to him. Clearly, we know more about the man than the pub that carried his name!

Prince Regent
Location: Birdport
Years active: 1811 – 1830

C4/45

Opened in 1811, the Prince Regent appears to be comparatively short-lived – barely surprising given the number of pubs in and around Birdport over the years. Only one licensee appears to be listed: John Stinton. The title is most commonly associated with George IV, Prince Regent during the incapacity of his father, George III (as in the film *'The Madness of King George)*. Regent's Park and Regent Street in London are named after him during the period now known as the Regency. The title was conferred by the Regency Act on February 5, 1811 so the pub must have been built - or was certainly in existence - around this time.

Fourteen Stars
Also known as Druids Head (1829)
Location: St Andrews ward
Years active: 1820s-40s

C4/46

Listed in Victuallers Recognizances in 1827 Licensee listed as 'Thomas Collis Crompton now William Butler'. Later became **The Druids Head** listed as Merryvale in St Andrews ward 1829. By 1835 licensee listed as Henry Southall (Pigot)

Leather Dressers' Arms
Location: Birdport
Years active: 1820s-1840s

C4/47

Another apparently short-lived inn in Birdport, listed in Victualler Recognizances 1827 and later Pigot's Worcestershire Directory 1829 and 1835. Licensee Thomas Holder (1827, 1829 and 1835).

Lamb
Location: Birdport
Years active: 1790 - 1800

C4/48

Listed in Grundy Royal Directory 1792 under 'Wm Sanders vict lamb 4 Birdport' with no further listings

Dragoon
Also known as Jolly Dragoon, Jolly Sailor
Location: Birdport
Years active: 1780-c1810

'Dragoon' is likely to be a shortened version of 'Jolly Dragoon' listed in Register of Victuallers' Recognizance of 1784 under Eliz(abeth) Price. Later, as 'Dragoon' in the care of William Savage (1790), then Mrs Savage – described as 'vict dragoon 2 Birdport (1795). Possibly re-emerged by 1814 as **Jolly Sailor,** listed under licensee Thomas Evans – location unknown except 'St Andrews ward'. No further details known, though possibly re-emerged as **The Jolly Trowman,** listed in Victuallers Recognizances in 1814 as 'St Andrews ward' under Samuel Griffin

Wool Pack
Location: Birdport
Years active:

Listed 1822, precise location unknown and shown only as 'Birdport', but possibly – though by no means categorically – a clerical error siting it here rather than nearby Dolday as there are no further references to a pub of this name in this area. The inference *(okay, guess!)* would have been stronger if it had said Merry Vale which could, at a stretch, have identified it as one and the same as its better-known Dolday namesake – all of which underlines the uncertainty of records for this location while also adding to the mysteries surrounding this tightly-packed maze of courts and tenements that were also right at the heart of Worcester's criminal activities

Nelson/Lord Nelson
Location: Birdport (2, Merryvale)
Years active: 1800 – 1958

Precise location known largely because of long life-span even up to the 1950s. Corner of All Hallows and Powick Lane, also Birdport. (left side from Broad Street). Listed in Worcester Lewis Directory 1820 as **Lord Nelson** Birdport, and then variously as Lord Nelson Birdport (1850), Lord Nelson Birdport Street , **Nelson Inn** All Hallows (1900); Nelson 2 All Hallows (1910) 2 Merryvale (1913). Ansells house bought by conveyance £11,800 on November 6th 1944. Licence surrendered 9th December 1958 when it closed.

Licensees: Joseph Wharton (also listed as Joseph Worton 1814 – c1835); Mary Worton (1835); Thomas Scott (1842); Henry Anderson, (1850); John Johnson (1855);Harry Groves (1872-81); Emma Groves (1881-2); Arthur Radford (1882-4); Henry Radford (1884-90);Henry Smith (1890-7); John Welch (1897-99); James Currin (1899-1902); Harry Wakefield (1902); Arthur W. Everton (1902-4); Ernest Muitland (1904); George Lamb (1904-7); Edward Crump (1907-11);Tom Ridlington (1911); John Roberts (1911-13); Arthur Busby (1913-14); Harry Gregory (1914-18); Frederick George Hale (1918–1944); Phillip Everett (1944-5); Henry Reginald Lees (1945-1954); Benjamin George Bradley (1954-5); William Frederick Ypres Rumsey (alter went to The Swan, St Johns) 1955-6; Christopher Payne (1956-8); William Evans (1958); Irene Kathleen Clay (1958)

Pewterer's Arms
Location: Merrivale
Years active: 1740 - 1830

Seemingly short-lived pub in Merry Vale (no2) cleared to make way for Deansway, and run for most of its 90-year life by a succession of Merediths. Listed in Register of Victuallers' Recognizance of 1766 under Martha Meredith (described as 'widow') who had succeeded her husband Samuel (a noted City property owner and landlord, particularly in and around Friar Street) and was later succeeded by Elizabeth and then, presumably, Elizabeth's son, Thomas.

Licensees: Samuel Meredith (1745); Martha Meredith (widow - 1766); Elizabeth Meredith (1790); Thomas Meredith (1792); John James (1814); Chas. Walter (1827)

Quiet Woman
Location: Birdport
Years active: 1790

One listing only Worcester Royal Directory 1790 licensee William Weaver (also described as 'bricklayer')

Hole in the Wall
Location: Merry Vale
Years active: 1820 – 1880

Makes first appearance in Worcester Lewis Directory 1820 but closed around 1880 and not shown in Ordnance Survey map 1886, so clearly gone by then

Licensees: John Jones (listed as 'vict and farmer' 1820); Samuel Barnes (1835); John Groves (1842–c1853); Harry Groves (1855– c1873). No further listings

Jolly Farmer
Location: 'All Saints'
Years active: 1760 - c1784

Listed in Register of Victuallers' Recognizance of 1766 as 'All Saints ward' under licensee Francis Harding but not listed after 1784, so assumed closed.

Press
Location: All Hallows
Years active: 1850 – 1860

First listed Billings Directory of Worcestershire 1855 and sited next to Potters Printing Press which, according to historian Bill Gwilliam, appears to have run along with the tavern and later became **The Malt Shovel Inn** – in turn transforming itself as the Empire Dining Rooms c 1920 . Only one licensee listed – John H. Stone - leading to the assumption that **The Press** was a very short-lived venture indeed though its successor enjoyed a rather longer existence

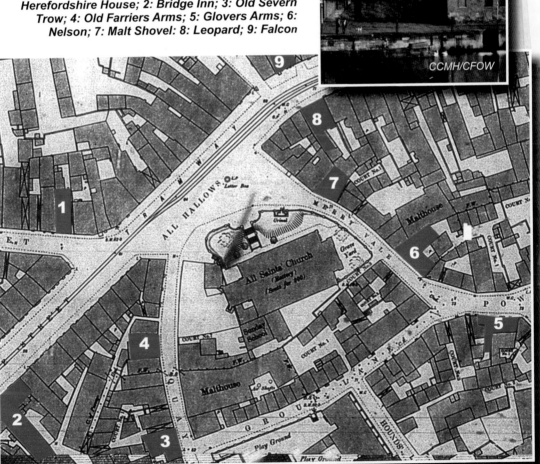

C4/57

**Malt Shovel
Location: All Hallows
Years active: 1870 – 1907**

Makes first appearance in Littlebury's Directory of Worcestershire 1873 at All Hallows (1873) and 3 All Hallows (1900). It closed in 1906 – just a short while after a damning report by the Chief Constable who said it was 'structurally deficient, not needed and sanitary conditions were inadequate'. He also noted that there had been three convictions 'against the house' in the previous seven years. It later became the Empire Dining Rooms, according to Bill Gwilliam

Licensees: William Hill (1872-82); John Carpenter (1882-3); Henry Roan (1883); Martin Boaz (1883-88); Richard Bradburn (1888-92 when he died); Sarah Bradburn (1892-3); Arthur Bradburn (1893-8); Charles Brown (1898 when he died); George Powell (1899); Frederick Guyatt (1899-1900); Ralph Major (1900-01); Alfred Hayes (1901); Walter Carnley (1901); Arthur Everton (1901-2); Richard Silk (1902-4); George Cleveley (1904-6); Charles Link (1906); Frederick Guyatt (1906)

OS map 1886 (reproduced with permission) shows 9 'live' pubs around All Saints Church: 1: Herefordshire House; 2: Bridge Inn; 3: Old Severn Trow; 4: Old Farriers Arms; 5: Glovers Arms; 6: Nelson; 7: Malt Shovel: 8: Leopard; 9: Falcon

CCMH/CFOW

H-A: South Quay – bridge

Bottle in Hand
Location: 'All Saints ward' (probably Quay Street)
Years active: 1820s - 1895

First listed Victuallers' Recognizances 1835 under Thomas Stalworth who is also listed elsewhere as licensee of The Queen Caroline – which suggests the two could be one and the same

Queen Caroline
Location: Quay Street
Years active: 1820 - 1895

Dating from the turbulent 1820s and thought to have changed from The Bottle in Hand to Queen Caroline at the time when there was great opposition to King George III. Caroline of Brunswick-Wolfenbüttel (Caroline Amelia Elizabeth; later Queen Caroline; 17 May 1768 – 7 August 1821) was Princess of Wales and later Queen consort of King George IV between 1795 and 1820.

Licensees: Thomas Collis Crumpton (1827); Thos. Stalworth (1832 – c1860s); William Hayden (1873); Joseph Sheen (1872-4); Joseph Birch (1874-6); William Bateman (1876-8); William Pritchard (1878-9); Henry Hannett (1879-80); George Leek (1880-2); William Birt (1882-5).

Severn Trow (and Old Severn Trow)
Also known as: The Pheasant (1820-30)
Location: Kain/Quay Street
Years active: c1780s - 1934

An old waterman's inn in the notorious quarter once the haunt of smugglers and the nearest thing to a dockside Worcester had, with a history apparently stretching back well over a century. First listed Worcester Royal Directory 1790 under Josiah Newman later in Victuallers Recognizances in 1814 as **The Severn Trow** but changed to **The Pheasant** in 1820, but had reverted to its original name before 1835 (Pigot's) and shown as **Severn Trow PH** in the Ordnance Survey First Edition of 1886 . A report by the Chief Constable in 1906 described the pub as 'structurally deficient, not needed, and sanitary conditions inadequate' – comments that don't appear to have unnecessarily harmed the pub as it continued in business for almost thirty more years!

*Licensees: As Severn Trow: Josiah Newman (1790); Mary Lloyd (described as 'widow' 1814); **As Pheasant:** Henry Mansell (1827). **As Severn Trow:** Willliam Jakeman (1835); Henry Southall (1842 – c1854); Mary Southall (Old Severn Trow, 1855): William Butcher (1872-5); Emma Butcher (1875-84); Elizabeth Little (1884-5); Arthur Ingles (1885-8); Richard Roberts (1888-1909 when he died); Mrs Mary Ann Roberts (1909-11); Bertram Roberts (1911-12); Frederick White (1912-13); William Tildesley (1913-14); William Green (1914-19); Herbert Jaynes (1919-22); Isaac Barker (1922-34); Elizabeth Barker (1934).*

A diversion...

Severn Swan
Also known as Black Swan or Swann
Location: Quay Street/Kain Street/South Parade
Years active: 1760 - 1880

Shown first white building (left) below. Listed as **Black Swann** in Register of Victuallers' Recognizance of 1766 under long-standing licensee Southall Bayley (1766 to c1814), **The Swan** by 1830, then and **The Severn Swan** by 1868. Another inn by the name of '**Old Swan**' also existed in the St Andrews ward area in 1766 under licensee George Mountford, and may well be the same premises, but there are no further details.

Licensees: Southall Bailey (1766, listed Grundy Royal Directory 1792 as 'merchant and innholder black fwan 8 Kain ftreet'); Edward Rees (1814); John Bennett (1827); Francis Woodward. Not listed Pigot's directory 1835 but then re-emerged as **Severn Swan** *1868 when it was run by one Thomas Ballard though there are no further references.*

Farmer's Arms
Location: Quay Street
Years active: 1850s

One listing only, Billings Directory of Worcestershire 1855.
Licensee: Stayt Thomas - beer retailer

Fountain
Location: Quay Street
Years active: 1700s

Listed in Noake as an ancient inn, but no further details

Farrier's Arms (and Old Farriers' Arms after 1952)
Location: Quay Street
Years active: 1827 - 1964

Appears in Victuallers' Recognizances 1827 and Pigot's Worcestershire Directory 1829 and listed as **Farrier's Arms (Old)**, Quay Street (1842), **Farrier's Arms, Quay Street** (1850); **Old Farrier's Arms,** Quay Street (1855), and later 6, Quay Street. Later Benjamin Kelsey house registered at Radford Hall Brewery Leamington (later Flowers, West Country, Whitbread). One noted landlord was Henry (better known as Harry) Davis who'd been a pro boxer before taking on **The Farriers Arms**. On 3rd September 1920, licensee Edgar Inight was fined £10 with £1.10s (£1.50) solicitor's fee for unlawfully selling rum above the maximum permitted price. On 21st February 1961, John Ralph Dunn was fined was fined £5 with 1gn (£1.05p) advocate's fee on both charges of aiding and abetting consumption after hours

Licensees: Edward Mayhouse (1827 - entry illegible); Thomas Maybury (1829–1876 though it's

Glorious panorama of South Quay in the snow c 1899.
The white building far left is The Black Swan (CCMH/CFOW)

almost certain later years were a different Thomas Maybury, possibly son); William Blundell (1876-1900); Richard Harman (1900-1908); Lewis A. Witts (1908-13); Edgar Inight (1913-31); Tom P Higgins (1931-2); George Dean (1932-3); Thomas Dexter (1933-6); Francis Robert Featherstone (1937); Henry John William Davis (1937-52); Beatrice Hudson (1952-3); Albert Lord (1953); Harold Juggins (1953-4); Herbert Walter Morton (1954-57); Harold Bayliss (1957-58); Margaret Clarke (1958); William John Llewellyn (1958-60); John Ralph Dunn (1960-2); Arthur Gilbert (1962-4)

Old Farriers Arms 12th January 1960 (RHS) and the same site (left) November 2013 (BB)

to London Vaults

The following pubs are mysteries: we know they existed because the documentary evidence says so and is there for all to see, but as with so many 'ancient' and pre-1850s pubs and inns, precise dates, location and further details are extremely elusive – more so in this historical and poorly documented area of the City. When 'Rambler' John Noake wrote... it's probably in connection with the proliferation of pubs in and around here but lost in the maze of alleys, courts and mean housing that he draws his exasperated and entirely justified conclusion with which I heartily concur. Rather than hazard an even educated guess – though the reality is likely to be considerably more haphazard given the available evidence at present – the best course is to lump them all together here for you to draw your own conclusions, though further research could, just possibly, throw more light on their whereabouts (for which, read 'retired hurt...')

Shoemakers Arms
Location: All Saints
Years active: 1760s

Listed in Register of Victuallers' Recognizance of 1766 as All Saints ward under licensee Mary Bowen (widow), but precise location and other details proving particularly elusive. Not included in the 1814 register, so presumably gone by then.

Barley Mow, All Saints
Location: All Saints
Years active: 1780s - 1800

Listed in Register of Victuallers' Recognizance of 1784 as All Saints ward under licensee William Piercey, but precise location and other details proving particularly elusive. Not included in the 1814 register so, again, presumably gone by then.

Salt Scales
Location: St Andrews ward
Years active: 1766

Listed in Register of Victuallers' Recognizance of 1766 as St. Andrews ward under licensee Eliz(abeth) Wilson described as 'widow'. Precise location and other details elusive but its name suggests it might have been in the Quay Street/Warmstry Slip area where boatmen loaded and unloaded goods for shipment up and down the river: salt from Droitwich being in demand all over the UK. Not included in the 1784 register of Recognisances so, yet again, presumably gone by then.

Crown & Canton
Location: St Andrews ward
Years active: 1766

Single listing - Register of Victuallers' Recognizance of 1766 under licensee John Loos, but no further listings suggesting it was either an ancient inn reaching the end of its days, or changed its name to something else, or just plain failed. Location unknown and no further details have so far come to light.

Black Hussar
Location: St Andrews ward
Years active: 1766

Single listing - Register of Victuallers' Recognizance of 1766 under licensee William Southall – but no further listings suggesting it was either an ancient inn reaching the end of its days, or changed its name to something else, or just plain failed. Location unknown and no further details have so far come to light.

Laurence's Mug House
Location St Andrews ward
Years active: 1760s-1814?

Single listing - Register of Victuallers' Recognizance of 1766 under licensee Laurence, but no further listings suggesting it was either an ancient inn reaching the end of its days, or changed its name to something else, or just plain failed. Location unknown – though the same index for 1814 lists 'Mug House' but no licensee's name, and no further details have so far come to light.

Kings Arms
Location: St Andrews ward
Years active: 1760s

Single listing - Register of Victuallers' Recognizance of 1766 under licensee Sarah Douglas described as 'widow', but no further listings suggesting it was either an ancient inn reaching the end of its days, or changed its name to something else, or just plain failed. Location unknown, though could possibly be the same as **The Kings Arms**, Lich (Leach) Street.

C4/72 King's Head
Also known as King David
Location: Birdport
Years active: 1760s - 1800?

An entry for The King's Head in St Andrews ward (Register of Victuallers' Recognizance of 1766) under licensee Joseph Showard or Sheward has been crossed out and replaced with 'King David' next referred to in Grundy's Royal Directory of 1790 under William

A very crowded South Quay 1880s (CCMH/CFO?)

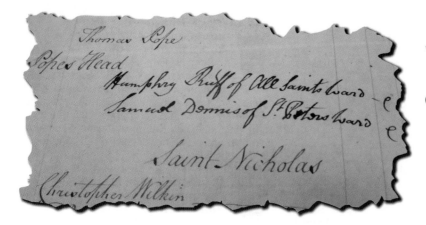

*Victuallers Recognizance
of The Pope's Head
1781*

*(Worcester City archives,
WRO)*

Sanders, but these the only references to either and no further details, including location, are known.

Pope's Head
Location: 'St Andrews ward'
Years active 1780s - 1800?

Shown in Victuallers Recognisances for 1780 under licensee Thomas Pope, but no indication to precise location and nofurther references.

Bricklayers Arms
Location: St Andrews ward
Years active: 1760s

Single listing - Register of Victuallers' Recognizance of 1766 under licensee Thomas Corbyn, but no further listings suggesting it was either an ancient inn reaching the end of its days, or changed its name to something else, or just plain failed. Location unknown.

Crispin
Location: St Andrews ward
Years active:

A single entry exists for this eccelesiastically-named inn (Register of Victuallers' Recognisance of 1766) under licensee Stephen Strickland whose name appears elsewhere – not least as licensee of The Dun Cow (also known as Hen and Chickens and Old Hen & Chickens in All Hallows Well, Merryvale. It's possible – though not very likely as it's listed in the generally reliable index of recognisances under its own name – that **The Crispin** was another name for either of these. It also indicates that Mr Strickland Esq was a very astute innkeeper and businessman

Well Sinkers Arms
Location: 'All Saints ward'
Years active: 1850

First listed Victuallers' Recognizances 1859 under Henry Evans, precise location unknown and no further listings. Not listed in the Ordnance Survey map of 1886 – though it may possibly have changed its name to something else.

12: City Centre 5

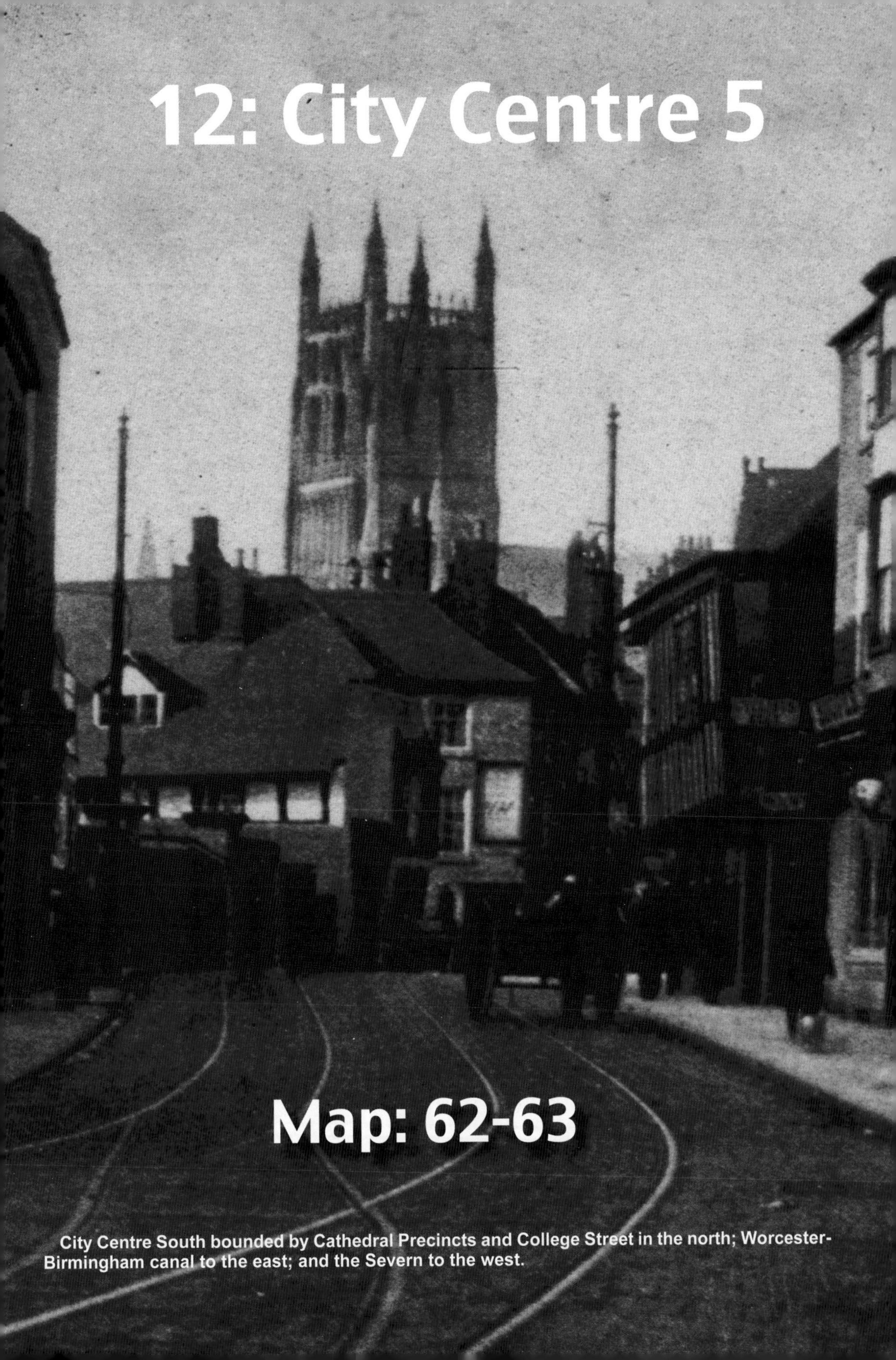

Map: 62-63

City Centre South bounded by Cathedral Precincts and College Street in the north; Worcester-Birmingham canal to the east; and the Severn to the west.

As is true of the previous seven chapters, a significant re-construction project – in this case, the development of College Street in 1792, cutting a swathe through what had been a very different-looking approach to the City – changed the face of this part of Worcester forever. It's an area dominated then as now by the cathedral – itself the latest in a long line of cathedrals on the same site. The first structure dates back to around 655 AD and the cathedral as we see it today is the third here – though the crypt and other sections pre-date the present structure by at least a thousand years. Inevitably, being the oldest part of the City by a wide margin, there's more history wrapped-up here than in any of the previous sections. Pick up any local history book and it – like the City it refers to – will almost certainly begin here and devote what might perhaps be considered a disproportionate number of pages to the cathedral and its surroundings. Curious to note this is where the pubs section ends – and it's the shortest chapter in the book! Typically though, being a historically-rich area, details are remarkably difficult to come by. Even so, from what *is* known with some certainty, there's a few surprises here...

A-B: College Street to Sidbury (south side)

Plume of Feathers
Location: cathedral
Years active: 1600 - 1700
　　Ancient inn apparently butting up to the cathedral. Known only through a single reference and mentioned by Hubert Leicester ('The east window of the cathedral reminds us that in the 17ᵗʰ century there was a dwelling house built close up to the cathedral and that Lord Somers (one of the counsel in the celebrated trial of Seven Bishops) was born there. The house afterwards was an inn, under the sign of 'The Plume of Feathers')

Where there's a churchyard or a cemetery – let alone a superstructure like a cathedral *(and let's face it, Worcester's is a super structure, right?)* – superstition and tales of the unexplained are never very far behind. There's rumours of a bear said to haunt the cathedral grounds, and another one of a severed hand making regular appearances, but there's a particularly haunting tale that concerns at

least one drinking establishment and it carries a salutary lesson for all young women in this area. It's the story of a mischievous poltergeist living in the City's Edgar Street/College Street area – as I wrote in an article in September 1987

City 'being' hates all the young women

In November 1718 Mary Bentall who worked in service 'without Sidbury Gate' was troubled with a poltergeist who caused stones to fall out of the air, narrowly missing the girl's head as she was at work. Her mistress fired her – more through fear than the trumped-up charge of a stealing a scarf, and Mary went into service in a house in College Churchyard (one of the houses in the wedge between today's College Street and Edgar Street). She was not there many days when stones, tiles and brickbats flew about her like hailstones to the great amazement of the family – so much so that the maid declared she was weary of her life implying that it had happened on several occasions before'. On January 20th 1804, a housemaid working in the same house – that of Mr Harris, an attorney was also the victim of flying bricks with fatal results. During a violent storm she'd joined the lawyer's two children in bed when the chimney-stack fell through the roof and killed her, though the two children were unharmed. Strangely in 1960 another girl was killed on the same spot by flying bricks when the chimney of The White Hart collapsed.

White Hart, right, 1972 (CCMH/CFOW)

C5/2   **White Hart**
Also known as: Shamus O'Donnell's.   Hand in Glove
Location: College St. and Sidbury
Years active: 1700s - present

Another 'ancient' inn in the old ecclesiastical centre of the City, taking its name from the arms of Richard II and mentioned by Noake (1877) as one of a number of 'ancient' City inns, some of which are 'probably not much less ancient than the eighteenth or even 17th century. At one time (1840s) one of seven City pubs owned by maltster James Portman Rea of Sidbury whose portfolio also included the **Ram Inn** in 'New Town Road' later Regent Street, **Red Cow** beerhouse, **Hen & Chickens, Apple Tree, Swan with Two Necks** (sic), and **Rising Sun**. Thought to be haunted by a misogynistic (female-hating) poltergeist claimed to have been responsible for several deaths in the College Street/Edgar Street triangle – including a young typist killed while passing the White Hart when the chimney collapsed, February 1960 and other incidents in and around the triangle. An inn has stood on this site for more than three centuries but the present structure is typical 60s (*It was rebuilt after the fatal accident*

The aftermath of the White Hart chimney collapse killing a young typist, 3rd February 1960 (RHS)

White Hart rebuilt 1965 (JAS) and (below) trendy Hand in Glove 2013 (BB)

here) and has since undergone two trendy name changes – though present landlords are having a good go at keeping it alive. It's thought the name '**Hand in Glove**' could be a reference to The Hand in Glove Club that used to meet for bowls games on Diglis Pleasure Gardens close by. Flowers (later Whitbreads) house. On 25th October 1899 licensee Frederick Bedford was fined 5/- (25p) with £2.11.6d (£2.57$^1/_2$p) costs for being drunk on his own premises.

Licensees: As White Hart: Martha Baylis (listed as 'vict.White Hart Sidbury' 1790); Samuel Tidmarsh (1820); Thomas Francis (1829); Thomas Yeates (now 'White Hart, College Street' 1842–1870s); William Perry (1872-80); Jane Perry (1880-3); Seth Robinson (1883-90); John Barnett (18901-1); Acton Roan (1891-8); Frederick Bedford (1898-1900); Frederick Cook (1900-01); Charles Martin (1901-2); Frederick Harding (1902-3); Mrs Louisa Morris (1903); Thomas Anderton (1903-4); Richard Silk (1904-5); James Tyler (1905-6); Alexander French (1906); Charles Lucas (1906–13); Charles Price (1913-22); Henry Baker (1922-3); Francis George Jenkins (1923–1940 when he died); Thomas Avery (1940-5); Joseph Arthur Powell (1945-60) Thomas Edwin Overbury (1960-62); Marie Louise Gregory (1962-8); Albert Moody (1968-9); Raymond Rainbow (1969-71); Leonard Profitt (1971-3); Robert Proffitt (1973); James Murphy (1973-5); John Palmer (1975-86); Brian McHale (1986-9); Michael Browne (1989). **As Shamus O'Donnells** *Alan Bendall (2000); Noel Butler (2001). As Hand-in-Glove Current (2013) licensee and dps: Matthew Bradley Pugh. Worcester City licence 1093*

Ye Cocke
Location: corner of Edgar Street and Sidbury
Years active: 1500s to 1750s

Mentioned more than three centuries ago as belonging to Hugh Adams *(John Noake Worcestershire Relics 1877, p119)*: 'Ye Cocke, Knowle-end, Sidbury at ye Knowle-end Sidbury the Knowle or Knoll's end was the corner of Edgar Street, by Sidbury the house is described in 1734 as a hall, a kitchen, a buttery, parlour, cellar, brew-house yard or court, stable four upper chambers and top lofts over them in the occupation of Mrs Elizabeth Stevens, widow'.

Angel (de la Trompe)
Also known as The Trumpet'
Location: Sidbury
Years active: 1730 – 1966 (re-built 1898)

Referred to by Noake in Worcestershire Relics *(printed March 1877 price 5/-)* 'in the most ancient records, 'Stodemaris' Knoll' is the name used to describe the place or street called le knoll in the reign of Richard II (1377-99); and a reference to 'the second tenement from the hospice or inn called **'The Trumpet'** in the reign of Henry VI (1421-71). The inn was certainly in existence in 1433 and documents survive from 1517 showing The Abbott of Bordesley as having reserved accommodation at **The Angel** at a cost of 2/6d (12$^1/_2$p) a year. The building was replaced in 1898 but retained its name though in later years it became more commonly known as The Angel. Hubert Leicester in his *Worcester Remembered* also wrote: 'The corner house at Edgar Street was for some years a public house known as **The Angel de la Trompe'**. Listed as The Angel St Peters ward in Victuallers Recognizances in 1766, 'Angel' 1820-47, Angel family and commercial hotel' 1855), Angel Commercial 1873, and Angel Commercial Hotel (1957). It was also occasionally used for inquests. On 9th December 1819, three inquests were held here: John Gorle trunk maker who died 'from a visitation by God'; Maria Gardner, aged 4, burned to death, and Amphlett *(first name unknown or illegible)* who 'fell into the Severn at Kempsey'. Not listed as 'one of (Worcester's) five principal carriers' Inns, even so, photographs show it to have been a fine imposing-looking building and it had a good reputation as a Mitchells and Butlers house in its day. On 5th November 1946, licensee Robert Cureton was fined a total of £10 for two counts of selling ginger beer to Worcester City Weights and Measures officer Joseph Henry Moore at a price exceeding maximum permitted. The building was demolished c1967 and the site is now the northwestern corner of King Street car park – though curiously, The Angel's original 1898 door and doorway still exist and they and the passageway that originally led to the ancient pub, now form an integral part of Benedicto's Italian Restaurant.

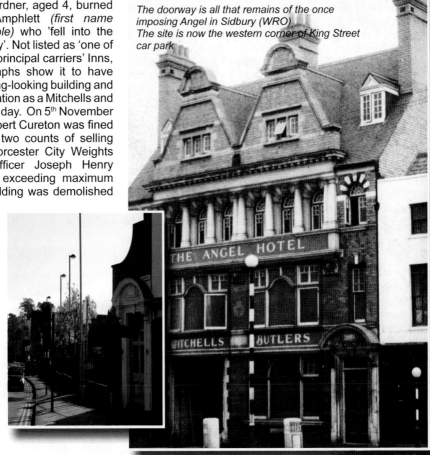

The doorway is all that remains of the once imposing Angel in Sidbury (WRO). The site is now the western corner of King Street car park

Sidbury 1910 (CCMH/CFOW) and the same view 2013 Note the 'Angel' door (BB)

Licensees: *R(ichar)d Poole (1734); Evan Jones (1763); Joseph Stevens Jnr (1790); Joseph Stephens (1814); John Thornes (1827); Catherine Day, (1842-c1870); John Edward Evans (1872-6): Thomas Cater (1876-7); Anne Cater (1877-8); Whitmore Jones (1878-80); Herbert Hallwall (1880-1); John Sidebottom (1881-3); Catherine Gibbons (1883); Edward Bennett (1883); Edwin Jones (1883-5); Maria Jones (18858); Elizabeth Hyde (1888-96); Annie Osborne (1896-8); Robert Davies (1898); John West (1902); Wm Chamberlain (1908); James Smith (1915); Steven Overall (1898-1939); Reginald Haines (1939); George John Green (1939 to 1946); Robert Cureton (1946); Stanley Sercombe (1946-48); Wyndham Edwards (1948-50); Ronald Philip Gadd (1950-52); Richad Puzey Hayden (1952-56); Max Cyril Klette (1956-57); Dennis Oliver Murphy (1957-59); Henry Howard (1959-60); George Charles Hedgecock (1960-3); Edward Bidwell (1963) John Fulton (1964);*

The ecclesiastical sign of the cross keys would have been seen on four Worcester pubs of that name: one, a several times re-named inn at this point in College Street, another less than 150 yards away at the bottom of London Road, a third in Friar Street (now the Tudor House Museum) and the fourth in The Trinity.

C5/5

Cross Keys (1600s)
Also known as: Horse and Groom (1770-1800);
Hare and Hounds (1800-1885)
Location: Sidbury

Long-standing commercial inn of 17th century origin initially sited in the cathedral churchyard, re-named twice. Originally The Cross Keys, according to John Noake in 1877: '...in 1776, the Cross Keys, so removed and described as 'near the Deanery Garden' changed its name to The Horse and Groom and 30 years afterwards to the Hare and Hounds. This was before the houses were removed to make way for the new College Street'. A sale notice in Berrows Worcester Journal 1717 gives this description: **'The Hare and Hounds**, a good inn with stables and garden thereto belonging, late in the possession of Nathaniel Morgan in Sidbury in the City of Worcester'. Listed in Victuallers Recognizances in 1766 under licensee Richard Ricketts. 'Rambler' John Noake records a Cross Keys in 1877: '...**Cross Keys** Sidbury,

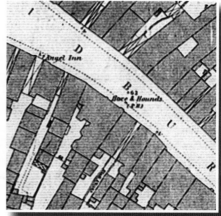

subsequently **The Hare and Hounds**, and now converted into a boot and shoe factory by Mr Willis, recently mayor of Worcester was a noted house more than two centuries ago. In 1690 was in the occupation of Harry Green maltster in 1719 Alan Malpas who then had for a neighbour on the south side Samuel Bryan, printer of the *'The Worcester Postman'*. Soon afterwards **The Cross Keys** appears to have been pulled down and built on a new site but near the old one as in 1744... a tenement and building lately erected on the ground where The Cross Keys formerly stood now in the tenure of Thomas Bourn apothecary, Thos Grinnell cork-cutter, John Bissell maltster, Ed Flavell gingerbread marker; bounded on the north part by several tenements now in the occupation of H.Mason blacksmith and Ann Speed widow and on the south by a messuage in the occupation of Stephen Bryan printer (first printer of the Journal originally called The Postman). He died in 1748 having printed that paper for nearly 40 years'.

The Cross Keys changed its name to **The Horse and Groom** and 30 years afterwards to **The Hare and Hounds**. Like many pubs, **The Hare and Hounds** was used for inquests. On 25th July 1816, the inquest was held here into 'a new born male child found in a privy' and on 19th June 1830 that of Edward Davies who 'threw himself into the Severn'.

Licensees: Nathaniel Morgan 1717, Benjamin Corbet hare and hounds Sidbury (1792); John Cotterill, Hare and Hounds College Street (1820); Job F Horniblow, Hare and Hounds Inn (commercial), College St (1842); Abel Pointon (listed as 'commercial inn' 1855); Frederick Burlingham Hare & Hounds (Commercial) Sidbury (1872-4); James Humphrey (1874-6); Henry Handley (1876-80); Edward Jones (1880-85)

Griffin
Location: 'beyond Sidbury Gate'
Years active: 1730-1800
Mentioned by Noake (1877) as one of a number of 'ancient' City inns and described as 'beyond Sidbury Gate' in a location opposite the Commandery gates. Mentioned in 1747 as an ancient inn and also listed in Victuallers Recognizances in 1766 under Thomas Williams but not in 1814 listings.

Rose and Crown
Location: Sidbury
Years active: 1850 - 1860
Position unclear and not shown in the 1886 Ordnance Survey map. Listed only once, in Billings Directory of Worcestershire 1855 under Thomas Jennings, listed as 'beer retailer'

C-D: Edgar Street to Severn Street

What's now Edgar Tower was originally called St Mary's Gate and it dates from the early 1200s after King John took a personal interest in the City and '...ordered The Sheriff of Worcester to obtain wood and stone of the best quality to rebuild the gatehouse (the original had been destroyed in a disastrous fire in 1202 that ripped through the City and also left the cathedral severely damaged). The massive wooden gates seen today are mostly original, a complete thirteenth century two-leaf door' (Bill Gwilliam – Old Worcester People and Places, p 8). It was here that the first of a few surprises occurs...

Coach and Horses
Location: St Mary's Steps, Edgar Street
Years active: 1751 - 1800
Originally (1751) adjoined the east side of Edgar Tower, near St Mary's Steps. Afterwards pulled down and part converted into a registry office which in turn met the same fate and is now enclosed with a wall.

Hubert Leicester in Worcester Remembered wrote: 'At the top of Edgar Street, St Mary's Steps are seen. These were the end of a pathway through the churchyard which extended from the Lich Gate. In the short space between St Mary's steps and Edgar Tower there was for many years a public house known as Coach and Horses'. Beyond that, little else is known.

C5/9 King of Prussia
Location: Edgar Street/Frog Lane)
Years active: 1750 -1800

Comparatively short-lived – 50 years – inn on the corner of Edgar Street and Frog Lane, mentioned by Noake (1877) as one of a number of 'ancient' City inns, some of which are probably not much less ancient than the eighteenth or even 17th century. Listed in Victuallers Recognizances in 1766 under licensee George Bott and occupied by William Allen, glover about 1780.

Fish, also and Old Fish Inn
Location: High Timber Street (now Severn Street)
Years active: 1780 – 1918

C5/10

Long-life inn stretching from around 1780 until 1918, situated on the east side, four doors down from Edgar Street. First appears in Victuallers Recognizances in 1767 under Thomas Jones but by 1792 Grundy Royal Directory lists the licensee as 'Sufannah Jones vict fifh (Fish) 9 High Timber Street and in 1814 as Susannah Howell described as 'widow'. Also run by Richard Edgington at the same time as he was listed as licensee of the nearby **Fish Inn**. Described as Diglis Street (1855), then Severn Street and also as 5, Severn Street.

Licensees: *Thomas Jones (1767); Sufannah (Susannah) Jones (1790 – she appears to have married or re-married and became Mrs Howell but is widowed, possibly for a second time, by 1820 when she appears to have taken over the nearby **Masons Arms**); Samuel Ottley (1820); John*

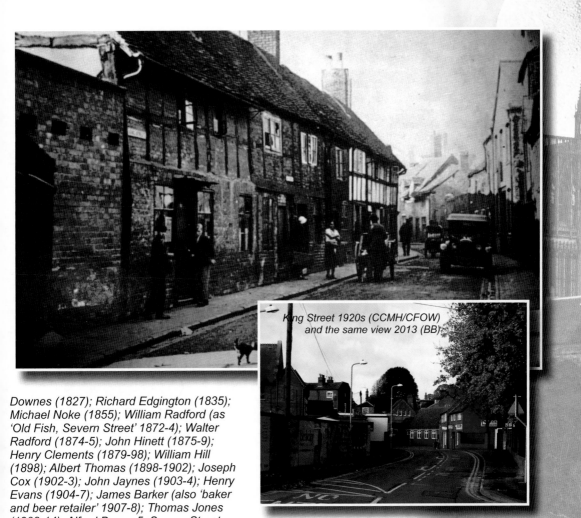

King Street 1920s (CCMH/CFOW) and the same view 2013 (BB)

Downes (1827); Richard Edgington (1835); Michael Noke (1855); William Radford (as 'Old Fish, Severn Street' 1872-4); Walter Radford (1874-5); John Hinett (1875-9); Henry Clements (1879-98); William Hill (1898); Albert Thomas (1898-1902); Joseph Cox (1902-3); John Jaynes (1903-4); Henry Evans (1904-7); James Barker (also 'baker and beer retailer' 1907-8); Thomas Jones (1908-14); Alfred Brown 5, Severn Street (1914-16); Alfred Cooper (1916); Alice Churchill (1916)

C5/11 Ring o'Bells
Location: listed as 'St Peters' - 1703
Years active: 1703 – 1760s

Precise location unknown, save 'St Peter's. Mentioned by Noake (1877) as one of a number of 'ancient' City inns, some of which are 'probably not much less ancient than...' the eighteenth or even 17th century'. Listed in Victuallers Recognizances in 1766 under James Jones but doesn't appear to have survived far beyond that date.

C5/12 Chequers
Location: King Street
Years active: 1820 - 1885

Little remembered inn butting up against the City wall close to what had been Frog Gate, listed as King Street, but accessed through an alleyway in Court Number 1 and set in a courtyard.well to the rear of the street. Later the site of St Peters School. In 1875, licensee here, William Wilkins was convicted for selling after hours and was fined 20/- £1) plus 9/- (45p) costs

Licensees: *Richard Edginton (1827 and 1835); John Andrews (1835); William Long – listed as 'beer retailer' (1855); James Goodyear (1873); Sarah Goodyear (1872-4); William Wilkins (1874-6); Thomas Payne (1876-80); William Garfield (1880-81); Sarah Thomas (1881-3); William Davis (1883-5)*

Severn Street to the river

For many years this was the site of Diglis Pleasure Gardens – according to Bill Gwilliam *(Old Worcester People and Places)* '...a fashionable resort in the 18th century and continued so until the 1830s. Here there were assembly rooms, a riding school, and a bowling green, all occupying the site of a bastion in the city defences where the wall abutted on to the river. The bowling green existed for a long time and was famed as 'The Hand in Glove Club'. Here the gentlemen played bowls on the green and afterwards joined the ladies in a dance in the long room on the ground floor. After dusk the members were accustomed to card playing and for the duration of the assizes and the Three Choirs public breakfasts and tea parties were very popular. Nearby in Frog Lane *(now Severn Street)* was a cockpit still in use in 1825. The downfall of the Pleasure Gardens was due to an unfortunate fracas in which a disagreement ended in violence, one member receiving a stab wound from which he died'. As a result, the Corporation closed it down and the green was abandoned.

The enforced closure of the Diglis Pleasure Gardens and the long-life inn that existed at its heart coincided with ambitious expansion plans by what was fast becoming a major force in the City, Worcester Porcelain (later conferred 'Royal' status) and when they shifted their original premises at Warmstry Slip *(now the site of Deansway car park)* to Diglis in 1840, the whole location changed its character from pleasant green fields and cherry orchards to one of smoke-belching industry. At the same time, the presence of so large a force as the porcelain works – a satanic mills-style mass of kilns and chimneys in direct contrast to the Royal Porcelain Works – sparked-off the construction of several pubs aimed virtually exclusively at catering for the growing number of workers at the factory that, alongside Lea and Perrins and Hardy and Padmore, had positioned Worcester firmly on the international map.

C5/13: Mason's Arms
Location: Frog Lane (also High Timber Street, also Severn Street)
Years active: 1750 - 1860

Stretching back believed to be as far as 1750s, listed in Victuallers Recognizances in 1766 under licensee Joseph Stephens who's still there in 1814 – though that's also the year he ended his tenancy as a separate listing also names William Allen as licensee. Also listed in Grundy Royal Directory 1792 under 'John Lloyd Mafons arms 47 Frog Lane' and Hunt & Co's Commercial Directory for Gloucester, Hereford and Worcester (1842). Susannah Howells (1820-30s) had previously been licensee of the nearby **Fish Inn**

The impact of the Porcelain Works is clearly felt in these atmospheric shots of industrial Worcester early 1900s (Photographs CCMH/CEOW)

Licensees: John Stephens (1766 - 1814); William Allen (1814); Susannah Howells (1820-1830s); George Griffiths (1835); Chas. Vaughan (1842 – 1850s)

Thought likely - largely on account of the numbering (no 47 – The Fountain opposite was no 42) to have been the forerunner of....

Porcelain Workers' (or Works) Inn
C5/14
Location: Severn Street
Years active: 1873 - 1900

Clearly well used with a captive clientele and prominently displayed on the 1886 Ordnance Survey map, The Porcelain Workers' (or Works) Inn was created by the porcelain company to re-circulate the cash they'd just paid their employees in much the same way that **The Gardeners Arms** in St Johns had been created by Smith Nurseries. First appears 1873 and clearly established to serve those suggested by its name. Probably not too successful though as only one licensee is recorded: Mrs M.A. Foss, Porcelain Works Inn, Severn Street.

Site of the Porcelain Works (or Workers) Inn

Old House at Home
C5/15
Location: High Timber Street
Years active: 1850 - 1860

Another seemingly short-lived inn in High Timber Street – later Severn Street – listed just once, and without any further clues to its actual location, in Billings Directory of Worcestershire 1855 under licensee John Yarnold described as 'beer retailer'.

Fountain
C5/16
Also known as: Potters Wheel (from 1979). Salmon's Leap
Location: Diglis (or Severn) Street. No 42
Years active: 1840-2004

Unusually shaped pub opposite Royal Porcelain Works, accordingly popular with its employees – hence the name change to Potters Wheel c1979. Had been Grigg and Brettell house, later Holt's then Ansells. Now demolished and the site is currently being developed into ??? Listed Hunt & Co's Commercial Directory for Gloucester, Hereford and Worcester (1842) also as Diglis Street (1842); Severn Street (1900), 42 Severn Street (1910). On 11th April 1961 licensee Emily Pengelly was fined a total of £3 with £1 advocate's costs on two counts of selling and allowing intoxicating liquor to be sold to a person under 18, with barman Eric Merry also answering the same charges and receiving the same penalty

Licensees: *(as The Fountain): John Isaac (1842-c1860s); James Hammond (1872-9); John Marriott (1879-80); Henry Warman (1880-88); Thomas Harber Senior (1888-90); William Bedford (1890-1); Andrew Carpenter*

The Fountain (aka Potters Wheel/Salmon's Leap) is no more. November 2013 BB)

(1891-5); Alfred H. Foakes (1895-1913 when he died); Emma Foakes (1914-20); Percy Edgar Collier (1920-39 when he died); Mrs Emma Jane Collier (1939-40); George Mills (1940-1); Henry Lees (1941-5); Sidney Arthur Rouse (1945-1957); Archibald McGregor (1957-58); Emily Elizabeth Pengelly (1958-67); Arthur Argust (1967-8); Ronald Edmond (1968-9); Arthur Harris (1969-71);.Albert Ketteringham (1971-4); Katherine Lance (1974-9) **As Salmon's Leap:** Arthur Smith (1979-82); Robert Field and Douglas Blake (1982); Robert Field and Ronald Perks (1982-3); Torias Klias (1983-5); Philip Habgood and Diane Habgood (1985); Bernard Walker (2000)

Shades
Also known as: Chequers
Location: Diglis (or Severn) Street
Years active: 1840 - 1906

Originally called **The Chequers** and, confusingly, a different establishment to the similarly-named inn in nearby King Street, it changed its name c1814 when under the tenancy of James Glover. Sited at the bottom of Severn Street on south side and first listed in 1842 (Hunt & Co's Commercial Directory for Gloucester, Hereford and Worcester) variously as Diglis Street and Severn Street, In 1877 licensee William Woodward was convicted for selling in prohibited hours and was fined £5 including costs. Licensee Samuel Hunt was convicted in 1893 for being drunk on the premises and fined 10/- (50p) plus costs, and was again convicted in 1894 for allowing gaming and was fined £2 plus £1/9/6 (£1.47^1/$_2$p) costs. This lesser-known **Shades** (the other was in Mealcheapen Street) appears to have thrived for about half a century up to c1906 when a report into the state of Worcester's pubs by the Chief Constable said that there were four (public) houses in the street, one 'only 52 yards away' and that the premises were the worst in the street. 'The licence has been transferred three times in three years' he noted – prompting justices to grant only a provisional licence which no doubt heralded its demise just a short while after

It was also occasionally used for inquests. On 5th June 1828, the inquest was held here on Peter Dudley aged who drowned while bathing in the Severn.

11

Site of a lesser-known Shades

(CCMH/CFOW)

The South View of the CITY of WORCESTER, from Digley Fields.

Licensees: *James Glover (1814); John Johnson (1827); Saml Garland (1842 – c1865); William Woodward (1872-9); Edwin McLachlan (1879-8); Kate McLachlan (1888-9); Samuel Hunt (1889-94); William George Cullin (1894-99); Thomas Prosser (1899-1900); John Howell (1900-01); Thomas Prosser (1901); George Jackson (1901-3); Alice Rowson (1903-5); Walter White (1905-6); Benjamin Ford (1906)*

Diglis House Hotel has a fascinating history attached to it

C5/18 Diglis House
Location: Portland Street (and Severn Street)
Years active: 1901 - present

Fine Queen Anne building with a historical background. It was the home of notable civil engineer Edward Leader Williams described as a 'non conformist dissenter' and Quaker Sarah Whiting whose marriage in an Anglican church resulted in them being disowned by the Society of Friends. They had eleven children of which the eldest was landscape painter Benjamin Leader Williams RA (12 March 1831–22 March 1923) much of whose work can be seen in Worcester Museum *(Interesting fact: in the 1980s a mystery donor bought a number of Leader paintings and donated them to the museum where they can still be seen. The benefactor's name has never been revealed).* Leader's father, also a keen amateur artist had been a friend of Joshua Reynolds and John Constable – and Benjamin would often accompany him and his noted friends on sketching trips along the banks of the River Severn *(Wikipedia).* His brother, also Edward Leader Williams, later became a notable civil engineer who was knighted for his work, and is now mainly remembered for designing Manchester Ship Canal. First listed as a licensed house in Worcester Trades Directory 1910. Harpers Hitchman House, registered at Lowesmoor Brewery later at 26 Bridge Street Banbury and taken into the M&B fold. As recently as 1969, manager Peter Aldrich reported some strange going-on here – even to the point that his pet alsatian showed signs of distress and refused to go near a bedroom recently converted from an attic. A psychic called in to solve the mystery is said to have sat in the room for three hours and had made contact with a former owner, who thought she was still in charge. In reality, according to the medium, she'd shown signs of mental disturbance so in true Jane Eyre fashion she was consigned to the attic where she was apparently forgotten, went blind and subsequently died. Frequented by visiting County and national cricket sides who were often accommodated at the Diglis House, it's now a popular wedding venue and summertimes in the garden by the side of the river are a delight. Licensed to Seymour Hotels Ltd and registered at Severn Street Worcester.

Licensees: *Andrew Carpenter (1901-12 when he died); Mrs A. Carpenter (1912-17); Albert Whensley (1917-25); Percy J. Aymes (1925-30); Silas Stewart (1930-32); Jessie Rowley (1932-4); Jerome Griffiths (1934); Edwin Lentell (1934-5); Edward Davenport (1935-6); Olive Gilbert (1936-8); Robert Gregory (1938-9); Olive May and Donald Harris (1937);Marie Louise Gregory (1939-1948); Robert Eustace Gregory (1948-52); Marie Louise Gregory (1952-57); Guy Gerald Darley Bentley (1957 listed as 'Diglis Hotel, Riverside, residential' 1957-59); Stefan Yan Lachkovic (1959- 63); Peter Bailey (1963-4); Harold Earp (1964-8); Peter Ovenden (1968-9); John Aldrich (1969); Brian Foote*

(1969-70); Brian Foote and Joseph Kimber (1970); Joseph Kimber and Peter Ovenden (1970-2); Richard Milner (1972-9); Jose Milner (1979-86); Roy Johnson (1986); john Bligh (1986-7); Greville Edwards (1987); Mary Bailey (1964); Sandra Alcorn (1980); Chris LaCroix (1990). Current (2013) licensee/dps: Julia Seymour. Worcester City licence

C5/19 Bowling Green Inn
Location: Diglis St
Years active: 1700s - 1830s

In 1723, City Corporation (councilors) spent £1.12s 2d on beer here 'during a perambulation of the City boundary'. Later listed in Victuallers Recognizances in 1766 under Mary Wythes and John Balcher 1814. By 1827 it was under the care of Mary Boucher – probably a different spelling of Balcher.

C5/20 Alma
Also known as King's Retreat
Location: 35, Mill Street
Years active: 1863 to 2000 (demolished 2008)

Unremarkable other than that it was run by the same landlord Henry Edward Matthews for almost 35 years and that two trees were planted either side of the door – intertwining as time went by to create a rather pleasant arboreal arch to the entrance. Originally listed as Diglis Gardens (1872-80), later as Mill Street Diglis (1900) and 35 Mill Street (1940), The Alma – one of three pubs of that name in the City built around the same time and named in commemoration of the British and French victory at the key Battle of Alma (20th September 1854) in the Crimean War – was originally built for workers from the surrounding porcelain works on land that had once formed part of Diglis Pleasure Gardens. A Flowers and Sons (later Whitbread) house, it was bought by City businessman Terry Carter who ran it for a short time and changed its name to King's Retreat but sold it for development by Kings School, closing about 2000 and standing empty for several years before being demolished with now no traces remaining. It is now part of King's School St Albans Preparatory Department

The Alma 1937 (Steve Agg)
Far left in 1985   Note the trees (BB)

Site of
THE ALMA INN
1863 - 2008

Licensees: Frederick Walters (1872-5); William Martin Bird (1875-1931 when he died); Frederick Slade (1931); Thomas Price (1931-2); George Price (1932-5); Henry Edward Matthews (1935 – 70); John Briggs (1970-2); William Edwards (1972-7); Brian Woodcock (1977-84); David Bolton (1984-6); David Morrison (1986); Jean Lowe (1986); Raymond Young (1986); David Merritt (1980); Adrian Ryder (2000)

Interiors of The Alma (Steve Agg) and below 1985 (BB)

Unicorn
Location: Mill Street
Years active: 1873 - 1908

Short-lived and little remembered inn on corner of Mill Street and Portland Street built on what had also been part of Diglis Pleasure Gardens but given over to housing in the industrial boom, largely serving the workforce for the booming Worcester Porcelain Works Listed 1883 as Unicorn, Diglis Gardens and shown on OS 1886 Portland St Diglis by 1900, but closed by 1908. Now a private house.

Licensees: Jas Hammond (listed as 'Unicorn, Diglis gardens' (1873); Andrew Carpenter (1900);

Two more pubs known to have existed but neither of them identified

Mug House
Location: 'St Peter's ward'
Years active 1760s- 1820s?

Listed in Victuallers Recognizances in 1766 under licensee Philip Moates. A separate listing for 'Mug House' in Friar Street (later **The Volunteer** and then **Eagle Vaults**) shows this to be a separate establishment. In 1814 Samuel Barnes is given as licensee but no further reference and no indication of precise location other than 'St Peters ward'.

Swan
Location: 'St Peter's ward'
Years active 1760s

Listed in Victuallers Recognizances in 1766 under licensee Jane Potter described as 'widow'. A separate listing for several others 'Swans' throughout the City indicates this to be a separate establishment but there's no no further reference and no indication of precise location other than St Peters ward.

Site of the Unicorn 2013 (BB)

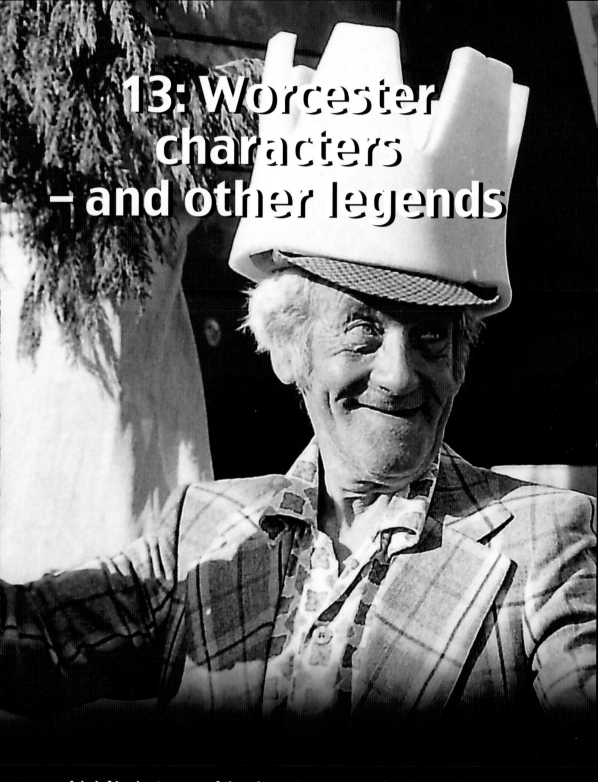

13: Worcester characters – and other legends

A brief look at some of the characters, rogues, hard-men, lookers, comics, clowns, spectacular fallers-over, streetwise kids, ladies-of-the-night and otherwise harmless scallywags and misfits who enlivened the centre and the pubs

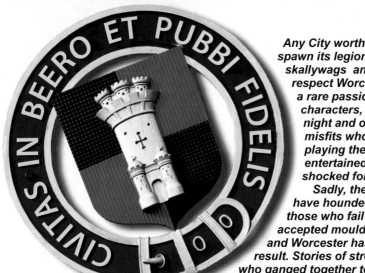

CIVITAS IN BEERO ET PUBBI FIDELIS

Any City worth its salt is bound to attract and spawn its legion of boisterous nutters, nuisances, skallywags and ne'ers-do-well – and in this respect Worcester rose to the challenge with a rare passion, producing as mixed a bag of characters, rogues, hard-men, ladies-of-the-night and otherwise harmless rogues and misfits who enlivened the centre and the pubs, playing their role in keeping the City cheerfully entertained, faintly amused and occasionally shocked for words...

Sadly, the do-gooders and the nanny state have hounded off the streets almost all of those who fail to conform or don't fall into the accepted mould of what is and isn't acceptable, and Worcester has become a lot less colourful as a result. Stories of street singers – even the Welsh miners who ganged together to form choirs and came to the City in the dark Depression-hit days of the 30s to sing on street corners in return for a few pennies to send home, were shooed-off by the hard-hearted City Council of the time who passed a bye-law making it illegal to trade or perform on the street. The likes of Chicken George and The Sherriff – two of the last faces, still fresh in many folks' memories – would appear to be the rump of a long line of characters that enlivened the street scene and made life in Worcester rather more fun than it might otherwise have been. Here's just a few...

Albert Thatcher: said to have been blessed with the broadest Wusterrrshurrr accent ever heard and fond of spouting old Worcestershire wives' tales

Alec Hayes: a paper seller whose pitch was outside the Cadena Café. His brother was Boots at **The Pack Horse** and **Star Hotels** and the two were reported to be different as chalk and cheese.

Arthur Sage: larger-than-life extravagantly moustachioed ex-mayor (1974-5) Tory councillor for All Saints ward, former publican – first as manager of the **King Charles** (Tubs) in the Cornmarket then, after a spell in his home town of Bristol, tenant of **The Dolphin** (Broad Street/ Angel Place) then a return to the King Charles II – a vocal, energetic and influential supporter of Worcester's pubs.(right the mayor's chain)

Arnie the Cobbler: who had shoes in his Charles Street cobbler's shop still unmended and unclaimed after 20 years – long after their owners had given up hope of ever having them returned. Instead, they lay in the window, yellowing and curling up in the sunshine.

The mayor of Worcester's chain of office (BB) See Arthur Sage (left). Mayor 1974-5, he was a larger -than-life Worcester publican and vigorous supporter of Worcester's pubs

Banana Joe often found on street corners in the City selling over-ripe bananas from a tall wicker basket

Banjo Bradshaw: said to have a jaw shaped like a wedge

Barrington Evans reputed to have a laugh '... like a sheep caught in a thornbush'

Bert Perry: ex-chimney sweep who owned a bike shop and made a tiny three-wheeler that he'd ride around town – much to everyone's amusement

Bert Probert: inveterate pub crawler whose tales got ever more lurid and fanciful the more beer he sank.

'Big Ausie' Austin, a carpenter said to possessed hands 'like a bunch of Fyffes' who could saw through wood like a knife through butter.

'Big Dennis': with a laugh like Robert Newton's Long John Silver and a penchant for bringing down bossy and actressy barmaids

'Big Malcolm' said to have a voice as big as his massive frame

'Big Reg': ex WRGS, Coldstream Guards, Military Police eccentric who'd expound his theories on the mysteries of life to all who'd spare him the time of day – and go on unbroken and uninterrupted, often for hours at a stretch

'Big Scouse': well educated, quietly spoken 6' 4" scouser who was the target of every up-and-coming hard-case who soon learned the hard way not to be fooled by looks and that there's truth in the adage that there's always somebody bigger and better than you. Said to remind folk of Gregory Peck in The Gunfighter, a popular film at the time

Billy Parrish. Black Countryman born 1868 who started work in a Dudley colliery at 5/-

(25p) a week, but progressed to become owner of several collieries and brickworks, as well as being proprietor of The Star Hotel, the Hop Pole and British Camp Hotel, Malvern. Keen sportsman who excelled in most sports including billiards and snooker (he also won the Empire ball-punching competition) he is reputed to have won a £100 bet by drinking a bottle of champagne in the lion's den at Dudley Zoo. A great horse racing punter, he went on to own several race horses including Golden Fleece which he offered any horse in the world t challenge for a £5,000 bet but found no takers. In 1928 he came to Worcester, bought the Star Hotel from George Spurr for £33,000 and also acquired the lease for the Hop Pole Hotel. He died in 1946.

'Bill the Bike' and his three-legged dog on the crossbar

'Blackflash': Irishman with a mass of back curly hair like Charlie Chaplin's, always ready for a fight, any time, anywhere, any size

"Bob the Bag': his great-grandfather was reputed to have invented Worcester Sauce and no-one had the faintest idea what was in the ever-present bag he toted around

'Brasso' whose party trick, usually in The Bridge' but then anywhere else that'd have him, was eating dimpled beer mugs

'Brasso' (2) far-from-untalented singer, all-round entertainer, ex-Womble and general genial nice guy Keith Brace who was usually to be found in The West Midland Tavern and who died aged 64 in August 2013. One half of duo Novak'n'Goode (with drummer Trevor Davey, also dec'd). "Say it quickly and that just about sums us up" he used to say. They even took on a third member and called themselves Still, Novak and Goode – wonder happened to 'Still'? Even solo, Brasso had the ability to get an entire bar up and singing at the drop of hat. Genuinely missed.

'Bruce' the 70-year old lift boy at the Co-op in The Trinity

Buttie (or Butt-End) Annie: real name Annie Handy who scoured every gutter and bin in the City for more than four decades on the rootle for discarded cigarette ends. She wore a shapeless grey felt hat like a schoolgirl's and green topcoat that was several sizes too big and could bandy obscenities with even the most sewer-mouthed trooper.

Cedric (Ceddie) Walls who sported a 14-inch handlebar 'tache

'Champagne Charlie': painter and decorator said to have won a fortune on the pools, lost it and had to go back to work, then spent the rest of his life dressed in overalls but with the ever-present dickie bow!

Charlie Warren: a patch-eyed barber from St Johns

Chicken George: George Webb *(pictured right)*: where the name Chicken George is heard, controversy is never very far behind - in life and in death. Fondly remembered by some as 'a free expression street dancer' he'd annoy buskers and the likes of the Salvation Army band by doing a crazy jig to the music. (One miffed busker from Birmingham lashed out at George but some Worcester lads tracked him down and returned the compliment – with interest). A recent website *'Chicken George and Memories of Worcester in the 1980s'* aims to preserve memories of George almost canonising him as a popular and loveable character when in reality he was a drunk, a sewer-mouth whose string of profanities would shock whole bus-loads of people, and frankly a nuisance – and I knew him better than most. Invited into his Warndon home in 1988 I interviewed him for a 2-page profile in Berrows Worcester Journal. Admittedly he never swore once and told me he hadn't had a drink in four days and confessed he'd found God – but I had warned him about his behaviour beforehand. The group seems to have hatched a misguided plan to have a statue of Chicken George erected in the City – even suggesting demolishing the Elgar statue and replacing it with George's a move that most folk would find utterly ludicrous. Me too.

'Chockie' Mason: bowler-hatted Angle Place sweetshop owner (and father of rock superstar Dave) always humming to himself

Below: comparatively recent feature (2011) on Chicken George as it appeared in Worcester Online Newsmag www.worcester-online-newsmag.co.uk

The Chorister described by F. H. Adams as 'a slim young man in his mid-twenties who used to lurk in doorways (but had...) the voice of a 12-year old choirboy as though his voice had never broken. His treble notes in renderings of popular songs of the day used to stop young women in their tracks, particularly if he sang one of Ivor Novello's hits. Every note was perfect'

'Codshead': a 20-stone giant who sold newspapers outside Foregate Street Station.
See also Sam Smith.
'Colonel Jim': immaculately dressed, impeccably groomed and beautifully spoken English gent

Costas Michaela: head-turning chef at The Oyster Bar

'Curly': Dennis Rosevere Philips one of a great line of character newspaper-sellers who also sold scorecards at the County Ground and amused spectators during intervals. He died as recently as 1988.

Dancing Dinah who frequented the St Andrews /All Saints area and is said '...after a few pints would dance most beautifully' and the tale was told that she had once been on the stage but had been shamed by a nobleman who left her in the gutter

'Danny the Pram': pushing his pram – usually empty but for a few comics – in the main stream of traffic when the High Street was the main A38 trunk road, the M5 of its day, wheeling through the jams, signalling his intended directions and waiting for the green light at traffic signals

Dave Tremellen a longhair hippie-style beat poet who ran a magazine 'New Expression' from a boat moored at Pitchcroft

Derrick William Bollen well-known character, dapper man-about-town and cathedral chorister, ever cheerful MC and manager of Worcester Co-operative Restaurant in St Nicholas Street

Desi and Norman Munslow – celebrated funny men

Dicky George who, it was said, never had a dull minute

Dickie Moon ('Ambassador to Hay-on-Wye')

Duke of Lowesmoor: Ron Hale had been a bookie with his father and went on to run **The Alma** in Lowesmoor and later The Lamp Tavern in Malvern. Described himself as 'The Duke of Lowesmoor' and claimed to be – probably with some justification – the only publican in the City who was also a tic-tac man. A charming gentleman

Drusilla 'Dru' Band who lived in Autumn Terrace a cul-de-sac at the end of Hillborough and had a reputation as a trouble-maker. According to local bobbies, she had the face and physique of a heavyweight boxer that hadn't been too successful

Eddie Harris, legendary haulage operator with his fore- and rear-end signs 'Here Comes Eddie' and 'There Goes Eddie' long before the other Eddie, Mr Stobart, had similar ideas

Eddie Ruddick, a notorious hard man said to 'ooze hate from every pore' who could menace innocent drinkers from across a crowded bar.

'Ephraim' who would throw down his cap, drop down to his knees talking loudly in some unintelligible nonsense and stamp on his cap before putting it back on his head and walking away as if nothing had happened.

Eric Twinberrow, noted osteopath only recently deceased – but a tall, straight, piercing eyed, immaculately turned-out gentleman with the most striking looks – even long after he retired and took up good deeds (like sleeping outside the Catholic church when in his 80s to drum-up support for the homeless)

Eugene van der Hoog: eccentric gnome-like artist in all media who looked like one of the seven dwarves and lived on a houseboat on the Severn. Especially noted for having painted the 20 foot mural of a one-legged pirate complete with parrot on his shoulder on the wall of The Jolly Roger Brewery (Brewery Tap) in Lowesmoor

Farmer Eden who'd drive round the City in supercharged pick-up truck with a boxer dog by his side

'The Ferry Man' – one of seven in the City

Flannel and Tony Francis: brothers with what's described as 'leonine good looks' and huge shoulders, both working as freelance bouncers (doormen they'd be called now) yet so popular and friendly they never actually got round to chucking anybody out

Eugene van der Hoog

'Fletch': said to have the most sparkling blue eyes in Worcester and always full of fun

Frank Kinchin: ex-fairground boxer who bragged of being the first man to test a parachute

Frank Roberts who operated the boats at South Quay and ate Vic chest-rub sandwiches

Frank Gunnell: a dustman who lived in a tree at Powick

Freddie Crump: whose address had been 6 Bromsgrove Street. Often seen on the City's streets, he cut a comical figure in silk top hat, frock tail coat, baggy pinstripe trousers, wing collar or cravat and Groucho Marx-like bendy-legged walk. Sometimes he'd been seen pushing a battered old pram and slung over his shoulders a bugle that he'd occasionally stop and blast like the Final Fanfare. He'd also sport

Eddie Ruddick

an impressive array of medals on his puffed-up chest – though closer inspection revealed most to be old cocoa tins, boot polish lids or silver paper from long-consumed chocolate bars. When he died, his home was found to be crammed floor-to-ceiling with old newspapers. Inspector George Lewis once told me of the time he was on duty in the City nick with noted prankster Sergeant Jack Holmes when they heard a shuffling from under the desk. Neither could see anyone there so the sergeant leaned over and sure enough there was Freddie, top hat and all, so small he couldn't be seen over the top of the counter. "Hello Mister Crump – and to what do we owe this pleasure?' asked Sgt Holmes. "I found this, sergeant' said Freddie reaching up on tip-toes to reach the desk and hand over a ball of blue wool the size of a cricket ball. The sergeant winked at George and gushed "Oh, well done Mister Crump, sir. You've saved us a lot of trouble you 'ave: I've got six bobbies out there looking for that there ball o' wool and now you've found it 'er Ladyship will be pleased" as Freddie visibly swelled up with pride. "You'll be rewarded for this: that there ball o' wool belongs to a titled lady and she's been worried sick. Now here's what you do..." and he told Freddie to be at the Public Hall the following Sunday Concert night and that no matter what was happening – be it a full-scale concert, a string quartet recital, drama or poetry readings – he should give out three loud blasts on his bugle at the very dot of 8 o'clock so that 'er Ladyship would know who he was so as to give him his just reward. To which, Freddie smartly saluted.

"Don't forget now, 8 o'clock on the dot" Sgt Holmes called after the delighted dodger. Sadly, it's not recorded what the concert goers' reaction was that following Sunday night as Freddie appeared on the scene and gave three hearty blasts on his bugle – though, no doubt the tipped-off copper on the scene almost certainly staved-off a lynching!

George Lewis, started off as a rookie cop with (then) Worcester City police in 1936 and rose to the rank of Inspector before retiring in 1966. In between pounding the streets and nicking more than his share of bad 'uns, he still found time to record his record of life 'in the magical hurly-burly back-water of dark alleyways, boisterous pubs and eccentric street characters that was – and some say still is – Worcester' (as I rather poetically wrote in Berrows Worcester Journal in 1989). In his memoirs he recalled many of the characters listed in this section, and had a particular fondness for what he called 'the squalid bob-a-night lodging houses' particularly those dotted

around Quay Street. He also made a note of those pub landlords whose names you'll find dotted throughout this book, jotting down his favourites with clear affection. They were, he told me 'just nice people who were first-class licensees': honest-to-goodness landlords like

Insp. George Lewis as a rookie cop 1936

Gladys Israel (Plough, Fish Street); Harry Dale (Golden Lion, High Street); Bill Hope (New Greyhound New Street); Bertie Witherford (Holly Bush, St Nicholas Street); "Gentleman" George Thorne (Shakespeare, Angel Street); Ernie Harding (Golden Hart, reputed to be the best pint of Spreckleys in town); Freddie Dean (Three Tuns, Castle Street); George Harrison (Green Man, Tything); Tom Higgins (Saracens Head); Arthur Vale (Coach and Horses, Tything); expert conjuror Will Curnock (Barbourne, New Bank Street); monumental mason Charlie Underhill (Bell, Droitwich Road); Bill Roberts (Mount Pleasant); Bill Blake (Park Tavern); Harry Hunt (Eagle Vaults); Walter Smith (City Arms); and a lady he called 'rather splendid', Bessie Sefton whose homebrew house, The Red Lion in Newport Street, he found especially to his liking.

George Portman: noted for a nose like an egg-plant

George Smith, gaffer of **The Union** in Lowesmoor and winner of the Croix de Guerre

'Gillie' Sales: who lived in Perry Wood and would wield his axe in Old Bill's Café in Infirmary Walk

Hackle Staite (centre) at either The Star Bransford Road or The Gun where he proved an amazing quoit thrower. BB article Berrows Worcester Journal 1989 (Pic: Derek Staite

Hackle — and team mates from The Star, Bransford Road — or was it the Gun Tavern? If you can place the faces in our photograph we'd like to hear from you.

'Guardsman Pat', described as 6'4" and straight as a board

Hackle Staite: amateur boxer with, as the sports writers describe it 'mixed fortunes' though reckoned to be winner of a hundred bare-knuckle scraps in the Cattle Market where he had a job cleaning down cows ready for auction. As somebody once said, give Hackle – real name Arthur – a bucket of water, a cloth and a curry comb and he'd put a fiver on the value of a cow. Once described as an expert kite-flier, some rookie Evening News journalist's mis-transcription of quoit player which it should have been (an aural clanger than would've had Hackle roaring over his pint in The Berwick, The Star, The Ewe & Lamb or The Gun), one of his party tricks was to turn a four-legged bar stool over and flip a quoit over each leg from the statutory chucking distance. Tales of Hackle's exploits throughout the 1940s, 50s and 60s are legion and he's best known for doing pretty much anything for a bet. Ready and always game for a laugh, more tales have been told of Hackle Staite than any other character and most of them are true. Like the time he set up as a tipster called 'The Major' selling hot tips at local point-to-points even though those in the know knew for certain that he couldn't tip a lop-sided wheelbarrow. With a ready wit, a prodigious thirst and amazing appetite, folk still tell of the time he ate a whole tray of Walls dripping cakes in **The Old Chapel;** eating a whole 14lb cow cabbage – raw stalks an' all, with a couple of celery sticks and a dozen ham rolls thrown in for good measure; eating a whole galvanised bucketful of chips with 27 fried cod; eating whole jars of pickled onions in a single

sitting, and eating all the lovingly laid-on bowls of onions and drinking a pint of vinegar at darts and quoits matches without so much as a hiccup. It's said the only time he met his eating come-uppance was when he was challenged to polish-off a 2d slice of hot fish sandwiched between two 2d bars of Cadbury's chocolate. Weekends would see him working the fruit and veg stalls in the Shambles where, come the end of a long hot Saturday, housewives couldn't believe it when Hackle's tomatoes and oranges still oozed juice: what they hadn't seen was the water-filled sponge under his arm!. Hackle died in October 1975. And his sons Tony and Derek are still seen in and around some of the remaining Worcester pubs, notably Saracens Head and Postal Order.

Hallelujah Lily whose claim to fame was a voice described as being 'of most exceptional range'. 'She would treat all who came to listen to pieces from grand opera and like Dancing Dinah had been brought up in different circumstances, but drink had brought her there (Bill Gwilliam – Old Worcester People and Places p 84)

Hannah Price is described as 'an old misery guts' who lived in one of the almshouses in the Chapel Walk/Powick Lane area of the City and pestered everyone and anyone young copper who had the misfortune to encounter her: nothing, it seems, was ever right for her – she just liked moaning and groaning

Harold Cook: a life devoted to closing gates that had been left open, picking up other folks' litter, and cleaning out telephone boxes without question of any reward or thanks.

Harry Witherford, said to have had the most hypnotic blue eyes

Horace Winwood: quick-fire cartoonist whose uncannily accurate sketches of darts, dominoes, skittles and other teams appeared in the Green 'Un on Saturdays and Monday editions of the Worcester Evening News

Hurdy-Gurdy man, with his barrel organ and small, but vicious monkey 'dressed in red jacket and sort trousers'.

Jack Goodyear a handy Worcester-born scrapper and friend of the boxing greats who always gave good value for money in the prize-fighting booths at the fairgrounds. A friendly and old-fashioned gentleman, he died as recently as 1988.

'Idris' Collins, a dramatic liar with a shock of black hair

'Jockey Mick' who wore jodhpurs, homburg hat with a huge feather, collarless shirt, knotted silk scarf, dinner jacket and spats and, at 5' 6" made out he was a jockey though he'd never ridden a horse in his life.

Jack Goodyear - who kept his boxing licence right up to his 70s (BB)

Joe Gibbs - former cabbie from the early horse-drawn days working from the rank outside the Shirehall. Once when he'd disappeared into the café opposite, some wag had put his horse in the shafts facing the wrong way and on another occasion he was offered a 5/- (25p) tip if he got his passenger to Shrub Hill station in time for the London train. Hammering hell-for-leather through Lowesmoor, he heard his passenger yelling from the hansom – which he and his horse both took as a signal to get an even faster spurt on, galloping up Shrub Hill Road at breakneck speed. Pleased with his effort, sweating Joe held out his hand to collect his five bob tip but the passenger was far from happy... His feet had gone through the floorboards of the rickety old cab – hence his frantic shouting – and he said that as he'd run most of the way, he had no intention of parting with promised five-bob tip. Even later when Joe's horse-drawn cab was replaced by a new-fangled internal combustion version, he still yelled 'whoa...' every time he applied the hand brake.

'H': said to have been a hilarious clown and 'goon' long before the radio show of the same name

Harold the Barman: outrageous poofter but brilliant barman by all accounts who kept the beer flowing at The Hopmarket but would occasionally burst into tears wailing 'It's no good, I've even tried boxing!' much to the delight of the assembled punters.

Harry Perks who sang – and some say looked – like a cockerel

George 'Honky' Fletcher. Legendary owner of the Lowesmoor fish'n'chip shop that bore his name and was as well known a landmark as the cathedral. When he retired, at 65 in April 1985, handing the reins of the shop to his daughter Carole, he told me he'd only ever had one job aside from fruit and fish'n'chips – he'd worked at Metal Castings and he said 'I packed that 'un up after about a week'. He reckoned he got his nickname from when he was lad of about fourteen delivering fruit on his bike to homes in St Johns. "I couldn't afford a horn like the other delivery boys but they knew it was me 'cos I'd come round the corner shouting 'honk-honk' as if I had a real horn. They knew it was me alright!". He started work in the same shop aged 15 'cutting taters', and took over as owner in 1943 – when chips were a penny, and fish was $1\frac{1}{2}$d, and he said 'as long as they keep coming, we keep serving. I work all the hours God sends'. He also claimed

48 MARCH 1985

The Trumpet
DROITWICH 776420

George calls it a day

TARRA HONKY!

W chip cos...

Worcester says a fond "tarra" to one of its best-known institutions this week.

As George Fletcher nuzzles 65 he's hanging up his chip pan for the last time and retiring from one of the best known fish 'n' chip shops in the whole world — Honky's in Lowesmoor.

Everybody — but *everybody* from Warndon, Wychavon or Wichenford — knows Honky like a favourite uncle.

But though he's retiring from the shop, the County's best known fish 'n' chip man won't be disappearing from the City centre scene altogether...

He and Muriel are retiring to the little bungalow they've built behind the shop and handing over the keys to their daughter Carole who was only two months old when the family moved to the Lowesmoor landmark.

"I'll tell you something," George told The Trumpet this week, "... I've loved every minute of it. I've only ever had one job apart from fruit and ...

I soon packed that up — lasted about a week I think . . . !" he said.

Honky — born just off Silver Street only yards from the Lowesmoor shop that for many is as well known a City landmark as the Cathedral itself — first started "cleaning tayters" and stoking up the coke fires in that same shop at the age of eight when it belonged to the Lewis family.

Fruit

By the time he was fourteen he had a full-time job delivering fruit, not long ... took over a f...

shop in St. Johns.

In 1945 he took over the Lowesmoor shop he'd first started work in — and since then, he told The Trumpet "... worked ...

every hour God's sent. Some nights he wouldn't close until after 2 a.m." "... as long as they kept coming we'd keep serving," he said.

'Honk, honk' tag

Honky got his nickname from the time he was a fourteen year-old, delivering fruit on his bike around the St. Johns area.

"I couldn't afford a horn like the other delivery boys, but everybody knew it was me 'cos I'd come round th... ner shouting 'honk, honk' as if I ... al horn.

"They knew I ... ing alright ..." he told The Tr...

---

the most he ever paid himself was 30/- (£1.50) a week, preferring to plough the profits back into his other businesses, and he described his chips as 'the taste of Worcester'. His side-kick, minder, fellow fish-fryer, bouncer (yet gentle as they came when off-duty) bull terrier lookalike **Derek Russell,** has also earned his place in this section on noted Worcester characters.

Ivor Drinkwater, a Ross-on-Wye artist who walked about Worcester 'like a train' – once measured at a constant 6 miles an hour (you try it!)

Jack the Canoe who'd paddle a Red Indian kayak up and down the river
Jack Price whose boxing club in Farrier Street was a popular haunt with pugilists

'Jakey' who walked like a penguin

Jim (real name Nicola) Capaldi – later rock drumming star with Traffic and as a solo artist (Love Hurts), now deceased – but an apprentice at Heenan and Froude's, always singing to himself, mostly 'scat'

Joey Brookes, for many the man with Worcester's greatest style

Article I wrote on George 'Honky' Fletcher 1985

Joe the Builder said to have the deepest, gravelliest voice ever heard, and a strawberry nose

Johnny Mole: an ex- fairground prize-fighter described as having 'exciting features'

Johnny O'Shea (and his brother Pete) paper sellers in Angel Place and Broad Street. Johnny, a regular in **The Arcadia** (later the Long Stop) and The Old Rectifying House had a winning way when it came to flogging his papers on a quiet day: he'd 'invent' news. "Shockin' murder.... read all abaht it..." would be one. Another, according to Dennis Smith, was 'man hen-pecked to death. Fowl play!' as a rule, rounded-off with a raucous 'Een'n newsanal' (Evening News and Final) in his inimitable style

John Stenson: brash, burly and big enough to break up a bar-room brawl on his own and mete out punishment of his own kind (see a personal recollection: **The Beehive**)

Kempsey Lily: lady-of-the night who patch was, like many others, Dolday

Kenny Arnold: reputed to know, and be able to tell at the drop of a hat, any joke on any subject – some even say every joke ever cracked

Kenny Burroughs: said to have been a charismatic comedian who'd liven-up any sagging bar-room

'Kipey' Jones: known for a hundred stunts including eating a whole bunch of flowers in one go, cocking a leg over every car parked in New Street, and for riding his bike into **The Royal Exchange** and asking for a pint the day after the gaffer had told him 'never walk in my pub again'. "But gaffer" he said "...you only told me never to walk in here: I'm on me bike!". His cheek paid off – he got his pint and got banned again for riding the bike out of the other door! Never, ever known to utter even a mild profanity and always a gentleman in front of the ladies, he lived in shed – more accurately, the flower store at the back of **The Old Greyhound** (now Charlstons)

Lenny the Ted

Sün ELVIS

Kipey Jones

Lenny the Ted: taxi driver (and other odd jobs - above, right) would-be Elvis clone changed name from Len Rhodes to Len Rhodes Presley. Much given to weaving fanciful tales, but a dedicated Elvis and a not unimpressive impersonator either

Long-haired Freddy: who walked as though he had springs on his feet, shock of shoulder-length red hair flowing in the wind

Maisey dynasty – Ernie, Ernie and Lyndon (grandfather, father and son) – the City's oldest paper-boys whose battered bike and bike clips were handed down from generation

to generation and must have carried about ten million copies of Worcester Evening News and Sundays in all weathers for well over half a century. Lyndon is still to be seen, still riding the same bike, still delivering the news!

Market Harry – aka Harry Fantham – who sold fruit from an unlicensed barrow in the Cornmarket and Shambles.. Said to be the dead spit of Bruce Bairnsfather's Old Bill he's described as a loveable old rascal with a spiky moustache and a winning way. Inspector George Lewis commented: "...he'd gush at me 'ow are you sir?' when I was sent to move him on for the tenth time that day. "On your way" I'd tell him for the umpteenth time. "Yes sir, right away sir" would come Harry's prompt reply, similarly for the umpteenth time that day and probably not the last either!"

'Marx': with a voice like a megaphone, always ready to shout down the Salvation Army when they played their religious gatherings in the Cornmarket. See also Nobby Guy (p 407)

Micky Baker – friendly as a bull terrier but ever ready for scrap. Father of the ever popular and feisty Worcester pro boxer of the same name

Mick the Ganger: never known to crack his face – even when confronted by celebrated funny men like Bill Edwards and Pat Watkins

'Mother' James café Newport Street (CCMH/CFOW) and inset today (BB)

'Mr. 1940': always dressed ready for the dance – even when shopping

"Mister' Hardman, the School Board Inspector who would call on the houses where children were thought to be playing truant (modern Worcester parlance, 'skiving')

Mr. Whatsisname: Francis Reynolds, boisterous, animated and ebulllient Irishman regularly seen in and around many Worcester pubs (notably Goodrest and Coach and Horses). Initially christened Maria, he was charming, lucid and coherent when sober, but notably less so when drunk. Later law lecturer who gained national recognition for changing his name in response to current circumstances. As a protest against the amount of tax he was being hounded to pay, he first changed his name to Watt Tyler II and settled up by paying the full amount in individual 1p coins. He later became Watt Tyler III and IV for subsequent tax demands. Later changed his name again – this time to Mister Whatsisname after setting up cut-price property conveyancing company in the wake of a national Law Society ad campaign saying 'When it comes to conveying your property, don't use Mister Whatsisname from down the pub'. When he asked me to write his biography in 2000, I thought I'd found a get-out when I asked him to give me 100 reasons why I should. He did – instantly. Sadly the biog never got written and he died at a comparatively young age around 2003. It would have made fascinating reading – though the writing would, I'm sure, have rendered me in the same state as the subject!

'Mrs O'Keeffe' constantly haggling over priceless antiques at the auctioneer's with the withering phrase 'I'll give ya threepence for it and not a penny more'

'Mother' James whose Newport Street café, (see Then and Now pix above) featured aspidistras in brass pots, tea cups the size of chamber pots and a couple of 3-wheelers parked outside

Mouth Organ Annie, 'dressed in Union Jacks and danced to her own accompaniment' in The Shambles, according to Bill Gwilliam: she also performed cartwheels in the middle of the street despite being over seventy

Muriel McGarrity, singing barmaid reputed to have a repertoire of more than 80 folk songs

The Music Man' who'd push a battered old barrow around town playing scratched old 78 records on an equally scratched and battered wind-up record-player in return for coppers tossed into his cap

Naughty Nora: for many a rookie copper used to handling the boozers, roughnecks and ex-

Army hard-men, the biggest challenge was a seemingly harmless flower seller by name of Nora Constance Shearon whose relatives still follow the same trade today in much the same location. At times she's reputed to have been so violent it would take four, five or even six uniformed bobbies to control her and even then not before most had been kicked, punched, gouged and walloped by the battling flower-seller whose pitch was at the top of Church Street. When Nora was roused, there was no such thing as the Queensberry Rules and the copper who'd been at the receiving-end of those swirling fists knew he'd been in a heck of a scrap the following morning. Inspector George Lewis who had many a dealing with Nora and reckoned he was one of only two coppers who could reason with her, says that tales of her stripped to the waist in a fisticuffs free-for-all are exaggerated – even though she may well have ended up that way after particularly hissy scrap, he reckoned. George described her as 'a really handsome, striking woman', and recalled having a cup of tea with her when she lived in a dingy room at the junction of Lich Street and College Street after lodging a more than justified complaint abut the condition of the premises. Sadly, he says, she seemed to have fallen into the wrong crowd who appeared to have something against policemen.
See also Ted Stanley.

The famous - most say infamous – hard-man Nobby Guy pictured on the steps of St Nicholas church (now Slug'n'Lettuce) (CCMH/CFOW)

'Navy Bill' Hector described as 'a walking jumble sale'

Nellie Matthews, one of several noted street-walkers living and plying their trade in and around the rabbit warren bob-a-night lodging houses that abounded in the Quay Street area. Others included Mary Malcolm, Biddy Virgo and Liz Creighton whose patch included Harmans Lodging House in Lich Street and those of 'Ma' Roberts, Sarah Ann Jones and Bill Redman in Quay Street lodging houses

Nobby Guy: hard man and habitual drunk that took several coppers to haul him off to the cells after his usual Saturday night session. It's said that his only source of income was the shilling (5p) thrown to him by Mr Kilburn Kay to open the doors for him on a Friday evening, though he was always prepared to throw himself off Worcester bridge, fully clothed, for a half-ounce of tobacco. After dozens of arrests and spells in prison, the police asked the Salvation Army to help save Nobby from himself: the Sally Ann, never the body to give up on hopeless causes, promised to house him and feed him on the conditions that he'd mend his ways and sing the praises of the Lord – and provided he gave up the booze and his pipe (seems he managed the former, but not the latter). One Saturday night some weeks later as the Salvation Army band was playing its heart out in the Cornmarket in the vain hope of rescuing sinners from the evils of drink, the Captain called on Nobby to tell the assembled 'congregation' how he'd turned his back on a lifetime of alcoholic excess, had found God and mended his ways, and how happy he now was as a result. "Sir" said Nobby to the crowd – amazed at the rapid change in Nobby, now sober, smart and no longer the hopeless hard-case rolling about in the gutter and knocking ten barrels out of five coppers – "Friends" he said "...I'm that 'appy I could put me fist through that fucking drum".

'Nurse Paterson': midwife often to be seen in black bonnet and cape carrying the ever-present black bag, in and around St Johns.

Old Man Jeavons in his Panama hat watching the world go by from his window seat in **The Bridge Hotel**

Old Nana: an old rogue usually frequenting the Cross despite frequent warnings and threats of imprisonment from local bobbies. Said to be a tall, thin, oldish man with a straggling beard wearing the same dirty old mac in summer and winter and battered old felt hat, he always carried on open wicker basket which contained a few bananas and several copies of Old Moore's Almanack. Though generally dismissed as a nuisance he was also reckoned to be a financial wizard with a reputation for having been 'something in the City'

Old Sam: in an overcoat heavier than he was that touched the ground, always trying to flog a watch that nobody ever saw and probably didn't exist anyway

Ossie and Algie Green: celebrated funny men

Percy Gormley: seasoned accordian player often found entertaining in many City pubs – notably **The Hollybush, Garibaldi, Alma, Goodrest, Farmer's Boy** near where he lived, **Five Ways** and in a regular slot for nearly 30

Percy Gormley
(pic: Margaret Joel née Gormley)

years every Sunday night at Rainbow Hill club. Born in Dolday last but one of 16 children he learnt to play the accordian in the 1940s when he persuaded his mum to buy one from a pawn shop instead of retrieving his dad's suit. Invalided out of army with severe epilepsy, he was widowed at the age of 30 and left with 5 children under the age of 8 years who he brought up in Tolladine then Rainbow Hill areas before moving back to Tolladine where he lived on the corner of Tolladine Rd and Christchurch Ave. Reputed to be able to play just about anything: all the old war songs, Irish songs and anything else he could get his audience to sing along to. He also played for 58 years on the Rotary Club's disabled people's river trip to Holt Fleet and back. Latterly he worked at the Quality Cleaners before going to work as a storeman at Kays – where he also set up a dry cleaning department. He was born in 1923 and died 2006 aged died 2006 age 83.

Peter Dowdeswell *(King of the Trenchermen.* Not strictly a Worcester man – he was actually from Earl's Barton In Leicestershire – but a regular visitor to the City where he set many of his amazing world drinking records. In March 1985, he visited The Brewery Tap, then owned by the Soden brothers Martin and Paul and where he set two new world drinking records. I covered the event for 'The Trumpet' newspaper and probably wouldn't have believed the tales of drinking featsmanship had I not witnessed and photographed them at first hand – sadly no video though. Among his amazing feats, several set at **The Glover's Needle** and **The Brewery Tap**, were drinking 34 pints of beer in an hour, and drinking a further 90 pints in 3 hours.

Other drinking feats include:
1 pint of beer: 0.45 seconds
1 lire of beer: 1.30 seconds
1 pint of beer upside down: 2.56 seconds
2 pints of beer: 2.30 seconds
2 pints of beer upside down: 6.40 seconds
2 litres of beer : 6.00 seconds
2 litres of beer upside down: 15.20 seconds
$2^{1}/_{2}$ pint 'yard of ale' in 5.00 seconds
3 pints of beer: 4.20 seconds
$3^{1}/_{2}$ pint 'yard of ale' in 6.26 seconds
4 pints of beer upside down: 22.10 seconds
4 pint 'yard of ale' in 8.90 seconds
5 pint 'yard of ale' in 10.00 seconds
5 pints of beer upside down: 29.06 seconds
$7^{1}/_{2}$ pint 'yard of ale' in 14.00 seconds
8 pints of beer (I gallon) upside down: 8 mins 35 seconds
1 pint of champagne upside down 3.30 secs
$3^{1}/_{2}$ pint 'yard of champagne' in 14.20 seconds
2 pints of milk in 3.20 seconds
1 Pint of beer through a 6mm straw: 11.00 seconds

The Soden brothers Paul and Martin help Peter Dowdeswell to another world record at The Brewery Tap 1985 (pic: BB)

Challenged to drink 12 pints of beer in the time it took Big Ben to strike the hour of twelve, he'd sunk all twelve by the eighth chime! When he arrived at **The Brewery Tap** for a charity exhibition drinking match, the first thing he asked for was a cup of tea!

Pete Westwood: never, ever, ruffled or seen to lose his rag however hard people tried

Phil Lannie: ever shooting his cuffs and tugging at his starched collar

'Plumber Bert' whose party piece was to imitate a terrier shaking a rat

Powick (or sometimes 'Pint') Nance: one of the most notorious of all Worcester's 'ladies of the night'. Wrapped up in a fox fur like her heroine music-hall songstress Nellie Wallace, her patch was Foregate Street, The Butts and the Cattle Market. By all accounts harmless, she's said to have acknowledged the decline of her offer of services with dignity, while welcoming acceptance with real enthusiasm. Described by F. H. Adams as 'tall, slim, wild-eyed, eccentric and funny' he said '...she wore a battered pair of high-heeled shoes and stockings which because the garters had failed became layered around her dirty, bony but shapely ankles. And old bonnet made of material that looked like an old dishcloth – yet saucy in appearance – lay on her wispy yellow hair. The hat often bore a bunch of daisies which always seemed to be wanting to droop down and obscure Nance's blue eyes. She had spent some time in Powick Asylum hence her nickname and was

a familiar figure on the road between Powick and Worcester and could often be seen in the Sidbury area'.

'Ptolemy': postal chess player who looked like Caesar and walked with abandonment, swinging his briefcase – probably containing nothing more than the details of his current chess game – contrariwise to his body

'Queequeg': said to have been the dead-spit of the tattooed Polynesian in the film 'Moby Dick'

Reg 'Happy' Starkey who'd hang himself up on a hanger on a coat rail in The Peep o'Day (then kept by his brother John) or years after, The Vine, and sing a passing selection from Jesus Christ Superstar, or for afters bash a tray over his head until it was shapeless mass of tangled tin while hollering out 'Mule Train Yee-Haa'

Reg the Pianist who'd have every customer in the George and Dragon warbling along like wandering minstrels

Reuben Smith, blond haired, blue eyed and with a physique that turned heads, said to be the biggest bird-puller in town

'Rocky' Rea, the City's vaccination officer. A little bald man who lived in the Arboretum, he was always immaculately dressed with pince-nez, spats and a mincing gait. But because he was eternally puffed-up with his own sense of self-importance, he was always fair game for the ragamuffin City kids who picked mercilessly on his speech impediment: "S'not Rocky, s'Mitter

Rea" he would screech back.

'Rocky' (Tony Oakes) – one of the City's Three Brushketeers (street sweepers, along with Ivor Bishop and Don Pugh) and at 71, still the oldest teddy boy in town.

The Salt Lady who plied her trade in a long dress several decades old, pushing a handcart laden with blocks of salt for sawing-off to order – with an old saw reckoned to be so rusty the salt it had come in contact with was brown! Also reputed to be called Annie on account of her cry 'Anny Salt?'

Sam Browne: described as having a smile as wide as the Severn

Sam Smith: smart, dark-hared, bespectacled, mutton-chop moustachioed paper-seller who must have read a million paperbacks while peddling the Evening News and Green 'Un outside Foregate Sreet Station

Old Sarah - a nickname earned from a million renderings of the old favourite 'Sarah, Sarah, Sitting in the Shoe-Shine Shop'

'Rocky' Oakes - at 71, the oldest teddy boy in town

Sarah: or Old Sarah, an ex-soldier by name of Boulton or Bolton. Best known and sweetest-voiced of all the street singers begging in the aftermath of the Great War. He'd earned his nickname from a million renderings of his favourite song of the day 'Sarah, Sarah, Sitting in the Shoe-Shine Shop' and locals reckoned he came from one of the villages west of the City, possibly Hallow. He's also said to have had an understanding with the local bobbies who'd turn a blind eye to his antics while for his part he'd

scarper as quick as he could on first sight of the boys in blue. Certainly active mid-1930s playing his banjo and regaling the crowds outside the Theatre Royal or serenading passers-by outside **The Horn and Trumpet.**

Saucy Sam: banjo player said to have been 6' 2" who plied his trade around the Blockhouse pubs in the 1920. Observer F.H.Adams described him almost lovingly thus: '..walking home one night through the gas-lit streets and clinging to my mother's arms, I suddenly heard the melodic strains of a banjo as we drew near a pub doorway and there he was, plucking vigorously away at the strings of his battered old banjo... wearing a shabby raincoat and a bowler hat perched at an angle on his beer-reddened face. He could hardly wait to finish playing his tunes and tapping out the rhythms with his foot before lurching back into the pub to pass his hat round, Sam was a master of his craft. I felt I wanted to put my arms around my mother's ample waist and dance along the pavement to his music, he was every bit as good as George Formby was to become in the next decade'.

The Sherriff: Ralph Gordon Banks, hairless, toothless and generally harmless, Scouse scrap-iron totter and mischievous scallywag, usually seen with a towering hulk of a minder, pushing an old pram full o' junk and blowing a plastic bugle. I wrote of The Sherriff in a recent blog (http://newsmagbobsblog.wordpress.com/2012/03): 'Today would have been The Sherriff's birthday. But then, every day was The Sherriff's birthday. Devoid of teeth, hair, or

The Sherriff -
Ralph Gordon Banks

the vaguest semblance of any of the social graces, Ralph Gordon Banks was a one-off. if he'd had a good day round the scrap yards, you'd see his handcart tipsily leant against a Worcester pub wall somewhere, and inside he'd be the same. "Ey, ar kid" he'd call over to me – his favourite reporter on account of the fact that I'd once written a whimsical little article about him in which I'd referred to him as 'a twinkly-eyed rogue', a description he relished every bit as much as being mentioned in dispatches: "...it's me berrrthday. Er, buy us a drink, like?" "Oh aye" I'd say, for the fourth time that week: "...so what's your birth sign then, Sheriff?" He hadn't a clue, but it didn't stop him trying again the next week. And the next. Best was the day I interviewed him outside the Magistrates Court just minutes after his ninety-eighth conviction – some for obstruction, but most for drunk-and-disorderly. "See, like, I'm waitin' fer me 'undredth so's I'll get me telegram from da Queen!" he said, before informing me that it was his berrrthday. Again. By my reckoning he'd be due about now the real telegram from E.R. Then again, if he'd had as many berrrrthdays as he claimed, he'd have been 946 today. They don't make 'em like that any more.

'Smiler' (also 'Old Jim') who ply his trade of odd-jobbing – usually knife-grinding or cutting hedges – in return for pennies to spend in the St Johns pubs

'Speedy' Brown described as 'a long haired likeable eccentric who'd pedal his bicycle up and down Foregate Street with his feet going like whirligigs yet travelling at half the speed of other cyclists at a time when Foregate Street was wash with bicycles. His distinct lack of speed and progress was due to some gimcrack flywheel mechanism he'd attached to his bike. As he rode, he'd turn round in his saddle, gurn at passers-by or even comb his hair – all the while putting the fear of God into motorists.

'Taffy' Herbert police sergeant reckoned to scrap on a par with all the City's hard-men and well respected as a result. The salutory tale of an altercation at the **Lamp Tavern** in Tybridge Street - one of many tales involving this old-fasjhoned copper meting out his own kind of rough justice .
See Lamp Tavern

'Tapper' William Earl – so called because he was always on the cadge, usually for cigarettes but at weekends he'd change his tack and steal boots and shoes hanging on display outside the 101 shoe shops abounding the city centre. Trouble was, he'd never quite cottoned-on to the fact that they were never hung out in pairs.

Ted Stanley, a flower seller and husband of Naughty Nora, who, despite his wife's violence, was gentle and fond of quoting from literature – especially Oscar Wilde.

Ted Wheatley – the singing bricklayer

Tex Tudge: another City 'looker' said to be big on style

'The Lud': who'd make ladies weep with his impersonation of Al Jolson yet could wang a brick clear over a house.

'Thirsty Martha'. On October 28th 1750, Berrows Worcester Journal recorded an incident at The Wheatsheaf 'without Sidbury gate' when a man offered to pay for as much ale as she could drink while he smoked a pipe of tobacco. She's reported to have drunk eight pints in the 15 minutes it took to smoke the fill, after which '...she went off, not at all disordered excepting that she complained she was still dry' *(Berrows Worcester Journal)*

Thomas Neary, a lodging-house dweller of the 1930s, beggar and boozer who claimed to have been in the Black Watch. Except that he barely reached 5 foot!

Tommy Aston who would sway down Foregate Street in the 1940s in his bowler hat, immaculately-pressed suit with the ever present carnation button-hole and giant watch chain en route to his job – which by all accounts he was brilliant at, apparently at some unknown estate agent and auctioneer's. No matter what time of the day he always reeked of the day's livener, resembling W.C Fields as Mister Micawber more than a little. He was also said to have been blessed with a bellowing voice reckoned to stop you in your tracks at 50 paces.

Tommy Baulch who'd dive off the railway bridge into the Severn

'Tussy': who was game for anything – piggy-back races down the High Street, walking backwards for miles, walking on beer bottles and a finger-wrestler fond of knitting

Vernie Challis: described as 'a lovable cheerleader' who could raise an entire pub's spirits with a single quip

Vic Young: said to have the face of a hero who'd offer to mend old folks' shoes for free

Wally (Alan Waller, pictured below): ex-military man (and looking like it) and the fairest traffic warden who'd only book erring drivers if he was left with little choice or if they gave him some lip. Typical exchange of words: '..if you can draw your car keys quicker than I can draw my pencil, I'll let you off!' I know – it happened to me!

The White Lady: Elsie Wood who, though already large and in later life notably portly, glided round the City like a schooner in full sail, dressed all in white, with her face also painted white rounded-off with shaped black fur eyebrows. Said to have been jilted as a young woman – a view not shared by some who knew her who just described her as 'eccentric' – her garb was completed with a bustle, huge boater replete

with dove's wings and cherries, and parasol. It's said she rarely spoke to anyone and finished her days at Hillborough where she worked as a seamstress. There's only one known photograph of Elsie, take by Michael Dowty in the mid-50s, almost uniquely showing her dressed in black!

Whisky Rose: a ruddy-cheeked blue-eyed bus conductress who helped everyone – able bodied and less so – off her bus regardless of whether they needed her assistance or not

'Wingy' Jack Anderson a one-armed ex-matelot who'd walk the streets with his sailor's gait in naval sweater, medals and peaked service cap. When sober he's described as the quietest of men but drunk he had the strength and ferocity of Long John Silver and Cap'n Hook combined *(as recalled by Inspector George Lewis in 1989)* and when he died in one of the cheap lodging houses of the time, his post-mortem revealed him to be the most physically well-developed man George – who'd joined Worcester City police in 1936 and served until 1966 when he retired with the rank of Inspector – had ever seen. He described the cadaver as 'a mass of sinew and muscle'

William Stuart Handley: a name that crops up again and again in reference to pub landlord prosecutions – usually in terms of being overcharged or being served during prohibited hours – implying that he was 'plant' or snoop for the licensing authorities.

'Wünderbar': who'd catch the last bus home to St Johns after closing time and within minutes have the entire bus-load, driver and conductor included, belting out the hits of the day

'Wünderbar' (pic: Dickie Moon)

Note: much of the information included here is extracted from articles I originally wrote during the 1980s appearing in Berrows Worcester Journal, Worcester Evening News, The Source and The Trumpet and others, and based on interviews held with self-styled wit, raconteur and barman Dickie Moon (so-called Ambassador to Hay-on-Wye) and former Worcester City Police constable-turned-inspector George Lewis.

...and that's when it all went

Where were we? Oh yes....

That Worcester won – and firmly retained – a reputation as something of a drinkers' paradise is barely surprising. As already discussed, the only wonder is that with so many inns, taverns, hotels, pubs and brewhouses crammed into so surprisingly compact an area, the good and faithful citizens of Worcester found much time to do much else but party!

In 1950 Worcester had twice as many pubs (198) as it has today (just under 100) with about half the population. The pubs and the brewers that supplied them were doing grand business and despite the austerity measures imposed in the aftermath of World War II, Brits in general were keen to shake off the gloom and despondency the war years had mired them with, and to celebrate their deliverance from evil. In just two short years they also had a new monarch and the new Elizabethan age to look forward to, and this for many was considered the golden age of the English pub.

But it was also a time of change: in part fuelled by the lessons learned from the more commercially astute Americans stationed over here during the war, aggressive marketing techniques began to creep in and change the face of the breweries and the pubs they owned, while burgeoning new production methods altered forever the way the traditional English pint was made, promoted, delivered, served and horror of horrors, tasted.

It's a Government-stated fact that the world changed direction dramatically in 1959. That's when, by universal agreement, the old was ditched in favour of the new – and for the most part it was a move for the better, resulting in a complete change of life affecting every continent, every nation, every industry, every community and every single individual within it.

We'd never had it so good – we know that because Prime Minister Harold Macmillan told us so. It may not have been true of everyone, but it was certainly true of the brewing industry.

But... the world was changing at a pace unimagined up to then and for the pubs, the very title of this chapter gives a inkling into what was about to hit them...

The 1960s

The 1960s was THE Golden decade, unquestioned. With typical thoroughness and drawing on a whole range of influencing factors, even Government statisticians have pin-pointed virtually to the day the time when it was luckiest to have been born in the UK: January 1948. What that means is that by the time the soul lucky enough to have been born at that time began to face adulthood, the 60s with its improved conditions, NHS, school meals, music, fashions, escalating economic prosperity, job opportunities, and racing-ahead technology was at the point of taking off big-time, and the world was

shaped

his/hers in a way it had never been for any other generation before or since.

Conversely however, this was also the time it all started to go pear-shaped for the pub that had formed the backbone of British character and society for nigh-on 1500 years.

The pub was still the very heart of the community and pub-going still formed a major role in folks' lives, shaping what Britain was fast becoming. But the pubs were changing, just as the whole world was changing – the most notable feature being that the pace of all this change was revving up and getting ready to deliver the knock-out blow that would quite soon spell the end of the old and the start of the new. Technology was in the driving seat and the food and drinks industries were about to be hit from every direction. In fact, it's probably no exaggeration to say that some of the biggest changes anywhere were about to turn both sectors on their respective heads...

Up to this time, British beer had been produced using only traditional ingredients, unfiltered *(even today old habits die hard and older drinkers will still swirl the beer in their glass to shake up the dregs in the bottom despite the fact that in most cases modern processes have eliminated the presence of any sediment, certainly by the time it reaches the consumption stage)*. The English pub was the envy of the world, and the beer that was its lifeblood flowed freely. It was delivered in wooden barrels (casks) held together with iron hoops, and served while the yeast was still active and without any mechanical aid save a beer engine manually operated by human muscle power.

But now the onset of new technology began to make steamroller inroads as the direct result of brewers – of which more later – pulled out all the stops in their all-out quest to maximise profits.

One of their targets was to slash wastage by making beer keep longer – and by calling advanced chemistry into the equation, the solution they hit on was about as radical as the science of the time allowed. Their response was to add one *further* process to the way beer had been made for at least 2,000 years, effectively sterilising it – a move calculated to halt the fermentation process in its tracks – and store it in metal casks hermetically sealed to prevent oxygen from reaching the brew and thus begin to shorten its active (ie: saleable) life. The new process also offered additional benefits, or so they claimed – not least that the new aluminium or stainless steel 'kegs' were cheaper to produce, required no specialist skills to maintain, had a longer life-span than the traditional wooden casks, and also resulted in economies being made in the brewery through sheer dint of speeding up and generally improving the cleaning and filling processes.

The resulting concoction, keg *(for which read 'dead')* beer, could also be chilled in order to even

further extend its shelf-life (to between 3 and 8 degrees, compared to room or cellar temperature of around 12 degrees for casks); it was flat, inert, kept under pressure and only artificially brought back to life by being fizzed-up with carbon dioxide at the point-of-sale.

Where dispensing conditions were difficult, nitrogen could also be added to the mix to keep up the dispensing pressure that would traditionally have been applied by muscle-power in the form of the hand-pump linked to a beer engine. But now even this die-hard relic of times gone past was temporarily faced with extinction by being replaced with new electric pumps – standardisation allowing the merest touch of a button or flick of a switch to dispense a precisely measured half: not a drop more, and not a drop less. Such was the demand for economy at every stage of the process.

On a par with that, one of the most enduring and attractive features of the traditional English pub was also suddenly put at risk of becoming an endangered species: the barmaid...

The joys of watching that eternal object of lust, a buxom barmaid, flex some ample muscles by pulling on a handle followed by a gentle rebuke to squeeze a bit more in, were now under very real threat and there was even talk of self-serve bars with no staff save a cashier and behind-the-scenes potman to make sure the kegs didn't run dry. (The still mind-blowing introduction to my all-time favourite film 'A Clockwork Orange', written in 1962 and filmed nine years later shows precisely how things were going – though the reality has only just been realised with the opening of the Britain's first all-mechanical bar in Manchester as recently as September 2012)

As I wrote in a recent blog:

Oh dear… is this a vision of the pubs of the future? Lord help us in that case. A mate put me on to what they're calling 'a unique experience' – the UK's first self-service beer venue, no less. Thankfully it's far away in Manchester and there, I hope, is where it'll stay. I'm talking about Taps Bar and Restaurant where you sit yourself down in a comfy booth and serve yourself from the shiny taps in front of you, to be presented with your bill after you've had your fill. Now I can see at least one flaw in this… what if, like some of my friends in the north (and

The biggest shake-up to modern licensing laws came about as recently as 2005 when control over licences was taken out of the hands of the police and magistrates - a partnership that had been a successful one for centuries – and placed in the hands of the local authority: ie the Council. You can argue with the Council: I don't think there'd be much arguing with the Worcester City Police Force seen here at the former Worcester City Police Station at the rear of the Guildhall (CCMH/

CFOW)

'not turning taps but pulling pumps, gave barmaids splendid busts and rumps'

round here for that matter) have been known to do when faced with an unlimited supply of ale, you hang one on and end up totally blotto? What're they gonna do, frisk you? Don't forget, too, that there's an art to pulling a pint. I forecast a lot of sopping tables, floors – oh yes, and trousers. And then, of course, the move means the loss of what for many remains one of the charms of pub-going: chatting-up the barmaid. What's more fun than some harmless banter with a gigglesome wench who's showing just enough cleavage to make it interesting, dangles a carrot sufficient to allow you to think you might stand half a chance when you know you stand no chance at all really on account of the fact her boyfriend is six foot five, and can put you down with a withering stare or even keep you waiting longer for your next pint than you want to. Nah... I can't see it catching on 'round yur.

A comment in 'The New Statesman' at the time summed it all up even more succinctly:

'not turning taps but pulling pumps, gave barmaids splendid busts and rumps'

The inevitable fall-out from the brewers' concerted drive for maximum returns had also by now resulted in the standardisation of the quality of their resulting brews: almost overnight, wastage was virtually eliminated, localised tastes were ignored in favour of the flat, uniform sterilised concoctions that needed few specialised skills to keep, had a life span of as long as it remained unsold, and looked and tasted the same whether it was pulled in Worcester, Wolverhampton, Workington or Worthing.

1967 also saw the introduction of a well-intentioned piece of legislation that carried in its wake the most serious threat to British pubs' continued existence since the Defence of the Realm Act 51 years earlier – the introduction of drink-drive laws...

Up to then the judgement of a benign (or otherwise) police sergeant was the deciding factor in whether you were capable of driving or not, but here again, technology was press-ganged to take away any element of guesswork or fortuitous frame of mind. Enter the breathalyser - aka 'the bag'. With the motor car now being viewed as a weapon of mass destruction – particularly when in the hands of a driver impaired by drink – the death-knell was now being sounded for thousands of country pubs unable to exist on the custom of punters from within the immediate community. The traditional British way of life with a day in the country followed by a drink in a charming countryside inn also changed with it. (Incidentally, one of the prime movers in the Act was Justice Blennerhassett who up to then had been

a circuit judge presiding over courts in Worcester. Possibly it had been the result of some of the cases he'd heard that prompted the introduction of the dreaded 'bag'. We'll never know.

The 1970s

Not only had the previous decade spawned the growth of marketing and promotion of flat, dead, chilled, fizzy chemical beer, but the period had also marked the introduction of foreign lagers – thus destroying at a stroke the uniqueness that had always been the hallmark of British brewing.

By the early 1970s most beer in Britain was keg, filtered, pasteurised and artificially fizzed-up with the infusion of gas. Not only that but the look of a bar – unique, and so often unchanged from one generation to the next *(so much so that a granddad would still recognise the shape and form of the bar his grandson was drinking in)* was rapidly changing out of all recognition This was the age of the now reviled Watneys Red Barrel and Worthington E and, perhaps less reviled – in fact, it has to be said, quite popular at the time, the Ansells Bittermen.

Ivor was an Ansells Bitterman

The Ansells Bittermen were the macho icons of the 1970 – and a Worcester man was one of them!
There was even a move to set up a fan club for the then 33-year old local builder who found fortune – after his rugged looks and physique wowed the women and made the men jealous of their appeal in one of the most famous advertising campaigns ever: "Ansells Bittermen – you can't beat 'em'

But 41 years on, builder Ivor Band of Ombersley Road thinks it was all just 'a bit of a laugh' that earned him just a £120 – all but £20 of it in overnight expenses ahead of the actual photo-shoot that took place in a London studio on Thursday September 3rd 1970.

He says his 20-year old daughter had no idea of his illustrious past as a national icon whose features beamed down from thousands of posters and print ads across the Midlands – and it was only lack of an equity card that prevented him from appearing in the TV ads too.

The campaign is still fondly remembered by Midlanders and memorabilia still comes up for auction on websites like e-Bay. Tucked away for four decades until last week, Ivor's first-hand collection includes posters, free standing ads, outtakes from the actual photo-shoot, and a running set of correspondence from Ansells Brewery, then based in Aston.

So how did his shot at fame start...?

Says Ivor, then living at 2 St Georges Square: "...I woke up one morning after a bit of a session in the Bull at Fernhill Heath

with an entry form in my pocket asking for blokes to send in their photographs for a competition to find typical Ansells drinkers. I thought 'why not?', won the audition held at the Swan at Yardley on Friday April 17th 1970 and was chosen as one of ten Bittermen.

"We did the shoot in London, I got paid £100 to cover expenses and that was pretty much it, really" he says. He adds that as far as he knows, no lasting friendships were struck up between the other competition winners – all amateurs from around the Midlands – and that he's had no contact with any of them since.

Despite numerous requests by people asking what had happened to the famous Bitterman, Ivor remains completely laid-back about his moment of fame that even resulted in Mrs M. Joyce from Bringsty asking the brewery at the time if she could set up a fan club for the builder from nearby Worcester: "...as far as a fan club is concerned, of course you may start one though perhaps you should contact Ivor himself first' wrote Ansells' Advertising Manager Graham Page.

Fascinating facts about the campaign:
● Ansells Mild was used at the audition in Birmingham and the Ansells Bitter you saw in all the advertising material was actually lager!
● Though ten Bittermen appeared in the campaign, only eight were amateurs.
● The two in the foreground, who also appeared in the TV ads, were professional models
● They all wore their own clothes
● The Bittermen all had to pay 5/6d (27½p) for personal photos from the session
● Ansells Bitter today is no longer brewed at Aston Cross, but at Burton-upon-Trent and is considered by many to be inferior to 'the original and the best'
● Another City link with Ansells is the 7-pint can launched In December 1960 and kn... a party can ...er' ... l Box at

It's a little known fact that a Worcester builder, Ivor Band, put himself up for selection as a BItterman and appeared on posters throughout the Midlands.
More on page 12-13 of Issue 9,
Worcester Online Newsmag

(http://www.worcester-online-newsmag.co.uk/issue9)

If by now Britain's die-hard boozers had reckoned that this was about as bad as it could get, they – as they saying went '...ain't seen nothing yet'. They were, in fact, in for a rude awakening....

The post-war blurring of the traditional demarcation line between the English classes was eating away at society, and the great public bar/lounge dividing line was slowly being eroded in favour of the all-in-one all-purpose lounge-bar complete with carpets and twee furniture – a trend that's continuing to this day though thankfully it seems to be slowing down and possibly even reversing as some brewers are beginning to realise that the decisions they made may not have been in their best interests after all.

The so-called 'march of progress' next saw the brewers who, through most of the first half of the century had set about preserving the continuity of sales by buying-up the previously privately-owned pub properties, decide to pool their collective muscle by forming large conglomerates. The exercise had not always been a success even when operated on a much smaller scale back in the 1930s: typically, Worcester's largest brewery **Lewis Clarkes** (founded in 1869, tag-line *'No better bitter, no bitter better'*), closed in 1937 just months after being taken over by Marstons.

Despite the warning signs, the brewers yomped over the rest of the drinking public and continued their merry way in the name of profit and efficiency. Net result? By the mid-1970s, virtually all beer production and most of the 70,000 pubs was in the hands of just six major conglomerates whose virtual monopoly left them not only free to increase the rent paid by hard-pressed tenants, but also the price of beer, as well as to tamper with its content and flavour entirely as they wished.

The period also saw the insides and in many cases the outsides of thousands of traditional old pubs gutted and replaced with plastic and formica all in the name of uniformity and corporate identity. *Well, what did tradition or the drinkers matter...?*

At the root of it was profit or depending on who your employer was, 'greed' – on which subject who am I to talk of greed? At the time of the greatest change – the early 1970's when many a classic old boozer, especially in the backstreets of Birmingham, was being changed to 'The Formica Arms' as I privately referred to the new-look results, I was handling a lot of the publicity for **Ansells Brewery**, the worst culprit of them all.   Oh, the utter crap I used to write in return for a few pieces of silver. 'Judas' comes to mind – or is it Fagin? Mind, it also got me some excellent free beer, sometimes even at coffee time of an otherwise cold Monday morning!

The corporate pub had arrived: dressed exactly the same as its cousins elsewhere – though, mercifully, not a complete clone as the essentially unique character of The English pub was proving just too strong to completely erode. They had a bloody good go, though.

Interesting to note that between 1950 and 1975 the number of pubs in Worcester actually decreased from 198 to 178. The next 25 years saw the number further fall by almost a third to 129 – only marginally more than the same figure it had been in 1700 when the City's population was six times less!

The 1980s

As habits changed – as like as not driven by the all-embracing whims of the brewers who were not only out of touch with the drinking public but were motivated by one thing only, a quick buck – pubs were now really starting to struggle, and yet again, as happened throughout the history of The Brits and the Booze, the Government played its part in unwittingly hastening the demise of many a once favourite outlet.

First, the restrictions allowing supermarkets to sell cheap alcohol initially introduced in the 1960s were even further relaxed, thereby making alcohol as much a part of the shopping trolley as sausages or washing powder; then they further relaxed the traditional pub licensing hours that had stood Britain in reasonable stead since their introduction in 1916. Outside London where pressure from increasing droves of tourists made the capital a special case, opening hours had been extended in April 1973 from 10.30 to 11pm on Fridays and Saturdays.

In November 1984 I wrote (in The Trumpet):

Sandra Wallace of the then newly-opened Portobello heralds the new extending drinking hours 1985 (pic BB)

As Worcester's licensees plan to push for 11 o'clock closing at the next Brewsters sessions in February, bringing the entire county in line on drinks hours, Worcester and District LVA Chairman Mike Stevens reckons all day drinking could be a fact of life over the next few years.   He told The Trumpet that though he is personally 100 per cent totally against all-day drinking he believes the vast majority of public house managers and tenants are in favour of flexi hours for pubs. And he said, he believes the next Government will be elected with a firm commitment to ease existing licensing laws. "No-one's bothered to ballot the licensees yet but as we see it, there's no argument for not reviewing a set of laws that go back 70 years and were designed to protect the production of bombs during the first world war. As far as I know, there's not too many bombs being made in the County right now so there's really no need for such outdated regulations today" the licensee of the Bridge in Lowesmoor said – adding that the one major fear of licensees is that brewers will force tenants and managers to stay open all permitted hours. Dismissing the claim that increased hours will increase drunkenness, he said that if someone wants to drink all day they already can: "...the supermarkets sell cheap wine and cider from 9am onwards – and they're not too fussy who they sell it to. A lot of the trouble makers just wouldn't get served in the pubs".

He said that a recent experiment in Scotland had smashed all all-day opening objectors'
arguments. "Prices have remained about the same, there's been no significant increase
in drunkenness and violence and drink driving is no bigger problem than it was before the
experiment" he said.

In the meantime, drinkers in Worcester had – as they had nationally – been able to enjoy an extra half hour's drinking every evening from February 25th 1985, as I reported in an article showing landlady Sandra Wallace with an 1899 clock (as lent by Jeff Hughes Antiques then in The Tything) at **The Portobello** which had re-opened just that month after a £300,000 facelift.

Now, as supermarket drinks sales began to make serious inroads into pubs' profitability – largely because their prices were not only notably lower but they were also unhampered by restrictions on how or when they could serve customers wanting to buy alcohol provided it was for consumption **off** the premises of course, came calls for the pubs to have their freedom from opening restrictions.

By March 1987 Mike Stevens was predicting that all day opening will be 'a fact of life in two years': "...the majority of my members are in favour and the sooner it happens, the better. In fact, it's the only thing that's going to keep some businesses in operation". And he repeated his assertion that claims of increased drunkenness '...just don't hold water.

But some ominous-looking storm clouds were gathering...

Against a backdrop of The Big Six breweries becoming virtually omnipotent with their stranglehold on the drinks industry, a top-level report of the time recommended that each of the national brewers should have no more than 2000 pubs in their control, sparking off real fears for the future of the English pub.

At the same time, the EEC was taking an interest in how the breweries were running their pubs – and decided to throw in their two penn'orth by recommending that licensed house tenants could be freed from the traditional brewery tie on liquor purchases from July 1988 – effectively allowing publicans to shop around for the cheapest deals from alternative suppliers like cash and carries. But there was a down-side to all this – Mike Stevens had already accurately forecast in another article I wrote at the same time:

County licenses are bracing themselves for major rents hike when restrictions come off
their wine and spirits purchases. According to the LVA, greedy breweries who last year
made record profits are set to push up rents to counter profit-loss on wine and spirit sales to
publicans. Mike Stevens, tenant at The Bridge in Lowesmoor, reckons the move could be
enough to force scores of local publicans to throw the towel in for the last time. According
to the LVA, brewers have been milking profits from successful pubs for years. "When it
comes to exacting rents, they've left Rachman behind" he said this week. Steeply rising
prices – again almost certain to be fuelled in the forthcoming budget and an oversubscribed
list of outlets in the area have all contributed to the tenants' plight and at worst, some are
working for less than a pound an hour. I have reason to believe that there are publicans in
the area who don't even earn enough to qualify for paying tax".

The 1990s

The precarious 'stop-go' situation affecting pubs actively escalated throughout the 1990s and the decade really brought home the sobering fact that, for any number of reasons, the pub was losing its mass appeal. It had been an Act of 1961 that provided for 'restaurant' and 'residential' licences (this was also the same Act that allowed for ten minutes of 'drinking-up time') and now supermarkets were increasingly being allowed to sell alcohol without many of the restrictions placed on pubs; not only that, but they could also undercut pub prices by a significant margin.

That and wage freezes combined with dramatically rising amounts of violence in town centres *(back to 'A Clockwork Orange' again: I saw it in London in the week it was released, but the film had been banned by the Watch Committee from showing in Worcester's cinemas though now it regularly appears on TV, admittedly late at night)*. Much of this stemmed not so much from the pubs but, as Mike Stevens had earlier predicted, from yobs getting cheap alcohol from the supermarkets and off-licences before descending on City centres for a night's mayhem with the net result that the already hard-pressed publicans were blamed.

The situation began to take a serious toll on many pubs: Worcester's experience is well-catalogued and is typical of many.

By now, food was also playing an increasingly vital role in the rapidly-shifting character of pubs, and while for some it was a good move, for others it spelled the end of the '7 pints a night man' that had traditionally kept many afloat. Many once old-fashioned pubs had already become pseudo-

(Worcester Online Newsmag 2011)

restaurants where the drinker *(and at that time, smoker too)* inevitably felt out of place with the eaters, while families were loth to eat where there's the risk of the kind of behaviour traditionally associated with drinking.

One of the measures sparked-off in the drive to distance themselves from a boozy past was the deeply disturbing new rush to change their names – a practise that to me should be declared if not illegal, at least ill-advised – which many now did. Lots of long-standing pub and inn names that had been in existence for years were now scrapped in favour of something twee and meaningless.

With hindsight, the move has been only partially successful and some, to their credit have reverted to what'd once been: **The Eagle Vaults** *(for a while,* **The Top Hat** *ugh!)* **The Imperial** *(***Tap and Spile***)* and **The Pheasant** *(***The Bishop's Rest***)* were just a few that traipsed that particularly ill thought out route.

It was around now too, that increasing publicity about the harmful effects of drinking also began to hit home. Drinks advertising had been banned on TV some years earlier – with the result that a significant proportion of hitherto 'hard-core' drinkers intentionally put themselves 'on the wagon' for proscribed periods and the number of adults describing themselves as 'teetotal' began to show a marked upwards trend. The same also applied to smoking and many gave up the habit in this period. For those that didn't, the Government would at least strive to limit the places they could indulge the habit and would soon take an even harder line.

The 2000s

The greatest shake-up in the drinks industry in the better part of a hundred years came about with the Licensing Act of 2003 that took control over licensing from the police and magistrates and placed it in the hands of local authorities. Coming into effect from the start of 2005, the Act made the Council, rather than the Magistrates' Court in conjunction with the local constabulary, responsible for dealing with all licensing matters. The Act also demanded the issue of a Premises Licence for which applicants were obliged to submit a plan of their building, an Operating Schedule (a brief description of how the premises will be operated safely); a fee of around £500, and a Personal Licence, naming – and licensing a designated premises supervisor (dps). Their main objectives were stated as being the prevention of crime and disorder, prevention of public nuisance, public safety and prevention of harm to children

Significantly, the Act also made provision for any council to apply for a licence to be revoked on the basis of a single complaint by a member of the public or any other body.

Sometimes, licensed premises can cause problems. Where this happens, the Council will try and resolve the issues by discussion with all those involved. However, any of the 'responsible authorities', a local resident, or a residents or business association, can apply for the Council to review a licence. Providing a complaint is not frivolous, vexatious or repetitive, a Council hearing will be held to consider the complaint. The Council may decide not to do anything, or to impose extra conditions on the licence. It can also suspend either all or part of the licence for up to three months.

As hinted earlier, in 2007 the smoking ban hit all licensed premises – many believing this to be a greater disincentive to visit the pub than the 1967 drink-driving laws. Personally, as a rabid non-smoker, I still feel a pang of conscience for the smokers huddled together outside pubs in all weathers. We always knew smoking kills – now it's just as likely to be from pneumonia.

So what of the future?

I have to state that even missing out on the magical January 1948 date as the best time to be born (admittedly only by a few days) some of my most cherished memories of the 1950s, 60s, 70s, 80s, 90s, 2000s and even more recently – and will, no doubt in the future – revolve around the pub.

As a lad I loved being taken, feeling very grown up among the adults who, though ash-speckled and reeking of stale ale always had a quip or a ready tale, a very healthy complexion and a lovely warm view of life. When my girls came along they loved to be taken too, and a walk on the hills or in the country always ended up at the pub. Now I take their children: the pattern is repeated and a good time is had by all. One of them, now on the point of being a Worcester licensee himself, made me feel all had not been in vain when, as little more than a toddler he was confronted by his Nan as we were about to nip off to the pub...

"What d'you want to be" she asked, "...a smart boy and stop here with me, or a scruffbag like Bob and go to the pub?" His reply: "I want to be a scruffbag like Bob and go to the pub".

All of which is a mildly amusing aside from the sobering facts facing licensees today.

The biggest challenge of all is not necessarily that pubs are in decline or that the world has moved on, but that the industry hasn't got a clue what to do about it.

Scarcely a day goes by without some lurid headline proclaiming X-number of pubs are closing every week. The most recent crop of bad news was that 'up to 4,000 pubs will close this year' – a dire-enough statement, but when it comes from CAMRA, an organisation specifically set up in the wake of the creeping trend towards keg beer to safeguard British pubs, it takes on a whole new meaning, not least when they say those most at risk are the ones 'stuck in the 1980s (and) offering indifferent drink and food'.

As I've said before, I was never a member of CAMRA and by making statements like that, I'd never want to be. What's wrong with being stuck in the 80s? *(I know... there was lots wrong with the 80s but at least you were faced with a wider choice of pubs, most of them good).*

Prices are now also overshadowing every other element in shaping the future – or conversely, the non-future – of pubs. It won't be long before somebody will look at this self-same sentence you're reading now and laugh out loud, but at the time of writing (October 2013) official reports state that the average price of a pint recently was £3.03p – a rise of 12p, or 3.9% on the price the same time last year; in the wake of which quickly followed dire warnings of £4 a pint.

Stop press: I paid £4 this week *(October 2013)* **in The Swan at Whittington. It was, admittedly, Guinness as none of the others brews particularly appealed, and I was captive – it being a family 'do'. Oh, and it was raining. I'd have walked out otherwise.**

Of course the pundits don't always get it right: I recall that at the time of decimalisation, *(February 1971)* there was hell to pay when the price of a pint rose from 1/10d *(about 9p)* and was rounded-up to 10p (2/-) an unheard-of amount.

At the same time, the *News of the World* forecast that by the turn of the century – that is, by the year 2000 – drinkers would be shelling-out the sci-fi figure of 10/- (50p) a pint, creating gasps of disbelief among the drinking fraternity (me included). They got that wrong, didn't they? They were at least 300% out!

Of course, prices will never come down: the only time that ever happened was in 1962 when Chancellor Rab Butler in those 'never had it so good' days slashed a whopping 2d off a pint, making it a snip at 1/2d (6p). But the harrowing truth remains that the root cause of the problem ultimately comes down to the fact that prices are just too high. Breweries counter that statement by arguing that it's not that their prices are too high, rather that the supermarkets' prices are too low, but that doesn't really stand up to any kind of scrutiny, does it?

Another 'shock, horror' headline recently (September 2013) informed the waiting world that two out of five pub and bar customers are now drinking out less often than they did a year earlier – categorically stating that two-thirds of Brits now reckon that drinking out has become just too expensive.

To find out why, you don't need to look too far: the blame has to be laid firmly at the feet of the brewers and their dogged insistence on tying licensees to unsustainable contracts – thereby forcing up beer prices to tenants and consumers alike while the pubcos drain the industry of resulting profits.

Rightly so, licensees have long been trying to free themselves of the crippling tie imposed by the breweries – correctly claiming that unless they're given the option of making their own supplier choices, the net result is inevitable: that the industry, already in decline, will slide deeper into the mire, reaching the point of oblivion in as short a time as the next decade or so.

There's no getting away from it, the industry is cripplingly blighted: the pub sector is in the grip of a national crisis created virtually exclusively by the brewers and the pubcos, and nobody has the solution – which in turn begs the question 'when it comes to pubs what are we going to leave for the next generation(s)?'

Sad to relate, the kids of the future are going to be missing out on the simple pleasures their parents and their parents before them enjoyed as a matter of course: they will, no doubt, find something to take its place – but the fact remains that the pub as we knew it may not even survive another generation. Another school of thought revolves around the question 'should pubs be kept artificially alive anyway'?

Well, of course they should. The pub is an essential part of the British character and every effort must be made to preserve them before it's too late.

At the heart of it all, there are several issues eating away at the very heart of the industry and eroding the very existence of the pub as we know – or at least knew – it, but three emerge as more critical than the rest...

1) Puubcos and property companies: themselves heavily in debt with the fall in property values, they own over half of Britain's pubs and their route to survival is also the pubs' sure-fire path to failure: they charge outrageous rents to tenants who are not only tied to their pubs but additionally have no choice but to buy their beer and spirits stocks from one supplier who in turn can charge similarly outrageous prices. Until this is reversed, or at least regulated, the decline into oblivion will continue

2) Prices. The industry is marred by its own business methods – not least that of continually finding new and ever more ingenious ways to pass products to their eventual target – ie the hard-pressed drinker – via as many intermediaries as they can drum-up, each one demanding his share of the spoils and apparently safe in the knowledge (false or otherwise) that the drinker will always dig deep enough whatever the price. Well, now's crunch time – and the drinker has gone about as far as he's prepared to go: hence the current crisis. At the same time, beer duty – that is, the amount the Government takes out of every £ taken over the bar is already the highest in Europe, and while recent measures have curtailed planned increases, the overriding view is that it's too little, too late

3) The number of outlets selling alcohol. In August 2013 I asked the City Council to let me have a list of all premises licences *(that is, on- and off-licences as well as occasional and music licences)* in Worcester. To their credit, almost by return I received a pdf document stretching to nearly 800 pages, listing over 700 premises licensed to sell alcohol.

This is the list covering St Johns and west of the river alone: in August 2013 just this one small part of the City is home to 65 premises licensed for the on- or off-sale of alcohol. They include:

18 pubs and on-licences: Herefordshire House *(Gary and Lorraine Kay Wainwright)*; Portobello Inn *(Edward William Joseph Salmon)*; Grosvenor *(William Dailly)*; Brunswick (*Christopher Walter Hankins)*; Crown Inn *(Peter Christopher Styles/Rosie Melville)*; The Mayflower *(closed - Cydell Annette Daniels); Manor Farm (Michael Anthony Wilton); Berkeley Arms (Colin Richard Kenwrick/Richard John Kenwrick); Brewers Arms (Deborah Louise Daniels)*; Crown & Anchor *(James Gavin Lavin)*; Fox Inn *(Kenneth Lamb)*; Coppertops *(Mark Wild)*; Maple Leaf *(Heidi Kirkham); Pavilion in the Park (Robert Neal Thompson)*; Bell Inn *(Phillip Stephenson); Wheatsheaf (Jonathan Guy Beech)*; Garibaldi *(Hellen Allan)*; Bush Inn *(closed -Tracy Wagstaff); Bedwardine (Hannah Batchelor)*.

6 Clubs and Social Centres: St Johns Working Mens Club; The Green Centre (Worcester City Council); Worcester Student Union *(Philip Glyn Roberts);* University of Worcester *(Thomas Anthony Taylor)*; Sketchley's Bar *(two licences Tracy Martin/Mandy Louise Smith and Robert Thompson)*.

8 Sporting Outlets: Worcestershire County Cricket Club *(David Anthony Leatherdale);* Worcester Golf and Country Club; University of Worcester Sports Centre *(Susie Hart);* Old Vigornians Cricket Club; 1st Bowl *(Eleanor Jane Perks);* Premier Inn, Worcestershire CCC *(Richard Frederick Walker);* Worcester Arena & Riverside Buildings *(Thomas Anthony Taylor);* St Johns Sports Centre *(Ian Jakeways)*.

5 supermarkets: Sainsbury's Swanpool Walk and 4 Co-ops (53 Gresham Road, 99 Henwick Road, 8-10 St Johns and 63-65 Canada Way

14 Convenience Stores: Dove Stores *(Nurul Haque)*; Bargain Booze Plus Convenience *(Paramjit Dhesi);* Broadway Express *(Santokh Singh Minhas)*; Tesco Express *(Mark Jason Hine)*; Costcutter *(Tirath Singh)*; 6 Hanbury Avenue *(Suzanne Edith Davis/Jeremy Mark Bedwell)*; Costcutter *(Mohammed

Alyas); Simply Fresh *(Nicholas Anthony Baxter)*; Boughton Stores *(Thiyagarajah Suresh)*; Red Mini Mart *(Navaratnarajah Menakan)*; Laugherne Road Stores *(Navaratnarajah Menakan)*; B & G Liquor Store *(Anthony Houlston)*; Simply Fresh *(Anil Pal/ Gurminder Singh Lola)*

4 Chinese resturants and takeaways: Golden Fortune *(Coong Sang Ung)*; Ruby Cantonese Restaurant *(Wai Hung Ho)*; Hing Tai Chinese Takeaway *(Hing Tai Ltd)*; Fortune House *(Koon Yu Hau)*

2 Indian restaurants and takeaways: Pasha Indian Restaurant *(Nurul Haque)*; Anaz Indian Takeaway *(Ahmedia Brothers Ltd)*

6 others: Perfect Pizza *(Al Wasey Traders Ltd)*; Little Acorns *(Simon Lloyd)*; McDonalds, Tybridge Retail Park; Marco's Fish Bar *(Pamela Ashcroft)*; Lower Wick Garage *(Jayaruba Vijithan)*; St Johns Newsagents *(Harjit Minhas)*

...and the pattern is repeated in the remaining 7 areas of the City listed in this book. Currently (November 2013) around 720 outlets are licensed are licensed to sell alcohol on or off the premises.

There's another issue that's having an unwelcome effect on the continuance of a tradition that's been uniquely ours for centuries...

In November 2012 and again three months later, I approached the gaffers of 100 pubs in Worcester and outlying districts with the offer of a **free** dedicated Worcester Pubs website which they can use to publicise themselves, **free** monthly Worcester pubs newspaper, **free** blog entries and all manner of sales-promoting initiatives, including a revival of sponsored games leagues, video and other high impact marketing initiatives at win:win prices.

The website was already in existence **(http://worcester-pubs.co.uk)** and they could easily gauge the impact it potentially offered. (***Note: it still is - see page 476***)

Result? First time, not one reply. Second, just eight.

Given the headlines, it's barely surprising the stuffing has been knocked out of many of the shell-shocked tenants and landlords – but at risk of giving offence to a breed of person that for the most part has my undying admiration, they could do more to help themselves.

It sparked off a blog on the Bob Backenforth blog-site **(http://bobbackenforth.wordpress.com)**

> *Why am I not totally gob-smacked by yesterday's 'shock, horror' headline that 26 pubs are shutting up shop every week? Or that the tally is a good third up on last year – itself the blackest year to date for pub closures? Having spent a goodly whack of the Bank Holiday weekend visiting several pubs I haven't set foot in for way too long – among them **The Vine, The Wheatsheaf, The Maple Leaf, The Brunswick and The Brewers Arms**, not to mention half a dozen or more I visit almost as a matter of habit (and a good one at that), the distinctly sad'n'sorry inference I can't help but draw is that too many Worcester landlords are a) devoid of any spark of imagination when it comes to promotion, b) sleepwalking into oblivion and taking their pubs with them, c) losing the battle with terminal apathy and d) worst of all, couldn't give a shot. T'ain't any wonder the words 'kiri' and 'hara' are swirling around in my mind – not necessarily in that order.*

The upshot to all this? Without some reform and some clear thinking and direction, the pub will continue in its terminal decline until it's gone forever.

Reform and fresh thinking are needed at every level. The industry can go on pretending that it's not so bad as it's painted with misguided PR about feel-good factors and international football and royal weddings and good weather bringing the punters out in droves, but the analogy with Nero fiddling while Rome burned is an apt one.

Although it's reckoned there's around 60,000 pubs still in existence in the UK today, four are closing every day of the week – and that's unacceptable. What's worse, hardly any are likely to re-open as pressures on land and the sorry state of the industry mean most are doomed to conversion for residential

or retail use.

At local level, Worcester's MP Robin Walker at least appears to be taking an interest. Describing himself as 'a passionate supporter of our local pubs' he recently *(August 2013)* held a constituency 'surgery' in **The Pheasant** in New Street – although several requests for him to join me on serious crawl of the City's remaining pubs to see the situation for himself, first-hand, and to talk to hard-pressed licensees and their equally hard-pressed patrons have been met with a polite 'yes, we must do that one day Bob'.

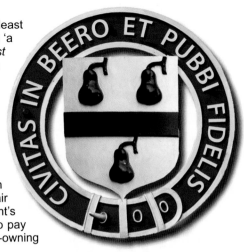

He means well but in modern-day parlance, I ain't holding me breath.

But at least, recent months have seen him go through some of the required motions: like signing up to the 'Fair Deal For Your Local' campaign calling for the Government's statutory code to include an option for tied publicans to pay a fair, independently-assessed market rent to the pub-owning company – effectively, a 'market rent only' option.

Another alternative to mass closure is a switch to community-owned 'co-operative pubs' whereby local investors pool their resources to buy their own threatened or even closed pub, put a tenant in place and run it as an on-going business.

There's no hard-and-fast solution to the decline in the once great British tradition of The Pub. What there is, is a pressing need for action and action now. Until that happens, the overbloated pubcos will continue to take more than their fair and sustainable share of pub profits and thus put even further out of reach any faint glimmer of hope of licensees being able to make a living from their craft.

In short, actively contributing to the failure of pub businesses up and down the country.

If the current situation is allowed to continue unchecked, then this book will be seen on the history shelves rather than in the reference section – which is where it's intended, and if – when – that happens, it'll be a sad day indeed and cause for national mourning.

If you want a beer or alcohol of pretty much any form, it's always going to be available – at a price. Funny though, how it loses almost all its appeal if you're drinking it anywhere other than that great – and now severely threatened – institution, the pub, and if drinking at home is all that's on offer, I'll stick to something else, thanks all the same.

On which note, I leave you with three drink-related quotes that bring into sharp focus what we're in danger of losing. No, we're not losing drink in general or beer in particular. But we are in very real danger of losing what makes drinking – especially drinking beer – rank among the most pleasurable of pastimes. As I've already stated, if all that's left is to drink beer at home, count me out.

From man's sweat and God's love, beer came into the world
(Saint Arnold of Metz patron saint of brewers)

It takes beer to make thirst worthwhile
(German Proverb)

He was a wise man who invented beer
(Plato)

Wushter's three unnedd an pubsh? That's the beer talking!

It's a rare day some beery soul doesn't lurch over and offer me – probably you too – the entirely unsolicited information that 'Wushter 'as got three unnedd an shishtyfive pubsh'.

It's usually preceded by a dig in the ribs and a well-intentioned 'Ey… did you know…?' and rounded-off with the entirely unnecessary kiss-off that 'thatsh one frevry day o' the yur'.   To which I say 'on yer bike'.

Now on one hand, you could argue that given the drink-driving laws these days, a bike is the only way you're realistically going to get to see all of them. But on the other, given that the tale is utter tosh, it's as good a response as any to offer anyone who trots out hearsay and rumour as cast-in-concrete.

The truth is, Worcester *doesn't* have three unnedd an shishtyfive pubsh. Nor at any time in its history has it ever rejoiced in being home to a pub 'frevry day o'the yur'.

Truth to tell, I first heard the myth on me auld granddad's knee about 60 years ago – and it was well shy of its pie-in-the-sky claim even then!

What I can offer with more than a degree of confidence following most of 2013 having been spent in The Hive conducting re (hic!!) search into Worcester's rich heritage of pubs, is that the City can lay claim to 656 between 1500 and now – whittled down to 515 if you discount the different monikers some have been blessed with over the years (I'm referring here to the likes of **The Coventry Arms, Cardinals Hat and Catherine Wheel** which were one and the same – as were the **Severn View, Steam Packet Tavern and Hope & Anchor; The Fort Royal Tavern, Ale & Porter Stores, London Vaults, Clock Tavern, and Little Sauce**

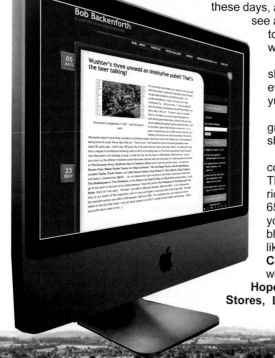

shishtyfive

Factory; **King Charles II, Tubs, Barrels, Slug'n'Lettuce** and today's characterless **Bar12**… oh, and please don't get me going on the utterly nonsensical switch from **The Shakespeare to The Cricketers**, or the **Alma to the Toad & Tulip and Pig & Drum** among others; I could go on but won't on account of my blood pressure.

Thank the Lord for **The Pheasant** and **The Swan with Two Nicks,** that's all I can say!

On a sobering note, you might just care to reflect on the fact that today I can just about stretch it to 100 if I include Fernhill Heath and Kempsey. What all this means is that one of Worcester's most enduring legends is now unarguably exposed as myth and hearsay.

Like most Worcester folks I also grew up believing the tale I'd heard that the City additionally rejoiced in the similarly fanciful claim that at one time you could go into a different pub every day starting on January 1st and not return to the same pub until the same date the following year.

Sadly, like most things pub-related, there's an element of exaggeration here and the truth is rather less romantic – but at least it's a measure of the pride with which Worcester folk still talk of their old pubs.

Another legend is that the City can boast more pubs per person than anywhere else in Britain – and here we might be on stronger ground...

As the following pages – The Chronology of Worcester pubs from 1600 – will show, in 1826 there was one pub for every 82.6 souls in the City. Today it's in the region of 1:1,000. But even so, Worcester remains a strong contender for the title of most pubs per head of population which goes some way towards explaining why the City remains a favourite with visiting hen- and stag-parties and organised pub crawlers.

As you've already seen, in 1500, Worcester was limited by statute to just three inns. Within half a century the number of licensed establishments stood at 10. The tally more than doubled to 110 in the half century between 1750 and 1800 when Worcester had about the same number of pubs as today though the population was then one-seventh of today's figure. The number of pubs listed then further doubled to 237 by 1900. From then to now there's been a steady decline: 178 between 1950 and 1975, 129 in the final quarter of the 20th century, and hovering just below 100 today. *(Sighs, and sniffs back a tear or two…)*

(Adapted from Bob Backenforth's blog: http://bobbackenforth.wordpress.com)

Chronology of Worcester pubs 1600-present

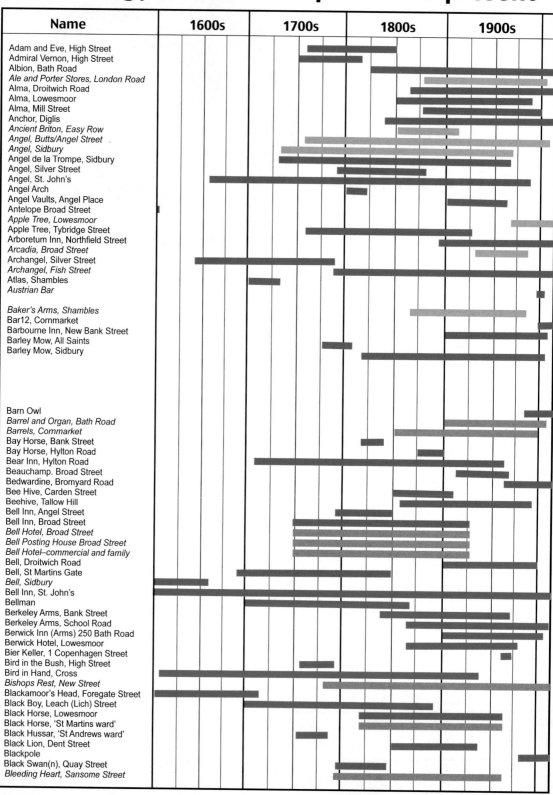

Name	1600s	1700s	1800s	1900s	
Adam and Eve, High Street					
Admiral Vernon, High Street					
Albion, Bath Road					
Ale and Porter Stores, London Road					
Alma, Droitwich Road					
Alma, Lowesmoor					
Alma, Mill Street					
Anchor, Diglis					
Ancient Briton, Easy Row					
Angel, Butts/Angel Street					
Angel, Sidbury					
Angel de la Trompe, Sidbury					
Angel, Silver Street					
Angel, St. John's					
Angel Arch					
Angel Vaults, Angel Place					
Antelope Broad Street					
Apple Tree, Lowesmoor					
Apple Tree, Tybridge Street					
Arboretum Inn, Northfield Street					
Arcadia, Broad Street					
Archangel, Silver Street					
Archangel, Fish Street					
Atlas, Shambles					
Austrian Bar					
Baker's Arms, Shambles					
Bar12, Cornmarket					
Barbourne Inn, New Bank Street					
Barley Mow, All Saints					
Barley Mow, Sidbury					
Barn Owl					
Barrel and Organ, Bath Road					
Barrels, Cornmarket					
Bay Horse, Bank Street					
Bay Horse, Hylton Road					
Bear Inn, Hylton Road					
Beauchamp. Broad Street					
Bedwardine, Bromyard Road					
Bee Hive, Carden Street					
Beehive, Tallow Hill					
Bell Inn, Angel Street					
Bell Inn, Broad Street					
Bell Hotel, Broad Street					
Bell Posting House Broad Street					
Bell Hotel–commercial and family					
Bell, Droitwich Road					
Bell, St Martins Gate					
Bell, Sidbury					
Bell Inn, St. John's					
Bellman					
Berkeley Arms, Bank Street					
Berkeley Arms, School Road					
Berwick Inn (Arms) 250 Bath Road					
Berwick Hotel, Lowesmoor					
Bier Keller, 1 Copenhagen Street					
Bird in the Bush, High Street					
Bird in Hand, Cross					
Bishops Rest, New Street					
Blackamoor's Head, Foregate Street					
Black Boy, Leach (Lich) Street					
Black Horse, Lowesmoor					
Black Horse, 'St Martins ward'					
Black Hussar, 'St Andrews ward'					
Black Lion, Dent Street					
Blackpole					
Black Swan(n), Quay Street					
Bleeding Heart, Sansome Street					

Name	1600s	1700s	1800s	1900s	

Blue Oyster, Lowesmoor.
Boar, 'St Clement ward'
Boar's Head, Newport Street
Boat, Lowesmoor
Boat House, St Clements
Bobby McGees, Blackfriars
Bottle in Hand, 'St. Andrews ward'
Boston Tea Party
Bottoms Up, Angel Street
Bowling Green Inn, Diglis St
Brewer's Arms, Comer Road
Brewers Arms, The Cross
Brewer's Arms, Moor Street
Brewer's Tavern, (St) Nicholas Street
Brewery Tap, Lowesmoor.
Bricklayers Arms, 'St Andrews ward'
Bricklayers Arms, Park Street
Bridge Commercial, Park Street
Bridge Inn Bridge Street
Bridge Inn, Lowesmoor
Bridge Inn, Lowesmoor Terrace
Bridge Inn, Lowesmoor Terrace
Britannia, Dolday ('Doldy')
Britannia Brewery (later Spreckleys)
Brunswick Arms, 50 Malvern Road
Bull, Hylton Road
Bull's Head, High Street
Bull & Sun, Bull Entry
Bush Inn, Cripplegate (Bull Ring)
Bush Tavern, Dolday
Bushwackers, Trinity Street
Butchers' Arms, Shambles

Cannon, Blockhouse
Cap 'n Gown, 45 Upper Tything

Cardinal's Hat, Friar Street
Carpenter's Arms, Dolday
Carpenter's Arms, Spring Gardens
Carpenters Arms, 5 George Street
Castle & Falcon, Broad Street
Cathedral Spirit Vaults, College Street
Catherine Wheel, Friar Street
Cavalier, St Georges Lane North
Cellar Bar, Foregate Street
Chapel, New Street
Charlston's New Street
Chequer, High Street
Chequer and Squirrel, Lich Street
Chequers, Leach (Lich) Street
Chequers, King Street
Chequers, Hylton Road
Cherry Tree, 'St Clements ward'
Cheshire Cheese, Foregate Street
Chestnut Tree, Lansdowne Road
City Arms, Church Street
City Arms, Cripplegate
City Arms, 'St Martins ward'
Clock Tavern, Fort Royal
Coach and Horses, Edgar Street
Coach & Horses, Shambles
Coach & Horses, Tything
Coach and Mares, Dolday
Cock, Copenhagen Street
Cock, (Cripplegate) Tybridge Street
Ye Cocke, Edgar Street and Sidbury
Cock & Cross St Johns
Cock and Magpie, Pheasant Street
Cocktail Club
Commercial, 5 Silver Street
Conservatory Café Bar, Friar Street
Coppertops, Laugherne Road
Cornucopia, Berkeley Way Warndon
County Bar, Foregate Street

Worcester Inns and Taverns — Timeline Chart

Name	1600s	1700s	1800s	1900s
Courtyard, St Nicholas Street		▬	▬	▬
Coventry Arms, Friar Street	▬	▬	▬	
Cricketers, Angel Street		▬		
Crispin, 'St Andrews ward'		▬	▬	▬
Crispin, Friar Street		▬	▬	
Crispin (and Crispianus), St Johns	▬	▬		
Croft Inn, James Street			▬	▬
Cromwells, Shrub Hill Road				▬
Cross, Cornmarket	▬			
Cross, 'St Clements ward'		▬		
Cross Keys, Friar Street		▬	▬	
Cross Keys, Sidbury		▬	▬	▬
Cross Keys, Trinity		▬	▬	
Crowle House, Hill Street		▬	▬	▬
Crown, Bransford Road			▬	▬
Crown Inn, Broad Street		▬	▬	▬
Crown, Droitwich Road			▬	▬
Crown, Friar Street			▬	▬
Crown, Pump Street			▬	▬
Crown, Tallow Hill			▬	
Crown and Anchor, Henwick			▬	▬
Crown & Anchor, Silver Street			▬	▬
Crown & Canton, 'St Andrews ward'		▬		
Crown & Sceptre ('near the Foregate)		▬		
Curriers' Arms, Angel St.			▬	
Dark Angel, Fish Street		▬	▬	▬
Deers Leap, Droitwich Road				▬
Diglis House, Portland Street				▬
Dingles, Broad Street				▬
Distillers Arms, Newport Street		▬		
Dive Bar, Blackfriars				▬
Dog and Duck, Henwick Hill		▬		
Dog and Duck, St Nicholas Street)		▬		
Dolphin, Queen Street		▬	▬	
Dolphin, Cooken (Copenhagen) St		▬		▬
Dolphin, Broad Street		▬	▬	
Dolphin, Angel Street				▬
Don Cossack, Doldy Street (Dolday)		▬	▬	
Dove, Lowesmoor			▬	
Dragoon, Birdport		▬		
Dragon Inn, Tything		▬	▬	▬
Drakes Drum, Tudor Way			▬	▬
Druids Head, Merryvale			▬	
Drum, All Saints		▬		
Drum, St Nicholas ward		▬		
Drum, Dolday		▬		
Dudfields, Foregate Street		▬	▬	▬
Duke of Cumberland, 'St Clements'		▬	▬	
Duke of Wellington, Birdport		▬		
Duke of York, Lich Street			▬	▬
Duke of York, Angel Place			▬	▬
Duke of York, Little Newport Street			▬	▬
Dun Cow All Hallows Well		▬		
Eagle, Pheasant Street			▬	▬
Eagle and Serpent, Dolday			▬	
Eagle Vaults, 2, Friar Street			▬	▬
Elephant and Castle, Sansome Place			▬	▬
Emperor of Russia, 'St Martins ward'			▬	
Ewe and Lamb, Angel st.			▬	
Ewe and Lamb, The Butts			▬	
Express (Tavern) Bransford Road			▬	▬
Express (Inn) Lowesmoor			▬	▬
Falcon (and Falcon Vaults) Broad St			▬	▬
Falcon, Sansom(e) Street			▬	
Falstaff, Silver Street		▬		
Farmer's Arms, Hylton Road			▬	▬
Farmer's Arms Quay Street			▬	
Farmer's Arms, Farrier Street			▬	

Name	1600s	1700s	1800s	1900s	
Farmer's Boy, Tolladine Road					
Farriers' Arms, Farrier Street					
Farriers Arms, Fish Street					
Farrier's Arms, Quay Street					
Feathers, The Tything					
Firefly, Lowesmoor, 54 Lowesmoor					
Fish Inn, Friar Street					
Fish Inn, Severn Street					
Five Ways, Butts/ Angel Street					
Flamingo, North Quay					
Fleece, Angel Street					
Fleece, Mealcheapen Street					
Foregate St Stn Refreshment Rooms					
Foley Arms, Salt Lane (Castle Street)					
Foresters Arms, Chestnut Walk					
Fort Royal Inn (Tavern) London Road					
Foundry Tavern, Park Street					
Fourteen Stars, 'St Andrews ward'					
Fountain, Bank Street					
Fountain, Angel Street.					
Fountain, Checketts Lane					
Fountain, Quay Street					
Fountain, Diglis (or Severn) Street.					
Four Ways Inn, Charles Street					
Fox, Pitmaston Road					
Freemason's Arms, Carden Street					
Freemason's Tav, Mealcheapen St					
Gardeners Arms Little Boughton St					
Gaiety Bar, Angel Street					
Garibaldi, 80 Bromyard Road					
Garibaldi (Tavern), Wylds Lane					
General Hill, Fish Street					
Gentlemen and Porter					
George, George Street					
George, Silver Street					
George Inn, Powick Lane					
George, The Tything					
George and Dragon, The Tything					
Georgian Lounge					
Globe, The Cross					
Globe Inn, 1 and 2 Friar Street					
Gloucester Arms, Copenhagen Street					
Glove, 'St Martins ward'					
Glovers' Arms, Powick Lane					
Glovers' Arms, Turkey (Tybridge St)					
Glover's Needle, Windermere Drive					
Golden Cross, The Cross					
Golden Eagle, Pheasant Street					
Golden Fleece, 'near Blackfriars'					
Golden Hart (also Heart) Sansome) St					
Golden Lion (also Lyon), High Street					
Goodfellows, Lowesmoor					
Goodrest, Barker Street					
Grandstand (1), Pitchcroft					
Grandstand (2), Pitchcroft					
Grapeshot					
Great Tolladine Inn, Berkeley Way					
Great Western Hotel, Shrub Hill					
Green Dragon, Cornmarket					
Green Dragon, Foregate Street					
Green Dragon, High Street					
Green Dragon, Tything					
Green Dragon, Newport Street					
Green Man,The Tything					
Greyhound, New St.					
Griffin, Sidbury					
Grosvenor Arms, Henwick Road					
Guildhall Tavern, 32 High Street					
Gun Tavern (Gun) New Town					

Name	1600s	1700s	1800s	1900s

Half Moon, Bransford Road
Hand and Heart, Clement Street
Hand and Sheers, Fish Street
Hand in Glove, College Street
Hare and Hounds, College Street
Hen and Chickens, Merry Vale
Herefordshire House, Bransford Road
Herefordshire House, Newport Street
Hero, Bridge Place (Hylton Road)
Hickock's House
Hole in the Wall, Merry Vale
Holly Bush, St Nicholas Street
Holy Lamb
Hope & Anchor Inn, Newport Street
Hop Market Inn, Hop Market
Hop–Pole Inn Royal Hotel, Foregate St.
Hoppers, Sansome Street
Horn and Trumpet, Angel Street
Horn and Trumpet, Little Charles Street
Horse and Groom, Sidbury
Horse and Jockey, Quay Street
Horse and Jockey, Pump Street
Horse and Jockey, The Butts
Horseshoe Bar Blackfriars
House at Home, Severn Street

Imperial (Hotel), St Nicholas Street

Jolly Dragoon, 'St Andrews ward'
Jolly Farmer, All Saints
Jolly Sailor 'St Andrews ward'
Jolly Sportsman, Tunnel Hill
Jolly Trowman, 'St Andrews ward'

Ketch, Bath Road
Keystones, 1 Copenhagen Street
King's Arms, 'St Andrews ward'
King's Arms, Leach (Lich) St.
King Charles, New Street
King Charles II, Cornmarket
King David, Birdport
Kings Head, Birdport
Kings Head, High Street
King's Head, Sidbury
King's Head, St. John's
King of Prussia, Edgar Street
King William (III), Dolday
King William (IV) Vaults, St Pauls St

Lakes, 29 Ambleside Drive
Lamb, Birdport
Lamb and Fleece, Tything
Lamb and Flag, Tything
Lame Dog, Blockhouse Lock
Lamplighter, Wylds Lane
Lamp Tavern, Moor Street
Lamp Tavern, Tybridge Street
Lansdowne Inn, Lansdowne Street
Lansdowne (Hotel), Lowesmoor Place
Laurence's Mug House, St Andrews
Leather Dressers' Arms, Birdport
Leopard, Broad Street
Lion, Cornmarket
Little Sauce Factory
Little Swan, New Street
Live and Let Live, Moor Street
Liverpool Vaults, Shambles
Lloydies Bar, The Tything
Lloyds No1, Broad Street
Locomotive Inn, George Street
    London Wine & Spirit Vaults, Broad St

Name	1600s	1700s	1800s	1900s
London Vaults, London Road			■	■
Long Sow Cutter, St Nicholas Street			■	
Long Stop, Broad Street				■
Lord Nelson, Birdport			■	■
Lucky's				
Luna Bar				
Luna Restaurant, High Street				■
Lyppard Grange, The Lyppards				■
Malt Shovel, All Hallows			■	
Manor Farm, Lower Wick				■
Maple Leaf, 49 Canada Way				■
Market Hall, Shambles			■	
Market Fountain			■	■
Market Tavern. Shambles		■		
Marquis of Granby 22 Copenhagen St		■		
Marquis Wellington, 'St Andrews ward'			■	■
Marwood, 40 Upper Tything				■
Masons Arms, Carden Street				■
Mason's Arms, St Nicholas ward				■
Mason's Arms, Severn Street		■		
Maximilian's Bar				■
Mayflower, Grenville Road				■
McBride's Mug House, St Nicholas		■		
Merry Fellow Copenhagen Street		■		
Metro Bar, 35 St Nicholas Street				■
Mitre, Lich (originally Leach) Street	■	■	■	
Mitre, High Street	■	■		
Mode (Tramps Nightclub)				■
Monroes Cellar Bar, 43 Foregate Street				■
Moors Ketch, The Moors				■
Mount Pleasant (Inn), London Road			■	■
Mouth of the Nile, Copenhagen Street			■	
Ms Monroes, 43 Foregate Street				■
Mug House, Claines 1600-present	■	■	■	■
Mug House, Friar Street		■	■	
Mug House 'St Peters ward'		■	■	
Mug House, Hylton Road		■	■	
Nag's Head, Blockhouse			■	
Navigation Inn, Lowesmoor			■	■
Nelson, 2 Merryvale (All Hallows)			■	■
New Butchers Arms, Shambles			■	
New Chequers (Inn), Astwood Road			■	
New Greyhound, New Street			■	
New Inn, Bath Road	■	■	■	■
New Inn, George Street			■	■
New Inn, Ombersley Road		■	■	
New Inn, Shambles		■	■	
New Market Tavern (or Inn), Shambles			■	■
New Pope Iron (Inn), Pope Iron Road			■	
New Punchbowl, Lich Street			■	
New Red Lion, Newport Street			■	■
Northwick Arms, Vine Street				■
Oak, (also Old Oak) Friar Street			■	■
Oak Apple, London Road			■	
Oddfellows				■
Odd Fellows Arms, Fish Street			■	
Oddfellows Arms, Carden Street			■	■
Old Apple Tree, Tybridge Street		■	■	■
(Ye) Olde Chappelle, New Street		■	■	
Old Cock, St Andrews ward		■	■	
Old Clock Tavern		■	■	■
Old Crown, Friar Street			■	
Old Crown, Pump Street		■	■	
Old Dog and Duck		■	■	
Old Dolphin, Copenhagen Street		■	■	
Old England, Little Angel Street			■	
Old England, Providence St			■	
Old Ewe and Lamb, 'St Nicholas ward'		■	■	■
Old Falcon, Sansome Street			■	■
Old Farrier's Arms, Quay Street			■	■

Name	1600s	1700s	1800s	1900s
Old Greyhound, New Street			████████████	████████
Old Hen and Chickens, Merry Vale			▪	
Old Holly Bush, St Nicholas Street		████████████████████████		
Old House at Home, Severn Street			▪	
Old Lamb and Fleece			████████	
Old Oak, Friar Street				
Old Peacock, Queen Street		████████████████████		
Old Pheasant New Street			████████████████	
Old Porter Stores, 15 Copenhagen St			████████████████	████
(Ye) Olde Punchbowl, College Street			████████████	████████
Old Rectifying House, N. Parade			████████	
Old Red Lion, Newport Street			████████	████████
Old Seven Stars, Quay Street			████████	
Old Severn Trow, Quay Street			████████████	
Old Spot				
Old Swan, St Andrews ward		▪		
Old Talbot, Sidbury	████████████████████████████████████			
Old Wherry, Quay Street			████████████	
Old Yorkshire House, St Nicholas St		████████████████████████████		
O'Neills, 8 St Nicholas Street				
Oscars, Foregate Street				████████████
Oyster Bar, Angel Street				▪
Pack Horse St Nicholas Street	████████████████████████			
Painter's Arms			▪	
Park Street Tavern, 18 Little Park St			████████████████	████
Park Tavern, Park Place			████████████████	
Parrot Inn, Broad Street	████████████████████████████████			
Parrot, Friar Street	████████████████████████████████			
Paul Pry, The Butts				
Pavilion in the Park				▪
Peacock Trinity			████████████████	████
Peep o' Day, 23 Cumberland Street				▪
Perdiswell House, Droitwich Road				▪
Perseverance, St Georges Lane North				▪
Pewterer's Arms, Merrivale			████████████	
Pheasant, Pheasant Street			████	
Pheasant, New Street			████	
Pheasant, Quay Street			▪	
Pheasant, Silver Street		▪		
Piaf's, Mealcheapen Street			████████████████████	
Pig'n'Drum, 53 Lowesmoor			████	
Plaisterer's Arms, Dolday			▪	
Pleasure Boat, Hylton Road		▪		
Plough, Fish Street			▪	
Plough, New Street,		▪		
Plough, Silver Street			████████████████	
Plumber's Arms, Friar St.		████████████████		
Plumbers Arms, Wylds Lane			████████████████	
Plume of Feathers (cathedral)	████████████████████			
Plume of Feathers, Copenhagen St			████████	████
Plume of Feathers, Sansom(e) St			████████	
Plume of Feathers, The Tything				
Poachers Pocket, Berkeley Way				▪
Pope Iron, Waterworks Road		████████████████		
Pope Iron, Pope Iron Road				████
Porcelain Workers' Inn, Severn Street			████████	
Porter Stores Copenhagen Street			████████████████	
Porter Stores, London Road			████████████████████	
Porto Bello, Henwick			████████████	
Portobello, Bransford Road			████████	
Postal Order, 18 Foregate Street				▪
Potters Arms, St Paul's Street			▪	
Potters Wheel, Severn Street			████████████	
Press, Allhallows			▪	
Prince Blucher, Birdport			▪	
Prince Regent, Birdport			▪	
Prince of Wales, The Moors			████	
Prince of Wales, Newport Street			████	
Prince of Wales, Shrub Hill			████████████	
Prince of Wales, Windermere Drive				▪

Name	1600s	1700s	1800s	1900s
Prince's Arms, Cornmarket				
Punch Bowl, College st.				
Punchbowl, Lichfield Avenue				
Queen Caroline, Quay Street				
Queen Elizabeth, Henwick				
Queen's Arms, The Park				
Queen's Arms, Powick Lane				
Queens Head, High Street				
Queen's Head, Tything				
Quiet Woman, Birdport				
Railway (Railway Arms), Shrub Hill				
Railway, Westbury Street				
Railway Bell, St Martin's Gate				
Railway Express, Pheasant Street				
Railway Refreshment Rms Shrub Hill				
Rainbow, Westbury Street				
Ram (Tavern), Regent Street				
Raven, Droitwich Road				
Rectifying House, North Quay				
Red Cow, Birdport				
Red Lion (also 'Lyon') Sidbury				
Red Lion, Tybridge Street				
Red Lion, Newport Street				
Reindeer, Mealcheapen Street				
Ring o'Bells (St Peter's)				
Rising Sun, Cripplegate				
Rising Sun, Powick's Lane (Bank St)				
Rodney, 14 Cornmarket				
Roebuck, St Paul's Street				
Roman Indian				
Rose and Crown, Foregate Street				
Rose and Crown, Easy Row				
Rose and Crown, Sidbury				
Rose and Jossamine, 'St Clement'				
Round of Beef, The Tything				
Rovers Arms, Little Charles Street				
Royal Exchange, 13 Corn Market				
Royal George, Tybridge Street				
Royal George, Tunnel Hill Road				
Royal Oak, Bransford Road				
Royal Oak, Carden Street				
Royal Oak, Dolday				
Royal Oak (1), 'St Martins ward'				
Royal Oak (2), 'St Martins ward'				
Royal Oak, York Place				
Salmon's Leap, Severn Street				
Salt Scales, 'St Andrews ward'				
Salutation, St Johns				
Sandpits, Bromyard Road				
St George's Tavern, St George's Lane				
Saracen's Head, Tything				
Sawyer's, Hylton Road				
Sebright Arms, London Road				
Sedan Chair 'St Martins ward'				
Seven Stars, Palace Street				
Seven Stars, New Street				
Severn Galley, Newport Street				
Severn Swan, South Parade				
Severn Trow, Hylton Road				
Severn Trow, Quay Street				
Severn View Hotel, Newport Street				
Shades (Tavern), Mealcheapen Street				
Shades, Diglis (or Severn) Street				
Shamus O'Donnell's				
Shakespeare, Angel Street				
Ship, Copenhagen Street				
Ship, Canalside Lowesmoor				
Shoemakers Arms, All Saints				
Slug'n'Lettuce, 12 Cornmarket				
Slug'n'Lettuce, The Cross				

Name	1600s	1700s	1800s	1900s
Silver Grayling, Powick Lane				
Smoke Stack (Swan, St Johns)				
Sow and Pigs, Dolday				
Spread Eagle Dolday				
Spread Eagle, Pheasant Street				
Stag (possibly Cornmarket)				
Star, Bransford Road				
Star, Newport Street				
Swenchard (Swinesherd?)				
Star Bar, Foregate Street				
Star & Garter Hotel Foregate Street				
Star Vaults, Farrier Street				
Stationers Arms, High Street				
Steam Packet Tavern				
Sun and Bull, Bull Entry				
Sun Beer House, Lowesmoor Terrace				
Sun Tavern, 'St Martins ward'				
Swan, Barbourne				
Swan, High Street				
Swan, Lowesmoor				
Swan with Two Necks/Nicks) New St.				
Swan, Newport Street				
Swan Powick('s) Lane				
Swan, Pump Street				
Swan, St Johns				
Swan, 'St Peters ward'				
Talbot, The Cross				
Talbot (and {Ye} Old Talbot), Sidbury				
Talbot, Tything				
Tap and Spile				
Telegraph (Tavern), George Street				
Ten Bells, Doldy				
Thistle Vaults, Charles Street				
Three Blackbirds, Tything				
Three Cranes, Lich Street				
Three Cranes, High Street				
Three Crosses, Friar Street				
Three Cuxxes				
Three Pyes, Lich Street				
Three Tuns, St Nicholas ward				
Three Tuns (Castle Street)				
Timberdine, Broomhall				
Toad and Tulip				
Toby Carvery, Bath Road				
Toby's Tavern, Sansome Street				
Top Hat				
Travellers Inn, New Street				
Trinity Inn				
Tubs, Cornmarket				
Turks Head, Lowesmoor				
Unicorn, Dolday				
Unicorn, Mill Street				
Unicorn Inn (and Hotel), Broad Street				
Union (Inn, Tavern) Lowesmoor				
Union, Union (or Carden) Street				
Vaults, 12 Cornmarket				
Vaults, 1 Little Angel Street				
Vaults, 51 New Street				
Vauxhall, Astwood Road				
Victoria (back of 85 High Street)				
Vine, Ombersley Road				
Vintorne, Broad Street				
(Ye) Virgin, Tolladine Road				
Volunteer, Friar Street				
Vulcan, St Paul's Street				
Wagon & Horses, Angel Street				
Washington (Arms), Washington Street				
Waterloo, Waterloo Street				

Name	1600s	1700s	1800s	1900s
Welcome Inn, Wylds Lane				
Well Sinkers Arms, All Saints ward				
Western Bar, Foregate Street				
West Midland Arms, Lowesmoor Place				
Wheat Sheaf, Sidbury				
Wheat Sheaf, Corn Market				
Wheat Sheaf, Henwick				
Wheelwrights Arms, Hylton Road				
Wherry, Quay Street,				
Whey Tavern, Lansdowne Road				
White Hall, Bransford Road (Rushwick)				
White Hart, College St.				
White Horse Cripplegate				
White Horse (Inn) Silver St.				
Whitehouse, Foregate Street				
White Lion (Lyon), Cornmarket				
White Lion, Lowesmoor Close				
White Swan(n) Powick Lane				
Wine & Brandy Vaults, Copenhagen St				
Wine Vaults, Bridge Street				
Winning Post, Pope Iron Road				
Woodman, Dolday				
Wool Pack, Birdport				
Wool Pack, Dolday (Doldy)				
Woolpack, Friar Street				
Wrens Nest, Henwick Road				
Yates Wine Lodge, Mealcheapen Street				
Ye Olde Chappell, New Street				
Ye Olde Punch Bowl, Lich Street				
Ye Virgin (Tolladine Road)				
York House, Moor Street				
Yorkshire House, St Nicholas Street				
Young's Mug House, Friar Street				

'...'Worcester is considered one of the most ancient and respectable cities in England; and there are but few reckoned superior to it in extent and population, and a less number in beauty. The streets of the city are handsome and regular.... indeed, for beauty, cleanliness, respectability, and as affording all the comforts of life, unsparingly, no visitor will be disappointed on his arrival at the city of Worcester, and but few will leave it without regret'

(Pigot's Directory 1842)

CIVITAS IN BEERO ET PUBBI FIDELIS

and index to
Worcester pubs

A

Adam and Eve
Location: High Street
Active: 1760s–1840s
C3/14 Page 296

Admiral Vernon
Location: High Street
Active 1750s–c1800
C4/20 Page 356

Albion
Location: Bath Road
Active: 1826 to present
E1 Page 160

Ale and Porter Stores
Location: London Road
See Fort Royal

Alma
Location: Droitwich Road
Active: 1864 to present
N46 Page 152

Alma
Location: Lowesmoor
Active: 1850s to present
C2/50 Page 279

Alma
Location: Mill Street
Active: c1860 to 2000
C5/20 Page 393

Anchor
Location: Diglis
Active: 1840s–present
E2 Page 161

Ancient Briton
Location: Easy Row/Severn Terrace
See Rose and Crown

Angel
Location: Butts/Angel St.
See: Five Ways

Angel
Location:Sidbury
Active: 1730–1966
C5/4 Page 382

Angel de la Trompe (Angel and Trumpet)
Location: Sidbury
Active: 1730–1966
C5/4 Page 383

Angel
Location: Silver Street
See: Plough

Angel
Location: St. John's
Active: 1660s–1985
W2 Page 71

Angel Arch
Location: High Street
Active: 1814
C4/19 Page 356

Angel Vaults
Location: Angel Place
Active: 1900–1966
C1/33 Page 222

Antelope ('Anteloppe')
Location: Broad Street
Active: ancient–1500–1600s

Apple Tree
Location: Lowesmoor
Active: 1970s–present
C2/52 Page 282

Apple Tree
Location: Turkey St (Tybridge Street)
Active: 1760–1926
W39 Page 100

Arboretum Inn
Location: Northfield Street
Active: 1890–2003
N23 Page 132

Arcadia (and Arcadia Restaurant)
Location: Broad Street
Active: 1930s–1985
C4/6 Page 350

Archangel
Location: Silver Street
See Plough

Archangel
Location: Fish street
Active: 1820–c 1830
See Farriers Arms

Atlas
Location: Shambles
Active: c1700–c1730?
Page 324

Austrian Bar
See Cardinals Hat

B

Baker's Arms
Location: Shambles
See: Liverpool Vaults

Bar12
Location: Cornmarket
See: King Charles II

Barbourne Inn
Location: New Bank Street
Active: c1900–2010
N44 Page 150

Barley Mow
Location: All Saints
Active: 1766 –?
C4/66 Page 377

Barley Mow
Location: Sidbury
Active: c1820–2006
E7   Page 168

Barn Owl
Berkeley Way Warndon
Active: 1984–present
E39 Page 198

Barrel and Organ
Location: Bath Road
See: The Berwick

Barrels
Location: Cornmarket
See: King Charles II

Bay Horse
Location: Bank Street
Active: 1820–1830
C4/11 Page 352

Bay Horse
Location: Hylton Road
See Wheelrights Arms

Bear Inn
Location: Hylton Road
Active: 1710–1967
W40 Page 102

Beauchamp (and Hotel)
Location: 42 Broad Street
Active: 1720–1960
C4/4 Page 348

Bedwardine
Location: Bromyard Road
Active: 1870–present
W5 Page 74

Bee Hive
Location: Carden Street
Active: 1850s to 1908
C3/66 Page 338

Beehive
Location: Tallow Hill
Active: 1860s to c2000
E22 Page 181

Bell Inn
Location: Angel Street
Active: 1792–?1850
Ref: C1 Page 218

Bell Inn
Location: Broad Street
Active: 1750s to 1927
Ref: C1 Page 218

Bell Hotel
Location: Broad Street
Active: 1750s-1912
C1/27 Page 218

Bell Posting House
Location: Broad Street
See: Bell Hotel

Bell Hotel–commercial and family
See: Bell Hotel

Bell
Location: Droitwich Road
Active: 1900–2000
N47 Page 154

Bell
Location: St Martins Gate
See: Railway Bell

Bell
Location: Sidbury
See: Kings Head

Bell Inn
Location: St. John's
Active: pre–1791–present
W11 Page 79

Bellman
Location: High Street (or Cornmarket)
Active: 1700s–1870
Unknown location
Page 269 and 294

Berkeley Arms
Location: Bank Street
Active: c1830s–c1970
C4/12 Page 352

Berkeley Arms
Location: School Road
Active: c1870–(present
W19 Page 84

Berwick Inn (Arms)
Location: 250 Bath Road
Active: from 1900– 2008
E3 Page 163

Berwick Hotel
Location: Lowesmoor
Active: 1870s-1980s

Bier Keller
Location: 1 Copenhagen Street
See Mouth of the Nile

Bird in the Bush
Location: probably High Street
Active: 1760s - 1790
C1/41 Page 234

Bird in Hand
Location: Cross
Active: 1600s–1934
C1/43 Page 234

Bishops Rest
Location: New Street
See: Pheasant

Blackamoor's Head
Location: Foregate Street
See Saracens Head

Black Boy
Location: Leach (Lich) Street
Active: 1700–1880
C3/23 Page 302

Black Horse
Location: Lowesmoor
Active: 1820–1965
C2/47 Page 276

Black Horse
Location: 'St Martins ward'
Active: 1760
C2/47 Page 276

Black Hussar
Location: 'St Andrews ward'
Active: 1766
C4/69 Page 377

Black Lion
Location: Dent Street
Active: 1850s –1930s
E19 Page 178

Blackpole
Location: Blackpole Road
Active: 1980–present
E41 Page 199

Black Swan(n)
Location: Quay Street
Active: 1790–1840
4/61 Page 374

Bleeding Heart
Location: Sanfom (Sansome) Street
Active: 1790–1965
See Golden Hart

Blue Oyster
Location: Lowesmoor.
See: Turks Head

Boar
Location: 'St Clement ward'
Active: 1760s
W53 Page 109

Boar's Head
Location: Newport Street
Active: 1800–1906
C1/5 Page 209

Boat
Location: Lowesmoor
Active: c1800 to 1965
C2/44 Page 274

Boat House
Location: St Clements
Active: 1700–1800
W49 Page 109

Bobby McGees
Location: Blackfriars
Active: 1969-80s
See Dive Bar

Bottle in Hand
Location: 'St. Andrews ward'
Active"
C4/58 Page 374

Boston Tea Party
See: Dolphin

Bottoms Up
Location: Angel Street
See: Fountain

Bowling Green Inn
Location: Diglis St
Active: 1700s
C5/19 Page 393

Brewer's Arms
Location: Comer Road
Active: 1900–present
W3 Page 72

Brewers Arms
Location: The Cross
Active: 1700s
C1/42 Page 234

Brewer's Arms
Location: Moor Street
Active: 1900–1960
N15 Page 123

Brewer's Tavern
Location: (St) Nicholas Street
See: Imperial

Brewery Tap
Location: Lowesmoor.
See: Turks Head

Bricklayers Arms
Location: 'St Andrews ward'
Active: 1760s
C4/74 Page 378

Bricklayers Arms
Location: Park Street
Active: c1873 to c1985
E18 Page 177

Bridge Commercial
Location: Park Street
See: Bricklayers Arms

Bridge Inn (and Bridge Hotel)
Location: Bridge Street
Active: 1790–1965
C4/1 Page 346

Bridge Inn
Location: Lowesmoor
(See Sun Tavern)

Bridge Inn
Location: Lowesmoor Terrace
Active: 1850 -1937
C2/60 Page 285

Bridge Inn
Location: Lowesmoor Terrace
Active: 1937- present
C2/60 Page 285

Britannia
Location: Dolday ('Doldy')
Active: 1750–1880
C1/12 Page 213

Britannia
Location: Barbourne Road
attached to Britannia
Brewery (later Spreckleys)
Active: 1930s–1962
N31 Page 138

Brunswick Arms
Location: 50 Malvern Road
Active: c1900–present
W25 Page 88

Bull
Location: Hylton Road
Active: 1830-50
W48 Page 109

Bull's Head
Location: High Street
See: Guildhall Tavern

Bull & Sun
Location: Bull Entry (also Bull
Square)
Active: 1792–1900
C4/41 Page 369

Bush Inn
Location: Cripplegate (Bull
Ring)
Active: 1780–to 2010
W31 Page 94

Bush Tavern
Location: Dolday
Active: 1790s
C1/19 Page 215

Bushwackers
Location: Trinity Street
Active: 1990-present
C2/3 Page 248

Butchers' Arms
Location: Shambles
Active: c1810–1955
C3/47 Page 322

C

Cannon
Location: Blockhouse
Active: 1850s – 1860s
C3/69 Page 338

Cap 'n Gown
Location: 45 Upper Tything
Active: 1898–present
N27 Page 134

Cardinal's Hat
Location: Friar Street
Active: 1500s–present
C3/32 Page 308

Carpenter's Arms
Location: Dolday
Active: 1750–1820
C1/18 Page 215

Carpenter's Arms
Location: Spring Gardens
Tything
Active: c 1840–1961
N11 Page 122

Carpenters Arms
Location: 5 George Street
Active: 1870s-1906
C2/65 Page 288

Castle & Falcon
Location: Broad Street
See: Falcon

Cathedral Wine and Spirit Vaults
Location: College Street
Active: 1873–1908
C3/28 Page 303

Catherine Wheel
Location: Friar Street
See: Globe Vaults

Cavalier
Location: St Georges Lane
North
Active: 1968–present
N37 Page 143

Cellar Bar
Location: Foregate Street
See: Monroes Cellar Bar

Chapel
Location: New Street
See: Old Chapel

Charlston's
Location: New Street
See: Old Greyhound

Chequer
Location: High Street
See Chequers Lich Street

Chequer and Squirrel
Location: Lich Street
See Chequers

Chequers
Location: Leach (Lich)
Street
Active: 1820–30
C3/24 Page 302

Chequers
Location: King Street
Active: 1820–1880
C5/12 Page 387

Chequers
Location: Hylton Street (also Hylton Road)
Active: C 1820–1928
W46 Page 106

Cherry Tree
Location: 'St Clements ward'
Active: c1760s
W54 Page 109

Cheshire Cheese
Location: Foregate Street
Active: 1750s–1820
N1 Page 114

Chestnut Tree
Location: Lansdowne Road
Active: 1870–present
N33 Page 140

City Arms
Location: Church Street
Active: 1760–1961
C3/1 Page 293

City Arms
Location: Cripplegate
Active: 1760–1870s

Clock Tavern
Location: Fort Royal
See: Fort Royal

Coach and Horses
Location: Edgar Street
Active: 1751–1800
C5/8 Page 385

Coach & Horses
Location: Shambles
Active: 1780s to 1960
C3/48 Page 322

Coach & Horses
Location: Tything
Active: 1790 to present
N28 Page 135

Coach and Mares
Location: Dolday
Active: 1790–1800
C/11 Page 212

Cock
Location: Copenhagen Street
Active: 1760s 1920
C4/29 Page 361

Cock
Location: Tybridge Street
Active: 1790 to 1966
W33 Page 96

Ye Cocke
Location: Edgar Street and
Sidbury
Active: 1500s to 1750s
C5/3 Page 383

Cock & Cross
Location: St Johns
Active: 1780–1800
W10 Page 79

Cock and Magpie
Location: Pheasant Street
Active: 1850–1906
C2/58 Page 284

Cocktail Club
(Keystones Cocktail Club)
Location: Copenhagen Street
See: Keystones

Commercial
Location: 5 Silver Street
Active: 1784
C2/31 Page 265

Conservatory Café Bar
Location: Friar Street
Active: 1985–present
C3/36 Page 313

Coppertops
Location: Laugherne Road
Active: 1970–present
W8 Page 77

Cornucopia
Location: Berkeley Way
Warndon
See: Barn Owl

County Bar
Location: Foregate Street
See: Star Hotel

Courtyard
Location: St Nicholas Street
See Pack Horse

Coventry Arms
Location: Friar Street
See: Cardinals Hat

Cricketers
Location: Angel Street
See Shakespeare

Crispin
Location: 'St Andrews ward'
Active:
C4/75 Page 378

Crispin
Location: Friar Street/ later
Union Street
See: Fish

Crispin (and Crispianus)
Location: St Johns
Active: 1600s –1780
W8 Page 79

Croft Inn (and House)
Location: James Street
Active: 1860s–1974
C3/79 Page 343

Cromwells
Location: Shrub Hill Road
Active: 1980-1990
See Great Western

Cross
Location: Cornmarket
Active: 1600s
C2/35 Page 266

Cross
Location: 'St Clements ward'
Active: 1780-1800
See Bell

Cross Keys
Location: College Street
Active: 1600s
C5/5 Page 384

Cross Keys
Location: Friar Street
Active: 1660s–1910
C3/34 Page 311

Cross Keys
Location: Sidbury
Active: 1870s-1960s
E8b Page 169

Cross Keys
Location: Trinity
Active: 1760s–1830
C2/26 Page 263

Crowle House
Location: Hill Street Tallow Hill
Active: 1850–1966
E21 Page 180

Crown
Location: Bransford Road
Active: 1790–present
W18 Page 83

Crown Inn (Posting House)
Location: Broad Street
Active: 1660s to present
C1/28 Page 218

Crown
Location: Droitwich Road
Active: 1780s to 1979 (see
also Deers Leap)
N45 Page 151

Crown
Location: Friar Street
Active: 1820–1938
C3/37 Page 314

Crown
Location: Pump Street
Active: 1760–1860
C3/43 age 318

Crown
Location: Tallow Hill
Active: c1850 to 1943
E20 Page 179

Crown and Anchor
Location: Henwick (also
Henick Hill Old Henwick Road
Lower Henwick Road and
Tybridge Street)
Active: 1790 to present
W45 Page 106

Crown & Anchor
Location: Lowesmoor/Silver
Street
Active: 1790–1962
C2/43 Page 273

Crown & Canton
Location: 'St Andrews ward'
Active: 1760s
C4/68 Page 377

Crown & Sceptre
Location: ('near the Foregate)
Active: 1700s
C2/6 Page 252

Curriers' Arms
Location: Angel St.
Active: 1814–1840
C1/37 Page 230

Dark Angel
Location: Fish Street
Active: 1790–1810
See Farriers Arms

Deers Leap
Location: Droitwich Road
Active: 1981-2010 (see also
Crown Droitwich Road)
N45 Page 151

Diglis House
Location: Portland Street
Active: 1908–present
C5/18 Page 392

**Dingles (also Dingle Son and
Edwards Wine and Spirit
Vaults)**
Location: Broad Street
See Dolphin

Distillers Arms
Location: Newport Street
Active: 1780-90
C1/9 Page 210

Dive Bar
Location: Blackfriars
Active: 1969-1984?
C1/32 Page 222

Dog and Duck
Location: Henwick Hill
Active: 1780s to 1840
W42 Page 103

Dog and Duck
Location: Garden Market
Active: 1820–1850
C2/14 Page 259

Dolphin
Location: Queen Street
Active: 1766–1800
C2/24 Page 263

Dolphin
Location: Cooken
(Copenhagen) Street
Active: 1780s to 1880
C4/23 Page 359

Dolphin
Location: Broad Street
Active 1790s
C1/25 Page 216

Dolphin
Location: Angel Street
Active 1927–2009
C1/26 Page 216

Don Cossack
Location: Doldy Street
See: Sow and Pigs

Dove
Location: Lowesmoor
Active: 1840s to 1870
C2/46 Page 276

Dragoon
Location: Birdport
Active: 1750s
C4/49 Page 371

Dragon Inn
Location: Tything
Active: 1790–present
N19 Page 127

Drakes Drum
Location: Tudor Way
Active: 1958–2008
W6 Page 76

Druids Head
Location: Merryvale
Active: (listed 1837)

Drum
Location: All Saints
Active: 1750s–c1780

Drum
Location: St Nicholas ward
Active:
C2/20 Page 259

Drum
Location: Dolday
Active: 1760-c1790
C1/21 Page 215

Dudfields (Bar/Wine Lodge)
Location: Foregate Street
Active: 1850s to 1980s
C1/36 Page 238

Duke of Cumberland
Location: 'St Clements ward'
Active: 1760s
W50 Page 109

Duke of Wellington
Location: Birdport
Active: 1829–1960s
C4/43 Page 369

Duke of York
Location: Lich Street
Active: 1820 to 1850s
C3/25 Page 302

Duke of York
Location: Angel Place (Little
Angel Street)
Active: 1810 to 1965
C1/31 Page 221

Dun Cow
Location: All Hallows Well
Active: 1780–1800
C4/3 Page 348

Duttons
See: Guildhall Tavern

Eagle (and Eagle Inn)
Location: Pheasant Street
Active: 1850 –1952
C2/56 Page 284

Eagle and Serpent
Location: Dolday
See: Spread Eagle

Eagle Vaults
Location: 2 Friar Street
Active: 1750–present
C3/39 Page 316

Elephant and Castle
Location: Sansome Place
Active: 1850–1971
C2/48 Page 278

Emperor of Russia
Location: 'St Martins ward'
Active: c1814
C3/5 Page 294

Ewe and Lamb (Vaults)
Location: Angel st.
Active: 1750–1990
C1/39 Page 231

Ewe and Lamb
Location: The Butts
Active: 1850–1972
C1/49 Page 239

Express (Tavern)
Location: Bransford Road
Active: 1900–1922
W17 Page 83

Express (Inn)
Location: Lowesmoor
Active: 1850–1910
C2/45 Page 275

Falcon (and Falcon Vaults)
Location: Broad Street
Active: 1760-1906
C1/24 Page 216

Falcon
Location: Sansom(e) Street
See: Old Falcon

Falstaff
Location: Silver Street
Active: 1790s
C2/33 Page 265

Farmer's Arms
Location: Bridge Place
(Hylton Road)
Active: 1850s–1909

Farmer's Arms
Location: Quay Street
Active: 1850s
C4/62 Page 375

Farmer's Arms
Location: Little Butts (Farrier
Street)
Active: 1850s
C1/53 Page 243

Farmer's Boy
Location: Tolladine Road
Active: 1957–present
(reduced size)
E33 Page 192

Farriers' Arms
Location: Farrier Street
Active: 1820–1964
C1/56 Page 244

Farriers Arms
Location: Fish Street
Active: 1870s to present
C4/36 Page 365

Farrier's Arms
Location: Quay Street
Active: 1840–1960
C4/64 Page 375

Feathers
Location: The Tything
See: Cap'n'Gown

Firefly
Location: Lowesmoor 54
Lowesmoor
See: Apple Tree

Fish Inn
Location: Friar Street
Active: 1780–1880
C3/17 Page 317

Fish (and Old Fish) Inn
Location: High Timber
Street (now Severn Street)
Active: 1780–1920
C5/10 Page 386

Five Ways
Location: Butts/ Angel Street
Active: 1760s-2012
C1/52 Page 242

Flamingo
See: Old Rectifying House

Fleece
Location: Angel Street
Active: 1600 to 1860s
C1/30 Page 220

Fleece (and Fleece Inn)
Location: Mealcheapen Street
Active: 1870–1929
C3/61 Page 333

Foley Arms
Location: Salt Lane (Castle
Street)
Active: 1850–1876
N5 Page 118

**Foregate Street Rly.
Refreshment Rooms**
Location: Foregate Street
Station
C2/7 Page 252

Foresters Arms Hotel
Location: Sansome
(Chestnut) Walk
Active: 1860–1990
N22 Page 132

Fort Royal Inn (Tavern)
Location: London Road
Active: 1880s–2007
E9 Page 170

Foundry Tavern
Location:
See: Bricklayers Arms

Fourteen Stars
Location: 'St Andrews ward'
Years active: 1827
C4/46 Page 371

Fountain
Location: Bank Street
Active: 1820s–1830
C4/10 Page 351

Fountain
Location: Angel Street.
Active: 1840s–1983
C1/38 Page 230

Fountain
Location: Droitwich Road/
Checketts Lane
Active: 1930–52
N 48 Page 155

Fountain
Location: Quay Street
Active: 1700s
C4/63 Page 375

Fountain
Location: Diglis (or Severn)
Street.
Active: 1840–2000
C5/16 Page 390

Four Ways Inn
Location: Charles (or
Foundry) Street
Active: 1870s–1923
Ref: C3 Page 340

Fox
Location: Pitmaston Road
Active: 1900–present
W26 Page 90

Freemason's Arms
Location: Carden Street
Active: 1850–1959
C3/64 Page 337

Freemason's Tavern
Location: Mealcheapen
Street
See Reindeer

Gardeners Arms
Location: Little Boughton
Street
Active: 1872–1911
W22 Page 86

Gaiety Bar
Location: Angel Street
See: Ewe and Lamb

Garibaldi
Location: 80 Bromyard Road
Active: 1900–present
W4 Page 74

Garibaldi (Tavern)
Location: Wylds Lane
Active: 1870–1986
E16 Page 175

General Hill
Location: Fish Street
Active: 1820–1830
C4/35 Page 366

Gentlemen and Porter
Location:
Active: 1780-90
C2/18 Page 259

George
Location: George Street
Active: 1850–60

George
Location: Silver Street
Active: 1850–60
C2/32 Page 265

George Inn
Location: Powick Lane
Active: 1600s
C4/14 Page 355

George
Location: The Tything
See Dragon Inn

George and Dragon
Location: The Tything
See Dragon Inn

Georgian Lounge
Location:
See: Apple Tree

Globe
Location: The Cross (also
listed as Powick
Lane)
Active: 1700s
C4/9 Page 351

Globe Inn (and Vaults)
Location: 1 and 2 Friar Street
Active: 1780–1971
C3/31 Page 307

**Gloucester (and Glo'ster)
Arms**
Location: Copenhagen Street
Active: 1820–1915
C4/27 Page 360

Glove
Location: 'St Martins ward'
Active: 1760s
C3/7 Page 295

Glovers' Arms
Location: Merry Vale (also
listed as Powick Lane)
Active: 1820 c 1919
C4/18 Page 356

Glovers' Arms
Location: Turkey (Tybridge
Street)
Active: 1820s
W34 Page 98

Glover's Needle
Location: Windermere Drive
Active: 1962 –present
E38 Page 197

Golden Cross
Location: The Cross
Active: 1700–1830s
C2/1 Page 247

Golden Eagle
Location: Pheasant Street
See: Eagle

Golden Fleece
Location: 'near Blackfriars'
See: Fleece

Golden Hart (also Heart)
Location: Sansom
(Sansome) St.
Active: 1750s- 1972
C2/10 Page 254

Golden Lion (also Lyon)
Location: High Street
Active: 1680–1986
C3/12 Page 296 and 297

Goodfellows
Location:
See: Brewery Tap

Goodrest
Location: Barker Street
Active: 1930s–present
E31 Page 191

Grandstand (1)
Location: Pitchcroft
Active: 1824–1901
N8 Page 121

Grandstand (2)
Location: Pitchcroft
Active: 1901–1960s
N9 Page 121

Grapeshot
Location: Foregate Street
See: Monroes Cellar Bar

Great Tolladine Inn
Location: Berkeley Way
Active
See Barn Owl

Great Western Hotel (also Vaults)
Location: Shrub Hill
Active: 1850–2004
E24 Page 183

Green Dragon
Location: Cornmarket
Active: 1720–1800
C3/59 Page 331

Green Dragon
Location: Foregate Street
Active: 1670s–1750
N4 Page 117

Green Dragon
Location: corner of Cooken
and High Street
Active: 1600–1700s
C4/21 Page 357

Green Dragon
Location: Tything
See Dragon Inn

Green Dragon
Location: Newport Street
Active: 1780s–1932
Ref: C1/3 Page 208

Green Man (also Green Man and Still also Green Man Inn)
Location: The Tything
Active: 1790-present
N20 Page 129

Greyhound
Location: New St.
See: Old Greyhound

Griffin
Location: Sidbury
Active: 1730–1800
C5/3 Page 385

Grosvenor Inn (and Arms)
Location: Henwick Road
Active: 1870–present
W29 Page 92

Guildhall Tavern
Location: 32 High Street
Active: 1780–1931
C3/11 Page 295

Gun Tavern (Gun)
Location: New Town
Active: 1850 - 2013)
E28 Page 187

Half Moon
Location: Bransford Road
Active: 1870–c1875
W20 Page 86

Hand and Heart
Location: Clement Street
Active: 1850–1870
W37 Page 100

Hand and Sheers (or Shears)
Location: Fish Street
Active: 1790–1810
See Farriers Arms

Hand in Glove
Location: College Street
See White Hart

Hare and Hounds
Location: College Street.
Active: 1750–1885
See Cross Keys

Hen and Chickens
Location: Merry Vale
Active: 1790–1880

Herefordshire House
Location: Bransford Road
Active: 1859–present
W21 Page 85

Herefordshire House
Location: Newport Street
Active: 1784–1965
C/10 Page 210

Herefordshire Tavern
Location: Newport Street
See: Herefordshire House

Hero
Location: Bridge Place
Active: 1860s
W59 Page 112

Hickock's House
Location: unknown
Active: 1500s

Hole in the Wall
    Location: Merry Vale
    Active: 1820–1880
    C4/54 Page 372

Holly Bush
    Location: St Nicholas Street
    Active: 1730s–1986
    C2/12 Page 256

Holy Lamb
    Location: Cornmarket
    Active: 1760s- 1770s
    C2/27 Page 264

Hope & Anchor Inn
    Location: Newport Street
    See: Severn View Hotel

Hop Market Inn (and Hotel)
    Location: Hop Market
    Active: 1750s–1964
    C2/5 Page 251

Hop–Pole Inn and Royal Hotel
    Location: Foregate St.
    Active: 1700–1865
    C1/46 Page 235

Hoppers
    Location: Sansome Street
    See Toby's Tavern

Horn Tavern
    Location: Angel Street
    See: Horn and Trumpet

Horn and Trumpet
    Location: Angel Street
    Active: 1760–present
    C1/35 Page 228

Horn and Trumpet
    Location: Little Charles St
    Active: 1850–1915
    C3/71 Page 340

Horse and Groom
    Location: Sidbury
    See Cross Keys Sidbury

Horse and Jockey
    Location: Quay Street
    Active: 1780–1830s
    C4/31 Page 362

Horse and Jockey
    Location: Pump Street
    Active: 1785–1915
    C3/41 Page 317

Horse and Jockey
    Location: The Butts
    Active: 1850–1860
    C1/50 Page 240

Horseshoe Bar
    Location: Blackfriars
    Active:
    See Dive Bar

House at Home
    Location: High Timber
    (Severn) Street
    Active: 1850–1860
    C5/15 Page 390

Imperial (Hotel)
    Location: St Nicholas Street
    Active: 1760 –present
    C2/23 Page 261

Jolly Dragoon
    Location: 'St Andrews ward'
    C4/40 Page 370

Jolly Farmer
    Location: All Saints
    Active: 1760-84
    C4/51 Page 372

Jolly Sailor
    Location: 'St Andrews ward'

Jolly Sportsman
    Location: Tunnel Hill
    See: Royal George

Jolly Trowman
    Location: 'St Andrews ward'

Ketch
    Location: Bath Road
    Active: 1600–present
    E5 Page 164

Keystones
    Location: 1 Copenhagen
    Street
    Active: 1969–present
    See Mouth of the Nile

King's Arms
    Location: 'St Andrews ward'
    Active: 1766?
    C4/71 Page 377

King's Arms
    Location: Leach (Lich) st.
    Active: 1820–1830
    C3/26 Page 302

King Charles
    Location: New Street
    Active 2013–present
    C3/58 Page 330

King Charles II
    Location: Cornmarket
    Active: 1850s–present
    C2/36 Page 266

King David
    Location: Birdport
    Active: 1760s-1800
    C4/72 Page 377

Kings Head
    Location: High Street
    Active: 1750–1800
    C3/10 Page 294

King's Head
    Location: Sidbury
    Active: 1600–present
    C3/30 Page 305

King's Head
    Location: St. John's
    Active: 1790–1911
    W13 Page 81

King of Prussia
Location: Edgar Street/Frog
Lane)
Active: 1750 –1800
C5/9 Page 386

King's Retreat
Location:
See: Alma Diglis

William (III)
Location: Dolday
See: Sow and Pigs

King William (IV) Vaults
Location: (King Billy) St Pauls
Street/Foundry Street
Active: 1859–1971
C3/73 Page 341

Lakes
Location: 29 Ambleside Drive
Active: 1963–2013
E36 Page 195

Lamb
Location: Birdport
Active: 1790–1800
C4/48 Page 371

Lamb and Fleece
Location: Tything
See: Lamb and Flag

Lamb and Flag
Location: Tything
Active: 1780–present
N21 Page 131

Lame Dog
Location: Blockhouse Lock
Active: 1870–1950
C3/67 Page 338

Lamplighter
See: Garibaldi

Lamp Tavern
Location: Moor Street
Active: 1850–1899
N17 Page 125

Lamp Tavern
Location: Tybridge Street
Active: 1896 –1965
W36 Page 98

Lansdowne Inn
Location: Lansdowne Street
Active: 1900–present
N34 Page 141

Lansdowne (Hotel)
Location: Lowesmoor Place
Active: 1880s –1925
C2/55 Page 283

Laurence's Mug House
Location: St Andrews ward
Active: 1766– ?
C4/70 Page 377

Leather Dressers' Arms
Location: Birdport
Active: 1820s–1840s
C4/47 Page 371

Leopard (and Leopard Vaults)
Location: Broad Street
Active: 1720-1855
See Beauchamp

Lion
Location unclear: possibly
Cornmarket
Page 269

Little Sauce Factory
See: Fort Royal

Little Swan
Location: New Street
See Swan with Two Nicks

Live and Let Live
Location: Moor Street
Active: 1850s–1860s
N16 Page 124

Liverpool Vaults
Location: Shambles
Active: 1840–1959
C3/49 Page 323

Lloydies Bar
Location: The Tything
See: Coach and Horses)

Lloyds No1
Location: Broad Street
*See: Crown Inn (and Posting
House)*

Loch Ryan Hotel
Location: Sidbury
E8 Page 169

Locomotive Inn
Location: George Street
Active: 1900–1972
C3/80 Page 343

London Wine and Spirit Vaults
Location: Broad Street
Active: 1870–1912
C4/2 Page 347

**London Vaults (London Spirit
Vaults)**
Location: London Road
See Fort Royal Tavern

Long Sow Cutter
Location: St Nicholas Street
Active: 1820–1840?
C2/15 Page 259

Long Stop
Location: Broad Street
See: Arcadia

Lord Nelson
Location: Birdport
Active: 1822–1955
C4/51 Page 372

Lucky's
Location: Fort Royal
See: Fort Royal

Luna Bar
See: Swan with Two Nicks

Luna Restaurant
Location: High Street
C3/13 Page 296

Lyppard Grange
Location: The Lyppards
(Ankerage Green)
Active: c1990–present
E40 Page 199

Malt Shovel
Location: All Hallows
Active: 1870–1906
C4/57 Page 373

Manor Farm
Location: Lower Wick
Active: 1990–present
W28 Page 92

Maple Leaf
Location: 49 Canada Way
Active: 1970–present
W27 Page 91

Market Hall (and Market Hall Vaults)
Location: Shambles
Active: 1870– 1896
C3/46 Page 322

Market Fountain
Location: Shambles
See: Market Tavern

Market Tavern (also New Market Tavern)
Location: Shambles
Active: 1850–1908
C3/44 Page 319

Marquis of Granby
Location: 22 Cooken (ie Copenhagen) Street
Active: 1770–1800
C4/25 Page 360

Marquis Wellington
Location: 'St Andrews ward'
See Duke of Wellington

Marwood
Location: 40 Upper Tything
See Green Man

Masons Arms
Location: Carden Street
See: Freemasons Arms

Mason's Arms
Location: St Nicholas ward
Active:
C2/21 Page 259

Mason's Arms
Location: Frog Lane (Severn Street)
Active: 1750-1860
C5/13 Page 389

Maximilian's Bar
See Great Western

Mayflower
Location: Grenville Road
Active: 1960–2010
W7 Page 77

McBride's Mug House
Location: 'St Nicholas ward'
Active: 1784–?
C2/16 Page 259

Merry Fellow
Location: Copenhagen Street
Active: 1780–1800
C4/28 Page 361

Metro Bar
Location: 35 St Nicholas Street
See Imperial

Mitre
Location: probably Lich (originally Leach) Street
Active: 1660s–1860s
C3/27 Page 302

Mitre
Location: High Street
Active: 1664–1776
C4/33 Page 363

Mode (Tramps Nightclub)
Location: Angel Row
Active: c1994-present
C1/34 Page 226

Monroes Cellar Bar
Location: 43 Foregate Street
Active: 1980s–present
N3 Page 117

Moors Ketch
Location: The Moors
Active: 1850–1924
N13 Page 123

Mount Pleasant (Inn)
Location: London Road
Active: 1870–present
E11 Page 172

Mouth of the Nile
Location: Copenhagen Street
Active: 1820–1930
C4/21 Page 358

Ms Monroes
Location: 43 Foregate Street
Active: 1980s–present

Mug House
Location: Claines
Active: 1600-present
N51 Page 156

Mug House
Location: Friar Street.
See Eagle Vaults

Mug House
Location: 'St Peters ward'
Active: 1750s-1820s

Mug (or Mugg) House also Old Mug House
Location: Hylton Road
Active: 1760s–1912
W47 Page 108

Nag's Head
Location: Blockhouse
Active: 1900–1912
C3/68 Page 338

Navigation Inn
Location: Lowesmoor
Active: 1820–1869
C2/54 Page 283

Nelson
Location: 2 Merryvale (All Hallows)
See Lord Nelson

New Butchers Arms
Location: Shambles
See Butchers Arms

New Chequers (Inn)
Location: Astwood Road
Active: 1932–present
E32 Page 191

New Greyhound
Location: New Street
Active: 1810–1965
C3/53 Page 325

New Inn
Location: Bath Road
See: Ketch

New Inn
Location: George Street
Active: 1840–1974
C2/67 Page 289

New Inn
Location: Ombersley Road
Active: pre-1870–present
N43 Page 148

New Inn
Location: Shambles
Active: 1760s–1880
C3/45 Page 321

New Market Tavern (or Inn)
Location: Shambles
See: Market Tavern

New Pope Iron (Inn)
Location: Pope Iron Road

See: Winning Post

New Punchbowl
Location: Lich Street
Active: 1870s–1909
C3/22 Page 301

New Red Lion
Location: Newport Street
Active: 1850–1952
C1/7 Page 209

Northwick Arms
Location: Vine Street
Active: 1890–2010 (re-opened 2013)
N41 Page 148

Oak (also Old Oak)
Location: Friar Street
Active: 1840s to 1880s
C3/38 Page 314

Oak Apple
Location: London Road
Active: 1984–present
E13 Page 174

Oddfellows
Location: Lowesmoor
See: Brewery Tap

Odd Fellows Arms
Location: Fish Street
Active: 1840s–1860
C4/37 Page 366

Oddfellows Arms
Location: Carden Street
Active: 1870–1964
C3/63 Page 336

Old Apple Tree
Location: Tybridge Street
See Apple Tree

(Ye) Olde Chappelle
Location: New Street
Active: 1900–1970
C3/51 Page 324

Old Cock
Location: St Andrews ward
Active:
C4/29 Page 360

Old Clock Tavern
Location: See Fort Royal

Old Crown
Location: Friar Street
See: Crown

Old Crown
Location: Pump Street
See Crown

Old Dog and Duck
See: Dog and Duck

Old Dolphin
Location: Copenhagen St
See: Dolphin

Old England
Location: Little Angel Street
Active: 1850–1860
C1/29 Page 220

Old England
Location: Providence St
Active: 1870–1964
C3/70 Page 338

Old Ewe and Lamb
Location: 'St Nicholas ward'
See Ewe and Lamb

Old Falcon
Location: Sansome Street
Active: 1810–1967
C2/11 Page 254

Old Farrier's Arms
Location: Quay Street
Active: 1827-1964
C4/64 Page 375

Old Greyhound
Location: New Street
Active: 1764-present
C3/54 Page 326

Old Hen and Chickens
Location: Merry Vale
See Hen and Chickens

Old Holly Bush
Location: St Nicholas Street
See: Holly Bush

Old House at Home
Location: High Timber (Severn) Street
See: House at Home

Old Lamb and Fleece
Location:
See Lamb and Flag

Old Oak
    Location: Friar Street
    Active: 1840–1880
    C3/38 Page 314

Old Peacock
    Location: Queen Street
    See Peacock

Old Pheasant
    Location: New Street
    Active: 1787 to present
    C3/56 Page 327

Old Porter Stores
    Location: 15 Copenhagen St
    Active: 1820–c1955
    C4/24 Page 360

(Ye) Olde Punchbowl
    Location: College Street
    Active: 1790s–1958
    C3/21 Page 301

Old Rectifying House
    Location: N. Parade
    Active: 1870s to present
    Ref: C1/1   Page 202

Old Red Lion
    Location: Newport Street
    Active: 1850–1952
    See New Red Lion

Old Seven Stars
    Location: Quay Street
    Active: 1842– 1850s
    C4/39 Page 368

Old Severn Trow
    Location: Quay Street
    See: Severn Trow

Old Spot
    Location: Lowesmoor
    See: Turks Head

Old Swan
    Location: St Andrews ward
    See: Swan Powick(s) Lane

Old Talbot
    Location: Sidbury
    See: Talbot

Old Wherry
    Location: Quay Street
    See: Wherry

Old Yorkshire House
    Location: St Nicholas Street
    See: Imperial

O'Neills
    Location: 8 St Nicholas St
    Active: 1990–present
    C2/22 Page 260

Oscars
    Location: Foregate Street
    See: Dudfields

Oyster Bar
    Location: Angel Street
    Active: 1947-1959
    Page 230

Pack Horse (and Pack Horse Hotel)
    Location: St Nicholas Street
    (orig. Garden Market)
    Active: 1700 to present
    C2/13 Page 257

Painter's Arms
    Location:Powick Lane
    Active: 1820-30
    C4/16 Page 355

Park Street Tavern
    Location: 18 Little Park Street
    Active: 1850–1961
    E17 Page 177

Park Tavern
    Location: Park Place (Little Park St/Upper Park Street)

Active: 1870–1990
E10 Page 171

Parrot Inn
    Location: Broad Street
    Active: 1600s–1800
    C4/7 Page 351

Parrot
    Location: Friar Street
    Active: 1600s–1800
    C3/33 Page 311

Paul Pry
    Location: The Butts
    Active: 1850–present
    C1/51 Page 240

Pavilion in the Park
    Location: Tybridge Street
    Active: 2012–present
    W38 Page 100

Peacock
    Location: Trinity
    Active: 1760s–1912
    C2/25 Page 263

Peep o' Day
    Location: 23 Cumberland St
    Active: 1870–1968
    N35 Page 142

Perdiswell House Hotel
    Location: 40 Droitwich Road
    Active: 1950s to present
    N49 Page 155

Perseverance
    Location: St Georges Lane North
    Active: 1900–1930
    N36 Page 142

Pewterer's Arms
    Location: Merrivale
    Active: 1892–1930
    C4/52 Page 372

Pheasant
    Location: Pheasant Street
    Active: 1853– c1880
    C2/57 Page 284

Pheasant
    Location: New Street
    See Old Pheasant

Pheasant
Location: Quay Street
Active: 1820–1840

Pheasant
Location: Silver Street
Active: 1760-1780s
C2/34 Page 265

Piaf's
Location: Mealcheapen Street
See: Shades

Pig'n'Drum
Location: 53 Lowesmoor
See: Alma

Plaisterer's Arms
Location: Doldy (now Dolday)
Active: 1810 –1850
C1/17 Page 215

Pleasure Boat
Location: Hinton Lane (Hylton Road)
Active: 1760
W51 Page 109

Plough
Location: Fish Street
Active: 1820–present
C4/38 Page 366

Plough
Location: New Street
Active: 1750–1798
C3/55 Page 327

Plough
Location: Silver Street
Active: 1873–1971
C2/40 Page 272

Plumber's (also Plummers) Arms
Location: Friar st.
See: Eagle Vaults

Plumbers Arms
Location: Wylds Lane
Active: 1870–present
E15 Page 174

Plume of Feathers
Location: (cathedral)
Active: 1600–1700
C5/1 Page 380

Plume of Feathers
Location: Copenhagen St
Active: 1820–1910
C4/30 Page 361

Plume of Feathers
Location: Sansom(e) St
Active: 1780–1800
C2/9 Page 254

Plume of Feathers
Location: The Tything
See: Cap'n'Gown

Poachers Pocket
Location: Berkeley Way
See: Barn Owl

Pope Iron
Location: Waterworks Road
Active: 1750s–1870
N39 Page 145

Pope Iron
Location: Iron Road
See Winning Post

Pope's Head
Location: 'St Andrews ward'
Active: 1770-1800?
C4/72 Page 378

Porcelain Work(er)s' Inn
Location: Severn Street
Active: 1873–1900
C5/14 Page 390

Porter Stores
Location: Copenhagen Street
See Old Porter Stores

Porter Stores
Location: London Road
Active: 1870–1880
See Fort Royal

Porto Bello
Location: Henwick
Active: 1790–1860
W41 Page 103

Porto Bello (Portobello)
Location: Bransford Road
Active: 1820–present
W23 Page 86

The Queen's Head stood on the north side at the top of Salt Lane (Castle Street) was owned by The Corporation of Worcester from 1876–77 and was lost in the widening of Castle Street in 1880. The census of 1851 lists then licensee James Davies described as 'innkeeper 38 as living here with his wife Charlotte 45. See page 118

Postal Order
Location: 18 Foregate Street
Active: 1997 to present
N2 Page 116

Potters Arms
Location: St Paul's Street
Active: 1870–1959
C3/78 Page 343

Potters Wheel
Location: Severn Street
See: Fountain

Press
Location: Allhallows
Active: 1850–1860
C4/56 Page 372

Prince Blucher
Location: Birdport
Active: 1815–1830
C4/44 Page 370

Prince Regent
Location: Birdport (also listed as Dolday)
Active: 1811–1830
C4/44 Page 371

Prince of Wales
Location: The Moors
Active: 1898–1939
N12 Page 123

Prince of Wales
Location: Newport Street
Active: 1870–1893
C1/6 Page 209

Prince of Wales
Location: Shrub Hill
Active: 1850–1963
E26 Page 185

Prince of Wales
Location: Windermere Drive
Active: 1963–present
E37 Page 196

Prince's Arms
Location: Cornmarket
Active: 1500s-1750
C2/37 Page 269

Punch Bowl
Location: College st.
Active: 1790s–1958
C3/21 Page 301

Punchbowl
Location: Lichfield Avenue
Active: 1958 to present
E29 Page 188

Queen Caroline
Location: Quay Street
Active: 1820 1894
C4/59 Page 374

Queen Elizabeth
Location: Henwick
(see Wheatsheaf)

Queen's Arms
Location: The Park
Active: 1850–1860
C3/3 Page 294

Queen's Arms
Location: Powick Lane
Active: 1840–1959
C4/17 Page 355

Queens Head
Location: High Street
Active: 1700–1800
C1/45 Page 234

Queen's Head
Location: Tything
Active: 1790–1877
N6 Page 118

Quiet Woman
Location: Birdport
Active: 1790
C4/52 Page 372

Railway (Railway Arms Railway Tavern also Railway Hotel)
Location: Shrub Hill

Active: 1850–1964
E25 Page 184

Railway
Location: Westbury Street
See Rainbow

Railway Bell
Location: Clap Gate (St Martin's Gate)
Active: 1850s–1912
C2/41 Page 272

Railway Express
Location: Pheasant Street/St Martins Gate
Active: 1850s
C2/68 Page 290

Railway Refreshment Rooms– Up and Down Platforms
Location: Shrub Hill Station
E27 Page 186

Rainbow
Location: Rainbow Hill (Westbury Street)
Active: 1859–1891
C2/62 Page 286

Ram (Tavern)
Location: Regent Street (Shrub Hill)
Active: 1843–1935
E23 Page 182

Raven (and Raven Inn)
Location: Droitwich Road
Active: 1820–present
N50 Page 156

Rectifying House
Location: North Quay
See Old Rec House

Red Cow
Location: Birdport
Active: 1870–1900
C4/40 Page 368

Red Lion (also 'Lyon')
Location: Sidbury
Active: 1760 to 1990
E6 Page 167

Red Lion Tybridge Street
Active: 1670–1730
W56 Page 110

Red Lion
 Location: Newport Street
 See: Old Red Lion

Reindeer ('Rein–deer' also Reined Deer Reign Deer and Reindeere) Inn
 Location: Mealcheapen St
 Active: 1673–1987
 C3/60 Page 333

Ring o'Bells
 Location: (listed as St Peter's 1703)
 Active: 1703–1750
 C5/11 Page 387

Rising Sun
 Location: Cripplegate
 Active: 1780–1865
 W35 Page 98

Rising Sun
 Location: Powick's Lane (later Bank Street)
 Active: 1790s to 1930s
 C4/13 Page 354

Rodney
 Location: 14 Cornmarket
 See: Royal Exchange

Roebuck
 Location: St Paul's Street
 Active: 1872 –1886
 C3/76 Page 340

Roman Indian
 Location: Henwick
 See: Wheatsheaf

Rose and Crown
 Location: Foregate Street
 Active: 1660–1780
 C1/44 Page 234

Rose and Crown
 Location: Easy Row
 Active: 1850–1913
 N10 Page 122

Rose and Crown
 Location: Sidbury
 Active: 1850–1860
 C5/7 Page 385

Rose and Jossamine
 Location: 'St Clement ward'
 Active: 1760s
 W52 Page 109

Round of Beef
 Location: The Tything
 Active: poss 1880s
 N25 Page 136

Rovers Arms
 Location: Little Charles Street
 Active: 1872-1906
 C3/72 Page 340

Royal Exchange (Wine and Spirit) Vaults
 Location: 13 Corn Market/ Mealcheapen Street
 Active: 1870–present
 C2/37 Page 267

Royal George
 Location: Tybridge Road (originally Old Bridge Street also Torcae Street also Turkey)
 Active: 1767–1939)
 W57 Page 111

Royal George
 Location: Tunnel Hill Road
 Active: 1930–1990
 E35 Page 194

Royal Oak
 Location: Bransford Road
 Active: 1820–1885
 W16 Page 82

Royal Oak
 Location: Carden Street
 Active: 1827-1937
 C3/65 Page 338

Royal Oak
 Location: Dolday
 See: Spread Eagle

Royal Oak (1)
 Location: 'St Martins ward'
 Active: 1760s
 C3/8 Page 294

Royal Oak (2)
 Location: 'St Martins ward'
 Active: 1760s
 C3/8 Page 294

Royal Oak
 Location: York Place
 Active: 1850–1962
 N29 Page 136

Salmon's Leap
 Location: Severn Street
 See: Fountain

Salt Scales
 Location: 'St Andrews ward'
 Active: 1760s
 C4/67 Page 377

Salutation
 Location: St Johns
 Active: 1700–1750
 W12 Page 80

Sandpits (and Sand Pits)
 Location: Bromyard Road
 See The Bedwardine

St George's Tavern
 Location: St George's Lane
 Active: 1910-1968
 N37 Page 143

Saracen's Head
 Location: Tything
 Active: poss.1500s–present
 N18 Page 125

Sawyer's
    Location: Hylton Road
    Active: 1987-1992
    See Bear

Sebright (also Seabright) Arms
    Location: London Road
    Active: 1840–2011
    E12 Page 173

Sedan Chair
    Location: 'St Martins ward'
    Active: c1760s
    C3/6 Page 294

Seven Stars
    Location: Palace Street (also Quay Street)
    Active: 1700–1860
    C4/39 Page 368

Seven Stars
    Location: New Street
    Active: 1790–1800
    C3/50 Page 324

Severn Galley
    Location: Newport Street
    Active: 1760–1800
    Ref: C1/4 Page 208

Severn Swan
    Location: South Parade
    Active: 1860–1880
    C4/61 Page 374

Severn Trow
    Location: Hylton Road (Street).
    Active: 1790–1850
    W44 Page 105

Severn Trow
    Location: Quay Street
    Active: 1840–1930
    C4/60 Page 374

Severn View Hotel
    Location: Newport Street
    Active: 1832-present
    Ref: C1/2 Page 207

Shades (Tavern)
    Location: Mealcheapen Street (Frog Lane)
    Active: 1820–1970
    C2/39 Page 269

Shades
    Location: Diglis (or Severn) Street
    Active: 1840–1905
    C5/17 Page 391

Shamus O'Donnell's
    Location:
    See White Hart

Shakespeare (Shakespear)
    Location: Angel Street
    Active: 1780–present
    C1/40 Page 232

Ship (fhip)
    Location: Cooken (later Copenhagen) Street
    Active: 1780–1908
    C4/26 Page 360

Ship
    Location: Canalside Lowesmoor
    Active: 1850–1860
    C2/64 Page 288

Shoemakers Arms
    Location: All Saints
    Active:
    C4/65 Page 377

Shrub Hill Station Railway Refreshment Rooms 'Up' and 'Down' platforms
    Location:
    Active: 1850–1960s
    E27 Page 186

Slug'n'Lettuce
    Location: 12 Cornmarket
    See: King Charles II

Slug'n'Lettuce
    Location: The Cross former St Nicholas Church)
    Active: 2004–present
    C2/4 Page 250

Silver Grayling
    Location: Powick Lane
    Active: 1850–1860
    C4/15 Page 355

Smoke Stack
    Location:
    (see Swan St Johns)

Sow and Pigs
    Location: Doldy
    Active: 1784-1909
    C1/13 Page 213

Spread Eagle
    Location: Dolday
    Active: 1780–1800s
    C1/20 Page 215

Spread Eagle
    Location: Pheasant Street
    See: Eagle

Stag
    Location:
    Active: 1500-1600s
    C3/4 Page 294

Star
    Location: Bransford Road
    Active: 1820–1990
    W15 Page 82

Star
    Location: Newport Street
    Active: 1780–90
    C1/8 Page 210

Star
    Location: Swenchard (Swinesherd?)
    Active: unknown
    E14 Page 174

Stag
    Location: possibly Cornmarket
    Active 1660s
    C2/38 Page 269

Star Bar
    Location: Foregate Street
    See: Star and Garter Hotel

Star & Garter Hotel
 Location: Foregate Street
 (and Star Bar)
 Active: 1740–present
 C1/47 Page 236

Star Vaults or Tap (Star Hotel Tap)
 Location: Farrier Street
 Active: 1840–1959
 C1/54 Page 243

Stationers Arms
 Location: High Street
 Active: 1870– 1910
 C4/33 Page 364

Steam Packet Tavern
 Location:
 See: Severn View Hotel

Sun and Bull ('fun & bull'– 1792)
 Location: Bull Entry
 See Bull and Sun

Sun Beer House
 Location: Lowesmoor Terrace
 C2/59 Page 285

Sun Tavern
 Location: 'St Martins ward'
 Active: 1830s-1850s
 C2/59 Page 285

Swan
 Location: Barbourne
 Active: 1850–present
 N38 Page 144

Swan
 Location: (104) High Street
 Active: 1896-1964
 C4/34 Page 364

Swan
 Location: High Street (below Russell and Dorrells)
 Active: 1965-1969
 C3/16 Page 298

Swan
 Location: Lowesmoor
 Active: 1827–1920
 C2/53 Page 282

Swan (Swan with Two Necks/ Nicks)
 Location: New Street
 Active: 1760–present
 C3/57 Page 329

Swan
 Location: Newport Street
 Active: 1770-80

Swan
 Location: Powick('s) Lane
 Active: 1790–1800
 C4/12 Page 354

Swan
 Location: Pump Street
 Active: 1870 to 1965
 C3/43 Page 318

Swan
 Location: St Johns
 Active: 1750–1990
 W14 Page 81

Swan
 Location: 'St Peters ward'
 Active: 1760s–1820s

Swan and Falcon
 Location: Friar Street
 See; Cardinals Hat

Talbot
 Location: The Cross
 Active: 1740–1850
 C2/2 Page 248

Talbot (and {Ye} Old Talbot)
 Location: Sidbury
 Active: poss pre-1400s to present
 C3/29 Page 303

Talbot
 Location: Tything
 Active: 1750–present
 N30 Page 137

Tap and Spile
 See: Imperial

Telegraph (Tavern)
 Location: George Street
 Active: 1850–1922
 C2/66 Page 287

Ten Bells
 Location: Doldy
 Active: 1830–1928
 C1/14 Page 213

Thistle Vaults
 Location: Charles (and Foundry) Street
 See: Four Ways Inn

Three Blackbirds
 Location: Tything
 Active: 1840–1870
 N26 Page 136

Three Cranes
 Location: Lich Street
 Active: 1601–1700
 C3/17 Page 300

Three Cranes
 Location: High Street
 Active: 1500-1600s
 C3/18 Page 300

Three Crosses
 Location: Friar Street
 Active: 1500s – 1600s
 C3/18 Page 300

Three Crowns
 Location: High Street (or Cornmarket)
 See Bellman

Three Cuxxes
 See Three Crosses

Three Pyes
 Location: Lich Street
 Active: 1601–1700
 C3/19 Page 301

Three Tuns
Location: St Nicholas ward
Active: c1810–1830?
C2/19 Page 259

Three Tuns (and Hotel) also Tunns
Location: Salt Lane (Castle Street)
Active: 1820–1958
N7 Page 120

Timberdine (also Harvester)
Location:
Active: 1986–present
E4 Page 164

Toad and Tulip
Location: Lowesmoor
See: Alma

Toby Carvery
Location: Bath Road
See: Ketch

Toby's Tavern
Location:
Active: 1990–2007
C2/8 Page 253

Top Hat
Location: Cornmarket
See: Eagle Vaults

Travellers Inn
Location: New Street
Active: 1820–1830
C3/52 Page 325

Trinity Inn
Location:
Active: 1700–1800

Tubs
Location: Cornmarket
See: King Charles II

Turks Head
Location: Lowesmoor
C2/51 Page 280

Unicorn
Location: Dolday
Active: 1760s
C1/22 Page 216

Unicorn
Location: Mill Street
Active: 1873–1908
C5/21 Page 394

Unicorn Inn (and Hotel)
Location: Broad Street
Active: 1760s-1930s
C4/5 Page 349

Union (Inn Tavern)
Location: Lowesmoor
Active: 1810–1971
C2/42 Page 272

Union
Location: Union (or Carden) Street
Active: 1820–1904
C3/62 Page 336

Vaults
Location: 12 Cornmarket
Location: Active:
See King Charles II

Vaults
Location: 1 Little Angel Street
See: Angel Vaults

Vaults
Location: 51 New Street
See: (Ye) Olde Chappelle

Vauxhall
Location: Astwood Road
Active: 1870–2005
E30 Page 189

Victoria
Location: (back of 85 High Street)
Active: 1900–1912
C4/42 Page 369

Vine
Location: Ombersley Road
Active: 1870–present
N42 Page 147

Vintorne
Location: Broad Street
Active: 1670–1720
C4/8 Page 351

'The Timberdine looks as though it should have been home to some wicked highway robber and could tell some tales of dastardly deeds and bodice-ripping lust and romance, Sadly it doesn't!' See page 164

(Ye) Virgin (and Virgin's Tavern)
Location: Tolladine Road
Active: 1840–present
E34 Page 193

Volunteer
Location: Friar Street
See: Eagle Vaults

Vulcan
Location: St Paul's (and Wellington) Street
Active: 1900–1973
C3/77 Page 342

Waggon (or Wagon) & Horses
Location: Angel Street
Active: 1790–1850
C1/36 Page 228

Washington (Washington Arms)
Location: Washington Street
Active: 1900–2002
N24 Page 133

Waterloo (Waterloo Tavern)
Location: Waterloo Street
Active: 1820–1962
C3/75 Page 341

Welcome Inn
Location: Wylds Lane
See: Garibaldi

Well Sinkers Arms
Location: All Saints ward
Active: 1850s-1870s
C4/76 Page 378

Western Bar
Location: Foregate Street
See: Dudfields

West Midland Arms
Location: Lowesmoor Place
Active: 1860s–present
C2/63 Page 287

Wheat Sheaf
Location: Sidbury
Active: 1780s–1860s

Wheat Sheaf
Location: Corn Market
Active: 1790–1840s
C2/29 Page 265

Wheat Sheaf
Location: Henwick
Active: 1780–present
W43 Page 104

Wheelwrights Arms
Location: Hylton Road (also Bay Horse)
Active: 1872–1922
W55 Page 110

Wherry
Location: Quay Street
Active: 1820–1905
C4/32 Page 362

Whey Tavern
Location: Lansdowne Road/ Flagge Meadow Walk
Active 1820s–40s
N32 Page 140

White Hall
Location: Bransford Road (Rushwick)
Active: 1840–present
W24 Page 88

White Hart
Location: College St.
Active: 1700s–present
C5/2 Page 381

White Horse
Location: Cripplegate
Active: 1780–1810
W32 Page 96

White Horse (Inn)
Location: Silver St.
Active: 1766–1880
C2/30 Page 265

Whitehouse
Location: Foregate Street
Active:
See Star Hotel

White Lion (Lyon)
Location: Cornmarket
Active: 1760s–1770s?
C2/28 Page 264

White Lion
Location: Lowesmoor Close
Active: 1842–1870s
C2/49 Page 279

White Swan(n)
Location: Powick Lane
Active: 1810-1830s
Ref: C4/12 Page 354

Wine and Brandy Vaults
Location: Copenhagen
Street
See: Old Porter Stores

Wine Vaults (also London Vaults)
Location: Bridge Street
See: London Wine and Spirit Vaults

Winning Post
Location: Pope Iron Road
Active: 1873–present
N40 Page 146

Woo Bar
Location: St Nicholas Street
See Imperial

Woodman
Location: Dolday
Active: 1850–1860
C1/16 Page 215

Wool Pack
Location: Birdport
See: Woolpack, Dolday

Wool Pack
Location: Dolday (Doldy)
Active: 1810–1968
C1/15 Page 214

Woolpack
Location: Friar Street
Active: 1500s
C3/35 Page 313

Wrens Nest
Location: Henwick Road
Active:1890s-1910?
W30 Page 94

Yates Wine Lodge
Location: Mealcheapen
Street
See: Reindeer

Ye Olde Chappell
Location: New Street
Active:
See Old Chapel

Ye Olde Punch Bowl
Location: Lich Street
Active:
See Punchbowl

Ye Virgin
Location: Tolladine Road
See Virgin

York House
Location: Moor Street
Active: 1830s–1965
N14 Page 124

Yorkshire House
Location: St Nicholas Street
See: Imperial

Young's Mug House
Location: Friar Street
See: Eagle Vaults

32 Club
Location:
See Turks Head

18: A tribute to all those I

Weird as it may sound, there are clear parallels with writing a book and going to the pub...

Both can be a hugely satisfying experience or ultimately a sad let-down: both call on all the senses demanding you keep your wits about you – or else; both can take over your life if you allow them to; both leave you thinking 'crikey, have I done the right thing here *(to which, in almost every case the answer is a resounding 'too bloody right it is');* both leave you losing all sense of time; both can leave you feeling woozy, dizzy and blurry-eyed unless you're careful; both can leave you either desperately down and bruised or with a fabulous sense of exhilaration once you're done, blinking in the sunshine and looking back on the experience; and both bring you into contact with some amazing people that leave you a) wondering why you hadn't started earlier and b) thirsting to do it all over again.

Another similarity, of course, is that both can be undertaken on a solo basis or in the company of others. Akin to many a drinking session, this one started off by venturing into some largely unknown territory alone but confident in the knowledge that experience and a certain street-savvy would see me through. Then, someone sidled over and said 'hi, what's you up to?". Then another and another and before I knew it, there was a party going on.

And that's exactly what happened here... what had started off as a solo affair from which I'd have tottered-off home pretty much fulfilled and essentially OK but maybe lacking a certain *(as they say round yur)* 'summat', was made infinitely more colourful and pleasurable with some good company – and as company goes, this has been some of the best: people who know more about their subject than I ever will, and without whom this book, like the drinking session (oh, alright then, glorious bender) I'm comparing it to would have been a very different proposition.

Thus, it's only fitting that I record and pay tribute to those that have kept me company – spiritually, if not physically – on this particularly pleasurable journey.

Without them, this book would bear a strong comparison to that saddest of all sad sights, an empty bar.

It's no coincidence that this section starts and ends with the Worcestershire Record Office – now, of course, housed in that most controversial of buildings The Hive in Worcester. While it was under

pestered!

construction, I compared it to three Crunchie bars that had had all the chocolate licked off, and even made a completely illicit video *(I tacked on to a private viewing by the mayor of Worcester – but in true journalist fashion, I was first to get a sneaky peek of the inside!)* of the newly-constructed shell, then of course, devoid of books or people. Whether you're from Worcester and visit the Hive daily or if you're from elsewhere and are wondering what all the fuss was about, a look here will perhaps fill in some of the gaps:

http://www.youtube.com/watch?v=axoKxB1IGD0

Now it's alive with people and tangible 'things', it's here I came into contact with some amazing folk. There's the day-to-day staff, of course – for the most part, just sound and very knowledgeable, happy to welcome you into their world of facts and figures and maps and books and documents and microfilm and photographs and paper and boxes and... well, for want of a better word, order (of which more later). Other words come strongly to mind too: efficient, helpful, keen, everywhere, friendly and *(assuming it's a word which somehow I'm not sure it is)* unruffleable: I know, I tried!

First to join the party – well, to be more precise, I joined theirs because, to call up an old drinking phrase much used my longest-standing drinking mate Billy Parish, they were 'in the chair' first. Ie: they were volunteering to get the first round in – were Messrs Pigot, Lewis, Hunt, Billings, Grundy, Kelly and Littlebury whose Worcester directories go all the way back to 1795.

Without them I'd have been left standing at the starting post.

At least, now the party had started and was starting to perk up no end! One by one we were joined by others every one of whom brought something new to what was shaping up as a monster session... Seeing as the 'conversation' exclusively centred on the Faithful City, it was only fitting two ex-mayors joined our merry throng...

'Rambler' John Noake (1816-94)

...had been a journalist with the local press (now there's a coincidence! It's often said the journalists prefer the company of other journalists and I must confess I did find this man's contributions particularly illuminating). His works are, by general consensus the starting point for any work looking back at any aspect of Worcester and this is the man who started off what I trust I am continuing – picking up the ball and running with it, as the modern idiom has it – by conducting research into Worcester's rich heritage of pubs. Seems we have more than another thing in common too: as he said as far back as 1877: '...sorry I am that the fragments of the history of this institution of Worcester are so scanty as to afford little beyond a dry list of names. But slight as this is, I deemed it worth preservation in the hope that some friendly correspondents might be enabled to throw further light upon the ancient Vigornian victualling fraternity'.

And as I responded earlier, 'enter this friendly correspondent and fully-paid up member of the ancient Vigornian victualling fraternity'!

Tired of the world of hackery (it happened then and it happens still) he put up for election to the City Council and was returned to represent Claines in 1875. Four years later, he was mayor. I think I'd have liked this man. A lot.

Hubert Leicester

Stepping into his shoes (and chain of office) was Hubert Leicester. He and Edward Elgar were, apparently, great mates... One of the leading Catholics of the Midlands, Alderman Leicester' had been mayor on five occasions, and in 1932 was made a Freeman of the city. His first year of Mayoralty was in 1904, a Three Choirs Festival year, when it was felt there was a peculiar fitness in the election of a man of his musical tastes and acquirements. He retained the office in 1905, and in 1913 he again accepted the office and remained mayor for three years. In recognition of his exemplary service to the City, the Corporation and magistrates presented Alderman Leicester with a portrait of himself to be hung in the Guildhall – not least for his support and leadership of large-scale slum-clearance in Worcester. He was a life-long friend of Worcester's most famous son Sir Edward Eigar – they'd been schoolmates and when the Alderman completed fifty years as choirmaster at Worcester Catholic Church, Sir Edward made a point of being present at the commemoration ceremony.

From the time of its formation, he was treasurer of the Festival Choral Society and several of his noted works on the City's history - notably 'Forgotten Worcester' and 'Worcester Remembered' – are extensively quoted throughout this book.

Bill Gwilliam

He'd been a printer, an engineer, a teacher and a university lecturer and his **'Old Worcester People and Places'** (Halfshire Books ISBN 0-9513525-8-x) could still be regarded as the major modern work on Worcester. A passionate and meticulous historian who made even the crustiest of events seem like a party, he was founder of the Worcester Industrial Archaeological and Local History Society and he too shared an interest in local pubs. His work in relation to this particular subject is unpublished, but I've seen his notes and have drawn from them extensively throughout my research – with due reference where extracts emerge here. Mind, it's a reciprocal thing as he 'lifted' some of my stories, photographs and passages from articles and not least Bob Backenforth reviews, and humbled I am that he should have chosen to have done so. I'd like to think that he'd have loved to have been even closer associated with this work: after all, he was in at the conception if not the actual birth. It's with affection that I recall a particular session – Bill was no boozer so it didn't quite qualify as a full-scale 'crawl' though it came mighty close – in 1986

When the City was home to more pubs php* than anywhere else

A few of the City's 100-year survivors: Brunswick Arms; Grosvenor; King Charles, Swan with Two Nicks and Pheasant; Eagle Vaults; Pack Horse (now The Courtyard)

City's 480 pubs
(now there's 50 - and dwindling)

100-year survivors

In the thirty five years from 1930 to 1965 the City Centre lost 49 of its favourite inns.

The casualty list includes two Royal Oaks, two Crowns and a Crown and Anchor and two Carpenters Arms

The full list reads...

Angel (Sidbury), Apple Tree (Tybridge Street), Beauchamp (Broad Street), Bird in Hand (Cross), Black Lion (Dent Street), Boat (Lowesmoor), Brewers Arms, (Broad Street), Bridge (Lowesmoor), Bulls Head (High Street), Butchers Arms (Shambles), Carpenters Arms (Spring Gardens), City Arms (Church Street), Coach and Horses (Shambles), Cock and Magpies (Pheasant Street), Cock (Copenhagen Street), Croft (James Street), Cross Keys (London Road), Crown and Anchor (Silver Street), Crown (Friar Street), Crown (Tallow Hill), Crowle House (Lower Street), Express (Bransford Road), Farriers Arms (Farrier Street), Freemasons (Carden Street), Green Dragon (Newport Street), Lame Dog (Canalside), Liverpool Vaults (Shambles), Moors Ketch (Moors); Nelson (All Hallows), Oddfellows Arms (Carden Street), Old England (Providence Street), Old Farriers (Quay Street), Old Peter Stores (Copenhagen Street. Old Red Lion (Newport Street), Old Severn Trow (Quay Street), Park Street Tavern (Park Street), Potters Arms (James Street), Prince of Wales (Shrub Hill Road), Queens Arms (Powick Lane), Ram (Shrub Hill), Railway Arms (Shrub Hill), Swan (High Street), Royal Oak (Carden Street), Royal Oak (York Place), Royal George (Hylton Road), Turks Head (Lowesmoor), Waterloo, Punch Bowl (College Street)

* per head of population

Off the rails

The coming of the railway to Worcester played a key part in the growth of pubs around Shrub Hill where travellers would welcome a pint or two of foaming Worcester ale without having to travel too far back to the station for the return trip home.

As a result, eight pubs with a railway theme appeared in the immediate area almost overnight and within at most 200 yards of each other. They were Railway Arms, Great Western, Midland Hotel, Great Western Vaults, West Midlands, Express, Railway Bell and The Locomotive. None exist today.

Historian Bill Gwilliam spent much of his time tracing the history of 480 Worcester pubs from 1860 up the mid 1980s

One-time university lecturer Bill, who published several works on the history of the City until he passed on to that great hostelry in the sky in 2002 aged 90, told me the research had taken him years and years and that he really enjoyed the – hic – crucial research involved!

"Pubs were the principal social aspect of the City. It's a great, great pity that so many of them have just vanished off the face of the earth" is a comment he made when he and I did a tour of several of his favourite pubs one spring day in 1985.

"The history of pubs in Worcester reads like the history of Worcester itself" he said.

He reckoned that up to 1948, the City had hardly changed since the eighteenth century and the pubs in existence even then reflected the City's changing fortunes.

"The rot really set in when the pubs became the great casualties of the Rape of Worcester and the slum clearance programme of the late 1950s – early 1960s.

He recalled an old Worcester saying that every other house in Worcester had been a pub at some stage and that it was almost true – especially around Friar Street and New Street.

In 1910 - precisely a century ago – the City was home to 158 pubs – in stark contrast to the current Yellow Pages that lists just 50 pubs at least six of which have since closed but also includes many built since the war on estates like Dines, Green, Ronkswood and Warndon and 'fun pubs' like The Postal Order.

The following two pages lists them all - and no doubt Bill would approve that among the survivors a hundred years on, there's still some recognisable names.

Fun on the Station Run

Up to the 1930s a great test of many a young man's virility was the famous Cross to Shrub Hill run...

It was said that if you could drink half a pint in every pub you passed and still read the timetable, then you were indeed one of the lads.

Today you could perform that feat by car and still be within the drink drive limit... The course started with the Hollybush in St Nicholas Street, then the Pack Horse, Dog and Duck, Imperial, Old Yorkshire House, Old Falcon, Union, Crown & Anchor, Boat, Black Horse, Alma, Express, Turk's Head, Swan, Navigation, Lamadowne, West Midland Arms, then on to the station with the Great Western, Midlands Arms, Prince of Wales, and finally, the Ram. A run of 21 pubs.

Naturally enough, Bill had his favourites among the historic old pubs that once graced the City in vast numbers –The Farriers Arms in Fish Street and the Old Talbot in Sidbury ranking among his favourites.

The Old Talbot was the City's great Jacobean headquarters where drinkers would secretly toast Bonnie Prince Charlie with their wine held over a glass of water 'to the King across the water'. Another Talbot toast was the Toast of Damnation where Jacobeans pledged to restore Charles to the Throne would raise a glass to the hated Hanoverian King George with the left hand as a gesture of derision.

The Paul Pry was another of Bill's favourites – particularly the amazing Edwardian ceramic tile work throughout the pub. He also rated the 'beautiful' sandblasted windows of the long-gone Beehive in Tallow Hill and the Star Hotel in Foregate Street, formerly the Star and Garter and now Whitehouse Hotel. It was famous all over the country as a coaching house and it was here that two famous old coaches, the Hirondelle and the Hibernia met during their historic race from Liverpool to Cheltenham in 1832 - clocking up 136 miles in 9 hours and 33 minutes including stops...

Bill also loved the now very-much altered Green Man in the Tything for its historical importance: formerly the Green Man and Still which was the meeting place of the

The Worcester Classified Directory for 1910 lists 158 working pubs in the City and the next page shows how they proliferated in and around the City centre.

But while they indicate a significant casualty list, they also indicate how pubs are natural survivors – with 49 still alive and kicking. The elite list, still operating though not necessarily under the same names are: Albion, Alma (Droitwich Road), Anchor, Bell (St Johns), Berkeley Arms, Berwick Arms, Bridge (Lowesmoor), Brunswick, Chestnut Tree, Coach and Horses, Diglis House, Eagle Vaults, Farriers Arms (Fish Street), Five Ways, Garibaldi (Bromyard Road), George and Dragon, Green Man, Grosvenor, Herefordshire House, Horn and Trumpet, Kings Head, Hatch, Lamb and Flag, New Inn (Ombersley Road), New Pope Iron, Northwick Arms, Old Greyhound, Old Rectifying House, Pack Horse, Pheasant, Plough (Deansway – then Fish Street), Plumbers Arms (Plume of) Feathers (now Cap'n Gown), Portobello, Raven, Royal Exchange, Sandpits (now the Bedwardine), Saracens Head, Sebright Arms, Swan (Barbourne), Swan with Two Nicks, Talbot (Barbourne and College Street) Vaults, West Midland Arms, Wheatsheaf, White Hart and Virgin (now temporarily closed because of fire)

Next page - all the pubs from 1910

At the commercial heart

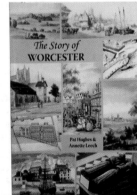

As the commercial heart of the City, the Cornmarket was the terminal for the carriers taking their passengers to and from outlying villages. As a result, pubs grew in abundance in the area, consequently assuming an agricultural theme as farmers and growers from all over the county converged o the City to sell their produce. With the Royal Exchange the centre of corn bartering, pubs in the immediate area assumed a partisan stance almost as extensions of the villages from which many of their customers came from.

Favourites in the area were The King Charles, Fleece, George (Silver Street), Wheatsheaf, Reindeer, New Greyhound, Old Greyhound, Plough, Shades, Queens Head, Old Pheasant, Swan with two Nicks, Royal Exchange and Railway Bell. And not more than 50 yards separating them all.

Bill Gwilliam in 1985

---

when he and I visited half a dozen pubs in pursuit of a feature I subsequently wrote on the subject. In each, and bearing in mind that these were for the most part my 'regulars', Bill told me some fascinating things about each one that I never knew before. A great man and a huge influence on all who came into contact with him. Me included.

Dr. Pat Hughes

I also interviewed Pat Hughes over the years and her recent (2011) book in association with Annette Leach **'The Story of Worcester'** (Logaston Press, ISBN 978-1-906663-567-5) is a towering work of reference on the origins of this fascinating and undeniably great City – made all the more fascinating and undeniably great through her deep and always reliable research. Again, I have drawn extensively on her work throughout, and when we chatted recently in The Hive *(where else?)* she was happy to allow me to use any part of her past work. As you will have no doubt seen and guessed by now, I dipped so freely, the words 'kid' and 'sweetshop' come firmly to mind. I'm in awe of what she's achieved and will ever remain grateful for her rich legacy of work and her readiness to share it with others

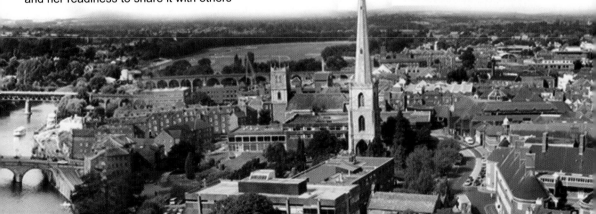

Derick Stephens

It was a chance introduction over photographs that I became re-acquainted with the name Derick Stephens whose work also plays a key part in the preparation of this work. Derick had been born and raised in Worcester and like many who grew up knee-deep in its history, he too fell under its spell and embarked on a lifelong mission to find out more – his approach benefitting greatly by being from the stance of 'passionate amateur' as opposed to the essentially academic starting-points of Bill Gwilliam and Pat Hughes. As such, his contribution is all the more powerful for being very hands-on and 'feet on the ground'. Derick's family owned a thriving local iron foundry within the city and if you look closely enough you'll still see the Stephens name on some of the city's drainage gratings. Like many growing up in Worcester – and as has been referred to several times throughout – the local pub scene and its history held a particular fascination for him and he started researching the rich heritage of inns, pubs, taverns and ale-houses as part of a wider research project into the general history of Worcester, an element made all the easier as in later life he worked out his pre-retirement years at the Guildhall where one of his many legacies was the editorial content for some of the pamphlets still used to guide visitors around this testament to so much of the City's past. His invaluable contribution to **'Bob Backenforth's Worcester Pubs Then and Now'** has

*Derick Stephens
(pic Tony Stephens)*

been the crucial filling-in of what would otherwise have been glaring gaps in the ranks of known listed licensees, and I'm indebted to his son, IT teacher Tony, for completing what would had been in grave danger of becoming an incomplete (for which read 'useless') element of this book. Tony – also born in Worcester and, despite a few years living in Birmingham now lives in the City with his family – not only inherited his father's love of his home town and its history, but was also doubly-blessed in being able to combine two family businesses into his research – his father's as already outlined and his mother's, the Green family business which employed a lot of Worcester folk prior to the last war, Interestingly, one of the Green family business' pieces of transport can still be seen in the Tudor House Museum (who incidentally, also play a role in the research for this book). 'It has been a pleasure to work on this book and to be able to put my father's archives to good use' Tony told me – a viewpoint gratefully reciprocated.

The Haines Brothers – Clive and Malcolm (CCMH/CFOW)

They say a picture's worth a thousand words – in which case, there must be nigh-on a whole library's worth in this book alone, all the work of, or where they remain custodians of someone else's work, reproduced with the kind permission of, the Haines brothers. Anybody with even the slightest interest in the history of Worcester will have heard – and like as not, seen the work – of Clive (the elder) and Malcolm Haines whose passion in bringing images of Worcester from days long since past ought by rights to have earned them both the Freedom of the City at the very least.

Those unfortunate enough never to have seen 'The Changing Face of Worcester' are missing a

vital chunk of their local knowledge, while those that were fortunate enough *(and that includes me, several times)* were probably altered by the experience.

The letters CCMH/CFOW (Collection of Clive and Malcolm Haines) throughout this book stand testament to what by any standards is a vast body of their output – all of it invaluable as a record of how Worcester has changed over the years. Interesting to note that when I attempted a similar project quite recently I succeeded only in showing how much it's remained the same!

http://www.youtube.com/watch?v=xf2_z75MkDs

The brothers' sharply-honed photographic skills stemmed from their father, a skilled toolmaker and engineer with his own workshop where, alongside the inevitable lathe and metal-working tools, he set up a simple darkroom for developing and printing photographs. In those days when photography was more of a science than an art, the brothers regularly helped with measuring and mixing the chemicals that dictated whether a picture was or wasn't worth exposing on then highly expensive photo-paper, and those now used to digital prints on a little inkjet machine or even nipping down to Boots for instant prints would no doubt be staggered at how fiddly, time-consuming and downright risky photography was in those pre-digi days. Says Clive: '...during my teens I went on many Youth Hostel cycling holidays and for these journeys I would borrow my father's Zeiss Ikon folding camera. Back at home I developed the films and made prints. Around this time my younger brother, Malcolm, also became interested in photography and we began to explore what was possible and expand our horizons'.

The first 'serious' *(Clive's word)* camera they had was an Ilford 'Sportsman' and a Canon 'Canonette'. In the early 60s they were far and away the youngest members of Worcestershire Camera Club – but this was a time that the City was undergoing sweeping changes, as has been remarked on more than once in the preceding pages. The brothers had early cottoned-on to the fact that while whole swathes of the city's historic core were being demolished and areas cleared for redevelopment this would make the perfect vehicle for their new-found new enthusiasm for photography – now enhanced by the latest gear, Praktica Vs that not only offered single lens reflex operation, but additionally opened up a whole new world of interchangeable and close-up lenses, extension tubes and tripods. The expanding new technology also allowed them to combine their increasing photographic ability and artistic confidence with their growing pictorial record and bring them all together with what was fast becoming a major bolt-on to traditional photographic techniques: audio-visual communications. The result was **'The Changing Face of Worcester'**

"My early employment and training was in radio and TV engineering and electronics, and my inclination towards sound-systems and control equipment. I was captivated by the first proper audio-visual show I saw: the combination of still images set to music was magical. It was also very accessible technology.

Clive Haines FRPS

"Our collection of pictures of Worcester, both old records and contemporary photographs was growing, then a camera club colleague, unable to give a talk at a local WI, asked if we could 'fill-in'" he said. This slide-show was the 90-minute *'Changing Face of Worcester'*, which ran for 35 years, always to sell-out audiences.

Now switching from Praktica Novas to the smaller and lighter Olympus system, more sophisticated a/v shows followed: a 90-minute in-depth look at Worcester Cathedral 'In Focus' in which Clive's wife Gill was also closely involved, and 'Three Part Invention', another 90-minute presentation involving numerous a/v modules of varying length, covering a variety of themes, using four projectors synchronised to a time-track controlled tape.

Since then, Clive further developed 'The Changing Face...' to involve seven computer-controlled projectors and 18 feet wide panoramic screen, to author several books on the City – the most recent just two years ago – and to work on more a/v projects and print-based talks with colleague Martin Addison.

In the early 1990's he qualified as a teacher and developed a number of photography courses, lecturing at three local colleges – one of the lasting results of which is his website **www.crhfoto.co.uk** covering many aspects of his photography as well as Worcester history and numerous 'Photoshop' techniques.

The Sargeants: Bob, Jim and Harry

Mention the name Sargeant at the Hive and even seasoned civilian archivists snap to attention.

A very large proportion of what's by any standards a massive photographic collection depicting Worcester and Worcestershire in all its moods bears the initials RHS, JAS and EHS as originators – *but that's just the starting point for a legacy of amazing material that's worth a book in its own right.*

RH (Robert Harry) and JA (James Andrew) are the sons of EH (Edgar Harry) Sargeant and when the talk gets round to Worcestershire, photographs and archives, talk of the Sargeants is never far behind – and never less than in the most respectful of terms.

In a brilliantly catalogued filing system of the Hive's massive cache of photographs. it's a fair bet that ownership details of at least one in three point to one of the Sargeant dynasty, and the work of the two sons makes up a large part of the imagery in this book while the entire project might not even have got off the starting block without the work of the father.

Which is where we started....

(right) Harry Sargeant as many will fondy recall him (pic courtesy RHS) and top right my first dealings with Sergeant Sargeant 1985 (BB)

Harry (Edgar Harry) Sargeant (EHS)

Harry was the County's first-ever Archivist – a role he was appointed-to at a particularly young age (33) and in which he continued right up to retirement – which in itself is a remarkable achievement. But that's nothing compared to the fact that not only did he position Worcestershire right at the forefront of initiating, logging and preserving a huge body of archival material, but that the systems he put in place as County Archivist still form the basis that all archivists still meticulously follow – even in this computerised age.

As such, he's viewed as one of the major formative influences in the field of archive storage and retrieval and is, even now, still universally viewed as an innovative and pioneering county archivist, setting the pattern that every County archivist since continues to follow.

Now while that in itself sounds very grand, it only comes into its own when you consider that Worcestershire's Hive alone has nearly twelve miles of shelving housing possibly millions of irreplaceable documents, maps and photographs. Repeat the pattern hundreds of times over in archive centres across the UK and possibly the rest of the world, and then you'll begin to get a picture of his huge influence.

Thus, it's also fair to say that without the assistance and efficiency of Worcestershire Record Office here in Worcester alone, research into the rich legacy of our old pubs and inns could possibly have been limited to living memory and a few scratched notes instead of going back to the 1400s – and for that I owe Harry a huge debt.

I first met Harry in 1985 when I went to interview him about something to do with archives – I forget quite what – but that he completely brushed that aside and asked me, as editor of one of the local newspapers, if instead I'd give some publicity to something infinitely more important, the Worcestershire branch of the Dunkirk Veterans Association, an organisation of which he was Chairman. Now, to say that an organisation exists is one thing, but making it appeal to a diverse readership aside from other like-minded members of the same organisation is another. But Harry was most insistent, and very persuasive – even though I had doubts...

'What have you got that'll make it interesting to somebody who might never have even heard of Dunkirk, Harry?' I asked. At first he was incredulous that such a no-brainer existed, but then relented and he brought down his tin hat – the actual tin hat he'd worn on the beaches all those 46 years earlier.

Nah, I said, 'you could have got that from the props department down at The Swan Theatre'. More incredulity: ha! The very thought that anyone could even contemplate so dastardly an act!

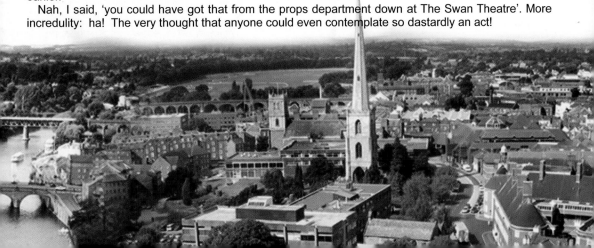

Harry (second right) with fellow Dunkirk veterans (l-r) Vernon Wiggin, Major Tom Averill, and Reg King open the 45-year old tin of Army issue bully beef in front of the TV cameras at County Hall in 1985

(pics BB)

'There's always *that*' he said, pointing to a tin box that had been kicked around and had served as a door stop at his meticulously neat Henwick Road home for nigh-on half a century.

'And what's that?" I asked, still wondering if or not I was going to get a story out of this and looking at the clock: it was a Friday afternoon and the pubs weren't far from opening, I recall.

'That, young man' he said, straightening up and fixing

me with a stare like a bayonet point, '...is the actual tin of bully beef issued to me on 25th May 1940'

And sure enough, a label he'd fixed to the tin read 'Bully Beef canned 1939, issued 1940 and brought back to the UK from Dunkirk, France, by E. H. Sargeant 25th May 1940'.

Now the story was taking shape: that and the helmet would give me a front page – and even the pub momentarily took a back seat as I sensed I could squeeze a bit more out of this...

'Tell me, Harry' I asked, thinking on my feet as all good journalists are supposed to do and sensing a scoop looming, no less: '...if I got some BBC mates to come and film it for TV, would you be prepared to open it and at least make it appear as though you were eating it?'

I don't think he was ever so keen – after all, this had been a treasured memento of a momentous event in his life: he'd have been 26 at the time of the historic evacuation. But then it was my turn to be insistent: '...it'd make great TV" I said 'and the Dunkirk veterans would get some great publicity'. To which he eventually relented.

Thus it was that a week or two after my front page story appeared, a TV crew came to County Hall and filmed Harry and three more Dunkirk veterans, 'Major Tom' Averill, Vernon Wiggin and Reg King, opening and apparently scoffing the 45 year-old meat ration for broadcast at a time that the rest of the Midlands TV region was sitting down to their no doubt fresher and more sumptuous dinners.

And I was right – it did make good TV!

There was a postscript to this: earlier in the day I'd asked County Analyst Geoffrey Keen to check out the 45 year-old Argentinian meat to make sure it was at least fit for human consumption – after all, these were ex-soldiers, all now in their 70s, and I didn't want to find myself pulling off something even Hitler had tried and failed to achieve. Geoffrey Keen had made a small hole in the tin and extracted some of the meat to test it – declaring it'd be fine provided they didn't eat great spoonsful of the stuff and that they avoided the bit that had been in contact with the tin.

The old soldiers survived. Just a few weeks later, Geoffrey Keen was dead.

When Harry also passed on, quite suddenly the following year aged 71, some big names in the fields of librarianship and archives – as well as even more rarified heights – filled St Johns church to pay tribute to the man and his work.

Christened Edgar Harry, but known by his middle name, he was born in Sutton Coldfield and educated at Bishop Vesey's Grammar School, not long afterwards joining Birmingham Reference Library where he was appointed assistant librarian. In October 1931 he moved to its Manuscript Section – already, according to one of his successors as County Archivist, recently-retired Tony Wherry, '...standards set by that institution, its insistence on order, accuracy and the priority of the user, were one of the major formative influences on his subsequent work'.

A colleague who worked with him at the time said that when he joined the staff of the Birmingham Reference Library in 1936, Harry Sargeant was well established as a member of the department responsible for the library's outstanding collection of archives and manuscripts...

'This was a department which can have few equals as a training ground for future leaders in the field of archives. I recall particularly his many aids to research and researchers – and not least the invaluable index to changes in Birmingham street names, which he produced as a by-product of his archival activities. I also recall the long thin scroll of key-words to his enormous repertoire of funny stories' – to which, it appears, Harry also applied the then standard archives indexing system KWIC (Key Word in Context viewed as '...a useful indexing method for technical manuals before computerised full text search became common [Wikipedia]).

By all accounts, Harry's subsequently remarkable career successes stemmed from the sound foundation of librarianship he'd mastered at Birmingham Reference Library – not least, insistence on order, accuracy and the priority of the user, all critical qualities that stood him in great stead for his next

One of Harry's photographs showing early development of Worcester's newest housing estate, Warndon 20th February 1960

great adventure, the Army, which began in March 1939 when he enlisted as a signalman in 48 Division Territorial Army Section D Army Reserve at Hall Green Birmingham.

Though classed as a reservist, he was called up with them at the very outbreak of war and almost immediately joined the BEF in France and Belgium – which is where we came in: Dunkirk. Not that that was the end of the Harry's war: he subsequently returned to France – this time as Sergeant Sargeant of the 79th Armoured Division and a member of the now-victorious allied army who had recognised his talents even to the point of mentioning him in despatches. Harry was subsequently demobbed at the cessation of the hostilities.

Now with an even greater-defined sense of leadership and discipline combined with his own natural inclinations towards meticulousness and attention to the minutest detail in organisational matters, he found himself restless in his former role at Birmingham and so applied – along with twenty-three others – for the newly-created post of Worcestershire County Archivist. He got the job and began work on 1 April 1947 commuting daily from Kings Norton to the Shirehall, a tedious drag in those pre-M5 days.

Tony Wherry picks up the tale: "...thus began one of the most innovative careers known to the archive profession. Order and discipline were paramount. The embodiment of his work is still to be seen today in the unique and extremely effective classification scheme which makes use of decimal notation. Based fairly and squarely on the most orthodox and Jenkinsonian archive principles, all records are classified according to provenance and their relationship one to another is fixed permanently. In the early days of record offices some colleagues found Harry Sargeant's system somewhat cumbersome, but it has stood the test of time. It is efficient, accurate and extremely useful. Its great strength lies in its supreme step-by-step logic, a virtue of considerable proportions in these days of pressure for instant retrieval".

Many also view it as typical of the man when he produced The Office Manual - a classic example of written classification of organisation and methods he demanded from everyone who worked with him.

'Each job in the office and the manner in which it was to be approached was outlined in detail and deviation was not permitted. Sadly, he found it difficult to renew the manual as expansion upon expansion took place in the workload of the office, and by the time of his retirement the manual was largely out of date. One or two specialised areas, however, remain in operation to this day' said a former colleague.

Then, as post-war change began to make its mark on all towns and villages in Worcestershire and elsewhere, Harry hit on a notion that, yet again, has subsequently been picked up and closely copied virtually everywhere else – WPS: the Worcestershire Photographic Survey.

It was his idea to record for posterity the rapidly-changing countryside at a time that the face of Britain was transforming like never before. Targeting a specific town or parish or even a general topic, Harry marshalled his 'troops' – first, friends and colleagues from Birmingham photographic clubs whose ranks were later swelled by teams of volunteer photographers whose only material reward was to have their film replaced. As Tony Wherry put it: '...those who questioned his activities in the 1940s and 1950s in commissioning volunteer photographers to record Worcestershire buildings and places parish-by-parish would not now doubt his wisdom exemplified by a magnificent photographic archive almost 70,000 items strong'.

Despite being still at school – in both cases Worcester Royal Grammar, another coincidence – sons Bob and Jim were also recruited into the team's activities.

The collection today – still regarded as the very model of how to initiate and conduct what has become a valuable photographic resource – is typical of Harry's vision and organisation.

In the 1950s he also masterminded and oversaw the re-location of the County Archive department and its collection to the newly-redundant St Helens Church.

Later, as director of a major new Postgraduate School of Librarianship, his lectures were '...always forcefully presented and highly informative' as one Sheffield University student still recalls 50 years on.

Locally, he became Chairman of local Rotary and Probus groups and The Archaeological Society.

In a glowing tribute in 1986, Tony Wherry summed it all up by stating that it was Harry Sargeant alone who laid the foundations of he present network of county record offices: '...he was an innovator in this field and the 'point of creation' was the area where his main professional interest and enthusiasm lay. Undoubtedly his pioneer work was entirely responsible for the substantial present day and county-wide records management programme operated at Worcester".

But even then, Harry Sargeant had the last word – penning the words of his own obituary...

'All tactics based on the military pattern. Autocratic but fair, even benevolent at times. Always admitted own errors, and sought advice from all sources when needed. Military type discipline, plus tactical conferences. Information to all staff. Intensely interested in the latest recruit'.

There are several of Harry's photographs re-produced with kind permission in this book. They are marked EHS.

Jim (James Andrew) Sargeant (JAS)

Harry's younger son Jim reckons he was about 16 and still at Worcester Royal Grammar School when he embarked on a largely solo project to record as many Worcester pubs as he could reach on his bike – and some of his work dating from that time, 1963-5, is re-printed here for the first time, with his permission: they are marked JAS.

Jim, now retired from his own business as an independent construction adjudicator High Trees Consulting operating from his adopted village of Crowthorne in Berkshire, clearly picked up his father's and brother's seemingly natural flair for photography and was also a regular 'volunteer' on the WPS projects systematically organised by his father and generally masterminded from the Sargeants' Henwick Road home. 'A large and enthusiastic group would gather with much merry-making, banter and humour as well as the important work in hand. We would focus on an area of the county and record specific categories of visual image, marking the evolution of the county life', Jim said – adding that he learned the craft of photography from the WPS trips with some highly-experienced photographers, often from several Birmingham photographic clubs, '...learning the ropes as a junior apprentice'. He adds that Record Office staff also played their part, generally helping out in their own time and without reward save having their film replaced and, if the photographs were deemed good enough, the honour of seeing their work included in the collection.

"I took many photographs around Worcestershire, making use of an incentive scheme giving a free film for every 8 photos accepted by the WPS. As I had a half-frame camera taking 16 photos on each roll, that kept me in free film!" Jim said.

Jim Sargeant and some of his photographs as seen elsewhere throughout this book.

He adds that he recalls being driven out to locations by his father in his diminutive A35 van like Wallace and Gromit, often accompanied by his keen and personable young assistant Stella Whitehouse – who went on to achieve fame in her own account as Stella Rimington, head of MI5 and her autobiography also describes the period she spent as Harry's assistant and the impact he made on her at the time.

Jim also told me he didn't think his father would have approved of him conducting his own personal survey into the Worcester pubs of the time: even so, the photographs he produced then are, so far a I've been able to tell, largely unique and a valuable inclusion in this book. "I'm glad they can be seen again and that you can bring them to a wider audience" he told me. Jims photographs are:

Alma, Droitwich Road (p153); Alma, Lowesmoor (278; Angel (p71); Arcadia (p350); Bell (St Johns) (p78); Bell (p154); Black Horse (p276); Bridge (p284); Bush (p94);Cardinals Hat and Globe (p307); Coach and Horses (p135); Dolphin (p216); Drakes Drum (p76); Dudfields (p238); Duke of York (p222); Ewe and Lamb and Fountain (p231); Farriers Arms (p244); Feathers (p134); Five Ways (p242); Golden Lion (p296); Great Western Hotel x2 (p182); Green Man (p130); Gun (p187); Horn and Trumpet (p226); King Charles (pp266); King William IV (p340); Kings Head (p306); Locomotive (p344); Lakes (p196); Lamb and Flag (p131); Loch Ryan and Cross Keys (p168); (old) Plough (p272); New Chequers (p192); New Bank Street (p150); Old Talbot (p304); Old Talbot (p303); Old Chapel (p325); Paul Pry (p240); Plough Deansway (p367); Plough Silver Street (p270); Park Tavern (p170); Red Lion (p166); Saracens Head (p126); Star Hotel (p236); Talbot (p3137); Vauxhall (p189); Vulcan (p342); White Hart (p382); Woolpack (p214);

Bob (Robert Harry) Sargeant. (RHS)

Bob, five years older than his brother, is now a highly-regarded road safety engineer and consultant whose interest in road safety and construction started with a holiday job working for Monks who were building the M5 through Worcestershire at the time (1960-1961). Bob was also heavily involved with WPS being enrolled as another 'volunteer' as early as 12, he said – adding, like Jim, that aside from the knowledge that he was actively recording a rapidly-changing image of Worcestershire, a huge incentive for him was that he'd be rewarded with free film which, as his was a half-frame camera, would give him

Bob Sargeant

maybe 16 exposures at a time when photography was a highly expensive profession – or in Bob's case, hobby. "I was keen – for me it was more than a passing interest" he told me. While Jim went off and did his own thing with Worcester's pubs, Bob – a lifetime teetotaller who reckons he's only ever once been inside a pub, and that was with his father who himself was no great frequenter of our various hostelries – specialised in photographing Worcestershire country houses and streets. Even so, his is also a valuable legacy of pub-related photographs often, he says, by way of accident as his main subject was the general street scene but the pubs got in there too!

"Jim and I were both aware that the early-to-mid 60s were a time of great change and we both wanted to save for posterity what we were seeing at the time". Bob even went so far as to strike up an arrangement with demolition companies to let him know what buildings and where were next up for a date with a bulldozer in return for photographic records of the event. This is the list of RHS and EHS photographs included in this book:

Brewers Arms, Moor Street 13616–RHS-11-01-58 R121.4 (p124); Mug House, Hylton Road 13031-EHS-20-04-57 E572.6a. EHS 20th April 1957 (p10) Crowle House Hill Street: 13708-RHS-25-01-58 R123.7 (p180); New Pope Iron Inn Pope Iron Road 13925-RHS-02-03-1958 R127.12 (p147); Black Horse, Lowesmoor: 13928-RHS-02-03-58 R127.10 (p277); Garibaldi, Wylds Lane: 13980-RHS-15-09-57 R112.7a (p176); Bricklayers Arms: 14001-RHS-15-09-57 R112.8a (p178); Eagle Vaults: 14057-RHS-23-03-58 R135.12 (p316); Bush, St Johns: 14916-RHS-02-08-58 R166.12; Crown and Anchor, Hylton Road: 14923-RHS-29-07-58 R165.8 (p107) ; Liverpool Vaults, Shambles: 15053-RHS-07-09-58 R190.7; Lamp Tavern, Tybridge Street: 15061-RHS-05-09-58 R187.8 (p98); Cock Inn, Tybridge Street: 15083-RHS-02-08-58 R166.10 ; Lame Dog, Canalside: 15637-RHS-01-09-58 R183.6; White Hart, College Street: 18518-RHS-03-02-60 R234.10 (p382); Old Farrier's Arms, Quay Street: 18531-RHS-12-01-60 R232.12; Warndon panorama: 18764-RHS-20-02-60 R248.6 (p194); Albion, Bath Road: 18906-RHS-27-02-60 R249.12 (p8); St Georges Tavern: 19349-RHS-20-04-60 R268.2; Freemasons Arms: 20854-RHS-31-05-60 R282.6; Oddfellows Arms: 20857-RHS-31-05-60 R282.8; New Inn, George Street: 24011-RHS-22-09-61 R327.5 (p290); Boat, Lowesmoor: 24018-RHS-21-09-61 R325.17 (P275); Union, Lowesmoor: 24020-RHS-21-09-61 R325.3 (p272); Pack Horse, St Nicholas Street: 24022-RHS-21-09-61 R324.8 (p258); Bedwardine, Bromyard Road: 24894-RHS-03-04-62 R338.3 (p.74; Prince of Wales, Shrub Hill (rear): 29685 26985-RHS-13-04-63R359.10 (p186); Prince of Wales, Shrub Hill (front): 29687-26987RHS-13-04-63 R359.12 (p186); Lamp Tavern Tybridge Street: 27950-EHS-25-01-64 E755.3a; Vulcan, St Pauls Street: 30852-EHS-31-10-64 E793.3b

Prints of Bob's photographs are available on application to Bob Sargeant at: 7 Richmond Road Aylesbury HP20 1PL, Tel 01296 482380

www.bobsarg.nildram.co.uk/wps.htm   Here's just four, seen elsewhere in this book

19: Worcester's Pubs - your

We're now almost at the end of this book – but that's not to say we're almost at the end of the subject.

In fact, there's more – lots more – and it's fair to say that this could even be the beginning.

By getting this far in 'Worcester Pubs Then and Now' you've already shown your interest in the subject – hopefully fuelled even further by what you've read in the past 475 pages. But the printed word is just the start and we're almost at the point of allowing technology to take over.

Not only that, but here's your chance to play your part in the continuing saga of Worcester pubs then, now – and better still, in the future.

The Worcester Pubs website

http://www.worcester-pubs.co.uk

is here to make sure you do just that - with actions, not just words.

Dedicated to the preservation of Worcester's pubs, it gives details of all the 'live' pubs in the City and immediate surroundings. What's more, it's globally-accessible, fully interactive and dynamic with your favourite pub's instantly updateable info pages.

It means that if you're a licensee you can post details of your pub, photographs, up-coming events, menus, special offers and reasons why people should visit. And if you're a local, a visitor, a casual drinker or a hardened boozer you're also welcome to post your own photographs, comments and views.

In short, if you have something to say about this book and/or any of the pubs included in it, the Worcester Pubs website is the place to air it. Information for inclusion in Volume II will also be readily welcomed!

It's a tribute to the everlasting appeal of British pubs in general and Worcester pubs in particular that despite the best efforts of the pubcos and the image-driven corporate chains, every pub, in every location, remains special, unique and a one-off. As I said in an earlier chapter, pubs are like people – but again, like people sometimes they need introductions: we are Brits after all!

http://www.worcester-pubs.co.uk

https://www.facebook.com/groups/worcesterpubsthenandnow

chance to get in on the act

That's why in addition to general information about Worcester pubs and instantly updateable pages, there's also videos, archive information and links to associated websites.

Access the website, click on the Worcester Pubs A-Z link and scroll down to the one you're interested in visiting. To add your views, photographs, comment and suggestions, click at the appropriate point.

In addition there's also the **Worcester Pubs Then and Now Facebook Friends' page**. It's lively Friends' forum on anything to do with Worcester's pubs and open for anyone to apply to join *(prove to me you have a genuine interested in Worcester pubs and you're in!)*

Apply to join now and you'll be in the company a friendly group of people who share the same interest: curiously enough, Worcester pubs then and now. Who knows... one day, there might even be a big get together which

might become an annual event – even monthly – and then... But first things first.

Join now and let's take if from there.

https://www.facebook.com/groupsworcesterpubsthenandnow

The Whole

Bob Backenforth's Worces___ Pubs Then and Now is the first title from a brand new publishing company – The Whole Pictu___ Publishing Company Limited.

And while a second volume on the fascinating subject of Worcester's pubs is already being considered, it doesn't necessarily mean that it will be title #2, #3 or even #4 in the stable – because The Whole Picture Publishing Company Limited is now actively on the lookout for more books to publish. And one of them could be yours.

As any would-be author will tell you, formulating the idea and knuckling down to perhaps months of writing is the easy part – yet far too many potentially successful authors with good ideas have given up their dream of being published after the umpteenth rejection slip proved just one too many.

Disheartening is scarcely the word and while all the 'How to' books advocate never giving in – with urges to try, try, try, and then try some more – the all too real disappointment of manuscripts being returned with monotonous regularity and letters that begin 'It is with regret...' is inevitably going to make even the most persistent artist wonder if it's all worth the while.

Essentially, it's the getting published that's the biggest hurdle of all and not the writing – and not just because of subject matter, either.

All too often – and assuming they're read, of course *(which isn't always the case)* – manuscripts are rejected and returned not so much on the grounds of content but just as often because their presentation has failed to do justice to the initial idea... poorly laid-out draft manuscripts and unnecessary grammatical errors are as often the cause of rejection than the actual words, and the adage 'first impressions count' is more true of publishing than probably any other sector.

But that may – just may – be about to change with the creation of The Whole Picture Publishing Company Limited.

They say everyone has a book in them – and not just advertising copywriters, journalists and other ilks of professional writers either. Accordingly, if you have a story, an idea, a vision and the will to make it work *(don't get too bogged down in the skill element – that's where the bolt-on services company comes in)* The Whole Picture Publishing Company can help you make it happen.

On one hand, it's a publishing services company specialising in presentation, design, layout, editing, proof-reading, ghost-writing, photo re-touching and photography, all the way up to cover design and top-tier marketing for other would-be authors. As a seven times award-winning journalist, designer